T0354367

Discovery
of
Prehistory Ancient India

Discovery
of
Prehistory Ancient India

Krishna & Radha

Dr. Jagat K. Motwani

DISCOVERY OF PREHISTORY ANCIENT INDIA
KRISHNA & RADHA

iUniverse books may be ordered through booksellers or by contacting:

iUniverse
1663 Liberty Drive
Bloomington, IN 47403
www.iuniverse.com
1-800-Authors (1-800-288-4677)

ISBN: 978-1-5320-3789-4 (sc)
ISBN: 978-1-5320-3790-0 (e)

Print information available on the last page.

iUniverse rev. date: 02/09/2018

Discovery
of
The Prehistory Ancient India
Dedicated
to
my parents
who taught me that I should consider
only
MYSELF
responsible for shaping my life
and
Nothing is impossible if there is determination

Preface

Will Durant in "Our Oriental Heritage" considers India important for modern mind and heart and it alerts the modern student about the inadequacy of his acquaintance with India and tells "This is the India that its patient scholarship is now opening up, like a new intellectual continent, to that western mind which only yesterday thought civilization an exclusively European thing." The birth of Indian (Vedic) civilization is too ancient for European mind to know its depth and varicosity of its knowledge.

This book addresses the history of India from pre-history ancient times when she[1] was known as 'Āryavarta'. Vedic people (Hindus) love the country of their birth as 'mother', therefore, 'she' for Āryavarta (India).

India is not her original name. It was given by her victors with their mischievous ethno-political agenda to disconnect her people 'Aryans' from their enviable Aryan heritage. The relationship of Indians (Aryans, Hindus) with their glorious 'Aryan heritage', as defined by the original name 'Āryavarta' of their motherland, has been sidelined as mythology. It has been mutilated, corrupted and selectively ignored. History, written by others, particularly by victors, can not be objective. Writing history of others is unethical. It is a literary sin. But the powerful colonialists consider it as their sacred duty to write whatever about the governed. Power makes a lie as truth and vice versa. Power mostly is insensitive to the feelings of the governed. The British opined that they wrote Indian history because history was not an Indian cup of tea. As a matter of fact, Hindus have been very particular about history, as evidenced by the Vedas, describing remote prehistory ancient events and the lessons by ancient Vedic gurus of various philosophical dimensions. Composers of Vedic hyms, being modest, have not publicized their names.

No other history is older than the history given in Vedas and other Hindu sacred scriptures, like Ramayana (app 5000 BC) and Mahabharata

---

[1]   Hindus consider their country as mother therefore she not it.

(app.3000 BC). The stories of Ramayana and Mahabharata are being played as dramas in temples and in open-air wall-less musical theaters, so that even small children know their proud heritage. Thus, the history of prominent events, culture and philosophical thoughts are being passed over from generation to generation through millennia-long Vedic oral traditions. This is the reason, why European historians were not able to influence common Indians by their Christian cultural ideology. They have been able to influence only some section, particularly the urbanite educated class, as per their taste for European party manners, dress, music, etc. Surprising, most of them, when in religious occasions, proudly behave and dress traditionally and enjoy traditional vegetarian food.

The book addresses the history of Aryans, presently known as Hindus, since their birth, yet unknown, because difficult to map the ultra-large geography of their original cottage of their birth which has been diminishing, last by loss of Pakistan and Bangladesh. It has been diminished as the result of foreign assaults, mainly, because of the adverse influence of *Ahimsa* and domestic rivalries and infightings based on caste, religion and language. Unfortunately, optimum military force, though possible, has rarely been used against foreign aggressors.

Hindus have their history, longer, more ancient than and different from the history, as recorded by modern historians who seem to have been purposefully ignorant, perhaps biased too. The real history of the ancient India has been misrepresented, ignored as myth and buried too deep. A country is defined by its geography, as marked by its present borders, susceptible to territorial greed of foreign aggressors.

History of the originality and antiquity of Aryans (present Hindus) has been distorted, thus made too complex to correct and reconstruct. Sickness of the history of ancient India is generally caused by the germs – bias, ignorance, and infightings – driven by ethnic rivalry and jealousy. Historians, particularly of imperialistic mentality, have been corrupting, distorting and abusing their only child HISTORY.

Myself, being Aryan (Hindu), have been lost, confused and too bewildered to decide which historian and which historical facts to trust. It is a difficult task. I have tried to use litmus test to see if the story is in congruence with the historically established basic facts or not.

Contradictions are to be objectively examined to establish believable facts. It is good to know both, positives as well negatives, because both would have some truth. Let the readers to discern truths.

Power dictates and redefines borders, which in case of almost all colonized countries, have not remained constant. The borders of India, as affected by Britain and other European colonialists – French, Portuguese, Spanish, and Dutch – have dwindled, fortunately some regained after independence.

Almost all the colonized peoples – Asian as well African – have recovered their lost geography, but unfortunately not India. Some countries, particularly India have been fragmented into pieces. Indians are much better than the Native American Indians who have lost their nationhood forever. Colonization, infested with slavery, has been the culprit. Colonization is shameless. Colonialists have yet to admit and regret for their guilt. Territorial greed can never be sated. Now with the UN shelter, weak countries sleep peacefully. But still there are some shameless hungry lions, particularly China, defying the UN, have been looking for some more land and water. Tibet is not sufficient to satisfy their territorial hunger.

With passage of time, the borders of Âryavarta (Bharat, India) have extremely shrunk to her bones, as the result of loss of several territories, like the Central Asian *'istan'* countries, Iran, Afghanistan, Pakistan, Bangladesh, Sri Lanka, Myanmar, Nepal, South Eastern region, Thailand, Malaysia, Singapore, Vietnam, Cambodia, and Indonesia. The names of people, towns, mountains, lakes and rivers have been too disfigured and distorted.

But the influence of Vedic culture and Sanskrit is still distinct there, little faded. Possible efforts have been made to piece together the known related circumstantial evidences to weave a meaningfully believable history.

Jagat K. Motwani, Ph.D. Fulbright
August 15, 2017

Foreword

The ancient Vedic culture is one of the most important and influential cultures known to humanity. Its philosophy, as elaborated in its highly regarded texts, such as the Vedas, the Upanishads, the Bhagavad-gita and Mahabharata, the Puranas, and others, is what no other country has to offer. This literature explains many aspects of life in order to assist and direct humanity to reach its fullest potential in all areas of life, especially its spiritual developments.

As philosophers around the world became aware of what these Vedic texts and its way of life had to offer, many of them studied and adopted it to their own outlook, understanding and teachings. Dr. Jagat Motwani has provided a great review of this information. It is like a reference of references of all kinds, something I would certainly use in my own research.

So, in a time when it seems like much of the importance of India's ancient Vedic culture is being forgotten, and the realizations of how much it had affected the world, Dr. Jagat Motwani has done a great job with his wide research in helping reestablish the significance of this tradition. He takes a look at countries around the planet and uncovers the historic influence the ancient Vedic tradition, especially its philosophy, had on other cultures. He also reviews some of the advancements, both social and scientific, that can be found in the timeless Vedic texts, like the Ramayana and the Mahabharata.

Therefore, herein the reader will find a wealth of information on how far back in time the Vedic culture can be traced, but also how beneficial it had been and still is, and how respected the Vedic tradition and its vast knowledge was by both historic and modern philosophers and scholars. Any reader will get a renewed admiration for what the Vedic culture of India has provided to humanity around the world.

Stephen Knapp

About author and the books authored by

Jagat K. Motwani, Ph.D., Fulbright

M.A. (Eco), M.S.W., University of Baroda, India., Ph.D. Fordham University, New York, and Fulbright Scholar.

- Associate Professor at graduate school of social work, M.S. University of Baroda, in India (1958-70).
- Asst. Director of Social Service, New York (1970-1988).
- Psychotherapist & family therapist (Pvt. practice, on PT basis) (1971-1995)
- Organized and Moderated several conferences on family and youth issues all over America and India (1981- 2009), under the auspices of National Federation of Indian Associations.
- Visiting scholar on Indian Diaspora and family issues to Delhi, Gujarat, and Patan universities.

Writer, Historian, Areas of interest:

History, Linguistics, Language, Indus Valley civilization, and Indian Diaspora.

Books by author

1. Sindhi Roots and Wings: New Perspectives on Mooanjodaro (2013)
2. India Reborn: Bharat Mahan, As Perceived by Westerners, Gandhi, Nehru, Tagore & Others (2012)

3. None but India (Bharat): The Cradle of Aryans, Sanskrit, Vedas & Swastika, 2010.

4. "Sindhu (Indus) Valley Civilization: Heritage of the Culture, Sindhyat, & Entrepreneurship of Sindhis" (2009).

5. "America and India: In a 'Give & Take' Relationship" (2003).

6. Global Indian Diaspora: Yesterday, Today and Tomorrow (1993), by Dr. Jagat K. Motwani, Dr. Mahine Gosine and Dr. Jyoti Barot-Motwani.

7. "Global Migration of Indians: Saga of Adventure, Enterprise, Identity & Integration" (1989).by Dr. Jagat K. Motwani and Dr. Jyoti Barot-Motwani

8. Discovery of the Prehistory Ancient India (2017)

Chief author of a column on family and youth issues for two Indian Weekly News Papers in America,1978-1988.

Acknowledgments

I salute the scholars of various disciplines – such as history, religion, culture, archeology, anthropology, language, economics, sociology, psychology, psychoanalysis, diplomacy, etc – for their contribution, direct as well as indirect, to make the book appropriately and adequately fruitful. Names of the scholars, referred to, are given in appendix.

I very much appreciate to have Mr. Stephen Knapp, author of over forty books, though over-occupied, found time to write the Foreword.

Without cooperation and assistance of my whole family – Jyoti, Neha, Daniel, Shilpa, Emad – it would have been uncomfortable to work long hours, several times at odd hours.

Last, not the least, I love my both grand children – Annika (6 yrs) and Remi (10) who have been recreating me when I need break, particularly Annika plays 'hide and seek.

Dr, Jagat K. Motwani, Ph.D., Fulbright

Contents

Chapter One

INTRODUCTION

The title of the Will Durant's book: *"The Story of Civilization: Our Oriental Heritage"*(1935) raised my curiosity to know the prehistory ancient India and what colonial European historians think about India and about her civilization. It is hard to understand why they think that their (European) heritage is in the East (India). Contradictions in host of their thoughts about India, her originality, antiquity and Vedic civilization have been confusing. This book with the help of several unbiased objective scholars – Indian as well as Westerners – will try to answer most contradictions.

This book "Discovery of the Prehistory Ancient India" is the continuing sequential story of the four known Eras (Yugas) of the Hindu life as reflected by – (i) Vedas (about 11,700 BC), (ii) Ramayana (about 5114 BC), (iii) Mahabharata (about 3112 BC) and (iv) *Kalyuga* (modern Era).

I would like to explain why we Indians address India as "Mother India", because India, like mother gives milk and all other basic necessities of life. Therefore, in this book "She and her", not "It and its" are used for India

Will Durant (p.391) inspired me to know my 'Mother India':

> "Nothing should more deeply shame the modern student than the recency and inadequacy of his acquaintance with India. ... an impressive continuity of development and civilization from Mohenjo-daro, 2900 B.C. or earlier, to Gandhi, Raman and Tagore; ... this is the India that its patient scholarship is now opening up,

like a new intellectual continent, to that Western mind which only yesterday thought civilization an exclusively European thing."

In its chapter '*The Foundations of India*' (page 391, footnote), Durant observes:

> "From the time of Megasthenes, who described India to Greece ca. 302 B.C., down to the eighteenth century, India was all a marvel and a mystery to Europe. Marco Polo (1254-1323 A.D.) pictured its western fringe vaguely, Columbus blundered upon America in trying to reach it, Vasco da Gama sailed around Africa to rediscover it, and merchants spoke rapaciously of 'the wealth of Indies'. But scholars left the mine almost un-tapped."

India, like several others, has been a mystery and a marvel to me too. The more I read, the more ignorant I find self and feel eager to know own birth cottage, more and more since her birth I know is too ancient to know. Colonial masters knew that it was important to keep colonized people ignorant of their heritage as long as possible to prevent rising of their feeling of freedom which is not possible. The British masters changed the name of the country from Amravati to India and from 'Aria" to Indian, saying that Aryans invaded India and brought with them Aryan civilization, Sanskrit, Aryan genes and Vedic religion, also claiming that Vedas were composed later by the invading Aryans. Black Dravidians were the original natives who were driven South by the fair skin invading Aryans. All such ill-based faulty history will be reconstructed based on irrefutable historical, linguistic and biological facts and evidences.

Aryans misrepresented

Most historians, knowingly or unknowingly, have misrepresented the ancient Aryans and the name of their birth land Âryavarta, now known

India to suit the colonial historical agenda. The names "Arya" and "Âryavarta", are familiar to Vedas and other Vedic scriptures. It is not known why they are considered myth. It is not explained why original name Âryavarta is changed to India, though it is neither Sanskritic nor does it reflect the culture of Âryavarta, now known as Bharat and India. The name 'India' does not reflect the heritage, nor the history of Âryavarta (India). Shamelessly it compares to the most disgraceful clan "Native American Indians" who could not hold on their territory which was swallowed by invading Europeans.

Some historians say that the name "India" has its origin in 'Indus', one of the prominent rivers of India. The name 'Hindu' has come from the name 'Sindhu', the Sanskritic name of the river Indus. Iranians pronouns 'S' as 'H', therefore Sindhu became Hindu and Sindhustan became Hindustan.

Whereas, Arya is the most civilized enviable race, white Europeans are crazy to have Aryan heritage which is Asian, particularly Indian (Hindu).

Sincere efforts are made to address almost all the following issues and try to discover the ignored, forgotten and buried facts related to ancient India, whatever possible:

- Vedas are the most ancient scriptures of the mankind.
- The sacred scriptures give history, but they are considered as mythologies to give historians freedom to write whatever they want to.
- Mythologies become history when written.
- Sanskrit, the man spoke first.
- Adverse historical implications of the two ill-based theories – (i) Aryan invasion of India and (ii) Indo-European Family of Languages.
- Both Aryans as well as Dravidians are the original natives of Âryavarta (India).
- Both Sanskrit as well as Dravidian languages are the original languages of India.
- There is close linguistic relationship between Sanskrit and Dravidian languages.

- Historical adverse implications of the change of the original name Âryavarta to India.
- History has been corrupted. In general it does not mirror appropriate picture of the ancient Âryavarta (Bhārat, India).
- Modern inventions, when objectively analyzed, will tell that their inventors got their ideas from ancient Vedic scriptures, meaning that the seeds of their ideas were already there in remote pre-history Vedic scriptures.

Knowledge, very important in Hinduism

Hinduism is based on knowledge (education), as evidenced by its first Ashram known as 'Brahmacharya'. During the first twenty-five years of life, the person needs to observe celibacy in pursuit of knowledge. The person, the society or the nation, based on knowledge, will always be guided by the light of the wisdom of knowledge. Education in ancient times was universal, meaning none was allowed to remain ill-literate. Hindu is a knowledge-based civilization. The Vedic texts should not be ignored, dismissed as mythologies or as the works of imagination or just containing some moral stories. The word Veda means knowledge. They contain relevant knowledge otherwise these texts would not have survived the millennia years of historical storm. It is for the people to keep their eyes, ears and minds open to understand the truth in them. Because of communal politics, the governments of India have been hesitant to be loud about their proud heritage, like the reality of Ram Setu, also known as Rama's bridge. It is discussed later in the Chapter Twenty Six, Ram Setu. It is irony in communal politics that one segment can not rejoice the godly achievement which is not endorsed by the religion of the opposition. The religion, endorsing negatives, rather opposing positives, is not religion in its true sense.

Images of 'Ram Setu' were globally flashed out by NASA, to put end to the hesitation. Ram Setu, so far known, is the oldest man-made bridge. It reflects the grandeur of the ancient Vedic (Hindu) civilization. It is a civil engineering marvel of 5076 BCE. This was built into the sea along the shore of the Bay of Bengal by the army of Lord Rama to pave its way to Sri Lanka to free Seeta from the cruel clutches of Rawana.

The Government of India seems to be awakened to accept the reality of Ram Setu and has decided to go ahead with its plans for building a shipping channel by breaking the bridge, believed to have been built by Lord Rama and his team. The research brings out to light that the layers of the bridge construction take us back to the period of Ramayana about 5200 BC. For more about Ram Setu, please refer to the Chapter 26 pp.356-360.

There is an interesting legend explaining the necessity of Ram Setu. It has been historically ignored or hidden. It happened during Ramayana period, the life of Lord Rama. In Ramayana there is mention about the bridge, which was built between Rameshwaram and Sri Lankan coast under the supervision of a dynamic and invincible figure called Rama who is known as the incarnation of Vishnu.

Seeta urged Rama to get for her the golden deer jumping near their kutir (cottage) in Panchvati near Nisik. It was actually the Rakshasha Maricha in disguise sent by Rawana. When Rama did not return for long time, Seeta became impatient and interruptedly cried and repeatedly pleaded Lakshmana to go in search of her husband. Lakshmana did not think wise to leave her alone in the ferocious Dandakaranya forest. Then Seeta accused him of ill-design to get her after Rama's death. Reluctantly and helplessly Lakshmana left her on the condition that she would not cross the line he drew as a protective line, known as Lakshman Rekha,[2] which would burn any intruder. The technology of the Lakshmana Rekha – Rawana did not dare to cross – is not explained in Ramayana.

Once Lakshmana left, Rawana, in the disguise of a mendicant appeared begging alms. Seeta did not know Rawana, and did not smell his trick. Seeta influenced by the Vedic culture of "अतिथि देवो भव" (Atithi Devo Bhava, meaning 'guest is like a god), crossed over the Lakshman Rekha (लक्ष्मण रेखा), to give alms to the beggar disguised as Rakshas Rawana. He forcefully kidnapped her and flew with her in his Pushpaka Viman, kept hidden behind bushes, to Sri Lanka.

Amazing! Hindus during the time of Ramayana (about 5114 BC) had technology to make small plane. All such information is not given in history, being taught in schools and colleges. Colonial historians

---

[2] Now it refers to a strict convention or a rule, never to be broken.

have not only buried such knowledge about ancient Bhārat (India), but also have misrepresented lot of Vedic ancient glory to defame the Vedic civilization.

Nothing grows out of zero. It seems that the modern scientists and technologists got the idea about their products – planes, Ram Setu, TV, guided missiles, fire missiles, and creation of night-like dark clouds and disperse them to bring the sun back, etc – from ancient scriptures, such as Vedas, Ramayana, Mahabharata, etc. Night-like dark clouds were created by Lord Krishna to bring Jaidrath – responsible for killing of Abhimanue, the son of Arjuna and Subhadra – out from his hide. The credit for research to translate all these ideas into reality goes to modern scientists and technologists. Colonial historians have ignored such information, branding it as mythology. This incident of Jaidrath and Arjuna has a moral lesson to learn that Arjuna would not have attemted to kill Jaidrath if found after the end of the day.

Mythology has some base. No mythology is born out of nothing. According to 'The New Oxford American Dictionary', 'myth' means "a traditional story esp. concerning the early history of a people."

Colonial historians have misrepresented, confused and defamed the heritages of the colonized peoples, sentimentally important to them. The title of Will Durant's book "Our Oriental Heritage" may enkindle desire in minds of all, particularly colonized, to know own heritage. To know own heritage, history is most precious. Shamelessly, most history has been distorted or hidden.

Will Durant (1963, p. 391) has alerted the sleeping Hindus to wake up to know own heritage, the torch on the path to the future. He has told that there is enviable scholarship to enable India to be "a new intellectual continent."

The sleeping magnificent "patient scholarship" of India seems to be awakening and opening up with recent surge of Indian professionals into America and in several others developed as well as developing countries. Indians, the carriers of varied scholarship, have proved to be effective global informal ambassadors of India. They have been significantly responsible for changing and enhancing the image of India from 'a country of poverty and snake-charmers' to the land of not only Gurus and philosophers, but also of scientists, high technologists, academics, doctors, engineers, IT wizards and professionals in various fields. India has bestowed gifts of such great technologists, academics, philosophers, scholars, doctors and diplomats to America, UK and several countries. The image of India has been enhanced so much that an Indian social worker in white robe in American hospitals is often mistaken as a doctor, meaning Americans perceive Indians as educated as doctors. This has happened because India's roots are in Vedas, meaning knowledge. Amazing! Great renowned scholars, like Swami Vivekananda, have been more interested in knowing self, rather than the physical world. Knowing self – inner-self – is the most difficult knowledge, no university can provide. Only long, uninterrupted *tapasiya* (lonely observation of penance) may help one to have deep introspection within self to realize union between *atma* and *Paramatma* (Supreme God).

You know India much better when you leave her and live somewhere overseas. You hear and read what foreigners and some great Indians have said about the glory of India. You identify holes in your knowledge and recognize the clouds darkening your perceptions about your Mother India. You see your misperceptions, perhaps self-induced by your own ethnic inferiority complex. You examine why you resist seeing truths about India, perhaps you choose not to see the positive and great aspects of India in order to justify why you left her. Many overseas Indians criticize and belittle India, though unconsciously love and adore.

This also is true that when any non-Indian wrongly criticizes India, we hit him / her back very hard. I, as a Fulbright student at the Smith School, North Hampton, and MASS in 1966-67, felt shy telling that I was from India, may be because of national inferiority complex. The Sociology professor remarked: "We got small pox from England." A British student Grace rose up and agitatedly said: "We got smallpox from India." I got up and said: "Thank God, we have been able to control smallpox since British left India." I was happily surprised to watch the professor and several students clapping hard, reflecting American lofty broad-minded bias-free attitude. When coming out of the class, Grace shouted at me: "Jagat, did you not know that I am from England?" I replied: "Grace, still you don't seem to admit that England has lost its lordship over several countries including India."

In such situations, suppressed love for Bharat Mata (Mother-India) bursts out. American liberal and broadminded ethos encourages objectivity and allows one to muster the courage to express self to relieve the guilt for ignorance of the grandeur of own heritage.

Discovery of great things about India evokes a sense of pride and strength. The things, other people say about our India, evoke a feeling of victory, like a win of a billion dollar lottery. Each day, since I landed at the JFK airport in 1970 as a Green Card holder, I have been learning more and more about the grandeur of India. While in India, I never felt interested to read what great people like Swami Vivekananda, Gandhi, Nehru, Tagore, and several western Indologists have said about India. What Durant has written in *"The Story of Civilization: Our Oriental Heritage"* (1963), particularly its title "Our Oriental Heritage" would inflate ethnic ego of every Indian.

All this enkindled my interest to know as much as possible the history of ancient Herat which has been misrepresented, hidden, buried or ignored as mythology. This is my modest effort to dig the hidden mine of the historical scholarship on prehistory remote ancient Bhārat which has been left untapped and most is misrepresented by colonial historians. Vedas and several other sacred scriptures are full of history regarding Aryans, philosophies on life, Sanskrit, Dravidian languages and Swastika, which have not found place in most history books. Most of the content, though historical, has been discarded as mythology, and thus has not been part of history. Great historical epics like Ramayana and Mahabharata are not being taught as history. The Bhagvad Gita, the ocean of secular knowledge – science and art of life – is branded as 'non-secular' (communal), thus is not being taught in schools and colleges of Bhārat, the country of more than 80 percent population of Hindus, Jains, Buddhists and Sikhs.

History, the picture and life-line of the nation, has been disfigured and has been drowned in the colonial flood of ill-representations and erroneous perceptions by invaders and colonialists. True objective history – full of both positives and negatives – is yet to be written. Negatives, if objectively viewed, have useful preventive lessons. Unfortunately, all the post-independence governments have given little attention to the history of India, the diagnosis and prognosis of the political health – domestic as well as diplomatic – of the nation.

Hope to dig into the mine of the historically relevant facts, the scholars have viewed or not, and also those which have been ignored or even buried intentionally or otherwise. Hope this book will unearth some diamonds which would shine the ancient India. It is hard to tell everything reader would like to know about the ancient India and in the manner he/she would like to know. I want to admit my possible subjective perceptions, may unconsciously be evoked by my affection for my Mother India, hard to control.

It would be interesting to know what some Western and Indian scholars have said about India and about her original natives (Aryans), language (Sanskrit), literature (Vedas), Swastika, culture, and also about courageous overseas adventures for trade and colonizations.

The book will address much more than the following, supported by irrefutable documented historical evidences:

- Aryans are from Âryavarta (India), the abode of Ayans
- World-wide spread of Aryans in ancient times.
- India, the enviable Aryan heritage, being stolen by Europeans.
- Aryan, the Jewel of the White Race?
- Theories; 'Aryan Invasion of India' and 'Indo-European Family' are illbased and corrupting history.
- Originality, antiquity and authorship of the Vedas.
- Sanskrit and Dravidian languages.
- Unity in India's amazing diversity.
- Ancient Hindu Astronauts, unbelievable but true.
- Hinduism, natural, eternal, origin-less and eternal.
- Hinduism, its origin and as perceived by Gandhi, Tagore, Swami Vivekananda, Greek and Western philosophers.
- Hinduism compared to Buddhism. And Zoroastrianism.
- Yoga, key to desirable health, physical as well as spiritual.
- Misperceptions of Hinduism, monotheistic or polytheistic.
- India's absorbing capacity

Sir William Jones (Asiatic Research, vol.1, p. 426) talks about the Hindu colonies all over the globe: "Of the cursory observations on the Hindus, which it would require volumes to expand and illustrate that they had an immemorial affinity with the old Persians, Ethiopians,

CRIES OF HISTORY

History of India has been crying for help to cleanse the mud over truths. History of India has been misrepresented, distorted, ignored and hidden. Colonially written histories are ill-based and vague. They are full of misperceptions and contradictions, as evidenced by complaints by several historians. Both Nehru and Dr. K. M. Munshi, the founder of the Bharatiya Vidya Bhavan, have complained that colonially corrupted history is being taught in schools and colleges. Holi should be celebrated by burning all such books in front of the pictures of stalwart historians like Nehru and Munshi, so that they get peace of mind in heaven that teachers and professors would not find any such poisonous misleading books to teach from, and students would read reconstructed history to feel proud of their heritage.

Several historians have similar complaints about history. Historian Herbert Butterfield[3] complains about the history, being taught in schools and colleges:

"The national history taught in schools has tended to encourage the most general and terrifying of existing evils, "human presumptions and particularly intellectual arrogance," or in other words self righteousness. Wrong history is being taught in all countries, all the time, unavoidably; while we have great need of history, our first need is to *unlearn* most of what we have been taught."

---

[3] Taken from Herbert J. Muller, "The Loom of History" New York: Harper & Brothers, 1958, p. 28.

Herbert J. Muller[4] writes that on a national scale, history becomes the kind of prejudice and conceit that led Paul Valery to call history the most dangerous product ever concocted by the chemistry of the brain:

Mark Twain[5] (1835-1910) complains: "We learn from history that we do not learn any thing from history." Aldous Huxley (1894-1963) encourages efforts to find hidden and ignored facts: "Facts do not cease to exist because they are ignored."

Herbert J. Muller (p.28) tells that Herbert Butterfield, himself a historian, feels that the national history taught in schools has encouraged the most general and terrifying of existing evils, faulty presumptions and intellectual arrogance. He concludes:"While we have great need of history, our first need is to *unlearn* most of what has been taught. A superficial, confused and distorted notion of history is far more dangerous than ignorance of it."

Adam Hochschild (NY Times, July 24, 2005), reviewing the book *"Dancing with Strangers: Europeans and Australians at First Contact,"* by historian Inga Clendenin, that she feels that because of their 'Divide and rule' tactics, the British colonizers did not meet heroic resistance in much of Africa, India and Latin America. They succeeded because they could make indigenous groups fight among one another, not against the strangers. History is not written by those who have lived the history, but by the victors: "History is always written by the victors and history remains a messy and complicated business."

… Yet history remains a messy and complicated business."

History, India made abroad, yet to be written

Nehru, in *'Discovery of India'* (1946, p. 200), while talking about 'Indian colonies and culture in South-East Asia,' expresses his disappointment that people don't know the great history, India made overseas:

"One has not only to go back in time but to travel, in mind if not in body, to various countries in Asia,

---

4   Ibid, p. 28.
5   Samuel Langhorne Clemens, better known by his pen name Mark Twain, was an American author and humorist.

where India spread out in many ways, leaving immortal testimony of her spirit, her power, and her love of beauty. How few of us know of these great achievements of our past, how few realize that if India was great in thought and philosophy, she was equally great in action? The history that men and women from India made far from their homeland has still to be written."

Amazing! What a keen insight Nehru had into India's spirit, power and love for the beauty in her diversity. He mourns our ignorance of India's great achievements and no appreciation of her great (Hindu) thought and philosophy. It is because her history is dominated by Europe. The history of ancient India has been given little attention and scant space to leave the pages for the history of Europe and Mediterranean countries closer to Europe than to India. Such histories also prefer to write about the history of Judeo-Christianity to the history about Vedas, Vedic philosophy and Hinduism. Whatever is written about India is distorted to suit their colonial agenda.

Nehru (p.20) writes: "The history, that men and women from India made far from their homeland, has still to be written. Most westerners still imagine that ancient history is largely concerned with the Mediterranean countries, and medieval and modern history is dominated by the quarrelsome little Europe. And still they make plans for the future as if Europe only counted and the rest could be fitted in anywhere."

Nehru (p.200) cites Sir Charles Eliot[6] who has complained about the injustice European historians have done to the history of ancient India:

"Scant justice is done to India's position in the world by those European histories which recount the exploits of her invaders and leave impression that her own people were feeble dreamy folk, sundered from the rest of mankind by their seas and mountain frontiers. Such a

---

[6] Eliot: 'Hinduism and Buddhism' (vol. 1, p. xii).

picture takes no account of the intellectual conquests of the Hindus."

Nehru (p. 201) appreciates that recently lot of light is being thrown on the history of South-East Asia (some times referred to as "Greater India"), but with lot of gaps and contradictions:

> "During the past quarter of a century a great deal of light has been thrown on the history of this widespread area in south-east Asia, which is some times referred to as Greater India. There are still many gaps and many contradictions. Scholars continue to put forward their rival theories, but the general outline is clear enough, and some times there is an abundance of detail. There is no lack of material, for there are references in Indian books, and accounts of Arab travelers and, most important of all, Chinese historical accounts. There are also many old inscriptions, copper-plates, etc., and in Java and Bali there is a rich literature based on Indian[7] sources, and often paraphrasing Indian epics and myths. Greek and Latin sources have also supplied some information. But, above all, there are the magnificent ruins of ancient monuments, especially at Angkor and Borobundur."[8]

One finds in history all of this – prejudice, conceit, false memories, exaggerations, absurdities, misrepresentations, arrogance, vanity – particularly in the case of the history of ancient India in regard to:

- origin of Aryans and their relationship with Dravidians,
- the identity of the original natives of India,
- the age and authorship of the Vedas,
- antiquity and originality of Sanskrit,

---

[7] Better to be specific – 'Hindu' instead of 'Indian', because the words 'India and Indian' came in currency only about two centuries back.

[8] Dr. R.C. Majumdar's 'Ancient Indian Colonies in the Far East' (Calcutta, 1927).

- antiquity and the origin of the Swastika,
- relationship between Sanskrit and Dravidian languages,
- the ages of the epics – the Mahabharata and the Ramayana,
- change of the name of the country, from Ârya-āvarta to India, and change of the names of the cities, rivers, mountains, etc.

Colonial historians have been successful to some extent in infusing ethnic inferiority complex in the minds and hearts of Indians, particularly Hindus, and crafting confusion around their identity. History has been confusing the originalities of Aryans, Sanskrit, Vedas, Hinduism and Swastika, telling that fair skin Aryans are outsiders who invaded India their own abode Ârya-āvarta in about 1500 B.C. and brought with them Sanskrit, Caucasian genes, a pantheon of gods, Swastika and composed Vedas. All such confusion has been produced by the two ill-based intermingled theories – 'Aryan invasion of India' and 'Indo-European family of languages'. The critique of both theories is discussed later. The British East India Company (BEIC), the colonial agency, created in London, thought that it was needed to weaken the great nation of Aryavarta (India, Bharat). It employed all possible means to distort India's history and misrepresent her great civilization, Europeans envied.

Europeans have been perceiving or searching their heritage in Aryans, as evidenced by the title of Will Durant's book: *"Our Oriental Heritage"* (1935). William James Durant (1885-1981) was an American writer, historian, and philosopher. He is best known for "The Story of Civilization", 11 volumes written in collaboration with his wife Ariel and published some time between 1935 and 1975. Pictures of Buddha and one Egyptian god decorate its cover.

Durant remarks that for an Occidental mind it is difficult to understand the Orient, particularly India and her philosophy. It took him eight years of study and travel to grasp the Oriental philosophy and culture. He (p. ix) remarks: "The metaphysical Hindu will mourn this superficial scratching of Indian philosophy."

Durant, in preface (p. viii) writes:

"Our story begins with the Orient, not merely because Asia was the scene of the oldest civilizations known to us, but because those civilizations formed the background and basis of that Greek and Roman culture which Sir Henry Maine mistakenly supposed to be the whole source of the modern mind."

Sir Henry James Summer Maine (1822-1888) was a British comparative jurist and historian. He spent some of his early years in India. According to some Europeans Aryans are jewels of European culture. It will be minutely discussed later.

It seems colonialists got the wisdom of the strategy how to stay longer in colonized countries from some seasoned politician:

"If you want to weaken a nation, confuse its identity, distort its heritage, belittle its achievements, highlight its failures, divide it into as many fragments as possible, tarnish its ancient scriptures, and rewrite its history according to your colonial agenda."

The British East India Company (BEIC) did all this. Colonial historians have tried their best to tarnish and distort the heritage of Hindus and distanced them from their glorious past. It is advisable that people have deeper sense of their **Past,** wrongs and rights of which can be an effective guiding torch for successful **Present,** paving path to desirable **Future.** Man, disconnected from his roots, will feel shaky without the mind and heart of his past. Hence, the texts of colonial histories have excluded Vedas, Ramayana, Mahabharata and Bhagvad Gita to deprive Hindus of their knowledge to guide them and the nation. Fortunately for Hindus they got little success because Vedas and other sacred scriptures have been disseminating the truth through the age-old Hindu oral traditions.

Uncontaminated history is essential for the health and strength of the nation. Unfortunately, most of the colonially contaminated histories, authored by copycat professors are being taught in schools and colleges as text books because of their ill-based professional clout. Such books have generous shelf space in book stores and libraries. Colonial history books, like contaminated drugs, should be outlawed and should be burnt. They should be replaced by well-researched objective true history books. History, the life line of the nation, should be corrected.

Falsification of history, even in 21st century!

After India's independence, the barometer of her national morale has been shooting up and up. Alarm against falsification of recent 20th century history has been loud when the events are supposed to be instantly documented, leaving little scope of any kind for the facts getting falsified. Yet, pen is gifted with amazing art of manipulation by misinterpreting and distorting what has come out of some one's mouth or pen. One should learn this from Russia. The case in point is: *"Russia: Kremlin Demands New History Lessons"* (NY Times, May, 20, 2009). It says:

> "The Kremlin is starting an official drive to try to reverse what it sees as an anti-Russian view of 20th-century history. President Dmitri A. Medvedev[9] issued a decree on Tuesday ordering "creation of a presidential commission to counter attempts to harm Russian interests by falsifying history."

Whereas, Oleg Orlov, a human rights advocate in Moscow, said the commission was an attempt "to halt any objective view of what really happened in Russia's past." Can you believe open proud war against truths in 20th century? Then, what would happen to history?

I am not here to say who is right and who is wrong. I am trying to underline that falsification of historical facts is possible even in 21st century when it is supported by power. Falsification of facts is unethical. It will live as long as historians lacking professional integrity thrive. Unfortunately, unprofessional mind seems to be immortal, so its pen too, perhaps because unethical historians are not interested in talking

---

[9]   The Russian name 'Medvedev', ending in 'dev' suggests some ancient Russia-India ancient relationship.

truths, fearing they may challenge alleged colonial facts given by them in their books which have been popular at universities.

I met one celebrated university professor of history in his office to understand contradictions in his book. The meeting was arranged by my friend Mr. Inder Singh who knew him as a friend. I brought out a few contradictions in his book, arising out of his misperceptions, related to origins of Aryans, Sanskrit, pantheon of Hindu gods and Vedas. He believed in the theory 'Aryan invasion of India' according to which Aryans invaded India in about 1500 B.C. and they brought with them Sanskrit, a pantheon of Hindu gods, Caucasian genes and composed Vedas later after about 500 years stay in India. On other page he writes about the peace treaty between two Aryan kings of a kingdom at Boghaz-koi in which Hindu gods – Indra, Varuna, Mitra and the Naksatras – were invoked as witnesses. I raised the question "Does it not suggest that both the Indo-Aryans kings were originally Hindu, and later, when in trouble, some of them might have been absorbed there, and some might have attempted to come back to India, their original abode. They, being from Royal families, might have been traveling in armed horse-driven chariots. Thus, they might have been mistaken as invaders and their return to India was mischievously theorized as invasion of India. To support my thesis that those Aryans were Indo-Aryans, present Hindus, I cited Max Müller who also on some page endorses Aryan invasion and on some other page – in 'The Science of Language" (vol. 1, 1891, p. 291), says that India was originally known as *Ârya-ârta*, meaning the land of Aryans. I also pointed that *'Dasa'* has been mistranslated by him as slave. In Hindi / Sanskrit, *Dasa* means *sevak* (Servant), not slave who is bought and sold. I asserted that Hindus have never practiced slavery. It was a proud tradition of Europeans and Americans. He got very angry. I left his office, saying: "Very sorry." His book, being a text book, is read by several students. It is full of misperceptions, misinterpretations, mistranslations, biases and ignorance. I got reminded what Gene D. Matlock[10] has said:

> "The person who claims to know every thing, or a lot, is more unforgivably ignorant and stupid than he

---

[10]   Gene D. Matlock 'India Once Ruled the Americas' (2000, pp.170-171)

who honestly admits that he knows nothing yet as he should know. But there is one type of human being even more disgustingly ignorant than the one who lets his knowledge "go to his head:" *he who doesn't want to know."*

It is shocking to know the presence of *'Kill the Truth Movement,'* as talked about by Matlock.[11] He feels confident that it will be defeated by his expanded linguistic evidence, he has been working on. Sorry to be pessimistic. In my opinion, Matlock's mission, though sacred, will not succeed completely. War against history (truths) is like breaking head against a stone, because man, socio-economically and ethnically rival, will find difficult to be an objective historian. Thus, most histories are not 100% correct.

Distorted history hurts the education, the nation and the morale of its readers. Objectivity (Truth) has been in trouble from its immemorial long past, only because man has been in trouble with self. TURTH (History has been increasingly getting in more trouble by declining professional ethics. Students of history feel disappointed and unhappy with the diminishing returns of the professional integrity. In most cases, misuse of the power by the ruling government, guided by its political concerns, is responsible. If truth is truth, why then, in most cases, the judgment is not unanimous. Almost all governments have two departments, politically opposing each other in almost all cases and rarely in agreement.

After independence, India's national will is required to get the corrupted history professionally reconstructed by rigorous research to find unbiased objective truths about our History, the mirror of the personality of the nation, should always be kept clean and untarnished for healthy morale of its people. History should always be kept out-of-reach of the criminal-like self-centered, unethical, greedy politicians. It is hard to understand why all the post-independence governments – from Nehru's (1947-1964) to present Modi's – have been enjoying *Kumbhakaran* long slumber, insensitive to the national need of reconstructed true history for youngsters, fathers of the future. Even

---

[11]   Ibid, p.49.

19

a minute should not be lost in getting the history of ancient Bhārat corrected and the books containing wrong history, like contaminated foods and drugs, be immediately outlawed. Colonial history is poison and harmful to the national ego, morale and ethos. History of Bhārat has been colonially falsified to tarnish Bharat's international image and her great civilization. History has lot of lessons to learn from. Even the mistakes of the past have great guiding lessons.

Name of country has lot of its ancient history

The colonialists have changed the name of the country from 'Bhārat' to India, and the name of her people from 'Bhāratvasi' to 'Indian' only to disconnect Bhāratvasies from their great heritage. History of a country can not be meaningfully expressive of her identity and of her past if its name is changed. The future is to be created on the basis of the past. The past (History) gives lot of lessons to guide the present to fruitful future. Yesterday, today and tomorrow may be different, but are inseparable: **Past → Present → Future.** The future will be disastrous, if based on confused past and shaky present.

   Colonialists knew that as the name tells the true story of the family, the name of the country has lot of history. If you want to weaken a nation, change its name to disconnect its people from their heritage. Colonialist rulers chose the name 'India' so that its Indians, be compared with the Native American Indians, most peoples would hate to be associated with. My both US-born daughters – Shilpa (born in August, 1974), and Neha (June 1976) – complained that they were ridiculed in their New York primary school by their American classmates by vocal and physical gestures, as of the native American Indians. Whenever I read any article in 'The New York Times' or in any other news paper or magazine with title 'Indians,' I have to read a few sentences to figure out if it is talking about Indians of India or about the native American Indians. Name of a country should not be confusing. No proper name should be changed or translated. In English papers in India, it is India, but in Hindi or in any vernacular paper, it is Bhārat or Hindustan.

Why still love for disgreatful name India?

It is shame that the name of the great country Bhārat – with a millennia-long history of enviable culture, most ancient literature (Vedas), with knowledge of various disciplines and the language (Sanskrit) with dynamic grammar – has been changed to India whose people 'Indians' are identified with the most degraded 'American Native Indians' who have been outlawed from their own land. It is hard to undertant, why the renowned educated leaders of independent Bhārat including her prime ministers are still charmed by such shameful name India for their great nation Bhārat.

Original name: Window to identity and heritage

The name, especially of a nation, speaks immeasurably of its history and culture. It defines the identity of its original people and the antiquity of their being. Because of loss of power, confounded by indifference of her people to her own history, may be due to colonial mentality still alive, Bhārat has been having a long **'awakened-slumber'** over the issue of restoration of her traditional name. Ceylon, immediately after her independence, did regain her traditional name Sri Lanka. So did Burma regain Myanmar, and so several other colonized countries might have celebrated their freedom by being reborn. But India is still waiting for her sons and daughters to wake up to help her to regain her traditional name.

Independence can not be complete without gaining back whatever was lost, robbed or buried by the colonial rulers. Independence can not be celebrated without correcting the history by removing all the wrongs have been recorded in. The traditional name of the country, being the most important treasure, should be restored. Who will not rebel if he is forced to change his name? Traditional name (Bhārat) speaks lot of her history. The foreign-given name "India" corrupts her history and cuts it short.

Traditional or original name of the country opens up various chapters of her ancient history, and lets her children have a deep peep into their remote heritage. Ancient history of the country, thus evoked by its original name, will alert historians – colonial as well as confused native – to check the truths related to the thoughts and events they are writing about, and not to do any mischief with history. For example, the antiquity of the name 'Aryavarta' would have told every body around the globe that the theory, 'Aryan invasion of India' is illogical, ill-based and mischievous. Why would Aryans invade their birth land **Aryavarta**? They could enjoy lullaby in her cradle, sung by Bhārat Mātā.

The name "India" doesn't tell full and true story of Bhārat

Would the politicians, who oppose or remain silent over the restoration of the original name Bhārat, tell what true history, the name 'India' is giving? The name 'India' is cutting short the history of India, to only a few centuries. That history is full of shame and disgrace. It omits, ignores or buries the facts, described in Ramayana, Mahabharata, Bhagvad Gita and other sacred scriptures, by labeling them as mythology. They are not myths. They are being devotionally sung. They glorify Bhārat's image. Name 'Bhārat' or 'Aryavarta' would open up numerous pages in her millennia-long ancient history connecting youngsters to their proud heritage. Rarely one would find a history book with Ramayana, Mahabharata and Bhagvad Gita in its contents. It reflects ignorance and narrow vision of most historians.

Bhārat, as the original name of India, is given in her Constitution. It has remained as merely a paper name. Only a few neighboring countries – Pakistan, Nepal, Bhutan, Bangladesh, Sri Lanka, and a few more at the United Nations – know about her name as Bhārat. If I tell any American that I am from Bhārat, the response would be"What?" The government of Bhārat, itself, has been promoting its foreign-given name India, by naming its internationally related agencies, such as 'Government of India', 'Air India', 'State Bank of India', 'Embassy of India', etc. It is hard to understand why independent Bhārat still loves her foreign given name India.

The name – of a country, a street, a school, a university, a library, a river or a mountain – evokes nationalism and gives desirable historical message, as explained by Sophia Kishkovsky's article *"Honor a Literary Giant, But Be Careful Where"* (NY Times, September 26, 2008, p. A10).

It is suggesting changing the name of the street "Bolshaya Kommunistic-heskaya Ulitsa" or "Big Communist Street" (Ulitsa means street) be changed to "Ulitsa Solzhenitsyna, or Solzhenitsyna Street, in honor of Mr. Aleksandr Solzhenitsyna for his extra-ordinary contribution to Russian culture. The article writes: "In death as in life, Aleksandr Solzhenitsyna remains a difficult, polarizing figure for Russia, a fierce critic not only of communism but also of the decadence and materialism of post-Soviet Russia." Changed names of rivers, cities, streets, etc confuse the originality of the natives of Bhārat. Shocking! The name of the country is changed from Bhārat to India and its leaders are least concerned about it. The natives of Bhārat are called Indians, the most disgusting name on the planet. Who will like to be known as Indian, a member of the most uncivilized natives of ancient America? Shockingly surprising that leaders of the independent Bhārat feel proud of being known as Indian and name so most national agencies, like Air India, Indian Embassy, etc.

Name of a country expresses its heritage

Colonial governments, in order to completely erase or confuse the history of the heritage of the colonized people, changed names of their colonized countries and the names of their mountains, rivers, lakes, etc which may remind the natives of their culture. Ganga has been changed to Ganges, Sindhu to Indus, *Lake Mansarover* to *Lake Mapam Yutso,* Gandhar to Kandahar, Pryaag to Allahabad, Karnnavati to Ahmadabad, etc. Pakistan changed the name of 'Ram Baug' in Karachi to 'Araam Baug'. Ram Baug would have opened the window to the *Ramayana.* I remember my childhood playful times in Ram Baug, very close to my uncle's home, when we were in Sindh before it became Pakistan.

Max Müller, in his book, *India: What can it teach us?* has written that the ancient names of the rivers of the Vedic Bhārat have been changed. Historians, in most cases, have not given in parenthesis, their original name. Thus history, particularly of ancient Bhārat, has been obscured and confused. This has been more adversely affected because of the attitude of indifference or helplessness on the part of Hindu historians towards history. Lieut. Col. F. Wilford – in the section '*On the Ancient Geography of India*' (Asiatic Researches, vol. xiv, pp.374-376) of the Asiatic Society of Bengal's research series, led by Sir William Jones (1746-1794) – says that some *Puranas* have information about the names of some mansions, geographical tracts, mountains, rivers, etc, but without any explanation about them. Wilford also described his difficulties and frustration in collecting relevant data, mainly because of lack of adequate cooperation from *Pandits* and Hindu historians. Sir William Jones was born in UK and died in Calcutta.

If Wilford had received full cooperation and if historians, over the years, referred to the ancient names of the rivers and towns in addition to their respective modern names, we would have been able to get clear picture of the history and geography of the ancient Bhārat's geographical spread. The history of ancient Bhārat, thus, has been erroneous and obscured. It has been infected with several misrepresentations and gaps. The question is: "What was the colonial intention behind changing the names of the places of cultural significance? Would Britain allow any body to change names of its cities, rivers, mountains, etc.?

A book, entitled as '*Five Thousand Years of Pakistan,*' was published in 1950 when Pakistan was only three years old, and Islam about 1500 years. Most of the pages of the book talk about Muslim dynasties, tombs, forts, Masjids, etc. Pakistan is shrewd. It got it authored by R. E. M. Wheeler, Archeological Advisor to the Government of Pakistan, and sometimes Director General of Archeology in India. It got it published by the Royal India and *Pakistan Society, London.* But inside, it clearly shows its ethno-political agenda. In the Preface, Fazlur Rahman, the Minister of Commerce and Education, Govt. of Pakistan writes:

> "It (the book) includes one of the great civilizations of Asia – the Indus Civilization of the third and second millennia B.C.; it shares with the borderland of Afghanistan the primarily glory of that remarkable and individual Buddhist art which flowered there in and after the second century A.D."

There is no mention of Hindu art or literature, but lot on art, exhibited by Masjids and Moghul fortresses. Rahman mentions Pakistan's border only with Afghanistan, but not with Hindustan. By the way, the Indus Valley civilization is 4500 years old or even much older. Rahman further writes in the Preface:

> "Its achievements after the arrival of Islam, extended from the tiled mosques of Tatta to the Moghul fortress of Lahore and the *Chhota Sona Masjid of Gaur*, are more vividly familiar. The story of these things is worth telling, in every school and university of the land. The heritage of Pakistan must be kept alive if the future is to grow strongly and healthily out of it. It will be no good to tie new leaves on to dead tree."

For Rahman, the Hindu (Vedic) heritage of the Indus Valley civilization is the dead tree. Then, why should the Indus Valley civilization is considered the heritage of Pakistan? But, it becomes necessary to explain the way the conquerors or the new occupiers highlight their culture by erasing the culture of the conquered. In a way, Pakistanis may be right to claim their heritage connected with the Indus Valley civilization, because most of them are converts. They should be commended for their patriotism. Pakistan has been doing lot of writing about the glory of the Indus Valley civilization – Mohenjodaro and Harappa – to present it as the heritage of Pakistanis.

History has been unfair to her sister 'Archaeology'

V. Gordon Childe, in *'What Happened in History'* (1942, p.12, section, *'Archaeology and History'*), has expressed that history has been unprofessional for being ungrateful to archaeology for the facts received from it. Unfortunately, several significant facts have been ignored, misrepresented and/or misperceived by several celebrated colonial historians, may be because of Europe's ethnic rivalry with the East (particulary Bhārat). West's tinted professional integrity or its scholarly fatigue to catch up with the fast-surfacing hidden facts glorifying ancient

Bhārat, being brought out by archaeological spades and professional dives into waters surrounding India. It is difficult to understand why historians have been tarnishing the image of their only child history.

Prof. Grahame Clark, in the Foreword to Prof. V. Gordon Childe's book *'What Happened in History: The Classic Study Which Opened up New Perspectives in History'* (1941), praises Childe for his appropriate use of archaeology and natural science:

> "More perhaps than any other man, he (Childe) showed how by using the data won by archaeologists and natural scientists it was possible to gain a new view of what constituted human history."

But, unfortunately, several historians have not adequately and appropriately availed themselves of the opportunity provided by the archaeology. Clark expresses Childe's concern about omissions and inadequate coverage of the important events, such as civilizations in the Far East, Sumer, Egypt, and Indus (Sindhu) Valley and about the gaps and contradictions in history:

> "The scope even of a work as comprehensive as *'What Happened in History'* is bound up with and limited by this concern: the New World, like Australasia, is omitted and only glancing references are made to the great focus of civilization in the Far East."

Clark also has expressed concern about historical contradictions the ancient urban civilizations were subjected to: "But the urban civilizations of Egypt, Sumer, and the Indus Valley were no more immune from the effects of inborn contradictions than the Neolithic peasantries had been."

Ignorance of the Indus Civilization has been a dark hole in the history of India. Archaeology opened windows to the Indus Valley civilization and other civilizations, hidden under the earth. The historian Graham Hancock, in *'Underworld: The Mysterious Origins of Civilization'* (2002, p.116), remarks:

"Almost every thing that was ever written about this (Indus) civilization before five years ago is wrong. Spades have brought out significant historical truths."

Hancock concludes that during most of the twentieth century, the archaeological record refused, rather ignored, to reveal evidence of the Indus Valley civilization's long period of development. This created a vacuum, a dark hole in history, European scholars took advantage of. Hancock remarks: "European scholars felt free to conclude that the Indus Valley civilization might, in its origin, have been alien to India."

Indus (Sindhu) Valley is an integral part of India. We know that the socio-cultural and religious landscape in the Indus Valley was very much similar, if not identical, to that in the rest of Bhārat.

Hancock (2002, p.169) explains how the culture of the ancient India has been misinterpreted and minimized, only based on the archaeological finds, not based on the civilization's own ancient texts, like Vedas, Ramayana, Mahabharata, Bhagvad Gita and other ancient Vedic literature:

"The Indus-Sarasvati civilization was a literate culture, but the archaeological interpretation of it has been strictly limited to excavated material remains and has never been able to draw upon the civilization's own texts. This is because all attempts to decipher the enigmatic 'Harappan' script have failed, and because (at least until very recently) the Sanskrit Vedas were regarded as the work of another, later culture and were assumed to have had nothing to do with the Indus-Sarasvati civilization. Well into the twentieth century, this approach simply meant that there was no Indus-Sarasvati civilization. It was not part of the archaeological picture of India's past and was never even contemplated. It was, in other words, as 'lost as Plato's Atlantis' until the material evidence that proved its existence began to surface when excavations were started at Harappa and Mohenjo-daro in 1920s."

Even now, for some or even larger section of the world society – the Eastern (particularly Indian) as well as the Western – the Indus Valley civilization has remained lost as Plato's Atlantis.

Unfortunately, when Sir William Jones first spoke of the early literature of India, it seems he had absolutely no idea of the antiquities of Hindu civilization, its Sanskrit and Vedas. If he had, he would have not written what would challenge his theory of *Indo-European family of languages*. Colin Renfrew, in *'Archaeology & Language: The Puzzle of Indo-European Origins'* (1987, p.183), remarks that historians had no knowledge about ancient India, prior to Ashoka's kingdom (3rd century B.C.):

> "For many years, the material record did not go back much before the time of King Ashoka in the third century BC, and the brief accounts of north India left by the commentators upon Alexander the Great's travels and conquests in the previous century. It was not till the year 1921 that Sir John Marshal[12] (with R.D. Banerji) made his great discovery of the Indus Valley civilization, with the investigation of two of its great cities at Mohenjodaro and Harappa. ... The civilization was already flourishing shortly after 3000 BC, but had gone into irreversible and rather rapid decline by 1800 BC. This was a literate civilization."

Historians knew about the grandeur of the Indus Valley (Sindhu Valley) civilization, before its few cities Mohen-jo-daro, Harappa, etc were archeologically unearthed in 20s of the 20th century, and some other later. It doesn't mean that only those cities were civilized, not the rest. How can times forgive historians, particularly of civilized societies, abusing their professional integrity? It is shame, that historians have been taking pride in their skillful maneuvers to hide, misinterpret, misrepresent, and distort the facts, hard-discovered by archaeology and ocean diving to fill-in the gaps and holes in the history. They will help

---

[12]   Marshal Sir John, "First Light on a long forgotten civilization, Illustrated London News, 1924.

in reconstructing the distorted history. Historians have been knowingly ignoring human life found under earth and oceans. For example, several post-Indus-excavation historians have been knowingly ignoring what the seals bearing the *Swastika* and the *Shiva Linga* have been telling about the origin of Swastika, Sanskrit, Vedas, and the Vedic religion (Hinduism). Sanskrit, Vedas, and Swastika have relationship with one another. Sanskrit is the language of the Vedas and Swastika is a Sanskrit word. Hence, it can be safely theorized that all the three – Sanskrit, Vedas and Swastika – are quadruplets, born to Mother Nature, the daughter of God. Their dates of birth are too ancient to know, as that of God.

Whatever was written by Sir William Jones and some other early historians out of their ignorance of such great civilization is being used as the basis of the history of the ancient Bhārat. It seems historians, in general, excepting a few, don't seem to realize that it is their professional responsibility to continue to keep themselves abreast of the fresh historical information given by archeology and by finds below oceans, so as to fill in the gaps and holes to correct what was written wrong. Scholars can/should not be forgiven for the ignorance of the facts, they are supposed to know. In light of the Indus Valley archaeological excavations, required corrections should have been made to keep the history fresh and clean. Scholarly ignorance, particularly knowingly, is a sin for keeping students and teachers in dark.

One, who doesn't admit his mistakes, is not a scholar

It needs scholarly modesty and courage to admit one's own shortcomings and mistakes, and then gracefully move further to correct them, whenever discovered. The NY Times (June 20, 2002) published Donald Foster's statement, as the'QUOTATION OF THE DAY':

> "No one, who cannot rejoice in the discovery of his own mistakes, deserves to be called a scholar, admitting that his work to establish Shakespeare as the author of an obscure poem was wrong."

This is the message to the post-Indus-Valley-excavations historians that they should correct whatever wrong has been written, though in ignorance of the facts which were brought out later by the finds, excavated at the Indus Valley cities, Mohenjodaro and Harappa.

Hindu Apathy to History

The Indian, rather Hindu apathy to history is historically talked about, and more so, on the part of the post-independence governments of India, seemingly because of their political concerns. Historically, Hindus were not apathetic to history. Lot of history has been given in the Vedic scriptures and epics. But colonial historians did not accept it as history, but mythology. The enslaved Hindu scholars have been helplessly timid and voiceless against powerful colonial pen.

Fortunately, some post-colonial scholars, particularly European, complain about the harm has been done to the history of ancient India. Stephen Knapp[13] writes what the Britain has done to demean the Vedic culture:

"As we have now investigated the rest of the world for remnants of the global Vedic culture, we must also focus our attention on India where it still thrives. However, now we will uncover some of India's real history. This will help us understand how much of its glory, beauty, art, music, architecture, and sciences have been falsely attributed to outsiders and foreigners. India has not been given credit where credit is due. India's skills in science, administration, art, architecture, and of course, spiritual under-standing were once the highest in the world. ... Furthermore, much of its real history has been pushed aside, distorted, perverted, and based on misinformation. ... The English attempted to divide and conquer India, to ruin the Vedic Aryan civilization, and to demean Indian culture, even to the point of

---

[13] Stephen Knapp in 'Proof of Vedic Culture's Global Existence' (2000, p.268)

30

trying to make its own person hate everything that is Indian."

Since her independence in 1947, India has been getting up – slowly but surely – from her long *Kumbhakaran*[14] slumber to show to the world her innate caliber, scientific and technological. The independent India has been digging deep to unearth the buried history of the wealth of her knowledge of science, technology, cosmos, astronomy, space, etc., which was pushed down deep by the powers had colonized her for over a millennium. India has been looking increasingly more powerful, knowledgeable, self-composed and beautiful, and has been soaring up to touch the sky. Colonialism, ironically by today's civilized peoples, has been the worst enemy of the humanity. India had in her prehistory ancient times colonized some peoples to enrich their cultures; not to impoverish and tarnish them as European colonialists and imperialists have done to Asian and African peoples and their cultures.

Dr. S. Venu Gopalacharya,[15] in his book *'Worldwide Hindu Culture'* (pp.165-6), writes:

"On July 3, 1835, Lord Macaulay suggested that the only statesmanship of the Britishers to establish permanent imperialist sovereignty over their richest colony, India, was to make the Indians "Englishmen by Taste." This was to be accomplished through "English Education," similar to bringing under control hundreds of elephants by taming a couple of wild elephants. By 1854 when the whole of India came under British rule, Charles Woodraffe, the Director of the Education Department of the Government of India, in his minutes dated July19, 1854, stated that it was the best opportunity to give effect to Lord Macaulay's suggestion."

That "Englishmen by Taste" effect is very much there even now sixty six years after India's independence, particularly in the metropolis

---

[14] Kumbhakaran used to sleep months. He was brother of Ravana, the Raja of Sri Lanka.

[15] Taken from Stephen Knapp, Proof of Vedic Culture's Global Existence (2000, p.268)

upper educated echelon. Because of their English fluency, they think themselves superior, meaning modern *Pundits*. English-medium schools are mushrooming and they are preferred to regular schools. Increasing number of families, particularly in cities, is encouraging their youngsters to speak English at home and among friends. It seems okay because English language has better employment prospects in India as well as overseas. But, they should be taught to think and feel as Indian, and not to create another type of caste system, hating English-illiterates as *achhoots* (untouchables), and demoralizing every thing which is traditionally Indian.

Stephen Knapp[16] writes:

> "We have to realize that there was a comprehensive strategy to overlook, cover, and falsify the real history of India. Not only did the invading Muslims try to do this over the centuries, but the British, while in India, also played a heavy hand in this."

To prove this, Knapp mentions what Major Gen. Cunningham[17] had suggested to the British East India Company to falsify India-related archaeology:

> "Major General Cunningham, a retired army engineer, was appointed in 1861 as the first archeological surveyor under the British administration in India, not because he had special knowledge but because as early as September 15, 1842 when he was a mere Lt. A.D.C. to the Governor General Lord Auckland, Cunningham had suggested in a letter to Col. Sykes (a director of the British East India Company) a scheme for falsifying Indian archeology as an 'undertaking of vast importance to the Indian Government politically and to the British public religiously (so that) the establishment of the

16   Stephen Knapp, Proof of Vedic Culture's Global Existence (2000, p. 271).
17   N. Oak in Some Missing Chapters of World History, in his book World Vedic Heritage, (p.16), Pune (India).

Christian religion in India must ultimately succeed.'
In pursuance of that political objective Cunningham
attributed a very large number of Hindu townships and
buildings to Muslim authorship."

Knapp (p.271) further writes that Max Müller also expressed
the same sentiment in a letter to the Duke of Argyll, who was then
the Secretary of State for India: "India has been conquered once, but
India must be conquered again and the second conquest should be by
education."

Fortunately for Hindus, but unfortunately for the BEIC, Hindus
used to get real education about their culture, religion and history
through their millennia-old oral traditions, which could not be polluted,
corrupted or hidden, neither by pen, nor by the formal education.

The BEIC's end objective was "to subvert Hinduism and whatever
was left of Vedic culture." It did not succeed. This was to be achieved
through education. But the British Government of India did not promote
education. On the contrary, the BEIC economically exploited India and
created utter poverty. Most Indians could not buy education, and thus
it increased illiteracy. Their strategy – outsourcing goods manufactured
in England, which were made out of the raw material imported from
India at bottom low prices, and exporting the finished products back
to India at much higher prices – backfired against their plan to make
Hindustan a Christian country through education. The mass illiteracy –
thus produced by utter poverty, created by British uncivilized colonial
exploitation – prevented them from reading ungodly things, taught in
schools and colleges. Definitely yes, the mini minority of the educated
elite echelon got misguided and brainwashed. Ironically they remained
illiterate of their own culture, thus aloof from the mainstream. On the
other side, the wide majority of English-illiterates remained immune
to the colonial anti-cultural virus, and thus became paradoxically more
educated about own culture and religion, and also about the science
and art of Hindu living through their oral traditions. The BEIC was
disappointed by Britain greed, thus fed by its uncivilized economic
exploitation.

Mention of melting of the late Pleistocene Himalayan glaciers in the *Rig Veda* evidences that Vedas were composed at least 10,000 years back when the Himalayas melted into seven mighty rivers (*Sapta Sindhu*). So it tells the age of Sanskrit, the language of Vedas.

All this challenges the validity of the two intermingled theories – (i) Aryan invasion of India (AII) and (ii) Indo-European Family of Languages (IE). The theories were mischievously created in Britain to distort the history of Bhārat (Aryavarta, present India) and confuse the identity and history of Aryans, India, Vedas, Sanskrit and Swastika.

Unfortunately, even now in present times, most history books are being written by copycat historians. Several renowned history professors are teaching what colonial missionary historians had written that Hindus are not the original Aryans; and that the Dravidian are the original natives, and so Dravidian are the native languages of India, not Sanskrit.

Lot of history has been hidden, ignored and corrupted. Aldous Huxley (1894-1963) remaks: "Facts do not cease to exist because they are ignored"

Several historians, like – Aldous Huxley (1894-1963), Jawaharlal Nehru (1889-1964), Dr. K.M. Munshi (1887-1971), Michael A. Cremo (1948-), Richard L Thompson (1947-) – and several others, have shocked the world about the colonially corrupted history. It has inspired me to try to find the ignored and hidden history of ancient Bhārat as much as possible.

History is misperceived as only the stories of kings, wars and changing maps. Such histories of India, as written, tell little about the people, their thinking and their aspirations, to learn lessons from to make a road map for better life of their future generations. Such histories with names of kings and dates of wars and of other events have little utility. Moreover, most historians seem to have been knowingly reluctant to cross the AD-BC border and tell selected little about pre-history ancient Bharat, and hesitant to address the literary, cultural, philosophical and heroic jewels to feel proud of.

History should talk about the people, their thoughts, values, aspirations and imaginations, building continuous bridges connecting generations, one after the other. History should be the stories of its people, its culture, its traditions from pre-history ancient times, its education system, its languages, and about the dynamics of various events and factors impacting culture, education and relationships, within and without. History should keep pace with the changing life and its ups and downs, not like the present history which talks only about the rulers and wars. Such histories have become unpleasant burden on the classroom of growing young brains.

History should be written by those whose life is touched by the events described in the history. How much truth can one expect from the stories written by the victors? History has been dominated by Europeans. During their global colonization they distorted ancient histories of Asia and Africa to suit their colonial agenda. The first print, particularly backed by the colonial might, has been too dark to erase.

Nehru[18] remarks:

"The history that men and women from India made far from their homeland has still to be written. Most westerners still imagine that ancient history is largely concerned with the Mediterranean countries, and medieval and modern history is dominated by the quarrelsome little Europe. And still they make plans for the future as if Europe only counted and the rest could be fitted in anywhere."

Nehru (same page 200) cites Sir Charles Eliot[19] who has praised Hindus for their intellectual and political conquests, colonization of several territories, etc.:

'Scant justice is done to India's position in the world by those European histories which recount the exploits of her invaders and leave the impression that her own people were a feeble dreamy folk, sundered from the rest of mankind by their seas and mountain frontiers. Such a picture takes no account of the intellectual conquests

---

18   Nehru, in Discovery of India, 1946, p.200.
19   Elliot, 'Hinduism and Buddhism', vol. 1, p. xii.

of the Hindus. Even their political conquests were not contemptible, and are remarkable for the distance, if not the extent, of the territories occupied. ... But such military or commercial are insignificant compared with the spread of Indian thought."

Dr. K. M. Munshi, in the foreword to 'The History and the Culture of the Indian People' (1951, pp.8, 9), remarks: "The central purpose of a history must, therefore, be to investigate and unfold the values which, age after age have inspired the inhabitants of a country to develop their collective will to express it through the manifold activities of their life. Such a history of India is still to be written." .... In the past, Indians laid little store by history. Our available sources of information are inadequate, and in so far as they are foreign, are almost invariably tainted with a bias towards India's conquerors. Research is meager and disconnected. ... Works by ancient Indian authors which throw light on history are few. ... The attempts of British scholars, with the exception of Tod, wherever they have taken these "histories" as reliable source-books, have hindered rather than helped the student.

Knowledge and History too powerful for any Empire

Hindus love *gyan* (knowledge). Knowledge, like time, has neither its beginning nor its end. Knowledge is eternal. Knowledge was born along with man. Knowledge is too powerful and so is the history for any empire to distort, destroy or hide. Empires may come and go, but their history survives. History can not be hidden. The books have appeared – "The Hidden History of Human Race" and "Forbidden History" – and several others. They seem to be in revolt against the empires that have been playing unholy mischief with history. History is the knowledge of time. It connects man with his heritage. It was being said, "Sun never sets over the British empire." Arrogant London did not know that it had power neither over the sun, nor over the history.

Chapter Three

LEGENDS & MYTHOLOGIES
ARE HISTORY

Happy surprise that the same Max Müller, who once said that the Vedas are mythology, has said later in his last book *'India: What Can It teach Us?'* (1999, p.139), that the Vedas are more primitive than any other document and they give lot of historical data. They give us trustworthy information of a period in the history of human thought of which we knew absolutely nothing before the discovery of Vedas. Max Müller,[20] in *'History of Ancient Sanskrit Literature'* (p.557), has said: "In the *Rig Veda* we shall have before us more real antiquity than in all the inscriptions of Egypt or Ninevah. ... the *Veda* is the oldest book in existence."

In the same book (p. 63), Max Müller has noted:

> "The *Veda* has a two-fold interest. It belongs to the history of the world and to the history of India. In the history of the world the Veda fills a gap which no literary work in any other language could fill. It carries us back to times of which we have no records anywhere."

It gives lot of pain to the students of the Indian history to find that colonially brainwashed native historians have failed to objectively research and rewrite true history of their ancient Mother India. Most Indian, like European scholars, have been colonially made to think that Vedas, Upanishads, Shastras, Epics, etc are mere mythology. Thus

---

[20]   Stephen Knapp's Proof of Vedic Culture's Global Existence (2000, p. vii).

colonial bosses got an opportunity to write whatever they thought would divide Indians on lines of North Indians as Aryans, and South Indians as Dravidians. They would not have been able to do this if the stories of the pre-history natives of the ancient India were considered true as history, not as mythologies. All ancient people – Asian, African, European and others – had mythologies which gave history so as to keep them connected with their ancestors.

Mythology, as perceived by Germans[21]

William L. Shirer writes that Hitler reiterated in his monologue that *'Tristan and Isolde'* was Wagner's masterpiece, and it was inspired by the great German epic myth, *Nibelungenlied,* "that gave Germany and especially the Third Reich so much of its primitive Germanic mythos." He further reiterates the significance of mythology: "Often a people's myths are the highest and truest expression of its spirit and culture, and no where is this more true than in Germany."

According to Shirer, Schelling believed:

> "a nation comes into existence with its mythology. ...
> The unity of its thinking, which means a collective philosophy, [is] presented in its mythology; therefore its mythology contains the fate of the nation."

Mythology means the same for Hindus as for Germans. Whatever was said in stories about India prior to the concept of history has been termed as mythology. In fact, pre-history mythology was history, as evidenced by lot of truth contained there in. There are some who would not hesitate even to designate a historical event as mythology. The line between mythology and history is too thin to completely curb historical trespassing. Historians are left free, to trespass. The border is being crossed over both ways – mythology → history→ mythology – by the historian depending on his own individual subjective perspectives. Better for historian to honestly know well what he is writing about with

---

21   William Shirer, The Rise and Fall of the third Reich. New York, (1959, p. 102).

what intention. If he is out to defame Hinduism, he would translate the word '*dasa*' as slave, not as 'servant' (sewak), as it really means, as it was done by Prof. Stanley Wolpert[22] and the same might have been done by many other historians. In my meeting with him in his office (LA), arranged by my friend Mr. Inder Singh, I raised question about the validity of 'Aryan invasion of India,' he has talked about when Max Müller himself has said that originally India was known as 'Aryavarta' or 'Aryabhoomi.' When I questioned if he had referred to a dictionary to confirm righteousness of his translation of the word 'dasa,' as a slave, he got agitated.

Several western scholars view the Vedas as mythology, product of sentimental subjectivity of Hindus. Paradoxically, the same scholars claim that the Vedas were composed by the alleged invading Aryans in about 1000 B.C., after about five hundred years of their arrival in 1500 B.C. Contradiction is apparent. Then how would Vedas be myth when they were composed by the invading Aryans, not by the prehistory Vedic people? Fortunately, cat is out of bag. Some prominent post-colonial European historians, like Max Müller,[23] have come out to tell the truth and cry about the abuse, the histories of the European colonies have suffered. He has said that originally India was the cradle of Aryans, known as *Aryavarta, Aryadesh* or *Aryabhoomi.*

What Smith said about the Pandvas would explain it:

> "The other features (of the Mahabharata) are clearly
> non-Aryan, notably the polyandry of the Pandavas who
> all shared the one wife, Drupadi, after the manner of
> the Tibetans and certain other Himalayan tribes in the
> present day. The name Pandava means pale face, and the
> conjecture seems to be legitimate that the sons of Pandu
> have been representatives of a yellow-tinted Himalayan,
> non-Aryan tribe, which practiced polyandry."

---

[22] Stanley Wolpert, 'A New History of India,' New York: Oxford University Press, 1977, p.25.

[23] Max Müller, in 'The Science of language' 1891, p. 291.

Before writing the above, Smith should have known that Pandavas were one of the most civilized royal families of the times. They were not a Himalayan tribe. Pandavas did not have custom of polyandry. This was the only instance of polyandry in the Mahabharata age, and even after until today. An unfortunate incident was responsible for this uncivilized act of polyandry, unfamiliar not only to this great royal family, but also to the whole Hindu society right from its birth. Raja Drupad, according to the royal custom, arranged *Swayamvar* (Swayam = self + var = husband) for his daughter Drupadi, to enable her to select husband of her choice. Eligible and appropriate princes were invited to compete in an extra-difficult feat to win the exemplary great bride. In this case, aspiring candidates had to arrow-shoot the eye of a fish, hanging from a tree over a clear water pool, by only looking at the image of the fish in the water. Only Arjuna, one of the five Pandu brothers, did it successfully. Arjuna was considered expert in arrow shooting. He got Drupadi. She reserved her right to reject Arjuna if she did not like him, and choose some one else of her liking.

On his return to his home, Arjuna jubilantly shouted at the door, "Maa, I have a great gift for you!." His mother Kunti, not knowing what the gift he was talking about, said: "Share, with your brothers." In those days, children, out of respect for their mother, did not feel right to argue back. "Obey your parents, especially mother" was more religious than the religion itself. He did what his mother told. I feel it was stupid. If he had told what the gift was, his mother would not have insisted on it. In present times, it looks ridiculous and unbelievable. Whatever it was, but it was not their custom. The five husbands lived strictly according to the clear-cut rules were set for such strange situation. Neither the Pandu family nor the society had any prior knowledge of polyandry. Smith should have spent a few minutes to talk to some one to know about this incident and the feelings of Hindus about it. Some western scholars think it is their right to interpret it as a custom among the Pandu tribe. No, it is not the right of any historian to subjectively interpret it as a custom, when unknown and unfamiliar, without knowing it fully, including its related circumstances. Culturally, the West is different from the East. No one thought, nor does any one think, that what, the Pandavas did, was right. But, they have high regard for Arjuna as an obedient son and as a great warrior. History is full of incidents showing that great people do stupid things. In present times, there have been some unfortunate incidents of raping daughter. They have not been considered as a custom. Smith would have criticized the incident as anti-social and uncivilized. But it was professionally wrong on Smith's part to describe one incident as a custom.

This incident gives rise to the question: "Should one write the history of others?" Because of cultural biases and ignorance, it would be unprofessional to write the history of the people, other than own, without adequately and respectfully consulting their scriptures. Unconsciously inter-ethnic comparative biases would creep in. Historians are human beings and human is to err. The historian should have identification with and adequate knowledge of the culture of the people, he is writing the history of. History is a story of a family, an organization, a company, or of a nation. It would not be accurate if it is written by some body who is not closely acquainted with the country and its culture he is writing about. It is surprising to see history of India, written by a European historian who has not lived in India, who does not have adequate knowledge about India, and respectful feel for Hindu culture and moreover little or no knowledge of Hindu mythologies. He collects information from the books; many authored by those who, like him, are ignorant of or partially knowledgeable about India and her customs. They copy the content they read, subjectively from European perspectives.

Sorry to say that some scholars, particularly colonial, have ethnic superiority complex in regard to most Asian and African cultures. Histories penned by such historians are bound to be subjective and ethnically biased with little respect for non-western cultures. May be the colonial lords did not give them correct facts or they told them what to write and how. Several colonial histories are witness. Their ignorance and contradictions are seen floating on their content like oil on fried food.

Biases and ignorance: Intolerable enemies of history

As a matter of fact, in the ancient prehistory period, legends were customary ways of recording history. Even for a great scholar, legends of others are hard to appropriately understand the history in them, particularly for the one who does not have adequate knowledge of the culture of the people he is writing about. It would be harder for the scholar who is subjective and ethnically biased, and particularly the one who has ethnic superiority complex. Good scholar needs to have respect for and sensitivity to the culture of the people he/she is writing about. Professional integrity expects that historian needs to be culturally unbiased and prejudice-free. Historian's ignorance of and bias against other cultures are the worst enemies of the history.

Herbert J. Muller, in *'The Loom of History'* (1958, p.3), has said about the legends and myths, as true history:

> "More important, the myths and legends are true history
> as the records of the mind of ancient peoples. They yield
> insights into prehistoric customs and beliefs, the growth
> of more civilized aspirations, and finally the realization
> of conscious ideals."

Herbert Muller[24] has correctly described legends and myths, as significant stores of historical facts. How could Jones adequately, objectively and accurately write history about Hindus by discarding their ancient scriptures, as mythology? Hindu legends – like those of Greeks, Romans and Germans – are not completely mythological. Most of the content of religious scriptures contains historical facts. The song or poetry sung by the fan would naturally be hyperbolic in praise of the act of his/her hero/heroine; but the act will be fact in its essence. It will be insensitively cruel to consider the act as a myth because of its exaggerated praise by a fan. The feelings and the sentiments, writers and poets have for their heroes, should not be blamed for exaggerations. They should be thanked for the facts they have given for historians to reconstruct an objective and reliable history for next generations.

If Sir William Jones complains that eastern cultures have used their mythology and fantasy in explaining their origins, why then did he thinks that Judeo-Christian tradition was an exception? Is the theory that whole humanity descended from the couple 'Adam and Eve,' not hopelessly obscured in the mists of mythology and fantasy? It will be

---

[24]   Herbert J. Muller. The Loom of History,

hard for any sensible person to believe that the global humanity has its heritage only in 'Adam and Eve' who were sent down on earth by God only about a few millennium years back. Jews and Christians have right to adore their mythology. So let others celebrate their mythologies. The civilized people, who have respect for their own mythologies, should have respect for mythologies of other peoples.

The concept of "science" came much later. Mythology, in general, is viewed as a product of fantasy. In my opinion, mythology is what is written in pre-history times. So it would be wrong to define mythology as a story of only myths. Almost all mythologies have lot of grains of historical truths. There is no society without its own mythologies and legends. In fact, they are needed as a source of definition of own identity and identification of heritage. Scholars, particularly western (several, not all), should develop ethnic sensitivity towards other cultures by monitoring their own ethno-cultural biases, particularly negative. It is the responsibility of historians to objectively sift myths from facts.

Ignorance of Indian mythology: Ignorance of India's global role

Gene D. Matlock, in *"India Once Ruled the Americas"* (2000, p.170), remarks about the significance of mythology:

> "The one and only reason why we don't know about India's true role in human history is our self-imposed ignorance of Indian mythology, history, and traditions!"

He also seems to subtly taunt the historians who think they know all and resist admitting that every mythology gives history of its people:

"The person who claims to know every thing, or even a lot, is more unforgivably ignorant and stupid than he who honestly admits that he knows nothing yet as he should know."

Chapter Four

ARYANS, WHO AND FROM WHERE?

T he colonial Europeans historians created the following two ill-based, mutually contradicting and inter-tangled theories to confuse the origin and identity of Aryans, and their culture, religion, and their original language Sanskrit:

(i)   Aryan Invasion of India (AII), and

(ii) Indo-European Family of Languages (IEFL).

The theories have disassociated Aryans from their roots in Ârya-āvarta (India). According to AII Aryans are not originally from Ârya-āvarta (Bhārat, India), but they had gone there as invaders in about 1500 BC, along with Sanskrit and a pantheon of Hindu gods. But, colonial historians have not been able to identify the country, the invading Aryans came from which had Aryans as its natives, Sanskrit as its language and where Hindu gods were worshipped. They also write that Swastika is found all over the planet, but not in India, though Swastika is a Sanskrit word and it has been used in almost all Hindu religious ceremonies since millennia.

Both theories are contradicting each other. According to AII, Sanskrit came into India in1500 B.C., and according to IEFL, in 3000 BC and according to some others in 6000 BC. Sanskrit is being falsely understood as an Indo-European language. How can it happen when India is geographically too distant from Europe and socio-culturally and historically too different? Sanskritic languages are linguistically too different from Germanic, Roman and Latin languages. Their roots and ancestors are different and their geography too distant and history too different.

Why would Aryans invade their mother land Ârya-āvarta (Bharat, India)? The origin of the Aryan race, like that of any race, can be only one and the same – either Indic or European – not 'Indo-European' as mischievously coined by colonial linguists and historians. So their proto-parent language has to be only one, Sanskrit for Indic and Roman/Latin for European languages. Languages are influenced by religion, Sanskrit by Vedic *Sanatan* Dharma (Hinduism) and European languages by Judeo-Christianity.

Both theories 'AII and IEFL' were ethno-mischievously engineered in London to divide Indians into two societies (i) fair-skin North Indian Aryans who allegedly invaded India and (ii) dark-skin South Indian Dravidians, the original natives of India. As a matter of fact, all the North Indians as well as South Indians are Aryans and are original natives of Aryavarta (Bhārat, India). Difference in complexion is due to difference in weather – cold climate in north and warm in south.

Only Hindus – North Indians as well as South Indians – are original natives of India. Buddhism and Sikhism are offshoots of Hinduism. Indian Muslims and Christians are not original natives of India. They are invaders, refugees or immigrants. Colonial history tells that the fair skin Aryans invaded India in 1500 BC, settled in North India and pushed the dark-skin original natives to south whom they called Dravidians. Complexion is influenced by geography and weather. In India, residents of Kashmir are fairer than those living in Punjab and as you go further south, complexion becomes increasingly darker and darker. Language changes by distance. Hence, India, being a large country like a continent, has several languages.

India originally was known as Ârya-āvarta

F. Max Müller[25] has said that the word 'Arya' means noble and it is a Sanskrit word and it has appeared frequently in Vedas. He also said that India originally was known as Ârya-āvarta, Âryabhoomi and Âryadesh,

---

[25] F. Max Müller (1823 –1900), a Germany-born philologist and Orientalist, p. 291.

meaning the nation of Aryans. All this clearly spells out that India (Ârya-āvarta) was the original home of Aryans. Hence, 'Aryan invasion of India' is a myth, rather a hoax.

Max Müller has said that the ancient Ariana, the district around Herat, was the cradle of the Aryan languages. In ancient times, Afghanistan, like Pakistan, was a part of India (see the Chapter, *Afghanistan, Its roots in India'*.

Max Müller[26] (p. 291) talks about the use of the word "Ârya" in the Rig Veda:

> "Ârya is a Sanskrit word, and in the later Sanskrit it means *noble, of a good family*. Teachers are frequently addressed as *Ârya*. It was, however, originally a national name, and we see traces of it as late as the law book of Mānavas, where India is still called Ârya-āvarta, the abode of Âryas. In the old Sanskrit, in the hymns of the Veda, Arya occurs frequently as a national name and as a name of honour, comprising the worshippers of the gods of the Brahmans, as opposed to their enemies, who were called in the Veda as Dasyus. Thus one of the gods, Indra, who, in some respects, answers to the Greek Zeus, is invoked in the following words (Rig–Veda i.51,8): 'Know thou the Aryas, O Indra, and they who are Dasyus; punish the lawless, and deliver them unto thy servant! Be thou the mighty helper of the worshippers, and I will praise all these thy deeds at the festivals."

Hymns of the *Rig Veda* were composed much earlier than the alleged *Aryan invasion of India.'* Max Müller (p. 292) writes: "In India, as we saw, the name of Ârya as a national name."

World knows the British colonial policy 'Divide and Rule'. They think they have right to write histories of their subjugated peoples. As the result, histories of most Asian and African peoples are written by their European bosses according to their colonial agenda. Thus history,

---

[26]   Max Müller. "The Science of Language" (1891, p.291).-

the Bible of humanity, has been shamelessly abused and corrupted by European colonial historians. History of ancient Bhārat has been shamelessly crucified by colonial scholars to the extent that they tend to deprive Aryavarta of the credit for being the cradle of Aryans, Vedas, Sanskrit and Swastika. They claim that India is not the home of Sanskrit and that it was brought in by the alleged invading Aryans who composed Vedas five hundred years after their stay in India. Historians and linguists have not found any country other than India which has or had Sanskrit as its native language.

Europeans envy the Aryan race and have been trying to misrepresent and steal the origin of Aryans. They ignore 'Aryavarta' as the cradle and heritage of the Aryans. To emphasize their point, colonial historians created the two ill-based theories (i) Aryan invasion of India and (ii) Indo-European family of languages. Both have confused the origin and heritage of Aryans and also the origins of Sanskrit, Swastika and Vedas. This has adversely affected and confused the history of the ancient India.

Fortunately, some historians of professional integrity have praised India as the heritage of humanity, as evidenced by the title "Our Oriental Heritage" by William James Durant[27] (1885-1981), an American writer, historian and philosopher.

The story of the origin of Aryans has been tampered by the colonial historians. Aryans have been a misunderstood and misconceived race, even by several anthropologists, ethnographers and historians. Wrong history is being taught in schools, colleges and universities, shamelessly under the nose of the leaders of independent India. The European, particularly the mighty British colonial pen, seems to have been getting indirect endorsement by India's submissive slavish silent scholarship and the prime ministers of independent India. Why are these false history books not barred from universities? Colonially corrupted histories have adversely influenced the Hindu history of ancient India.

Fortunately, several historians – Indian, African, European as well as American – have been interested in cleansing the dirt sitting over the history of ancient Bhārat and diging out the mischievously burried history.

---

[27]   William James Duran, American historian, (MJF Books, New York, (1935)

The dugout history, so far partly, tells that in pre-history ancient times, Aryans, now in different ethno-cultural and linguistic attires, have been found widely spread all over the planet.

Arya is a Sanskrit word. It has appeared often in the Rig Veda, Upanishads and in several Hindu sacred books. According to Dr. Poonai,[28] Rig-Vedic Aryan clans established their respective city-states in ancient Mesopotamia and neighboring lands where they used Sanskritic dialects, tailored according to local languages. In ancient times, because of absence of communication and transportation means, large states were not practical. Dr. Poonai on the same page writes that *Sarvagun* (man of all virtues), also called *Sargon* 1, was the leader of the Aggar or Akkad clan of Indo-Aryans. He annexed the Sumerian states in 2750 B.C. The Akkads adopted a modified Sumerian language, which like their own was Rig-Vedic in origin. In about 2100 BC, the Sumerian–Akkadian Empire was attacked and defeated by other two Rig-Vedic clans: (i) Amar or Amarites who under Amaravi was called Hummurabi and (ii) Babylonian Empire over the Bhupalans. Aryans were learned. They knew Sanskrit and its grammar. They were cultured and fond of spirituality.

In pre-history ancient times, Aryans (Hindus) from Ârya-āvarta had gone out all over the planet and had established their kingdoms all over the north-western region including Mesopotamia and had given to them Aryan (Hindu) culture and Sanskrit language in modified form, to suit the local language.

Aryans, because of their culture and achievements, have been so popular and enviable that every people, they lived with, have been eager to claim Aryan heritage. White European claim Aryans as their proud heritage. Hitler claimed that Germans are Aryans. He adopted Aryan Swastika as the symbol for his army. Max Müller in 'What India can teach us' (p.137), has praised the Aryan race: "... the Aryan race, that the race we and all the greatest nations of the world belong." Its use by Nazi Germans has confused the world about the origin of the Aryan race and their proud symbol Swastika. There were attacks by Jews on Hindu Temple in Queens, New York, because its external wall bore the image of Swastika. Swastika was borrowed by Hitler, as explained

---

[28] Poonai, M.D., Ph.D. in "Origin of Civilization and Language" (1994, p. 171).

by William L. Shirer in his book *'The Rise and Fall of the Third Reich: A History of Nazi Germany'* (1959, p. 43). He writes that the Swastika (hakenkreus) is as old, almost, as the man on the planet. It is true that Swastika is as old as Vedas, at least over ten thousand years. If Swastika is so old, how then it could be of Nazi Germans?

It has been historically established that *Swastika* is at least older than 10,000 years. It, in turn, reflects the age of Sanskrit, because Swastika is a Sanskrit word. Then, how could the alleged invading Aryans bring Sanskrit and Hindu godly pantheon into India? Aryans are connected with Vedas. They are often mentioned in Vedas, Ramayana (earlier than 5114), Mahabharata (earlier than 3138) and Bhagvad Gita.

Aryan connection with Vedas

Religion of Aryans is described in the Reader's Digest's *'The World's Religions'* (1993, p.130): "Knowledge of the Aryans is mostly derived from the heritage of their sacred literature, known as the Vedas, especially the Rig Veda, a collection of hymns." This clearly suggests that the Aryans practiced the Vedic religion (present Hinduism), worshipped Hindu pantheon of gods and knew Sanskrit long before the alleged 'Aryan invasion of India' in 1500 BC.

Antiquity of the Rig Veda challenges Aryan Invasion

The antiquity of the *Rig Veda*, as given by various scholars, ranges from 7,500 B.C. to 3,000 B.C., though it is much older. Considering the latest date 3,000 B.C., Vedas were composed at least 1,500 years prior to the year of the alleged Aryan invasion. This challenges the validity of the Aryan invasion, according to which Sanskrit was brought into India in 1500 B.C., and the Vedas were composed by the invading Aryans about 500 years later than their arrival. This also refutes the IEFL (Indo-European Family of Languages), according to which Sanskrit came into India from outside in about 3,000 B.C., according to some others 6000 B.C. The IEFL, time wise contradicts the AII. Both theories (AII and IEFL) contradict each other to establish that any colonial theory regarding Aryans is baseless. The truth is that Hindus are Aryans, the original natives of Ârya-āvarta (Bhārat, India).

Europeans stealing Aryans Heritage

Europeans seem to be so jealous of Aryan (Hindu) culture and origin that they have been trying to steal their Aryan identity and their heritage. They say that Hindus are not original Aryans. According to them original Aryans are only those who invaded India in 1500 B.C. and brought along with them Sanskrit, Caucasian genes and a pantheon of gods. They also claim that the alleged invading Aryans composed Vedas in 1000 B.C., about 500 years after their stay in India. But the colonial history does not identify the country; the invading Aryans came from where they spoke Sanskrit and worshipped a pantheon of gods. It is too difficult to believe such a bizarre colonial ethno-political baseless story about the origin of Aryans. The word 'Aryan' has its origin in Sanskrit. Aryan means noble. Are there any other people, excepting Hindus, who spoke Sanskrit and whose sacred scriptures (Vedas) were composed in Sanskrit? Is or was there any nation, other than Âryāvarta (Bhārat, India) which had Sanskrit or any Sanskritic language as its native tongue? This has been confusing only because Hindus are not considered as Aryans, who because of their adventurous ethos, had gone out all over and had culturally and linguistically touched the hearts and minds of several peoples so significantly that they invited jealousy and rivalry, particularly from Europeans who have been addicted by superiority complex.

The Aryan, the Jewel of the White Race?

William L. Shirer, in *'The Rise and Fall of the Third Reich'* (1959, pp. 103-104), talks about Count Joseph Arthur de Gobineau, a French diplomat and a man of letters who wrote a four volume book entitled *'Essai sur l'Inegalite Des Races Humaines'* (Essay on the Inequality of the Human Races), which was published in Paris between 1853 and 1855. Gobineau believed that race was the key to history and civilization and Aryan was the jewel of the White race. He believed that the racial question dominates all the problems of history:

> "There were three principal races, white, yellow and black, and the white was the superior. History shows that all civilization flows from the white race that no civilization can exist without the cooperation of this race. The jewel of the white race was the Aryan, this illustrious human family, the noblest among the white race, whose origin he (Gobineau) traced back to Central Asia."

The Encyclopedia Americana (2003, vol. 2, p.426) writes the same for Gobineau:

> "In a book published in 1854, the French writer Count Joseph-Arthur Gobineau gave a racial meaning to Aryan. Gobineau held the White race to be superior to all others and the Aryan race to be supreme among whites. This theory aroused interest in Germany and was espoused by the composer Richard Wagner among others. In the 20th century it was taken up by the German dictator Adolf Hitler, who equated Aryan with Nordic race and used the theory to justify his persecution of Jews. Modern anthropologists reject the theory that there are "pure" or inherently superior human groups."

Elizabeth E. Bacon, Hofstra University

The Europeans are craving to be known as Aryans. In fact, they are not. Only Vedic people (present Hindus) are Aryans. How could Gobineau say that the White is the superior race, when he himself says that the 'Aryan' is the jewel of the White race, and that the Aryan is the "noblest among the White race? Historically, it has been established that Aryans are from Ārya-āvarta (Bhārat, India). I, as an Aryan, will be happy if Germans call themselves Aryans, but I will not like if Gobineau claims that the Aryans are not originally from Ārya-āvarta.

He seems to believe that the origin of the Aryans is traced back to Central Asia, not to Europe, the principal abode of the White. Then, in no way, White European can be original Aryans. It would have been more accurate if he had said that the origin of the Aryans is traced back to Ârya-âvarta (Bhārat, India), instead of Central Asia. He can be right if he says that originally Central Asia was a part of ancient India.

It is hard to understand why European scholars hesitate to give credit for the greatness in the Aryan race to Ârya-âvarta (Bhārat, India) where it legitimately belongs. How and why does Gobineau think that the origin of the Aryan race be traced to Central Asia, not to Aryavarta (India)? Why did he ignore the Brown (Wheatish) race, while talking about the white, yellow and black, as the principal races of the world? Perhaps, because by Gobineau Aryans (Indians of India) are considered 'White', not 'brown'.

It would be a dirty sinful blot on a civilized race to justify persecution of the members of any other race. Each and every race has its birth right to believe whatever, it thinks, is right about itself. It is not right to consider any other race to be inferior, and hate it because it is different. I, being an Aryan (Hindu), would not like Aryan association with any race which feels itself superior. It is OK if it calls itself 'a great civilized race.' Civilized people should not feel ashamed of admitting learning from any other race.

Count Joseph Arthur de Gobineau,[29] a French diplomat and a man of letters, has said:

> "The jewel of the White race was the Aryan, this illustrious human family, the noblest among the White race, whose origin he traced back to Central Asia."

How could Aryans who originated in the Sanskrit-speaking land India, be members of White race?

The Encyclopedia Americana (2003, vol. 2, p. 426) writes the same about Aryans, as the 'Jewels of the White race':

---

[29]   William L. Shirer. "The Rise and Fall of the Third Reich, A History of Nazi Germany. New York: Simon and Schuster, 1959, pp.103-4.

"Gobineau held the White race to be superior to all others and the Aryan race to be superior among Whites. This theory aroused interest in Germany and was espoused by the composer Richard Wagner among others. In the 20th century it was taken up by the German dictator Adolf Hitler, who equated Aryans with Nordic race and used the theory to justify his persecution of Jews. Modern anthropologists reject the theory that there are "pure" or inherently superior human groups."

It has been shown above that Western historians, particularly European, have envied Aryans (in fact Hindus) and have tried to steal their treasure possessions, such as Aryan race, Vedas, Sanskrit and Swastika. History shows that Aryans have been all around, in Asia, Europe, Africa, Australia, SE Asia, etc. as traders since millennia, but their roots are only in Ârya-āvarta (India, Bharat). Will Durant (American historian), in "Our Oriental Heritage' (p.479), praises India as a great manufacturer and international trader:

"Europe looked upon the Hindus as experts in almost every line of manufacture, wood work, ivory-work, metal-work, bleaching, dying, tanning, soup making, glass-blowing, gunpowder, fireworks, cement, etc. China imported eyeglasses from India in 1260 A.D. Bernier, travelling in India in the seventeenth century, described it as humming with industry. Fitch, in 1585, saw a fleet of one hundred and eighty boats carrying a great variety of goods down the river Jumna."

Will Durant, on the same page, describe India as a manufacture and international trader:

"Internal trade flourished; every roadside was-and-is a bazaar. The foreign trade of India is as old as her history; objects found in Sumeria and Egypt indicate a traffic between these countries and India as far as 3000 B.C.

53

> Commerce between India and Babylon by the Persian
> Gulf flourished from 700 to 480 B.C.; and perhaps the
> "ivory, apes, and peacocks" of Solomon came by the
> same route from the same source. India's ships sailed
> the sea to Burma and China in Chandragupta's days;
> and Greek merchants, called *Yavana* (Ionians) by the
> Hindus, thronged the markets of Dravidian India in
> the centuries before and after the birth of Christ. Rome,
> in her epicurean days, depended upon India for spices,
> perfumes and unguents, and paid great prices for Indian
> silks, brocades, muslins and cloth of gold."

European colonial historians, being universally powerful, seem to claim that the achievements of Aryans are as of Europeans. Several objective and honest historians have been increasingly appearing to talk about the East (India, Hindus), as evidenced by the titles of the two books out of several, such as Will Durant's *"Our Oriental Heritage"* and Harvard Prof Diana L. Eck's *"India: A Sacred Geography."*

In order to show that they are not blind and that they are knowledgeable, historians write that Aryans were semi-nomadic Nordic Whites, perhaps located originally on the steppes of southern Russia and Central Asia, who spoke the parent language of the various Indo-European languages, meaning. Proto-Indo-European (PIE). The PIE is the lost ancestral language from which, it is said, those languages ultimately have been derived. Why are linguists going too far back to talk about the lost language about which they have zero knowledge? They don't know why, when and how it (PIE) got lost. Even a word of the lost PIE has not been found. How can it happen? Languages have been lost, but gradually, not like the alleged PIE, totally disappearing in a second, not leaving any of its signs or words behind. Historians have knowledge of several extinct languages. Vedic oral traditions, being too ancient, should have some information about the PIE, which, if spoken any time, would have been related to Sanskrit in some way. How can linguists talk about the language which was never spoken? This seems to be a colonial hoax to deprive Sanskrit of its philological supreme seniority.

This has been making students confused and disappointed that they know nothing about, not even the name of the alleged great-grand mother of Sanskrit. Now cat is out of bag. Awakened linguists of professional integrity have been coming out to admit that the PIE was colonial ethno-political hoax to deny India the credit for being the cradle of Sanskrit, the supreme language of the mankind. How can it happen that the PIE, if the great-grand mother of all languages including Sanskrit, would completely disappear leaving no trace of its being? The language, which has never been heard being spoken, can not be considered lost, but never born. Linguists have been pretending their pride in claiming to have found the language which was never spoken.

Despite distortion of their history, Aryans (present Hindus), by way of their millennia-long oral traditions, know all – their origin, their cradle, their sacred scriptures (Vedas) and their most ancient language Sanskrit, all Indian vernaculars have sprung from. It is an Indo-European philological ethno-political web, mischievously entangling Aryans and Sanskrit. It was created by the colonial masters to realize their colonial agenda that India's civilization is due to its relationship with Europe, by creating the ill-based "Indo-European Family of Languages" theory to stress that Sanskrit is the cousin of European languages and that the Indian civilization is not older than the European.

The concept of the 'Indo-European family' is wrong, impractical, ill-conceived and mischievous. Each language has its own well-defined geography. Both Europe and India are geographically too distant and socio-culturally and historically too different to make a family of languages. Colonial historians want to stress that Indian civilization is contemporary of the European. Vedas are much older than Bible and the Vedic philosophy is too ancient for Christianity and Judaism. The fact is that Europe owes to India lot for its spiritual orientations, as talked about by Max Müller in his book *'India: 'What Can it teach us?'* and by several other scholars including the ancient Greek philosopher Plato (427-347 BC).

Europe has been far ahead in material scientific development. This also is fact that India had ideas of air ships (*Vimans*), fire missiles (*Agni baans*), TV, navigation, shipbuilding, bridge building (Ram setu) as evidenced by Ramayana and Mahabharata. But in terms of research to realize them in their final form, Europe has been in fore-front of almost all other countries. India's backwardness, in my opinion, was due to short of resources, India has never wanted to amass resources by robbing her colonized people as European colonialists did, and multiplying it by slavery. India did colonize several territories in her distant past. She did not rob their people, but gave them civilization, knowledge and language. European captivating buildings are the mirror of the Afro-Asian destruction.

Originality of Aryans

If any one wants to know the originality of Aryans, he should read what Max Müller has said in his book *The Science of Language* (p, 291) about them, their abode and language. The book is based on his lectures, delivered in 1861-1868. He has clearly said Ârya-âvarta (Bharat, India) is the original home of Aryans and Sanskrit, the parent language of all the Indian vernaculars.

William L. Langer[30] introduces Aryans:

> "Strange to say, the ruling class of the Hurrians bore not Hurrian but Indo-Aryan names. Evidently the Aryans drove both the Hurrians and the Kassites before them in the 17th century, overrunning the former and establishing them-selves as an aristocracy. Probably they won their position as chariot warriors, since it seems likely that the horse-drawn chariot, introduced in the 18th century, and widely used in the 17th century, originated among Aryan peoples. The symbiosis of Hurrian and Indo-Aryan elements at all events is characteristic of Hurrian society wherever we come upon it."

Langer tells that the Hurrians in Asia Minor region were originally Indo-Aryans, meaning Aryans from India. They bore Indo-Aryan (Sanskrit) names. Langer's characterization of Aryans as Indo-Aryans, clearly suggests that the alleged invading Aryans were originally from

---

[30] "The New Illustrated Encyclopedia of World History" (vol. 1, 1896, p.34).

India. Since (i) the word 'Arya' has its origin in Sanskrit, (ii) it has appeared several times in Vedas and (iii) India in ancient times was known as Ârya-āvarta, there can not be any country other than India, as the cradle of Aryans.

Langer further tells that in 18ᵗʰ century B.C., Aryans were known as "chariot warriors" who had established themselves as an aristocracy. Chariot was not new in 1800 BC. It was used in the Mahabharata war in 3067 BC. Langer's observation that the Hurrians bore Indo-Aryan names and that there was symbiosis of Hurrian and Indo-Aryan elements, suggests that Hurrians too were from India. It seems, that a few *Kshatriya* (warrior) tribes, such as Hurrian, Kassites, Mitannies, etc, had gone out of India in about 18ᵗʰ century B.C. or even earlier and had established their kingdoms in the Middle East region, comprising of Mesopotamia, Egypt, Syria, Anatolia, Palestine, and others. It is possible, that the three – Hurrians, Kassites, Mitannies – though Indo-Aryans from India were fighting among themselves. They might not knowing that they all were Aryans and were original from Ancient India, because in those pre-history ancient times, there was no sense of geography, there were no maps marking or defining international borders, crossing of which visa was required. There was no sense of international borders. There were small city-like kingdoms, as evidenced by hundreds of tiny states governed by Rajas and Nawabs during the British rule in India which were abolished immediately after India's independence in 1947. All were merged into one consolidated nation by Sardar Vallabbhai Patel, the first Home Minister of the independent Bhārat. He has been rightly recognized as 'Iron Man.' He understood that a few foreigners, particularly the British were able to rule over giant nation, only by dividing the vast territory into hundreds of small states. I remember how Patel consolidated the shattered India into a solid nation with his determined iron mind. The stories I heard about Patel are amazing. He called a meeting of the rulers of states and told them that in the interests of India all states are to be abolished and be merged with the nation. He distributed a copy of agreement to be signed by them. There was loud uproar, saying they needed time to think. He said "Okay! You have five minutes to decide and walked away. Only the Nizam of Hyderabad defied.

I was 21 year old, living in Birsi refugee camp, which was on the northern border of the Hyderabad Deccan state. In the morning buses came and took us away because Sardar Patel thought military action if the Nizam defied. We heard that Nehru telephoned Sardar not to take military action. He lied and told Nehru that Nizam has surrendered. Really the Nizam after little military resistance yielded and Hyderabad became, like other states merged with India. Pakistan was disappointed because it had eye on Hyderabad. I think the last Nizam was Osman Ali Khan who had amassed so much wealth that he was considered one of the world's richest men in 1930s. India has been dominated by foreigners because of disunity and rivalry among Hindu kings.

Disunity and Rivalry: Invitation to invaders

Pages of history ink that disunity and rivalry among Hindu rajas were responsible for repeated invasions and constrictions of the vast Indian geography of the *Viraat* Bhārat (Greater India) since pre-history ancient times. Alexander the Great entered into India via Afghanistan's Hindu Kush Mountains in 327 B.C. when Afghanistan was an integral part of Bhārat, culturally as well as administratively. Alexander would not have been able to stay in Hindustan even one day, rather would not have been able to enter, if rivalry-driven Hindu kingdoms were united to jointly fight back against the invaders from north-west. Unfortunately, north-western borders – Indus Valley, Sind and Punjab – were left unprotected to welcome foreign intruders. Both powers, Nandas and Mauryans, were enough to seal the north-western borders to arrest any unwanted foreign intrusion. Nandas were a militarily powerful kingdom with large army of brave soldiers, elephants and horse-driven chariots. Mauryans, under Chandragupta were strong enough to seal the north-western borders. Hindustan would have remained different and larger. Afghans and Baluachs would not have been able to create Afghanistan and Baluchistan. The Raja of Takshashila (Taxila), feeling alone and insecure, yielded to Alexander without putting up a fight. Helplessly, he became a generous host to Alexander and his army. Shamelessly, he provided food for his army and sizeable soldiers to help him fight

58

against his rival neighbor Raja Porus,[31] belonging to the Pauravas tribe, descending from the Puru. He has been mentioned in the *Rig Veda*. Alexander had fierce battle with King Porus, one of the most powerful Hindu kings by the river Hydaspes (Beas) in the spring of 326 B.C. Porus was defeated although he fought with a large army, assisted by elephants. Alexander had never seen elephants in battle. Porus was captured. I have a faint remembrance reading some where that the wife of Porus tied *rākhi* on Alexander's wrist. He knew its significance that the woman considers the man, on whose wrist she ties *rākhi*, as her brother Alexander allowed him to retain his kingdom.

Alexander got lot of success in Bhārat which would have given him fortunes, but he could not hold. Fierce battles in Bhārat with several kingdoms fatigued him and his army. In ancient times, Bhārat was fragmented into hundreds of small kingdoms, Alexander had to fight with. Credit goes to Sardar Vallabhbhai Patel (31 Oct.1875 – 15 Dec. 1950) who tactfully with his iron fist consolidated and integrated all into a giant strong Bhārat. Patel was a barrister and statesman, one of the few top leaders of the Indian National Congress Party.

Alexander was wounded several times during his violent confrontation with the Malli,[32] known to be one of the most warlike Indian tribes. He was seriously wounded when an arrow pierced his breastplate and his ribcage. His army officers rescued him in a narrow escape. Alexander, seeing his army's shaken morale, gave up pursuit of his next goal to reach about 250-miles-distant Ganga Valley because his army heard tales of powerful tribes, they had to fight against. Bhārat, as divided into hundreds of tiny city kingdoms, looked as a weak country; but it became difficult for a foreign invader to fight numerous battles, as happened in case of Alexander the Great.

Moreover, with fatigued army and inadequate decreasing supplies, Alexander felt utterly depressed. Indian Territory was unknown to him. Day by day increasing depletion of the supplies – food, entertainment, prostitutes, etc. – made his army unhappy. At the top of all this, Alexander's horse Bucephalus got wounded and died. He loved Bucephalus so much that he founded a city in its name.

---

[31] Wikipedia, Free Encyclopedia
[32] Ibid, Wikipedia

Nehru: "Aryan India."

Nehru has rightly called India **'Aryan India'** (p. 202). As per V. Gordon Childe, Indo-Aryans had established their kingdoms in the Middle East region. They were considered as chariot warriors. When they were overpowered by some other forces, almost all of them got socio-culturally and linguistically absorbed there. Because of centuries-long separation from their roots, it was not only difficult, but impractical and inadvisable to contemplate about their return to the home of their forgotten ancestors. Childe[33] writes:

> "In Palestine the Aryan names have totally disappeared by 1000 B.C., and even in the Mitanni region they have scarcely a vestige behind them. Here at least Aryan speech succumbed to Semitic and Asianic dialect, and small Aryan aristocracies were absorbed by the native population."

The remaining few might have attempted to return to India, the country of their ancestors. They, being Kshatriya (warriors) of royal families, might have traveled in armored horse-driven chariots. They might have been initially mistaken as invaders, the theory of "Aryan invasion of India" might have been based on.

Return of Aryans

In my opinion, Aryan return, after centuries-long stay away from their cradle, seems inconceivable and impractical, particularly in so ancient times when there were no maps to guide them back to their starting point. Because of about three centuries (1800-1500 B.C.) of separation, remembrance of and feelings for kith and kin would be little if not zero, particularly because of absence of telephone and post office services. Moreover, they might have stepped out from Ârya-āvarta as a whole family, leaving behind any close kith and kin.

---

[33] V. Gordon Childes, in The Aryans: A Study of Indo-European Origins (1987, p.30

Historically, Aryans have been the most misunderstood people, or I may say "victim of colonial historical terrorism" to the extent that their origin has been historically confused and distorted by contradicting characterizations of Aryans and their origin.

Captain A.H. Bingley [34](p.1), talking about 'The cradle of Aryan Race' writes:

> "The original home of the Aryan race was on the banks of the Oxus in Central Asia. From thence they migrated into two directions. One branch moved north-west towards Europe, the other south-west towards Persia and India. It is with the latter that we are here concerned."

On the same page, Bingley writes:

> "The earliest records of the Aryans are contained in the *Vedas*, a series of hymns composed in the Sanskrit language from the 15th to the 10th century B.C. by the *Rishis*, devout sages, devoted to religious meditation."

Contradiction is evident. If "the Aryans are contained in the Vedas," how could be their roots in Central Asia? The Rig Veda was composed long before 15th B.C. as evidenced by the mention of the melting of the Himalayan glaciers in Rig Veda which happened about 10 thousand years back. Graham Hancock[35] (2002, p.169) quotes B.B. Radhakrishna of the Geological Society of India (1999), who writes that the *Rig Veda* talks about the break-up of Himalayan glaciers releasing water which flowed out in seven mighty rivers (*Sapta Sindhu*). The early inhabitants of the plains burst into songs praising Lord Indra for releasing water they very much needed. This happened during Late Pleistocene glaciations, about 10,000 years ago. Radha- krishna had said:

---

[34] Captain A.H. Bingley. "Hand book on Rajuts," Delhi: Low Price Publications, 2010.

[35] Graham Hancock. "Under World:The Mysterious Origins of Civilization" (2002:169).

"Geologist record indicates that during Late Pleistocene glaciation, water of the Himalaya was frozen and that in place of rivers there were only glaciers, masses of solid ice. ... When the climate became warmer, the glaciers began to break up and the frozen water held by them surged forth in great floods, inundating the alluvial plain in front of the mountains. ... No wonder the early inhabitants of the plains burst into song praising Lord Indra for breaking up the glaciers and releasing waters which flowed out in seven mighty channels (*Sapta Sindhu*). ... With the hindsight we possess as geologists, we at once see that the phenomenon described in the *Rig Veda* was no idle fancy but a real natural event of great significance connected with the break up of Himalayan glaciers and the release of pent-up waters in great floods."

The mention of the break up of the Himalayan glaciers in the *Rig Veda* suggests beyond any doubt that the *Rig Veda* was composed at least 10,000 years back. How then would Vedic Aryans come to India from outside and that in 1500 B.C.?

The archeologically excavated seals at Mohenjo-Daro and Harappa, in early 1920s, shed historical light to awaken historians to the truths about the prehistory ancient Bhārat, her native *Aryans*, and the antiquity of the *Rig Veda*, and of its language Sanskrit. Unfortunately, the wrong history, written by colonial Westerners, has not yet been corrected. Encyclopedias and several text books continue to carry on the same wrong texts as written by them prior to the Indus Valley civilization saw the sunshine in 1920s.

History has been kind to Aryans by giving them an enviable global ethnic status to the extent that some envious European people have been proudly claiming Aryan heritage, but unkind to them, by misconceiving, distorting, and confusing their origin, their original native country, and denying them authorship of their sacred scriptures (Vedas) and their language Sanskrit. Colonial historians have attempted in vain to deprive India of the pride for being the cradle of such a great race and authors of the Vedas, the most ancient scriptures of the humanity, containing knowledge pertaining to various aspects of life, mankind needs for healthy and happy survival. Because of the Hindu oral traditions, colonial historians have not been able to distort or bury Vedic knowledge, man needs.

All the misconceptions and conscious deliberate ignorance and omission of several historical facts seem to be deliberate maneuvers on the part of colonial historians and linguists for their hidden agenda to belittle non-European civilizations, particularly Asian and African, and validate their both ill-based inter-twined theories, (i) *Aryan Invasion of India* (AII) and (ii) *Indo-European Family of Languages* (IEFL).

Clouds can not hide the existence of the sun. It would be idiocy if any one, particularly a philologist or historian, would write that Sanskrit and a pantheon of Hindu gods came from outside into Ârya-āvarta (India), the cradle of all the four – Aryans, Sanskrit, Swastika and Vedic gods. The Aryan influence has been subtly felt and vibrations recognized almost every where on the planet, including Americas, Asia, Southeast Asia, Africa, and in several other regions. Arya and *Swastika* are Sanskrit words. According to 'The Practical Sanskrit Dictionary' by Vaman Shivram Apte (p.229), the word Arya means "worthy, venerable, respectable, honourable, and noble." None, but Ârya-āvarta (present India or Bharat) is the original abode of all the four – *Aryans*, Vedas, Sanskrit, and *Swastika*. In my opinion, because Aryans have gained global face, it has been therefore difficult for historians to confine them to only India.

The name "Ârya-āvarta" was not given to ancient India after the name of the alleged invading Aryans. She has been known as "Ârya -āvarta" for millennia, too difficult to know her birth, may be since the birth of the mankind which is too ancient to know. Hinduism, unlike all other religions, is too ancient. It was not founded by a person. India's name Bhārat came much later.

. The Columbia Encyclopedia (1993, pp.163-4) talks about the glory of ancient Sanskrit literature, as contained in its three major Oriental dramas:

"Of the three major Oriental dramas – Sanskrit, Chinese, Japanese – the oldest is Sanskrit, although the dates of its origin are uncertain. Sanskrit drama is a part of Sanskrit literature, the classical literature of India, which flourished from about 1500 B.C. to A.D.1100. The earliest extant critical work on Sanskrit drama is attributed to Bharata, the legendary formulator of the dramatic art in India. ... The earliest-known Sanskrit playwright was Bhasa (c.3d cent. A. D.), while among the most renowned were Kalidasa, Bhavabhuti (c.8th cent. A.D.), and King Harsha."

Kalidasa wrote Shakuntala. She was daughter of Rishi Vishwamitra (विश्वामित्र) and Apsarā (अप्सरा) Menkā (मेनका). Maharaja Dushyanta, while on hunting in forests, got mesmerized by the beauty and innocence of the rustic dame Shakuntala. They fell in love and had a son who was named Bhārat, the name, our great ancient country has adopted. It is mentioned in the Constitution of Bhārat. Dushyanta, due to some curse and/or his busy royal engagements, forgot his meeting with her and his promise to return to the forest to take her to the palace. She lost the royal ring Dushyanta had given her, while playing with water in a river. Fortunately, the ring was brought to the palace by a fisherman who found it in a fish. It helped the reunion and majestic celebrations of Shakuntala-Dushyanta wedding, and enthroning of their brave son Bhārat, the prince. Bhārat's main sport was playing with lions and tigers and counting their teeth. This is the story, how ancient Ārya-āvarta came to be known as Bhārat, as given in the Constitution of Bhārat.

The name "India" was given to Bhārat only a couple of centuries back, with a hidden mischievous British agenda to disconnect Bhārat from her long great enviable heritage. The name of a country has history. Aryans were there in Bhārat, long before the alleged Aryan invasion. Rather, Aryans were there from the day, the country was named as Ārya-āvarta. So, in no way, history can say that Ārya-āvarta was named after the alleged invading Aryans or Aryans because of Ārya-āvarta. Who cares: "If hen came first or egg?" History is happy to know that both, Ārya-āvarta and Āryans, are closely related to each other since remote pre-history ancient times.

Some historians say that the alleged invading Aryans came from Central Asia. It is true that Central Asia had Aryans only because whole Central Asia, comprising of all its 'stan / istan'countries, was part of Bhārat, as explained in the Chapter "*Central Asia: Original abode of Aryans* (Hindus). *Ancient Bhārat.*" Takshashila University gets its name from Taksha, son of Bharat, the brother of Lord Rama. Taksha ruled over the kingdom of Taksha Khandan which extended even beyond modern Uzbekistan, in Central Asia.

Is Aryan a race or a language?

Almost all scholars feel Aryans are a race, a society, a community. Few feel Aryan is a group of languages. In my opinion, Aryan is a race. Their languages can be called as Aryan languages, which include Sanskrit and all Indian vernaculars as its children.

It is disappointing to see how the history, supposed to be a true and objective story of mankind, has been treated unprofessionally by several scholars, ironically historians too. Different and contradicting versions on some sensitive socio-cultural and religious aspects of several communities, particularly of the East – Asian and African – by several Western historians, have confused students of history about Aryans, their identity and ancestry. Colonial pen, backed by British might, has not been fair to history. Hope the post-WW-II freedom-spirit will awaken some historians, if not all, to correct whatever wrongs have been written, and encourage free Eastern peoples to reinterpret and reconstruct their respective distorted ancient histories. It may not be easy for many historians to identify the wrongs they themselves have done – knowingly or unknowingly – to their own history; and thus it would be difficult to clean the colonial mud has been sitting for a couple of centuries over the remote eastern ethnic histories. Hindus can get lot of insights into their ancient history – corrupted, hidden or ignored – by their oral traditions as contained in their various ancient sacred scriptures, like Vedas. Most ancient Vedic mythologies have lot of historical truths, enveloped within them. Only a nationalistic x-ray eye is needed to be objective enough to weed out improper sentiments and myths.

The Random House Webster's College Dictionary writes that in Sanskrit 'Arya' means noble and a person of high rank. It defines Aryan as "a speaker of the languages ancestral to the Indo-Aryan or the Indo-Iranian languages." Indo-Iranian, because in ancient times Iran was a culturally, linguistically and administratively part of India. It is discussed in detail later in the Chapter *"Iran, the Cradle of Aryans."* The dictionary also defines it as "(formerly) a speaker of Proto-Indo-European; an Indo-European." It gives confusing and vague versions on the identity of Aryans, as "Indo-Aryan", "Indo-European" and "Indo-Iranian." Since the 'Arya' is a Sanskrit word and Sanskrit is originally linked with none but India, then why not to associate the origin of the Aryans only with India, the land of Sanskrit-speaking people? Why to confuse it with Indo-Iranian or Indo-European?

Max Müller (1891, p. 291), talks about the use of the word "Arya" in the *Rig Veda*: "In the old Sanskrit, in the hymns of the Veda, Arya occurs frequently as a national name and as a name of honour, comprising the worshippers of the gods of the Brahmans, as opposed to their enemies, who were called in the Veda as Dasyus. Thus one of the gods, Indra, who, in some respects, answers to the Greek Zeus, is invoked in Vedas."

Max Müller cites the hymn:

> 'Know thou the Aryas, O Indra, and they who are Dasyus; punish the lawless, and deliver them unto thy servant! Be thou the mighty helper of the worshippers, and I will praise all these thy deeds at the festivals.'"
> (Rig Veda i.51.8):

Are Aryans: Ancestors of Europeans?

J. P. Mallory, in the Epilogue of his book *"In Search of Indo-Europeans"* (pp. 266-272), vehemently talks about the 'Aryan Myth':

> "We cannot examine the legacy of the Indo-Europeans without first dispelling the spectre of the 'Aryan Myth'.

The world is all too familiar with how the concept of racial supremacy was implemented by the National Socialists in Germany, and we would be quite mistaken to imagine that the grotesque obsession with the Indo-Europeans or, as they were then more popularly known, the Aryans, was merely the creation of a handful of Nazi fanatics."

Mallory is half-right that the problem of the homeland of Aryans has been created by a handful of Nazi fanatics. I feel the term 'Indo-European' was current long before the birth of Hitler, as evidenced by the theory of *Indo-European Family of Language'* which was created earlier. India is geographically too distant, and culturally and historically too different from Europe to contemplate an Indo-European family or language. It was mischievously theorized to validate ill-based 'Aryan invasion of India' to deny Hindus the credit for such a great Aryan race. Europeans envy Aryan race. They have been trying to steal Aryan heritage as their own, claiming that Aryans are the jewels of White race.

Europeans: In search of their ancestors

Mallory seems to give an impression that Europeans – English, Germans, Anglo-Saxons, Vikings, Normans, etc. – seem to have been confused about their legacy and ancestry. They have been in serious search of their ancestors. The vague broad-based term 'Indo-Europeans' doesn't indicate exactly the people it is referring to. It can be any one of the several members of the IE family, such as – Indo-Aryans, Iranians, Germans, French, English, etc. In my opinion they are not confused, but not satisfied about their ancestry. Some seem to think that Aryans are their ancestors. They have been unable to reach a consensus on the homeland of Aryans, whether Europe, Asia (India) or Indo-Europe. It is hard to understand why unable to accept Aryavarta, historically known as the home of ancient Aryans. The quarrel seems to be between two mothers – (i) real mother (Aryavarta) and (ii) the fascinated mother (Indo-European). Let the readers decide.

Mallory (p. 269) talks about Max Müller's confusion around Aryan, whether it is a race or a language:

> "The great Indologist Max Müller, annoyed by the madness he had helped to create, blasted the anthropologists who spoke of an 'Aryan race, Aryan blood, Aryan eyes and hair' as a lunacy comparable to a linguist who spoke of 'a dolichocephalic dictionary or a brachycephalic grammar'. But it was too late: the Indo-Europeans and racism had become inseparable in the minds of many scholars. Although there would always be linguists and anthropologists to protest, the superiority of the ancient Aryan Nordic race had entered popular political culture."

This problem is created by racially biased and confused European scholars. Students of history and language have been concerned about that confusion, ironically created by historians themselves, particularly by colonial Europeans. They have been confused because of their self-induced ignorance of and bias against the cultures of the societies, particularly Eastern, they are writing about. The Western ethno-political agenda has induced Western scholars to write histories of the Eastern (Asian and African) societies and their cultures to put them down, so that Europeans look ethnically superior. Unfortunately, ethno-biased European scholars feel desperately failure to claim their superiority over Aryans who have proved to be superior on two counts, race and language. Some Europeans have been craving to be Aryans.

Some European scholars, like Gobineau, call Aryans a White race. They have been desperately connecting themselves with Aryans and seeking their heritage in the Aryan race. They have fabricated the two baseless theories – 'Indo-European' and 'Aryan invasion of India' according to which, Aryans and their language Sanskrit came into India from outside and the Vedas (scriptures of knowledge) were composed by the alleged invading Aryans, not by the original natives (Hindus) of *Aryavarta* (present India).

It is always advisable to feel proud of own ethnic identity. No race is absolutely perfect. Each race (European, Asian or African) has some characteristics to feel proud of and some to feel ashamed of. Aryans can not be Europeans, and Europeans can not be Aryans.

They have been confusing (i) the identity of the Aryans, (ii) their homeland and (iii) originality and homeland of Sanskrit, the language of the Aryan Vedas. The original homeland of Aryans, according to history and common sense, can not be any country other than "Aryavarta" (India). None, but Hindus, can be the people of the Aryan race. None but Hindustan (India, Bharat, Aryavarta) can be the cradle of Aryans and of Sanskrit, the language of Aryans and of their Vedas. Max Müller, as explained earlier in this chapter, believed that none but *Aryavarta* (India) is the original home of Aryans, their Vedas and their language Sanskrit.

John Gunther, in his *'Inside Asia'* (1939, p. 373), has remarked about the Aryan invasion:

> "About 1500 B.C. or earlier, a series of invasions of India began by light-skinned nomads who came through the Afghan passes and settled in the Ganges plains. ... These nomad invaders were the Aryans; in Sanskrit the word "Arya" means gentleman or one high born. The Aryans had their own literature; their early books are called Vedas, or scriptures. Veda literally means knowledge. ... The Aryans very early developed an exceedingly complicated form of worship, which became Hinduism."

Does Gunther mean to say there was no Hinduism (in its original form, i.e. Vedic religion) prior to 1500 B.C.? Does he mean that the invading Aryans had Vedas, prior to their alleged invasion in 1500 B.C.? Is he trying to say all the Aryans of Asia Minor or any other country left for India in around 1500 B.C., leaving none behind? History has not talked about any country, outside India, with Sanskrit-speaking Vedic Aryans, as its natives. History has not talked about any country, other than India, had Sanskrit as its native language, nor Sanskrit as a dead language.

Osborne & et al (1988, p. 59) have said: "From 1500 to 500 B.C., the Aryans brought the Sanskrit language, the horse, and iron products." They contradict themselves on the same page: "Since its origin around 3000 B.C., Hinduism has had great influence on Indian society. .... Gods, they chiefly worshiped are: Brahma, the creator; Vishnu, the preserver; and Shiva, the destroyer."

If Hinduism originated in India in about 3000 B.C., how then the alleged invading Aryans, with knowledge of Sanskrit and the Vedas, be considered outsiders or invaders? They must be returning to India (*Aryavarta*), the country of their ancestors who were Aryans, practicing Vedic religion (Hinduism). Such an apparent serious contradiction on the same page by historian reflects their ignorance or a conscious historical mischief.

It would not be contradiction, only if Osborne & et al mean that Hinduism originated some where else, the Aryans came from. Then, the difference of 15 centuries (3000 BC minus 1500 BC) should be the life of Hinduism outside India, where the invading Aryans practiced Hinduism before arriving in India. In such situation, several questions arise, such as:

- Does any country, outside India, show that Hinduism or Hinduism-like religion was practiced there any time in the past?
- What are the name of that country and the name of the religion? All must have not left for India. What happened to those who did not leave?
- Does history of that country talk about that religion, Vedas and Sanskrit?

Will Durant, in his book *"Our Oriental Heritage"* (1935, p. 406), clearly seems to suggest that if the invading Aryans were not original Indo-Aryans from India, *Sanskrit* could not be their spoken language.

Stanley Wolpert (1993: 24) says that around 2000 B.C. (not 1500 BC), the ancestors of the Italic, Greek, Germanic, English, Celtic, Iranian, Sanskritic, and modern Hindi-speaking peoples were forced to flee from the southern Russia to survive by some life threatening natural disaster and Mongol invasions from Central Asia. Wolpert further writes:

> "These tribes moved in every direction, splitting up into smaller, more cohesive units, driving their herds of cattle, sheep, goats, and domesticated horses with them, and opening a new chapter in the history of Europe, as well as of India. .... By about 1500 B.C., however, they appear to have split once more and pastoral tribes known to history as the Indo-Aryans, or simply Aryans, advanced still further east, across the perilous Hindu Kush Mountains, into India."

Multiple splitting of the migrating group from the alleged birth place of the reconstructed proto-Indo-European (not real/original) suggests that the final group of India-bound Aryans would have been too small to be able to overwhelm linguistically and culturally the massive population of India.

When according to Wolpert, the immigrating Aryans were known to history as Indo-Aryans or simply Aryans, they should not be considered as foreigners to India. Wolpert does not say they were invaders. In fact, they might be returning to India, the country of their ancestors. It makes it clear that they knew about India and they also knew that their ancestors belonged to India. They knew an Indic language, Sanskrit, Hindi, or any other. If Sanskrit was their native language while they were in Central Asia, Southern Russia, or Asia Minor, etc., the history of languages would have mentioned Sanskrit, as one of the ancient languages of that region, alive or dead. The 'Arya' is a Sanskrit word. History vouches that Sanskrit is the language of the Vedas, the oldest religious scriptures of *Aryavrata*, now known as Bharat or India. In the Chapter on Vedas, it has been shown, based on irrefutable evidences that the *Rig Veda* is older than ten thousand years, and so its language Sanskrit.

Stanley Wolpert[36] (1993, p. 27) has said:

"In 1909 excavations at the Hittite site of Boghaz-
koi in Cappadocia yielded tablets containing a treaty
concluded between the Hittite king Subiluliuma and
his Mitanni neighbor to the east, King Mattiwaza, who
reigned in about 1400 B.C. invoked as divine witnesses
to this treaty were four gods, Indara, Uruvna, Mitira,
and the Nasatiya, whose Sanskrit names in the *Rig Veda*
were spelled virtually the same (Indra, Varuna, Mitra,
and Naksatras), proving that by this date the Vedic
pantheon had acquired its identity. This confirmation
of Müller's estimates leads us to assume that, since the
Rig Veda itself does not mention the Aryan invasions of
India, the process must have begun at least a century
earlier, or probably around 1500 B.C. The final wave of
tribal invasions may have come centuries after the first
Aryans started over the northwest passes. This was the
most important invasion in all of India's history, since
the Aryans brought with their Caucasian genes a new
language – Sanskrit – and a new pantheon of gods, as
well as the patriarchal family and the three-class social
structure (priests, warriors, and commoners) into which
their tribes were organized."

Wolpert is right about the treaty. History tells it happened in about
1300 -1400 B.C. The invocation of Hindu gods – Indra, Varuna, Mitra,
Naksatras – suggests that both Hittite and Mittani kings were of Vedic
(Hindu) origin, and history confirms it. Wolport writes that they were
Rig Vedic gods. Then how would Max Müller, Wolpert and others say
that the Vedas were composed by the alleged invading Aryans in 1000
B.C. or later? Since the Vedas were composed by the alleged invading
Aryans, then the Vedas would have talked about the alleged Aryan
invasion of India.

---

[36] Stanley Wolpert. A New History of India, (1993, p. 27).

Wolpert has not explained what the two Aryan kings of Indian origin – Hittite and Mitanni – were doing there. As a matter of fact, they were of the *Kshatri* (warrior) tribe. They must have gone out of India earlier than 1300 B.C. and had established there their kingdoms. When in trouble around 1500 B.C. they might have attempted to return to India, the country of their ancestors. Since, from Royal family, they might be traveling in armored horse-driven chariots, thus might have been mistaken as invaders, the theory of 'Aryan invasion of India' could be based on. Invasion of their own cradle is ill-conceivable; it could be their return to home. Idea of invasion was mischievously contemplated by colonial strategists to deprive Hindus of the credit of Aryan world-wide glory. Aryans were Hindus and Hindus were Aryans.

According to the above statement by Wolpert that the invading Aryans, while as Hittite and Mitanni kings in the Asia, Minor region had Sanskrit, the Vedas and Vedic religion. Then, history would have mentioned Sanskrit, as the native language and Vedic religion of the natives of the Asia Minor region. As a matter fact, Aryans had gone there as traders and had established their kingdoms, and when overpowered by the natives or other powers, almost all of them might have got culturally and linguistically absorbed. The thought that some of them attempted to return to Aryavarta (India) seems inconceivable and impractical.

If this historical claim is true, why has history been completely silent about this? Did all the Sanskrit-speaking people of Asia Minor move to India, leaving no sign of their Sanskrit and Vedic religion there?

Wolpert has not said that Sanskrit originated in Central Asia or in India. In my opinion, whatever Wolpert has said that Aryans were in Asia Minor is true. But it is not true that the Aryans were natives of Asia Minor region. It is also not true that their language Sanskrit was the native language of that region. It is also not true that the Vedic religion originated there. Sanskrit was spoken there and the Vedic religion was practiced, but not by its native. It was practiced only by the Indo-Aryans (Hittites and Mitannis) who had gone there as traders. Wolpert should have explained all this.

Sanskrit was spoken in Asia Minor when Indo Aryans were there. Now it is dead there. The linguistic history is witness that no language has died in the place of its origin and survived somewhere else. Sindhi is dying among Sindhi Hindus living outside Sindh, the birthplace of the Sindhi language. It will not die in Sindh, the birthplace of Sindhi.

It may die in Sindh only when all Sindhi-speaking Sindhis (Hindus as well as Muslims) living in Sindh die or leave Sindh. Yet, it will leave its signs there in form of some literature, or at least its name among the dead languages of the region. Sanskrit is not mentioned among the dead languages of Asia Minor, nor of any other country in the region. Parsi (Farsi/Persian), as a spoken language, has died among Parsis living in India, but not in Iran. In present India Persian is being taught in schools and colleges, as a classical language, few opt because it has little employment and literary value.

According to Max Müller (p. 291), the word 'Arya' has been often mentioned in the *Rig Veda* which is older than 6,000 B.C.

Edward C. Dimock, Jr.[37] and his associates have said about the Aryans, Indo-European family, Sanskrit, the Dravidian and Austric languages:

> "Let us turn back to the beginning, when the wandering Aryan tribes, with their cattle and their great possession, the Veda, were drifting through the high passes into the fertile plain below. For they must have collided almost at once with representatives of two other major language families, with which their tongue, the south-eastern-most branch of the Indo-European family, had not a word in common. Those two families were Dravidian and Austric."

It is interesting to note that the invading Aryans came with "their great possession, the Veda." Dimock & et al seem to suggest that the invading Aryans had the Vedas and that they knew Sanskrit while in the country they came from. Some other scholars, including Wolpert, have also said the same. Such misrepresentations and contradictions – on part of several scholars, like Dimock and Wolpert, about the originality of the Vedas and Sanskrit, and also about the authorship and date of

---

[37]   Edward C. Dimock, Jr. 'The Literature of India: An Introduction' (1974, p. 6)

the Vedas – confuse students as well as teachers of history related to Aryans, Sanskrit and Vedas. The irony is that the scholars who claim that Sanskrit was brought into India by some invading Aryans, have yet to identify the country outside India which had Aryans as its natives, Sanskrit as its native language and a pantheon of Hindu gods they worshipped. Those historians need to stop chasing the mirage of 'Aryans *outside Aryavarta.'*

Historians have not yet been able to tell who those Aryans were and the country they came from. Some scholars say that the alleged Aryans brought the Vedas too. The same scholars say that the Vedas were composed by the invading Aryans after their arrival. The invading Aryans with the Vedas must have practiced Vedic religion in the country they came from. Which is that country other than India where Vedic religion was practiced any time in the past? It is unbelievable that a scholar, particularly a historian would contradict himself. All those Vedic people, it is understandable, must have got converted into some other religion. But history should tell who those Aryans were, and the country or region they came from where they spoke Sanskrit, and practiced Vedic or Vedic-like religion. It is understandable Sanskrit can be dead there. But its name "Sanskrit" should be among the dead languages of that region.

Sentimental significance of native language

Language is the most precious possession one would not like to lose. I am an immigrant in America from India. I know very well my all the three languages:

1. **Sindhi,** my mother tongue; I spoke while in Sindh, now in Pakistan, until I left for India in 1947, when the British India was partitioned into Bharat (India) and Pakistan.
2. **Hindi,** the national language of India, I spoke until I left India in 1970 for America, and
3. **English,** the language of my adopted country America.

Mother tongue too precious to lose!

In migration, understaningably there will be gains and losses. I still love to speak Sindhi, my mother first spoke to me in, whenever possible. I am married to Gujarati. We speak Hindi quite often at home and in Indian social gatherings. But mostly English. We love to hear Hindi songs and watch Hindi movies. I always feel concerned if my America-born daughters Shilpa and Neha would preserve at least Hindi. I feel happy when I hear them speaking it even a little bit. If they don't, how would their children and grand children speak?

I was amazed to read the article *"To save Its Native Tongue, Tribe Teaches the Young"* (NY Times, October 17, 2008), written by Dan Frosch. It vividly paints the sentimental concerns – of the elders and youngsters of the Arapaho Native Indian tribe living on the Wind River Reservation in Wyoming – how to preserve their native language ARAPAHO. Frosch writes that they (Arapahos) have schools, although with thin attendance, because they know that their language has little employment prospects. But, they attach other precious value to their native tongue. Ms. Inee Y. Slaughter – the Executive Director of the 'Indigenous Language Institute,' a group in Santa Fe, N.M. that works with the tribes on native languages – says that it provides a safe place where a child's roots are nurtured, its culture is honored, and its being is valued. Ms. Kayla Howling Buffalo (25 yr young) happily voiced: "My son talks nothing but Arapaho to me and my grand parents." She herself took Arapaho classes because her grand mother no longer has any one to speak with and fears she is losing her first language.

Language dies with its speakers. Who will like to relate with or associate with one who does not have a language? Mr. Ryan Wilson, a member of a National Indian Education Association Board, said: "If we lose that language, we lose who we are." According to Dan Frosch, the author of this article, only about 200 Arapaho speakers are still alive. Language defines the ethno-cultural identity of its speakers. Ellen Lutz, the Executive Director of Cultural Survival, remarks: "Language seems to be a healing force for Native American communities."

I am referring to this article only to show the significance of the native language and how difficult it is for a community to let it die even facing so many odds. This is to prove that Sanskrit would not have died in the region, the invading Aryans allegedly came from, if it was any time its native language. Even after all the Arapaho speakers are dead, the name of Arapaho will remain among the dead languages.

Vedic (Hindu) traditions are the oldest in the history of humanity. In remote ancient times, there was no concept of history. Significant events were given in sacred scriptures. So much history, given in the Hindu legends, has been ignored, and wrong history, guided by European ethno-cultural competitive agenda, is being taught. Subjective interpretations of the significant historical events are being recorded. History is being shamelessly abused by its creators, the historians. Every religion is basically good. Better be broad minded and open to learn from other religions and cultures.

Fortunately for Hindus, and unfortunately for several biased Western historians, history is being given down to Hindus orally from generation to generation in temples, through traditional street Ram/Krishna *leelas* (plays), and now through cinema, radio and TV. It has prevented Hindu minds and hearts, particularly of the mass illiterate villagers, from getting infected by the colonial history virus. The rest of the educated-elite seniors, who have been adversely brainwashed against their own culture, are speeding to their cremation ground. It would be advisable for Western historians to admit the abuse of their beloved child history, and rewrite correct histories, particularly of Asian and African societies. Deliberate distortion of the history is described in the Chapter *'Cries of History.'*

Both the inter-twined theories – Aryan invasion of India (AII) and Indo-European family of languages (IE) – have created lingual, cultural and political rift between the North Indians and the South Indians. As a matter of fact, South Indians are as civilized as the North Indians. South Indians, as per their names, seem to have been more inclined to Vedic religion and culture. It may be because the North Indians have been more vulnerable to the West, thus slightly brushed by Christian and Islamic paint. Basically, both North and South Indians, have similar socio-cultural orientations.

With increasing education and national ethos, enflamed by Indian parliament, music and cinema, the wall between the North and the

South has started trembling down, and its foundation loosening. Fortunately, increasing number of Western scholars have been surfacing to call a spade, and talk about the abuse of Asian and African histories at hands of Western scholars.

The *Rig Veda* has not talked about the alleged Aryan invasion. Its last hymn was composed long before 1500 BC, the year of the alleged Aryan invasion. The invasion has not been mentioned even in later Vedic scriptures because of the fact it did not happen. Why would Aryans invade their own motherland Aryavarta? Their attempt to return, if happened, has been mistaken as invasion.

Colin Renfrew[38] seems to suggest that the Aryas were not strangers in the Punjab; the land of the Seven Rivers, Wheeler thinks was invaded by Aryans:

> "When Wheeler speaks of 'the Aryan invasion of the Land of the Seven Rivers, the Punjab', he has no warranty at all, so far as I can see. If one checks the dozen references in the *Rigveda* to the Seven Rivers, there is nothing in any of them that to me implies invasion: the land of the Seven Rivers is the land of the *Rigveda,* the scene of the action. Nothing implies that the Aryans were strangers there. Nor is it implied that the inhabitants of the walled cities (including the Dasyus) were more aboriginal than the Aryas themselves."

Renfrew clearly asserts that none of the several references to the *Rig Veda* suggests invasion of India. Ainslie T. Embree (ed.)[39] talks about the Aryans who they were and about their alleged invasion of India:

> "The major source of the Brahmanical tradition is related to the migration into the Indian subcontinent from the northwest, sometime around 2000 B.C. of

---

[38]   Colin Renfrew. Archaeology & Language (1987, p.188).
[39]   Ainslie T. Embree (ed.), in 'Sources of Indian Tradition' (2nd. edition, vol. 1, 1988, p. 4),

people who spoke an Indo-European language. These
people, whose original homeland may have been around
the Caspian Sea, are known in the Indian tradition
itself as "Aryans," a term that has been misunderstood in
European history. ...The Aryan migrants brought with
them religious concepts and a pantheon of naturalistic or
functional gods, ritualistic cult involving the sacrificial
use of fire and an exhilarating drink called soma, as well
as the rudiments of a social order."

Whatever, Prof. Embree has said above, needs to be minutely analyzed
to see if he is implicitly endorsing my theory that these immigrants or
invaders were Indo-Aryans whose religious concepts were similar to
those of the native Aryans of India. Aryans have been misunderstood
and misrepresented. Embree seems to admit that the immigrants "spoke
an Indo-European language" which can not be other than Sanskrit or
a Sanskritic language. Whatever they brought with them – "religious
concepts and a pantheon of naturalistic or functional gods, ritualistic
cult involving the sacrificial use of fire and an exhilarating drink called
soma" – clearly suggest that immigrants were Vedic Hindus. He also
says, "(they) are known in the Indian (Hindu / Vedic) tradition itself
as "Aryans," a term that has been misunderstood in European history."
Only Embree failed short of explaining why, when, and where, those
returning Aryans had gone out of India.

History is full of well-evidenced accounts of several emigrations of
Aryans to almost all regions of the world, as described in the Chapter
Vishaal Bharat (Greater India): Borderless World of Vedic Culture.

Opposed to most other historians who say that Aryans invaded
India, Prof. Embree talks about Aryan migrants, not as invaders. He
also gives different time frame, 2000 B.C., as opposed to 1500 BC,
given by most scholars. If the Brahmanical tradition, Embree is referring
to, is related to immigrants who brought with them Hinduism-related
religious concepts, it can be said beyond any doubt that the immigrants
must have practiced Hinduism-like religion in the country/region they
came from. They must have spoken an Indo-European language; I think
the reference is to Sanskrit. In my opinion, Aryans might have migrated

to some where around the Caspian Sea and might have practiced their Hindu religious concepts during their long stay there. Some of them might have attempted to return to India, the country of their origin. This can be understood better if we compare them to the people of Indian origin who have migrated about a couple of centuries back to the Caribbean region, Africa, Mauritius, Fiji, and even to Americas. They have preserved and will continue to preserve their Indian culture through several of their Mandirs (Hindu temples), *Gurudwaras* (Sikh temples) and *Masjids* all around. Most of the families have a prayer room in their house to practice and preserve Indian philosophy. Some are returning to India. They are not considered as invaders.

Embree's characterizing of the gods, Aryans worshipped, "as a pantheon of naturalistic or functional gods" clearly suggests that the gods, Aryans worshipped, were Hindu gods. Only Hinduism is a naturalistic religion, as it was not founded by an individual, as all other religions have been. Thus, the name of its founder and date of its birth are not known. Hinduism is as ancient as man. Nature and mankind are twins. Hindu gods are functional. Brahma is creator, Vishnu caretaker, and Shiva destroyer of the worn and torn out body to be reborn to enjoy another full life.

History does not talk about any country around the Caspian Sea and in the Middle East region (Egypt, Mesopotamia, Asia Minor, etc.) whose natives spoke Sanskrit and practiced Hinduism or a Hinduism-like religion. It clearly suggests that those Sanskrit-speaking were Vedic people (Hindus or Indo-Aryans). They were travelers or immigrants there. They were not natives. They must be speaking Sanskrit and practicing Hindu religion among themselves, as in America, immigrants speak their own respective languages and practice their respective religions among themselves. When out of their home – in school, office, or shopping mall – they speak English. If Sanskrit was the native language of any country in the region, it would have been still there or would have been mentioned among the dead languages of the region.

By saying: "These people, whose original homeland may have been around the Caspian Sea, are known in the Indian tradition itself as Aryans," this could rightly be interpreted that these migrants were Indo-Aryans who might have gone from India to the Caspian Sea region for trade or for some other reason; or even as invaders who might have established their kingdoms there. They must have settled there, and some of them might have returned to India, the country of their origin. History tells that Aryans (Hindus) from India had gone to that region and beyond, and had established their kingdoms there, as mentioned in the Chapter *"Vishaal Bharat (Greater India): Borderless World of Vedic Culture."* Embree seems to confirm it by saying that the term *'Aryan'* has been "much misused and misunderstood in European history." I fully agree with him that European scholars have been completely confused about the term "Aryan", therefore its misuse. Unfortunately, Embree didn't come out to say that he is not convinced about the validity of the theory of Aryan invasion of India.

To be honest, some times I feel that European historians were not confused around the term Aryan. They knowingly have done it so as to be able to validate their ill-based theory of Aryan invasion, and also to deny Hindus of their traditional ethnic identity as Aryans. I wish I am wrong thinking that the term "Aryan" – along with the history associated with it – has been knowingly misinterpreted by most historians with colonial and missionary agenda.

Prof. Embree (p.5) says: "The religion thus developed by the Aryans from the time of their migration into India until roughly 500 B.C. was embodied in a collection of hymns, ritual texts, and philosophical treaties called the Veda." It clearly suggests that the seeds of the Vedic religion were already sown in the minds of the returning Aryans which they started developing from the time they reached the Vedic land India. The Vedic seeds bloom when they are nourished by Vedic land and nurtured by Vedic atmosphere. This happens with Hindus who return to India after their long stay away from India. I hope I am not wrong if I say that Embree confirms the historically evidenced fact of the prehistory antiquity of the *Rig Veda* and its language Sanskrit, as proved with irrefutable evidences in the Chapters on Sanskrit and Vedas, that the *Vedas* were composed long before the arrival of the alleged invading Aryans. Mention of melting of the Himalayan glaciers in *Rig Veda*, testifies that the *Rig Veda* was composed before ten thousand years, because glaciers melted about ten thousand years back. If the alleged invading Aryans came with Vedic orientations, they should be

Indo-Aryans who must be returning to India. They did not compose the Vedas after their arrival. The Vedas were already composed long before their arrival.

The historians who still claim that the Vedic religion surfaced in India only after the alleged arrival of Aryans in 1500 B.C., seem to be ignorant, rather pretend to be ignorant of the ages of Sanskrit and the Vedas. Juniors (recent students) of the world history know that none but India is the cradle of Sanskrit, Aryans and the Vedas. Most Indian school children know that Sanskrit and Vedas have close association with India from pre-history ancient times. The Vedic religion, as measured by the ages of the Swastika and *Shiva Ling*, is much older than at least 5000 years. Seals depicting *Swastika* and the *Shiva Ling*, which have been excavated from the Mohenjodaro, were at least one thousand years older than the year of alleged Aryan invasion. The age of the *Rig Veda* has been determined much older than 1900 B.C. when the *Sarasvati* River was completely dried up, and the *Rig Veda* contains several hymns talking about the life on its banks.

The *Swastika* is a Sanskrit word and it has been used in almost all the Vedic religious ceremonies and *Pujas*, even in present times. It has been found among some Native American Indians. It suggests that their ancestors must be none other than Vedic Aryans from ancient India who must have taken Swastika along with them to Americas about ten thousand years back. This proves that Sanskrit is at least ten thousand years old, and the *Rig Veda* must be about seven or eight thousand years old.

Stephen Knapp[40] emphatically refutes the theory of 'Aryan invasion of India': "In light of this, the belief of an "Aryan Race" coming from outside India is, indeed, a blunder of historical research. All references to the Aryans as a race who migrated to India should be deleted from history. There is no evidence that upholds this theory."

How would the hymns glorify the alleged invading Aryans as heroes in the *Rig Veda*, which was composed before 4,000 B.C.,[41] at least 2500

---

[40]   Stephen Knapp. 'Proof of Vedic Culture's Global Existence' (2000, pp. 270, 271).

[41]   In the Chapter, "Sanskrit and Vedas', the age of the Rig Veda has been ascertained longer than 6,000 years.

years before the alleged invading Aryans entered India? The age of the *Rig Veda* has been shortened by Western historians to validate the ill-based theory of the 'Aryan Invasion of India.'

Max Müller: The Age of Vedas and Aryan Invasion

Max Müller (1823-1900) – the strong supporter/architect of the theory of 'Aryan Invasion of India' – eventually came to realize that the *Vedas* were much older than what he himself and others thought. Müller has graciously admitted the misrepresentation of the birth-date of the *Vedas*.

The World Book Encyclopedia (1983, p. 728) writes about Aryans:

> "Aryans were a group of people who settled in Iran and northern India about 1500 B.C. Their language is also called *Aryan*. In Sanskrit, an ancient language of India, the word Arya means noble."

Since, according to the encyclopedia, the word 'Arya' has its origin in Sanskrit, and Sanskrit is the ancient language of India (former *Aryavrata)*, then how could the Encyclopedia suggest that Aryans came from outside and settled in India, their own native country? The above can be interpreted that in ancient times Iran and India were together as one country. In the Chapter *'Vishaal Bharat* (Greater India), this has been established with irrefutable historical evidences that in ancient times, Iran was administratively as well as culturally a part of Greater India, and that Sanskrit and Avestan were linguistically too close to each other to distinguish one from the other. Aryans were neither immigrants nor invaders. They were the natives of Aryavarta (India).

The World Book Encyclopedia (p. 728) states:

> "During the 1800's, language experts used the term *Aryan languages* for a group of related Asian and European languages. This group included English and most European languages; Bengali; and Persian. Today, scholars call these the Indo-European languages. The term *Indo-Aryan* refers to the Indo-European languages

of India. These languages include Sanskrit, which is no longer used in everyday conversation, and Hindi."

As said earlier that the two theories (i) Aryan invasion of India and (ii) Indo-European Family of Languages have confused and distorted the history of ancient India. The term 'Indo-European' has been too vague, therefore confusing. How can the languages of Europe are termed as 'Aryan languages? Aryans were from India, and that they were speaking Sanskrit, the ancient language of Aryavarta (India). Since Sanskrit, the language of the Vedas is a very ancient language, much older than 1500 B.C. and its documents are older than the documents of the ancient European languages, such as Latin, Greek, German, English, etc. The word "Arya" has repeatedly occurred in the *Rig Veda,* the oldest piece of literature of the world. How then would Sanskrit be considered as Indo-European and brought into India from outside? It has not been explained to the satisfaction of the readers why "Indo" has been prefixed to various families of languages. In my opinion, the word "Indo" (Indo-European, Indo-Iranian, Indo-Aryan, etc) has been senselessly floating in the ocean of linguistics. Talk specific. It has been confusing the students of linguistics and language too deeply to be able to understand the origin of Sanskrit and Aryans and relationship between the two. Thus, it is difficult to see any sense in both ill-based theories – 'Aryan invasion of India' and 'Indo European langages'.

The Columbia Encyclopedia on Aryans

According to the Columbia Encyclopedia (1993, p. 159), Aryan is a Sanskrit term meaning noble. The term formerly was used to designate the Indo-European race or a family of languages or Indo-Iranian subgroup. It further writes:

> "Aryans were part of a great migratory movement that spread in successive waves from S. Russia and Turkistan during 2nd millennium B.C. Through out Mesopotamia and Asia Minor, literate urban centers fell to their warrior bands."

The above statement clearly suggests that Aryans were warriors migrating to various places, S. Russia, Turkistan, all Mesopotamia and Asia Minor. But, history, biased to India and Indo-Aryans puts their reverse travel route. Migrations have been from south-east to north-west. Since Aryan is a Sanskrit term, as said by the Encyclopedia, Aryans should be from Aryavarta, not from some where else. Encyclopedia is right that "literate urban centers fell to them." Rather it would be more correct that the region occupied by Aryans became literate centers because Aryans were from India, the land of Vedas, the ocean of knowledge. Veda means knowledge.

Dr. Poonai[42] has talked about ancient migrations from India to north-western regions. He says that several Rig-Vedic Sanskrit-speaking Aryan clans emigrated north-westward beyond the Aegean area. In the early part of the third millennium B.C., the states of Caria, Miletus, Lydia, Troy and Phrygia, and neighboring lands were already occupied by Aryans who spoke Sanskritic dialects.

In ancient times, as early as 2500-3500 B.C., when the Indus Valley civilization was flourishing, adventurous and enterprising Aryans went out from India to so many regions of the world, as mentioned above, for trade; and at several places they established their Vedic/Hindu kingdoms. Historians, seeing Aryans at several places in north-west of India, think Aryans came to India from outside. But, they don't see the origin of the word 'Arya' in Sanskrit, the ancient language of India. Historians are putting Aryan movements from opposite direction – from north-west to south-east – instead from south-east to north-west. Always, even now in present times, human movement has generally been from south-east to north-west. They didn't move out from S. Russia and Turkistan as suggested above by the Columbia Encyclopedia. On contrary, the migratory Sanskrit-speaking Aryans went out from India to S. Russia and Turkistan. In about 1500 B.C. when they were militarily overpowered by some other forces, some of them might have attempted to return to India, the country of their origin. Because they, being royal warrior families might be traveling in horse-driven armored chariots, they might have met military confrontation from the natives of India who mistook them as invaders. If they were other

---

[42] Dr. Poonai. Origin of Civilization and Language (1994, pp: 157-8).

than Indo-Aryans (Vedic Hindus), how could they speak Sanskrit? This was misinterpreted as Sanskrit was brought by those alleged invading Aryans into India. Prehistory ancient Vedas evidence that Sanskrit was already being spoken in India.

The Columbia Encyclopedia further confuses its readers by writing: "Archeological evidence corroborates the text of the Veda by placing the invasion in India by the Aryans at c.1500 B.C." As a matter of fact, there is no mention of Aryan invasion in Vedas, because perhaps the last hymns of the Vedas were composed long before 1500 B.C. This has been made clear in the Chapter on Vedas. How would the Vedas mention the invasion which did not happen? The Aryan invasion is a historical myth, or it can be called a colonial mischief.

The Encyclopedia (p.159) seems to correct itself: "Before the discovery of the Indus Valley sites in 1920s, Hindu culture had been attributed solely to Aryan invasion." It clearly says that before excavations at the Indus Valley in 1920s, historians, out of their ignorance, attributed Hindu culture and religion to the alleged invading Aryans. The excavations confirm that Vedic culture current in India long before the Indus Valley civilization, which flourished before 3000 B.C. Excavations at Indus have discovered Shiva Linga and Swastika, implicitly refuting both the theories, AII and IE.

The Columbia Encyclopedia (p.2420) seems to admit that Sanskrit is the ancient language of India, not an import, as suggested by both the AII and IE theories. But it fails short of admitting that the Vedas were composed long before 1500 BC:

> "Sanskrit was the classical standard language of ancient India, and some of the oldest surviving Indo-European documents are written in Sanskrit. ... The Vedas probably date back to about 1500 B.C. or earlier, many centuries before writing was introduced into India."

It would have been clear to the point, if the Columbia Encyclopedia used "Sanskrit documents" instead of Indo-European documents.

The Encyclopedia Britannica defines 'Aryan' as:

"a people who, in prehistoric times, settled in Iran and northern India. From their language, also called Aryan, the Indo-European languages of South Asia are descended. In the 19th century the term was used as a synonym for "Indo-European" and also, more restrictively, to refer to the Indo-Iranian languages (q.v.). It is now used in linguistics only in the sense of the term Indo-Aryan languages."

Indo-Aryans did not settle in Iran or in Northern India, but they were born and raised there. Aryans were natives of India and Iran. In ancient times Iran was a part of India – culturally, linguistically, historically as well administratively. It is hard to understand why histories and encyclopedias are not specific when talking about languages. Why vague and in broad-based terms like, Indo-European, Indo-Aryan and 'Indo-Iranian' are used for Sanskrit. It should be termed as Sanskrit. It is hard to understand the historians, who despite, after the Indus Valley excavations in 1920's, having clear knowledge about the origin and the antiquity of Sanskrit, and the *Rig Veda* still continue to talk about Aryan invasion, import of Sanskrit, and wrong authorship of the *Rig Veda*.

Aryans were in Iran too in ancient times when Iran was a part of India. History will one day forget that Pakistan was once a part of India.

Historians need to use the specific name of the language when talking about it. They confuse readers by using a broader term (IE) for Sanskrit which can be interpreted as talking about any language, a member thereof. For example, use "Indo-European" or "Indo-Iranian" for Sanskrit is not appropriate. The term 'Indo-European' can mean any language member of the IE family, and 'Indo-Iranian' means any Indian or Iranian language. Why not call it by its specific name? It is difficult to understand why historians are shy of using the specific name of the language they are talking about. History should be specific and clear, not vague and confusing, like what Sarah Weir (ed.), in *'Webster's 21st Century Concise Chronology of World History'* (1993, p.28), has said:

"Nomadic Aryans migrated to the Indus Valley (in 1500 BCE), bringing with them (from the Russian steppe) the horse, the chariot, and the Sanskrit language. The origins of Hinduism can be found in the fusion of the Aryans' Indo-European creed with indigenous Harappan theology."

History tells that Aryans were never nomads. Aryans always have been civilized people with their home, family and stabilized establishment. They have been moving around for further advancement and for better life. How would Aryans bring Sanskrit from any where to their Sanskrit-speaking homeland India? Horses and chariots were there in the Indus Valley and the rest of India in ancient times. Multiple-horse-driven chariots were used in the Mahabharat war in around 3067 B.C. The picture of the chariot driven by four horses showing Lord Krishna and Arjuna would be found in Hindu temples and in most Hindu houses.

Hinduism has its origin Vedic philosophy which originated in India thousands of years back and is still flourishing. Weir's perception of the origin of Hinduism is too broad, vague and confusing.

As I understand, Max Müller believed that 'Aryan' was the name of a people, not of a language or of a family of languages. Obviously, their languages can rightly be called Aryan languages. But, it is hard to understand how languages of non-Aryans, like Europeans, can be called as Aryan languages. Europeans are not, and can not be Aryans by calling themselves so.

Max Müller makes it clear that 'None but Aryavarta (Aryadesh, Aryabhoomi, Bharat, India) is the original home of both, the Aryans and their language Sanskrit. It is unfortunate, that some confused and or biased scholars confuse the meaning and origin of the words 'Arya' and 'Aryan' to unjustifiably validate their unfounded theory of 'Aryan invasion of India'. How can the Aryans, the natives of Aryavarta (India), be considered foreigners to Aryavarta? How can scholarship say that Sanskrit, which was never a native language of any country outside India any time, was brought into India from outside?

America seems to be perfect analog of Central Asia. New York is its miniature. Immigrants from almost over hundred countries, including European, Asian, and African, have settled in America. They speak several Indo-European languages. If IE languages are called Aryan languages, would we say that these immigrants are Aryans and that America is the native land of Aryans? Or can we say that America is the native land of all those languages or all those languages are native languages of America?

The history of the ancient world is full of migrations, and so is the present history. It shows that in remote ancient times, Aryans (Vedic people) were every where on the planet, and had established Vedic (Hindu) kingdoms in the Middle East – Egypt, Mesopotamia, Asia Minor, Syria, Palestine, etc. – and in Central Asia in the countries with names, suffixed with 'stan' or 'istan'. Their histories have been buried too deep, and too disfigured to be able to know their original names. Their names have been changed.

The colonial historians felt free to represent the events as they wanted to, and hide lot of related history. Thus, they have abused their only child, 'history'. Lot is happening to history in the present open world; but comparatively much less. Now it will not be that easy, because the historically significant events are immediately documented by pen, internet and TV. The world has become very small, open and transparent. But, smart language jugglers can twist and misrepresent the event, though it has been documented.

According to Isaac Taylor[43]:

> "ARYAN, a term invented by Professor Max Müller, is almost as objectionable as Sanskritic, since it properly designates only the Indo-Iranian languages, in which sense it is used by many continental scholars. Moreover, it tacitly implies or suggests that the ancient Ariana, the district round Herat, was the cradle of the Aryan languages, and thus begs the whole question of their European or Asiatic origin."

The term "Aryan" was identified, not invented, by Max Müller, as Taylor thinks. It has been there in the *Rig Veda* and other Vedic/Hindu scriptures, long prior to the Indus Valley excavations of 1920s.

---

[43] Isaac Taylor, 'The Origin of the Aryans", pp. 2-3

Unfortunately, the ethno-politically engineered distorted history of ancient India was already written by the European colonial mighty pen. First written history has always longer shelf life and more favorable place in libraries, university as well public. It becomes too hard to get it repealed or erased.

History has not yet been corrected, despite professional confessions of wrong doings on the part of its writers. Such books have not been recalled and not removed from the library shelves as it happens in case of contaminated drugs and food products. Contaminated books, particularly on history and culture, are injurious in ethno-cultural ego formation.

Surprisingly, since Europeans realized the beauty – linguistic, philological, and grammatical – of Sanskrit, they have started playing linguistic games by creating the theory of the Indo-European family of languages to include Sanskrit as its member and to disregard India as being the original home of both "Aryans" and their great language Sanskrit. They have been vague and have been confusing readers by affixing "Indo" to most of the language families, such as Indo-European, Indo-Germanic, Indo-Iranian, Indo-Aryan, etc. Some say that most European languages have evolved from Sanskrit. Hence they are termed as'Aryan' languages. Thus, they feel justified that Aryans and their language Sanskrit came to India from outside. Unfortunately, European colonial historians consciously ignore logic, reason and their ethnic bias in their senseless thinking that Aryans are strangers to their cradle (Aryavarta), and that they are not speaking their own native language, but the language allegedly brought in from outside.

Isaac Taylor[44] writes what Max Müller thought about 'Aryans' and 'Aryan languages,' which, he feels, doesn't seem to be acceptable to some Europeans:

> "Professor Max Müller, owing to the charm of his style, to his unrivalled power of popular exposition, and to his high authority as a Sanskrit scholar, has done more than any other writer to popularize this erroneous notion among ourselves. Thus, in his *Lectures on the Science of*

---

[44] Isaac Taylor. "The Origin of the Aryans" (1889, pp.3-4).

language, delivered in 1861, instead of speaking only of a
primitive Aryan language, he speaks of an "Aryan race,"
an "Aryan family," and asserts that there was a time
"when the first ancestors of the Indians, the Persians,
the Greeks, the Slaves, the Celts, the Germans were
living together within the same enclosures, nay, under
the same roof," and he argues that because the same
forms of speech are preserved by all the members of the
Aryan family, it follows that ancestors of Indians and
Persians started for the South, and the leaders of the
Greek, Roman, Celtic, Teutonic, and Slavonic colonies
marched towards the shores of Europe, there was a
small clan of Aryans, settled probably on the highest
elevation of Central Asia, speaking a language not
yet Sanskrit or Greek or German, but containing the
dialectical germs of all."

There are two schools of thought about the cradle of Sanskrit and
its relationship with some European languages, particularly Greek,
Roman, German, etc.:

1. India (Ârya-āvarta) is the cradle of Aryans and their language
   Sanskrit.
2. Sanskrit is a member of the Indo-European family of languages,
   meaning that in prehistory distant past, as mentioned above that
   Sanskrit did not enjoy its own exclusive cradle, separate from
   European languages.

As said earlier that the two theories, *'Aryan invasion of India'* and
'Indo-European family of languages' were mischievously created by
colonialists to confuse, rather distort the origin of Aryans and their
language Sanskrit, the ancient history of India is based on.

Max Müller did not invent the term Arya, as Taylor thinks. The
word 'Arya' has been already current among Hindus (Aryas or Aryans)
of India for millennia years before Max Müller wrote this. Max Müller
correctly identifies and defines the term "Aryan" as it philologically,

linguistically and ethno-culturally means. Several scholars have been misidentifying Aryans, and so have been wandering around in vain to find Aryavarta, the original abode of the Aryans. Müller makes sense, since Arya is a Sanskrit term, the original home of Aryans can not be different from the original abode of their language Sanskrit. Taylor, citing what Müller wrote in his *'Lectures on the Science of Language'* (1861), criticizes Müller: "instead of speaking only of a primitive Aryan language, he (Max Müller) speaks of an Aryan race and Aryan family." Aryan, as a matter of fact, is a race or a people, not a language. Their languages can be called as Aryan. Sanskrit is well developed and has a great grammar. See in the chapter on Sanskrit what Sir William Jones has said about Sanskrit that "Sanskrit is of a wonderful structure; more perfect than the Greek, more copious than the Latin, and more exquisitely refined than the either."

Several Western scholars, in order to validate their two ill-founded theories, AII and IE, changed the authorship of the *Rig Veda* from the ancient native *Rishies* to the alleged invading Aryans, and reduced its age by saying that it was composed by invading Aryans in about 1000 B.C. and even later. All this has confused the origin and the antiquity of Aryans and their language Sanskrit.

'Arya', being basically a Sanskrit word, can / should not be associated with any race other than the Vedic people (present Hindus). Hence, any Aryan language can/should not be associated with any non-Indic language or race. Hitler[45] picked up *'Arya'* and *'Swastika'* in 20th century as a propaganda gimmick. He, himself, has said that the *Swastika* was borrowed as a symbol to boost the morale of his army.[46] Is or was there any people other than Hindus; the *Swastika* was originally associated with? Is or was any country other than India *(Aryavarta)* whose natives were known as Arya who spoke Sanskrit? Hitler chose the word Aryan for his race, but all Germans do not consider themselves as Aryans; nor do they believe in the *Swastika* as Hindus do. Germans do not speak Sanskrit. Some Germans do appreciate the qualities of Sanskrit and its grammar.

---

[45]   William L. Shirer. The Rise and fall of the Third Reich. (1959, p. 43)

[46]   Ibid, p. 43.

Hitler's *Swastika* was shaped different from the *Vedic Swastika*, may be because of his oversight or ignorance. It seems that the Hindu *Swastika* was not copied correctly. Because of absence of his religious sentiments associated with the *Swastika*, it was difficult for Hitler to identify the difference between the two. Thus, it would be historically erroneous to consider *Aryans*, the Vedic people of India, as invaders of their *Bharat Mata* (Mother India). The returning Aryans were always welcome to their home.

Glynnis Chantrell, in *The Oxford Dictionary of Word Histories* (2002, p. 31), has given the origin and the history of the word *Aryan*. He says that later the term *Aryan* race was revived and used as propaganda in Nazi Germany:

> "Aryan (late 15th century) is based on Sanskrit Arya 'noble'. Aryan is used by some as equivalent of the term Indo-European for a language family. In the 19th century, the notion of an Aryan race corresponding to a definite Aryan language became current and was taken up by nationalistic historical and romantic writers. One of these was De Gobineau (1816-82), an anthropologist who linked the idea to a notion of inferiority of certain races. Later the term Aryan race was revived and used as propaganda in Nazi Germany (1933-45)."

Nazis claim being Aryan and Aryan supremacy

Nazis were not Aryans. Hitler, like some other Europeans, felt great being Aryan. They were neither Asians nor Indo-Aryans. They were Europeans. Mallory (1989: 269-270) remarks about Hitler and Aryan race:

> "One hardly needs to emphasize that the implementation of Aryan supremacy by the Nazis was wholly inconsistent with Aryan as a linguistic term; Yiddish is as much an Indo-European language as any other German dialect, while Romany-speaking Gypsies had a far better claim

on the title of Aryans than any North European. Thus, the myth of Aryan supremacy was neither a direct nor necessary consequence of the philological discoveries of the nineteenth century, but rather the misappropriation of a linguistic concept and its subsequent grafting onto an already existing framework of prejudices, speculations and political aspirations. The Indo-Europeans leave more than the legacy of Aryan supremacy."

I think Nazis don't consider Aryan as a language. They consider Aryan as a race. Nazis, as some Europeans, felt great by considering themselves as the members of the Aryan race. Hitler was not talking about the German language as an Aryan language. In order to be on the top of the racial Mount Everest, they claimed Aryan supremacy. Historical records show that there has been a very tough war around conflicting controversy among scholars over the homeland of the Aryans, because of the universally acclaimed supremacy of the Aryan race. Since most of the scholars are European, they feel that Europe is the homeland of Aryans. Only few feel India, though Arya is a Sanskrit word and it is frequently used in the *Rig Veda*. Europe's fallacious victory over India is only due to its colonial power. Might is right.

It is hard to understand why Europeans claim that Europe is the original homeland of Aryans, though they know that the "Arya" is a Sanskrit word, and that the Vedic scriptures have generous use of the word 'Arya'. In fact, though history books talk about Europe, because of European clout, but informally outside libraries and university classrooms, the Europe-hypothesis has scant and shaky acceptance.

The *Webster's New Universal Unabridged Dictionary* (1996) defines 'Indo-Aryan' as "A member of people of India who are Indo-European in speech and Caucasoid in physical characteristics."

The dictionary is correct that the Indo-Aryans are natives of India. Indo-Aryans are Caucasians, but not the cognates of the European Caucasians. Indians and Africans are also Caucasian. If two geographically distant peoples can not have similar physical characteristics without cognate relations, then it would be historically fair to say that Europeans received their Caucasoid characteristics from

Indo-Aryans, not the opposite way, because of the following three evidences:

1. As history suggests, migrations have been from south-east (Asia and Africa) toward north-west (Europe), not the opposite way.
2. The Indo-Aryan (Indus) civilization is much older than the European.
3. The sculpture of Hindu and Buddhist deities in ancient caves reflect their Caucasoid features.

J. Mallory[47] writes:

> "But it was too late: the Indo-Europeans and racism had become inseparable in the minds of many scholars. Although there would always be linguists and anthropologists to protest, the superiority of the ancient Aryan Nordic race had entered popular political culture."

I feel the linguistics, though a welcome science of language is some times used with some hidden agenda – ethnic, racial, political, or colonial. In several instances, words are stretched too far with the help of the linguistic maneuvers to show their resemblance to words of a geographically distant, as well as historically different language. For details, please, read the Chapter, *'The Indo-European Family: Too Diverse to be One.'* The theory of the Indo-European family of languages is ill-based because the IE family includes even non-genetic languages as its members. For example, Indic languages have no genetic relationship with European languages. How could the parents of the too geographically distant and culturally and historically different families, the Indic and the European, meet and marry to give birth to Sanskrit, Latin, and Greek? The fairy tale of the Indo-European family was created, that in remote ancient times, the speakers of Sanskrit, Latin and Greek met somewhere, lived together under the roof of their parent language PIE (Proto Indo-European), and later in about 3000 B.C. (some say

---

[47]   J. Mallory. "In Search of the Indo-Europeans" (1989: 269),

in 6000 B.C.), they dispersed and took three different routes to their respective desired destinations, India, Italy, and Greece and gave birth to Sanskrit, Roman and Greek, thus claiming that the three are genetic siblings. Who and how many intelligent persons would buy that fairy tale as a scientific thesis? The story goes that IE family has its children too ethno-culturally varied, historically different and geographically too distantly scattered all over, as a well-knit one family. Is it a fairy tale for children or a historical fact for scholars?

All IE are not Aryan languages and no Aryan language can be European. Hence, the word Indo-European is senseless and illogical. All Indo-European can be neither Indic, nor European. Thus, no place can be homeland of neither European nor of Indic languages. No country can be homeland of all the Indo-European languages, because the term 'Indo-European' is too broad to be confined to only Europe or India. Cradle of a race or of a language has to be only one. The IE suggests two cradles – India and Europe – for each language. Thus, the IE is a misnomer.

Mallory (p.268) explains what should be the homeland of Aryans:

> "But even if superiority of physical type, language, and culture were all being united under the name of Aryan, there was still one essential element missing – with the singular exception of Roger Latham's claim that the Indo-European homeland lay in Europe, the common opinion of most scholars prior to the later nineteenth century was that the Aryan homeland must lie in Asia. While no one doubted that the Aryans belonged to the white race, up until the end of the 1860s most believed that this race originally dwelt somewhere in the vicinity of the Hindu Kush or Himalayas. There was no reason to seek their home in Northern Europe."

It seems there is confusion around the two terms, Indo-European and Aryan. According to Mallory (p.266), the Indo-Europeans are also known as Aryans. The confusion was the result of the European fascination for Aryan supremacy, as reflected by the following statement by Mallory:

> "The blond, blue eyed Aryan, fathered in Northern Europe, convinced of his superiority and obsessed with his racial superiority, was the product of numerous intellectual currents of which the development of Indo-European linguistics was but one. Leon Poliakov has shown that the roots of this caricature reach back into the near-universal longing of the peoples of Europe to secure for themselves an illustrious ancestry."

The longing of the Europeans to secure for themselves an illustrious ancestry of Aryans suggests that they are not happy with their own European ancestry. Perhaps, they seem to be more fascinated by the Aryan ancestry. This confusion has arisen because the people (may be some) of the Northern Europe how and why considered themselves as Aryans. As a matter of fact, Aryans, in general, are not blond and blue-eyed, as Northern Europeans are.

But Europeans seem to be confused to decide who Aryans are and what their homeland is. Some think Europe and some Asia, most in favor of Europe. Different scholars suggest different homeland of Aryans or Indo-Europeans[48]: Roger Latham (Europe), Isaac Taylor (Finns), Lazarus Geiger and Theodor Poesche (Germany), Poesche (Easter Europe), Penka (Southern Scandinavia), Charles Morris (Caucasus), Tilak (north Pole), etc.

Al this reflects nothing but confusion created by linguists around the IE, Sanskrit, Aryans, and racism. Scholars, including linguists, are not clear if the IE is a family of languages or of different races. This is reflected by Max Müller's anger, as reported by Mallory (p.269):

> "The great Indologist Max Müller, annoyed by the madness he had helped to create, blasted the anthropologists who spoke of an 'Aryan race, Aryan blood, Aryan eyes and hair' as a lunacy comparable to

---

[48] Mallory: 'In search of the Indo-Europeans (pp. 268,269).

> a linguist who spoke of 'a dolichocephalic dictionary
> or a brachycephalic grammar'. But it was too late: the
> Indo-European and racism had become inseparable in
> the minds of many scholars."

The problem is about the homeland of the IE. The idea of its different places, as suggested by different scholars (as given on an earlier page) is questionable. It has created confusion. The concept of any one homeland for the IE would be irrational and illogical, because it is a grand family of several families of languages, which are scattered around Europe and the Indian subcontinent. Each language would have its homeland, for example: England for English, France for French, India for Sanskrit, and so on. Aryan languages have their home in Aryavarta (India), and European languages have their home in Europe. Aryans are historically seen in enviable status in India as well as in Europe; therefore historians feel that their home land is Indo-Europe. Confusion will be cleared only when linguists, anthropologists and historians teach themselves that no language will have more than one homeland, as no child can have more than one biological mother. Let me tell them Aryavarta (Aryabhoomi, India) is mother of Aryans.

The Aryan race is not European. It is Asian, specifically Indian. India and Europe can not be squeezed – historically, geographically, culturally, or linguistically – into the ONE HERITAGE to be possessed by both – Europeans and Aryans (Indians). Hence the term 'Indo-European' is a misnomer. The homeland of the Indo-European can be neither India nor Europe, because it is a grand family of two different families – Indic and European – which are geographically too distant and historically too different from each other. No Aryan language enjoyed lullaby in a European cradle; and no European language would ever enjoy a Sanskrit lullaby. Aryan (Vedic/Hindu) culture is very different from the European. Some Europeans seem to crave to have Aryan heritage. May be, they feel Aryans are superior because of their spiritual culture. I, being Hindu (Aryan), don't like to be considered as belonging to the White race, only because I don't want to be considered different from what I am. I am proud being Aryan. In my opinion, each race has some great traits others may envy. Every one should feel proud of whatever he/she ethno-racially is. Racism is the worst socio-cultural cancer. It causes human pain, both sides suffer. It is difficult to cure. Racism doesn't reflect civilization. A civilized person can not be racist.

I would have agreed with Mallory if he had said that Aryan homeland must lie in India, instead of Asia. Historians need to be specific. There is difference between 'India' and 'Asia'. All Indians are Asian, but all Asians are not Indians.

The sentence – "One group settled in northern Greece and another in Iran (whose name is derived from "Aryan") – reflects conflicting statements given in one and the same paragraph. If the name of Iran is derived from "Aryan", Aryans were already there. It has been historically proved in the chapter on Iran, and that its ancient language *Avestan* was linguistically close to Sanskrit.

It becomes confusing when the same book gives conflicting narrative picture of Aryans, their Sanskrit and their religion similar to that of the people of the much older Indus civilization. When the knowledge about Aryans came from the Vedas, as written by Clarke and other scholars, how then could those Aryans be from some country other than India, the cradle of the Vedas and Sanskrit? When Arya is a Sanskrit word and it is found several times in Vedas and Vedas are the most ancient documents of the world, then how could the home of Aryans be other than India?

Aryan contribution to Russia and Europe

Childe, in the Chapter *'Role of the Aryans in History'* of his book *'The Aryans'* (1926, pp. 210-212), has written:

1. "… graves covering the remains of a people, who, whether they were come from South Russia or represented a section of the pre-dolmenic population, were, we believe, Aryan in character."
2. "The gulf between French and Scandinavian culture at the beginning of the 2nd millennium is enormous. The superiority of the former is the measure of the contribution made by the Aryan element to European civilization."

3. "Thus the Aryans do appear everywhere as promoters of true progress and in Europe their expansion marks the moment when the prehistory of our continent (Europe) begins to diverge from that Africa or the Pacific."

4. Aryan genius found its true expression in Greece and Rome."

5. The lasting gift bequeathed by the Aryans to the conquered people was neither a higher material culture nor a superior physique, but a more excellent language and the mentality it generated.

Childe, in the First Chapter *'Language and Prehistory'*, emphasizes the significance of spiritual unity, and the concept of Divine Law or Cosmic Order in Aryan culture which was bequeathed to Europeans through their language (I believe Sanskrit) which has ability of abstract thinking. Spirituality, the gem of the Aryan (Vedic or Hindu/Buddhist/ Sikh) culture, is too complex for most European thinkers. This was the reason why the scientist Albert Einstein wrote to Nehru that the first part of his book *'Discovery of India'* was not easy reading for a Westerner

Chapter Five

INDO-EUROPEAN FAMILY, TOO DIVERSE TO BE ONE

History of India has been distorted by the two ill-based theories, (i) Aryan invasion of India and (ii) Indo-European family of languages. According to both, Sanskrit is not the native language of India, but it was brought in by alleged invading Aryans in about 1500 BC. This chapter will address the futility of the concept of the 'Indo-European Family of languages.' Origin of Aryans is discussed in the chapter on Aryans. The history of Ancient India, rather of Bhārat, will be rightly reconstructed only when origins of both – 'Aryans' and 'Sanskrit' are correctly established.

> "An archaeologist of the distant future would be grossly in error if he took the worldwide occurrence of huge quantities of Coca-Cola bottles as an indication of a unified world language."

Garharo Herm[49]

Presence of some similar words in Indian and European languages is being theorized that all these languages are Indo-European, they share common parentage and they have their origin in a Proto-Indo-European (PIE) language, yet to be identified and yet to be found. It is a colonial mischief to support the two ill-based intermingled theories – (i) Aryan Invasion of India (AII) and (ii) Indo-European Family of

---

[49]   Garharo Herm, 'The Celts" (1975, p. 71).

Languages (IE). According to AII, Aryans came into India in about 61500 BC and brought along with them Sanskrit, a pantheon of Hindu gods and authored Vedas about 500 years later after their arrival. It was created to deny Hindus the credit for their most enviable gifts – Aryans, Sanskrit, Vedas and Swastika – to mankind. World knows the British strategic policy "Divide and Rule." The 'Aryan invasion of India' was also created to divide India into alleged "North Indian Aryans and South Indian Dravidians." As a matter of fact, all Indians, excepting immigrants and invaders, meaning the rest Hindus[50] are Aryans, and Sanskrit is an ancient language of Bhārat, as old as Vedas. Sanskrit does not have its origin in ill-founded PIE (Proto Indo-European).

PIE is a fairy tale that in pre-history unknown distant times, great-grand parents of the speakers of Sanskrit, Latin, Greek and some other European languages lived together under the same roof (I think understanding is of Central Asia) and spoke the languages which had several philological (words) similarities.

Linguists write further that later in about 3,000 BC (some say (6,000 BC), the speakers of Sanskrit, Latin and Greek, dispersed and marched toward three different destinations – Sanskrit speakers went to India, Latin speakers to Italy and the Greek-speaking to Greece. It is not explained why and how these three destinations were selected. In my opinion, they knew that they were immigrants there from their respective native lands – India, Italy and Greece. It should be noted that all the three countries are geographically distant from one another, particularly India is too distant from Italy and Greece and Sanskrit has little linguistic correspondence with Roman and Greek languages. It is said, that language changes every 30 Kos/koh (about 60 miles). Moreover, India is culturally, linguistically and historically different and geographically too distant from Italy and Greece.

The theory of *'Indo-European Family of Languages'* (IE) has been mischievously created by European colonialists to confuse the origins of Aryans, Sanskrit and Vedas. PIE is ill-based. Linguists have not yet been able to find even a little piece of its text, nor even its name. It has been hypothetically named as 'Proto-Indo-European' (PIE). No

---

[50] Hindu means Hindus, Buddhists, Jains and Sikhs, because Buddhism, Jainism and Sikhism are offshoots of Hinduism.

linguist knows how it was spoken or written. Not even one sentence of the PIE has been traced. There are also contradictions, such as some say 3000 BC, some 6000 BC and some other say 1500 BC of the arrival of Sanskrit in India. Sanskrit was in India long before twelve thousands years, as evidenced by the mention of Himalayan melting glaciers in *Rig Veda* which happened before 12,000 B.C.

In order to test the validity of the PIE thesis that its member languages share common parentage, a table of about 150 words of common use is given to see that there is little or no linguistic correspondence between Sanskrit and European languages – English, German, Latin and Greek. This may help in studying the factors affecting the linguistic difference between Sanskrit and European languages. The primary purpose of this study is to prove that the IE is too diverse to be a family of languages. Sanskrit is geographically distant, and linguistically, culturally and historically different from European languages, such as English, German, Greek and Roman.

This also be noted that the scholars do not have consensus on the time of their dispersion, and on the original abode of the PIE. With all these gaps, contradictions, and absence of consensus among linguists, can the IE be considered as a linguistic phenomenon in form of a family of languages?

How would scholars have consensus on the matters related to the PIE when it has not been known as a spoken language, nor as a written language? Linguists have not been able to tell what were the native languages of India, Italy, and Greece before they got Sanskrit, Latin and Greek respectively from the people of Central Asia. What happened to those original languages of India, Italy and Greece? Hindus, Romans and Greeks do not accept that their respective languages – Sanskrit, Latin, and Greek – were imported.

Sir William Jones, one of the strong proponents of the IE, has remarked:

> "The Sanskrit language, whatever be its antiquity, is of a wonderful structure, more perfect than the Greek, more copious than the Latin, and more exquisitely refined than the either, yet bearing to both of them a stronger

affinity, both in the roots of verbs and the forms of grammar, than could possibly have been produced by accident; so strong indeed, that no philologer could examine them all three, without believing them to have sprung from some common source, which, perhaps, no longer exist: there is similar reason, though not quite so forcible, for supposing that both the Gothic and Celtic, though blended with a very different idiom, had the same origin with the Sanskrit, and the Old Persian might be added to the same family."

I agree with Jones that Sanskrit has affinity with Latin and Greek, but not of the kind, not of the quality, not of the extent and not linguistically close to Latin and Greek so as to qualify both – the Indic and European languages – as cognate members of one and the same family. Moreover, other prerequisite qualifying factors – sameness of geography, history, and culture – are also not satisfying for such relationship. The main thing, Jones seems to have ignored that there can be factors other than common parentage which can cause philological resemblances, such as long cohabitation of the speakers of various languages due to travel, tourism, trade, colonization, migrations, etc, as has been happening now mainly in America, Canada, U.K, Australia, etc. Several English words are floating so commonly in India and in other non-European countries, and several Asian words in European countries that it is advisable to understand the global visa-free migration of words to make international communication easier and effective. It will be linguistic fallacy to theorize that all global languages share common parentage.

Readers should seriously examine what Jones has said "... have without believing them to have sprung from some common source, which, perhaps, no longer exist." How can 'common parenthood' be theorized when the parent has never been identified and no longer exists?

It is too hard to agree with Jones that such affinity is due to their common source which doesn't exist. Sanskrit has not sprung from the Latin and Greek roots which are geographically too distant and culturally and historically different. Had Sanskrit sprung from the same roots, the philologically resembling common texture would not have faded so dim. This has happened because their linguistic roots, culture, geography and history are different.

Some linguists agree with my thesis. Russian linguist N. S. Trubetskoy[51] argued that the presence of the same word or words in number of languages need not suggest that these languages descend from a common parentage. Colin Renfrew, in *Archaeology & Language* (1987, p.108), talks what Trubetskoy felt about this:

"This indeed was the interesting position adopted by the Russian linguist, N.S. Trubetskoy in 1939. He argued that the presence of the same word in a number of languages need not suggest that these languages descend from a common parent."

Renfrew (pp.108-109) writes that Trubetskoy severely criticized the ill-based and illogical assumptions which led to the construction of the Proto-Indo-European (PIE) language:[52]

"The homeland, the race and the culture of supposed Proto-Indo-European population has been discussed, a population which may possibly never have existed."

There are several lingual families, as members of the grand IE family, as designated by linguists. Affinity – semantic as well as syntactic – is natural among the members of the same linguistic family, but the family-membership-qualifying affinity between any two languages would depend on significant close linguistic correspondence, geographical proximity, cultural and historical propensity of their speakers. Word similarities between any languages of different origin – for example Indic and European – can be accidental and/or as the result of borrowing. Because of over four thousand languages, some languages can have a few words, which may have same or different meaning. Borrowing is possible only because of cohabitation which may happen

---

51 Trubetscoy 1939 in Scherer 1968, p.216, taken from Colin Renfrew, Archeology & Language, 1987, p.108.

52 Ibid, pp.108-109.

due to colonization, trade, tourism, or migrations. History speaks lot about prehistory global migrations of Sanskrit-speaking Indo-Aryans. Mutual linguistic influence between Indic and European languages, particularly Greek and Latin, has been described by E. Pococke, in his book *'India in Greece* or *Truth in Mythology.'* Pococke has established with host of irrefutable evidences that in ancient times, India had colonized Greece in about 2448 BC, leaving not only philological influence of Sanskrit on Greek, but also influence of Vedic philosophy on Greeks. Understandably, it must have influenced neighboring Latin too. But the lingual correspondence was not that much and not of the kind that it should be interpreted as the result of their common origin. If Sanskrit and Greek had same parentage, the lingual resemblance between the two would not have been completely washed out. Pococke, in the Chapter One, *'Evidences of Indian Colonization'* (p.12) talks about Indian influence on the philosophy, religion, language, arts of peace and war, etc. of Greeks. Surprisingly, so much is written by Pococke about socio-cultural 'give and take' between India and Greece in distant ancient times:

> "Now, the whole of this state of society, civil and military, must strike every one as being eminently Asiatic; much of it specifically India. Such undoubtedly is; and I shall demonstrate that these evidences were but the attendant tokens of an Indian colonization, with its corresponding religion and language. I shall exhibit dynasties disappearing from Western India, to appear again in Greece: clans, whose martial fame is still recorded in the faithful chronicles of North-Western India, as the gallant bands who fought upon the plains of Troy; and, in fact, the whole of Greece, from the era of the supposed god-ships of Poseidon and Zeus, down to the close of the Trojan war, as being *Indian* in language, sentiment, and religion, and in the arts of peace and war."

The same is confirmed by Dr. Ravi Prakash Arya in '*Indian Origin of Greece and Ancient World*' (pp.23-24).There doesn't seem any justification to deny what Pococke and Dr. Arya are talking about India's impact on Greece. But, it is hard to accept that Sanskrit has as much and kind of linguistic resemblance to Greek that both can qualify to be cognate lingual sisters. Sanskrit, as the result of long stay of Sanskrit-speaking Indo-Aryans in their worldwide colonies, including Greece, must have globally influenced several languages. Sanskrit-speaking Indo-Aryans (now known Hindus) had colonized some European, African and several SE Asian countries and had influenced their languages. This explains why Sanskrit has philological resemblance to several languages of the world. But, it should not be postulated that Sanskrit has genetic relationship with them. Thus, the hypothesis of the Indo-European family of languages that Sanskrit shares common origin with Latin, Greek and some other European languages is erroneous. As said earlier, word resemblances were caused by borrowing and some were accidental or by chance.

How could IE without religion, be a family?

History tells that Indo-Europeans do not have a common religion nor even the concept of religion. It evidences that IE can not be a family. Emile Benveniste,[53] in his book '*Indo-European Language and Society*' (1973, p. 516), writes:

"One fact can be established immediately; there is no term of common Indo-European for religion. Even in the historical period there are a number of Indo-European languages which lack such a term, which is not surprising."

How can there be a family without religion? Peter B. Clarke, in "*The World's Religions*" (1993, p.7), remarks:

"From the dawn of civilization, religion has played an indispensable role both in people's private lives and in

---

[53] Émile Benveniste (1902-1976), a French structural linguist and Semiotician was best known for his work on IE languages.

the realm of society. In prehistoric times, evidence from Stone Age cave paintings of animals suggests religious rituals may have been used to ensure the success of hunting."

The origin of the religion of the Aryans in Vedas is described in the Reader's Digest's *'The World's Religions'* (1993, p.130):

"Knowledge of the Aryans is mostly derived from the heritage of their sacred literature, known as the Vedas, especially the *Rig Veda*, a collection of hymns."

This clearly suggests that the Aryans practiced the Vedic religion (present Hinduism). How, then Aryans be considered foreigners to Bhārat, the cradle of Vedas? The Vedic religion is the oldest religion, may be of over 12,000 years. It suggests that the man had the concept of religion from remote pre-history times. It was understood that God was invisible, thus God was identified with NATURE which had both ultimate power and mystery. Hinduism, like Christianity, believes in one GOD, with a number of His secretaries or assistants in form of *Devtas* (gods), and *Devies* (goddesses). Similarly, there are several Roman and Greek gods and goddesses, known as saints. See Roman and Greek gods in 'Mythological gods and goddesses of East and West.

Benveniste further remarks:

"Since the Indo-Europeans did not conceive of that omnipresent reality which religion represents as a separate institution, they had no term to designate. In those languages which do present such a term it is of great interest to trace the process by which it was constituted. ... Nothing has been the subject of a greater or longer dispute than the origin of the Latin word religion."

Benveniste's above observation regarding religion does not seem to be based on all the IE speaking societies. It seems he is talking only about a few societies, may be European only. The fact is that all societies have religion, right from their birth, but known by different names, depending on their language, for example *"threskeia"* in Greek, *"dharma"* in Hinduism, and *mazahib* in Islam, etc. More than 12,000 years old *Rig Veda* talks about the Vedic Dharma (present Hinduism). It talks about Hindu gods and about the relationship of man with God. Man can not live without religion, meaning without his relationship with Ishwar, God, Allah, etc.

Since the members of the IE family do not cherish the concept of religion or do not have one common term for religion, it can not be considered as a family.

Man was born with religion and vice versa. Both – man and religion – are twins. Man can not live without religion, and religion can not survive without man. God is known to all societies, of course with different names because of their different languages. Even atheism is a religion, because it talks about God, of course in a negative way. Some people, rather few, like the German philosopher Friedrich Nietzsche (1844-1900), do not believe in God. Nietzsche pronounced: "God is dead" in his book *'Joyful Wisdom.'* He didn't know or didn't understand that only wisdom can not bring joy. Joy comes from knowledge of self, known as self-awareness. It primes in almost all religions. *Atmagyan* (self awareness) has been the paramount goal for God-seekers. Only serious meditation can move one closer to **'self-within-self'** where one can meet or feel God.

Who is creator – man[54] or God?

Always there has been conflict between God and science, rather between God and man, on the question: who is the creator of the things to meet the needs of man, "Man or God?" Due to emergence of science and technologies during last few centuries, the question about the entity of God has been perplexing. Scientists should try to realize that the man has not created any thing, but has discovered what was already there; such learnt the ways and means how to create things man needs for his life. The knowledge of all the science and technologies is already there, man has been discovering little by little according to the growth of his

---

[54]   Man implies both "man and woman."

mind, opportunities and circumstances available to him. Man needs to understand that God is ultra-scientist, as evidenced by scientific nature of every thing, created by Him – all planets accident-proof hanging in space since millennia years, man's physiology, animal physiology, varying flying caliber of various kinds of birds and insects, multi-color flower plants, etc.

Man should not shamelessly take the credit for creating them from the five basic elements – earth, wind, water, fire and ether or space. Man does not create, but discovers little by little. Man has spent millions of years from Stone Age until today to get the civilization which is not yet optimal.

What, Colin Renfrew (1987, p.42) writes as given below, seems to raise the question if there is really genetic relationship between Sanskrit and European languages. He also talks about the "prolonged contact" affecting philological resemblance. He doubts the righteousness of the IE family:

> "Few scholars today would go so far as Trubetskoy in suggesting that there is no genetic or family-tree relationship at all among the Indo-European languages, and that they just came to resemble each other through the effects of prolonged contact. And very few indeed would agree with the French archaeologist, Jean-Paul Demoule,[55] that there really is no Indo-European language group at all, or that the similarities observed are un-important, insignificant and fortuitous."

Karl Menninger[56] seems to question the righteousness of the PIE, as a language:

---

[55] Demoule 1980 Jean-Paul Demoule is professor of later European prehistory at Paris 1 University (Panthéon-Sorbonne) and member of the Institut Universitaire De France.

[56] Karl Menninger, in "Number Words and Number Symbols: A Cultural History of Numbers" (1969, p.101).

> "If all these languages are sisters, they must have a
> common ancestor, an original language from which
> they have developed. But we know of no people that
> spoke or wrote such a mother language nor have we any
> direct evidence or written documents concerning it."

It is hard to understand why and how such a concept of the IE languages and their invisible mother PIE has been theorized and has been endorsed by celebrated linguists like Sir William Jones. No document written in PIE has been found; even her name and home address are not known.

Inter-lingual borrowing has been a well known inevitable global phenomenon. Language, culture and religion owe lot to migration for their respective development and enrichment. But resemblances of any magnitude between two languages should not be presumed as evidence of cognate relationship without examining their other legitimate linguistic parameters – age, geography, culture, and genesis – required to qualify for membership of a family.

Did European languages evolve from Sanskrit?

Victor Stevenson[57] feels that the European languages have evolved from Sanskrit:

> "Evidence that the languages of Europe had, with a few
> exceptions, evolved in stages from a common source,
> was found neither in Greece nor Rome, nor any where
> in Europe, but in an ancient and distant language, the
> Classical Sanskrit of India. Enshrined and unchanged
> for more than 2,000 years in the ritual speech of its
> scholars, it was shown to possess massive similarities to
> Greek and Latin. Only one conclusion could be drawn;
> all three had come from a common source."

---

57   Victor Stevenson, in Words: The evolution of western languages (1983, p.10),

Scant linguistic correspondence between Indic and European languages has been misperceived as massive. It would be erroneous to interpret scant or even massive lexical or vocabulary similarities between any two languages as one's evolvement from the other. Exceptions are there. Evolvement, between two languages which are spatially, temporally, culturally, and historically different from each other, is not linguistically acceptable.

Evolvement between two geographically distant languages which are culturally and historically different is not possible and is not linguistically acceptable. There seems contradiction between Stevenson's following two statements:

1. Most languages of Europe had evolved in stages from the classical Sanskrit of India.
2. All the three – Latin, Greek and Sanskrit – had come from a common source.

Contradiction is apparent. When all the three have come from a common source, how then can any one of them evolve from any of them? How can one be born of a sister?

There are similarities, but not that massive, and not of the kind required for Sanskrit's cognate relationship with Latin and Greek. Even if the similarities were massive, they should not be considered as the basis for qualifying them for a cognate relationship, because some other possible causes – such as age, geography, grammar, culture, and history – are not taken into account. The degree and the kind of linguistic affinity of Sanskrit with Greek and Latin do not seem to be appropriate to qualify Sanskrit as their sibling. If both, Latin and Greek had really evolved from Sanskrit, there would have been massive vocabulary similarities and the kind of similarity would have been different. History, geography, and culture are also main attributes, required for membership of the same family. Sanskrit is different from any of the European languages including Latin and Greek in terms of their geography, culture and history.

Max Müller (1891, p.232) writes that August Wilhelm von Schlegel, the brother of Frederick Schlegel, used his influence which he had acquired as a German poet, to popularize the study of Sanskrit in Germany.

Fourteen scholars have suggested nine different places for the birthplace of PIE. The scholars also differ about the date when the PIE family of languages split and spread around, ranging from 6000 B.C. to 3000 B.C. Stevenson (1983) suggests 6000 B.C. and both Gimbutus (1970) and Baldi (1983): 3000 B.C. Such a wide range difference in the scholarly opinion – about the homeland of the PIE, and the timing of departure of the speakers of Latin, Greek and Sanskrit from the PIE homeland – challenge the reliability and the validity of the IE family. Mythologies have better integrity and logic than such a fragmented, baseless, and subjective thesis of the IE and the PIE.

The two theories, IE and AII conflict

If, according to IE, Sanskrit-speaking people reached India in or before 3000 B.C., how then scholars say that the invading Aryans brought Sanskrit with them to India in about 1500 B.C.? This tells that both the theories Indo-European family (IE) and Aryan Invasion of India (AII) are illogical, irrational and ill-based.

Two Exceptions to PIE

Renfrew (1987, p. 35) talks about the two exceptions who do not believe that the IE languages have same ancestral parent language. The Russian scholar N.S. Trubetskoy and much more recently Jean-Paul Demoule have "questioned the whole notion of an ancestral IE language." Trubetskoy suggests "Such critical examination of our assumptions is necessary if a solution to the problem is ever to be found."

The scholarship seems to be too obsessed with the two theories to feel free to explore other avenues to find answers to resolve the problem and test the reliability and validity of both, IE and PIE. Renfrew (p.35) stresses:

Relationship between culture and language

Culture, is what the language is heavily consumed with. Speakers of every language have their own culture keeps them connected. Language reflects their artistic, intellectual, literary and philosophical pursuits. Geography makes difference in the culture. Difference between oriental and occidental cultures is enormous. Each culture has great art but the subjects of the art differ from society to society. They may reflect their history. Each culture has its great literature but their content is distinctly different, mostly influenced by their history and the way of their life. Philosophies are different. Language helps in defining the socio-cultural identity of its speakers and in distinguishing them from other peoples. Language helps in preservation of the culture of its people, and the culture feeds the language with lot of stuff to talk and write about. Similarities, as said earlier, could be accidental and/or due to borrowing. The minds of most western linguists seem to have been programmed to blindly interpret even scanty vocabulary similarities between Sanskrit and a European language as an evidence of Sanskrit's membership of the IE family.

Stevenson seems contradicting what other scholars have said about the homeland of the PIE. They have not reached a consensus on one *Urheimat*. About ten different locations for the homeland of the PIE have been suggested by about thirteen scholars as would be discussed later in this chapter. It is because the PIE is not the language any body has heard the speech of. It is a fictitious or hypothetical term for the language which did not exist any time.

T. Burrow, in *The Sanskrit Language* (2001, p.9), observes that the original home of the IE family has been still a question. The original home of the IE family will remain as a question until the concept of the IE family is declared as a myth.

Words of IE are stretched too far to show resemblance. Gerhard Herm, in *The Celts* (1975, p.72), has claimed resemblance of the Sanskrit word *"raj"* with *"rex"* (Latin), and *"rix"* (Celtic). Does 'raj' resemble to 'rex' or 'rix'? Only 'r' is common.

Is Linguistics a science?

Linguistics, as to be a science in its real sense, should be objective and free from the colonial clutches. Unfortunately, the thrust of linguistics has primarily been to validate the colonially corrupted theory of IE (Indo-European family of languages) which is trying to prove that linguistically East and West share common parentage. Rather, it should have been to examine if the factors, the IE has been based on, are appropriate. Is it right to theorize that the IE is a family of languages – Indic and European – only because there is scant philological affinity between a few words? Linguists have responsibility to research and ascertain if resemblance of some words is enough for two languages to qualify for cognate sisterhood, meaning common parentage, and that between the two who are geographically too distant and culturally historically different from each other.

Linguistics can be a science in its real sense, if it objectively examines the origin, geography, culture, grammar and history of the various languages of the world to determine which languages belong to a cognate family of languages, not only based on philological resemblance of a few words. Thus Sanskrit and European languages can not form as a linguistic family because of only a few philological (word) similarities. Sanskrit is geographically too distant from Europe and its culture, grammar and history are too different from those of Roman and Greek languages.

Holes in Linguistics and IE

Some scholars have identified holes in the IE theory. P. H. Matthews, in *'Linguistics: A Very Short Introduction'* (2003, p.49), responding to the question, "What is the evidence?" replies:

> "The answer lies in the 'comparative' method. This
> involves a step-by-step comparison of different languages,
> in which we look for detailed correspondences that can
> not reasonably be explained unless a common ancestor

existed. The great problem is: what sorts of details are convincing?"

How can one be considered as a child of 'some body,' when that 'some body' has never been seen living, in other words does not exist? If that 'some body' died, where is his/her grave? Let linguists first find the PIE, then talk about its children, the IE languages. It is hard to understand how linguistics can be considered a science without ascertaining the existence of its elements it is talking about.

Matthews (p.53), talking about Greek and Sanskrit, writes: "Why should there be correspondences? These languages were spoken thousands of miles apart, in societies historically different. The statement by Matthews implicitly rejects the IE hypothesis that since Sanskrit-speakers once lived together with the speakers of Latin and Greek, the linguistic correspondence among their languages was due to their common origin. According to the science of language, the hypothesis that there can be more than one native language on one and the same land is invalid. Speakers of non-native languages could be immigrants, traders or tourists. For example, French is the native language of France. The languages, other than French, spoken in France are the languages of its immigrants, not of its original natives. So many languages are being spoken in England, only English can be considered as its native language.

Each language has its own geographical enclosure and close relationship with the culture of its speakers. India has over twenty different vernaculars and hundreds of different dialects. Since the advent of matured grammar, systemization of the vernaculars by universities, increasing literacy, wide-spread reach of schools, television and cinema in rural India, dialects have been immersing into vernaculars. In a way, dialects have been enriching vernaculars and vice versa. Such mutual immersing process would continue until dialects are completely consumed by vernaculars. Dialects are still there in their vocal forms, particularly among the senior population who have not gone to school. Their dialects have been approaching towards their grave, along with their speakers.

Various scholars on the Indo-European family

Philip Baldi, in his *'An Introduction to the Indo-European Languages'* (1983, p. 3), writes that Sir William Jones (1746-94), in late 18th century, postulated that the languages spoken by the majority of the peoples of Indian sub-continent, Europe and Iran have a common ancestral language, known as the Proto-Indo-European (PIE) which has been hiding itself from linguistic historians right from its hypothetical birth. May be its birth never occurred. How can it be considered born when no body has been ever known speaking it? Linguistic historians write that in Eurasia there existed a population who spoke a language directly ancestral to all of those we now recognize as the languages of the Indo-European family. How can it be called a family when all its members do not have one and the same origin or parentage?

In my opinion, it was the native language of Eurasia which contained some words from various languages being spoken by immigrants there, like American English has been picking up words from various languages of immigrants. Linguists are putting it in opposite way – calling the effect as the cause, only to validate the IE hypothesis. It was not ancestral to those languages being spoken in Eurasia. It was its native language – developed by additional words from the immigrant languages. The resemblances among those additional words and also some other words, particularly from Sanskrit, Latin and Greek, were used by Sir William Jones to propound the theory of the IE family of languages.

Malmkjær (ed), in *The Linguistics Encyclopedia* (1991, p.191), states that long before William Jones' discovery, the first known reference to Sanskrit in the West occurred at the end of the sixteenth century when: "F. Sassetti wrote home to his native Italy about the *Lingua Sanscruta* and some of its resemblances to Italian. Others too, such as B. Schulze and Pere Coedoux, made similar observations on the resemblances of Sanskrit to Latin and European languages."

It is educationally interesting to identify such lexical resemblances between languages, particularly with different ethnic and historical backgrounds, and far distant from each other. It would be real education if the causes for their resemblances are objectively examined whether resemblances are because of their common origin or because of borrowing or by chance. Resemblances between Sanskrit and European languages can not be due to their common origin, because they were geographically too distant and culturally too different to make a family. They are because of borrowing, as explained earlier. Historically, it has been established that in pre-history ancient times, Sanskrit-speaking Indo-Aryans had gone out around and had established their colonies in several regions including Europe, particularly Greece, as vouched for by E. Pococke in his book *India in Greece*.

Mother tongue and IE Languages

According to the definition of mother tongue, one would have only one mother tongue, he learns from his parents. Mother tongue is tied to the native place of its speakers. No place has more than one native tongue, and no person has more than one mother tongue. It is possible, that one may also speak a couple of languages other than his mother tongue, when he lives and has been brought up at a place where speakers of some other languages have immigrated. For example, a child of parents from India, born and raised in New York, where several languages are being spoken, may be able to speak a few languages. Most probably, he would be significantly exposed to three languages – (i) at home his mother tongue (Sindhi, Gujarati, Bengali, etc, (ii) Hindi (national language of India), and (iii) English, the native language of America. It is possible, his speech may have fluency in English, even more than his mother tongue and Hindi, because of the simple reason that he spends his time more in school with English-speaking people – his classmates, teachers, friends, and people he meets in restaurants, on the street, and media, such as TV, radio, papers, school books, etc. – much more than he spends at home with his family. The magnitude of such socialization may vary from individual to individual, depending on the individual's interests and engagements. It is possible that child's speech and thought process may be more English-oriented. This may not be true among some immigrant families who try to confine their children within their own lingo-cultural walls. All this I am talking about languages, one can speak, only to emphasize that in no way, on the basis of cohabitation, it should be theorized that Hindi, English and any other immigrant language have common origin, as several linguists have been mis-theorizing that Sanskrit, Latin, and Greek have their origin in one and the same parental language, hypothetically named as PIE.

I am not denying that there could be a place in Eurasia or some where else, where peoples, speaking three or even more different languages, were living together. I also would not deny that there is similarity between few or many words of those three languages, Sanskrit, Latin and Greek. But it is too hard to accept the theory that those languages had sprung from one and the same origin, and that the speakers of those different languages were the original natives of that place. Thus, it would be wrong to theorize that Sanskrit, Latin, and Greek share common origin (parentage) because they were spoken by the people who once lived in Eurasia like a family and because some words of the three languages have philological resemblances.

It is difficult for human mind to accept the fairy tale that the speakers of the three languages separated and later dispersed for three different destinations – India, Italy, and Greece – leaving their missing mother (PIE) behind, who is still wandering around to find her home. No Linguist knows her name and even one word of the language their mother PIE spoke or wrote. Linguists have been in vain wandering all around the world for over two centuries to identify the *Urheimat* (PIE residence).

The PIE: Its residence and year of birth

Karl Menninger (1969, p.101) expresses the need to identify the ancestor of the IE family, and asserts that the ancestor has not yet been found:

> "If all these languages are sisters, they must have a common ancestor, an original language from which they have developed. But we know of no people that spoke or wrote such a mother language nor have we any direct evidence or written documents concerning it."

How can it found when it not exist, not even was born? Since Sanskrit is older than twelve thousand years, as explained in the Chapters on Sanskrit and Veda. It would be erroneous and illogical to say that Sanskrit developed from the PIE which never existed. Several different places have been suggested as *Urheimat* by different scholars, depending on their BLIND subjective perspectives. This can be better explained by the following anecdote. A few curious blind boys were taken to a zoo to see what an elephant would be like. The first one happened to touch a waving ear of the elephant. He announced: "Oh! It is like a fan." The other one, who touched its leg, shouted: "No! It is like a trunk of a tree." The third one, who touched its body, said that it was like a wall. So, the elephant was different for different blind boys. So has the homeland been different to several PIE-blind linguists who have never seen, nor read the PIE. The linguists need to have objective, rational and realistic mind. How can they have it when they have been ethno-politically entangled by mischievous colonial concept of IE to confuse the real origin of Sanskrit and Vedas?

Different Urheimat to different linguists

So many different *Urheimats* suggest the fallacy of the theory of the IE family. In order to ascertain any truth, if any, in the concept of IE family, the following table of about one hundred fifty words of common use – consisting of family relations, foods, colors, nature, religion, numbers, animals, and common verbs, etc – has been given to ascertain if Sanskrit has adequate and appropriate linguistic affinity with any of the European languages, such as English, German, Greek, Latin, etc. This will establish the truth, if any, in the concept of IE family of languages, Eastern and Western, which are culturally and historically different and geographically too distant from each other to make a family.

Linguistic affinity between Sanskrit and European languages

English	Germanic	Greek	Latin	Sanskrit
family	familie	eekoyeneea	familia	kutumba
mother	mutter	meetera	mater	maata, amba
father	vater	pateras	pater, parens	pita, janak
son	sohn	yos	filius, natus	putra, suta
daughter	tochter	koree	filia	putri,
sister	schwester	athelfee	soror	sodarya,
brother	bruder	athelfos	frater	bhratur
cousin	vetter	ksothelfos	patruelis	pitruvyputra
uncle	onkel	theeos	patruus	piturvyah
man	mann, Stein	anthras	vir, homo	nar, purusha
woman	frau	gynaika	femina	naari
child	kind	paidi	filius, infans	baal, baalak
religion	religion	threeskeea	religio	dharma
God	Gott	Theos	Deus	Dev, Ishwar
prayer	gebet	prosefhi	preces, votum	prarthna,pooja
prophet	prophet	profitis	vates	sidhah, avataar
sin	sunde	amaritia	peccatum	paapam
temple	tempel	naos	templum	mandir, decgraha
saint	heilige	agios	sanctus	sadhuha, sant, muni
body	korper	somatos	corpus	sariram
arm	arm	kheree	bracchium	bhujah, bahuha
back	rucken	platee	tergum	prishtham
ear	ohr	aftee	auris	karnah
eye	auge	matee	oculus, ocellus	netram, chakshu
finger	finger	thakhteelo	digitus	angulee
foot	fut	pothee	pedes	padam, charan
hand	hand, zeiger	kheree	manus, palma	hastah, kar
hair	haar	maleea	pilus, saeta	kesh, baalah
head	kopf,oberhaupt	kefalee	caput, vertex	siras
leg	bein, keule	pothee	crus	jangha
mouth	mund	stoma	os	mukham
nose	nase	meetee	nasus, nares	naassaa
shoulder	schulter	omos	humerus	skandhah

English	Germanic	Greek	Latin	Sanskrit
stomach	magen, vertragen	stomakhee	stomachus	jathrah, udaram
English	Germanic	Greek	Latin	Sanskrit
---------	-----------	-----------	------------	-----------
thumb	oaumen	andeekheeras	pollex	angushtah
food	esser	fayeeto	cibus	aahaar,bhojnam
bread	brot	psomee	paris	apupah
fruit	frucht, obst	frooton	fructus,frux	falam
milk	milch	ghalo	mulgere	dugdham, kheeram
rice	reis	ryzi	-------	dhanah
vegetables	gemuse	lakhaneeko	planta, holus	shakah, shakam
water	wasser	neero	aqua	jalam, neeram
fire	feuer	fotia	ignis, flamma	agni
oil	ol	ladi	oleum	tailam
colors	farbe	khroma	color, pigment	rangah, varnah
white	weib	aspros	albus	shukla, shweta
black	schwarz	skoto	niger, ater	krishna, kal, shyam
blue	blau	ble	caeruleus	neelah
green	grun	prasino	viridis	harit
red	rot	aspro	ruber	rudhir, rakta
yellow	gelb	keetreenos	flarus	peelo
Seasons	jahreszeit	epohi	tempus	Irutah
spring	fruhling	aneeksee	ver	vasant
summer	sommer	kalokeree	aestas	grishamaha
autumn	herbst	ftheenoporo	autumnus	sharad
winter	winter	kheemonas	heems	sheetkalah, hemantah
Animals	Tier	Zoo	Animas	Pranin, Jeevah
bear	baer	arkouda	ursus	------
bull	bulle, stier	tavros	taurus	vrushah
buffalo	buffel	voualos	bos	mahish
cat	katze	gata	feles	biralaha,marjar
cow	kuh	agelada	vacca	dhenu, go
dog	hund	skylos	canis	shvan,kukkurah,
horse	pferd	alogho	equus	ashva, turgah
lion	lowe	liontari	leo	sinha
mouse	maus	pontiki	mus	undra

English	Germanic	Greek	Latin	Sanskrit
snake	schlange	fidi	serpens, anguis	sarpaha, bhujagaha

Nature

nature	natur	fysi	natura	Prakrutiha

English	Germanic	Greek	Latin	Sanskrit
earth	erde	gi	terra, solum	pruthivi, mahi,
moon	mond	selini	luna	chandrah, shashi
sun	sonne	ilios	sol	rohit, surya, ravi,
mountain	berg	opec, voono, ores	mons, montanus	parvat, giri
planets	planet	planitis	stella, erans	graha, nakshatra
rain	regen, regnen	vrekhee	pluria, unber	varshah
river	flub	potamos	flumen, amris	nadee, nadah
sky	himmel	ouranos	caelum	nabhas, ambaram
stars	stern, star	asteria	stella, astrum	nakshtra, taaraa
wind	wind, atem	anemos	ventus	samir
east	osten	anatoli	oriens	purvadish, prachi
west	westen	theeteeka	occidens	pashchima
north	norden	vorras	septentrio	uttara
south	suden	notos	meridies	dakshina

Numbers

English		Germanic	Greek	Latin	Sanskrit
one	1	einz	enas	unus	eka
two	2	zwei	theeo	duo	dvi
three	3	drei	tpio	tres	tri
four	4	vier	tesara	quattuor	chatur
five	5	funf	penda	quinque	pancha
six	6	sechs	eksee	sex	sas
seven	7	sieben	epta	septem	sapta
eight	8	acht	okta	octo	asta
nine	9	neun	enea	novem	nava
ten	10	zehn	thoka	decem	dasa
hundred, 100		hundert	ekato	centum	satam

Verbs in common use

English	Germanic	Greek	Latin	Sanskrit
eat	essen	tro-o	edere, vesci	khad, baksha
feed	futtern	taeezo	pascere	bhujoo
drink	trinken	pino	bibere, potare	paa
catch	haken, fang	perno	capere, exupere	grah
clean	sauber	katharo(adjec)	purgare	pavitra

English	Germanic	Greek	Latin	Sanskrit
come	kommen	erhomai	venire, redire	aagam
go	energie	pame	ire, vadere	gam, chal
bring	bringen	ferno	ferre, portare	aanee
hear	hohen	akouo	audire	shru
English	**Germanic**	**Greek**	**Latin**	**Sanskrit**
---------	-----------	-----------	------------	-----------
learn	lernen,enfahren	matheno	discere	shikshoo,abhyas
play	spiel	pezo	ludere	khel,rama, keed
love	lieb, null	agapo	amare,diligere	snehah, preman,
lose	verlieren	khano	amittere	tyaj, apahra
see	sehen	tho	videre, visere	drish
sit	sitzen	kathome	sedere	upavish, aas
forget	vergessen	keekhno	oblivisci	vismra
sing	singen	--------	conere,contare	gai (geet =song)
sleep	schlaf	keemame	dormire	swap,shayanam, nidra
speak	sprecher	meelo	dieere, loqui	vad, bhash
here	hier, hierher	etho	hic, adesse	atra, ihi
there	da, dahin	ekei	ibi, illie, istic	tatra
where	wohin,woher	poo	ubi, qua	kutra
now	jetzt, wo	tora	nune,iam,	adhuna, idanin
when	wann	pote	cum,ubi,quando	kadaa, yadaa
then	dann, damals	tote	tum, tune	tadaa
day	tag	imera	dies	dinam, divasah
week	woche	evdomada	septem dies	saptah
year	jahr	etos	anni, annus	varsha
morning	morgen	proi	tempus, matutinum	usha,arunoudya
evening	abend	vradi	vesper	sandhya,sayumkaal
night	nacht	nyhta	nox, nocte	ratri, rajani
yesterday	gestern	khtes	heri	purvehyoo, hyustan
today	heute	seemera	hodiernusdies	talee
tomorrow	morgen	avreeo	crastinus	parehyavi
inside	inner	mesa	interior, intus	antaram, udaram
good	gut, brav,artig	kalo	borus,probus	bhadra, shreshta
bad	schlect,schwer	kako	malus,pravus	nirdit, ashubha,
beautiful	schon	oreo,omorfo	pulcher,formosus	sunder,kant,

English	Germanic	Greek	Latin	Sanskrit
dirty	schmutzig	vromeeko	spurcus,turpis	malin, kalkam
short	kurz, klein	meekro,kondo	brevis,humilis	alpa, laghu.
tall	hoch	pseelo	longus,proccrus	ucha, dirgha
ugly	ubel	askheemo	deformis, turpis	vikurta,kuvaproop,
cave	hohle	-------	hohle	guha, ruhakm
house	haus	spectee	domus, aedes	girham, vasah
English	**Germanic**	**Greek**	**Latin**	**Sanskrit**
---------	-----------	-----------	------------	----------
king	konig	vassilias	rex	rajan
queen	konigin	vassiliassa	regni	rajyee, rajpatni
road	strabe,weg	dromos	via, iter	margah,
student	student	feeteetes	discipulus	vidyarthin, chhatra
teacher	lehrer	thaskalos	doctor,magister	shikshaha, adhyapakaha
servant	diener	ypiretis	servus, famulus	sevakaha,dasaha
town, urban	stadt	khoryo	urbs, oppidum	nagaram, puram
village	dorf	khoryo	pagus, vicus	gramaha
friend (he)	freund	feelos	amicus, sodaus	mitram
friend (she)	freundin	feelee	amica	sakhi
enemy	feind	ehthros	hostis, inimicus	shatruha,ariha,
neighbour	nachbar	geitonas	vicinus	prativeshin
stranger	fremde	xenos	hospes, advena	paraki

Surprisingly, even Greek and Latin do not seem to be closely related to each other. Mutual borrowing, technical or otherwise, should not be misconstrued. There is significant affinity between the parent language German and its child English. When the correspondence English has with Latin and Greek is so poor, how can one claim significant linguistic correspondence between Sanskrit and its two alleged linguistic sisters Latin and Greek?

The IE, in fact, is not one family. It is a group of families of languages, not confined to one home. The speakers of the IE languages live in several homes as many as its member languages, bordered by oceans, culture and history. It would not be difficult for the ultra-ambitious subjective linguists to prove world-wide diffusion of the IE family and the whole planet as its home. They are out to prove any language, even with affinity of only a few words, as the member of the IE family. Linguistics has been revolting against the constitution of the language. Linguists seem resisting to understand that the affinity could be caused also by borrowing and or mere chance. They ignore the variables, such as geography, culture; grammar and history also influence lingual correspondence.

With these notable exceptions, however, the various theories differ primarily in the location of the *Urheimat*, the area where the Proto-Indo-Europeans supposedly lived before splitting and setting off in their different ways. They differ also about the time when the split occurred.

Why would they not differ when the base of the theory itself is shaky and unbelievable? The PIE, the assumed ancestor of the IE, is dead and unidentifiable. In the case of the PIE, neither it was ever seen alive nor found dead. No history has recorded its birth, nomenclature, or its life. What is the name of the mother of Sanskrit, Greek and Latin? Where was she born? Where did she live? How long did she live? What happened to her? How did she disappear or die before the history could know her name and her whereabouts? All these questions are yet to be answered. No scholar seems to be optimistic to be able to trace her alive or dead. All this suggests that the IE family of languages is a myth. Beyond any doubt it seems to have been mischievously created by colonialists to confuse the originality of Sanskrit.

Conclusion

Several scholars addressing the IE concept have established beyond any doubts that the Indic and European are linguistically two different families of languages and also that European languages have not evolved from Sanskrit, as being misconceived. There are some philological similarities between the two, but not appropriate and adequate enough to qualify Sanskrit and European languages as cognate sisters. Some similarities could be accidental, and more due to borrowing, because of cohabitation as a result of massive migrations of Sanskrit-speaking Indo-Aryans to almost all regions of Europe and also because of Hindu (Vedic) colonization of some regions, particularly Greece in prehistory ancient times, as documented by Pococke in *'India in Greece; Truth in Mythology.'*

SANSKRIT

Lullaby, the first child enjoyed, was in Sanskrit

Hard to tell in what form and structure Sanskrit was spoken by the first Aryan in Âryavarta. No thing – human, animal or botanical – is born in its youth. It takes time to grow and develop into youth, decline in old age and then end by death. But, in case of language it is different. In general, language goes on blooming with new buds, developing into various philological flowers and later branches, becoming more expressive. No language completely dies, not leaving behind any words or phrases.

Sanskrit, the great-grand mother of world languages, as claimed by various linguists, has been generously productive, bearing several languages at home, and donating words to other languages, particularly European, to be more emphatically and meaningfully more expressive.

Because of inter-lingual intercourses due to globalization, most languages, being philologically fattening with increasing number of new words, phrases and proverbs, have made man more effectively expressive. Borrowings have been welcome because they make languages adequate, more expressive, more meaningful and beautiful. Colonial walls between Sanskrit and Dravidian languages have been cracking down, and they are becoming increasingly more Sanskritic (Hindi) by regaining ethos of nationalism, rekindled by independence. Hindi, the Cinderella of Indian vernaculars, is being welcome by all, including Dravidians and

Muslims, all around India. Amazing to see what Shaheena,[58] a Muslim graduate in Sanskrit has said about Sanskrit: "Sanskrit is the most apt language for Indians since most Indian languages are its offshoots."

Prof. Satya Vrat Shastri[59] has talked about the relationship, Sanskrit has with Bharatiya (Indian) vernaculars:

> "The languages of the Aryan family are direct descendents of Sanskrit through Prakrit and Apabhrasas. The languages of the Dravidian family have not come down from Sanskrit. Even with this difference the languages of both these families, the Aryan and the Dravidian, have strong presence of Sanskrit, the only dividing line from the point of view of Sanskrit, in them being that while in the languages of the Aryan there is more of Sanskrit in *tadbhava*, derivative, form while in the languages of the Dravidian family like Telugu, Kannada, Tamil and Malayalam, there is more of *tatsama*, the words in their original Sanskrit, form."

According to some specialists, as Dr. Shastri sees that around 70% Malayalam, 50 to 60% Telugu and Kannada, and 30% Tamil have philological congruence with Sanskrit and with one another. It is surprising that the Dravidian languages as they move towards east and north have been getting increasingly more sanskritized. It seems with time, because of occupational inter-mobility – south → north → south – and also because of Hindi, as increasingly being used as the national official language (written as well as vocal), there will be increasingly significant mutual linguistic congruence between Hindi and Dravidian languages. There were times when there was resistance from some quarters of south to Hindi as the national language. Ironically, some southerners considered Hindi as foreign, not English, perhaps because several southerners did not know Hindi. Several confused southerners

---

58 Shaheena, a graduate in Sanskrit - Satya Vrat Shastri, 'Sanskrit Studies: New Perspectives' (2007, p. 26)

59 Ibid, pp. 166-167).

preferred foreign language English to Hindi as the national language of Hindustan.

Prof. Shastri writes that the Dravidian languages have adopted Sanskrit words as borrowings, but the structure is different. The Sanskritic shade in Dravidian languages varies from language to language – overwhelming in Malayalam, just strong in Telugu and Kannada, but weak in Tamil. Since independence, because the Central Government is jointly administered by Hindi and Dravidian ministers, influence of Hindi (Sanskrit) on Dravidian languages and vice versa has been increasing.

During the British rule, guided by the world-known British policy of 'divide & rule,' the South was distanced from the North by infusing in them the colonial notion that Sanskrit-speaking north Indians are descendents of the alleged invading Aryans, and the south Indian Dravidians are original natives who were allegedly pushed down to south by the invading Aryans. This was done to validate the ill-based theory 'Aryan Invasion of India.' The words 'India' and 'Indian' were mischievously introduced by the colonial British to politically confuse the identity of Hindus,[60] the only true natives of Hindustan. Others are immigrants or invaders, but if and when citizens, they have the same and equal rights as Hindus have. Hats off to London for its shrewdness, foresight and sharp understanding of the Bible of colonialism. They sowed seeds infusing immortality of the ever green 'Hindu-Muslim Conflict' by creating 'The Indian National Congress' long before leaving India.

In May 1885, Allan Octavian Hume, with approval of the Viceroy and with support of some educated Indians created "Indian National Congress" to discuss issues concerning the common public interests. It created communal rift. Many Muslim community leaders, like the prominent educationalist Syed Ahmed Khan, viewed the Congress negatively, owing to its membership being dominated by Hindus, ignoring Hindu majority over 80%.

All Hindus of north as well of south are Aryans, as evidenced by the original name of Bharat, as Aryavarta and common culture,

---

[60] The word Hindu includes the followers of religions, offshoots of Hinduism, like Jains and Sikhs.

religion, mythologies and history. There is/was no country other than Aryavarta (present Bharat, India) which has or had Aryans as its natives and Sanskrit as its native language. It is unbelievable that all Indians of north were pushed down to south. Their complexion is dark because of influence of warm weather of south. All Indians, southern as well northern, were and are Aryans, as evidenced by their similar culture and their basic philosophy of life, as based on Vedic religion (Hinduism), all Hindus of north as well of south believe in.

Millennia-old ancient (prior to 1500 BC) names of the rivers, mountains, hills, lakes, towns, villages would vouch their origin in Sanskrit, excepting some which were later changed or given by Muslim and Christian rulers.

Sir William Jones praises Sanskrit:

> "The Sanskrit language, whatever be its antiquity, is of a wonderful structure, more perfect than the Greek, more copious than the Latin, and more exquisitely refined than the either, yet bearing to both of them a stronger affinity, both in the roots of verbs and the forms of grammar, than could possibly have been produced by accident; so strong indeed, that no philologer could examine them all three, without believing them to have sprung from some common source, which, perhaps, no longer exits: there is similar reason, though not quite so forcible, for supposing that both the Gothic and Celtic, though blended with a very different idiom, had the same origin with the Sanskrit, and the Old Persian might be added to the same family."

I agree with Sir William Jones that Sanskrit has some affinity with Latin and Greek. But it is not as close as, and not of the kind as required to qualify Sanskrit to be cognate sister of any European language. It is too hard to agree with Jones that such affinity is due to their common parentage, Proto-Indo-European (PIE). Philological similarities can be caused by borrowing or by accident. Sanskrit has not sprung from the same source, as Latin and Greek have. Speakers of Sanskrit are ethno-culturally and historically too different and geographically too distant from Europeans to have a cognate relationship. Moreover, their religion and mythologies are too different. Hinduism, the religion of the speakers of Sanskrit is much older than Christianity and Judaism. Hinduism is the most ancient religion, as ancient as the mankind. The name of its founder is yet not known. Language is associated with the religion of its speakers. Thus, their languages – Indic and European – can / should not be considered as the members of one and the same family. The theory of 'Indo-European family of languages' has been mischievously created to confuse, rather distort, the origin and antiquity of Sanskrit, which is the most ancient language with a refined grammar. Philological resemblances can not make them cognate siblings. Some philological resemblances are caused by borrowing due to cohabitation, chance, tourism or by lingual accidents.

According to Wikipedia, "Sanskrit is a historical Indo-Aryan language and the primary liturgical language of Hinduism and Buddhism. Today, it is listed as one of the 22 scheduled languages of India."

Will Durant[61] (p. 406) remarks:

> "The Sanskrit of the Vedas and the Epics has already earmarks of a classical and literary tongue, used only by scholars and priests; the very word Sanskrit means 'prepared, pure, perfect, sacred.' The language of the people in the Vedic age was not one but many; each tribe had its own Aryan dialect. India has never had *one* language."

Durant (p.555) talks about the transformation of Sanskrit into Prakrit – from its use by scholars to its use by public in form of various vernaculars, such as Hindi, Bengali, Punjabi, Gujarati, Marathi, Sindhi, etc.:

> "JUST as the philosophy and much of the literature of medieval Europe were composed in a dead language

---

[61] Will Durant, in Our Oriental Heritage (p.406).

unintelligible to the people, so the philosophy and classic literature of India were written in a Sanskrit that had long since passed out of common parlance, but had survived as the *Esperanto* of scholars having no other common tongue. Divorced from contact with the life of the nation, this literary language became a model of scholasticism and refinement; new words were formed not by the spontaneous creation of the people, but by the needs of technical discourse in the schools."

Durant (pp.574-575) talks about the literary beauty of the play *'SHAKUNTALA'* of Kalidasa which was translated into English by Sir William Jones, and praised by Goethe. Kalidasa was nominated as one of the 'Nine Gems' – poets, artists, and philosophers – by Raja Vikramaditya (380-413 A.D.)

Celebrated playwright Girish Karnad[62] emotionally expresses his amazement at "Sheldon Pollack's work, revealing how the umbra and penumbra of Sanskrit culture spread." He is right that Sanskrit has developed as a culture rather than as a language. Sanskrit, being the language of the Vedas, oldest scriptures of human mind, has amazing wealth of man's wisdom and culture. The relationship between language and culture is of 'Give and Take' friendship. They feed each other and get nourished.

Dr. Sheldon Pollock[63] (Arvind Raghunathan) was celebrated as India Abroad's 'Person of the year 2013.' He was the Professor of Sanskrit and South Asian Studies from 2005-2011 at Columbia University. Before that he served as the Professor of Sanskrit and Indic Studies at the University of Chicago (1989-2005).

Max Müller (1999, p.40) talks about Sanskrit, its antiquity and its relationship with other languages:

"First of all, its antiquity – for we know Sanskrit at an earlier period than Greek. But what is more important than its merely chronological antiquity is the antique

---

[62] India Abroad, M126 June 2014 "India Abroad Person of the year 2013.
[63] Wikipedia

state of preservation in which that Aryan language has been handed down to us. ... Sanskrit was the eldest sister of them all and could tell of many things which the other members of the family had quite forgotten."

It is hard to understand how Sanskrit could be handed down to Europeans when it was an Aryan language, meaning the language of Aryavarta (Bharat, India). He has not explained how it was handed down to Europe. Max Müller seems to indirectly suggest that Sanskrit is a member of the IE family. In my opinion, Sanskrit can not be genetically related to any European language because it is culturally and historically different and geographically too distant from all European languages. The IE is linguistically too diverse to be one family. Particularly, Indic languages are not and can not be genetically related to European languages. Philological similarities between some – even several – Sanskrit and European words can / should not qualify them as linguistic genetic sisters. Similarities, as said earlier, are caused by borrowing due to long cohabitation of their speakers and/or by chance.

Max Müller, in *'Science of Language'* (1891: 225-6), writes that the discovery of Sanskrit struck Lord Monboddo, like a thunderbolt just after he had finished his great work *'Of the Origins and Progress of Languages'* (2nd edition, 6 volumes, Edinburgh, 1774). In this work, he says all the dialects of the world were derived from a language originally framed by some Egyptian gods. Later in 1792, Monboddo writes:

"There is a language (Sanskrit) still existing, and preserved among the Brahmins of India, which is richer and in every respect a finer language than even the Greek of Homer. All the other languages of India have a great resemblance to this language, which is called the Shanskrit. ... I shall be able clearly to prove that the Greek is derived from the Shanscrit, which was the ancient language of Egypt, and was carried by the Egyptians into India, with their other arts, and into Greece by the colonies which they settled there."

133

If Sanskrit is the language of the Brahmins of India, how then do some linguists say that it came to India from outside? I do agree that several Sanskrit words have resemblance to Greek, but disagree with Monboddo that that Greek is derived from Sanskrit or Sanskrit from Greek. I also disagree that Sanskrit was the ancient language of Egypt. As a matter of fact, history vouches that Sanskrit-speaking Aryans had established their kingdoms in Egypt, other middle-east countries and Greece in remote ancient times. Thus, due to long cohabitation of Sanskrit-speaking Aryans with Egyptians and Greeks, Sanskrit philologically influenced the languages of Egypt and Greece. It is explained later that in ancient times that the Vedic Aryans had gone out of India for trade and had established their kingdoms in various regions all over the planet. In those days, Sanskrit could be a popular language in Egypt and Greece, but it was not their lingua franca. India, the land of Sanskrit, is historically and culturally different and geographically too distant from Greece and Egypt to make European, Egyptian and Indic languages a family.

A few years later (1795), Lord Monboddo (Max Müller, 1891, p.226) realized that Sanskrit is not a dialect of Greek, nor Greek of Sanskrit. But, still he does not seem to be clear about the origin of Sanskrit and its relation with Greek and with some Egyptian language. He writes:

> "Mr. Wilkins has proved to my conviction such a resemblance betwixt the Greek and the Shanscrit, that the one must be a dialect of the other, or both of some original language. Now the Greek is certainly not a dialect of the Shanscrit, anymore than the Shanscrit is of the Greek. They must, therefore, be both dialects of the same language; and that language could be no other than the language of Egypt, brought into India by Osiris, of which, undoubtedly, the Greek was a dialect, as I think I have proved."

It seems, both Max Müller and Sir William Jones were so much emotionally and intellectually engrossed to prove the validity of their ill-founded theory of IE (Indo-European family of languages). Hence they engineered also the theory of Aryan Invasion of India (AII), according to which Aryans invaded India in about 1500 B.C. and brought with them Sanskrit and a pantheon of Hindu gods; and composed the Vedas in about 1000 BC and even later. Who is going to believe all this? Even a school-going youngster in India will laugh at this. Both the theories (IE and AII) were guided by the European missionary agenda to prove that all the three – Aryans, Sanskrit and the Vedas – were not originally from Aryavrata (India).

Unfortunately for them, cat is out of bag. Both the theories, AII and IE, contradict each other on both counts – (1) the story the way they came to India, and (2) on the year of entry of Sanskrit in India. According to the AII, Aryans invaded India in about 1500 B.C. and brought Sanskrit; and according to IE, speakers of Sanskrit and European languages lived some where (no consensus on their abode), and after their separation in 3000 B.C (some say 6000 B.C.) Sanskrit-speaking came to India and Europeans went to Greece, Italy, etc. All this looks like a fairy tale.

According to *Samvad* (December, New Delhi, 1997, p.3), the German scholar Kurt Schildmann claims that his study of ancient inscriptions, discovered in Peru and USA, show that they are similar to ancient Sanskrit, suggesting sea fares from India might have reached Americas long back.

Glory of Sanskrit

The Columbia Encyclopedia (1993:163-4) talks about the glory of ancient Sanskrit literature, as contained in its three major Oriental dramas:

> "Of the three major Oriental dramas – Sanskrit, Chinese, Japanese – the oldest is Sanskrit, although the dates of its origin are uncertain. Sanskrit drama is a part of Sanskrit literature, the classical literature of India, which flourished from about 1500 B.C. to A.D.1100. The earliest extant critical work on Sanskrit drama is

attributed to Bharata, the legendary formulator of the dramatic art in India. ... The earliest-known Sanskrit playwright was Bhasa (c.3d cent. A. D.) while among the most renowned were Kalidasa, Bhavabhuti (c.8th cent. A.D.), and King Harsha."

The book *India: What Can It Teach Us* (1999) contains the text of the seven lectures, Max Müller delivered to the European candidates for civil service in India. He addressed several issues to help them to have clear idea of Hindus, Vedas, Vedanta, Vedic deities, significance of the study of Sanskrit and its literature. He also has addressed European misconceptions of and prejudices against India, Hindus, their deities and Vedic literature.

Max Müller (1999, p.137) has emphasized that India deserves European attention and respect because:

"(India), both by its language, the Sanskrit, and by its most ancient literary documents, the Vedas, it can teach us lessons which nothing else can teach, as to the origin of our own language, the first formation of our own concepts, and the true natural germs of all that is comprehended under the name of civilization, at least civilization of the Aryan race, that the race we and all the greatest nations of the world – the Hindus, the Persians, the Greeks and Romans, the Slaves, the Celts, and last, not least, the Teutons, belong."

Max Müller, (1999, p.138), writes that the ancient literature of the Vedic period of India deserves careful attention, not only of Oriental scholars, but also of every educated man and woman, any where, even in England. He wishes to know how we (Europeans) came to be what we are. He talks about the significance of meditation and transcendentalism in which Hindus excel:

"I wish to point out that there is another sphere of intellectual activity in which the Hindus excel – the meditative and transcendent – and that here we might learn from them some lessons of life which we ourselves are but too apt to ignore or to despise."

Max Müller (1999, p.22) makes a pleasing remark about the respect Sanskrit commands in Germany:

"A scholar who studies Sanskrit in Germany is supposed to be initiated in the deep and dark mysteries of ancient wisdom, and a man, who has traveled in India, even if he has only discovered Calcutta, or Bombay, or Madras, is listened to like Marco Polo. In England a student of Sanskrit is generally considered a bore."

Max Müller (1891, p.232) writes that August Wilhelm von Schlegel, the brother of Frederick Schlegel, used his influence which he had acquired as a German poet, to popularize the study of Sanskrit in Germany.

Sanskrit in China

Max Müller, in 'The Science of Language' (p. 196), talking about 'Chinese accounts of India,' observes that the next nation after the Greeks that became acquainted with the language and literature of India, was the Chinese. Though Buddhism was not recognized as a third-religion before the year 65 A.D., under the Emperor Ming-ti, Buddhist missionaries had reached China from India as early as the third century, 217 B.C. He further writes: "The very name of Buddha, changed in Chinese into Fo-t'o and Fo, is pure Sanskrit, and so is every word and every thought of that religion. The language – which the Chinese pilgrims went to India to study, as the key to the sacred literature of Buddhism – was Sanskrit."

Tedd St Rain,[64] in the Preface to Max Müller's *'What India Can Teach Us'* (1999), praises Max Müller for his accomplishments by translating

---

[64] Tedd St. Rain, author of 'Mystery Of America'

the Upanishads and editing a massive collection of the work, called *The sacred Books of the East*:

> "Some of the most valuable and instructive materials in the history of man are treasured up in India, and in India only. In her classic dialect, the Sanskrit, we may read with what success ancient India conquered the elements and the world as it was then known."

He further remarks about the significance of Sanskrit:

> "The study of Sanskrit, and particularly a study of the Vedic Sanskrit, is able to enlighten us and illuminate the darkest passages in the history of the human mind."

Max Müller (1999, p.39), writes that no one supposes any longer that Sanskrit was the common source of European languages:

> "I am not speaking as yet of the literature of India as it is, but of something far more ancient, the language of India, or Sanskrit. No one supposes any longer that Sanskrit was the common source of Greek, Latin, and Anglo-Saxon. This used to be said, but it has long been shown that Sanskrit is only a collateral branch of the same stem from which spring Geek, Latin, Anglo-Saxon; and not only these, but all the Teutonic, all the Celtic, all the Slavonic languages, nay the languages of Persia and Armenia also."

Linguists should appreciate the scholarly realization that Sanskrit and European languages do not share a common origin. But, I don't agree that Sanskrit is a collateral branch of the same stem from which Sanskrit and European languages have sprung. The Indic and European are two distinctly different families of languages, culturally as well as historically. They are geographically too distant to make a family, not even a tree of languages having branches of Indic and European languages. On no tree both mangoes and apples are grown. Moreover,

Sanskrit is much older than all the European languages. Some philological resemblances between Sanskrit and European languages, as seen, are caused by borrowing and or by long close cohabitation, but not by alleged common parentage. It is historically known that in ancient times, Vedic people had gone out of India for trade to several countries including European. They had established Vedic kingdoms and had colonized some countries including Greece, as shown by E. Pococke in his book, *'India in Greece* or *Truth in Mythology'* (1856). It is hard for many to believe that in distant ancient times Greece was colonized by Indians (Hindus and Buddhists), only because history has been distorted, hidden and buried. Europeans did not want the future generations know all this.

Sanskrit adored by Muslims too

Dr. Satya Vrat Shastri, in his book *"Sanskrit Studies: New Perspectives"* (2007, p. 18), remarks:

> "The pursuit of Sanskrit by Muslims is not limited to the medieval or the early modern period only, it is carried on even now. The number of Muslim Sanskrit scholars pursuing Sanskrit may not be very large but it is not too small either to be ignored."

Dr. Shastri has given quite a few examples of Muslim scholars in Sanskrit, such as Shri Ghulam Dastgir of Bombay, Shri Habibur Rehman Shastri, known as Pandit Habibur Rehman, Prof. Fatehullah Mojtabai, Ms. Shaheena S., etc. Three of them need mention to emphasize Muslim interest in Sanskrit.

Sanskrit scholar Shri Ghulam Dastgir was honored in 1976 by the Government of Maharashtra. He had so much deep and abiding love for Sanskrit that he sent out invitation in Sanskrit for the marriage of his younger brother.

Ms. Shaheena, a 25 year young woman topped in the Kerala University M.A. (Sanskrit) examination. She is the second of the three daughters of Shri Shahul Hamid. She opted for Sanskrit with her parents' blessings. Dr. Shastri (p.26) talks about her that when asked by some people as to why she did not choose Arabic in place of Sanskrit, Shaheena replied: "Sanskrit is the most apt language for Indians since most Indian languages are its offshoots." Dr. Shastri writes that Shaheena wants to launch a Sanskrit magazine to help Sanskrit lovers in India express their creativity. She wants one day to teach Sanskrit. She mourns: "It is shame that this beautiful language is reduced to a Cinderella in her own land."

Prof. Fatehullah Mojtabai, former Cultural Counselor of the Embassy of Iran in India, was a noted scholar of Sanskrit and a well-known exponent of Hindu philosophy. He has translated Gita into Persian the Gita, the *Laghuyogavāsistha* and *Mahopanisad*. Translation of Gita into Persian suggests that Prof. Mojtabai was so much impressed by the philosophy of Hinduism, as contained in Gita, that he wanted his countrymen (Iranians) should also benefit from the Gita philosophy. May be his ancestors were Zoroastrians whose language Zend-Avestan was very similar to Sanskrit.

Hindus are so much in love with poetry that almost all ancient sacred scriptures – Vedas, Upanishads, Bhagvad Gita, Rāmāyanā, Mahābhāratā. – are composed in poetry form. Dr. Shastri (p.51) has remarked that poetry has been with Bharat from the times of the Vedas, and that from time to time its character has been undergoing change – from religious poetry of the Vedas to narrative poetry of the Rāmāyanā, the Mahābhāratā and the Purānas to the highly sophisticated and ornate poetry of the Mahākāvyas.

Shaheena's family finds Sanskrit *shlokas* melodious when she recites them at home. She herself says that there is poetry in every syllable of them." When a non-Hindu (particularly a Muslim) feels so much melody in Sanskrit *shlokas*, it is difficult to estimate the feelings of a Hindu devotee to the god / goddess he adores. Such millennia long poetry traditions have been evident in all Indian walks of life. Surprisingly, present modern cinema seems to follow the traditions. Love is expressed through song, supported by dance. Indian classical dances are expressive of love and beauty. Some movies are stuffed with songs and dances too much at the cost of story, thus become boring.

Edward Pococke, in his book *'India in Greece',* writes that Hindus had colonized Greece in ancient times. Every thing including mathematics was expressed in a poetry form.

Language talks about both culture and religion. For some times culture is confused as religion. Any culture is much wider than religion. Therefore, the members of the same culture, though followers of different religions, may speak the same language, as is happening in India. This also is true that each culture has some of its ingredients related to various religions. Some conservative and narrow-minded persons become too sensitive to the choice of words, to insure that the word is from the language related to his/her religion.

Several ethnicities can be associated with one culture. Culture, unlike religion, doesn't have any defined restricting borders. Hence, associates of the same, rather similar culture may follow different religions. Followers of various religions – Hinduism, Jainism, Buddhism, Christianity, Zoroastrianism, Islam, Sikhism, Sufism, etc. – are associated with Indian culture in varying ways and in varying degrees, and so are various languages of India. This can be understood better if American culture is seen in relation to various religions and various languages of its people.

Sanskrit is primarily related to Hinduism, and then to its offshoot religions – Jainism, Buddhism and Sikhism – in varying degrees.

How did Sanskrit influence most of the world languages?

Several books, authored by European scholars, would vouch that India, with her Vedic culture expressed in Sanskrit, was all over the globe. Because of cohabitation between Sanskrit-speaking Aryans and speakers of other languages, mutual borrowing of words would be inevitable. As the result, it is natural that there would be some linguistic correspondence between Sanskrit and European languages, including Greek and Latin. But it will be wrong to interpret it as cognate or genetic relationship Sanskrit has with Greek, Latin and some other European languages.

Breakup of Himalayan glaciers → age of Sanskrit → age of स्वि

Swastika, being a Sanskrit word, tells the age of Sanskrit, and that Bharat was the original home of Sanskrit, the Vedas and Vedic religion. The Swastika, found among Celts and American Indians, tells that Bharat had trade and/or travel relations with them since too remote pre-history times.

Graham Hancock (2002, p.169) quotes B.B. Radhakrishna of the Geological Society of India (1999), who writes that the *Rig Veda* talks about the break-up of Himalayan glaciers releasing water which flowed out in seven mighty rivers (*Sapta Sindhu*). This happened during Late Pleistocene glaciations, more than 10,000 years ago. Its mention in *Rig Veda* evidences that the age of Sanskrit and also of Swastika. This challenges the validity of both the theories – 'Aryan invasion of India' (1500 B.C.), and 'Indo-European family of languages' (3000 B.C.). As a matter of fact, Sanskrit was in India long earlier than 10,000 years, as evidenced by mention of 10,000 old warming up of the Himalayan glaciers in *Rig Veda*, written, rather composed in Sanskrit. This also proves that Sanskrit did not come into India from outside.

According to Forbes Magazine, Sanskrit is a suitable language for computer software.

Chapter Seven

SANSKRIT AND AVESTAN

I t is true that the Persian, the language of Persia (Iran), has its origin in Sanskrit. The authors of the Vedas and worshippers of Ahuro Mazdao did live together in early ancient times. India, including Persia (Iran), was the original home of the Aryans and of the Persians (Iranians). Iranians were originally Aryans. As a matter of fact, in remote ancient times, Iran was a part of Greater India (Vishaal Bharat). Both the languages, Sanskrit and Zend-Avestan, were linguistically too close to consider them as two different languages. J. P. Mallory, in *'In Search of Indo-Europeans'* (1989, p.35), has shown close linguistic relationship between Sanskrit and Iran's Avestan:

Avestan:	tem amavantem yazatem
Sanskrit:	tam amavantam yajatam
Avestan:	surem damohu sevistem
Sanskrit:	suram dhamasu savistham
Avestan:	mithrem yazai zaothrabyo
Sanskrit:	mitram yajai hotrabhyah

Mallory (p. 35) remarks:

"The concept of a common Indo-Iranian language is indicated by the close similarities between this Indic (Sanskrit) translation of an early Iranian hymn. The god Mitra / Mithra was common to both Indians and Iranians."

In fact, these are not translations. The same Sanskrit was spoken in Avestan with little difference in phonetic pronunciation of some letters. For example:

Sanskrit	Avestan
'j'	'z'
'h'	's'
'dh'	'd'
'th'	't'
'bh'	'b'

Same way, Iranians pronounced 'Sindhu' as 'Hindu', and 'soma' as 'homa.'

Dr. Poonai[65] writes about the relationship between Sanskrit and the Zend-Avestan:

> "It has also been shown on the basis of statements which have been made in the oldest of the Gathas of the Zend Avesta, about mantras and personalities of the *Rig Veda*, that the *Rig Veda* predates the Gathas by several millennia and that the Vedas appear to have contributed to the content of the earliest Gathas by accumulation of concepts."

The word *'Gathas'* has its origin in Sanskrit. It literally means stories. Nehru[66] writes about the relationship between Sanskrit and Avestan:

> "Even the language of the Vedas bears a striking resemblance to that of the Avesta, and it has been remarked that Avesta is nearer to the Veda than the Veda is to its own epic Sanskrit."

Max Müller,[67] in *'Science of Language'* (1861, p.289), remarks:

---

[65] Dr. Poonai (Origin of Civilization and Language, 1994, p. 220).
[66] Nehru, in 'Discovery of India' (1946, p.77).
[67] Max Müller, in 'Science of Language' (1861, p.289).

"Sanskrit and Zend share certain words and grammatical forms in common which do not exist in any other Aryan languages; and there can be no doubt that the ancestors of the poets of the Vedas and the worshippers of A*huro Mazdao* lived together for some time after they had left the original home of the whole Aryan race."

Hard to understand what Max Müller meant by the "original home of the whole Aryan race." I think, Max Müller meant Greater India when Iran remained as its part, until Iran was captured and occupied by other forces. Aryans (Hindus) and Persians (Iranians) did not leave India (the original home of the whole Aryan race). Some Avestan-speaking Zoroastrians had to leave Iran for Sanskrit-speaking India, when Iran was captured by Muslims around 900 AD. Most of them stayed there in Iran.

It can be understood better from the event 'Partition of India in 1947' when Muslims had Pakistan. Many Muslims opted to continue to live in India, and even some migrated back from Pakistan to India. So it happened with Zoroastrian Iranians. The ancient relationship between Iran and Bharat (India) is discussed in detail later in Chapter "Iran: Cradle of Aryans."

Dr. Poonai (p.226) gives genealogic time trend of some important IE languages:

Language Group	Approximate time of origin
Rig-Vedic Sanskrit	9000 B.C.
Zend	1500 B.C.
Greek dialects	800 B.C.
Latin languages	400 B.C.
Celtic languages	500 B.C.
Germanic languages	350 A.D.
Baltic languages	1100 A.D.

Sanskrit is much older than 9,000 BC, as evidenced of the description of melting of Himalayan glaciers in *Rig Veda* which happened about 11,700 B.C.

Chapter Eight

GRAMMAR ENJOYED
SUNSHINE IN INDIA

J. Ludolf[68], in 1702, seems to believe different from Jones. He stated: "affinities between languages must be based on grammatical resemblances rather than vocabulary, and among vocabulary correspondence, the emphasis should be on simple words such as those which describe parts of body."

Kirsten Malmkjær (ed.), in *'The Linguistics Encyclopedia'* (1995, p.191), praises the Indian grammarian scholarship, being centuries ahead of the European:

> "Ancient Indian grammarians were centuries ahead of their European counterparts in language studies and from their best-known scholar Panini, whose studies, still extant, date back to the second half of the first millennium BC, we see brilliant independent linguistic scholarship in both theory and practice."

The linguistic quality of a language depends on its grammar. It guides in writing a correct and clear language. Max Müller (1891, pp.124-5), praises the Panini grammar:

> "The Hindus are the only nation that cultivated the science of Grammar without having received any

---

[68]   Kirsten Malmkjær (ed.), The Linguistics Encyclopedia (1991, p. 190).

impulse, directly or indirectly, from the Greeks. ... Sanskrit grammar arose from the study of the Vedas."

Michael Coulson[69] talks about the Panini grammar:

"The grammar of Panini, the Astadhyayi, usually attributed to the fourth century BC, is evidently the culmination of a long and sophisticated grammatical tradition, though the perfection of his own work caused that of his predecessors to vanish."

Such recognition of Sanskrit grammar by Max Müller and Michael Coulson seems to question the reliability and validity of linguistic congenital sisterhood of Sanskrit with Greek, Latin, and/or any other European language.

Among more than 4,000 languages, it is possible that quite a few languages, if not several, would have similar basic grammar. Two languages having similar grammar may not necessarily have vocabulary affinity, and vice versa.

Grammar of a language gives rules how we say or write, change and arrange words to express ourselves correctly. It is possible that some languages may have some aspects of grammar similar. It would not be appropriate to consider those languages as genetic sisters, meaning having common parentage because grammar is not hereditary. Even two languages, though of the same linguistic family, may have some aspects of their grammar different, and some languages of different families may have some aspects of their grammar similar, only because grammar, unlike words, is not hereditary. All this will be clear when we examine grammars of both the Indic and European languages. Language gradually evolves and develops in response to increasing demand for coining words to define the emerging objects and concepts to meet the human needs to express the feelings, hopes, aspirations and despairs of the humanity. Sense of grammar came later when the people realized the need for systemizing, regulating, and disciplining language,

---

[69]   Michael Coulson, in 'Sanskrit: Introduction to Classical Language' (1992, p. xv),

so as to be able to create literature in an adequate and appropriate manner.

In a language, it is important to examine the seven main basic paradigms of a sentence – subject, object, verb, adverb, preposition, adjective and inflection, etc. – to understand the systematic order of their placement to express what the writer or speaker wants to say and distinguish the grammar of one language from that of any other language. The order of the 'subject-verb-object' is considered as the most basic paradigm of a sentence. Each sentence must have at least subject and verb. In almost all languages, subject comes first, excepting in interrogatory sentences, which may begin with verb. In passive voice object comes first. Or in case of emphasis on object, it can come first. In some languages, mostly European, subject is followed by verb and then object. In most Indic languages, subject is followed by object, and then verb. The paradigm of 'subject-verb-object' is prevalent in most western languages, such as Greek, Germanic, English, French, etc. In Latin, unlike most western languages and like Sanskrit, the standard word order is 'subject-object-verb'. For example, *John Portiam amat* (John loves Portia). In Latin, word order is more flexible than in other western languages. In case of emphasis on object, Portia would come first *(Portia John amat),* and in case of emphasis on verb, amat would come first *(Amat Portiam John.)*. In Sanskrit and most eastern languages, the word order generally is 'subject-object-verb *(Aham pustakam pathaami* = I am reading a book).

Even if we think that each of the three – subject, verb, and object – would change its place three times, maximum total number of different computations would be six. There would be at the most six different paradigms of placement order of subject, verb, and object:

1. subject, verb, object
2. subject, object, verb
3. object, verb, subject
4. object, subject, verb
5. verb, subject, object
6. verb, object, subject

In other words, according to the rules of probability out of about 4,000 languages of the world, approximately 666 languages can have one and the same word order. It would be even a larger number of languages with different paradigms, in case of position of preposition and adjective in relation with their nouns, pronouns, etc.

In conclusion, grammatical similarity should not be considered as a determinant of linguistic affinity between any two languages. It is interesting to note that there is no grammatical correspondence between Latin (the parent of the Romance family) and its members, such as French and Spanish. French and Spanish languages have the word order (subject-verb-object) different from that their parent language Latin (subject-object-verb) has. Latin has its word order (subject-object-verb) similar to what Sanskrit has.

Sanskrit: Aham (I) ekam pustakam (one book) pathaami (read)
            (Subject, object, verb)

Latin: Canem (dog) homo (man) mordet (bites) :
            (Subject-object-verb)

Spanish: Yo (I) bebi (drank) vino (wine) enmi (in my)
            casa (house).
            (Subject-verb-object)

French: Je (I) responds (am answering) a la lettre.
            (Subject-verb-object)

Greek: Ekhasa to (I have lost) kleeTHee (key) moo (my)
            *(***Subject, verb, object)**
            (possessive adjective comes after its noun)

Germanic: Mein (my) bruther spielt (plays) klavier (piano).
            (Subject, verb, object)

English: My brother plays piano.
            (Subject, verb, object)

There are other grammatical paradigms, such as of the position of preposition and adjective in regard to the nouns they are associated with. In these cases, the probability would be 50%.

Adjective and Noun

In most western languages (Greek, English, Germanic, French, etc.), as well as in eastern languages (Sanskrit, Hindi, etc), adjective comes before its noun or pronoun. For example:

Hindi: Sunder larki (Beautiful girl)
                (Adjective before noun)
English: Beautiful girl
                (Adjective before noun)

But in Latin and Spanish, it is different. Generally adjective comes after its noun. For example:

Latin: John nobilis (noble John)
                (Adjective after noun)
Spanish: vino blanco (wine white).
                (Adjective after noun)

But, in Spanish possessive adjective comes before the noun: "en mi casa" = in my house.

Preposition and Noun

In case of preposition, in some languages, preposition comes before, and in some cases it comes after the noun/pronoun. In most western languages – English, German, Latin, Greek, French, etc. – preposition is followed by its noun. Where as, in most eastern (Indic) languages including Sanskrit and Hindi, preposition follows its noun. For example:

Sanskrit   Aham mam grahe (grah-e) nivsaami. Prep. "e" (in)
                after noun "grah" (house)
Hindi: (ghar mein) preposition (mein = in) comes after its
                noun (ghar = home).

Greek:	sto thomateeo moo = in room my (prep. "sto" before, but adj "moo" after noun)
Latin:	John in horto (in garden) cum Mary (with Mary) est (is).
Spanish:	Yo (I) bebi (drank) un vaso (a glass) de vino (of wine) blanko (white) en (in) la restarante Italaina (restaurant Italian).
French:	Marie cherche (is looking) le (for) livre (book).
English:	John is with Mary in the garden.
Germanic:	Meine (My) schwester (sister) ist (is) in der schule (in school)

In case of placement of adjective, the mother Latin is different from her daughter Spanish, also in case of placement of subject, verb, and object; Latin is different from her two daughters, Spanish and French. How, then, can one claim that the members of the same family will have grammar similarities? This also is proved that languages with grammar similarities may not have genealogical linguistic affinity.

We have seen above that there is no correspondence among the three ancient languages, Sanskrit, Greek and Latin, in case of the three grammar counts:

(1) Word order of subject, verb and object,
(2) Placement of adjective and its noun, and
(3) Position of preposition and the noun it governs.

In short, all the three ancient languages, allegedly considered as daughters of one and the same parent language 'Proto-Indo-European,' have failed to pass the Grammar DNA test. They are partially different as far as their grammar is concerned.

Inflection

Languages differ from one another on the basis of inflections. Most modern European languages, including English, are least inflecting. In most modern Indo-Aryan languages – Bengali, Hindi, Gujarati,

Punjabi, Sindhi, etc., like Sanskrit – verb inflects to reflect the gender, the number and the case of its subject. Verb inflections in English are less than those in Latin, Sanskrit and modern Indian languages. In English, verb does not inflect to reflect the gender of its subject as it does in Sanskrit and in some other Indo-European languages. Would English, therefore, be considered as a non-Indo-European language? In Latin, unlike in English, noun inflects to show whether it is used as subject or object. In conclusion, grammatical differences do not suggest whether language is IE or non-IE.

Hindus: First in cultivating Science of Grammar

Max Müller, in *'The Science of Language'* (1891, pp.124-5), praises the Panini grammar:

> "The Hindus are the only nation that cultivated the science of Grammar without having received any impulse, directly or indirectly, from the Greeks. ... Sanskrit grammar arose from the study of the Vedas, the most ancient poetry of the Brahmans. ... These supplied the solid basis on which successive generations of scholars erected that astounding structure which reached its perfection in the grammar of Panini. There is no form, regular or irregular, in the whole Sanskrit language, which is not provided for in the grammar of Panini and his commentators. It is the perfection of a merely empirical analysis of language, unsurpassed, nay even un-approached, by anything in the grammatical literature of other nations."

Sanskrit grammarian Pāṇini[70] (पाणि नि, 4th century BCE) gave grammar to Sanskrit. Pāṇini is known for his Sanskrit grammar, particularly for his formulation of the 3,959 rules of Sanskrit morphology, syntax and semantics in the grammar known as 'Aṣṭādhyāyī' (अष्टाध्यायी), meaning eight chapters. The Aṣṭādhyāyī is one of the

---

[70] Wikipedia, Pāṇini's comprehensive and scientific theory of grammar,

earliest known grammars of Sanskrit, although Pāṇini refers to previous texts like the Unadisutra, Dhatupatha, and Ganapatha. It is the earliest known work on descriptive linguistics, and together with the work of his immediate predecessors (Nirukta, Nighantu, Pratishakyas) stands at the beginning of the history of linguistics itself. His theory of morphological analysis was more advanced than any equivalent Western theory before the mid 20th century, and his analysis of noun compounds still forms the basis of modern linguistic theories of compounding, which have borrowed Sanskrit terms such as bahuvrihi and dvandva. Pāṇini was born in Pushkalavati, Gandhara, in the modern-day Afghanistan. Amazing that ancient Bharat knew the science of linguistics.

Michael Coulson, in his book '*Sanskrit: Introduction to Classical Language*' (1992, p. xv), talks about the Panini grammar:

> "The grammar of Panini, the Aṣṭādhyāyī', usually attributed to the fourth century BC, is evidently the culmination of a long and sophisticated grammatical tradition, though the perfection of his own work caused that of his predecessors to vanish."

Such recognition of Sanskrit grammar by Max Müller and by Michael Coulson seems to question the reliability and validity of linguistic congenital sisterhood of Sanskrit with Greek and Latin.

SANSKRIT AND DRAVIDIAN
LANGUAGES

According to the ill-based theory "Aryan invasion of India" (AII), Dravidians are the original natives of India, thus only Dravidian languages, not Sanskrit, are the native languages of India. The AII theory further tells that Aryans came into India from outside in around 1500 B.C., who brought along with them Sanskrit and a pantheon of Hindu gods and who composed the Vedas about 500 years after their arrival.

The theory 'AII' was mischievously engineered in London by the British colonialists to distort the ancient history of Bhārat and to confuse the originalities of all related to Hindus, including their religion, Vedas, Sanskrit and Swastika. This has been the basic strategy of all European colonialists, particularly British to disconnect the colonized people from their heritage. The same Russians did with the peoples they colonized. No one, even little conversant with history would believe that Sanskrit, pantheon of gods, Aryan race; Vedas and Swastika are not related to Hindus. Yet, I am writing this only because the colonially corrupted history is being taught in schools and colleges and library shelves are loaded with such books. Like contaminated drugs, they should have been recalled.

The four Indian Dravidian languages – Tamil, Telugu, Kannada and Malayalam – when keenly examined, would exhibit their philological congruence with Sanskrit in varying degree from language to language, as shown in the Table later in this chapter.

According to Random House Webster's Dictionary, The Dravid is eth-no-nym in Sanskrit.

The Columbia Encyclopedia remarks:

> "There are many words of Indic origin in the Dravidian languages, which in turn have contributed a number of words to the Indic tongues."

Aryan (Sanskritic) as well as Dravidian languages have linguistic and philological congruence with one another of varying degree, as shown in the Table later in this chapter. They all have their origin in Bharat and all are Aryan languages because all of their speakers – Northern as well Southern – are Hindu, the original natives of Bharat having same religion, culture, heritage and history. All are Aryan and no Aryan came into Bharat from outside, as explained in the chapter on Aryans. Thrust of this chapter is to challenge the following ill-based linguistic hypotheses related to Dravidian languages, as pronounced by colonial historians:

- Only Dravidians are the natives of India, and so only Dravidian are native languages of India, not Sanskrit.
- Sanskrit was brought in from outside.
- The four Dravidian languages – Tamil, Telugu, Kannada and Malayalam – were spoken in south because the Dravidian-speaking natives were pushed to south allegedly by the invading Aryans who stayed in north of India.
- The Dravidian languages do not qualify for the membership of the Indo-European family of languages (IE), because they do not have a word in common with Indo-European family of languages, Sanskrit is a member of.

Edward C. Dimock[71], Jr., et al (1974, p.6), write that the writing on the seals recovered from the ruins of the Indus Valley is Dravidian. They (pp. 7-9) suggest that only the Dravidian languages – Brahui (northern), Gondi (central), Tamil, Telugu, Kannada and Malayalam (southern),

---

[71]   Edward C. Dimock, Jr., et al, The Literatures of India (1974, p.6)

and also Austric languages – were being spoken in India before invading Aryans arrived in about 1500 B.C. They believe that Sanskrit was not the native language of India, nor were the Aryans its natives. Sanskrit was brought in by the alleged invading Aryans.

Dimock ignores the seals bearing the images of Shiva, Swastika, sacred bathing pool, un-deciphered texts etc, found in the ruins of the Indus Valley. The following image of Swastika, excavated from the Indus valley, will speak the true story of the Indus Valley that the natives of the Valley spoke both, Sanskritic as well as Dravidian languages, philologically and linguistically congruent to one another.

```````

India (Aryavarta, Bhārat) is the original abode of Aryans, Sanskrit and Vedic religion. The four South Indian Dravidian languages – Tamil, Telugu, Kannada and Malayalam – have significant linguistic relationship with Sanskrit, as shown in the Table, given on next few pages, but they do not qualify for the membership of the Indo-European family of languages because the Indic languages are linguistically, culturally, ethnically and historically different and geographically too distant from all the European languages. Whatever correspondence is accidental or due to borrowing. There is no genetic relationship between Indic and European languages. Genetic relationship between Sanskrit and European languages is being erroneously theorized by some. Brahui, being spoken in Baluchistan, is not of the Indian origin, even Austric.

Sanskrit has significantly greater correspondence with Dravidian languages than it has with any European language – Latin, Greek, English or German – as it is shown in the Chapter *'The Indo-European Family: Too Diverse to be One.'* Both theories (i) Aryan invasion of India and (ii) Indo-European family of languages were mischievously created to distort the origins of Aryans, Vedas, Sanskrit and Swastika.

### The word 'Dravid' has its origin in Sanskrit

It may be tempting for readers to know that the word *'Dravid,'* itself, has its origin in Sanskrit. According to the Random House Webster's Dictionary, the word 'Dravid' is 'eth-no-nym' in Sanskrit. According
```````

to *The Columbia Encyclopedia,* "There are many words of Indic origin in the Dravidian languages, which in turn have contributed a number of words to the Indic tongues." Sanskrit and Dravidian are twins. This is evidenced in the Table, *'Linguistic Affinity between Sanskrit and Dravidian Languages'*, given in this Chapter later.

Dravidian Scripts connected with Devanagri

The scripts of the Dravidian languages, except Brahui, have their ancient connection with Devanagri, the script of Sanskrit: "the Dravidian languages – Tamil, Telugu, Kannada and Malayalam – have their own alphabets, which go back to a common source that is related to the Devanagri, the script of Sanskrit."[72]

Brahui is written in the Arabic script.[73] Brahui adopted Arabic script recently only after Baluchistan was captured by Muslims. The same happened with the script of Sindhi. Arabic script was imposed on Sindhi in 1853 A.D. by the British Government at the insistence by Muslim majority in Sindh. Prior to pre-Arab invasion of Baluchistan, the land of Brahui-speaking people, Brahui, like other Dravidian languages, was written in a Devanagri-related script, because the region – on the north-western border of India, stretching from Baluchistan to Hindu Kush, including Afghanistan – was under the administrative control of Hindus and Buddhists.

The Table of over 100 words, given below, will show that the Dravidian languages have significant philological similarity with Sanskrit.

---

[72]   The Columbia Encyclopedia, p.794.
[73]   Ibid. p. 794.

Linguistic Affinity between Sanskrit and Dravidian Languages

English	Sanskrit	Tamil	Telugu	Kannada	Malayalam
Family	kutumba	kudumbam	kutubham	kutumba	kudumbam
Mother	maata, janani, amba	amma, tai	amma,talli	amma,taai	mathave
Father	pita, janak	appa, tapanar	pitrudu, tandri	tande	pithave
Son	putra, suta	magan	putrudu, koduku	maga	putram
daughter	putri, kanya	sagodhari,maghal	putri, kuturu	magalu	puthri
sister	sodarya, svasa	sagodari,thangai	sahodari, aaka	tangi, akka	sahodari
brother	bhratur	sagodaraa,anna	sahodarudu	anna,tamma	sahodaran
man	nar,purusha, manusha	manidhan	manishi, purushya	manushya, purosha	purushan
woman	naari, stree	mangai,pombalai	naari, ammani	hennu	sthree
child	bal,baalak, shishu	kulandhai, sisu	....	....	Kunju, balan
religion dharma	dharmam, madham	dharmam, madham	dharma	matham	
God	Parmatma,Prabhu, Bhagwan,Ishwar,Dev	Deyvam, Bagwan Kadavul, Ishwaran	Dayvudu, Devi	Devaru, Deva	Daivom
prayer	prarthna,pooja,japa	prarthanai, poojai	japaun, prarthna	puja,japa,prarthana pravachakam	prarthna
prophet sidhah, avataar	avtaar, avatharam	sidhudu	avatara		
sin	paapam	pavam	paapam	papa	papam

English	Sanskrit	Tamil	Telugu	Kannada	Malayalam
temple	mandir, decgraha	kovil	mandiram, goodi	devasthan, goodi	ambalam
saint	sadhuha,muniha,	sadhu, munivar	muni	sadhu, dasaru	puniavalan, sanyasi
sanyasi					
body	sariram, kaya, deha dheham	kayam, sariram,	sariram	deha	sariram
arm	bhujah, bahuha	kayyi, kai	chetulu	kai, bhuja	kai
back	prishtham	moodhav	nadumu	bennu	purake
ear	karnah	kaad,kaadhu,chevi	karnaun, chevvi	kevi	chevi, karnam
eye	netram, chakshu,	kann, nayanam	kannu, netram	kannu	kanne, netram
nayan					
finger	angulee	viral	vaylu	bekalu, bottu	viral, angulam
foot	padam, charan	padam, kaal	padaun	kaalu, paada	kal, padam
hand	hastah, kar	kai	cheyya	kai	kai,hastham, karam
hair	kesh, baalah	mmodi	zutu	kudalu, kesha	moodi kesan
head	siras	thalai	talakai	shirassu, talee	thaly, sirasu
leg	jangha	kal	kaalu	kaalu	kal
mouth	mukham	vai	norue	bai	vai

English					
nose	naassaa	mookku	muku	moogu	mook, nasam
shoulder	skandhah	thol	bujaun	bhuja	thole
thumb	angushtah	kattviral	botakanavelu	hebbattu	thalaviral
food	aahaar, bhojnam	bhojnam,chappadu	bhoinam,aaharam	bhojana, aahara	aharam,bhojnam
bread	apupah	rotti	rotilu	chapaati, Rotte	rotti
fruit	falam	param	falam, pallu	falla, hannu	pazham, phalam
milk	dugdham, kheeram	pal	ksheeram, paalu	haalu	pal
rice	dhanah	sadam	hanaalu, annam	anna	ari
vegetable	shakah, shakam	kai kurry	kooralu	palya	pachakari
water	jalam, neeram,	thanni, neer	neelu, jalam	neeru	vellam,neer,jalam
paaniyam					
fire	agni	neruppu, thee	agni, munta	agni, Kenda	thee, agni
oil	tailam	tailam, yenn	nooni	enni	yenna, thailam
colors	rangah, varnah	varnaam	rangulu	banna	varnam
white	shukla, shweta	vella, veluppu	tella	bili	vella, swetham
black	krishna, kal,shyam	karup, karuppu	nalla	kappu	karuppu
blue	neelah	neelam, ootha	neelam	Neeli	neelam
green	harit	pachchai	pachcha	Hasiru	pacha
red	rudhir, rakta	sivappu' manga	rudhram, yerra	Kempu, Kenchu	chuvappu, rudra
yellow	peelo	manjal, manga	pasupu	Halaadi	manga
Seasons	Irutah	kalangal	kaalaalu	vrutu	-------

English	Sanskrit	Tamil	Telugu	Kannada	Malayalam
spring	vasant	vasantha, vasantam	vasanta kaalamu	vasantha vrutu	vasantam
summer	grishamaha	kodaikalam, chood kalam	vesavi kaalamu	Beesige kala	chood kala
autumn	sharad	ilaiyuthirkalam	sharadum	sharada vrutu	-------
winter	sheetkalah,hemantah	kulirkalam	seeta kaalamu	sheetha,hemantha	hanoopa kala
animal	pranin, jeevah	mirugam	pasuvu, jantuvu, mrigamu	praani	karady
bear	-----	karadi	elugubunt	karadi	kala
bull	vrushah	kalai, madu	yeddu	ettu	yerumy,rishabam
buffalo	mahish	erumai	gedi (F),dunna (M)	emmi	poocha
cat	biralaha, marjar	poonai	pilli	bekku	pashy
cow	dhenu, go	pasu, maadu	aavu	aakalu	go
dog	shvan, kukkurah	nay	kukka, sunakamu	naai	nayu, shawanam
horse	ashva, turgah	kuthirai	ashvam, gurram	kudure	kuthira, ashvam
lion	sinha	singam	simham	sinha	simham
mouse	undra	yelli, munjur	elaka, mooshkam	Elee	yeli
snake	sarpaha, bhujagaha	pambu	paamu, sarpamu	Haavu	pampu, sarpam
nature	prakrutiha	iyarkai	prakruti	prakruthi	-------

English	Sanskrit	Tamil	Telugu	Kannada	Malayalam
sun	rohit, surya, ravi bhaskar	surya, suriyan	suryudu, bhaskaram	surya, ravi	suryam
earth	pruthvi, mahi, vasundhara,dharitri, dhara,bhoomi	bhoomi, man	bhumi, pruthivi	bhoomi, jagiathu	bhoomi,pruthvi
moon	chandrah,shshi, indu	chandhran, nila	chandrudu	chandappa	chandran, chanoham
mountain	parvat, giri	malai	parvatam, giri	parvatha, giri, gudda	parvatham, giri
planets	graha, nakshatra	ghirakam, graham	grahamull	nakshatru, griha	grahangal,graha
rain	varshah, megha	amarai, malai	varsham, vaana	male	megha
river	nadee, nadah	nadee	nadee	nadee	nadee
sky	nabhas,ambaram, aakasha	aakaayam,vanam	aakasam	aakasha	akasham
stars	nakshtra, taaraa	nakshatram	nakshatrams, taaralu	nakshatra	nakshathram
wind	samir	katru, kaat	gaali	gaali	kattu
English	Sanskrit	Tamil	Telugu	Kannada	Malayalam
east	purvadish, prachi	kilakku	toorpu	poorva	kighake
west	pashchima	merku	pascham, patamara	paschima	padinjaru, paschiman
north	uttara	vadakku	uttara	Uttara	vadaku,utharam

south	dakshina	therkku	dakshina	dakshina	theku
zero, 0	sunya	pujiam	sunna	shunya	poojiam
one, 1	eka	onru, won	okati	vandu	onnu
two, 2	dvi	erandu, rend	rondu	eraadu	rande
three,3	tri	moonru, moon	moodu	mooru	moone
four,4	chatur	nangu, naal	naaligu	naalku	nale
five, 5	pancha	iyandu, anji	aidu	eidu	anchu
six, 6	sas	aru, aar	aaru	aaru	aaru
seven,7	sapta	elu, yer	yedu	eelu	yejhi
eight,8	asta	ettu, yett	yeimidi	entu	yettu
nine, 9	nava	onbadu	thomidi	vanbattu	ompathy
ten, 10	dasa	pathu, patt	phadi????	hattu	pathu
hundred	satam	noor, nooru	satam, nooru,vanda	nooru	nooru
eat	khad, baksha	sappad, thinnu	tinu, bakshinchu	oota	thinnuk
feed	bhujoo	------	pettuta, tinipinchuta	bhojana	kaghikuka
drink	paa	kudi	taagu, taaginchadam	Paana	kudickuka
clean	pavitra, shubha	sudam, suththam	subhamu, pavitram	pavitra, Swacha	vruthy,pavitram

English	Sanskrit	Tamil	Telugu	Kannada	Malayalam
come	aagam	wa	raa	Banni	varuka
go	gam, chal	po	vellu	hoogiri	povuka
bring	aanee	koduva	teesukura	tanne	konduvaruka
hear	shru	kelu, kel	vinuta	keelu	kelkuka
learn	shikshoo,abhyas	paddi, katrukkol	nerchuta	sheekshana	padikuka, abhyasam
play	khel,rama, keed	vlaiyadu	aata	aata	kalikuka
love	snehah, preman	kaadal, nesam	prema	prema	snehickuka, premam
lose	tyaj, apahra	taut, ilathal	povata	apaharisu, tyaga	nashtapeduka
see	drish	paar	drishti, choodu	drishti	kanuka
English	Sanskrit	Tamil	Telugu	Kannada	Malayalam
sit	upavish,aas (aasan=seat)	wokar, utkar	koorcho, aasnam	koodiri, aasana	irikuka
forget	vismra	marandhi	marchi, povuta	maruvu	marakuka
sing	gai (geet = song)	paad, padu	paadu, geetam	hadu, bhajpani	paduka
sleep	swap, shayanam, nidra	toong, thoongu	nidra	nidra	uranguka,nidra
speak	vad, bhash	pesu, chol, urayadu	matladu	bhasha, maatu	somsarikuka
here	atra, ihi	ingey	ikkada	illi	ivide

there	tatra	angey	akkada	alli	avide
where	kutra	yengey	ekkada	elli	yevide
now	adhuna, idanin	ippo	ippuda	eega	ippol
when	kadaa, yadaa	eppo	yeppuda	yavaaga	yeppol
then	tadaa	appo	appuda	matthe	appol
day	dinam, divasah	naal	dinam, rozu	divasha,dinna,belagu	divisom,dinam
week	saptah, saptadinam	varam	vaaramu	vaara	aaghcha
year	varsha	varshon, varudam	varsham,	varusha	varsham
morning	usha, arunoudya	kalai, kaartaale	udayamu, pratakalam	sooryodaya, belagu	ravile
evening	sandhya, sayumkaal	malai, sangyalo	saayantram, sayamkalam	sayankala	vaikunneram, sandhya
night	ratri, rajani	iravu raatri, rajni	raatri	raatri	raatri
yesterday	purvehyoo, hyustan	net, netru	ninna, poorvam	ninne	innale
today	taalee	inru, innik	ivala, eerozu	evathu, eedina	innu
tomorrow	parehyavi	nalai, naalik	repu	naale	naale
inside	antaram, udaram	ulle,ullo,ulpakkam	lopala, antaramu	valage	akutha
good	bhadra, prashast, shreshta	nalah	shrestamu, manchi	shresta, chennagide	nallatha
bad	nirdit, ashubha,	ketta	nirudhu, chedhu	ashubha, Kettadu ashubham,abhadra	

English	Sanskrit	Tamil	Telugu	Kannada	Malayalam
beautiful	sunder,manoj,manjul	sunder, arag, alagu	sundaramu, manjulamu	sundara, soundarya	sundaram
short	alpa, laghu.	Kuttai, kulgh	potti, vaamanu	chikadu, Sannadu	cheruthe
dirty	malin, kalkam	arak, alukku	malinamu, asubhramu	malinna, holasu	azhuku
Tall	ucha, dirgha	uyaram, niglon,	podugu	doddadu, Ettarro	valuthe, dirga
ugly	vikurta,kuvaproop	asseeng	vikaari, kuroopi	vakra	vruthykeltathu
cave	guha, ruhakm	gohai	guhastomach	jathrah, udaram	vayiru
house	girham, vasah	veedu	gruhamu, illu	griha, Manee	veedu, griham
king	rajan, samrat	raja	raaju	raja, Samrat	rajam
queen	rajyee, rajpatni	Rani, raassati	raani	raani, rajpatni	ranee
road	margah	chalai, theru	maargamu, daari	marga, Haade	vaghi, margam
student	vidyarthin, shishyaha	shishyan	vidyarthi, sishyudu	vidyarthi	vidyarthi
teacher	adhyapaka,shikshaha	asiriyar, vaadyar	guru, upaadyayudu	adhyapaka, guru	adhyapakan
servant	sevakaha, dasaha	velaikaran	sevakudu, daasudu	dasa, sevaka	sevakan
town	nagaram, puram	nagram	nagram, puramu	nagara, ooru	nagaram,patana
village	gramaha	graamah	graamamu, palli	grama, halli	gramam

friend	mitram (he)	snehidan, nanban	mitrudu, snehitudu	mitra, gelaya	kootukaran, mitram
friend	sakhi (she)	snegidhi	snehituraalu,	sakhi, gelathi	kootukari, sakhi
enemy	shatru, ariha, vairin	shatru	satruvu	vairi, shatru	shatru
neigbbor	pratieshin	pakkathu	pakkavallu	pakkadamane,	ayalvasi
stranger	parakiya	veliyur	parayivadu	hosabaru	aparichichan

The above Table evidences that the four South Indian Dravidian languages have significant linguistic correspondence with Sanskrit. Benjamin Walker, in *'The Hindu World: An Encyclopedic Survey of Hinduism'* (1968, p.353), observes that Dravidian elements are strong in Sanskrit. The similarities between Sanskrit and the Dravidian languages, as shown in the above Table, would convince any body that all the five – Tamil, Telugu, Kannada, Malayalam, and Sanskrit – are native languages of India.

Siva, the Ancient Daksinamurti (God of South) and Dravidians

Graham Hancock, in *'Underworld: The Mysterious Origins of Civilization'* (2002, p.281), tells that Siva is being worshipped in South India for longer than 5000 years, and so in the Indus Valley. The natives (Hindus) of Hindustan, from the Himalayas in north to Kanyakumari in south, and from the Indus Valley in the east to Bengal in west, have been practicing Vedic religion, worshipping the same pantheon of Vedic gods (Brahma, Vishnu, Siva and others), speaking an array of Indic vernaculars, and reading and believing in the same Vedic scriptures, including all the four Vedas, Upanishads, Puranas, Gita, Ramayana, Mahabharata, etc, from pre-history ancient times. It is hard to understand if there is difference – lingual, racial and cultural – between the North Indians and the South Indian Dravidians, the history has been harping on. All the North Indian and the South Indian Hindus are Aryans.

Chapter Ten

VEDAS, OCEAN OF WISDOM

Breakup of Himalayan glaciers → age of Vedas → age of Sanskrit → age of Swastika (卐)

Graham Hancock (2002, p.169) quotes B.B. Radhakrishna of the Geological Society of India (1999), who writes that the *Rig Veda* talks about the break-up of Himalayan glaciers releasing water which flowed out in seven mighty rivers (*Sapta Sindhu*). The early inhabitants of the plains burst into songs praising Lord Indra for releasing the water they very much needed. This happened during Late Pleistocene glaciations, about 10,000 years ago. Radha- Krishna had said:

> "Geologist record indicates that during Late Pleistocene glaciations, waters of the Himalaya were frozen and that in place of rivers there were only glaciers, masses of solid ice. ... When the climate became warmer, the glaciers began to break up and the frozen water held by them surged forth in great floods, inundating the alluvial plain in front of the mountains. ... With the hindsight we possess as geologists, we at once see that the phenomenon described in the *Rig Veda* was no idle fancy but a real natural event of great significance connected with the break up of Himalayan glaciers and the release of pent-up waters in great floods."

Break up of Himalayan glaciers happened over 10,000 years. Its description in the *Rig Veda* suggests that Vedas were composed at least 10,000 years back and so the age of their language Sanskrit and also the age of Swastika, as it is mentioned in the *Rig Veda*.

The Swastika, being a Sanskrit word, tells the age of Sanskrit, and that Bharat was the original home of Sanskrit, the Vedas and Vedic religion. The Swastika, found among Celts and American Indians, tells that Bharat had trade and/or travel relations with them since too remote pre-history times.

Sarasvati River: Age of the Rig Veda

Several historians have written that the Sarasvati River dried up in about 1900 B.C. and that the *Rig Veda* has described life on its banks. It evidences that the *Rig Veda* was originally composed at least before 1900 B.C. How then, several historians have been still writing that the *Rig Veda* was composed by the alleged invading Aryans after their arrival in India in about 1,000 B.C., and even later.

Vedas: Ocean of knowledge and wisdom

Hindus have numerous sacred scriptures. Vedas are the earliest sacred scriptures of Indo-Aryans (present Hindus). They are the oldest documents of mankind. They are being sung with devotion and are being orally transmitted down from generation to generation. Now they are written and computerized. They contain teachings and wisdom of ancient sages. The word Veda means knowledge and wisdom. Vedas describe almost all aspects and needs of life – physical, spiritual, philosophical, cosmic, agricultural, medicinal, etc. as contained in four primary Vedas – Rig Veda, Yajur Veda, Sam Veda and Atharva Veda. There are several other scriptures, such as Upanishads, Upaniyās, Upaveda, Shastras, Brahmanas, Ayurveda, etc. Vedic literature also talks about social, legal, family and religious customs of Vedic people. Vedic sages – *Rishis* and *Munis* – had all-pervasive knowledge; they wanted to share with common man to make society appropriately adequate and productive. In short, the Vedic literature covers all the knowledge related to all human needs and aspirations.

Vedic emphasis has been on knowledge, starting from self. It is believed that if you know self, you know every thing. God is within self, so knowing self is knowing every thing. Vedic sages understood that only *Gyān* (knowledge), particularly *Âtmagyān* (knowledge of self), would brighten darkness, has been causing human misery. Man, charmed by bodily comforts, doesn't realize that physical luxury can be appropriately and adequately enjoyed only by healthy mind and pious soul. This can be understood only by objectively answering the question "Why are billionaires, despite all luxuries, not happy?" Physical comforts are also essential, but not by ignoring righteous bites of conscience. Real happiness lies in the peace of mind. Physical comfort can not be enjoyed when soul is not at ease. Pain of soul speaks through mind. Uncomfortable mind (thinking) would not let one to have peaceful sleep. It is surprising that millennia-old sages had the knowledge of Freudian psychology, psychotherapy and psychoanalysis, as evidenced by its use by Lord Krishna to help Arjuna in his conflicts, to enable him to perform his duty towards self, his country and people. Bhagvad Gita has lot of psychoanalytical knowledge for every body, irrespective of his/her religion, to understand the inner conflicts as obstacles in *Dharma* (duty). Hindu Dharma is misperceived only as a religion of various rituals worshipping multifarious gods and goddesses, but ignoring their teachings. Each god and goddess is an enviable un-buyable book, worth billions of dollars, if converted into a check book. Peace of mind, Dharma gives; no Bank – Chase Manhattan, Citibank or any other Bank – can give. Dharma means duty. The person, who rightly performs his duties, will be happy and make every body around happy.

Education: Fountain of Wisdom & Mine of Literary Diamonds

Education has proved itself not only as the fountain of wisdom, but also as a mine of literary riches to make life full of soul tranquility, comfortable and secure. Education has always been secular for all humanity, irrespective of its ethnic or religious background. If the whole humanity has right secular education, there would be peace on the planet. There would be no Talibanism, the product of illiteracy and absence of right understanding of God and religion. All religions are compassionate and peace-loving, because they all talk about the merciful, compassionate loving God – omnipresent, omnipotent, and omniscient. God is one and the same for His vast providence. Unfortunately, God is being misunderstood and divided as humanity has been variedly fractured on basis of religion, ethnicity, language, etc. Almighty God, though only ONE for all mankind, is being mischievously, rather ignorantly disfigured as MANY, resulting in irreligious fights to abuse religion, the wealth of mankind to remain peaceful and happy. No religion wants fights, but ironically, the men in high religious attire fragment God on the basis of religion, ethnicity, language, region, etc.

Veda means knowledge. In Sanskrit, education is known as Vidya, student as *'Vidyarthi'*. The paradigm of – Vedas, Vidya, and Vidyarthi – would explain why Indians, particularly Hindus, have been productively successful all over the planet. Vedas have multifarious knowledge responsive to all quests and needs.

In addition to the four primary Vedas – Rigveda, Atharvaveda, Yajurveda and Samaveda – there are several subsidiary sacred scriptures, such as Upanishads, Samhita, Aranyaka, Brahmana, Vedanta, Ayurveda, Vyakarana, Artha-shastra, Jyotish-shastra, several Puranas (Brahma, Vaishanva, and several other) and *shastras* which cover information about almost all human needs and concerns – medicine, psychology, meditation, psychiatry, sculpture, economics, finance, grammar, poetry, agriculture, navigation, dance, and astronautics. In short, Hinduism (Vedic religion) has information about everything, man would like to have.

Respect for knowledge

I, as a child, read an essay in an early school text book, that the interviewing committee to select a teacher for its school, deliberately, left a book in the room on the floor on the way from its entrance to the table where interviewing officials were sitting. Only one candidate picked it up, kissed it and respectfully placed it on the table before she took her seat to be interviewed. She was selected because the selection committee was convinced that she had respect for the knowledge, she was being selected for, to give to her students.

Max Müller,[74] talking about the various systems of Vedic thought on life, has said that the Vedas are guide for man in every walk of life and they are most primitive:

> "Whatever the Vedas may be called, they are to us unique and priceless guides in opening before our eyes tombs of thought richer in relics than the royal tombs of Egypt, and more ancient and primitive in thought than the oldest hymns of Babylonian or Acadian poets. If we grant that they belonged to the second millennium before our era, we are probably on safe ground, though we should not forget that this is a constructive date only, and that such a date does not become positive by mere repetition. It may be very brave to postulate late 2000 B.C. or even 5000 B.C. as a minimum date for the Vedic hymns, but what is gained by such bravery? Such assertions are safe so far as they can not be refuted, but neither can they be proved, considering that we have no contemporaneous dates to attach them to."

Max Müller[75] praises Vedas as the earliest fervent mind on life:

> "Whatever may be the date of the Vedic hymns, whether 1500 or 15,000 B.C., they have their own unique place, and stand by themselves in the literature of the world. They tell us something of the early growth of the human mind of which we find no trace anywhere else."

All this was written by Max Müller in his latest book: "*The Six Systems of Indian Philosophy*" which was first published in 1899, shortly before his death in 1900. His remark "They (Vedas) tell us something of

---

[74] Max Müller Six Systems of Indian Philosophy: Samkhya & Yoga; Nyaya & Vaiseshika" (1899, p. 33).
[75] Ibid (p.34)

the early growth of the human mind of which we find no trace anywhere else" suggests that the antiquity of the Vedas is beyond the imagination of human mind. If printing technology was available in those pre-history remote ancient times, we would have known the names of the authors of their various hymns. The sages of those thoughts were great and too modest to see their names publicized. The Vedas were composed during long span of time, may be even more than a couple of millennia. It seems this was the reason why Vedas were considered by some as revealed.

Max Müller[76] praises India, as endowed with all the paradise-beauty, the nature can bestow:

> "If I were to look over the whole world to find out the country most richly endowed with all the wealth, power, and beauty that nature can bestow – in some parts a very paradise on earth – I should point to India."

Pundit Jawaharlal Nehru, in *'The Discovery of India'* (1946, p. 93), talks about the influence of the *Upanishads* on self: "The study of the Upanishads has been the solace of my life; it will be the solace of my death." He (p.79) remarks:

> "The Vedic hymns have been described by Rabindranath Tagore as 'a poetic testament of a people's collective reaction to the wonder and awe of existence.' The Vedas have given us a deep peep into the philosophy of mind which has been increasingly broadening its horizon along with the advancing time.

Feuerstein & et al., in *"In Search of the Cradle of Civilization"* (1995, p. 39), observe that great philosophers around the world have been very much impressed by the *Upanishads*. They remark that the *Upanishads* are magnificent Gnostic treatises in the broad sense, from the capstone

---

[76] Max Müller, in "India: What can it teach us?" (p. 24)

of the Vedic edifice. They are the best known aspect of Vedic literature and have been lauded by great thinkers through out the world.

It is soul-soothing to know that western scholars read Hindu sacred scriptures with great interest. Feuerstein & et al. (p.39) write that the German philosopher Arthur Schopenhauer has said that the *Upanishads* were comfort to him in his life and his death. Schopenhauer has remarked about the *Upanishads* in German in his book, *Upanishaden, Altindische Weisheit* (1964, p.8):

> "How every line is of such strong, determined, and consistent meaning! And on every page we encounter deep, original, lofty thoughts, while the whole is suffused with a high and holy seriousness."

R. E. Hume, in *'The Thirteen Principal Upanishads'* (1921, p. vii), has remarked:

> "In the long history of man's endeavor to grasp the fundamental truths of being, the metaphysical treatises known as the Upanishads hold an honored place. ... they are replete with sublime conceptions and with intuitions of universal truth."

Feuerstein & et al (1995, p.40) write that Max Müller, who was critical of many aspects of the Vedic heritage, confessed toward the end of his life: "The conception of the world as deduced from the Veda, and chiefly from the Upanishads, is indeed astounding."[77]

Nehru (pp.92-93) quotes Arthur Schopenhauer (German scholar, 1788-1860), the pessimist, what he has said about the Vedic influence on the whole world:

> "From every sentence (of the Upanishads) deep, original and sublime thoughts arise, and the whole world is pervaded by a high and holy and earnest spirit. ... In

---

[77] Max Müller, The Six Systems of Indian Philosophy, (First published in 1899, reprinted in 1916, xlv).

the whole world there is no study ... so beneficial and as elevating as that of the Upanishads. ... (They) are products of the highest wisdom. ... It is destined sooner or later to become the faith of the people."

Every heart, irrespective of religious orientation, is welcome home of Divine light. Romain Rolland[78] (French writer, 1866-1944) – in a note *'On the Hellenic-Christian Mysticism of the First Centuries and its Relationship to Hindu Mysticism,'* as an appendix to his book on Vivekananda – writes: "A hundred facts testify to how great an extent the East was mingled with Hellenic thought during the second century of our era."

Nehru (p.93) writes that the most eloquent tribute to the Upanishads and the Bhagavad Gita was paid by A.E. (G.W. Russell), the Irish poet:

"Goethe, Wordsworth, Emerson, and Thoreau among moderns have something of this vitality and wisdom, but we can find all they have said and much more in the grand sacred books of the East. The Bhagavad Gita and the Upanishads contain such godlike fullness of wisdom on all things that I feel the authors must have looked with calm remembrance back through a thousand passionate lives, full of feverish strife for and with shadows, ere they could have written with such certainty of things which the soul feels to be sure."

Vedic people of ancient times had knowledge of psychology, as evidenced by the Bhagavad Gita[79] and the Vedas, which are much older than the Gita.

---

[78] Nehru, Discovery of India, p.92, foot note.
[79] Bhagvad Gita was the live conversation between Lord Krishna and Arjuna while the Mahabharata War between Pandwas and Kaurvas was in progress in about 3067 B.C.

What do Vedas teach Europeans?

Max Müller, though in his earlier life misrepresented Vedas, got very much influenced by Vedas, Upanishads, and other sacred scriptures. He, in *'India: What Can It Teach Us?'* (1999, p. 136), writes that Vedas can teach us lessons which nothing /no one else can. He, talking to the candidates for Civil Service in India, apprises them of the importance of Vedas for Europeans:

> "Therefore, before opening the pages of the Veda, and giving you a description of the poetry, the religion, and philosophy of the ancient inhabitants of India, I thought it right and necessary to establish, first of all, certain points without which it would be impossible to form a right appreciation of the historical value of the Vedic hymns, and of their importance even to us who live at so great a distance from those early poets."

Max Müller (1999, p.137) talks about the grandeur of Vedas, and of their language Sanskrit, to which, he believed, Europeans owe lot:

> "Secondly, that the ancient literature of India is not to be considered simply as a curiosity and to be handed over to the good pleasure of Oriental scholars, but that, both by its language, the Sanskrit, and by its most ancient literary documents, the Vedas, it can teach us lessons which nothing else can teach, as to the origin of our own language, the first formation of our own concepts and the true natural germs of all that is comprehended under the name of civilization, at least the civilization of the Aryan race, that race to which we and all the greatest nations of the world – the Hindus, the Persians, the Greeks and Romans, the Celts, the Slaves, and last, not least, the Teutons, belong."

Max Müller (1999, p.138) writes that the ancient literature of India "deserves careful attention, not of Oriental scholars only, but also of every educated man and woman who wishes to know how we, even we here in England, and in this nineteenth century of ours, came to be what we are." He adds that Hindus excel in the transcendental meditation; the westerners should learn and practice.

Max Müller (1999, p. 161), talking about the lessons India can teach, writes: "Although there is hardly any department of learning which has not received new light and new life from the ancient literature of India, yet nowhere is the light that comes to us from India so important, so novel, so rich as in the study of Hindu religion and mythology."

Max Müller (1999, p.160, footnote), talking about the progress in the research on India and her Vedas observes: "It is in the general line of progress in research that more evidence may be expected to connect Vedic thought with other cultures."

Max Müller,[80] captivated by the Upanishads, writes:

> "The Upanishads are the sources of the Vedanta philosophy, a system in which human speculation seems to me to have reached its acme. ... I spend my happiest hours in reading Vedanta books. They are to me like the light of the morning, like the pure air of the mountains – so simple, so true, if once understood."

French philosopher Francois Voltaire (1694-1778) remarks on Vedas: "Vedic metaphysics is the perennial philosophy that is at the core of all religions - a precious gift for which the West is ever indebted to the East."

According to S.D. Kulkarni, "Our civilization, Vedic or Hindu, has a continuity of more than 31092 years before present period,[81] and he pinpoints "21788 B.C. as the period, at least, of the origin of the *Rigveda.*"[82]

The archeologically excavated seals at Mohenjo-Daro and Harappa, beginning in early 1920s, shed historical light to awaken historians to the truths about the prehistory ancient Bhārat, her native *Aryans*,

---

[80]   Ibid p. 93

[81]   Bhishma, vol.2, p.14.

[82]   Bhishma, vol. 1, p. 128.

antiquity of the *Rig Veda*, and of *Sanskrit*. Unfortunately, the wrong history, written by Western colonialists, has not yet been corrected. Encyclopedias and text books continue to carry on the same text as written by colonialists prior to the Indus Valley civilization saw the sunshine in 1920s. Ignorance of the history of the Indus civilization, caused by the mischievous colonial historians was a great black hole which confused the history of the ancient Bhārat, her original natives Aryans, Vedas and Sanskrit.

Max Müller (1899, p.39), talking about Gaimini's support of the eternal character of sound (*Shabda)*, remarks:

> "Having thus, established to his own satisfaction the eternity of sound, Gaimini proceeds to defend the sounds or words of the Veda against all possible objections. These arguments were examined by us before, when the authorship of the Veda had to be discussed, and when it was shown that the author of the Veda could not have been a personal being, but that the Veda could only have been seen by inspired Rishis as revealed to them, not as made by them."

Nehru (1946, p.79) praises the productive mind (thinking process) of the composers of the Vedic hymns. Nehru did not like that the Vedas be considered as "revealed scriptures," because, then, Nehru rightly thinks that we wouldn't value the quality of the mind of the composers of the Vedic hymns which have the depth, too difficult for the common mind to dive into to peep.

In Nehru's opinion, the *Rig Veda* unfolded the human mind, in earliest stages of thought which has opened windows to the Vedic philosophy which has been increasingly blooming along with the time all over the planet:

> "Many Hindus look upon the Vedas as revealed scripture. This seems to me to be peculiarly unfortunate, for thus we miss their real significance – the unfolding

of the human mind in the earliest stages of thought.
And what a wonderful mind it was."

Vedas reflect lofty thought with its immortal life; the humanity should continue to use to keep on improving their life. The Vedic prescriptions have no expiry date, good for indefinite future. Nehru praises the mind – deep and wide mine of guiding thoughts – of the composers of the Vedas. Nehru understood that behind the *Rig Veda* lay ages of civilized existence and thought, during which various ancient civilizations – the Indus, the Nile and Tigris-Euphrates – had grown. Therefore, it is appropriate that there should be dedication to the seers, and our ancestors who were the first path-finders.

If the Vedas are considered as revealed to the *Rishis* of Bhārat, not composed by them, the antiquity of the Vedas can not be measured. The time of authorship of the *Rig Veda* is too ancient beyond human imagination. In such situation when the names of the composers of the various hymns of the Vedas are not known, there would be no option other than saying that the Vedas were revealed. But it is not correct. The fact is that the hymns were composed by several *Rishis* who were modest to publicize their names.

The *Rig Veda*, like other three *Vedas*, is a collection of *Mantras* (*Hymns*). They were composed in remote prehistory ancient times by several *Rishis*. Since the *Vedas* were not written to start with, the names of the composers are not known. Several *Rishis* might have contributed their thoughts in poetry-form-hymns which came down from generation to generation by Vedic oral traditions. Technology of writing came much later. We do not have the names of the authors of the *Puranas, Brahmanas, Aranyakas, Upanishads, Sutras, Shastras, Samhitas,* etc. In those ancient times, those great *Rishis* were not egocentric, crazy about their name, they were happy to share their thoughts and feelings. Moreover, there was no sense of copyright. They were happy that they contributed some thing, the humanity needed and the future generations would love to know.

There is such a recent example, similar to the *Vedas*. The *Guru Granth Sahib* of Sikhs (around 1469 AD) was not composed by only one person. It contains what the ten *Gurus* of Sikhs – from Guru Nanak to

Guru Gobind Singh – and some other similar-thinking devotees have sung. Unlike the *Rig Veda*, the names of most of the composers of Guru Granth Sahib are known, because of its recency.

Nehru (1946, p. 93) talks about the individualistic philosophy of wholesome life, as contained in the Upanishads:

> "There is, in the Upanishads, a continual emphasis on the fitness of the body and clarity of the mind, on the discipline of both body and mind, before effective progress can be made. The acquisition of knowledge, or any achievement, requires restraint, self-suffering, self-sacrifice. This idea of some kind of penance, *tapasya*, is inherent in Indian thought, both among thinkers at the top and the unread masses below. It is present today as it was present thousands of years ago, and it is necessary to appreciate it in order to understand the psychology underlying the mass movements which have convulsed India under the Gandhiji's leadership."

Positive constructive thinking helps the people, individually as well as collectively, to always move in right direction..

xxxxxxxxxxxxxxxxx

Resemblance between Vedas and Persia's Avesta

Nehru (p.77) talks about the resemblance between Vedas and the Persia's Avesta and between their languages, Sanskrit and Avestan respectively:

> "The Vedas were the outpourings of the Aryans as they streamed into the rich land of India. They brought their ideas with them from that common stock out of which grew the Avesta in Iran, and elaborated them in the soil of India. Even the language of the Vedas bears a striking resemblance to that of the Avesta, and it has been remarked that the Avesta is nearer the Veda than the Veda is to its own epic Sanskrit."

I agree with Nehru that Persia's Avesta and its language Avestan resemble to Bhārat's Vedas and Sanskrit respectively, but hard to agree that Aryans came to India from outside and that the Vedas were brought or composed by the alleged invading Aryans. Nehru's sentence "The Vedas were the outpourings of the Aryans as they streamed into the rich land of India" is self-contradictory. How can the Vedas be outpouring of Aryans who came to India from outside?

It has been historically proved that in ancient times Iran was a part of Bhārat, culturally as well as administratively. This is discussed in the Chapter, 'Iran: A part of Ancient India.'

Arya is a Sanskrit word

Aryans were the original natives of Ârya-āvarta, now known as Bhārat, India). The originality of Aryans has been confused by the ill-based theory 'Aryan invasion of India.' Not even one historian has yet been able to identify the country outside India which had or has Aryans as its natives and Sanskrit as its native language. Even India, in pre-history ancient was known as Ârya-āvarta.

The ill-based theory "Aryan invasion of India" has confused the originalities of Aryan race, Sanskrit and Vedas.

Max Müller was trying to correct what he himself had misrepresented the originalities of Aryans and Sanskrit, and also about the authorship of Vedas, Max Müller (1899, p.34) talks about the age of the Vedas:

> "Whatever may be the date of the Vedic hymns, whether 1500 or 15,000 B.C., they have their own unique place and stand by themselves in the literature of the world."

Break up of Himalayan glaciers happened over 10,000 years. Its description in the *Rig Veda* suggests that Vedas were composed at least 10,000 years back and so the age of their language Sanskrit and also the age of Swastika, as it is mentioned in the *Rig Veda*.

The Swastika, being a Sanskrit word, tells the age of Sanskrit, and that Bharat was the original home of Sanskrit, the Vedas and Vedic religion. The Swastika, found among Celts and American Indians, tells that Bharat had trade and/or travel relations with them since too remote pre-history times.

Sarasvati River refutes Aryan invasion

Several historians have written that the Sarasvati River dried up in about 1900 B.C. and that the *Rig Veda* has described life on its banks. It evidences that the *Rig Veda* was originally composed at least before 1900 B.C. How then, several historians have been still writing that the *Rig Veda* was composed by the alleged invading Aryans after their arrival in India in about 1,000 B.C., and even later.

Stephen Knapp[83] talks about the antiquity of the *Vedas*:

> "In the same line of thought, it has been determined that the Sanskrit *Rig-Veda* is the oldest piece of literature in the world. Reverend Morris Philip, in his book *The Teaching of the Vedas* (p.213), concludes: "After the latest researches into the history and chronology of the book of Old Testament, we may safely now call the *Rigveda* as the oldest book not only of the Aryan community, but of the whole world."

Harry H. Hicks and Robert N. Anderson[84] have given years of the antiquity of the *Rig Veda*, as given by different scholars:

* David Frawley, in *"Gods, Sages and Kings"*, on the basis of astronomical references in the *Rig Veda*, corroborating the work of other earlier scholars such as Tilak and Jacobi, go back to ca.6500 B.C.
* Probably beginning shortly after the major Indo-European "Kurganian" migration of ca 4,400 to 4,300 B.C., as described

---

[83] Stephen Knapp, in his book "Proof of Vedic Culture's Global Existence" (2000, p.66),

[84] Bhu Dev Sharma and Nabarun Ghose (ed.)., "Revisiting Indus-Sarasvati Age and Ancient India", WAVES, (1998, 348-350).

by Gumbutas, the Rig Vedic age, apparently with its inspired concepts, was conceived in India.

- According to Cambridge, "The hymns of the *Rig Veda* were composed in the NW of India, the country of the seven rivers in about 3700 B.C.

- Hicks and Anderson have given a historically convincing evidence of Vedic Aryan Head from the collection of the Hicks Foundation for Cultural Preservation. They remark that extensive tests and mutually corroborative and interrelated physical, stylistic and historical evidence indicate it was cast in the 4th millennium B.C., dating 3700 B.C. It was life sized, hollow, copper-based head in a human likeness. It may be the first hard evidence relating to the original Vedic Aryans in India. They tend to emphasize: "The Head's natural style and eye treatment also provide evidence of the continuity of Vedic Aryan art styles of the 4th/3rd millennium B.C., the Harappan and Mesopotamian art, and evolution into later Hellenistic and classical Indian art."

- Feuerstein & et al (1995: 29) write about the *Rig-Veda*: "The *Rig-Veda* is the oldest book in Sanskrit language, indeed in any Indo-European language. More than that, if we are correct, it is the oldest book in the world, and for this reason alone deserves our attention.

Feuerstein & et al (1995: 29) write that the *Rig-Veda* has a total of 1,028 hymns comprising 10,589 verses which were composed in various periods. The other three younger *Vedas* are *Sama Veda, Yajur Veda,* and *Atharva Veda.* In addition to the four *Vedas,* there were various subsidiary *Vedic* scriptures – *Puranas, Brahmanas, Aranyakas, Upanishads, Sutras, Shastras, Samhitas,* etc.

The antiquity of the *Rig Veda,* as given by various scholars, ranges from 7,500 B.C. to 3,000 BC. Considering the latest date 3,000 BC, the age of Sanskrit should be much much older than the age of its literature. Vedas were composed long prior to 1500 BC, the year of the alleged Aryan invasion. This challenges the validity of the Aryan invasion, according to which Sanskrit was allegedly brought in and the

Vedas were composed by the invading Aryans. This also refutes the IE, according to which Sanskrit came into India from outside in about 3,000 B.C., according to some 6,000 B.C.

Nehru (1946, p. 93) talks about the individualistic philosophy of wholesome life, as contained in the Upanishads:

"There is, in the Upanishads, a continual emphasis on the fitness of the body and clarity of the mind, on the discipline of both body and mind, before effective progress can be made. The acquisition of knowledge, or any achievement, requires restraint, self-suffering, self-sacrifice. This idea of some kind of penance, *tapasya,* is inherent in Indian thought, both among thinkers at the top and the unread masses below. It is present today as it was present thousands of years ago, and it is necessary to appreciate it in order to understand the psychology underlying the mass movements which have convulsed India under the Gandhiji's leadership."

Has cosmic religion been any where outside India?

Embree (p.7) rightly describes the Vedic religion as the cosmic religion. But his dating of the hymns later than 1500 B.C. is creating confusion:

"The earliest hymns of the Vedic Aryans, accordingly, pertained to this cosmic religion, to which they (Aryans) gave expression through such mythological concepts as those of the divine parents, Heaven and Earth, the cosmic law (rta), and the sustainer of that law, Varuna. Side by side with this cosmic religion, the Vedic Aryans had also developed a kind of fire worship. ... The Aryans finally emerged as victorious colonizers of that part of India known as the land of the seven rivers, the modern Punjab. Many of the hymns glorify the heroic and marshal virtues of the conquerors, with an emphasis on success in battle as proof of divine favor. Particular reverence is paid to (god) Indra."

The age of the *Rig Veda,* as based on irrefutable evidences given earlier, has been ascertained older than the Indus Valley civilization. Keeping the age of the *Rig Veda* in mind, what Prof. Embree has said in the above paragraph needs to be examined. All – including cosmic religion, god *Indra,* and worship of fire – have been talked about in the *Rig Veda.* Sanskrit is the language of the *Rig Veda.* Historians, including Embree, need to identify any country other than India, which could be the original homeland of the invading Aryans, where such cosmic religion was practiced and god *Indra* and goddess fire (*Agnidevi*) were worshiped any time in the past. Or does Embree feel that this cosmic religion was created by Aryans after their arrival in India? Then Embree needs to answer all these questions:

- What was the country, other than Aryavarta (India) where Aryans lived as its natives?
- What was their religion while in their assumed original homeland outside India?
- Has there been any society other than the Hindu that practiced such cosmic religion and worshiped *Indra* and *Agni* (fire)?

Max Müller, in *Six Systems of Indian Philosophy; Samkhya & Yoga, Naya & Vaiseshika* (1899, p.33), showers flowers in praise of the *Vedas* and recognizes his concern about their antiquity:

"Whatever the Vedas may be called, they are to us unique and priceless guides in opening before our eyes tombs of thought richer in relics than the royal tombs of Egypt, and more ancient and primitive in thought than the oldest hymns of Babylonian or Accadian poets. If we grant that they belonged to the second millennium before our era, we are probably on safe ground, though we should not forget that this is a constructive date only, and that such a date does not become positive by mere repetition. It may be very brave to postulate late 2000 B. C. or even 5000 B.C. as a minimum date for the Vedic hymns, but what is gained by such bravery? Such assertions are safe so far as they can not be refuted, but neither can they be proved, considering that we have no contemporaneous dates to attach them to."

Vedas, most ancient scriptures and source of history

Max Müller[85] writes that the Vedas are more primitive than any other document and that they give lot of history about India and the world:

"The Veda may be called primitive, because there is no other literary document more primitive than it; but the language, the mythology, the religion and philosophy that meet us in the Veda open vistas of the past which no one would venture to measure in years. Nay, they contain by the side of simple, natural, childish thoughts, many ideas which to us sound modern, or secondary and tertiary, as I called them, but which nevertheless are older than any other literary document, and give us trustworthy information of a period in the history of human thought of which we knew absolutely nothing before the discovery of the Vedas."

Nehru[86] writes about the age of the *Vedas:*

"The usual date accepted by most scholars today for the hymns of the *Rig Veda* is 1,500 B.C., but there is tendency, ever since the Mohenjo-daro excavations, to date further back these early Indian scriptures. Whatever the exact date may be, it is probable that this literature is earlier than that of either Greece or Israel, that, in fact, it represents some of the earliest documents

---

[85] Max Müller, in 'India: What Can It Teach Us?' (1999, p.139).
[86] Nehru in 'Discovery of India' (1946, p.77).

of the human mind that we posses. Max Muller has
called it: 'The first word spoken by the Aryan man."

Nehru further writes that in the *Rig Veda* we shall have before us
more real antiquity than in all the inscriptions of Egypt or Ninevah.
The *Rig Veda* is the oldest book in existence.

Nehru (pp. 76-77), talking about the earliest records, scriptures and
mythologies of Hindus, writes about the age of the Vedas:

> "Before the discovery of the Indus Valley civilization,
> the Vedas were supposed to be the earliest records we
> possess of Indian culture. There was much dispute
> about the chronology of the Vedic period, European
> scholars usually giving later dates and Indian scholars
> much earlier ones. ... Prof. Winternitz thinks that
> the beginnings of Vedic literature go back to 2,000
> B.C., or even 2,500 B.C. This brings us very near the
> Mohenjodaro period."

In fact, Vedas were composed earlier than 2,500 B.C., as it would
be shown later. Nehru (p.79) makes a very interesting observation about
the antiquity of the human civilization and its civilized thoughts, as
reflected in the *Rig Veda*, the earliest of the Vedas:

> "Yet behind the *Rig Veda* itself lay ages of civilized
> existence and thought, during which the Indus Valley
> and Mesopotamian and other civilizations had grown.
> It is appropriate, therefore, that there should be this
> dedication in the *Rig Veda*: 'To the Seers, our ancestors,
> the first path-finders.'"

The Vedas are the oldest and the most prominent Hindu sacred
scriptures. The word 'Veda' means knowledge. Hinduism puts
extraordinary emphasis on *Vidya* (education) to earn knowledge to make
life fruitful, fertile and comfortable. *Brahmacharya* is the first and the
most important of the four Ashrams, during which, one has to give the
first fertile 25 years of life to education, while remaining *brahamchari*

(unmarried). Ancient *Rishis* (sages) rightly thought that education would lay down strong foundation for useful and fruitful life. Education is the only wealth which doesn't decrease. It multiplies with years. It can not be lost nor stolen.

Unfortunately, due to non-Hindu immigrants by way of centuries of foreign domination – 9ᵗʰ A.D. until 1947 – the *Brahmacharya Ashram* was replaced by the *Grasth Ashram* due to early marriages, because of change in socio-cultural environment. Education of girls suffered lot. Now, because of independence, the education plant, particularly co-ed, has started growing jubilantly, with storming number of students in colleges and universities, more interested in modern non-traditional disciplines, so as to internationally compete.

Drying up of Sarasvati River: Age of the Rig Veda

The *Rig Veda* has described life on the banks of Sarasvati River. In ancient times, when population was thin, people preferred to live on the banks of rivers where water most important for life was easily available. This is the reason why most ancient civilizations – Indus, Nile and Tigris-Euphrates – developed near rivers. Several historians have written that the Sarasvati River dried up in about 1900 B.C. It evidences that the *Rig Veda* was composed at least 400 years before 1500 B.C., the alleged year of Aryan invasion. How then, several historians have still been writing that the *Rig Veda* was composed by the alleged invading Aryans, not by the original natives of Aryavarta (Bhārat, India) long before 1500 BC.

The antiquity of the Vedas and a source of history

Max Müller talks about the antiquity of the Vedas:

> "The Vedas are older than any other literary document, and give us trustworthy information of a period in the history of human thought of which we know absolutely nothing before the discovery of the Vedas."

Max Müller,[87] in *"History of Ancient Sanskrit Literature"* (p.557), has said:

> "In the *Rig Veda* we shall have before us more real antiquity than in all the inscriptions of Egypt or Ninevah. ... The *Veda* is the oldest book in existence."

In the same book (p. 63), Max Müller remarks, that the *Rig Veda* be considered as the oldest source of history, not only of India, but of the world too:

> "The *Veda* has a two-fold interest. It belongs to the history of the world and to the history of India. In the history of the world the Veda fills a gap which no literary work in any other language could fill. It carries us back to times of which we have no records anywhere."

Pliny and Arrian: Starting point of Vedic Chronology

Such an early date – 6676 BC or 6777 BC, as suggested by Greek historians Pliny and Arrian for the starting point for Indian (Hindu/ Vedic) chronology – challenges the validity of the theory of 'Aryan invasion of India'. Feuerstein and et al (p.246) write that Greek historians Pliny and Arrian based this on the reports they got from the ambassadors at the Maurya courts that the native historical tradition of India knew of 154 kings who ruled over a period of 6,450 years. Feuerstein and et al (p.246) remark: "When we reconstruct this tradition, it appears that during the Mauryan times the calendar was taken to commence in 6676 B.C."

Nehru (1946, p.79) talks about the *Rig Veda*, as the earliest book of the humanity which gives history of those who sought to discover the significance of the world:

> "The *Rig Veda*, the first of the Vedas, is probably the earliest book that humanity possesses. In it we can find

---

[87]   Taken from Stephen Knapp's Proof of Vedic Culture's Global Existence (2000, p. vii).

the first outpourings of the human mind, the glow of poetry, the rupture at nature's loveliness and mystery. And in these early hymns there are, as Dr. Macnicol says, the beginnings of the brave adventures made so long ago and recorded here, of those who seek to discover the significance of our world and man's life within it. ... India here set out on a quest which she has never ceased to follow."

Hindu Calendar & the Age of Rig Veda and Sanskrit

According to the Oxford Dictionary (p.541): "Hindu calendar, a lunar calendar usually dating from 3101 B.C. and used especially in India," is roughly the same (5116 Yugabda = 3101 B.C. + 2015) as Hindus, at present, have been celebrating. This tells that Hinduism (Vedic religion) should be much older than 5116. Realization of the calendar must have come later than the birth of Hinduism (original Vedic religion). So the Vedas and their language Sanskrit should be much older than 5,116 years.

David Frawley (Sharma & Ghose, 1998, p. 140) talks about the Vedic astronomical references related to the calendar: "The Vedas contain various astronomical references relative to the calendar.

Such astronomical data suggest that the Vedas and Sanskrit are at least 4,500 years old. But they, both Vedas and Sanskrit, are much older, as would be explained later. B.G. (Lokmanya) Tilak[88] proved on the basis of astronomical reference in the *Rig Veda*, that the composition of the Rig Veda commenced around 4500 B.C. or so and bulk of hymns were composed between 3500 B.C. and 2500 B.C."

But as per other geographical evidences appeared later, it can be said beyond any doubt that the hymns of the *Rig Veda* were composed much earlier than 10,000 years, as evidenced by the appearance of the mention of the event of the bursting of the frozen Himalayan glaciers in the *Rig Veda*.

---

[88] Shrikant G. Talageri, "The Rigveda A historical Analysis" (2000, p.363).

Break up of Himalayan glaciers: Age of the Rig Veda

Graham Hancock (2002:169) quotes B.P. Radhakrishna of the Geological Society of India (1999), who writes that the *Rig Veda* talks about the break-up of Himalayan glaciers releasing water which flowed out in seven mighty rivers (*Sapta Sindhu*). The early inhabitants of the plains burst into songs, praising Lord Indra for releasing the water they very much needed. This happened during Late Pleistocene glaciations, about 10,000 years ago.

Geologist record indicates that during Late Pleistocene glaciations, waters of the Himalaya were frozen and that in place of rivers there were only glaciers, masses of solid ice which broke up by sun and started flowing as seven rivers (*Sapta Sindhu*).

This description of the break up of the Himalayan glaciers in the *Rig Veda* suggests beyond any doubt that the *Rig Veda* was composed at least 10,000 years back.

According to S.D. Kulkarni, "Our civilization, Vedic or Hindu, has a continuity of more than 31092 years before present period[89], and he pinpoints "21788 B.C. as the period, at least, of the origin of the *Rig Veda.*"[90]

First break up of Himalayan glaciers happened over 10,000 years back. Its description in the *Rig Veda* suggests that Vedas were composed at least 10,000 years back and so the age of their language Sanskrit and also the age of Swastika, as it is mentioned in the *Rig Veda*. All this challenges the validity of the two intermingled theories – (i) 'Aryan invasion of India' and (ii) 'Indo-European family of languages.' They were mischievously created in Britain to confuse and distort the history of Bhārat (Aryavarta, present India), particularly to reduce the ages of Vedas and their language Sanskrit.

The archeologically excavated seals at Mohen-jo-daro and Harappa, in early 1920s, shed historical light to awaken historians to the truth about the prehistory ancient Bhārat, her native *Aryans*, antiquity of the *Rig Veda,* and of *Sanskrit*. Unfortunately, the wrong history, written by colonial Westerners, has not yet been corrected. Encyclopedias and text

---

[89]   Bhishma, vol.2, p.14.
[90]   Bhishma, vol. 1, p. 128.

books continue to carry on the same text as written by colonialists prior to the Indus Valley civilization saw the sunshine in 1920s.

'Arya' is a Sanskrit word. Aryans were the original natives of the ancient *Aryavarta* (Bhārat, India). The originality of the Aryans has been confused by the ill-based theory, 'Aryan invasion of India.' Not even one historian has yet been able to identify the country outside India which had or has Aryans as its natives and Sanskrit as its native language.

Max Müller[91] talks about the age of the Vedas:

> "Whatever may be the date of the Vedic hymns, whether 1500 or 15,000 B.C., they have their own unique place and stand by themselves in the literature of the world. They tell us something of the early growth of the human mind of which we find no trace anywhere else. ... in the eyes of the historian and the psychologist they will always retain their peculiar value, far superior to the oldest chronicles, far superior to the most ancient inscriptions, for every verse, nay every word in them, is an authentic document in the history of the greatest empire, the empire of human mind, as established in India in the second millennium B.C."

Stephen Knapp, in his book *"Proof of Vedic Culture's Global Existence"* (2000, p.66), talks about the antiquity of the *Vedas*:

> "In the same line of thought, it has been determined that the Sanskrit *Rig-Veda* is the oldest piece of literature in the world. Reverend Morris Philip, in his book *The Teaching of the Vedas* (p.213), concludes: "After the latest researches into the history and chronology of the book of Old Testament, we may safely now call the *Rigveda* as the oldest book not only of the Aryan community, but of the whole world."

---

[91] Max Müller, "Six Systems of Indian Philosophy; Naya & Vaiseshika (1899, p.34)

Harry H. Hicks and Robert N. Anderson[92] have given dates of the antiquity of the Rig Veda, as given by different scholars:

David Frawley, in *'Gods, Sages and Kings'*, on the basis of astronomical references in the *Rig Veda*, corroborating the work of other earlier scholars such as Tilak and Jacobi, goes back to ca.6500 B.C. Probably beginning shortly after the major Indo-European "Kurganian" migration of ca 4,400 to 4,300 B.C., as described by Gumbutas, the Rig Vedic age, apparently with its inspired concepts, was conceived in India.

According to Cambridge, "The hymns of the *Rig Veda* were composed in the NW of India, the country of seven rivers in about 3700 B.C.

Hicks and Anderson have given an interesting evidence of Vedic Aryan Head from the collection of the Hicks Foundation for Cultural Preservation. They remark that extensive tests and mutually corroborative and interrelated physical, stylistic and historical evidence indicate that it was cast in the 4th millennium B.C., dating 3700 B.C. It was life sized, hollow, copper-based head in a human likeness. It may be the first hard evidence relating to the original Vedic Aryans in India. They tend to emphasize: "The Head's natural style and eye treatment also provide evidence of the continuity of Vedic Aryan art styles of the 4th/3rd millennium B.C., the Harappan and Mesopotamian art, and evolution into later Hellenistic and classical Indian art."

Feuerstein & et al (1995: 29) write about the *Rig-Veda*: "The *Rig-Veda* is the oldest book in the Sanskrit language, indeed in any Indo-European language. More than that, if we are correct, it is the oldest book in the world, and for this reason alone deserves our attention."

Max Müller, in *"History of Ancient Sanskrit Literature"* (p.63), remarks, that the *Rig Veda* be considered as the oldest source of history, not only of India, but of the world too:

As based on linguistic and philological evidence, the Rig Veda is the oldest surviving literature (1700-1100 BC) of the Vedic religion, now known as Hinduism[93], God Rudra (Shiva) is mentioned in the

---

[92]   Bhu Dev Sharma and Nabarun Ghose (ed.)., "Revisiting Indus-Sarasvati Age and Ancient India", WAVES, (1998, 348-350).

[93]   Wikipedia.

Rig Veda (RV 2.33). Shiva is described as the "Father of the Rudras", a group of storm gods.

> "The *Veda* has a two-fold interest. It belongs to the history of the world and to the history of India. In the history of the world the Veda fills a gap which no literary work in any other language could fill. It carries us back to times of which we have no records anywhere. ... Before the discovery of the Indus Valley civilization, the Vedas were supposed to be the earliest records we possess of Indian culture. There was much dispute about the chronology of the Vedic period, European scholars usually giving later dates and Indian scholars much earlier ones. ... Professor Winternitz thinks that the beginnings of Vedic literature go back to 2,000 B.C., or even 2,500 B.C. This brings us very near the Mohenjo-daro period."

The other three younger Vedas are Sama Veda, Yajur Veda, and Atharva Veda. In addition to the four Vedas, there are various subsidiary Vedic scriptures – Puranas, Brahmanas, Aranyakas, Upanishads, Sutras, Shastras, Samhitas, etc.

Chapter Eleven

STATUS OF ANCIENT VEDIC WOMEN

Vedas show that women occupied important positions in ancient Bhārat (Âryavarta), far superior position to the men of those times, as evidenced by the feminine term 'Shakti', applied to the 'power or strength' to protect the nation. Durga, riding a lion, was assigned 'Defense', the most important portfolio. Other two important portfolios were assigned to Lakshmi (Finance) and Saraswati (Education). Woman was considered powerful, not physically as man, but mentally, emotionally and spiritually, better than man to think, feel and act right in complex situations. I saw my grand father consulting his bed-ridden mother in regard to the *Panchaiti* issues. Man is prone to see them from his own narrow selfish concerns. This may be the reason why some parliamentary decisions don't bear desired fruits for the common man.

Vedic wisdom suggests that all male power comes from the feminine. History tells that kings and towns were destroyed when a ruler insulted or troubled a woman. For example, Ramayana tells that Ravana and his entire kingdom were wiped out because he abducted Sita. Mahabharata teaches us that all the Kauravas were killed because they humiliated Draupadi in public.

Elango Adigal's Sillapathigaram teaches us Madurai, the capital of the Pandyas was burnt because Pandyan Nedunchezhiyan mistakenly did harm to Kannaki.

During Vedic times women and men were equal in many respects. Women participated in public religious rituals alongside men. One script mentions a female rishi Visvara was known for her vision and wisdom. Some Vedic hymns, are attributed to women such as Apala, the daughter of Atri, Ghosa, the daughter of Kaksivant and Indrani, the wife of Indra. Apparently in early Vedic times women also received the sacred thread and could study the Vedas. The Haritasmrti mentions a class of women called *brahmavadinis* who remained unmarried and spent their lives in study. Panini's distinction between acarya (acharya, a preceptor) and acaryani (acharayni, a lady teacher), and upadhyaya (a preceptor) and upadhyayani (a lady teacher) indicates that women during those ancient times could not only be students but also teachers of sacred Vedas. There were several noteworthy female scholars of the past such as Kathi, Kalapi, Bahvici and several others.

Upanishads refer to several women philosophers, who disputed with their male colleagues such as Vacaknavi, who challenged Yajnavalkya. The *Rig Veda* also refers to women engaged in warfare. One queen Bispala is mentioned, and even as late a witness as Megasthanese (fifth century B.C. E.) mentions heavily armed women guards protecting Chandragupta's palace.

Hindu religion has been occasionally criticized as encouraging inequality between men and women, towards the detriment of Hindu women. This presumption is inaccurate and wrong. In the Vedic period, we come across female scholars like Ghosha, Lopamudra, Romasha, Indrani and several others. In the Upanishad period, names of women philosophers like Sulabha, Maitreyi, Gargi are encountered.

In religious matters, Hindus have elevated women to the level of divinity. One of the things most misconstrued about Bhārat is that it is a male dominated society and Hinduism also a male-dominated religion. The truth is exactly opposite. Bhārat is considered 'Bhārat Mātā'. It is the religion that has attributed the words for the strength and power to feminine. "Shakti" means "power" and "strength". All male power comes from the feminine. The Trimurti Brahma, Vishnu and Shiva are all incomplete and powerless without their female counterparts Sarasvati, Laxmi and Parvati respectively.

In Vedas, Devi is worshipped as the Great Goddess, as echoed by the Devi-Mahatmiyam prayer:

"By you this universe is borne, by you this world is created; By you it is protected, By you it is consumed at

197

the end, O Devi! You are the Supreme knowledge, as well as intellect and contemplation."

In ancient Vedic Bhārat, women were held in higher respect than in other ancient countries. The epics and the old literature of the ancient Vedic Bhārat assign higher position to women than the epics and literature of other religions. Hindu women enjoyed rights of property in the Vedic Age, participated in social and religious rites, and were sometimes distinguished by their learning. There was no seclusion of women in ancient Vedic times.

Professor H. H. Wilson remarks: "And it may be confidently asserted that in no nation of antiquity were women held in so much esteem as amongst the Hindus." In Ancient Bhārat, however, Hindu women not only possessed equality of opportunities with men, but enjoyed certain rights and privileges not claimed by the male sex. The chivalrous treatment of women by Hindus is well known to all who know anything of ancient Hindu society. Knowledge, intelligence, rhythm and harmony are all essential ingredients for any creative activity. These aspects are personified in Saraswati, the Goddess of Learning, Music and Fine Arts. By the blessings of Saraswati, Hindus have been welcome all over the planet as the successful members of their adopted lands, not only from financial point of view, but also as messengers of peace, spirituality and Yoga.

Without the grace of Saraswati, or Saraswati Kataksham, as it is called, Brahma would not be able to do a worthwhile job as the Creator. Any maintenance activity needs plenty of resources, mainly fiscal resources, given by Lakshmi, the goddess of wealth, the consort of Vishnu.

Shiva, the destroyer, is paradoxically Brahma

The contribution of Parvati – as the consort of Shiva, who is being misunderstood as 'destroyer' – is amazing if rightly understood.

In Hinduism, death is not considered as the end of life, but the beginning of a new life, as explained by the Hindu basic dogma "rebirth and reincarnation." This can be better understood by the Sanskrit word "*dehant*" for death. It means end of body, *deh* = body + *ant* = end means end of the body, not of the soul. At death, body perishes and soul transmigrates into other body of a new-born innocent child. This is the reason why Hindus don't bury the body to worship his / her grave, but remember him / her during the month of "*Shradha*" to gather as family and talk about his / her great virtues and teachings, in presence of a Brahmin / or a Brahmini (depending upon the gender of the departed soul) representing god or goddess.

Shiva derives power and energy from Parvati, or Durga as she is called Shakti.

It is only the Hindu tradition, which provides, even at the conceptual level, the picture of the male and female principles working together, hand in hand, as equal partners in the society. This concept is carried further to its logical climax in the form of Ardhanareeswara, formed by the fusion of Shiva and Shakti (Parwati) in one body, each occupying one half of the body, denoting that one is incomplete without the other.

Just the *shloka* that is commonly recited during prayers is enough to show the status of the woman, respected as a Devi (goddess): "*Yaa Brahma Achyuta Sankara Prabhrudibihi Devaissadaa Poojithaa.*" It means: "O Devi! Brahma, Vishnu, Shiva and other Gods always adore you."

In Hinduism, all power (Shakti) is female. Shakti is the fundamental strength that infuses all life. Shakti, as the divine feminine power, is found in everything. Shakti is worshipped as a Goddess. In Hinduism Kali is worshipped as the great divinity. Hindus hold rivers, all having feminine names – Ganga, Jamuna, Sindhu, Narbada, Kaveri, Saraswati, etc – are held in great reverence. The rivers are worshipped as divine mothers, bestowing water, food and all life-sustaining necessities.

Ganga is the most holy, the most honored and the most gracious river to accept the ashes. Ganga is worshipped as mother. She rises from the snow bed, at the top of Himalaya, 13,800 feet above the sea level. Jamuna, Saraswati and other rivers are revered as goddess-mothers.

Devisukta, one of the most important of all Vedic hymns, is addressed to Vak (speech, revelation), the goddess who is described as the instrument that makes ritual efficacious: "I am the queen, the gatherer-up of treasures."

199

In Sanskrit, earth – which bears the load of mountains, oceans, rivers and all humanity – is considered female, addressed as 'Prithivi' or 'Dharti Mātā'. Even the giver of education is female, known as Saraswati. In ancient Vedic times education for girls was regarded quite important. Bramhavadani girls were taught Vedic wisdom and the Kshatriya girls were given warrior training, the use of the bow and arrow. Patanjali mentions the spear bearers (saktikis). Megasthanese speaks of the Amazonian women as the bodyguards of Raja Chandragupta. Kautilya mentions women archers (striganaih dhanvibhih). Similarly, Kautilya, in Artha Sastra, a document of Mauryan history, refers to women soldiers armed with bows and arrows.

Buddhism maintained the traditions of *Brahmanical* religion, according to which women held honored place in social life. Women were eligible for admission to what was known as the *Bhikshuni-Sangha*, the Order of Nuns, which opened to them avenues of culture, social service and ample opportunities for public life. Girls had Upanayana performed for them and they carried out the Sandhya rites.

In Gurukulas, the ancient Universities of Bhārat, there was a coed system of education; boys and girls were educated together. Atreyi studied under Valmiki along with Lava and Kusha, the sons of Rama. Curriculum of fine arts including music, dancing, drama and painting was available to both boys and girls in coed schools and colleges so that both socialize together to be great fathers, mothers, husbands and wives. I experienced gender walls in my high school in Muslim-majority Sind and also in the college; hence few girls took advantage of education. In Gurukulas, the content, as given in modern economics, sociology and psychology was taught, as Artha-Shastra, Samaj-Shastra, etc.

Academic gender equality in marriage

According to Yajur Veda (VIII.I), a young girl, who has observed *brahmacarya* and then received education, should be married to a boy who like her is learned. Such marriage of right togetherness will be happy, constantly producing wisdom and joy by constant exchange of high ideas of humanity and civilization.

Seclusion of women by *parda* (covering face) in public and even at home was unknown in Vedic times. It came in India during influx of Muslims after 7th century AD. The Atharva Veda refers to daughters remaining with their parents until their marriage. A part of the ancestral property was given to them as dowry, which became their own property and was called *stridhana*, property of woman.

Vedas say: "*Na grham kasthapasanair dayita yatra tad grham – Nitimanjari*", meaning "Home is not what is made of wood and stone; but where a wife is, there is the home."

It is significant to know that only Hindus worship God in the form of Divine Mother. In Hinduism the deities for knowledge, material wealth and defense are female – Saraswati, Laxmi and Durga – not male. The past social inconsistencies and injustices that did not arise from Hindu scriptures, but from humans who failed to correctly incorporate the teachings of the ancient scriptures, such as Vedas, Upanishads, Bhagavad Gita and several other scriptures talking about various institutions including family, society and nation. In Sanātan Dharma, even modern times, main thrust has been on spirituality, rightly believing that if man, in general, is spiritual, the humanity will be at peace and happy. The ancient Vedic ethos of 'spiritual equality between man and woman' would drive away the darkness of inequality in all other spheres of life at all level. Modern man, if civilized in its real sense, should wake up to realize the sin of the gender superiority ethos which has been causing marital conflicts, adversely affecting the security and happiness of innocent helpless children. Family in ancient timess was happy because of gender equality.

Was Manu anti-women?

Some gender secularists make the allegation that Hinduism, as represented by Manu, is anti-woman. Actually on objectively reading all the text about Manu felt about woman, one would realize that neither dowry (*dahej*) nor self-immolation of widows (sati) figure in what Manu felt about women:

- "Where women are honored there the gods are pleased; but where they are not honored no sacred rite yields rewards," (Manu Smriti, III.56, a text on social conduct).

- "Women must be honored and adorned by their fathers, brothers, husbands and brothers-in-law, who desire their own welfare." (Manu Smriti III, 55).

- "Where the female relations live in grief, the family soon wholly perishes; but that family where they are not unhappy ever prospers." (Manu Smriti III, 57).

- "The houses, on which female relations, not being duly honored, pronounce a curse, perish completely as if destroyed by magic." (Manu Smriti III, 58).

- "Hence men, who seek their own welfare, should always honor women on holidays and festivals with gifts of ornaments, clothes, and dainty food." (Manu Smriti III, 59).

In an old Shakti hymn it is said: *"Striyah devah, Striyah pranah"* meaning "Women are Devas, women are life itself." Manu (Manu, chapter IX, verse 77) has also said: "If husband dies, wife may marry another man" and "If husband deserts his wife, may marry another."

Wonderful and exciting! Manu, the lawgiver, has stressed: "A woman's body must not be struck hard, even with a flower, because it is sacred." It may be for this reason why Hindus do not like capital punishment for woman who is respected as mother. In India, an elderly woman on street is addressed as 'Maa' (mother) and a youngster as 'Ben' (sister).

According to the Atharva Veda (xiv. i. 43-44), woman after her marriage is invited into her new family 'as a river enters the sea' to rule there along with her husband, as a queen, over the other members of the family.

The idea of M / W equality was clearly expressed in the *Rig Veda* (Book 5, hymn 61. verse 8): "The wife and husband, being the equal halves of one substance, are equal in every respect; therefore both should join and take equal parts in all work, religious and secular." No other sacred scripture of the world has ever given to the woman such equality with the man as the Vedas of the Hindus.

A Vedic woman whose name was Romasha revealed the 126th hymn of the first book of the *Rig Veda*; the 179 hymn of the same book was by Lopamudra, another inspired Hindu woman. There have been several women such as Apala, Romasha, Lopamudra, Shashvati, Gargi, Visvara, Maitreyi, Ghosha, Aditi and several other who have significantly contributed their wisdom in Vedas. Visvavara instructed Indra, one of the Devas, in the higher knowledge of Brahman, the Universal Spirit. All of these gem women lived the ideal life of spirituality, not seduced and untouched by the things of the bodily comfort. Such women are called in Sanskrit Brahmavadinis, the speakers and revealers of Brahman. Vedic women were so much learned that one, who was well versed in almost all the scriptures, was requested to act as a judge when Shankaracharya, the great commentator of the Vedanta, was debating on philosophy with another philosopher.

Married man would not perform any religious rite, ceremony, or sacrifice without being joined in by his wife; as the partaker and partner in the spiritual life of her husband; in Sanskrit called as *Sahadharmini* (spiritual helpmate). Such tradition has survived even in modern times. *Rig Veda* (I-122-2; 131-3; III-53-4-6; X-86-10 etc) suggests that wife is a regular participant in prayers and the sacrificial[94] offerings of the husband.

In the whole religious history of the world a second Sita will not be found. Her life was unique. Still in modern times Sita is worshipped as an honored wife, as an incarnation of God. Bhārat is the only country where prevails a belief that God incarnates in the form of a woman as well as in that of a man.

In Ramayana we read the account of Sulabha, the great woman Yogini, who came to the court of King Janaka and showed wonderful powers and wisdom, which she had acquired through the practice of Yoga. This shows that women were allowed to practice Yoga.

Motherhood is considered the greatest glory of Hindu women. The Taittiriya Upanishad teaches *"Matridevo bhava"*, meaning "Let your mother be the god to you."

---

[94] Sacrificial offerings are misinterpreted by colonialists to defame Hinduism. These sacrifices mean offerings of fruits, sweets and grains, not of animals.

The popular 'Hindu Drama', called 'Shakuntal' shows that Shakuntala successfully pleaded her own case and claimed her wife rights in the court of King Dushyanata who had forgotten his intimate joyous nights with her, when captivated by her innocent beauty and charm while hunting in a forest. Similar instances are mentioned in the 10th book of the *Rig Veda*. As early as 2000 B.C. Hindu women were allowed to go to battlefields to fight against enemies. A king sent his wife Sarama, along with army in search of robbers. She was one of the most powerful women of her day. She caught them from their hiding place.

Hinduism offers some intriguing and unique examples of strong women in the form of Goddesses. Two thousand years ago Saint Tiruvalluvar observed: "What does a man lack if his wife is worthy? And what does he possess if she is lacking worth?"

In Hinduism God is genderless

In several Hindu philosophical texts, God is referred to a 'Tat', meaning 'it', suggesting that God is genderless. One would find a comparable goddess for every god.

Emphasis on education of ancient women

Gobhila Gruhya Sutras (Gobhila Gr. S. I-3) state that wife should be educated to appropriately participate in the prayers, knowing the meaning of the shlokas recited at prayers. It is amazing to know the significance of equal joint gender participation in prayers in ancient Vedic times, as evidenced by prayers of Brahma along with Saraswati, Vishnu with Lakshmi and Siva with Parwati, Rama with Sita, and so on. Woman in the role of wife occupies a position of pre-eminence in ancient Hindu tradition. Hindus from the Vedic times believed in dual joint H & W worship. In this dual worship, the names of Radha and Sita get precedence over the names of their companions Krishna and Rama, like 'Radha-Krishna' and 'Sita-Ram.

The *Rig Veda* places woman on a high pedestal of sublimity: '*Yatr nariyastu poojayante ramante tatr devah*', meaning 'Gods preside where woman is worshipped.'

Upanishads describe that women enjoy honored position, performing active role in the society and conversing freely and actively with men. In ancient times young girls led free life and had a decisive voice in the selection of their husband, as evidenced by the ancient tradition of '*swayamver*'. Girls and young women enjoyed freedom in participating in festive occasions and contesting at tournaments (*samana*). Women were more independent and freer in every respect. Ancient scriptures suggest that women did not lead a secluded life, like that of their descendants in later times. Ancient Vedic literature tells that women, like some modern women, delayed their marriage and some never got married to pursue their academic goals to satisfy their literary thirst. It is wrong impression that most ancient women remained uneducated.

Ancient tradition of swayamver: Freedom to select husband

Several hymns of the *Rig Veda* were composed by female *Rishis* (sages). Young ladies of the time had a voice in their marriage. A verse in the *Rig Veda* suggests gender equality: "The woman who is of gentle birth and of graceful form selects among many of her loved one as her husband." Ramayana (earlier than 5114 BC) and Mahabharata (before 3138 BC) cite numerous cases of *Swayamver*, tradition of freedom of woman to select her own husband.

Widow marriage encouraged, and Sati unknown in the Vedas

The *Rig Veda* (X, 18.8) appeals to widows to remarry:

> "Rise up woman, thou art lying by one whose life is gone, come to the world of the living, away from thy husband, and become the wife of him who holds thy hand and is willing to marry thee."

Every hymn of the *Rig Veda* is attributed to a *Rishi*. Majority of its hymns are the work of male *Rishis*. The *Rig Veda* also contains numerous hymns revealed by women seers, as called *rishikas* and *brahmavadinis*. The *brahmavadinis* were products of educational discipline of *brahmacarya*, for which women were also eligible. The *Rig Veda* (V, 7, 9) refers to young maidens completing their education as *brahmacharinis* and then getting married, like modern practice to marry after completing education and getting work, as guided by the second *Ashram*, '*Grastha Ashram.*' *Rig Veda* (iii, 55, 16) mentions that learned unmarried young women be married to learned young men.

Self-burning of widows (Sati) was not sanctioned by the Vedic religion. During about 7th century AD when Mohammedans conquered India, they treated widows of the Hindu soldiers brutally and tried to sexually abuse them. Helpless widows preferred death, by getting burnt along with their husbands, they loved and adored. Later the practice of Sati died with change in demography and change of government. It is often said that the British government has suppressed Sati; but the truth is, that the initiatives in this direction was taken by the noble Hindu, Raja Ram Mohan Roy. In my opinion, the real truth is that the 'Sati' died its natural death when women felt safe and secure in change of communal demography and children could not bear the sight of their mothers being burnt alive. They revolted against such inhuman, cruel and uncivilized custom. The law also became civilized, along with man. Law didn't find such inhuman practice in Ramayana or in Mahabharata. Neither of the three wives – Kaushalya, Sumatra and Kekayi – of Dashratha got burnt along with their husband they loved the most. In Mahabharata, Kunti, mother of Pandavas did not commit Sati.

Ancient Vedic women philosophers[95]

It is hard to understand why women, in modern Bhārat in general, all are not so educated as they used to be millennia years back in remote ancient Vedic times. May be because of infiltration of dominating non-Vedic peoples from outside who have not been so much fond of education, particularly of women. I remember there were only about five girls in 300+ schools in Muslim majority town Mehar, Dadu

---

[95]   Subhamoy Das, Wikipedia.

district. Most schools, colleges and hostels in Sind were sponsored by Hindu philanthropists who were fond of education. Even the number of Muslim boys was less than 20% of the school population. Since independence, face of Indian schools and colleges has been changing with increasing number of girls and women. Vedic scriptures tell that women of (circa 1500-1200 BCE) were epitomes of intellectual and spiritual attainments. The Vedas have volumes to say about several Vedic women, who both complemented and supplemented their male partners. It will need too long space for this book to talk about the wisdom and scholarship of all the learned women of ancient times. Better to talk abut the few selected female scholars of the Vedic period – Ghosha, Lopamudra, Sulabha, Maitreyi and Gargi – who represent their significant contribution to the socio-cultural history and concerns of women.

Ghosha

Vedic wisdom is encapsulated in myriad hymns and 27 women seers emerge from them. But most of them are mere abstractions except for a few, such as Ghosha, who has a definite human form. She was grand daughter of Dirghatamas and daughter of Kakshivat, both composers of hymns in praise of Ashwins. Ghosha has two entire hymns of the tenth book, each containing 14 verses, assigned to her name. The first eulogizes the Ashwins, the heavenly twins who are also physicians; the second is a personal wish expressing her intimate feelings and desires for married life. Ghosha suffered from an incurable disfiguring disease, probably leprosy, and remained a spinster at her father's house. Her implorations with the Ashwins, and the devotion of her forefathers towards them made them cure her disease and allow her to experience wedded bliss.

Lopamudra

The *Rig Veda* has recorded long conversations between the sage Agasthya and his wife Lopamudra that testifies to the great intelligence and goodness of the latter. As the legend goes, Lopamudra was created by sage Agasthya and was given as a daughter to the King of Vidarbha. The royal couple gave her the best possible education and brought her up amidst luxury. When she attained a marriageable age, Agasthya, the sage who was under vows of celibacy and poverty, wanted to marry her. Lopa agreed to marry him, and left her palace for Agasthya's hermitage.

After serving her husband faithfully for a long period, Lopa grew tired of his austere practices. She wrote a hymn of two stanzas making an impassioned plea for his attention and love. Soon afterwards, the sage realized his duties towards his wife and performed both his domestic and ascetic life with equal zeal, reaching a wholeness of spiritual and physical powers. A son was born to them. He was named Dridhasyu, who later became a great poet.

Maitreyi

The *Rig Veda* contains about one thousand hymns, of which about 10 are accredited to Maitreyi, the woman seer and philosopher. She contributed towards the enhancement of her sage-husband Yajnavalkya's personality and the flowering of his spiritual thoughts. Yajnavalkya had two wives Maitreyi and Katyayani. Maitreyi was well versed in Hindu scriptures and was a 'brahmavadini'. Yajnavalkya's other wife Katyayani was an ordinary woman.

One day the sage decided to make a settlement of his worldly possessions between his two wives and renounced the world by taking up ascetic vows. He asked his wives their wishes. The learned Maitreyi asked her husband if all the wealth in the world would make her immortal. The sage replied that wealth could only make one rich, nothing else. She then asked for the wealth of immortality. Yajnavalkya was happy to hear this, and imparted Maitreyi the doctrine of the soul and his knowledge of attaining immortality. This tells that in those ancient Vedic times only a few people would sacrifice material wealth for spirituality and immortality.

Gargi

Gargi, the Vedic prophetess and daughter of sage Vachaknu, composed several hymns that questioned the origin of all existence. When King Janak of Videha organized a 'Brahma Yajna', a philosophic congress centered around the fire sacrament, Gargi was one of the eminent participants. She challenged the sage Yajnavalkya with a volley of perturbing questions on the soul (*atman*) that confounded the learned man who had till then silenced many an eminent scholar. Her question was: "The layer that is above the sky and below the earth, which is described as being situated between the earth and the sky and which is indicated as the symbol of the past, present and future, where is that situated?"

It bamboozled even the great Vedic men of letters. It is amazing to see so much education among ancient women which has been hidden or deliberatively ignored.

It is amazing and heartening to know that in prehistory millennia-long distant ancient times Vedic (Hindu) women were so much interested in education and more so that the society encouraged them to pursue education in coeducation institutions, *gurukulas* (schools) at local level and co-ed universities like Nalanda (5th century AD) and Takshashila (Taxila), 5th century BC.

Chapter Twelve

HINDUISM: TOO ANCIENT, VAST AND UNIQUE

Hinduism, unlike almost all other religions, does not have any known founder, nor known date of its birth. It is too vast and too inclusive to feel need to borrow any dogma from other religions. On the contrary, Hinduism has been liberal and generous to offer to new religions, like Jainism, Buddhism, Sikhism and more to come to modify and redefine fundamental principles of Hinduism, leaving its basics original and pure. Hinduism is an ocean of philosophical and spiritual gems of varied colors and fragnarences to choose from and too varied to disappoint any new aspirant.

Hinduism is away from controversies, exceopt one that it is different from all known religions and that it is unique. This is perhaps the reason why most theologians call Hinduism not a relgion, but a 'way of life'. The year of its birth is yet to be known. It will never be known because it is too ancient for the humanity. Some historians think that Vedism (modern Hinduism) is over two million years old.

Hinduism, like some other religions, does not mandate that its adherents must accept or deny any particular dogma or tradition. Hinduism is a culture with flowers of various colors and fragrances. Hinduism is too liberal to be tied by any dictator. Hinduism is also marked by an attitude which seems to accommodate religious and cultural perspectives other than one's own, and so is characterized by a rich variety of ideas and practices resulting in what appears as a multiplicity of religions under one term 'Hinduism'.

The traditions and practices of Hinduism are too diverse, particularly for Westerners to see unity and oneness in it. Its diversity confuses them too severely to consider Hinduism monotheistic, it really is. Practical expressions of its various premises give a sense that Hinduism is like a compilation of religions. In my opinion, Hinduism can not be neatly slotted into any particular belief system – monism, theism, monotheism, polytheism, pantheism, pane theism – for all these systems are reflected in its many facets.

Origin of humanity is too ancient, so is the antiquity of Hinduism. Man can't live without religion, and religion cannot be religion without man. Both – man and religion – are twins and God is their father. God, though considered omnipresent, is never visible, anywhere. Only a sincere worshipper can feel Him with closed eyes in privacy, whenever and wherever, on lawn, bedroom or even on train to his office.

When man opened his eyes, he was overwhelmed by the variety and beauty of the nature. He wants to know and see its Creator, but yet not successful, and he will never be. Helpless man has given up the hope. Man helplessly wandered around all over, but no success to find its Creator. When too tired he fell down and dreamed Him. A few, out of frustration have fired God and have become atheist. Man, it seems, has realized that it would be futile to pursue the search, which definitely is infeasible. Man has been satisfied to leave it, as a mystery.

Aldous Huxley (1894-1963) has rightly said: "Facts do not cease to exist because they are ignored." David Lewis[96] writes: "The world is full of mysteries. And given its mystical traditions no place in the world remains more mysterious than India, a country and culture said to be rooted in primordial timeless."

Lewis further writes:

> "Westerners have frequently tried to fathom the mysteries of Mother India. Western scholars, relative newcomers on the world stage, have consistently tried to date Indian civilization according to Western time lines, assuming an intellectual superiority that routinely

---

[96] David Lewis, in 'Forbidden History', edited by J. Douglas Kenyon (2005, p.180), under the title "India 30,000 B.C.E".

> dismisses the accumulated wisdom of millennia, including cultural traditions that speak of humanity's origin, lost continents, and advanced prehistoric civilizations."

Geologists seem to agree that the roots of Indian (Hindu) culture lie drowned beneath oceans. Lewis adds: "Today, mainstream science still theorizes that landmass such as Gondwanaland and Pangaea must have existed, although they are relegated to extremely ancient epochs: 180 to 200 million years ago."

Michael A. Cremo and Richard L. Thompson[97] take us to over 2 million years back when or earlier, it is presumed that Hinduism might have been born. Geologists have been able to trace Hindu heritage over two million years back. Hundreds of crude stone tools have been found in 1961. Cremo and Thomson in "The Hidden History of Human Race' write that according to a 1984 report by two Russian scientists A.P. Okladinov and L.A. Ragozin, 1.5 to 2.5 million years old stone tools have been found. It is supported by Prof. Anek Ram Sankhyan[98] of the Anthropological Survey of India who found a stone tool in 1981 near Haritalyangar village, in the late Pliocene Tatrot Formation, which is over two million years old.

In 1982, K. N. Prasad[99] of the Geological Survey of India discovered a "crude unifacial hand axe pebble tool" in the Miocene Nagriformation near Haritalyangar, in the Himalayan foothills of northwest India.

Geologists talk about the two million old stone tools which have been found in Sivalik Hills[100] region of the north-western India. It is said that the Sivaliks derive their name from the demigod Siva (Shiva). It shows that Shiva worshippers were there two million years ago. Some other geologists may find Hindu roots still earlier. Hindu roots may be still remote, because the humanity – the twin of the ancient Vedic religion, presently known as Hinduism) – is too ancient. Lynn

---

[97] Michael A. Cremo and Richard L. Thompson in 'The Hidden History of the Human Race', p.50).

[98] Ibid, pp 50-51.

[99] Ibid, p. 51.

[100] Ibid, p.50.

Thorndikehas observes: "Thus we see that India's marvels were not always false."

The word *'Dharma'* means duty. Hindu Dharma is neither a religion nor an 'ism' because it doesn't dictate what to do and what not to do. Dharma has no dos, nor any don'ts. Do whatever your conscience tells you, and don't do whatever it prohibits. So your inner self – God within – is your guide. You will commit mistake only when you ignore and don't listen to your conscience, instantly reachable because all the time available in his office within you. Vedic philosophy is too delicate to understand, but when understood, it looks very simple and easily practicable. This makes life rich with tranquility; one can buy it with zero dollars.

Hindu Dharma is scientific, well-thought and well-designed to guide how life should be arranged and lived to its optimum satisfaction. Life is divided in four 'well-thought' stages, known as Ashrams, stages of life. All ashrams are meaningfully interrelated to live a happy and fruitful life – (i) Brahmacharya first 25 years (for education) to solidify the foundation for rewarding future life, (ii) Grihasatha (marriage and family life, (iii) Vanaprastha (community service) and (iv) Sanyas for meditation and own soul upliftment.

Sannyas is the last stage of life. When it becomes difficult to physically exert, the person needs to be spiritually active, so as have peaceful life with *moksha* (freedom) from the 'kith & kin attachments and also free from the financial greed, cause for emotional and sentimental distress. Then it is better for the *sanyasi* to meditate for spiritual development and be able to share wisdom with others, particularly younger generation.

In some situations, elderly persons get involved by unwanted irritable suggestions and advices. Better to make own life rich with spirituality and prayers. It is wrong to characterize *Sanyas*, as inactivity to live life of a wandering monk to live a useless life. The fruits of life at any stage should not be wasted. There have been several renowned *rishis* and *munis*, who in their *sanyas*, have thrown so much guiding light on various paths to satisfying and productive life, may not be material, but literary, spiritual or sharing wisdom with others. *Sanyas* has wealth, not to be ignored.

Some theologians and philosophers have misrepresented *Sannyasi*, as a wandering useless monk. No body is completely useless at any stage of life. Even after death, one does not stop contributing to the society. In several cases, it is historically seen that one's contribution, particularly after his/her death magnifies and multiplies and remains cherished by younger generations for ever, for example contribution of Lord Rama (about 5114 BC), Lord Krishna (about 3138 BC), Vardhamana Mahavira[101] (599-527 BC), Gautama Buddha[102] (563-483 B.C.), Guru Nanak (1469-1539 AD), Swami Vivekananda (1863-1902 AD), S. Radhakrishnan (1888-1975), Annie Besant (1849-1933), Sister Nivedita (Margaret Noble, 1867-1911), Sister Gargi (Marie Louise Burke, 1911-2004) and of several others. In Hinduism, 'age' has lot of respect, as an ocean of knowledge. Hindu Dharma is based on knowledge, as reflected by its first Ashram *Brahmacharya* to earn knowledge to lay down strong foundation of life.

Dharma (Hinduism) was not founded by an individual, so to follow his/her dictates as written in his/her Bible. It is hard to say how it came up. Dharma was born with man. It will not die because man is immortal. Therefore, so many curves, turns, and ups and downs, as man has experienced, Hinduism will continue to brave along in company of its eternal companion man.

Bhagvad Gita is not the Bible of Hinduism, as is being understood by many. Gita is an ocean of knowledge, not only is being read by several non-Hindus, but is even translated into several non-Sanskritic languages, European as well as Asian, Iranian and African. Prof. Fatehullah Mojtabai, former Cultural Counselor at the Embassy of Iran in India, was a noted scholar of Sanskrit and a well-known exponent of Vedic philosophy. He has translated Gita into Persian.

Conscience, not Gita, is the Hindu Bible

Conscience is the Hindu Bible every one has in his/her inner-self, known as *Atma*, connected with *Parmatma*. Hence, one doesn't need to go to temple. One can sit any where, on the ground, on bed, in chair

---

[101] Vardhamana Mahavira (599-527 B.C.) was the founder of Jainism.
[102] Not certain about the birth of Gautama Buddha, some say (480-400), age 80.

or on the train to office, any time of his/her convenience, to pray and meditate. God is kind and always with you, wherever and whenever you need Him. God is omnipresent and is of and for every body, even of an atheist, because he recognizes God in different way. Hindus don't believe in congregations to pray together in temple or anywhere. Hindus, unlike several other religions, prefer individual private union with God, union between *Atma* and *Parmatma*, believing in zero distance between the two.

Ironically, this has not politically helped Hindus, because they, unlike others (Muslims, Christians, Sikhs, etc), do not feel one and are not seen as one and united. Hindus prefer to be one with God in His temple within one's inner-self.

Hindus, unlike most others, please God also by dance and devotional songs. This has become common in cinema. Love is expressed by songs, music and dance. This seems to be traditionally coming down from the way the young Krishna, Radha and *gopis* were enjoying their youth. This shows that Hinduism, since millennia, has been liberal, broad-minded and co-ed. This has helped in promoting co-ed education and scholarship, keeping in tune with the mission of the first Ashram, *Brahmacharya*. But, such congregation does not enliven feeling of political oneness.

Hindu Dharma is not an 'ism' with dictatorial 'dos' and 'don'ts'. It is the philosophy of life, being continuously updated / modified to keep pace with the changing time. Hinduism is not rigid, as being misconceived. It is elastic, flexible and adaptable to meet the changing needs of the time. As said earlier, Hindu Dharma is scientific, defining duties and responsibilities of man according to his age (*Ashram*), one is living in. Man is committed to perform his duties and responsibilities until his death.

Life immortal, death tired to end it

Amazing! In Hinduism, death is not considered as the end of life, but the beginning of new life, as per the Hindu basic dogma 'Rebirth and reincarnation.'

Sannyasi – at the last stage of his life when he has completed his family obligations – has yet to perform the utmost important duty to share his wisdom guiding the younger generation with the light of knowledge on the path for the union with Almighty God for peace. Man may need help from such a learned sadhu (Rishi) during the last moments of his life, may become unbearably painful because of thoughts being separated from the loving kith and kin. In some or even several cases, remembrance of the wrongs done with the loved ones becomes unbearably painful.

Hinduism basically believes in knowledge (*gyan*, education), as understood by why '*Brahmacharya*' as the foundation, the life be erected on. Knowledge is useless if not used or not activated by *karma* to produce desired fruits. Despite millennia-long threatening jolts from within as well as from outside, Hinduism has survived amazingly taintless with new fresh philosophical multi-color flowers and fruits to make life happier, increasingly more beautiful and more productive. Amazing, Hindu Dharma has been continuously blooming with fresh multi-color flowers of philosophy, knowledge and wisdom, activated by desired *karma*. Mahatma Gandhi has advised to keep windows open for the light of other cultures to come in, but has warned not to let them wipe out our culture, we are proud of.

The Vedic Dharma is based on knowledge, as the word 'Veda' means. Knowledge is the light of mind, without which man will not be able to understand the desired mission of his life, nor to be able to map the path from soul (Atma) to the Supreme Soul.

Origin of gyan (knowledge), not yet known, nor its end

Origin of *gyan* (knowledge) has been un-identifiable, not even in Vedas, the most ancient scriptures of mankind. Vedic *rishis* must have got knowledge from some thing or from some event. Ignorance of some thing doesn't mean its absence or non-existence. Knowledge is pure like Ganga, flowing and merging with the streams of several kinds of other aspects of the same thought, making it more vivid and better understandable.

Gyan and Karma bear fruit, only when married

Knowledge (*gyan*) without action (*karma*) is worthless, so is the Guru who doesn't practice what he sermonizes. The relationship between *gyan* (thought) and *karma* (action) is as old as the mankind. Wisdom is too precious to ignore. The Vedic Dharma (present Hinduism) is birthless and deathless, immortal because of wealth of knowledge (gyan), particularly its emphasis on self (self-awareness) and its close relationship with *karma*. The western societies with knowledge of science and technologies are financially rich and are leading comfortable physical life, but searching peace of mind in the East. Life with both – practical external knowledge of the world and tranquility – will be wonderful, but very difficult. Only few can achieve, because of 180-degree pull between the two.

Hindu Dharma is a way of life to be expressed, not through rituals, but by one's duties, as defined by the five *Ahrams* of life – towards various institutions – family, community, nation and mankind – and also spiritually to the inner-self. SELF is the most important institution, the foundation of all other institutions. SELF needs to be strong, not only to bear the weight of all kinds of responsibilities, but also to cooperate with others to collectively function optimally to make all happy. The relationship between self and others is very important for the tranquility of the whole mankind and inner-self. The strength of self depends on the knowledge of self (self-awareness) which is too delicate for any university to explain. Only the 'University of SELF' can do it. This is a delicate concept, only great philosophers, like – Swami Vivekananda, Tagore, Gandhi, and several other philosophers, Western as well as Eastern – understand and have given their perspectives on Hinduism, basically not different, but emphasizing its different aspects, different ways.

Hinduism immortal and continuously fresh

Hinduism has been immortal and always fresh only because Hindus have been deeply committed to their millennia-long basic tenet *'rebirth and reincarnation.'* According to Hinduism, death is beginning of a new fresh life. Such optimism has kept Hinduism rosy and fresh. Shiva has been misunderstood as the god of death and destruction. As a matter of fact, Shiva becomes Brahma after man's body becomes worn and torn out. Body is cremated and the soul transcends into a new-born fresh body. On this philosophical doctrine 'transcendentalism' has been based. It is a millennia-old Vedic philosophy.

Several Western scholars and philosophers, such as Ralph Waldo Emerson (1803-1882), Henry David Thoreau (1817-1862), Herman Melville (1819-1891), Walt Whitman (1819-1892), Sir Charles Eliot (1862-1931) were attracted by this. Now Europeans are clamming that the doctrine of 'transcendentalism' is recent one and originated in Europe and it is not ancient Vedic. As a matter of fact, the ancient Greek philosopher Plato (427-347 B.C.) was influenced by this. He believed in the doctrine of rebirth and reincarnation.

There are five main kinds of Yoga (paths) leading to God:

i. **Gyānā Yoga** (yoga of knowledge) is for those who are interested in knowledge – basically knowing self (soul, atma) and its relationship with the Supreme Soul (*Paramatma*) through meditation. Atma gyān (knowing self) is the most difficult and tedious yoga. India was up, is up and is going to soar to touch sky, only because of her eternal relationship with *Gyan* (knowledge). Both Bhārat and Gyan were born as twins. It is difficult to know when. Research into their millennia-long relationship is not humanly possible, though humanity is also that old.

ii. **Karma Yoga** (deeds, activity) essential for every body to please God through good *karmas* (acts, behavior), in service of the family, community and others. Swami Vivekananda primes this yoga. The word *'Karma'* is being misconceived by many as destiny. *Karmasheel* person designs his/her own destiny only if circumstances cooperate. It is wrong to think that destiny of every body is already written and can not be changed. Opportunities are already every where – in America as well in India – as evidenced by the fact that all Americans are not rich and all people living in India are not poor. Destiny is a maid servant of a *karmasheel* person. Be optimistic and enjoy the fruits of your Karmas, meaning work, not of destiny, and get freedom from the misconceived web of destiny.

iii. **Rājā Yoga** is more close to Gyānā Yoga. It is for those who are interested in self-realization through meditation.

iv. **Bhagti Yoga** (Devotional Yoga) for those who want to please God through devotion. Meera Bai is very popular for this.

v. **Shakti Yoga** (power, strength) is for those who are for power to protect self, family and nation. They are devotees of goddess Durga, very important for the protection of the nation. They are members of the most important caste 'Kshattriya' (warriors). Surprising both most popular non-mythological gods – Shri Rama and Lord Krishna – were *Kshattriya*. They were not Brahmins, the top Hindu caste. Hindus seem to rightly understand the significance of Durga, the goddess of power. Because of this, Hindustan doesn't need drafting her people for army, as America does. *Kshattries* are born to whole-heartedly volunteer to fight for the nation.

The main ingredients of all the above five Yogas seem to be intermingling, meaning a member of any category has some ingredients of all the rest four Yogas. Hindu, in order to be a happy and useful member of the society, would need all the five Yogas – knowledge, activity (*karma*), self-realization, devotion and power. In other words, all the five Yogas are needed to coexist in each and every person to be worthy of God's love.

Hindus believe that all paths lead to one and the same Almighty God (*Paramatma*). Different devotees are seeing or feeling *Paramatma* (God) in His various manifestations – Brahma, Vishnu, Shiva, Ram, Krishna, Durga, Parvati, Sarasvati, Sai Baba, or any other divine personality. What difference does it make if a person seeks God in any form? Truth is one: "Ekam Sat Viprah Bahuda Vadanti," meaning "truth is one; the wise call it by various names." Hinduism is monotheistic, but misperceived by others as polytheistic, because they see Hindus worshipping God in His various manifestations. Several deities are His various manifestations, representing His various forms and functions, giving various guiding messages, as required by His devotees. God is one and the same for all, irrespective of their religious orientations. But, His message of love for all, though same, is unfortunately being interpreted differently by followers of different religions. Then, how can any religion be monotheistic, if different religions have different God? God is not dividing mankind, but man is dividing God and piecing His global providence, based on religion. God will be happy to see unity in His providence. How can God be multiple or be divided into many?

Nehru (1946, p.341) has said that Gandhi, Tagore, Vivekananda, Sir S. Radhakrishnan, etc. have enhanced Hinduism by their progressive and practical perspectives on it.

Several western scholars, philosophers, theologians and historians of 18th - 21st centuries were influenced by Hindu philosophy. Their literary works have enhanced the image of Hindustan by propagating her philosophies and culture, as reflected in the ancient sacred scriptures, such as Vedas, Upanishads, Bhagvad Gita, Rāmāyanā, Mahābhāratā, etc. Some of those scholars and philosophers are Annie Besant (1849-1933), Sister Nivedita (Margaret Noble, 1867-1911), Sister Gargi (Marie Louise Burke, 1911-2004), Ralph T. H. Griffith (1826-1906), Will Durant (1885-1981), Sir Charles Eliot (1862-1931), Francois Voltaire (1694-1778), Mark Twain (1835-1910), Romain Rolland (1866-1944), Henry David Thoreau (1817-1862), V Gordon Childes (1892-1957), Aldous Huxley (1894-1963), Lynn Thorndike (1882-1965), Arthur Schopenhauer (1788-1860, Albert Einstein (1879-1955), Amos Bronson (1799-1888), Ralph Walden Emerson (1803-1882), Walt Whitman (1819-1892), Max Müller (1823-1899), Sir William Jones (1764-1794), David Frawley, Stephen Knapp, Edwin Bryant (1948-), Michael A. Cremo (1948-), and several others. The description of their works about Bharat and her culture will need a big book. Some of them were so much fascinated by Hinduism that they became Hindu; and some of them lived and died in Hindustan. Some are living in India, and some more will be pouring in to know more about Hindu philosophy which has been blooming with refreshing flowers of various philosophical colors and fragrances.

Hinduism as conceived by Mahatma Gandhi

Mohandas Karamchand Gandhi[103] (1869 - 1948), 'Father of the Nation', was deeply spiritual and yet rational in his thoughts. He is known for his famous words of wisdom on God, life and religion. Mahatma Gandhi[104] explained the meaning of God:

> "There is an indefinable mysterious power that pervades everything. I feel it, though I do not see it. It is this unseen power which makes itself felt and yet defies all proof, because it is so unlike all that I perceive through my senses. It transcends the senses. That informing power or spirit is God. For I can see that in the midst of death life persists, in the midst of untruth, truth persists, in the midst of darkness light persists. Hence I gather that God is Life, Truth, Light. He is love. He is supreme good. But he is no God who merely satisfies the intellect. If He ever does, God to be God must rule the heart and transform it."

Three years later, in October 1931, when Gandhiji was speaking at the Kingsley Hall in London, he revisited the above idea about God but this time reasoning it out with anecdotes and rational thoughts.
Mahatma Gandhi to answer "Does God exist?" thought:

> "But it is possible to reason out the existence of God to a limited extent. Even in ordinary affairs we know that people do not know who rules or why and how He rules and yet they know that there is a power that certainly rules."

Mahatma Gandhi has talked about the role of Hinduism in identifying and mitigating the *Bhaya* (fears) of life, too difficult to know and difficult to deal with:

---

[103] Subhmoy Das
[104] The Young India magazine of October 11, 1928.

> "Hinduism has saved us from *Bhaya* i.e. peril. If Hinduism had not come to my rescue, the only course for me would have been suicide. I remain a Hindu because Hinduism is a leaven which makes the world worth living in. ... Hinduism teaches me that my body is a limitation of the power of the soul within."

In Hinduism life has been characterized as *'Bhaya Sagar'* (ocean of fears). *Bhaya* (fear of life) is the main cause of miseries and unhappiness of life. *Bhaya* arises from the ignorance, particularly of self, arising from the distance between self and inner-self. The distance increases, when one gets more involved in materialism, rather not in spiritualism. Man, in pursuit of material successes, is always preoccupied with fears of failures, hence little relaxation and no peace of mind, creating sleepless nights leading to illnesses.

Gandhiji[105] talking about materialism of the West and spirituality of the East, remarks:

> "Just as in the West they have made wonderful discoveries in material things, similarly, Hinduism has made still more marvelous discoveries in things of religion, of the spirit, of the soul. But we have no eye for these great and fine discoveries. We are dazzled by the material progress that Western science has made. ... After all, there is some thing in Hinduism that has kept it alive up till now. It has witnessed the fall of Babylonian, Syrian, Persian and Egyptian civilization. ... Yes, I see here ancient India still living. True, there is dung heaps, too, here and there, but there are rich treasures buried under them. And the reason why it has survived is that the end which Hinduism set before it was not development along material but spiritual lines."

---

[105] M.K. Gandhi (ed. by Anand T. Hingorani), "My Varnashram Dharma", Bombay: Bharatiya Vidya Bhavan, 1965, (pp.64, 65).

Mahatma Gandhi[106] considered religion as duty, not privileges:

> "A life of religion is not a life of privileges, but of duty. Privileges may come, as they do come to all, from a due fulfillment of duty. In the book of God, the same numbers of marks are assigned to the *Brahmin* that has done his task as well as to the *Bhangi* who has done likewise."

Religious significance of work (*Karma*)

Gandhiji, like all other theologians, primes work (*karma*) of any kind. He says that the work of a Brahmin earns the same number of marks as the work of *bhangi* (toilet cleaner, scavenger). In other words, a working *bhangi* should get more respect than a lethargic Brahmin.

Hinduism looks as a complex religion because it suggests several denominations, worship of various mythological gods and goddesses, such as Vaishnavism (Vishnu worship), Saivism (Shiva worship), Shaktism (Durga/shakti worship), Gyanism (Sarasvati worship), worship of *Lakshmi* for wealth and several other gods, depending on deity's interests and needs. I saw one worshipping tree in Juhu, Mumbai. When asked why worshipping tree, he appropriately responded "Tree provides shelter against intolerable heat to every body, irrespective of his/her caste and religious orientation." Pointing to apples, he said tree gives fruits too.

But, when viewed with unbiased positive mind, Hinduism is simple and easy to practice, and rituals are always welcome to enjoy delicious *prasaad* and fruits they come with. Hinduism is complex for only those who are ethnically biased against other religions, ignoring their own religious rituals, observed only in their places of worship, not among family and friends, as Hindus do.

Each deity has attributes, the devotee admires. But, all the ways (paths) eventually merge leading to meet at the point, known as the abode of Almighty God.

---

[106] Ibid, inside cover.

In Hinduism, there are two schools of Vedanta (goal of Vedas) – Advaita (अद्वैत वेदान्त) and Dvaita (द्वैत वेदान्त) – understanding distinction and distance between self (soul, *atman*) and God {Supreme-Soul, Paramatma (परमात्मा)}.

Advaita (अद्वैत वेदान्त)

According to Advaita, there is no distinction, no distance between self (soul, *Atma*) and God (Supreme Soul, *Paramatma*). God is omnipresent, thus resides in each *Atman* (soul). One can feel Him, by a deep peep within self with closed eyes. When a Hindu is in front of a stone god / goddess or a picture image of a god / goddess, his eyes automatically get closed to feel God within self. He does not worship the stone god, but God, omnipresent every where. Because of the belief of God's omnipresence all the time, Hindus don't feel religiously obliged to go to *Mandir* (temple). Devotee can sit in *Samadhi* position (cross-legged) any where in the house, on lawn or in office, at the time and place convenient. God is liberal to consider devotee's convenience, because He knows devotee has several other essential responsibilities of life. I have seen some one meditating with his eyes closed on the train towards his office.

Dvaita (द्वैत वेदान्त)

According to Dvaita (duality), there is distinction and distance between self and God, between soul (Atman) and Supreme Soul (Paramatma, परमात्मा), meaning God is not within self. Mostly Hindus believe in *Advaita*, evidenced by the way of their meditation – closed eyes peep to have a warm feel of God within self. Modern philosophers – Bharat Ratna Shri Atal Bihari Vajpayee, Gandhi, Tagore, Vivekananda, Paramhans Ramkrishna, Ghosh, Sir S. Radhakrishnan, etc. – seem to practice Advaita Vedanta.

God and man would not be different and distanced from each other, only when man cleanses his soul to make it worthy for God to come and be within. Because of Advaita, devotees don't feel essential to go to temple and they don't believe in rituals. For them God is within, always with them and talks to them through their conscience.

These two theories should not confuse us, thinking that Hinduism does not have a clear perception of God. The persons, believing in Dvaita, also feel that in reality, the distance between the two – God and man or between *Parmatma* and *Atma* – is zero. God doesn't need time to travel any distance to be with His devotee. Only man should not waste time to be with God. I love this coincidence that this moment I am listening on radio that lover is singing to his beloved: "My beloved, what can I do, I am seeing God in you." Hinduism fundamentally is based on man's union with God all the time, at all places, as evidenced by Hindu worship not only in temple. Hindus[107] really believe in God's omnipresence. What will man get from separation? Hindu, like others, would like to pursue his union with God. Hinduism may be understood better when seen how scholars – Indian as well Westerners – feel about it.

Bharat Ratna Atal Bihari Vajpayee, Secular Nationalist Selfless BJP Soldier

Vajpayee (December 1924 - …) the only non-Congress leader who served the nation as the Prime Minister and completed his full term, He was felicitated with country's highest civilian honor 'Bharat Ratna' on March 27, 2015. His birthday is also celebrated as Good Governance Day.

Vajpayee began his career in politics as a freedom fighter. He took active role in the 1942 'Quit India' movement. Later he joined the Bharatiya Jana Sangh (BJS), a Hindu right-wing political party, under the leadership of Dr Syama Prasad Mookerjee. He became national secretary of BJS in charge of the Northern Region.

As the new leader of BJS, Vajpayee was elected to the Lok Sabha for the first time in 1957 from Balrampur. He rose to become the national president of the Jana Sangh in 1968. Supported by his colleagues Nanaji Deshmukh, Balraj Madhok and Lal Krishna Advani, Vajpayee took the Jana Sangh to greater glory.

---

[107] Hindus, mean also followers of Jainism, Buddhism and Sikhism.

Vajpayee participated in the 'Total Revolution Movement' launched by Jayaprakash Narayan (JP) against the Internal Emergency imposed by the Prime Minister Indira Gandhi in 1975. In 1977, Jana Sangh became a part of the Janata Party, the grand-alliance against the Indira Gandhi government.

Vajpayee became a Union Minister in 1977 when Morarji Desai-led Janata Party coalition came to power. He became the Minister of External Affairs. As foreign minister, Vajpayee became the first person to deliver a speech at the United Nations General Assembly in Hindi. Therefore, he is recognized as 'nationalist'.

His career as a minister was short-lived as he resigned from his post following the resignation of Morarji Desai in 1979. But by then, Vajpayee had established himself as a national political leader.

Vajpayee along with Lal Krishna Advani, Bhairon Singh Shekhawat and others from the BJS and Rashtriya Swyamsevak Sangh (RSS) formed the Bharatiya Janata Party in 1980. He became a strong critic of the Congress (I) Government, particularly in matters related to religion and worship places. Vajpayee strongly criticized the 'Operation Blue Star' because he rightly felt that it was not a secular step. He raised his voice against the anti-Sikh violence after the assassination of Prime Minister Indira Gandhi in 1984 by two of her Sikh bodyguards. As a matter of fact the 'Operation Blue Star' was not necessary. The militant Sikhs could have been compelled to come out from the Gurudwara in a couple of days by cutting off the supply of water, food and electricity. She should have respect for religious worship place of any community. It should be divorced from politics.

Atalji is a poet and a captivating orator. He is a writer, the author of 'Decisive days, Meri Ekyavan Kavitayen" and more,

Vajpayee's second term as PM is known for Bharat's nuclear tests conducted at Pokhran desert in Rajasthan in May 1998. Delhi rightly realized that in the jungle of nuclear tigers, better to have nuclear preventive shield. How can you have peace with brainless nuclear powers, particularly neighbors, threatening nuclear attack, foolishly ignoring Bharat's counter nuclear response, resulting in horrendous loss of lives in both countries. Vajpayee also pushed for peace process with Pakistan. He inaugurated the historic Delhi-Lahore bus service in February 1999. He also pitched for resolving the Kashmir dispute and other conflicting issues with Pakistan. But Pakistan would not understand the demography as the result of the exchange of population on bases of religion, as after the independence of India in 1947. At present Bharat has Muslims more than 14%, where as Pakistan has less than 1% Hindus. Moreover Muslims in Bharat have effective political clout and in Pakistan Hindus are voiceless and always fearful. Pakistan is talking about only religious demography of Kashmir, not about the post-independence religious demography of both Bharat and Pakistan. Yes Kashmir issue[108] should be and can be resolved only (i) when the 'Pakistan-occupied Kashmir' is returned to Bharat and (ii) religion-based equitable exchange of population is resolved.

Atalji is secular in its real sense. I realized this when I saw him, prior to his Prime Ministership, in his meeting with about 50 community activists at my residence on Long Island, admonishing a fundamentalist youngster to understand that Muslims are part of the multi-religious integrated independent Bharat, and that unity among all will make Bharat strong. This awakened me to peep within to find if I was secular. Secularism will solidify Bharat and will take her to the Everest of unity and oneness.

Prime Minister Vajpayee's following quotes will explain Bharat's helpless compelling necessity of nuclear weapons, as deterrent to the adversaries, particularly neighbors, Pakistan and China:

- Our nuclear weapons are meant purely as a deterrent against belligerent hostile adversary neighbors.
- You can change friends but not neighbors.
- Global interdependence today means that economic disasters in developing countries could create a backlash on developed countries.

On Mar 27, 2015 *Atalji* was presented the highest Bharatiya award 'Bharat Ratna' at his residence by PM Narendra Modi, Lal Krishna Advani and several BJP leaders. It is shame that on such occasion

---

[108] This is my view point, hope Delhi would be loud about this.

opposition leaders did or could not be there on such occasion, as if he was not their Prime Minster.

Prime Minister Narendra Modi and Foreign Minister Sushma Swaraj hand overed the Liberation War award to Vajpayee's family members. Vajpayee also received several awards, mentioning a few, Padma Vibhushan in 1992, D. Lit. from Kanpur University in 1993, Lokmanya Tilak Award in 1994, Best Parliamentarian Award in 1994, Bharat Ratna Pandit Govind Vallabh Pant Award in 1994 and Liberation War award (Bangladesh Muktijuddho Sanmanona) in 2015.

Atalji authored 'Decisive days, *Meri Ekyavan Kavitayen*' and more. Atalji received awards 'Bharat Ratna' and 'Padma Vibhushan'. Atalji remained unmarried to serve the nation roundthe clock. He adopted a daughter, named Namita.

Prime Minister Narendra Modi wished veteran BJP leader Atal Bihari Vajpayee on his 91st birthday, praising his exemplary service and his 'politics of agreement. Politics was his love. He has M.A. in political science. He has political vision, domestic as well as international.

The Vajpayee government introduced many economic and infrastructural reforms, including encouraging the private sector and foreign investments. It also undertook National Highway Development Projects and Pradhan Mantri Gram Sadak Yojana. Vajpayee adopted pro-business, free market reforms approach to boost India's economic development. In March 2000, Vajpayee signed the Historic Vision Document during the visit of the US President Bill Clinton. The Declaration incorporated several strategic issues, apart from pitching for expansion in trade and economic ties between the two countries.

I am fortunate that my relationship with Shri Atalji started long before he became Prime Minister and remained the same even while he was Prime Minister. He used to call me from his private telephone. Therefore, his office did not know my appointment with him to wish him "Happy Birth Day' on the eve of his mini-vacation in Kerala. To be honest, without my continued relationship with the secularism-icon Atalji, it would have been difficult for me to remain secular.

xxxxxxxxxxxxxxxxxxxxxx

The main reason for our continued long relationship was RSS, with which we both are closely associated. Because of Atalji's physical limitations, meetings and phone conversations have been impractical.

The main reason for our continued friendly relationship was RSS (Rashtra Swayamsevak Sangh) with which we both were closely associated. We shared lot of stuff about RSS, the brain child of Dr. Keshav Baliram Hedgawar, to unite Hindus in the jungle of anti-Hindu monsters. Now, Hindus enjoy peaceful sleep under the strong protedtive umbrella of RSS, armored by generations of dedicated soldiers, like Guruji M. S. Golwalkar who assumed the charge of RSS, as the Sarsangha Chalak in 1940 when Dr. Hedgawar died. I had fortune of enjoying two annual lectures by Guruji at Karachi in 1945 and 1946. When I remember the effective Hindu climate in the Pre-partition Muslim majority Sindh, my blood boils. I was an RSS Pracharak and had fortune of having Baba Saheb Apteji, the then Sursangha Karyawah, at lunch with my parents at our hometown Mehar, Sindh in 1946.

Shri Atalji was happily surprised to know that I, as an RSS member, was imprisoned in Baroda jail for four months for protesting against the ban of RSS in 1948 because Nathuram Godse, who assassinated Mahatma Gandhi, was assassinated by Nathuram Godse. RSS was banned because Nathuram was a member of RSS. Why should the whole organization (RSS) be punished for the crime of its member Nathuram? What a shameful justice! Father can not punished for the crime of his son.

Shri Atalji has similar contacts with several other Indians to infuse in them the spirit of secularism and Dharma (duty) towards Bhārat Mātā. It is certain that when Atalji is up out of his sick bed, he will continue to do the same. Atalji never took it easy and never ignored his Dharma (duty) toward his people who elected him again and again for some national office. Shri Atal Bihari Vajpayee is a man of principles and he would like to continue to do the best, until alive to serve to safeguard the integrity of Bhārat. Better to understand Hinduism through other scholars on Hinduism.

As an academic, philosopher, and statesman, Dr. Sarvepalli Radhakrishnan[109] (1888-1975) was one of the most recognized and influential Indian thinkers in academic circles in the 20th century. Throughout his life and extensive writing career, Radhakrishnan sought to define, defend, and promulgate his religion, a religion he variously identified as Hinduism, Vedanta, and the religion of the Spirit. He sought to demonstrate that his Hinduism was both philosophically coherent and ethically viable. Radhakrishnan's concern for experience and his extensive knowledge of the Western philosophical and literary traditions has earned him the reputation of being a bridge-builder between India and the West. He often appears to feel at home in the Indian as well as the Western philosophical contexts, and draws from both Western and Indian sources throughout his writing. Because of this, Radhakrishnan has been held up in academic circles as a representative of Hinduism to the West. His lengthy writing career and his many published works have been influential in shaping the West's understanding of Hinduism, India, and the East. He was President of India 1962-1967. He authored:

i. The Hindu view of life,1926
ii. An idealist view of life,1929
iii. Dharmma,1950
iv. The Principal Upanishads, 1953.
v. A source book in Indian philosophy, 1957.
vi. Several articles on Hinduism, Vedanta and philosophy

A. C. Bhaktivedanta Swami Prabhupada

Swami Prabhupada[110] (अभय चरणारविन्द भक्तिवेदान्त स्वामी प्रभुपाद) (1896 –1977) was a Gaudiya Vaishnava spiritual teacher (guru) and the founder preceptor (acharya) of the International Society for Krishna Consciousness (ISKCON), commonly known as the "Hare Krishna Movement." His mission was to propagate Gaudiya Vaishnavism, a school of Vaishnavite Hinduism that was taught to him by

[109] Wikipedia, Google
[110] Wikipedia, Google

his guru, Bhaktisiddhanta Sarasvati, throughout the world. Born Abhay Charan De in Calcutta, he was educated at the prestigious local Scottish Church College. Before adopting the life of renunciation (vanaprastha) in 1950, he was married and owned a small pharmaceutical business. In 1959 he took a vow of renunciation (*sannyasa*) and started writing commentaries on Vaishnava scriptures. In his later years, as a traveling Vaishnava monk, he became an influential communicator of Gaudiya Vaishnava theology to India and specifically to the West through his leadership of ISKCON, founded in 1966. As the founder of ISKCON, he "emerged as a major figure of the Western counterculture, initiating thousands of young Americans." Despite attacks from anti-cult groups, he received a favorable welcome from many religious scholars, such as J. Stillson Judah, Harvey Cox, Larry Shinn and Thomas Hopkins, who praised *Bhaktivedanta* Swami's translations and defended the group against distorted media images and misinterpretations. In respect to his achievements, religious leaders from other Gaudiya Vaishnava movements have also given him credit.

Swami Prabhupada has been described as a charismatic leader, in the sense used by sociologist Max Weber, as he was successful in acquiring followers in the United States, Europe, India and elsewhere. After his death in 1977, ISKCON, the society he founded based on a type of Hindu Krishnaism using the *Bhagavata Purana* as a central scripture, continued to grow and is respected in India, though there have been disputes about leadership among his followers. In February 2014, ISKCON's news agency reported to have reached a milestone of distributing over half a billion books authored by Bhaktivedanta Swami Prabhupada, since 1965. He became very popular in America, though some loud criticism and opposition from narrow-minded segment of America. Later it calmed down when they realized it was in praise and worship of Almighty God, one and the same for the mankind. Amazingly the movement became world-wide popular, in India, and more so in western world, particularly in Europe and America. They have beautiful temple in Juhu, Mumbai where every day Aarti is performed with hundreds of dedicated devotees, dancing and singing.

Dayanand Saraswati

Dayanand Saraswati[111] (1824 – 1883) founded the **Arya Samaj,** a Hindu reform movement of the Vedic tradition. He was a profound scholar of the Vedic lore and Sanskrit language. He was the first to give the call for *Swarajya* as "India for Indians" in 1876, later taken up by Lokmanya Tilak. He denounced the idolatry and ritualistic worship prevalent in Hinduism. He worked towards reviving Vedic ideologies. Subsequently the philosopher and President of India, S. Radhakrishnan, called him one of the "makers of Modern India," as did Sri Aurobindo.

Madam Cama, Pandit Lekh Ram, Swami Shradhanand, Pandit Guru Dutt Vidyarthi were influenced by and followed Dayananda. Shyam Krishan Verma established India House in England for Freedom fighters, like Vinayak Damodar Savarkar, Lala Hardayal, Madan Lal Dhingra, Ram Prasad Bismil, Mahadev Govind Ranade, Swami Shraddhanand, Mahatma Hansraj, Lala Lajpat Rai and others. One of Dayanand's most influential works is the book *Satyarth Prakash,* which contributed lot to the Indian independence movement. Dayananda was a sanyasi (ascetic) from boyhood, and a scholar, who believed in the infallible authority of the Vedas.

Maharshi Dayananda advocated the doctrines of Karma (Karmasiddhanta) and Reincarnation (Punarjanma). He emphasized the Vedic ideals of brahmacharya (celibacy) and devotion to God. The Theosophical Society and the Arya Samaj were united from 1878 to 1882, becoming the Theosophical Society of the Arya Samaj. Among Maharshi Dayananda's contributions are his promoting of the equal rights for women, such as their right to education and reading of Indian scriptures, and his intuitive commentary on the Vedas from Vedic Sanskrit was in Sanskrit as well as in Hindi so that the common man be able to read them. Dayanand was the first to give the word of Swadeshi and Harijan to the dalits and Pariahs (Outcastes) long before Mahatma Gandhi.

Dayanand Saraswati was born in a Brahmin family, but he did not believe in caste system. His father was a follower of Shiva and taught Dayanand Saraswati the ways to impress the Lord Shiva. Dayanand was

---

[111] Wikipedia

also told the importance of keeping fasts. On the occasion of Shivratri, Dayanand had to sit awake the whole night in obedience to Lord Shiva. One such night, he saw a mouse eating the offerings to the God and running over the idol's body. After seeing this, he questioned himself, if the God could not defend himself against a little mouse then how could he be the savior of the massive world.

The deaths of his younger sister and his uncle from cholera caused Dayananda to ponder the meaning of life and death and he started asking questions which worried his parents. He was to be married in his early teens, as was common in nineteenth-century India, but he thought marriage was not for him and in 1846 ran away from home. Dayananda Saraswati spent nearly twenty-five years, from 1845 to 1869, as a wandering ascetic, searching for religious truth. As an ascetic, he gave up material goods and lived a life of self-denial, devoted to spirituality. He lived in jungles, in retreats in the Himalayan Mountains, and at a number of pilgrimage sites in northern India. During these years Dayananda practiced various forms of yoga. He became a disciple of a well-known religious teacher Virajanand Dandeesha, also spelled Birajananda. Virajanand believed that Hinduism had strayed from its historical roots and that many of its practices had become impure. Dayananda promised Virajanand that he would devote his life to restoring the rightful place of the Vedas in the Hindu faith.

Dayanand's mission was not to start or set up any new religion but to ask humankind for Universal Brotherhood through nobility as spelt out in Vedas. For that mission he founded Arya Samaj enunciating the Ten Universal Principles as a code for Universalism *Krinvanto Vishwaryam* meaning the whole world be an abode for Nobles (Aryas). His next step was to take up the difficult task of reforming Hinduism with dedication, despite multiple repeated attempts on his life. He traveled the country challenging religious scholars and priests to discussions and won repeatedly on the strength of his arguments based on his knowledge of Sanskrit and Vedas. He believed that Hinduism had been corrupted by divergence from the founding principles of the Vedas and that Hindus had been misled by the priesthood for the priests' self-aggrandizement. Hindu priests discouraged the laity from reading Vedic scriptures and encouraged rituals, such as bathing in the Ganges River and feeding of priests on anniversaries, which Dayananda pronounced as superstitions or self-serving practices. By exhorting the nation to reject such superstitious notions, his aim was to educate the nation to *go back to the Vedas.* He wanted the people who followed Hinduism to go back to its roots and to follow the Vedic life, which he pointed out. He exhorted the Hindu nation to accept social reforms, including the importance of Cows for national prosperity as well as the adoption of Hindi as the national language for national integration. Through his daily life and practice of yoga and *asanas*, teachings, preaching, sermons and writings, he inspired the Hindu nation to aspire to *Swarajya* (self governance), nationalism, and spiritualism. He advocated the equal rights and respects to women and advocated the education of a girl child like the males. Swami Dayanand did logical, scientific and critical analyses of faiths i.e. Christianity & Islam as well as of other Indian faiths like Jainism, Buddhism and Sikhism. In addition to discouraging idolatry in Hinduism, as may be seen in his book *Satyarth Prakash.* He was against what he considered to be the corruption of the true and pure faith in his own country. Unlike many other reform movements of his times within Hinduism, the Arya Samaj's appeal was addressed not only to the educated few in India, but to the world as a whole as evidenced in the sixth principle of the Arya Samaj. In fact his teachings professed universalism for the all living beings and not for any particular sect, faith, community or nation.

Arya Samaj allows and encourages converts back to Hinduism. Dayananda's concept of dharma is stated in the "Beliefs and Disbeliefs" section of *Satyartha Prakash.* He said: "I accept as Dharma whatever is in full conformity with impartial justice, truthfulness and the like; that which is not opposed to the teachings of God as embodied in the Vedas. Whatever is not free from partiality and is unjust, partaking of untruth and the like, and opposed to the teachings of God as embodied in the Vedas—that I hold as adharma. ... He, who after careful thinking, is ever ready to accept truth and reject falsehood; who counts the happiness of others as he does that of his own self, him I call just."

Satyarth Prakash

Sri Aurobindo (1872 –1950), nationalist, philosopher, yogi, guru, and poet, joined for a while the movement for independence from British rule, became one of its influential leaders and then became a spiritual reformer, introducing his visions on human progress and spiritual evolution.

Aurobindo studied for the Indian Civil Service at King's College, Cambridge, England. After returning to India he took up various civil service works under the Maharaja of Baroda and began to involve himself in politics. He was imprisoned by the British for writing articles against British rule in India. He was released when no evidence was provided. During his stay in jail he had mystical and spiritual experiences, after which he moved to Pondicherry, leaving politics for spiritual work.

During his stay in Pondicherry, Aurobindo developed a method of spiritual practice. He called it Integral Yoga. The central theme of his vision was the evolution of human life into a divine life. He believed in a spiritual realization that not only liberated man but transformed his nature, enabling a divine life on earth. In 1926, with the help of his spiritual collaborator, Mirra Alfassa ("The Mother"), he founded the Sri Aurobindo Ashram in Pondicherry.

His main literary works are:

- *The Life Divine*, which deals with theoretical aspects of Integral Yoga,
- *Synthesis of Yoga*, which deals with practical guidance to Integral Yoga, and
- *Savitri: A Legend and a Symbol*, an epic poem which refers to a passage in the *Mahabharata*, where its characters actualize Integral Yoga in their lives.

Aurobindo's works also include philosophy, poetry, translations and commentaries on the *Vedas*, *Upanishads* and the *Bhagavad Gita*. He was nominated for the Nobel Prize in Literature in 1943 and for the Nobel Prize in Peace in 1950.

Although Aurobindo was a scholar and philosopher his aim was not to develop any religion, but to attempt an inner self-development by which each human being can perceive oneness in all and procure an elevated consciousness that will externalize the godly attributes in man. This can be understood by his ten selected quotations:

1. **Indian Culture:** "More high-reaching, subtle, many-sided, curious and profound than the Greek, more noble and humane than the Roman, more large and spiritual than the old Egyptian, more vast and original than any other Asiatic civilization, more intellectual than the European prior to the 18th century, possessing all that these had and more, it was the most powerful, self-possessed, stimulating and wide in influence of all past human cultures."

2. **Hinduism:** "Hinduism ... gave itself no name, because it set itself no sectarian limits; it claimed no universal adhesion, asserted no sole infallible dogma, set up no single narrow path or gate of salvation; it was less a creed or cult than a continuously enlarging tradition of the God ward endeavor of the human spirit. An immense many-sided and many staged provision for a spiritual self-building and self-finding, it had some right to speak of itself by the only name it knew, the eternal religion, Santana Dharma..."

3. **India's Religions:** "India is the meeting place of the religions and among these Hinduism alone is by itself a vast and complex thing, not so much a religion as a great diversified and yet subtly unified mass of spiritual thought, realization and aspiration." (*The Renaissance in India*)

4. **Hinduism as a Law of Life:** "Hinduism, which is the most skeptical and the most believing of all, the most skeptical because it has questioned and experimented the most, the most believing because it has the deepest experience and the most varied and positive spiritual knowledge, that wider Hinduism which is not a dogma or combination of dogmas but a law of life, which is not a social framework but the spirit of a past and future social evolution, which rejects nothing but insists on testing and experiencing everything and when tested and experienced, turning in to the soul's uses, in this Hinduism, we find the basis of future world religion. This Sanatana Dharma

has many scriptures: The Veda, the Vedanta, the Gita, the Upanishads, the Darshanas, the Puranas, the Tantras ... but its real, the most authoritative scripture is in the heart in which the Eternal has his dwelling."

5. **Ancient India's Scientific Quest:** "... the seers of ancient India had, in their experiments and efforts at spiritual training and the conquest of the body perfected a discovery which in its importance to the future of human knowledge dwarfs the divinations of Newton and Galileo, even the discovery of the inductive and experimental method in Science was not more momentous..."

6. **India's Spiritual Mind:** "Spirituality is the master key of the Indian mind. It is this dominant inclination of India which gives character to all the expressions of her culture. In fact, they have grown out of her inborn spiritual tendency of which her religion is a natural out flowering. The Indian mind has always realized that the Supreme is the Infinite and perceived that to the soul in Nature the Infinite must always present itself in an infinite variety of aspects."

7. **Hindu Religion:** "The Hindu religion appears ... as a cathedral temple, half in ruins, noble in the mass, often fantastic in detail but always fantastic with a significance - crumbling or badly outworn in places, but a cathedral temple in which service is still done to the Unseen and its real presence can be felt by those who enter with the right spirit ... That which we call the Hindu religion is really the Eternal religion because it embraces all others."

8. **Inner Strength:** "The great are strongest when they stand alone. A God-given might of being is their force."

9. **Gita:** "The Bhagavad-Gita is a true scripture of the human race a living creation rather than a book, with a new message for every age and a new meaning for every civilization."

10. **Vedas:** "When I approached God at that time, I hardly had a living faith in Him. The agnostic was in me, the atheist was in me, the sceptic was in me and I was not absolutely sure that there was a God at all. I did not feel His presence. Yet

237

something drew me to the truth of the Vedas, the truth of the Gita, the truth of the Hindu religion. I felt there must be a mighty truth somewhere in this Yoga, a mighty truth in this religion based on the Vedanta."

To many, particularly to Westerners, Hinduism, though simple, appears complex, only because, like most other religions, it has not been created by an individual and because it has no one book like Bible. Hinduism is a natural religion with flowers of various philosophical colors and fragrances keep changing with the changing philosophy of life. Hinduism is not rigid. Hinduism, unlike most other religions, does not have one representation of God, nor one sacred book to describe the totality of the religion. Hindus believe that religion can or should not be bordered. It should be free, flexible, progressive, stretchable, and boundary-less to meet the changing needs of mankind, keeping pace with time without any guilt. This is the reason why Hinduism is like culture to keep pace with the time. Hindu culture does not remain static. It has been flexible and open to incorporate desirable cultural and philosophical orientations from other cultures. Mahatma Gandhi wanted to keep the windows of his house un-blinded to let the light of other cultures come in: "I don't want my house to be walled on all sides and the windows are blinded. I want all cultures of all countries to come into my house. But I refuse to be wiped away by any culture what-so-ever."

Ramakrishna Paramahansa

Ramakrishna Paramahansa[112] (1836 – 1886), was a Hindu mystic and yogi during the 19th-century. His religious school of thought led to the formation of the Ramakrishna Mission by his chief disciple Swami Vivekananda. Among the women, Ramakrishna emphasized service to other women rather than *tapasya* (practice of austerities). Gauri Ma founded the Saradesvari Ashrama at Barrackpur, which was dedicated to the education and uplift of women.

Ramakrishna was born in a poor Brahmin Vaishnava family in rural Bengal. He became a priest of the Dakshineswar Kali Temple, dedicated to the goddess Kali, which had the influence of the main strands of Bengali *bhakti* tradition. The most widely known amongst his first spiritual teachers was an ascetic woman, called Bhairavi Brahmani, who was skilled in Tantra and Vaishnava *bhakti*. He had 12 years of school education. But he did not develop any interest in school education and literature. He became well-versed in *Puranas*, *Ramayana*, *Mahabharata*, and *Bhagavata Purana*, hearing them from wandering monks and the *Kathaks* – a class of men in ancient India who preached and sang Puraānas.

Sarada Devi (1853–1920), his wife and spiritual counterpart outlived Ramakrishna by 34 years and played an important role in the nascent religious movement.

Ramakrishna was known for his principles:

- "Worship of God as Mother"
- "All religions as true" and
- "Assimilation of Hindu polytheism into Brahmoism

Ramakrishna's teachings in the journals of *New Dispensation* over a period of several years were instrumental in bringing Ramakrishna to the attention of a wider audience,

---

[112] Wikipedia

especially the Bhadralok (English-educated classes of Bengal) and the Europeans residing in India.

Ramakrishna, entitled *The Hindu Saint* in the *Theistic Quarterly Review* (1879), played a vital role in introducing Ramakrishna to Westerners like the German indologist Max Müller. Newspapers reported that Ramakrishna was spreading "Love" and "Devotion" among the educated classes of Calcutta and that he had succeeded in reforming the character of some youths whose morals had been corrupt.

Ramakrishna also had interactions with Debendranath Tagore, the father of Rabindranath Tagore, and Ishwar Chandra Vidyasagar, a renowned social worker. He had also met Swami Dayananda. Ramakrishna, considered as one of the main contributors to the Bengali Renaissance.

Principal Dr. W.W. Hastie of the Scottish Church College, Calcutta was among several Europeans who were influenced by Ramakrishna. In the course of explaining the word *trance* in the poem '*The Excursion*' by William Wordsworth, Hastie told his students that if they wanted to know its real meaning, they should go to "Ramakrishna of Dakshineswar." This prompted some of his students, including Swami Vivekananda), to visit Ramakrishna.

Swami Vivekananda (Narendranath Dutta) was one of the main *monastic disciples* of Ramakrishna who renounced their family and became the earliest monks of the Ramakrishna order.

A small group of women disciples including *Gauri Ma* and *Yogin Ma*. A few of them were initiated into *sanyasa* through *mantra deeksha*. As his name spread, an ever-shifting crowd of all classes and castes visited Ramakrishna.

Swami Vivekananda

Swami Vivekananda[113] did not believe in rituals. He believed that God is within: "Where can we go to find God if we can not see Him in our own hearts and in every being?" He clearly said that one has not to wander around to find God, when He is sitting in own soul. It will be like a *hiran* (deer), madly wandering around for *khasturi* (perfume), it is carrying with self in its nābh (navel). What a great philosophy! Vivekananda said spirituality grows from one's own inner self:

> "You have to grow from the inside out. None can teach you, none can make you spiritual. There is no other teacher but your own soul. You can not believe in God until you believe in yourself."

God is not different from self: "The first sign of your becoming religious is that you are becoming cheerful. One can be cheerful only when one sees God within self. In order to know God, you have to know yourself, meaning *ātmagyān* (self-awareness)."

Vivekananda believed that *loka-seva* (community service) is religion:

> "To devote your life to the good of all and to the happiness of all is religion. Whatever you do for your own sake is not religion. ... The more we come out and do good to others the more our hearts will be purified, and God will be in them." Mahatma Gandhi also believed the same.

Vivekananda believed that God lives in pure hearts: "If you want to have God with you, you have to make your heart pure." He talked about religion:

> "Religion is the manifestation of the Divinity already in man. The greatest religion is to be true to your own

---

[113] Wikipedia, Google

241

nature. Have faith in yourself. ... You can not believe
in God until you believe in yourself."

Vivekananda believed in **karma** (action, work) to get desired results. *Karma* is not destiny, as is being misperceived by many who do not have trust in self. America is a country of opportunity only for the one who creates opportunity for self. Otherwise, no American will be poor. You can make yourself what you want to be, only by *Karma*. In order to make *karma* effective and productive, Vivekananda suggests positive thinking:

> "If you think about disaster, you will get it. Brood about death you hasten to demise. You think positive and masterfully with confidence and faith, life becomes more secure, more fraught with action, richer in achievement and experience."

Hinduism primes optimism and positive thinking, as reflected by the Hindu concept of death – body dies, not soul – thus unending continuity of life. Hindus see in death rebirth of a sinless beautiful infant. Do good deeds (*karma*) to beget happiness in this life and also in the next life.

Vivekananda recommends selfless prayer, as reflected in his following quotations: "It is good to love God for hope of reward, but it is better to love God for love's sake. Prayer goes:

> "O Lord, I do not want wealth, nor children, nor learning. If it be Thy will, I shall go from birth to birth. But grant me this, that I may love Thee without hope of reward – unselfishly for love's sake."

Vivekananda observes: "God is to be worshipped as the one beloved, dearer than everything in this and next life."

Vivekananda, talking about *moksha / nirvana* (freedom) from the continuing cycle of birth and death, also meant freedom from the attachments (*moha*) with dear ones which may give grief after separation:

"The moment I have realized God sitting in the temple of every human body, the moment I stand in reverence before every human and see God in him, that moment I am free from bondage, every thing that binds vanishes, and I am free."

Nirvana is the prime pursuit of Hindus, Jains, Buddhists and Sikhs. It is not easy. It needs long sincere meditation and severe *tapasiya* (penance).

Swami Vivekananda on Hindu Dharma

Amazing, unbelievable the way Swami Vivekananda has described Hinduism. He asserts that Dharma is a practical way of life, not as an 'ism':

- You have to grow from the inside out. None can teach you, none can make you spiritual. There is no other teacher but your own mind and soul.
- Take up one idea. Make that one idea your life - think of it, dream of it, live on that idea. Let the brain, muscles, nerves, every part of your body, be full of that idea, and just leave every other idea alone. This is the only way to success.
- Arise! Awake! And stop not until the goal is reached.
- We are what our thoughts have made us; so take care about what you think. Words are secondary. Thoughts live; they travel far.
- You cannot believe in God until you believe in yourself. (This is too delicate to understand.)
- Truth can be stated in a thousand different ways, yet each one can be true.
- External nature is only internal nature writ large.
- When an idea exclusively occupies the mind, it is transformed into an actual physical or mental state.
- The more we come out and do good to others, the more our hearts will be purified, and God will be in them.

- Condemn none: if you can stretch out a helping hand, do so. If you cannot, fold your hands, bless your brothers, and let them go their own way.
- The moment I have realized God sitting in the temple of every human body, the moment I stand in reverence before every human being and see God in him - that moment I am free from bondage, everything that binds vanishes, and I am free.
- Our duty is to encourage every one in his struggle to live up to his own highest idea, and strive at the same time to make the ideal as near as possible to the Truth.
- God doesn't help those who do not help themselves.
- All the powers in the universe are already ours. It is we who have put our hands before our eyes and cry that it is dark.
- The whole secret of existence is to have no fear. Never fear what will become of you, depend on no one. Only the moment you reject all help are you freed.
- Never think there is anything impossible for the soul. It is the greatest heresy to think so. If there is sin, this is the only sin; to say that you are weak, or others are weak.
- The world is the great gymnasium where we come to make ourselves strong.
- The will is not free - it is a phenomenon bound by cause and effect - but there is something behind the will which is free.
- Where can we go to find God if we cannot see Him in our own hearts and in every living being.
- May He who is the Brahman of the Hindus, the Ahura-Mazda of the Zoroastrians, the Buddha of the Buddhists, the Jehovah of the Jews, the Father in Heaven of the Christians give strength to you to carry out your noble idea.
- If money helps a man to do good to others, it is of some value; but if not, it is simply a mass of evil, and the sooner it is got rid of, the better.
- All differences in this world are of degree, and not of kind, because oneness is the secret of everything.

- If faith in ourselves had been more extensively taught and practiced, I am sure a very large portion of the evils and miseries that we have would have vanished.
- That man has reached immortality who is disturbed by nothing material.

Swami Vivekananda has very well explained that Hinduism is not an 'ism' because there are neither 'dos' nor 'don'ts', but practical ways of life to make self closer to inner-self, (atma) the abode of *Paramatma*. Vivekananda emphasized knowledge of self, which according to him is the abode of God, therefore no need to go to temple or any where else to be with God. It is very difficult, but not impossible. It needs sincere serious long *tapasiya* and penance.

The influence of Vedic thought on Plato and Plotinus is one example of India's philosophical contribution to America via Europe. In return to West's scientific and technological contribution to India, the West has received from India the science and art of spirituality, Yoga, and vegetarianism, the West needs the most.

The present trend in the West seems to be focused on the soul's solace along with bodily pleasures. The increasing awareness among westerners – that their psychological pain is caused by family disintegration and their over-indulgence in bodily pleasures and material pursuits – has led them to look toward the East for answers. Meditation, Yoga, and vegetarianism are gaining popularity in the West. Indians, like Deepak Chopra, are gaining attention of the West and several westerners have been influenced by the Vedic (Hin

Chapter Thirteen

BUDDHISM[114]

Hinduism and Buddhism: A 'Mother-Daughter relationship

B uddhism has its roots in ancient Vedic Dharma, presently known
as Hinduism. Gautama Buddha, the founder of Buddhism, was
born of Hindu parents – Suddhodan and Maya Devi. Gautama
and his wife Yasodhara had a son Rahula. Yasodhara was daughter of
King Suppbubuddha. It is interesting to note that almost all Hindu
gods – Rama, Krishna, Gautama and others – have been *kshtriya*,
meaning of warrior race. Their primary *Dharma* (Sacred responsibility)
has been to protect the nation. Gautama, seeing so much bloodshed in
battles, got depressed and realized *'Ahimsa'* (nonviolence) as the only
path to ultimate true peace and tranquility of soul, not pleasures of
body and not in the glory of name, earned by victories in battles which
cause deaths. The origin of Buddhism is deeply rooted in and as guided
by the Vedic traditions.

According to early texts Gautama was born as Siddhārtha
Gautama in Lumbini and grew up in Kapilavasthu, a town in the region
of modern Nepal-India borders, and that he spent his life in what is now
on the borders of Bihar and Uttar Pradesh. Some hagiographic legends
state that his father was king, named Suddhodana, his mother queen
Maya, and that he was born in Lumbini gardens.

Buddha gave his first sermon at the Dhamek Stupa which was
built by Ashoka. Buddhism originated in prehistory distant ancient
Bhārat, sometime between the 6th and 4th centuries BCE. From there

---

[114] Wikipedia.

it spread throughout much of Asia and beyond. It declined in Bhārat because most Buddhists migrated out of Bhārat, but not forgetting their roots and their birth cottage in Bhārat, as evidenced by Dalai Lama seeking shelter in Bhārat and hearty welcome by their mother (Bhārat), despite threats by civilized, but in true sense uncivilized China, not recognizing and respecting its own lofty heritage.

Buddhism[115] is the world's fourth-largest religion, with over 500 million followers or 7% of the global population, known as Buddhists.

Practices of Buddhism include: (i) taking refuge in the Buddha Dharma and the Sangha (ii) study of scriptures (iii) observe moral precepts, (iv) renunciation of cravings and attachments, (v) remaining calm to develop self-awareness to be able to peek deep into inner self to feel oneness with God to cultivate wisdom, love, kindness and compassion for all others.

There are three traditions of Buddhism – Theravada, Mahayana and Hinayana. Theravada is most conservative. Hinayana is being practiced in Sri Lanka, Myanmar, Cambodia, Thailand and Laos.

Nirvana, the ultimate goal of life

Buddhists consider *Nirvana* as the ultimate goal of life. Nirvana is the transcendent state of life in which man seeks complete freedom from the bondage (jail) of desires, sorrows, sufferings, fears, happiness, and fortunately also freedom from the effects of *Karma*, and from the continuous 'cycle of birth and death'. In the Nirvana state, one does not have sense of self. It is too difficult, but not impossible to attain *Nirvana*. One can attain it by severe *tapasiya*, meaning non-stopping continued perseverance.

Buddha was moved by the sufferings of humanity as result of bloody battles and long painful illnesses. He secretly left home, leaving his family asleep, in search of peace and tranquility of soul. He meditated alone for an extended period of time, in various ways including asceticism, on the nature of suffering and means to overcome it. One can not imagine unbearable load of conflict, whether to abandon the pleasures of princely life in search of unknown *Nirvana*. He used

---

[115] Wikipedia

to sit in meditation long hours under a *Ficus religious* tree, now called the Bodhi Tree in the town of Bodh Gaya in Gangetic plains region. He attained enlightenment, discovering self, what Buddhists call the Middle Way (Skt. *madhyamā-pratipad*), a path of spirituality losing self (*Ahankar*), and feeling one with inner-self ending suffering (*dukkha*), expected from the non-stopping continuous rebirths. Gautama became enlightened, being known as *samyaksaṃbuddha (Skt)*. He founded a *Sangha* (monastic order), now being known as Buddhism. Buddha spent the rest of his life teaching the *Dharma* he had discovered. He passed away at the age of 80 in Kushinagar, Bhārat

Buddha's teachings have been propagated by his followers all over the planet, particularly more in eastern countries, with different philosophical interpretations, but strictly related to the basic authentic teachings of Buddha, known as Buddhism, with its roots in Bodh Gaya. The five precepts (*pancha-sila*) are moral behavioral and ritual guidelines for lay devotee in Buddhism, while those following a monastic life have rules of conduct (*patimokkha*). The five precepts apply to both male and female devotees, and these are:

1. Abstain from stealing;
2. Abstain from sensual (including sexual) misconduct;
3. Abstain from lying;
4. Abstain from intoxicants
5. Abstain from killing (Ahimsa)

Mostly they seem to have come from the Hindu five principles of life to distance self from the five basic vices of life – *Kaam* (lust), *Krodha* (anger), *Lobha* (greed). *Moha* (attachments) and *Ahankar* (pride) – which would help in distancing self not only from the five vices, but also free in search of God within inner-self. Almighty God always resides within at zero distance from soul. Keep soul pure for God. Interesting, Gautama is worshipped in all countries, particularly more in eastern. Buddhists strictly believe in *ahimsa* (nonviolence) and hate adultery. Gautama Buddha attained <u>Nirvana</u> under the Bodhi Tree at the Mahabodhi Temple in Bodh Gaya, Bhārat.

Vinaya is the specific Buddhist code of conduct for a *sangha* of monks or nuns. It includes the Patimokkha, a set of several offences including rules of decorum for monks, along with penalties for transgression. Buddhism is practiced in several countries, mostly in the east.

Mandala are used in Buddhism for initiation ceremonies and visualization. Idols of deity and icons have been a part of the historic practice, and Buddhist texts such as the 11th-century *Sadanamala*, wherein a devotee visualizes and identifies himself or herself with the imagined deity as part of meditation. This has been particularly popular in Vajrayana meditative traditions, but also found in Mahayana and Theravada traditions, particularly in temples and with Buddha image. In Tibetan Buddhism tradition, mandala are mystical maps for the visualization process with cosmic symbolism. There are numerous deities, each with a mandala, and they are used during initiation ceremonies and meditation. The mandalas are concentric geometric shapes symbolizing layers of external world, gates and sacred space. The meditation deity is in the centre, sometimes surrounded by protective gods and goddesses. Visualizations with deities and mandalas in Buddhism is a tradition traceable to ancient times, and likely well established by the time the 5th-century text *Visuddhimagga* was composed.

Throughout most of the Buddhist history, meditation has been primarily practiced in Buddhist monastic tradition, and historical evidence suggests that serious meditation by lay people has been an exception. In recent history, sustained meditation has been pursued by a minority of monks in Buddhist monasteries. Western interest in meditation has led to a revival where ancient Buddhist ideas and precepts are adapted to Western mores and interpreted liberally, presenting Buddhism as a meditation-based form of spirituality. Buddhists are interested in seminars and debates to get clear picture of their religion and also of its founder Gautama.

Serious Buddhists are interested in *Prajñā* (Sanskrit), meaning insight, self awareness or knowledge of self, inner-self where one can be at zero distance away from soul, the true nature of God's cottage. The Buddhist traditions regard ignorance (*avidyā*), a fundamental ignorance, misunderstanding or misperception of the nature of reality, as one of the basic causes of *dukkha* (sorrows) and *samsara* (circumstances).

For overcoming ignorance and misunderstandings, one should get enlightened, meaning develop knowledge of self and get liberated from the attachments with 'kith and kin' and also with the worldly possessions. This overcoming includes awakening of impermanence and non-self nature of reality and develop dispassion for the objects of clinging, and liberates self from *dukkha* and *saṃsāra*. *Prajñā* is considered important in all Buddhist traditions, and it is the understanding of *dharma*, functioning of *karma* and rebirths, realms of *samsara*, impermanence of everything, no-self in anyone or anything. Man can be happy only when he feels free of all worldly desires and is completely independent.

In Theravada Buddhism, also in Tibetan Buddhism, two types of meditation are practiced, namely *śamatha* (keeping "calm") and vipassana (insight). Buddhism wants the devotee to keep calm while meditating so that devotee can develop insights to be able to peep within to have union with soul, the home of God. The focus of Vipassana meditation is to continuously and thoroughly know impermanence of everything (*annica*) and no-self in anything (*anatta*). According to Buddhism there is nothing independent, except the state of nirvana. All physical and mental states depend on and arise from other pre-existing states, and in turn from them arise other dependent states while they cease.

Mahayana

Chanting during <u>*Bhatti Puja*</u> (Bhagti devotional worship) is often a part of the Theravada Buddhist tradition. Devotion is an integral part of the various practices of most Buddhists. Guru devotion is a central practice of Tibetan Buddhism. Guru is essential in any devotional prayer. Guru is the "enlightened teacher and ritual master" in Vajrayana spiritual pursuits.

Chapter Fourteen

WEST INFLUENCED BY HINDUISM

Plato and the Upanishads

M.P. Pandit[116] has highlighted a study by Dr. Vassilis Vittaxis, a former Greek ambassador to India. Dr. Vittakis brings to light the similarities and differences between Vedic philosophy and the philosophy of Plato. For example, he likens the *nous* (mind) of Plato to the *Atman* of the Upanishads. He further draws parallels between Plato's *Division of Society* and the caste system, "Plato's Guardians, Warriors, Craftsmen have a close resemblance to the Hindu Brahman, Kshatriya, Vaishya."

According to the Columbia Encyclopedia (p.2171), Plotinus (205-270), a Neo-Platonist philosopher, traveled in the Eastern expedition of Gordian III, the Roman emperor in c.242 to study the philosophies of India and Persia.

There is persuasive evidence that his cosmological conception, which is the chief tenet of Neo-Platonism, was influenced by the *Vedanta* philosophy.

Plato, influenced by Vedanta

Surprisingly, Plato (427-347 B.C.) was long back influenced by Vedic philosophy. Talking about the triumph of the East and the Hellenistic Age, Herbert J. Muller (1958, p.15) has elaborated on how Greeks profited immeasurably from spiritual trade with the East, more typical of India:

---

[116]   M.P. Pandit, 'Traditions in Mysticism' (1987, p.121)

"At the same time, Plato's own thought was so fertile because it was not a classically ordered system but an exploration of various possibilities, a sensitive response to various influences, including Oriental thought. Its historic influence has stemmed chiefly from his inclination to a transcendental idealism, another worldly kind of spirituality that is more typical of India than of Greece in its heyday."

Plato[117] believed in the immortality of the soul and reincarnation:

'Plato believed that though the body dies and disintegrates, the soul continues to live forever. After the death of the body, the soul migrates to what Plato called the realm of the pure form. After a time, the soul is reincarnated in another body and returns to the world. But the reincarnated soul retains the dim recollection of the realm of forms and yearns for it. Plato argued that people fall in love because they recognize in the beauty of their beloved the ideal form of beauty they dimly remember and seek."

A popular love song from an Indian movie echoes the Hindu belief in reincarnation, *"Aisa lagta hai ki ham agle janam men kahin mile honge.* (It seems we must have met somewhere in our previous life). Both doctrines, immortality of the soul and reincarnation, are the ancient basic doctrines of Hinduism and of its offshoots – Jainism, Buddhism and Sikhism. Buddhism was founded by a Hindu prince Siddhartha Gautama (563 to 483 B.C.).

Sister Nivedita

Sister Bhagini Nivedita born as Margaret Elizabeth Noble, Oct 28, 1867 in UK and died on October 13, 1911 in India. She was a Scots-Irish social worker, author and teacher.

---

[117] World Book Encyclopedia (1993, vol.15, p.504),

Sister Nivedita met Swami Vivekananda in 1895 in London and traveled to Calcutta in 1898. Swami Vivekananda initiated her into the vow of *Brahmacharya* on 25 March 1898 and gave her the name *Nivedita* (meaning "Dedicated to God"). She believed that Dharma means service of the mankind. Swami Vivekananda believed the same about the religion, as service, not as rituals of worship in temples. In November 1898, she opened a girls' school in Bagbazar area of Calcutta. She wanted to educate those girls who were deprived of even basic education. During the plague epidemic in Calcutta in 1899, Nivedita nursed and took care of the poor patients.

Nivedita had close association with the newly established Ramakrishna Mission. However, because of her active contribution in the field of Indian Nationalism and service of the people, she had to publicly dissociate herself from the activities of the Ramakrishna Mission under the president Swami Brahmananda. She was in a very close relationship with Sarada Devi, the spiritual consort of Ramakrishna and one of the major influences behind Ramakrishna Mission and also with all brother disciples of Swami Vivekananda. Her epitaph reads, "Here reposes Sister Nivedita who gave her all to India".

Dr. Annie Besant

Dr. Annie Besant (1847-1933), daughter of William Wood and Emily Morris was born in London in 1847 and died in India in 1933. She rejected Christianity in 1874, and became like an atheist. In 1890s, she became supporter of Theosophy, a religious movement founded by Helena Blavatsky in 1875. Theosophy was based on Hindu-Buddhist ideas of karma, reincarnation and *Nirvana*. She went to live in India. She got actively involved in the 'Indian Home Rule' movement. Dr. Annie Besant, a friend of Swami Vivekananda, has talked about the contribution of Hinduism to the theosophical philosophy:

> "After a study of some forty years and more of the great religions of the world, I find none so perfect, none so scientific, none so philosophical and so spiritual as the great religion known by the name of Hinduism. Make

no mistake, without Hinduism, India has no future. Hinduism is the soil in which India's roots are stuck and torn out of that she will inevitably whither as a tree torn out from its place. And if Hindus do not maintain Hinduism who shall save it? If India's own children do not cling to her faith who shall guard it? India alone can save India, and India and Hinduism are one."

Henry David Thoreau, Transcendentalist

Henry David Thoreau (1817–1862), an American philosopher, journalist, and poet believed in transcendentalism, civil disobedience, and was a dedicated abolitionist. Mahatma Gandhi learnt civil disobedience from him. Transcendentalism means thinking beyond the range of human mind and experience, in Sanskrit meaning *antardhyan*, deep dive into the inner-self (meditation). This is a too delicate concept for a westerner, though philosopher to understand. Therefore, transcendentalism, though ancient as man, is entering now in theological realms of western philosophy.

Controversy surrounds the question of miracles, or whether God communicates His existence to humanity through miracles as performed by Jesus Christ. Western transcendentalists think that this position alienates humanity from divinity. In my opinion, Emerson rightly leveled the charge forcefully in his scandalous Divinity School Address (1838), asserting that "the word Miracle, as pronounced by Christian churches, gives a false impression. Hindus, like several western transcendentalists rightly believe that God displays His presence all the times in every aspect of the natural world, not just at isolated times. True transcendentalists are liberal and democratic. They believe that truth lights its torch in the inner temple of every man's soul. Truth is core element of Hinduism, as of several other religions too. What I am stressing that transcendentalism is not a new religious concept, as Christians claim, as introduced by them.

Sister Gargi (Marie Louise Burke)[118]

---

[118] Wikipedia, Google

Sister Gargi (1911-2004) born as Marie Louise Burke, was an eminent researcher on Swami Vivekananda. She is known for her six volume work, *Swami Vivekananda in the West: New Discoveries*, highly acclaimed in India and in Vedanta circles worldwide.

Burke was initiated into the Ramakrishna-Vivekananda movement in 1948 by Swami Ashokananda, the abbot of the Vedanta Society of Northern California in San Francisco. Burke took her first vows in India from the Ramakrishna Order in 1974 and was given the monastic name "Gargi" after the Vedic scholar in recognition of her brilliant accomplishments as researcher and writer. In 1983, the first Vivekananda Award was given by the Ramakrishna Mission for her research on Vivekananda. Later on, she took her final vows of "sanyas" and was given the name Pravrajika Prajnaprana.

Dr. Diana L. Eck

Harvard Indologist Diana Eck has been very much interested in Hinduism, as a researcher on religions, not like Sister Nivedita, Gargi and some others who were so much influenced by Hinduism that they left their European abodes and got settled in India until their death. Diana has toured India wide and visited several Hindu temples and talked to several Hindu monks tto understand Hinduism. But, in my opinion she has not understood Hinduism as conceived by Hindu philosophers like Swami Vivekananda, Ramkrishna, Dr. S. Radhakrishnan, Sister Nivedita, Sister Gargi, David Frawley who really had deep understanding of Vedas and Vedic religion (Hinduism). Prof Eck considers India's as a sacred geography which has held in common and revered its mountains, forests, rivers, hilltop as shrines. She remarks that for Hindus, as also for many Indian Buddhists, Muslims, Christians and Sikhs, India is a holy land. For many India is Mother Goddess. According to Diana, Hindu mythology consistently visualizes India as a spiritually charged and living landscape in which mountains, rivers, forests and villages are elaborately linked to the stories of gods and heroes.

Prof Eck has authored several books, related to religion, particularly the following three, where-in she has talked lot about Vedas and Vedic religion (Hinduism):

    i.   Daršan: Seeing the Divine Image in India (1981)

    ii. A New Religious America (2001)

   iii. India A Sacred Geography (2012)

In Daršan (p.3), Eck writes "The central act of Hindu worship from the point of view of the lay person is to stand in the presence of the deity and to behold the image with one's own eyes, to see and be seen by the deity." Eck is right as seeing the Hindu worshipping in front of a stone or a picture deity. But, it seems she doesn't understand that the stone replica of God is a link, spiritually connecting the worshipper with God, who doesn't have any shape (*Nirākār*, meaning shapeless). This is too hard for most non-Hindus to understand that Daršan can be done only with deep peep with closed eyes within inner-self (soul, the abode of God). Eck doesn't see that the worshipper's eyes instantly get closed when he/she wants to have His Daršan. Christians in Church worship Christ with open eyes. Hindu doesn't meditate with open eyes. How can one see God, who does not have any shape? God is to be felt with deep peep within self where He stays with every human being. This is the reason why Hindus prefer to meditate (worship God) in complete privacy. In congregations, Hindus worship through devotional singing and dancing. This is called *Bhagti Yoga*, the way Mira and Radha were worshipping Lord Krishna. Worship of Lord Rama is different. His *Daršan* can be had only by deep peep within self, because Almighty God is omnipresent, no need to search Him in temple or church. His pictures and stone replicas are only medium. The eyes of the worshiper automatically get closed when seriously seeking His *Daršan*. Rishis and Munis don't go to temple. They sit any where, preferably in silent lonely environment, to have His *Daršan* deep within self. Spirituality needs silence and loneliness to enjoy the unknown sparkling union with beloved God. Thinkers and philosophers of the west feel such light when they read ancient Vedic scriptures. Hindu ancient Vedic scriptures have vast deep ocean of knowledge, that no body, irrespective of his sociocultural and religious orientation, will be disappointed to get what he is looking for.

- **Henry David Thoreau, American Thinker & Author:**
  "Whenever I have read any part of the Vedas, I have felt that some unearthly and unknown light illuminated me. In the great teaching of the Vedas, there is no touch of sectarianism. It is of all ages, climbs, and nationalities and is the royal road for the attainment of the Great Knowledge. When I read it, I feel that I am under the spangled heavens of a summer night."

- **Will Durant, American historian:**
  "India was the motherland of our race, and Sanskrit the mother of Europe's languages. She was the mother of our philosophy; mother, through the Arabs, of much of our mathematics; mother, through the Buddha, of the ideals embodied in Christianity; mother, through the village community, of self-government and democracy. Mother India is in many ways the mother of us all."

- **R.W. Emerson, American Author:**
  "In the great books of India, an empire spoke to us, nothing small or unworthy, but large, serene, consistent, the voice of an old intelligence, which in another age and climate had pondered and thus disposed of the questions that exercise us."

- **Hu Shih, former Ambassador of China to USA:**
  "India conquered and dominated China culturally for 20 centuries without ever having to send a single soldier across her border."

- **Mark Twain, American author:**
  "India is the cradle of the human race, the birthplace of human speech, the mother of history, the grandmother of legend, and the great grand mother of tradition. Our most valuable and most instructive materials in the history of man are treasured up in India only."

- **Albert Einstein, American scientist:**
  "We owe a lot to the Indians, who taught us how to count, without which no worthwhile scientific discovery could have been made."

- **Max Müller, German scholar:**

  "If I were asked under what sky the human mind has most fully developed some of its choicest gifts, has most deeply pondered on the greatest problems of life, and has found solutions, I should point to India."

- **Romain Rolland, French scholar:**
  "If there is one place on the face of earth where all the dreams of living men have found a home from the very earliest days when man began the dream of existence, it is India."

- **Keith Bellows, National Geographic Society:**
  "There are some parts of the world that, once visited, get into your heart and won't go. For me, India is such a place. When I first visited, I was stunned by the richness of the land, by its lush beauty and exotic architecture, by its ability to overload the senses with the pure, concentrated intensity of its colors, smells, tastes, and sounds... I had been seeing the world in black & white and, when brought face-to-face with India, experienced everything re-rendered in brilliant technicolor."

- **A Rough Guide to India:**
  "It is impossible not to be astonished by India. Nowhere on Earth does humanity present itself in such a dizzying, creative burst of cultures and religions, races and tongues. Enriched by successive waves of migration and marauders from distant lands, every one of them left an indelible imprint which was absorbed into the Indian way of life. Every aspect of the country presents itself

on a massive, exaggerated scale, worthy in comparison only to the superlative mountains that overshadow it. It is this variety which provides a breathtaking ensemble for experiences that is uniquely Indian. Perhaps the only thing more difficult than to be indifferent to India would be to describe or understand India completely. There are perhaps very few nations in the world with the enormous variety that India has to offer. Modern day India represents the largest democracy in the world with a seamless picture of unity in diversity unparalleled anywhere else."

The main praise-worthy thrust in Hinduism is to enkindle the deep (light) of knowledge which is within self. According to Vedas knowledge is within self, it doesn't come from outside. Knowledge is *roshini* (light) which should never be extinguished. It is not extinguished even by death, because death is not end of life, but it is the beginning of new light in a new-born baby with clean non-polluted mind and heart. Whole mankind, particularly Europeans and Americans are open to such Vedic (Hindu) philosophy of life.

Chapter Fifteen

YOGA: ANSWER TO ALL AILMENTS

Yoga is not a religion, nor a religious thing. It was introduced by Vedic *Rishis* and *Munis* who realized its health-related – physical, emotional, psycho-social and psychiatric – benefits during millennia-long ancient times. It is rightly said "Necessity is the mother of invention." It is a blessing in disguise that advanced medicine was not available in ancient times which would have nipped Yoga in the bud. Rishis developed Yoga, as remedy of several ailments, not of only body, but also of mind, psyche and soul. Yoga is a broad-based answer to varied kinds of suffering of body as well of soul. Both body and soul suffer together and enjoy life together. The line between the two is too thin to separate body pains from psychic sufferings. Rishis understood it very well. Hence, Yoga addresses the sufferings not only of body, as commonly understood, but also of mind, psycho and soul. Yoga meditation helps in bringing *Atma* closer to *Paramatma*. Yoga helps man / woman to be one with self. It helps in controlling body and mind from slipping away from self, the abode of God.

Yoga is a broad-based effort to diminish the distance between self and the inner-self, the abode of God. Yoga helps in reestablishing one's relationship with God. Yoga helps in controlling mind and soul from drifting away from self. Yoga addresses not only the problems of the mind and the soul, but also the comprehensive needs of man, as evidenced by the following various kinds of Yoga:

- Jnāna (Gyan, knowledge) Yoga.
- Karma Yoga means desirable activity without which man is useless.

- Bhakti Yoga, Yoga of love and devotion. Without love, one would not love life.
- Rāja-Yoga is a *melāp* (comprehensive compound) of about eight actions and qualities to realize peace and tranquility of mind and soul.
- Hatha Yoga

Jnāna (Gyan, knowledge) Yoga

The fountain of knowledge is deep rooted within self, flooded with the wealth of wisdom, one would feel proud of. All knowledge – botanical, scientific, technological, warfare, social, psychological, political, cosmic, etc – is already within self which comes out whenever man makes adequate and appropriate effort. Only some gifted persons discover the knowledge within self and share it with mankind. These are called discoveries or inventions, not creations. Man has discovered lot, not yet all. There is still lot hidden within self. Man would need millennia years to unearth all the knowledge hidden within.

This reminds me of an incident in the classroom, I was teaching at the Faculty of Social Work, M.S. University of Baroda in about 1964. I told the students "Today I am going to teach you what you know." I fragmented the concept 'Listening' into pieces and put related questions – why difficult, why mis-listening, why and how it gets mis-listened and polluted, etc. I wrote answers on the Black Board. Then, I raised the question: "What did you learn about the concept 'Listening' as the tool for making right diagnosis?" Several students raised their fingers to answer. One student said "Listening gets corrupted by unconsciously associating its contents with own life experiences and relationships." It proves that they knew various aspects about 'Listening,' needed to be pulled out of their unconsciousness.

Thus, it can be theorized without any doubt that the knowledge of all the modern scientific and technological products had their seeds in the minds of earlier people, as evidenced by the following few:

- Plane, Rawana flew Sita to Sri Lanka.
- Sanjavini shrub, used to awaken fainted Lakshman.

- Shrubs like these modern medicines are made of.
- Lakshman Rekha, unable to understand what technologically it was to prevent Rawana from walking over.
- Ramsetu, under water tunnel to help Rama's army to walk through to reach Sri Lanka.
- TV, Sanjaya narrating happenings on the Krukshtra to the blind King Dhrutrashtra.
- Fire missiles, Agni Baans (fire arrows) used in Mahabharata war.
- Missiles to create night-like darkness to bring Jayadratha from his hide.
- Missiles to remove darkness, purposefully created by Krishna for Arjun to kill Jayadratha, the main agent of the Kaurva group to kill Abhimanyu, the son of Arjuna and Subhadra, nephew of Krishna. Subhadra was the sister of Lord Krishna.
- Target-designated missiles (Arrows). They had technology that the arrow, shot against Arjuna, would not hit Krishna, the Gdriver of the chariot, Arjuna was standing on. Amazing technology, used in the Mahabharata war (about 3138 B.C.).
- TV, plane, etc had their seeds in too distant ancient times, as evidenced by such examples in Ramayana (about 5114 BC and Mahabhharata (about 3228 BC).

Still several inventions are on the way to be realized as the products of earlier seeds of knowledge, yet to bloom as desired flowers.

Swami Vivekananda has vividly explained all yogas, with more emphasis on *Karma* Yoga and Jnāna (Gyan, knowledge) Yoga. Both yogas are connected too closely to separate them. The knowledge without karma becomes useless if not used to serve self, family, community and mankind. It has significant bearing on not only own life, but connecting self to serve the mankind. Without Karma (activity) man is useless. Bhagvad Gita emphasizes *Karma*, the right Karma, detached from *moha* for self or for the kith and kin. Lord Krishna, while on Mahabharata *krukshetra,* helped drowning Arjuna to come out from the deep well of *moha* (attachments with kith and kin) and do *Karma* in the interest of the society and mankind.

Swami Vivekananda, in the booklet "Karma Yoga and Bhakti Yoga (p.1) explains the mission of *Karma Yoga*:

> "The word Karma is derived from the Sanskrit Kri, to
> do; all action is Karma. ... But in Karma Yoga we have
> simply to do with the word karma as meaning work.
> The goal of mankind is knowledge; that is the one ideal
> placed before us by Eastern philosophy. Pleasure is not
> the goal of man, but knowledge."

Hatha Yoga[119] is an easy-to-learn basic form of yoga that has become very popular in the United States. Hatha Yoga is the foundation of all Yoga styles. It incorporates *Asanas* (postures), *Pranayama* (regulated breathing), meditation (*Dharana* & *Dhyana*) and kundalini *(Laya Yoga)* into a complete system that can be used to achieve enlightenment or self-realization. It has become very popular in America as source of exercise and stress management. The ideal way to practice the *Hatha Yoga* poses *(asanas)* is to approach the practice session in a calm, meditative mood. Sit quietly for a few moments, then begin the series, slowly, with control and grace, being inwardly aware as the body performs the various poses selected for the practice session. Do not overdo the *asanas* or try to compete with others. Take it easy and enjoy.

Ancient Rishis and Munis are also known as Yogi. Later, due to sophisticated knowledge of various kinds of illnesses, Yoga has come to be recognized as the 'science and art' of non-medicinal preventive approach to some illnesses. For example:

- Asthma can be prevented, reduced and even cured by some respiratory Yoga. Several years back, I was hospitalized for a few days because of asthma attacks. Now, it has been reduced to almost zero, due to regular morning breathing exercises (Yoga).
- Old-age aches and pains due to Arthritis can be reduced or even cured by regular exercises (Yoga) by relaxing and mobilizing joints of limbs.

---

[119] Wikipedia.

Yoga, if started in early childhood or young age, would prevent several old age sufferings. Medical, repertory and orthopedic doctors will be able to explain better the benefits of Yoga.

Origin of Yoga is in the millennia-old Vedas. If translated into English, Yoga means 'exercise' and if in Urdu (Persian-Arabic), it is *kasrat* or *varzash*. Yoga is a science and art of physical health and mental and psychological hygiene. Yoga is a wholesome system of exercises, designed to prevent various kinds of ailments, particularly orthopedic, respiratory and emotional. Yoga prevents rigidity of limbs and joints, cause for arthritis. It also teaches respiratory exercises to cure or prevent further asthma. Yoga rejuvenates the body, mind and psyche, prevents illnesses and prolongs healthy life. There is nothing of religion in it.

Moksha-nirvāna Yoga helps in achieving freedom from attachments, the common cause of emotional distress affecting mobility. Significant use of *Moksha Yoga* was historically done by Lord Krishna to relieve Arjuna from the *moha*-web which might have immobilized him to fight on *kurukshetra* for truth. Swami Vivekananda and several other philosophers have talked lot on '*moksha*' (*nirvana*). It is a quite common emotional or sentimental ailment.

Swami Vivekananda has talked about all kinds of Yoga, including Hath and Raj Yoga. Surprisingly, all this about Yoga, and much more is given in all other sacred scriptures, in different way and in different languages.

The scientific advantage of 'Surya Namaskar' needs to be understood. Looking at the rising sun through pouring water improves eyesight. There is no religion in it. The sun is globally beneficial to all irrespective of their religious orientations.

In conclusion, Yoga is irreligious and secular, beneficially affecting every man and woman, irrespective of their ethnic and religious orientation.

Prior to the UN declaration of June 21 as 'International Day of Yoga,' formal and informal groups of yoga teachers and enthusiasts have celebrated 'World Yoga Day' on various other dates. It was in a conference organized at 'The Art of Living International Centre' that a proposal for observing 21 June as the 'World Yoga Day' was made.

The conference, titled 'Yoga: A Science for World Peace' was held on December 4 and 5, 2011. It was organized by 'The Art of Living Foundation' and Deemed University, Bengaluru jointly with Portuguese Confederation of Lisbon, Portugal. According to Jagat Guru Amrta Suryananda, though the idea of observing World Yoga Day originated 10 years ago but this was the first time yoga gurus from India were endorsing it in large numbers. On that day, under the leadership of Sri Sri Ravi Shankar a proclamation was signed for having UN and UNESCO declare June 21 as the World Yoga Day.

UN Declaration of 'World Yoga Day'

On 11th December, India's Permanent Representative Asoke Mukherji introduced the draft resolution in UNGA. The draft text received broad support from 177 Member States who adopted the text without a vote. This initiative found support from many global leaders. A total of 175 nations co-sponsored the resolution and had the highest number of co-sponsors ever for any UNGA Resolution of such nature.

Following the adoption of the UN Resolution, Sri Sri Ravi Shankar lauded the efforts of PM Narendra Modi, stating:

"It is very difficult for any philosophy, religion or culture to survive without state patronage. Yoga has existed so far almost like an orphan. Now, official recognition by the UN would further spread the benefit of yoga to the entire world."

Emphasizing the importance of yoga, Sri Sri Ravi Shankar said: "Yoga makes you like a child again. When there is yoga and Vedanta, there is no lack, impurity, ignorance and injustice. We need to take yoga to the doorstep of everyone and free the world of misery."

First International Day of Yoga

The first international day of Yoga was observed world over on June 21, 2015. About 35985 people, including Indian Prime Minister Narendra Modi and a large number of dignitaries from 84 nations, performed 21

Yoga asanas (postures) for 35 minutes at Rajpath in New Delhi. The day devoted to Yoga was observed by millions across the world. The event at Rajpath established two Guinness world records awarded to 'Ministry of Ayush' received by Ayush Minister Shripad Yesso Naik.

It is so far historically the largest event, involving over 84 participating nations. It is believed that it will remain largest for centuries to come. When proposing the date, the PM Modi had said that the date was the longest day of the year in the northern hemisphere, having special significance in many parts of the world. However, June 21 also coincides with the death anniversary of Dr. Keshav Baliram Hegdewar, the founder of the Hindu Nationalist organisation the Rashtriya Swayamsevak Sangh (RSS) which is incidentally the ideological godfather of the ruling BJP party.

Yoga Culture in America[120]

Prime Minister, Narendra Modi, during his address to UN General Assembly in September 2014, had asked world leaders to adopt an international Yoga day, saying "Yoga embodies unity of mind and body; thought and action; restraint and fulfillment; harmony between man and nature; a holistic approach to health and well being." On December 11, 2014, the 193-member UN general assembly adopted a resolution by consensus, proclaiming June 21 as 'International Day of Yoga. 'The resolution was introduced by India's ambassador to UN and had 175 UN members, including five permanent members of the UN Security Council, as co-sponsors. Smithsonian, on October 19, 2013 opened an exhibition on Yoga, 'The Art of Transformation,' featuring temple sculptures, devotional icons, manuscripts and court paintings, created in India over the past 2,000 years was introduced. Several artifacts, displayed in the exhibit, were borrowed from 25 museums and private collections in India, Europe and the United States. Smithsonian also arranged guest teachers to teach Yoga on Wednesdays and Sundays during the exhibit days. A symposium on Yoga's visual culture was organized for scholars and enthusiasts. The exhibit was kept on view

---

[120] Mr. Inder Singh, Chairman of GOPIO, has vividly described how Yoga received popularity in America.

through Jan. 26, 2014, and then taken to the San Francisco Asian Art Museum for three months from February 21, 2014 to May 25, 2014. The Cleveland Museum of Art had the exhibit from June 22, 2014 to September 7, 2014. The White House has embraced Yoga as a worthy physical activity. The annual Easter Egg Roll is the largest public event held at the White House. President Barack Obama and First Lady Michelle Obama made 'Be Healthy, Be Active, Be You!' as the theme for the April 1, 2014 event. They also included a 'Yoga Garden' on the Presidential lawn for children and their parents who attended the traditional Easter Egg Roll festivities and arranged a Yoga session by professional instructors. The Obama family has turned the traditional event into an active family-oriented day, and included Yoga since 2009 as part of the celebration.

For the last several years, Yoga and meditation are becoming more acceptable in America. Americans have witnessed increase in Yoga-related studios, meditation centers and vegetarian restaurants, all of which have roots in Bharat. Several New Age gurus, who travel across the globe and the best-selling author Deepak Chopra have significantly enhanced the popularity Bharatiya meditation, philosophy and Yoga in America. Yoga was first introduced to America by Swami Vivekananda who came to USA in 1893 to address the World Parliament of Religions in Chicago. He made a lasting impact on the delegates and lectured at major universities and retreats during his stay of about four years. He started the Vedantic centre in New York in 1896 and taught Raja Yoga classes. He focused on the religious aspect of yoga, which dealt with how to use meditation to become closer to God. Paramahansa Yogananda came as India's delegate to the International Congress of Religious Leaders in Boston. He established Self-Realization Fellowship in Los Angeles. Today, there are seven SRF centers in California where Yogananda's meditation and Kriya Yoga techniques are taught on regular basis. Again, his Kriya yoga technique is for self-realization to reach God within. Maharishi Mahesh Yogi brought Yoga to the United States in 1959 in the form of Transcendental Meditation (TM). TM offered tangible Yoga and became popular in reducing stress and fatigue. During 1960s and 1970s, TM became most widely practiced self-development program in the United States. Yogi Bhajan came to California in 1969 and started teaching Kundalini Yoga, the 'Yoga of Awareness.' He was an inspiring teacher and developed a large following. Several of his followers became yoga teachers and some opened their yoga studios in various parts of the world, popularizing Yoga for health and fitness. Thus began Yoga evolution from spiritual to physical during the 1970s and 1980s. B.K.S. Iyengar, as considered one of the foremost Yoga teachers in the world, was the founder of "Iyengar Yoga." He was author of many books on Yoga and was often referred to as "the father of modern Yoga." His book 'Light on Yoga' is called the Bible of Yoga and has been the source book for yoga students. Iyengar brought yoga to the west in the 70s and started hundreds of Yoga centers, teaching Iyengar Yoga which focuses on the correct alignment of the body within each yoga pose, making use of straps, wooden blocks, and other objects as aids in achieving the correct postures. He was awarded the Padma Shri in 1991, the Padma Bhushan in 2002 and the Padma Vibhushan in 2014. Sri Sri Ravi Shankar established the international Art of Living Foundation in 1981, which is claimed to be operating in 140 countries. He has been promoting the Sudarshan Kriya, a rhythmic breathing Yoga exercise. Choudhary has earned fame and fortune by teaching Yoga to Americans by opening heated Yoga studios. His style of Yoga is practiced in a room that has been preheated to a temperature of 105 deg F. Bikram Yoga is the 26 postures Sequence selected and developed by Bikram Choudhary from Hatha Yoga and is taught in 500 certified yoga studios all over the world. Swami Ramdev is the most celebrated Yoga teacher and has following which runs into millions. He has revolutionalized people's thinking about yoga exercises. In 2003, India based Aastha TV began featuring him in its morning yoga slot. Within a few years, he attained immense popularity and developed a huge following. His yoga-camps are attended by a large number of people in Bharat and abroad. His *Pranayam* exercises, a set of breathing exercises are promoted to bring the balance between the body and mind. Regular practitioners claim numerous benefits. Yoga, once an elusive practice has surged in popularity and its impact is everywhere – in movies, television, advertising, and schools. Yoga is marketed as a series of *asanas* (postures) that make you fit and help in weight loss. Many Americans have incorporated Yoga routines as an essential part of their work out routine. America is now dotted with Yoga gyms and studios providing easy access to everyone, including business executives and Hollywood celebrities. Several studies have shown that yoga also reduces blood pressure, back pain, relieves stress and improves overall health. Several doctors recommend yoga to their cancer patients during and after treatment. As per a study by Yoga Journal in 2012, over twenty million people in America practice Yoga. Walking has also become as mainstream of an exercise. There are countless people who are seeing positive difference in their health through Yoga. Hundreds of Yoga websites have all kind of information about Yoga, from health and wellness to spirituality and show simple to complex poses. Yoga studios are mushrooming in cities across America. Several entrepreneurs are flourishing in this $30 billion industry. They publish Yoga magazines, Yoga books, produce TV shows, make DVDs, video games and apps, manufacture yoga clothes, Yoga artifacts, Yoga furniture and furnishings, Yoga foods, Yoga tea, Yoga energy bars, and hundreds of products and services, popularized as Yoga. There are also many Yoga experts and teachers who have gained prominence in this multi-billion dollar industry. The proliferation of Yoga schools, DVDs, and internet has made yoga easily accessible by one and all.

Yoga has gone through several ups and downs during the last fifty years but now has earned well deserved respect and recognition. At its core, Yoga is both a physical and spiritual practice. But for most Americans, Yoga is an exercise system that consists of a series of poses, postures and positions. Over twenty million Americans regularly practice some form of Yoga to stay fit and healthy.

About 17,000 people including people from the United Nations set out their mats and stretched into Yoga exercises in New York's Times Square to celebrate the first International Day of Yoga. The UN Secretary-General Ban Ki-moon, dressed in white, joined the Yoga gathering late in the morning in one of the most recognizable squares in the world. Ban hailed the many benefits, the ancient yoga exercises could bring to people around the world:

"To all of you I say: Namaste! My hope is that Yoga will give people everywhere the sense and the oneness

269

we need to work together to live in harmony and usher
in a life of dignity for all."

The UN had declared in December, 2014 that June 21 would be
International Yoga Day, highlighting its "health benefits" for the public.
New York City is seen below enjoying yoga celebration.

Controversies

Because of the intelligent wandering mind of man, nothing has been
without controversies and nothing will remain so for centuries to come,
rather until man is alive. Even God has not been spared. God has
been inflicted by controversies. For some God is dead. To avoid the
controversy over *'Surya Namaskar,'* though ill-based, it was removed
from the official yoga program. The government of India declared that
chanting *'shlokas'* during 'International Yoga Day' was not "compulsory"
and appealed to Muslims to participate in the event. Shripad Naik,
Minister for AYUSH, said Muslims can "take the name of Allah instead
of reciting *'shlokas'* during the event. The All India Muslim Personal
Law Board was against performance of *Surya Namaskar,* because it was
against their religion. It is said that God has been divided into several
different entities, as many as languages. If God is one, Allah can not be
different from God or Ishwar. Even in Urdu or Arabic, God is known
differently by different names, like Allah, Khuda, Parvardigar, etc.

'Surya Namskar' means salutation to the sun or 'Sajda to Suraj' in
Urdu. The sun, like God, is secular. There is only one sun. In Sanskrit
it is Surya, in English it is sun, in Urdu it is Suraj and so on different
in different languages; so 'Surya Namaskar' in Sanskrit, 'salutation to
sun' in English, and 'Salaame Suraj' in Urdu. There is no sun – Hindu,
Christian or Islamic – as communally perceived. The sun gives light and
warmth to whole mankind, irrespective of any religious, linguistic or
ethnic orientation. The sun is communal only when God is communal.
Only communal-minded persons subjectively perceive 'Surya Namaskar'
as Hindu. It is said that narrow-minded devotees of God subjectively
constrict down God's providence as based on religion. Allah, God and
Ishwar are different names of one and the same Almighty God of all

the mankind. Language should not constrict His providence. Hindus salute the sun in early morning by pouring water it is scientifically true that looking at the sun through pouring water, would help eyesight.

Prior to the UN declaration of June 21 as International Day of Yoga, formal as well as informal groups of yoga teachers and enthusiasts have celebrated the 'World Yoga Day' on various other dates. It was in the conference organized at 'The Art of Living International Centre' that a proposal for observing 21st June as the 'World Yoga Day' was made. It was attended by the representatives of 84 nations. When proposing the date, PM Modi said that the date was the longest day of the year in the northern hemisphere, having special significance in many parts of the world. However, June 21 also coincides with the death anniversary of Keshav Baliram Hegdewar, the founder of the Hindu Nationalist organisation the Rashtriya Swayamsevak Sangh (RSS) which is incidentally the ideological godfather of the ruling party the BJP.

To avoid controversy over the 'Surya Namaskar,' it was removed from the official Yoga program. Chanting 'shlokas' during 'International Yoga Day' was not compulsory so that Muslims would participate in the event. Shripad Naik, Minister for AYUSH, said Muslims can "take the name of Allah instead of reciting 'shlokas'" during the event.

The All India Muslim Personal Law Board was against performance of Surya Namaskar, perceiving it as against their religion. 'Surya Namaskar' (salute to the sun), if objectively seen, is secular because *surya* (the sun) is universal and secular. The sun gives *roshni* (light) and warmth to all mankind, irrespective of their religious orientations.

HINDUISM, ZOROASTRIANISM, CHRISTIANITY

The Zoroastrianism of Iran can be understood better only in the light of ancient historical relationships (i) between India and Iran, (ii) between Sanskrit and Avestan and (iii) Vedas and Avesta.

The Avesta is close to the Vedas. Its language Avestan was too close to Sanskrit to distinguish one from the other. It is a historical fact that the Persian, the language of Persia (Iran), has its origin in Sanskrit. The authors of the Vedas and worshippers of Ahuro Mazdao did live together in early ancient times. India, including Persia (Iran), was the original home of the Aryans and the Persians (Iranians). As a matter of fact, in remote ancient times, Iran was a part of Greater India (Vishaal Bharat). Both the languages, Sanskrit and Zend-Avestan, were linguistically too close to consider them as two different languages.

J. P. Mallory[121] has shown close linguistic relationship between Sanskrit and Iran's Avestan:

Avestan:	tem amavantem yazatem
Sanskrit:	tam amavantam yajatam

Avestan:	surem damohu sevistem
Sanskrit:	suram dhamasu savistham

---

[121] J.P. Mallory, Search of Indo-Europeans (1989, p.35) and Burrow, T. The Sanskrit Language. Delhi: Motilal Banarsidas Publishers, (2001, p.4).

Avestan: mithrem yazai zaothrabyo
Sanskrit: mitram yajai hotrabhyah

Mallory (p. 35) remarks:

"The concept of a common Indo-Iranian language is indicated by the close similarities between these Indic (Sanskrit) translations of an early Iranian hymn. The god Mitra / Mithra was common to both Indians and Iranians."

In fact, these are not translations. The same Sanskrit was spoken in Avestan with little difference in phonetic pronunciation of some letters. For example:

Sanskrit	Avestan
'j'	'z'
'h'	's'
'dh'	'd'
'th'	't'
'bh'	'b'

Same way, Iranians pronounced 'Sindhu' as 'Hindu', and 'soma' as' homa'. Dr. Poonai[122] writes about the relationship between Sanskrit and the Zend-Avestan:

"It has also been shown on the basis of statements which have been made in the oldest of the Gathas of the Zend Avesta, about mantras and personalities of the Rig Veda, that the Rig Veda predates the Gathas by several millennia and that the Vedas appear to have contributed to the content of the earliest Gathas by accumulation of concepts."

---

[122]   Dr. Poonai, Origin of Civilization and Language (1994, p. 220)

The word *'Gathas'* has its origin in Sanskrit. It literally means 'stories'. Nehru[123] writes about the relationship between Sanskrit and Avestan:

> "Even the language of the Vedas bears a striking resemblance to that of the Avesta, and it has been remarked that Avesta is nearer to the Veda than the Veda is to its own epic Sanskrit."

Max Müller[124] remarks about Sanskrit and Avestan:

> "Sanskrit and Zend share certain words and grammatical forms in common which do not exist in any other Aryan languages; and there can be no doubt that the ancestors of the poets of the Vedas and the worshippers of A*huro Mazdao* lived together for some time after they had left the original home of the whole Aryan race."

Very close linguistic correspondence between Sanskrit and Avestan words, as shown above, will puzzle many to think if Avestan and Sanskrit are two different languages.

Will Durant, in *'Our Oriental Heritage'* (p.406), remarks that Sanskrit was a near relative of the early Persian dialect in which the Avesta was composed.

Benjamin Walker[125] writes about inter-mixing of Old Iranian and Indian (Hindu) gods and deities.

Max Müller[126] talks about close relationship between Sanskrit and Avesta's Zend:

> "Sanskrit and Zend share certain words and grammatical forms in common which do not exist in any other Aryan languages; and there can be no doubt that the ancestors of the poets of the Vedas and the worshippers of A*huro*

[123] Nehru, in 'Discovery of India' (1946, p.77).
[124] Max Müller, in 'Science of Language' (1861, p.289),
[125] Benjamin Walker, in 'The Hindu World: An Encyclopedic Survey of Hinduism' (vol. 2, p 353)
[126] Max Müller, 'The Science of Language' (1891, p. 289).

mazdao lived together for some time after they had left the original home of the whole Aryan race."

Max Müller (1891, p. 293) remarks: "Now *Airya* in Zend (like in Sanskrit) means venerable, and is at the same time the name of the people."[127] He (p. 292) remarks: "In India, as we saw, the name of Arya, as a national name."

Max Müller (1891, p. 287) writes that Pushtu was more closely related with languages of India;

> "The language of the Afghans, the Pushtu, and Paktyes of Herodotus, which was formerly classed as an Iranian dialect, has been proved by Trumpp to be more closely related with the vernaculars of India than of Persia."[128]

'Gāthās' (hymns/mantras of the Avesta) is a Sanskritic word, meaning stories. Both Hindus and Zoroastrians worship fire, and both wear sacred thread – *Janeoo* (Hindus) and *Kasti*[129] (Zoroastrians). Hindus wear *Janeoo* hanging from the shoulder, and Zoroastrians wear *Kasti* around the waist. Unlike Hindus, Zoroastrian (Parsi) girls also wear Kasti. Like Hindu Brahmin, Parsi 'Dastur' performs the rituals. Zoroastrians, like Hindus, believe in 'after life.' Both Hindus and Zoroastrians, unlike Christians, sit on the floor to pray.

Avestan "Vohu Mana" means good mind. 'Mana', in Sanskrit, means mind. The Avestan 'Asha' (the spirit of truth) means 'hope' in Sanskrit. Iran was a land of Aryans.

Hard to understand what Max Müller meant by the "original home of the whole Aryan race." I think, Max Müller meant Greater India when Iran remained as its part, until Iran was captured and occupied by other forces. Aryans (Hindus) and Persians (Iranians) did not leave India (the original home of the whole Aryan race). Some Avestan-speaking

---

[127] Lassen, Ind. Alt. b. i. s. 6.

[128] Trumpp, in the Journal of the German Oriental Society, vols xxi and xxii; also Grammar of Pushtu, 1878.

[129] Grateful to my friend Mr. Rustam Alamshaw for this authentic information.

Zoroastrians had to leave Iran for Sanskrit-speaking India, when Iran was captured by Muslims. Most of them stayed there in Iran.

It can be understood better from the event 'Partition of India in 1947' when Muslims had Pakistan. Many Muslims opted to continue to live in India, and even some migrated back from Pakistan to India. So it happened with Zoroastrian Iranians. The ancient relationship between Iran and Bharat is discussed in detail later in Chapter "Iran: A Part of Ancient India.".

Dr. Poonai (p.226) gives genealogic time trend of some important IE languages:

Language Group	Approximate time of origin
Rig-Vedic Sanskrit	9000 B.C.
Zend	1500 B.C.
Greek dialects	800 B.C.
Latin languages	400 B.C.
Celtic languages	500 B.C.
Germanic languages	350 A.D.
Baltic languages	1100 A.D.

Mallory (1989, p.15) also has placed Indo-Iranian (Iranian and Indic) as the oldest group of the Indo-European languages, around 1500 B.C., along with Anatolian languages, such as Luwian, Hittite and Palaic.

Hinduism and Christianity: Freedom compared

Pope Benedict XVI, addressing the American visiting Catholic bishops at the Vatican City on January 19, 2012, expressed his concerns about the "grave threats" to Christianity, posed by what he called radical religious secularism, challenging the roots of Cat holism. Pope stressed that Roman Catholics in the U.S. need to understand the "grave threats" to their faith posed by what he calls radical secularism in the political and cultural arenas, referring to gay marriages, which, in his opinion, is marginalizing their religious freedom. It is hard to understand whether he was preferring 'religious freedom' or 'religious dictation'.

In my opinion, both Hinduism and Christianity are liberal and champions of religious freedom. Conservatism in a religion should not confuse us about the freedom in it. Religion should be well understood only when measured on the scale ranging from conservatism to liberalism.

Chapter Seventeen

SIGNIFICANCE OF FIRE, EDUCATION AND VENERATION OF ANIMALS

Hindus[130] and the followers of Buddhism, Jainism and Sikhism – the offshoots of Hinduism – use cremation as the way of disposal of the dead. According to the Columbia Encyclopedia, cremation, as a mode of disposal of a corpse by fire is often related to the belief in the properties of fire as a purifying agent. The manner of disposal of the ashes varies in different parts of the world. Hindus, for whom cremation is the typical form of the disposal of the ashes, place them in urn and after some religious rituals; immerse them into a river, preferably the sacred Ganges. If possible, now some Hindus, living abroad may immerse them into the near by sea, river or lake.

I would like to talk about Hindu respect for knowledge and worship of fire as a sacred purifying agent, on the basis of my childhood experiences and observations. My father would insist that a page or pages from a book, especially from a religious book, should be disposed off only in fire. Same way, when a bit of food or of *persād,* blessed by religious rituals, like *Kanah Sahib*, the religious *persād* of Sikhism, accidently falls down on the floor, it should be disposed off in fire, not in a garbage can. It is not only for purifying reason, but also for our respect for the religious food. Hinduism puts extraordinary emphasis on knowledge or *vidyā* (education). Veda means knowledge. I, as a child, read in an early school text book, that an interviewing committee to select a teacher for its school, deliberately, left a book in the room on the floor on the way

---

130 Hindus, when talked about, mean Hindus, Jain, Buddhists, and Sikhs, the followers of Jainism, Buddhism and Sikhism, the offshoots of Hinduism.

from its entrance to the table where interviewing officials were sitting. Only one candidate picked it up, kissed it and respectfully placed it on the table before she took her seat to be interviewed. She was selected because the selection committee was convinced that she had respect for the knowledge, she was being selected for, to give to her students. In Sanskrit, student is known as *'Vidyārthi'*. The paradigm of – 'Vedas', 'Vidyā', 'Vidyārthi' – would explain why Indians, particularly Hindus, have been productively successful all over the planet. Other religions, which are open and broadminded, might have learnt the significance for knowledge from the Vedas, the oldest scriptures of the humanity.

Religious Significance of Fire

All Vedic (Hindu) religious ceremonies – nomenclature, *Janeyoo* (sacred thread), wedding, funeral and the rest – are not performed without invocation of the goddess *Agni* (fire).

S. R. Rao, in *'Dawn and Development of the Indus Civilization'* (1991, p.121), talks about the worship of the 'Goddess Fire' and Mother Goddess. He makes a very interesting remark:

> "There is no evidence for assuming a religion-dominated state in the Indus Empire though fire worship and veneration of animals were common."

How could the animal sacrifice be practiced among the pre-history Vedic people (Hindus) who venerated animals, and people in general were vegetarian? Present Vedic people (Hindus) in general, even after millennia-years of Vedic customs, have retained their tradition of vegetarianism and ahimsa. In present times, non-vegetarianism is not considered a celebrated habit among Hindus. Vegetarianism is considered as a virtue. In matrimonial matter, the candidate groom, if vegetarian, earns more marks.

Non-vegetarianism has been there since the birth of the humanity in varying degrees from society to society. Most Hindus, unlike Christians and Muslims, are generally vegetarian. Globali-zation, with its emphasis on healthy food, has been influencing eating habits with increasing emphasis on vegetarianism. Among Hindus, non-vegetarianism has been increasing as the result of the Christian and Islamic influence and the knowledge of its benefits. Each cuisine has good as well as bad effects, depending on the amount and frequency of its intake. Among Christians as well as Muslims there may be some vegetarian.

Hindus, Jains, Buddhists and Sikhs believe in Ahimsa (non-violence). They don't serve non-veg food on sacred days and never in temples and Gurudwaras. Mahatma Gandhi was a world-known champion of Ahimsa and vegetarianism. For Hindus Ahimsa is 'paramo-dharma', meaning 'Prime religion'. It is not known which word has been miss-interpreted or miss-translated as 'animal sacrifice' in Hinduism. In ancient times some were non-vegetarian. Butcher slaughter places, as archaeologically excavated in the Indus Valley, have been wrongly viewed as sacrificial altars. Were not those sacrificial animals eaten? Why then killing animals in present times is not considered as 'animal sacrifice'? What is the difference? Does archaeology show any religious rituals associated with the killing mode of the sacrifice animals? Does any Hindu sacred scripture describe 'Animal Sacrifice' along with religious rituals? This seems to be another way to demean Hinduism by colonial historians. Would God, the giver of life and the protector of the living creatures, be happy to receive the meat of a slaughtered animal as an offering? Only the historian, who thinks that way, could qualify to be a butcher of knowledge.

Interpolations in Manu Smrities regarding Meat-Eating[131]

It is historically known that the colonial British rulers wrote the histories of their colonized peoples to demean them and their heritage to weaken their ethnic ego so as they could rule them for ever, at least longer. They did more with the history and the sacred scriptures of Hindus. They very well knew that India, when independent, will rise and surpass every country, even the mightiest Britain. In order to make the corrupted history believable, they got it written by some prominent scholar, but greedy, who would be willing to reinterpret some content to demean

---

[131] "The True History and the Religion of India" by Swami Prakashanand Saraswati (2000, pp. 220-332).

the sacred Vedic scriptures, he himself is proud of. Money can do any thing; even buy the integrity of the historians. The British government did not buy it with British pounds, but by Indian rupees and to get the enemy be killed by him with his own gun. The British were getting Indian freedom fighters killed by Indians with the guns, bought by Indian rupees. Over and above they looted India to its bones. This way the British and other Europeans – French, German, Portuguese and Spanish – ruled India for over two centuries with little loss of their funds and lives. This impossible turned out to be possible only because of Hindu infighting, mostly on the basis of language and more so by the ill-based theory of 'Aryan invasion of India', according to which only the dark skin Dravidians were the original natives and their Dravidian languages were the original languages of India. Fair-looking North Indians were Aryans who invaded India in about 1500 BC and brought in Sanskrit and a pantheon of gods and later they composed the Vedas. Aryans (present Hindus) were the original natives of India and thus India in prehistory ancient India was known as Aryavarta or Aryadesh. The word 'Arya' has appeared in Vedas several times and it has not appeared in Bible or in any other sacred book. No other country has or had Aryans any times as its nationals.

Manu Smriti misrepresented and distorted

In Manu Smriti, there is description of some meat-eating people. Impious statements of animal killing and meat eating were interpolated in Manu Smriti telling that meat was served during *Shradh,* a pious religious ceremony related to the appeasement of the soul of the deceased elderly member of the family. In the pious *Shradh* ceremony, Brahmins are invited to dine. Only vegetarian food and fruits are served. But, the statements related to some meat-eating people in the *Smriti* were interpolated to show that meat was served at even the *Shradh* ceremony.

Every year, we have *Shradhs* in our family to remember our dear departed souls. This is the occasion when the whole day we eat and serve only vegetarian food and fruits, though we are non-vegetarian. I remember *Shradhs* from my childhood. This is a way to let children know our heritage – who were our great-great-grand parents, what their great attitudes were and what great things they did. History of family has lessons for children. Absence of such family ceremony will put an end to the knowledge and remembering of the family ancestors.

But the Britain erred. It failed to understand the significance of the oral traditions of Hindus which protected Vedic knowledge from being corrupted by mischievous interpolations. Moreover, the British rulers wanted to anglicize Hindus through English education. But, English education was too expensive for rural and for most urban people.

Is non-vegetarianism, animal sacrifice?

It would be wrong to characterize non-vegetarianism as a custom of animal sacrifice. It is hard to believe that any civilized society would like to entertain the custom of animal sacrifice, mean that a slaughtered animal be solemnized by some religious rituals to offer it to God. No religion would pronounce killing as sacred. Religion should not be maligned. Religion teaches to protect life and it prescribes civilization.

Western historians – some because of their absence of correct understanding of the main Indic language (Sanskrit), and some with their missionary agenda – have misinterpreted Sanskrit words to justify their biased perspectives on Hinduism. For example, the word *'Ashvamedh'* has been miss-interpreted. *Ashvamedh* is a very well known *Yagya*[132], mentioned in various Vedic scriptures. It was a well-known royal custom in ancient times when country was divided into several town-size small kingdoms. A horse – well adorned and ritually worshipped with Vedic Mantras – was let free by a mighty king to roam around in nearby small kingdoms to assert his lordship over them. The horse was followed by a group of well-armed warriors. The king in whose territory the horse entered had either to accept subordination or to put up fight.

It is well known that European colonialists, particularly British, used to mistranslate or to get mistranslated the sacred scriptures of their colonized peoples to pursue their mischievous colonial agenda by disgracing their culture to infuse in them low self-image to make it easier to get own European moral and cultural superiority accepted, the first step to get royal authority accepted. Political pundits have

---

[132]   3.Swami Prakashanand Sarswati, 'The True History of the Religion of India'

said: "If you want to establish your rule over some people, you have to weaken them by maligning their culture and heritage." So Britain did with the people they conquered. They were smart. They used to heavily bribe Sanskrit pundits to interpret words and sentences to suit their missionary agenda. They even got Sanskrit Vachaspatyam (dictionary) authored by some bribed Pundit. Max Müller wrote about the Vedas according to such dictionary[133]. Out of many, I am giving only two words –'*ashhvamedh*' and '*goghn*' – will explain my point.

Ashvamedh (Ashva = horse and medh means to kill) the horse to kill not be killed. How the king will order to kill the horse which made his mission successful.

The other word 'goghn' has also been misinterpreted to demean Hinduism. In fact, in Sanskrit 'go' means cow and 'ghn' means receiver of cow in charity. But it has been miss-interpreted as the 'killer' of the cow. How would Hindus kill cow which is being worshipped as mother from the birth of Hinduism? Hindus adore cow as mother because it gives milk? In Hindustan slaughter a cow is crime.

Money can buy any thing, even conscience and religion. The renowned Pundit Taranath of Calcutta Sanskrit College, in his *Vachaspatyam* (Dictionary) defied the accepted meanings of both the words, '*Ashvamedh*' and '*goghn*'.

Surprising, history professor Stanley Wolpert, in *A New History of India*' (1997, p.25), miss-translates the word '*dasa*' as 'slave'. The professor of history should have known the history and antiquity of the slavery. It does not have a long history. The shameful inhuman slavery is mainly associated with the Western people of Europe and America. Only rich and strong man or nation can have courage to do such shameful thing. Moreover, Wolpert should have known the exact dictionary meaning of '*dasa*' and the education system of ancient India. In Hindu educational traditions, the word '*dasa*' means '*sewak*' or servant who voluntarily stayed at the residence of his guru for education during the first stage (ā*shram),* known as *Brahmcharya,* of his life during which he was supposed to strictly observe celibacy to earn the knowledge of the Vedas and other sacred Vedic scriptures with uninterrupted guidance of his learned guru. He stays at Guru's house as a student, not as a slave.

---

[133]   Ibid. p. 274.

He returns home after his education is over to start the second ashram of life, known as 'Grahsta' (family). The Dasas were not slaves, sold and bought. They were shewaks (servants), rather students to learn Vedic knowledge. Their service to their guru was as if the tuition for their vidya (education).

Hindu life is divided into four *āshrams* – Brahamcharya, Grahastha, Vaishya and Sanyas. During his *brahamcharya āshram,* one is supposed to live at his guru's (teacher's) residence. Naturally he, as his student, would serve his guru at whose house he is staying as a member of the family. Misrepresentation of such an important historical institution of *Brahmcharya* as slavery is abuse of history.

Wolpert's (p.25) statement that the *Rig Veda* is "the world's earliest surviving Indo-European literature" contradicts his conviction in the theory of 'Aryan invasion of India', according to which Sanskrit, the language of the Rig Veda, came to India from outside.

Yueh-chi: "Wonderful assimilative power of Hinduism."

It would be interesting to know what Nehru[134] has said about Dodwell and Yueh-chi who have explained how the basic Indian culture has been growing because of Indian processes of synthesis, fusion, inclusion, absorption and assimilation:

> "Out of this synthesis and fusion grew the Indian races and the basic Indian culture, which had distinctive elements of both. In the ages that followed there came many other races: Iranians, Greeks, Parthians, Bactrians, Synthians, Huns, Turks, (before Islam), early Christians, Jews, Zoroastrians (Parsee); they came, made difference, and were absorbed. India was, according to Dodwell, 'infinitely absorbent like the ocean'. It is odd to think of India, with her caste system and exclusiveness, having this astonishing inclusive capacity to absorb foreign races and cultures. Perhaps it was due to this that she retained her vitality and

---

[134] Nehru, op. cit. pp. 73-74.

rejuvenated herself from time to time. The Muslims, when they came, were also powerfully affected by her. 'The foreigners (Muslim Turks),' says Vincent Smith, 'like their forerunners the Sakas and the Yueh-chi, universally yielded to the wonderful assimilative power of Hinduism, and rapidly became Hinduised."

Immigrant whosoever from India was called Hindu

It seems Nehru did not approve Smith's use of the words 'Hinduism' and 'Hinduised'. Nehru remarked: "I do not think that Smith meant to associate these words with a narrower, specifically religious concept." Earlier in 20th century, in America, France and some other Western countries, 'Hindu' was synonymously used for 'Indian', meaning a native of India, not a person who practices Hinduism. Who-so-ever came from India, irrespective of his/her religious affinity, was called 'Hindu'. This also is true that foreigners (Christians, Muslims, Parsees, Jews), who have settled in India permanently, have significantly (not completely) assimilated in the mainstream Indian (Hindu-like) culture. They have not assimilated in those cultural areas which are closely associated with their religion. The Indian constitution allows them full freedom to practice their religion completely the way they want.

Some, like Zoroastrians, have been in India for numerous generations, having faint memory of their heritage. They have no intention of returning to the country of their roots which have distanced from their mind and heart. They even do not know 'what' and 'where' their roots are. This has been the main reason for their easy assimilation, as Zoroastrians (Parsies) have done. They have faint sentiment for their distanced forgotten roots.

Therefore, some Parsies, like Ratan Tata, have willingly accepted Hindu names. There has been little resistance to intermarriages. In addition to their long cohabitation, religio-cultural resemblance between Hinduism and Zoroastrianism has provided impetus to their increasing closeness. Both worship fire and both wear sacred threat, Hindus Janeoo from shoulder and Parsis wear 'Kasti' around waist. Both believe in 'after life'. Both have heavy sentiment for their respective religion and origins.

Other reasons for their assimilation are conversions, inter-marriages, cinema and development of a few 'inter-religion' religions such as Sikhism, Sufism and Ismailia, which, in my opinion, have diluted the communal poison. I am using the word 'inter-religion' for them, because their philosophies were created with their sacred intention to narrow down the distance/differences between India's two major religions Hinduism and Islam, whose adherents, some times, get into violent conflict with each other. Sindhi Hindus as well as Sindhi Muslims were significantly influenced by both – Sikhism and Sufism – which bettered relations between them, much better than in other states. In Sind, the communal relations made undesirable turn which was effected by foreign elements in Sindh – immigration of Muslims from other states – as the result of the partition of India.

I would like to call it unconscious assimilation. If you make a Muslim conscious that he has adopted such and such thing from Hindus, he would vehemently and angrily deny it. So is true with Hindus and others. There is a very thin line between religion and culture. In India, religion has been a problem, though culturally Hindus and Muslims are not much different.

AYURVEDA

Ayurveda, known as the "science of life" in ancient Sanskrit, has been a key part of a comprehensive natural system of living in ancient Bhārat and Sri Lanka for centuries. The basic tenet of Ayurveda is that illnesses be treated with holistic, natural therapies, meaning by natural Ayurvedic herbs, messages and Yoga, balancing the mind and soul in harmony. The Ayurvedic approach keeps the patient psychologically distant from worrying about his / her illness. Psychology has minimal place in allopathic therapies. On the contrary patient and his / her family legally are supposed to know all about the nature and prognosis of the illness.

Most Allopathic medicines, unlike the Aurvedic and Homeopathic, have side effects which may create other problems. Natural therapy, by its herbal ingredients, has no side effects. Its effect may be slower than the use of allopathic medicine. In addition to supplementing the physical body with herbs, Ayurveda focuses on balancing the mind and soul to achieve inner harmony.

Ayurveda teaches that each person is a blend of three doshas (vital energies) within the body – Vata, Pitta and Kapha. Each person is born with an optimal balance and a unique harmony among the three doshas. Later in life, negative health may arise from an imbalance in the three doshas, and the science of Ayurveda is used to bring back this essential harmony.

Unlike the Western approach to health which tends to be more reactive, Ayurveda is used to strengthen and nourish the body *before* the onset of negative health conditions. Ayurvedic practitioners typically recommend a natural course of herbs, diet, exercise and meditation to bring harmony back to the individual. This may be accomplished with a regimen of natural herbs which focus on bringing the three doshas back into balance. In returning the mind, body and spirit back to its original dosha balance, Ayurvedic practitioners believe that an individual is better able to strengthen the body's health while living a more pleasant, harmonious life.

The world seems increasing interested in Ayurveda, as evidenced by the 6th World Ayurveda Congress, organized by the World Ayurveda Foundation in New Delhi from November 6-9, 2014, overarching the theme of 'Health Challenges and Ayurveda.' More than 4000 delegates from around the world congregated to discuss various topics on Ayurveda with the goal of making it an integral part of the global healthcare system because it has no side effects as allopathic medicines in general have.

PM Narendra Modi on Ayurveda

At the 6th World Ayurvedic Congress, India's Prime Minister Narendra Modi, explained vividly the ancient Ayurvedic health system to give a major impetus to the advance and adoption of Ayurveda.

In his valedictory address, India's Prime Minister Narendra Modi spoke about the ways we can bring acceptance and recognition for Ayurveda as a complete healthcare system adoptable in countries across the world. Ayurvedic healer Charaka studied at Taxila University.

Valedictory Address by Hon. PM Narendra Modi

My colleague and Cabinet Minister Dr. Harsh Vardhan ji, all the respected members sharing the stage and gathering dedicated to Ayurveda! It was being announced that a brainstorm-churning has happened here for three days and elixir of life has been found. So I have also come to take this elixir so that few drops would come in my fate and I don't know whether I would get it a full pitcher or not. This time the theme is something like "Health Challenges and Ayurveda". Isn't it? You must have discussed on a variety of points but to me the biggest challenges are we, the people attached to Ayurveda. It is hard to find

Ayurveda-doctor who is 100% dedicated to it. Even they realize that they can't make it through this path and that they have to take the path to Allopathy. So they ask patients to start with Allopathic medicines for first three days and Ayuvedic treatment can be taken care of in successive stages. I feel this mentality is the extraordinary challenge against Ayurveda. If these persons practicing Ayurveda would not be committed, devoted and confident then how those patients would trust them?

When I was a kid, there was a joke in circulation that a traveler went to a city. He visited a restaurant and asked to see the owner. He was told that the owner has gone to take a meal in a restaurant across the road. Now think who would like to eat in such restaurant? They can't win the trust of others, who don't believe in themselves and their traditions. Crisis is not of the "Ayurveda", but its practitioners. I don't know how do you take this discussion, in a pleasant or bitter way? But if it is bitter, then I think that I am referring the matter exactly according to the norms of Ayurveda because in Ayurveda what tastes bitter at first turns sweet ultimately.

I have been meeting many people and talking to them. Last time when I was Chief Minister of Gujarat, I had called meeting of specialists of Ayurveda. This was not my domain at that time and I was working within the state of Gujarat, but there was a need of awareness about Ayurveda. Ayurveda is not a field to be limited to a certified doctor. Our ancestors have made health, a part of our life. Today we have outsourced our health and lifestyle. Those days, health was not outsourced. It was part of lifestyle and due to that every person, every family was aware about wellness of body. If any problem would pop up, then what could be possible solutions, people were conscious about that too. Even today you must be feeling that experience.

At times when you are travelling in a train or bus and suppose a baby is crying a lot, you must have observed that 12-15 persons would come there and they would provide a variety of suggestive measures. One would say to give a dose of something, another would suggest some different dosage and third would even take out some packet asking to give a dose of that. We don't even ask who that person was, whether he was a doctor or not. But when he assures us, we believe him that by giving that dose would bring relief to her as the baby is in pain and crying and he might have a solution to this. We see these very often in course of our journey in a train or bus that if a co-passenger falls sick then one or other passenger would come over and treat him, even when he or she is not a designated doctor or specialist in Ayurveda, nor a graduate in Ayurveda from Jamnagar University. But because this has been a natural practise in India and a habit incubated under traditions, we have some knowledge of it. Gradually we outsourced the complete health sector. If any medical problem crops up, we have to take advice and consultation and we have to go according to prescription. If that treatment is successful then it alright otherwise we go to other practitioner...we change the consultancy.

The first and only necessity for the solution of this problem is that we should not compromise our core sector, let me be a student of Ayurveda, a teacher of Ayurveda or engaged in manufacturing of Ayurveda medicine or a promoter of holistic healthcare. We should be 100% committed to what we do, only then we will start seeing the results. Some negative circumstances have been encountered, due to which tired and desperate people are traversing back to the basics in the name of "Holistic health care". They are feeling that modern era medical science might give instant relief but it doesn't guarantee a healthy body as a whole. If at all we want the assurances of health, we would have to choose holistic approach. Be it naturopathy, Ayurveda, strict diet-control method or homeopathy; there is always a way in that direction and perhaps that is why Ayurveda is known to us as "Panchamveda". It has been valued and nurtured as such. There is not a part from the root to the fruit of a tree in nature which doesn't find a valuable position in Ayurveda. From the root to the fruit is a great deal and it means our ancestors must have had a microscopic study of attributes, its nature, its utility in practice. And after all those extraneous work they would have reached the miraculous position. How do we keep that great resource in modern times is the second challenge to us. It is not possible for us to wait for this world to learn Sanskrit language and then accept the preparative. But the least we could do is to translate the exalted resource in the language this world understands. So the workforce engaged in this industry should be motivated to do the research in the area with a time limit under an institutional framework and present all the research works.

Third point is regarding research articles published in science magazines all over the world. Can't we altogether launch a movement and try to put some pressure and also encourage people involved in this sector to publish a research article in every Ayurvedic session...make them a part of curriculum. One should be made to write an essay or article in modern terminologies with a profound study on a subject for once at the interval of every two year if he or she is a professor and in case of a student, in the final year of their education. And it should be published in international magazines or we should better say that 10% of all the space in the magazines of international medicine should be dedicated to Ayurveda. We would have our research articles at par though differently. If we could find a place for our research articles in at international forum then world working on medical science would notice it. If we would dedicate 20% of our work and 20% of spaces would be dedicated to Ayurvedic research articles then the world reading modern medical science would notice it eventually, and may be this would change the perspective of modern medical scientists in a positive way. I feel this might crystallize into a new stimulant to give new directions to Ayurveda.

But for this there should be a proper follow-up and identification of medical science magazines available globally. We also need to find out if among all those magazines whether or not Ayurveda has a place. And if Ayurveda is to given some space right there, then someone would have to discuss this and keep following it up with the concerned. In a sense we have to launch a movement that where there is a global acceptance, how we carve a niche for us there. Till a matter doesn't reach to us via America, we don't usually accept the same, and it's become a human tendency and in particular a feature of our fellow countrymen after 1200 yearlong slavery it has penetrated deep into our veins. So if an article is published in an international magazine then rest assured that the Ayurvedic doctor would adorn his drawing room wall with his photo frame. I don't know if people associated with Ayurveda have studied these or not. When Pundit Nehru was the Prime Minister, then these matters were dealt with differently in those social conditions.

Government then looked for an approach to promote Ayurveda on grounds that why such a massive stream of ours is getting destroyed. Then a Hathi commission was constituted. There was a Cabinet minister named Jai Sukhlal Hathi and commission was assigned a task to come up with suggestive measures to rejuvenate and promote Ayurveda. It's perhaps a report of year 1960 and quite a marvelous one. In that report there is an interesting suggestion on the first page itself. In that, it's been said that there is a need to change the packaging, because that packet… all those herbs is to be taken a bag full…get the same boiled, re-boil with two litres of water, and the next time it is to be halved…then keep it overnight…boil again to reduce it to half. These practises were not swallowed by common people. He further writes that it needs to be packaged as such that common people find it easy to use. Gradually there has been some change. Today people opting Ayurvedic medicine don't face such challenges of taking the herbs back home, boiling them and then make use of it. Now they find it readymade, in medicinal forms, in tablet forms and likewise. That mean these are available in all the forms at par with an allopathic medicine. We are in need of such developmental changes.

So there should be joint efforts in a year to two consisting of researchers, students and manufacturers in Ayurvedic field and not for doctors to prescribe the medicine manufactured for some specific company. Please understand the point I am referring to and inculcate it. It should be ensure how the production of medicine can be improved. Likewise, whether the herbs we have studied in Vedic texts are available and this is a field of intense research. There would be many medicines written in Vedic texts that would prescribe a root of a specific tree or plant to be used for medicinal purposes. Today it would seem difficult to find those trees and plants if searched in accordance with the description illustrated in those texts. I have this experience because when I was the Chief Minister of Gujarat, I had ordered to construct a "Teerthankar-forest" for all the 24 Teerthankars as they got their enlightenment under some or other tree. So I thought constructing a "Teerthankar-forest" and plant those 24 trees right there in that forest. When I started searching for the trees, I was shocked. I went as far as Indonesia to find those trees but couldn't find them all. It means one of the biggest challenges before us is the basic of Ayurveda, which is Herbal Plantation. How do we proceed in that direction and how do we plan a movement in that field?

If you get an opportunity to visit Bhavnagar, then also visit Palitana Jain shrine. There we have built a "Pavak-Van", back then when I was in Gujarat. It's situated at the base, right before the elevation of Palitana. That garden landscape is built in shape of a human body. Its extent is vast enough almost 200 meters in length. Relevant plants and trees have been planted in accordance to the parts of human body which is treated by that particular type of herb. If it's the heart, then the trees related to the cure of heart diseases have been planted there. If it's the problem and pains related to knee, then herbal plants and trees related to the cure has been planted at the place of knee in the garden. If a person visits that garden, he would easily identify the relevant herb and that the medicament from that very herb would help me in cure of a disease related to this very part of my body. The purpose to be fulfilled is an easy behaviour to describe an ancient knowledge in modern perspectives. Later when students tour the places, they also learn about the particulars of diseases and its curative medicinal plants. If we see the things around us, we learn faster.

According to our Shastras also, India is a country where crore of God-forms have been excogitated, and here we have devotee for each type of God. If the devotee is a wrestler, then the God is Hanuman and if the devout are adorer of money, then the Goddess is Lakshmi. If the devotee is interested in knowledge, then the Goddess is Saraswati. So here the state of affairs is as many Gods as the number of devotees. So let's keep one thing in mind, the number of God being worshipped in our country, each one of them has a tree associated. Observe how marvellous the environment friendly society was and the imagination of such environment friendly society. There is no form of the God which is not associated with a tree or plant, and a bird or animal...we don't have any God as such. These were the ways to broadcast the knowledge with ease. On these ways only, Ayurveda was a part of common people. We can change the things around if we have devotion like that. That's why people trust Ayurveda, however educated they are and if the body is to be purified internally, Ayurveda is the best way to go. This is a perception amongst almost everyone. They accept that if internal cleansing is to be done, then take a shelter of Ayurveda and it would be achieved quickly.

But many a time Ayurveda is mocked also. Once, a guest was invited in a family of Ayurveda practitioner. The lady of the house asked her husband to bring some vegetables from the market place for the guest. The practitioner husband went to market to buy vegetables. He returned with leaves of Neem tree. When the wife asked reasons, he said that he had gone to market. When he saw potatoes, he thought of illness related to the consumption of same. He saw brinjals, again he realised some diseases related to them. Then he realised he is not looking at vegetables, but the diseases themselves all around. And at last, he returned with Neem leaves. So at times we have to search a practical application of knowledge. If there is no practical approach to the knowledge, it gets ditched in the interstices of time. That is the reason that the focal area for us should be to develop an accepted and easy norm.

I acknowledge that a great deal of time has passed around the world and since last 50 years allopathy has captured the medicinal world. But people frustrated with Allopathy have turned towards holistic health care. All the institutions of the world are talking about food grain repertory and health funds and medical science is seeing itself in a new form. We have this inheritance. But it is important to see this inheritance in modern perspective. If a change is required then we ought to change it. And if we can achieve this then we would respond aptly to the challenges posed to us which could develop the trust factor in people. Lifestyle has been associated with Ayurveda. In many ways Ayurveda is connected to a way of life. Perhaps we never thought of this. Today few people sitting around here are clapping also. At the back, there are many students. Their mind must be deliberating… how will I make my career, how these small packets of herbs would help me going around with my professional life. This must be dwelling in their minds. After they go back from this discussion, then also this confusion won't fade away, given that now we could not become a doctor, but becoming a Vaidyaraj- an Ayurveda practitioner. But something needs be done to run a life. In spite of that, I would suggest that there is no reason for them to be disheartened. I am saying this especially to this new generation. We have examples and we can learn from those examples.

Even in our country which is the genesis of Yoga, the India which imparted knowledge of Yoga to the world, we had assumed that yoga is no more of our use. This is a project for sages in caves of the Himalayas who sit and meditate. And in a way common people kept themselves aloof from it. Does anyone imagine that how yoga has become a point of central discussion all over the world, keeping in mind the state of yoga 30 years back? What is the reason that big multinational companies have a space for a Stress management institute in their company in the same way as keep CEOs? Why? The moments of crisis brought about by reasons of frustration and depression leads a person to search a way for an eternal peace and for them Yoga comes as a reliever...as a rescue. I have tried so many ways; I tried even drugs, but could find any satisfaction. Now if I traverse back to this path, I would find the specific. Even though we had detached ourselves from The Yoga, the world now is connected to it, then the Ayurveda to which we are acting indifferent today, may be tomorrow the world would get connected to it too. We have a live example here. We can sprout the faith in common man about Ayurveda only after we have confidence of this stature. So if we try for this and I am confident it would certainly be helpful.

Even today, the exported herbal medicines are prescribed all over the world as additional food supplements due to hindrance in the laws of herbal medicines. It is sent in the name of additional food supplements. It has not been accepted as a prescribed medicinal form. Do you know the powers of these pharmaceutical companies? They would not let you enter so easily in the market. They would not provide certification of global acceptance norms for these medicines. The challenge is arduous, but if common man starts to believe in it then nobody can stop you, however huge the organization is.

I am looking at yet another problem. Blessed be Ayurveda and it should do well. But what is we have created a contrasting relationship between Ayurveda and Allopathy. Such is our complete Terminology and these terminologies need to be changed. Even we argue that Ayurveda is what cures a disease from its root, Allopathy provides only superficial relief and we follow the same. We say that Allopathy is a path, whereas Ayurveda is a lifestyle. We should focus on changing the emphasis of Ayurveda. It would not be beneficial for us if we take a contrarian view of Allopathy. Our benefit is in the fact that as yoga has carved a niche for itself, Ayurveda too can do so. If a new disease comes in picture, then Allopathy would take care of it. But if new disease doesn't show up then only Ayurveda can handle that. And this is a belief of all common man that this is the solution. You see, how so ever famous a doctor or surgeon be, in case of loose motion at the advent of sprouting of teeth to grandchildren, they take the kids to a Homeopath doctor. He takes the kids for medicines so that when teeth come, they don't suffer with loose motion… do you agree with me. For the wellbeing of their kids, they leave their way of treatment. This faith is too big a thing.

I am very well versed with an event. There was a doctor named Vanikar, where I lived in Gujarat. Now he is no more now. He was very famous, perhaps first M.S. in Pathology from Gujarat and had studied abroad. He used to run a pathology laboratory. Once in his family relations, a kid got severely ill. He was infant aged approximately 2-3 months old. Time passed but there was no sign of improvement. He was taken to a Vaidyaraj- an Ayurveda practitioner. Whole family was there and many people from pathology world were also present. When they got tired of their trials, the kid was taken to Vaidyaraj. I had known that practitioner. He examined the kid and asked his wife to bring some sweet halwa. Then these men requested the Vaidyaraj that they had their breakfast, so did not want to eat halwa. Vaidyaraj replied that he was not asking halwa for them but for the kid. But the question was that the infant was of 3 months, how can he eat halwa? But whatever the herbs to be mixed must have been known to the wife, so she brought a spoonful halwa and Vaidyaraj himself fed the halwa to baby from his fingers. Almost after half an hour of effort, little by little some amount of it was fed. Within three days the infant started showing improvement. These doctors would tell me that we being a big name in the field of Allopathy, but we couldn't treat own grandson. This Vaidyaraj amazed me by a spoonful of medicinal halwa.

The moral of this story is there is certainly some power in this knowledge. The problem is of our faith. Once we start believing, this strength will multiply four-fold and this world would accept it as a way of life and because of it from health point of view for a healthy society and secondly the biggest advantage is that it is one of the cheapest medicines it is not at all costly. Nowadays, I am engaged in giving speeches at elections and it hurts my throat. I receive hundreds of calls suggesting me to take some turmeric. Now those people don't know what effects does turmeric has. But when they know that there is sore throat, they know turmeric powder can be taken and I can continue delivering speeches. Such a simple and easy mechanism had developed in our society, we need to revitalise it.

I understand that in these 2-3 days of discussion many of such points must have caught your attention. On that basis formulate a plan. I would certainly cooperate in such ambitious projects as the Government of India and my support would always be there with you. I wish you all a healthy life, because doctors need to be healthy to treat patients. Secondly, I request you all to take up Ayurveda with sense of devotion only, not only on grounds of a profession. It is for the wellbeing of a society at large and for a great leap of developmental changes. March forward with this faith in you. I am blessed to have shared the space with you. This occasion is coming to a close.

I wish you all the best. Thank you.

Can people rely on Ayurvedic treatment?

The biggest challenge for the people seeking Ayurvedic healing is two-fold:

i.   Difficult to find Ayurvedic doctors who offer 100% Ayurvedic treatment.

ii.   There is a pervasive belief that they cannot heal patients with just Ayurvedic therapies. Rather, they ask patients to start with allopathic medicines for the first couple days and there after Ayurvedic treatment. This is the biggest challenge for Ayurveda. If these Ayurvedic doctors are not committed, devoted or confident about Ayurveda's ability to heal, then how would the patients trust Ayurveda?

In conclusion, I would like to stress that it is fortunate that the Ayurveda, as a medical system, is getting international attention. It needs time to get itself recognized as a mode of medical treatment. Practitioners need to show confidence in Ayurveda. Research is needed, papers on Ayurvedic studies be published in international journals and seminars be organized to develop mass awareness of and trust in Ayurvedic diagnostic and therapeutic tools. Emphasis be laid on the fact that the Ayurvedic remedies are side-effects-free, economical and affordable even for the poor population. Thanks to Swami Sadashiva Tirtha, D.Sc. and the author of The Ayurveda Encyclopedia for editing and summarizing Mr Modi's speech.

Chapter Nineteen

HINDUISM: MONOTHEISTIC OR POLYTHEISTIC?

Hinduism is being misperceived as polytheistic, because Hindus worship several mythological gods and goddesses. Hindu temples are crowded with pictures and sculptures of gods and goddesses to provide every devotee one of his choices. In some other religions also there is worship of their mythological gods and goddesses, but not to that extent. Every god represents some powers, qualities and attributes, his devotees would love to incorporate. When devotee meditates in front of a picture or stone sculpture, his eyes instantly get closed to have a deep peep within self to be with Almighty God. Picture, as a medium, zeroes the distance. Hindus believe in one-to-one meeting any where, any place, and any time, because God is omnipresent. It is a common scene of a man meditating with his eyes closed on a moving train rushing to an office or any other destination. Hindus, in general, do not believe in ritual worship. God is omnipresent. No need to go to a temple. No body can see God with his/her open eyes. They know that no one can have His *darsan* (sight) in a crowded congregation. Hindus prefer a lonely one-to-one VIP meeting with God. One can feel Him only within self with his/her meditating closed eyes.

Wilkins in the preface of his *'Bhagvat-geeta, or Dialogues of Kreeshna and Arjoon'* (London: Nourse, 1785) argued that the Gita was written to encourage a form of monotheist "unitarianism" as given in Vedas and to draw Hinduism away from the polytheism.

Vedic religion (Hinduism) is monotheistic or polytheistic would depend on the way a person perceives God:

1. God is one with all responsibility and all authority to look after His vast global providence, like a benevolent President or Prime Minister in modern democratic secular countries.

Or

2. God, with multitude administration with responsibility distributed among His trusted deputies, as given in all the mythologies – Judeo-Christian, Greek, Roman and Hindu.

No religion is, rather can be, polytheistic, because all people, irrespective of their religious orientations, worship only the One and the Same God. How can one worship two or more Gods, when there is only one God? Some persons – like Rama, Krishna, Jesus Christ, Mohamed, Sai Baba and some others – who although have ultra wisdom, divine attitudes and powers are not God, but are being worshipped as gods (small 'g'). Jesus Christ is a god, not God, so Rama is a god, not God. They, unlike God, were born, lived their life and died. The misperception, arising out of failure of distinguishing God from gods, has been cause of considering Hinduism as polytheistic.

If difference between the two – God and Jesus Christ – is rightly understood, no society will be, rather should be, considered polytheistic. There are several gods and goddesses in mythologies of most religions. Greeks and Romans, like Hindus, have several mythological gods and goddesses. Almighty God will be happy if His assistants, agents or representatives – saints, gurus, *sadhus, devtas, pegambors* – are also respected and worshipped. God will never like to be in competition with them, because they are His representatives. Dr. Michael S. Heiser[135] (Biblical scholar), explaining the consensus view of his peers, talks about their idea of "a divine council of multiple gods," as featured in the Old Testament. He further observes:

> "This evolution [monotheism], according to the consensus view, was achieved through the zealous commitment of Israelite scribes who edited and reworked the Hebrew

---

[135] Wikipedia.

Bible to reflect emerging monotheism and to compel the laity to embrace the idea. One specific feature of Israelite religion offered as proof of this development is the divine council. Before the exile, Israelite religion affirmed a council of gods which may or may not have been headed by Yahweh. During and after the exile, the gods of the council became angels, mere messengers of Yahweh, who by the end of the exilic period was conceived of as the lone council head over the gods of all nations."

This is not Michael Heiser's personal view. He is an evangelical Christian. He is simply describing the "consensus view" of his peers, mainstream biblical scholars. As a matter of fact, it is view of almost all peoples, all over the planet, irrespective of their religious orientations, who have heard and have been worshipping only One God. It is not only biblical view, but it is universal, including Vedic.

Hindus believe in Wholesome and Oneness of God

In the usual sense of literal meaning of the word monotheism, Hinduism is being viewed as polytheistic because of swarm of its gods and goddesses. It is a wrong perception of Hinduism. On similar lines, most religions would be considered as polytheistic, because most mythologies talk about several gods and goddesses. As explained earlier, that in almost all mythologies – Judaism, Greek, Roman, and Hindu – there is description of several gods and goddesses. Hindus have always insisted on their affirmation of oneness of God.[136] Totality of Almighty God is not complete if He is seen alone, separate from His various manifestations. Hindu God, like Roman and Greek, is not alone by Himself without His various manifestations. A god or goddess is recognized only if introduced as a manifestation of Almighty God.

All gods and goddesses are He, as His various manifestations. The gods and goddesses will be unidentifiable, when seen in isolation of Him, because each one is He in disguise. No god or goddess is a

---

[136] Diana L. Eck, "Daršan, Seeing the Divine Image in INDIA", (1985, p. 24).

part of Him, but one of His several representations. God can not be divided into gods and goddesses. For example, His various powers and attributes are symbolically shown through the multiple arms and vehicle of the god or goddess. Main Hindu mythological gods – Brahma, as creator, Vishnu as care taker, Shiva, as giver of birth, through death. Most westerners and even many Hindus will find difficult to see birth in death.

Durga (also known as Kali) – with her symbolical multiple arms, carrying various kinds of weapons to kill evil monsters and riding a lion – is worshipped as a great warrior to protect the integrity of Bharat Mata. Various powers and attributes of the invisible Almighty God would not be easily understood without showing His multiple manifestations, as expressed through Durga (Goddess of power), Lakshmi (Goddess of wealth), Sarasvati (Goddess of knowledge and wisdom), Indra, Varuna, and so on. It has been difficult for most western philosophers to see the multitude powers in the big ONE, exhibited by the symbolical arms of Durga.

The concept of *'Multitude within ONE'* is too delicate a concept to understand, particularly for Westerners who see God up in the sky, far away from self, not within self, as Hindus see. One doesn't need eyes to see the 'Only Truth' which is within inside self. One needs to close his eyes to have a deep peek within self to enjoy the panorama beauty of the ONENESS in the midst of God's multiple manifestations. The German Indologist Betty Heimann[137] uses the image of a crystal to explain the multiple images of God in His oneness that it depends on the angle, which would provide correct viewpoint of "a true all-comprehensive picture." Hindus don't need prism to see the multitude image of God. Even a child – Hindu, Buddhist, Jain and Sikh – knows that God is within self, not up in the sky, nor in the stone, he is praying in front of. Automatically his hands are folded and eyes closed to have His Daršan within self.

In his lecture, delivered in London on Nov. 3, 1896, Vivekananda[138] suggested to turn the senses inward to perceive DIVINITY within

---

[137] Ibid, p. 25.
[138] Vivekananda, "JNANA-YOGA", Ramakrishna-Vivekananda Center, New York (1955, pp.88-105).

SELF: "Each soul is potentially divine. The goal is to manifest this divinity within by controlling nature: external and internal." He says:

> "... that the reality of things is not to be found in the external world; it is to be found not by looking outward, but by turning the eyes, as it is expressed literally inward. And the word used for the Soul is very significant: it is He who has gone inward, the innermost reality of our being, the heart centre, the core from which, as it were, everything comes out; the central Sun, of which the mind, the body, the sense organs, and every thing else that we have are but rays going outward."

Amazing philosophy! One doesn't need to travel far from self. Man has within self the thing required for tranquility and peace of mind. Unfortunately, man has been confused and lost like the *hiran* (deer), wandering around in search of the *khasturi* (perfume) it has in its own *nabh* (navel, belly button). I am giving Hindi words – *hiran, khusturi and nabh* – for deer, perfume and navel respectively, because, in Hinduism, this is considered appropriate philosophical simile to a confused wandering person in search of the TRUTH, though it is within self. Where is the question of polytheism in Hinduism when both – Divinity and the devotee – are one, submerged into each other?

Mark Twain, overwhelmed by the beauty expressed by the unity in the divine diversity of Bhārat, wrote in his diary: "In religion, all other countries are paupers. India is the only millionaire."[139]

Nehru, in *'Discovery of India'* (1946, p.107), cites Sister Nivedita's perception of India's unity in her diversity:

> "The foreign reader ... is at once struck by two features: in the first place its unity in complexity; and, in the second, its constant efforts to impress on its hearers the

---

[139] Mark Twain, "Following the Equator", p. 397. Taken from Diana Eck's 'Daršan', p. 24.

idea of a single centralized India, with a heroic tradition
of her own as formative and uniting impulse."[140]

Sister Nivedita (Margaret Noble, 1867-1911), although a foreigner,
understood India's vivid phenomenon of 'unity-in-its-diversity.' Unity
in India's diversity' is too delicate a concept to see truth in it, especially
by foreign mind and eyes.

The visible diversity in India as reflected by various – languages,
religions, castes, complexions, political parties, and historical traditions,
etc. – has bewildered the West to recognize any underlying unity in
the Indianness of India (Bhāratiyata of Bhārat). In fact it is there. The
West needs to learn to see others from their own angle, not from the
West's subjective and colonially biased viewpoint. This is the main
reason why histories of Asia and Africa, particularly more of India, have
been distorted and mutilated. European superiority complex, colonial
mentality and ethnic rivalry have hurt the histories of the world. World's
ethnic politics, in disguise, has been playing historical mischief.

This was the reason, why the British civil servant John Strachey,
speaking to an audience at Cambridge University in 1859, was not able
to appreciate the unity underlying the immense floating diversity in
India. The West will understand the Indian 'Divine Oneness' only when
it understands the calmness below the roaring and dancing waves and
tides safeguarding the pearls in the ocean. Western scholars, writing
about India, need to keep aside their European colonially-biased glasses
to be able to see the truths, being distorted by the mischievous colonial
mind and heart.

Unfortunately, untruths have been fabricated by religious politics,
being played by renowned theologians to push own religion ahead of
other religions. How can any religion be ahead of other religions, when
the religion is the story of God, only One and the Same for the whole
humanity? Religions are many, but all their devotees sing various songs
in the praise of the only One and the Same God in various languages.
There can not be more than one God. Theologians should see the
Oneness, needed to unite all religions, despite apparent diversity.

---

[140] Nehru, Discovery of India (p.107), taken from Sir S. Radhakrishnan's book
'Indian Philosophy'.

Hinduism is polytheistic, only if Christianity is

History tells that like Hindus, both Romans as well Greeks have uncountable numerous swarms of mythological gods and goddesses. From the Olympian gods and goddesses right down to several minor gods and goddesses can be traced in almost all mythologies. From remote distant pre-history times, God, as omnipresent and omnipotent, is seen in each and every phenomenon of the nature, because man is amazed to see its beauty along with its uncontrollable power. Man can not understand nor influence the nature, and thus helpless. Therefore, man has been worshipping the nature, thinking several gods, as imagined in each and every piece of nature. This is seen not only in rural area. In 1997, I saw a person worshiping a tree in cosmopolitan Bombay. When asked why he was worshipping a tree, he said that tree, like God, is merciful and is giving comfort to every body without any bias. Such belief has been decreasing due to education, being given in formal schools and by formal as well as informal media. Following few examples of Roman and Greek mythology gods will prove my thesis that a religion can not be called polytheistic because it has several gods and goddesses.

Greek gods and goddesses[141]

Ancient Greek name	English name	Description
Αἰθήρ (*Aithḗr*)	Aether	The god of the upper atmosphere and light.
Ἀνάγκη (*Anánkē*)	Ananke	The goddess of inevitability, compulsion, and necessity.
Χάος (*Cháos*)	Chaos	The nothingness from which all else sprang. Described as a void.
Χρόνος (*Chrónos*)	Chronos (Chronus)	The god of time. Not to be confused with the Titan Cronus, the father of Zeus, Poseidon and Hades.

---

[141] Wikipedia.

Ἔρεβος (*Érebos*)	Erebus	The god of darkness and shadow.
Ἔρως (*Eros*)	Eros	The god of love and attraction.
Ὕπνος (*Hypnos*)	Hypnos	The personification of sleep.
Νῆσοι (*Nḗsoi*)	The Nesoi	The goddesses of the islands and sea.
Οὐρανός (*Ouranós*)	Uranus	The god of the heavens (Father Sky); father of the Titans.
Γαῖα (*Gaîa*)	Gaia	Personification of the Earth (Mother Earth); mother of the Titans.
Οὔρεα (*Oúrea*)	The Ourea	The gods of mountains.
Φάνης (*Phánēs*)	Phanes	The god of procreation in the Orphic tradition.
Πόντος (*Póntus*)	Pontus	The god of the sea, father of the fish and other sea creatures.
Τάρταρος (*Tártaros*)	Tartarus	The god of the deepest, darkest part of the underworld, the Tartarean pit (which is also referred to as Tartarus itself).

Roman gods and goddesses	Hindu counterpart
Jupiter, king of gods,	Indra
Juno, the queen of gods,	Every god has his wife
Neptune, god of the sea	
Pluto, god of death	Shiva
Apollo, god of sun,	Surya devta
Diana, goddess of moon	Chandra
Mars, god of war	
Venus, goddess of love,	
Cupid, god of love,	
Mercury, messenger of gods,	
Minerva, goddess of wisdom	Saraswati
Ceres, goddess of earth,	Dharti mata
Proserpine, goddess of	

the underworld,	
Vulcan, the smith good,	
Bacchus, god of wine,	
Saurn, god of time,	Kāl devta
Vesta, goddess of home,	
Janus, god of doors,	
Mala, goddess of growth,	
Flora, goddess of flowers,	
Plutus, god of wealth, etc.	Lakshmi

Harvard University Prof. Diana L. Eck's book *"A New Religious America"* (2001) will promote global awareness that religion, like God, is universal, and that it is the story of the theologian garland of flowers of all religions. Readers will love to see the stars on American Flag (cover of the book) have been replaced by the symbols of all religions to depict America, as the country where all religions are equally respected. How can one religion be better than any other religion when all religions talk the same about God, one and the same for all? Prof. Eck expresses her happiness: "How a Christian country has become the world's most religiously diverse nation!"

The universal divinity has been rightly projected by also Swami Vivekananda, the way he addressed the audience at the *World's Parliament of Religions*, held in Chicago, in 1893: **"Brothers and Sisters of America."** Such is the traditional way to address a crowd to show 'family relationship among all.' My grand uncle Shewaram addressed a political crowd: "Dear brothers and sisters, excepting one…"His wife was in the crowd. Hinduism and most other religions believe in the extended family of religions.

According to Vedic scriptures, the whole world is a family, as expressed by "वसुधैव कुटुम्बकम्" (*vasudhaiva kuṭumbakam*), meaning whole humanity is a family. It is contained in the "Mahopanishad". The verse is also found in V.3.37 Panchatantra (3rd century BCE), and also in verse 1.3.71 of Hitopadesha (12th century CE).[142]

---

[142] Wikipedia Dictionary.

Such salutation defines and explains the core theme of the World's Parliament of Religions, that all, despite followers of various religions, are brothers and sisters, meaning members of one and the same family. Vedas believe in and affirm 'Universal Divinity.' God can not be God if the whole humanity, w/o any exception, doesn't believe so. Prof. Diana L. Eck[143] has explained it better by quoting Vivekananda:

> "It is the same light coming through different colors. ... But, in the heart of every thing the same truth reigns; the Lord has declared to the Hindu in his incarnation as Krishna, "I am in every religion as the thread through a string of pearls. And wherever thou seest extraordinary holiness and extraordinary power rising and purifying humanity, know yet that I am there."

Hinduism affirms 'Oneness in variety'

Diana further observes that Vivekananda, in his speech "called for a universal religion which would have no place for persecution or intolerance in its polity, and would recognize a divinity in every man or woman, and whose whole scope, whose whole force would be centered in aiding humanity to realize its Divine nature."[144]

Humanity will be peaceful when people recognize that in all religions, it is "the same light though different colors" and listen to God: "I am in every religion." It is interesting and educative to see why Eck[145] feels that Hindu monotheism can not be aptly compared with that of the West. She, explaining the Hindu polytheistic imagination, writes:

> "In entering into the Hindu world, one confronts a way of thinking which one might call "radically polytheistic," and if there is any "great divide" between the traditions of India and those of the West, it is in just this fact.

---

[143] Diana L. Eck, "A New Religious America" (2001, p. 97).

[144] Richard Hughes Seager, ed., The Dawn of Religious Pluralism; Voices from the World's Parliament of Religions, (1893, p. 431.)

[145] Diana L. Eck, in Daršan, pp. 22-24.

Some may object that India has also affirmed Oneness as resolutely and profoundly as any culture on earth, and indeed it has."

Eck has explained why and how the "great divide" between the West and Hindu perceptions of the 'Divine Oneness' happened. Every body believes that there is only one God. It is of great comfort that both – the West and India – have not divided God into two or many. I don't think that there is even a single person on the planet – East, West, North, or South – who does not believe in Oneness of God. How then any polytheism? Those, who believe that Hindus are polytheist, are not able or do not want to differentiate God from mythological gods and goddesses, who are His manifestations. They are not Gods, with capital 'G'. Like Hindus, Greeks and Romans have numerous mythological gods and goddesses too. Denial of gods and goddesses is in a way, denial of God. They are not separate entities, meaning that they don't have existence only if God doesn't have. They define the totality, oneness and wholesomeness of God. Theological history needs to work harder to save God from being ethnically and communally fragmented. God is secular and biases-free, One and the same for all, irrespective of their religious orientations. God does not have religion. He, Himself, is the true religion, ignorance of which would make the humanity confused about His Oneness and about His Universality.

Prof. Diana Eck (Daršan, p.24) explains why the West has difficulty to see 'India's affirmation of Oneness':

> "The point here, however, is that India's affirmation of Oneness is made in a context that affirms with equal vehemence the multitude of ways in which human beings have seen that Oneness and expressed their vision. Indian[146] monotheism or monism cannot, therefore, be aptly compared with the monotheism of the West. The statement that "God is One" does not mean the same thing in India and the West."

---

[146] 'Hindu', for 'Indian' would be more appropriate.

Ethnically biased philosophers seem to have difficulty in understanding the concept of monotheism that the people, despite worshipping mythological gods and goddesses, can be considered as monotheistic because mythological gods are not Gods (with capital G). They are His assistants or His various manifestations, expressing His various epithets and his multifarious roles. The totality of God can not be adequately and appropriately realized by separating Him from His deputies. As a matter of fact, Hindu monotheism is not different from that of the West. It is deliberately made to look different by the mighty West by forgetting or discarding the multitude of the Judeo-Christian, Roman and Greek mythological gods and goddesses, and thus negating the concept of multiple manifestations of the Almighty God. Like Hindus, Romans and Greeks worshipped a mythological pantheon of gods and goddesses. It doesn't negate the oneness and wholesomeness of God. Mythologies – Roman, Greek and Hindu – have lot of truths and lessons to guide us to understand the relationship between God and mythological gods who, as a matter of fact, have kept us connected with God. Attributes and powers of mythological gods and goddesses educate us about God.

Mythologies of several religions, particularly Judeo-Christianity and Hinduism, talk that God in His various manifestations takes care of the basic needs of humanity – food, clothing, roof – and also of various other needs and concerns. God, through His messengers in human attire, like Rama, Krishna, Gautama Buddha, Zoroaster, Christ, Mohamed, Guru Nanak and others have helped in the problems, stemming from within such as the fears, anxieties, confusions, etc and also in several external problems. Religion has answers to several questions and concerns. Thus each mythology – Greek, Roman, Hindu, etc – talks about various gods and goddesses who have knowledge and powers how to appropriately address them. Mythological gods and goddesses have different names in different languages. In English they are called 'god' and 'goddess' with small 'g' or they are known as 'saints'. In Sanskrit, they are known as देवता (Devta) and देवी ('Devi') or *'Mātā'* (mother). Hindu goddess is respected as Mātā (mother), because no body, other than mother, can be so protector, affectionate giver and strong. It is why in Hinduism, Durga Mātā is given the charge of the defense.

Durga's multiple arms with various weapons and her ride on lion symbolically show her strength and various powers to fight against various evils. Man is threatened by the adversaries, hidden within inner self such as – *kaam, krodha, lobha, moha* and *ahankar* – (lust, anger, greed, attachments and ego) more than the outwardly enemies. The inner unseen conflicts cause hidden unbearable anxiety and restlessness. The problem becomes serious because all the adversaries – *kaam, krodha, lobha, moha* and *ahankar* – are too charming and too pleasurable to distance from. History is full of examples of mighty kings and presidents who have been easily defeated by lust within their palace without use of sword. The mighty Rawana would not have been defeated if he had controlled his lust.

Other two important portfolios – education and finance – are also assigned to two goddesses, Saraswati, goddess of knowledge and education and Lakshmi, the goddess of wealth of various resources to meet the various basic needs and necessities of living.

Saraswati, Goddess of Knowledge

Because of the blessings of goddess *Sarasvati*, India, particularly Hindus have come up to the Everest in areas of knowledge, education, wisdom, culture, music, arts, technology and civilization. There is respect for Guru who gives the knowledge. My father explained why the first school, I went to, was on *Guruvar* (the day of Guru, Thursday). Because of respect for guru (Teacher), there would be discipline in classroom, conducive atmosphere for learning. There were no lawsuits against a teacher who used corporal punishment. I am not recommending it. The parent should report it to the principal who should talk to the teacher. But, the case to court would hurt the education and discipline in the classroom. Punishment of mischief in the classroom is necessary for discipline, but not corporal. School has to decide what. I, as a teacher, used to tell the student to stand up in the back of the classroom for a few minutes, so that he/she should feel ashamed of his/her behavior. I would not like to order student to leave the classroom. Then he/she would miss what is being taught. It would, then be punishment to Saraswati.

Worship of goddess *Saraswati* has been prevalent since remote prehistory ancient times as evidenced by several scriptures – the four Vedas, Upanishads, several Shastras, Bhagvad Gita, and the two epics, Rāmāyanā and Mahābhāratā – in which all kinds of knowledge, including medicine and *vimans* (airplanes), etc is given. The word 'Veda' means knowledge. This affirms truth in mythologies. Mythologies should not be discarded as myths, but be respected as the history of the mankind, being given through oral traditions.

Almost all Hindus, excepting a few atheists, worship Lakshmi as goddess of good luck, wealth and prosperity, both material and spiritual. Money is very important for life. It is needed for every thing – life, education, defense, economic health and protection of the country. It would not be fair to say that Saraswati and Durga do not depend on Lakshmi and vice versa. All the three goddesses need one another. Lakshmi can not make money without education and protection from foreign aggressions.

Brahma is considered the creator of the universe, Vishnu, life sustainer and Shiva as the god of death, which is unavoidable. In Hinduism, death is seen as a 'new life', meaning *'punner janma'* (rebirth, reincarnation). Body is mortal. Hence in Sanskrit death is called as देहान्त (*dehant*), meaning end of body (देहा = body + न्त ant = end). Cremation, it seems, is based on the fact that since body is mortal, why then to preserve it in a grave?

Brahma, Vishnu, Shiva, Durga, Saraswati, Laxmi and several other gods and goddesses are various manifestations of Almighty God. When a devotee prays to any deity in form of a stone or a picture, he doesn't see the deity in isolation of the Almighty God. Since God can not be perceived in isolation of His multiple manifestations, no religion can or should be considered polytheistic. Eyes of the devotee worshipping in front of a stone god or a picture god get automatically closed as soon as he starts praying. He enjoys a deep peep within self to have His Daršan or feel of God. Hindu meditates with closed eyes to see God within. Christians may not understand this, because in Church, their eyes remain open when praying to Christ. Other prominent difference is that Hindus pray or meditate individually, mostly privately, not in a congregation. In Hinduism, no day, place or time is designated for prayer. Time, 'convenient, silent and lonely', is the best time for prayer. God, though invisible, is present always and everywhere to give blessings to the praying devotee. Same way a Muslim, when unable to go to Mosque, performs *Namāz* any where, any time convenient – home, airport, railway station, school, etc – only being certain that he is facing *Qiblā* (*Kabah*), in East or West. The place, wherever Namaz is performed, becomes pious and sacred.

It is too difficult to list all mythological gods and goddesses, Roman, Greek or Hindu. Each Hindu god and goddess has several names. How can the invisible God, with numerous attributes, powers and functions, have only one name? Elephant was touch-perceived different by various blind men, depending on what part each one was touching. God is real, but His devotees / worshippers are blind, rather ignorant. It is said that each Hindu god / goddess has 108 names. Thus, it is said that there are millions of Hindu gods. The number '108' has some religious connotation. Only an expert theologian can explain it. I would like to say only that reader of Hinduism should not get lost in the confounding web of multiple names of mythological Hindu deities. Like Hindus, Romans and Greeks have also uncountable number of mythological gods and goddesses. Unlike Christians, most Hindus, particularly rural, have not been able to sentimentally separate themselves from their remote mythological heritage. Hindus are known as traditionalists. Therefore, most Hindus still like to remain connected with their mythological gods and goddesses, hence still temples are swarmed with gods and goddesses. Some or several Hindus did not like this. Therefore they became Buddhists and some later Sikhs. Hinduism needs several Vivekanandas to explain 'One in diversity'.

But in true sense, Hindus, like Romans and Greeks, are monotheistic. Hinduism, though monotheistic, is being misperceived as polytheistic because of its varied rituals, and worshipping numerous representatives of Almighty God – gods and goddesses – reflecting elements of polytheism and *but-pooja* (idolatry). No religion can/should be considered as polytheistic, because it is difficult to find even one individual, excepting an atheist, who doesn't worship Almighty God. Humanity recognizes only One Lord of the universe with army of His assistants or manifestations.

Un-repairable loss of histoiry, if mythologies ignored

If seen with unbiased eyes and objective mind, one will find treasure of wisdom given by mythological gods and goddesses and also lot of knowledge pertaining to theosophy, psychology, science, technology, history, geography and thoughts of pre-history peoples, modern scholars would envy. As a face-saving game, historians have dumped it as useless mythology. Historians would not be able to tell what washistory prior to history, if mythology was not history. Mythologies kept pre-history humanity connected with the modern.

Man can not live at peace without knowing his YESTERDAY, so as to build his TODAY upon, and plan his FUTURE. Historians need the **'third eye'** to identify truths in mythologies; his ancestors have left for their descendents to know their heritage. Hindus – though some illiterate, have been fortunate to know thoughts of their remote prehistory renowned ancestors, like Sri Rama, Krishna, Buddha and several other heroes through street plays, like Ram-leelas, and Krishna leelas, enacted on streets, in *Mandirs* (Hindu temples), cinema, etc. Most Hindu lullabies have some religious story. Some western scholars may not admit that their scholarship has its roots in the scholarship; they have inherited from the wisdom, given in mythologies.

Brahma, Vishnu and Shiva are primary gods to assume responsibility for the humanity, its birth, life and death respectively. Who will say that God did not manifest Himself through Brahma, Vishnu and Shiva to appropriately discharge His primary duties towards mankind? There are several other human needs, to be taken care of by Him, through His other manifestations. Important among them are knowledge, wealth, defense, fire which have been assigned to goddesses – *Saraswati, Lakshmi, Durga* and *Agni* respectively. Without help from goddess Agni, all the gods and goddesses will feel helpless.

Wonder! Prime portfolios assigned to goddesses

It is heartening to know that in ancient India, all the four most important portfolios – education, finance, defense and fire – were assigned to goddesses. Defense was given to goddess Durga. I consider

Late Indira Gandhi, as an incarnation of Durga. She successfully invaded West Pakistan (present Bangladesh) in 1971 to prevent cruelty over Bangladeshis, particularly extremely more over Hindus. In ancient times, woman was rightly considered wise, honest, powerful and smart manager of all kinds of affairs, domestic as well as international. This is evidenced by the poor and dishonest management of most governments in the West as well in the East, only because almost all are governed by men. Woman, because of her prime responsibility of childrearing and home-management, has not been able to actively play outdoor roles, but significance of her proxy role can not be minimized. Ancient Hindu scriptures tell that a great successful raja (King) had shrewd minister at home in his wife and/or mother. I very vividly remember, my grandfather, used to heed his bedridden elderly mother's counseling in his town politics.

Chapter Twenty

AGNI, THE MOST PROMINENT GODDESS

Agni (Goddess fire or *Agni Mātā*, अग्नि माता) seems to have prime role, humanity can not live without. Food, the basic need of life, is cooked by fire. Fire keeps us comfortably warm in shivering winter. Agni is purifying goddess. Fire helps in keeping environment clean, therefore cremation, not grave. Cremation has saved lot of land for farming, needed to feed the humanity. For respect for knowledge, a page from a book, particularly from a sacred scripture, is not to be thrown in garbage, but in fire. A grain, particularly from a holy *prasad* (food), like Kanah Sahib (Sikh Prasad), accidently dropped on the floor, is to be respectfully immersed into fire. All Hindu ceremonies and celebrations from birth to death – nomenclature, *Janeyoo* (Sacred thread), wedding, prayers for peace, health, long life, easy death, protection against wrath of nature and even protection of country – are performed around fire.

Hindus, Buddhists, Jain and Sikhs, use cremation as the way of disposal of the dead. According to the Columbia Encyclopedia, cremation, as a mode of disposal of a corpse by fire:

> "(Cremation) is often related to a belief in the properties of fire as a purifying agent. ... Disposal of the ashes varies in different parts of the world. Hindus, for whom cremation is the typical form of disposal, place them in urns or immerse them in a river, preferably the sacred Ganges."

Cremation is friendly to the environment and saves lot of land for several other uses for better human life, particularly for farming the food for life. In Hinduism, fire (Agni) is worshipped as a goddess of life and more important as goddess for the protection of the nation.

Agni Missiles of Bhārat

In addition to several kinds of missiles, the Agni Missiles are the most important because Bhārat has bloody enemies, nearby like Pakistan and distant like China. Agni missiles have wide range to cover all:

Agni I

It has range capability of up to 750-1250 Km.

Agni II

It weighs 16 tons and can carry 1 Ton of Nuclear warhead. It has a range of 2000-3000 Km.

Agni III

Agni III has a range of up to 5000 Km.

Agni IV

It has a range of 4000 Km and weight of 17 Ton. It defers from the early series of Agni missiles by the fact that a lot of new technologies were introduced in this variant. The new technologies introduced were Re-Entry to atmosphere heat shield, Composite rocket motor, modern avionics with full digital control system providing very high level of accuracy in hitting the target.

Agni V

It is a three stage type ICBM having weight of 50 tons and warhead capacity of 1.5 ton. Exact range of this missile was never disclosed but as per estimates it is considered to be between 5000 – 8000 Km. this is an upgraded version of Agni III. This missile has the capability to hit the across Asia and reach farthest ends of Europe.

Agni VI

It is four stage type ICBM which is still in developmental stage. It is expected to have a weight of 55 to 70 Tons and warhead carrying capacity of 3 Tons. The expected range of this missile is 8000 to 12000 Km.

They are named as 'Agni Missiles' to underscore the significance of 'agni' (fire) for the defense of the nation. In Mahabharata *Agni baans* (fire arrows) were used to protect the truth. Modern missiles, as per Lockheed Martin Missiles and Fire Control (MFC), suggest use of fire in modern missiles. It seems modern fire missile got its idea from Mahabharata. In addition to Aakash, Trishul, Nag, and Prithvi missiles, Agni Missiles have been developed to enforce the power of Bhārat to scare the neighboring adversaries, including the most distant belligerent neighbor, to remain at arm's length:[147]

Name	Type	Stage(s)	Range
Agni-I	MRBM	One	700 km – 1,200 km
Agni-II	IRBM	Two	2,000 km – 2,500 km
Agni-III	IRBM	Two	3,000 km – 5,000 km
Agni-IV	IRBM	Two	2,500 km – 3,700 km
Agni-V	ICBM	Three	5,000 km – 8,000 km
Agni-VI	ICBM	Three	10,000 km – 12,000 km

---

[147] Wikipedia

In shastras, Agni is worshipped as goddess of warriors. Missiles of India have been named as 'Agni' to reflect her ancient warrior culture. Caste classification tells that *kshatriya* (Warrior) is number two caste after *Brahmin* (Knowledge, *Saraswati*). Historically, *kshatries* are honored the most, because they protect the nation against enemies. Both non-mythological gods – Rama and Krishna – were *kshatiya*. Both are being worshipped as gods since millennia. They will continue to be worshipped until humanity is alive. Hinduism is eternal, so it will not die until humanity is alive.

Hindus consider Agni as अग्नि माता (*Mother Fire*), who protects her children at any cost. Fire, like mother, can be too ferocious to be controlled, when the issue of protection of children arises. India (Hindustan, the land of Hindus) is not wrong to name her missiles as *Agni*. Long range international ballistic Missile "Agni V" was successfully launched on April 19, 2012. It has a range of over 5,000 kilometers, as a credible deterrent to China, the mighty untrustworthy hostile neighbor. Then, Agni-VI, covering 10,000 to 12,000 km, covering all China, was developed to remain safe and secure in the untrustworthy jungle of civilized lions. Paradoxically, it is safer to be in the jungle of lions than in the jungle of civilized lions in attire of a gentleman.

With this, India has joined an elite group of nations which have mastered such technology of ballistic missiles. India also yanked open the door to the super-exclusive ICBM (Intercontinental Club of Ballistic Missile) that counts only US, Russia, China, France and the UK as its members.

Guided Missiles of India[148]

The use of rockets in India, for warfare, dates back to the 18th century. These rockets (also known as Mysorean rockets) were the first iron-cased rockets that were successfully deployed for military use. The British reverse-engineered these and introduced the technology to Europe (see *Congreve rocket*). When India became a British colony, scientific R&D in India was restricted and military science in India naturally lagged.

---

[148] Wikipedia

Research in missile technology resumed again in the late 1950s under the political leadership of Jawaharlal Nehru, independent India's first prime minister. Successive Indian governments, after his continued providing consistent political backing to the program in 1982, India's political and scientific leadership, which included Prime Minister Indira Gandhi, Defence Minister R. Venkataraman, V.S. Arunachalam (Scientific Advisor to the Defence Minister), Dr. Abdul Kalam (Director, DRDL) accelerated and gave new dimensions to the missile program, under the 'Integrated Guided Missile Development Program' (IGMDP) during the Atal Bihari Vajpaee BJP (Bharatiya Janta Party) government. The IGMDP is one of India's most successful defence research project, as all the missiles – Prithvi, Akash, Trishul, Nag, Agni – have been successfully tested and inducted by the Indian armed forces.

After the end of the IGMDP (on 8 January 2008), India has been developing missiles, and wherever possible, with private industries and foreign partners. Brahmos is an example of one such successful collaborative project, between India and Russia.

Significance of the 'Surya Pooja' (Sun Worship)

Next importance in Hinduism seems to have been given to *roshni* (light). Both the sun (*Surya Devta*) and the moon (*Chandrama*) are worshipped. Religious Hindus worship the sun, at its rise in the morning by pouring water while reciting Vedic mantras. It has a scientific reason too. It is believed that looking at the 'rising sun' through water, improves eyesight and the worshipper enjoys *shanty* (peace).

Chanda Pooja (worship of the moon)

Moon is worshipped two times every Hindu month:

1. *Poornma*, night with full moon, and
2. *Amavas*, complete dark night.

Both days are observed as religious days. Hindu calendar is lunar, different from the solar, as in use almost all over the planet. Several

Hindu women observe fast on both days. Fast is good for health and peace of mind. Fast also generates good, positive and constructive thinking and love for others. Hindu fasts are not too strict, meaning not allowing drink of water. Alcohol consumption is strictly prohibited. Fruit juices are allowed. Hinduism doesn't prescribe any punishment-like practice in religious fasts. All planets are being worshipped as gods or goddesses. Varuna and Mitra are worshipped as gods of societal affairs and law.

Tree, worshipped by some

Several years back in Juhu, Mumbai, I saw one person worshipping a tree. When asked why, he responded, "Only tree, without any bias and discrimination, gives protection against scorching heat of the sun to all persons, irrespective of their religion, status, or caste. The lesson, tree gives, if heeded by the mankind, there will be peace all over the planet.

Only One Truth!

It is difficult to identify and enumerate all Hindu deities, as it is difficult to identify actors in the nature, cosmology and astronomy. The Rig Vedic hymn "The One Truth the sages call by many names" explains it. The truth is that there is only one God, Hindus and all others worship. His various manifestations, in form of gods and goddesses, should not confuse us that Hinduism as polytheistic. Romans, Greeks, Germans and several others have also numerous gods and goddesses. The learned theologians and historians should discard their color glasses so as to be able to realize that there is only one TRUTH, only expressed by only one God.

Max Müller[149] remarks about monotheism and polytheism:

> "I could not even answer the question, if you were to ask it whether the religion of the Veda was *polytheistic* or monotheistic. Monotheistic, in the usual sense of the word, it is decidedly not, though there are hymns

---

[149] Max Müller, 'India: What Can It teach Us?'(1999, pp. 163-4).

that assert the unity of the Divine as fearlessly as any passage of the Old Testament, or the New Testament, or the Koran. Thus one poet says (Rig Veda I-164- 46): "That one, sages name it in various ways – they call it Agni, Yama, Matari8van."

Max Müller further remarks: "That which is one, sages name it in various ways – they call it Agni, Yama, Matarisvan."

Max Müller talks about another poet who says: "'The wise poets represent by their words Him who is one with beautiful wings, in many ways" (Rig Veda X. 114.5.).

Vedic people (Hindus) are respecting Biblical perception of God. Why then are Christians not respecting Vedic perception of God? Every one has right to have his own view. Vedic and Biblical perceptions do not seem to be basically different. Both believe in oneness of divinity. Hindus see God in His totality, along with His assistant gods and goddesses.

The fact is that not even one person on earth believes that there are more than one God. Few persons are atheists who believe that there is no God. Confusion has arisen because some deny multiple mythological manifestations of God, though most mythologies, including Roman and Greek talk about numerous gods and goddesses.

Hindus see in God numerous images representing His various attributes, functions and powers. Why to minimize Him? No religion can be polytheistic if people believe that there is only one God with various powers and functions. Hindus see His various powers being exercised by His varied symbolical images and manifestations.

In conclusion, I would like to say that all peoples, irrespective of their various religious orientations, worship only one God, Who, takes care of all under the sun. His different names in different languages should not confuse us and divide God. All on the planet are His

WAS THERE ANIMAL SACRIFICE IN HINDUISM?

ANIMAL sacrifice[150] is the ritual killing of an animal and offering it to appease a god or goddess. Historically, it has been practiced in many religions all around the world in almost all cultures, including those of the Sumerians, Hebrews, Greeks, Romans, Germanics, Celts, Aztecs, and Mayans. Remnants of ancient animal sacrifice can also be found in various contemporary practices, for example the kapparos and shechita of Judaism and ḍabīḥah of Islam, It is happening even in America too. Linda Greenhouse (June 12, 1993) writes: "The Supreme Court ruled today that a Florida city's ban on ritual sacrifice violated the religious freedom of the followers of an Afro-Cuban religion in which the sacrifice of animals plays a central role."

It is unthinkable that Hindus, who, for millennia years, have been globally known as vegetarian, did any time or would practice unholy ritual of animal sacrifice to please their vegetarian God. I don't mean that non-vegetarians are unholy. It doesn't make sense that any religion, particularly Hinduism, Jainism, Buddhism and Sikhism, would like to offer a slaughtered animal as an offering to God, creator and protector of life.

Hindu scriptures forbid animal sacrifice

Vedas, Upanishads, Bhagvad Gita and other sacred scriptures tell that ancient sages were vegetarian and lived primarily on fruits and

---

[150] Wikipedia.

vegetables. Unfortunately, such unholy practices are yet happening in present India, particularly in some remote rural sections of the society, more so among some tribal aboriginals who have been socio-culturally and educationally distanced and isolated from mainstream. Education among them and improved communication and transport means have been diminishing their socio-cultural isolation, helping them to realize that sacrifice of animals has no humanitarian or religious sense, thus the practice of animal sacrifice has been shrinking. Their awakened interest in sacred scriptures is helping them to know that Vedas, Bhagvad Gita, and Purans forbid animal sacrifice.

The Hindi-English-Hindi Dictionary by Joseph W. Raker and Rama Shukla defines sacrifice: "to offer to a god *balidan* (sacrifice), *bhet chadana* (give gifts) or *tyaag karna* (sacrifice). It clearly says that sacrifice means to do sacrifice of own things in the interest of some one or society, not to sacrifice some body or some animal to please God because of own guilt.

Manu Smriti misrepresented and distorted

In Manu Smriti, there is description of some meat-eating people. Impious statements of animal killing and meat eating were interpolated in Manu Smriti telling that meat was served during *Shradh,* a pious religious ceremony related to the appeasement of the soul of the deceased elderly member of the family. In the pious *Shradh* ceremony, Brahmins are invited to dine. Only vegetarian food and fruits are served. But, the statements related to some meat-eating people in the *Smriti* were interpolated to show that meat was served at even the *Shradh* ceremony.

Every year, we have *Shradhs* in our family to remember our dear departed souls. This is the occasion when the whole day we eat and serve only vegetarian food and fruits, though we are non-vegetarian. I remember *Shradhs* from my childhood. This is a way to let children know our heritage – who were our great-great-grand parents, what their great attitudes were and what great things they did. History of family has lessons for children. Absence of such family ceremony will put an end to the knowledge and remembering of the family ancestors.

But the Britain erred. It failed to understand the significance of the oral traditions of Hindus which protected Vedic knowledge from being corrupted by mischievous interpolations. Moreover, the British rulers wanted to anglicize Hindus through English education. But, English education was too expensive for rural and for most urban people.

Is Non-vegetarianism, Animal Sacrifice?

It would be wrong to characterize non-vegetarianism as a custom of animal sacrifice. It is hard to believe that any civilized society would like to entertain the custom of animal sacrifice, mean that a slaughtered animal be solemnized by some religious rituals to offer it to the vegetarian God. No religion would pronounce killing as sacred. Religion should not be maligned. Religion teaches to protect life and it prescribes civilization.

Western historians – some because of their absence of correct understanding of the main Indic language (Sanskrit), and some with their missionary agenda – have misinterpreted Sanskrit words to justify their biased perspectives on Hinduism. For example, the word *'Ashvamedh'* has been miss-interpreted. *Ashvamedh* is a very well known *Yagya*[151], mentioned in various Vedic scriptures. It was a well-known royal custom in ancient times when country was divided into several town-size small kingdoms. A horse – well adorned and ritually worshipped with Vedic Mantras – was let free by a mighty king to roam around in nearby small kingdoms to assert his lordship over them. The horse was followed by a group of well-armed warriors. The king in whose territory the horse entered had either to accept subordination or to put up fight.

It is well known that European colonialists, particularly British, used to mistranslate or to get mistranslated the sacred scriptures of their colonized peoples to pursue their mischievous colonial agenda by disgracing their culture to infuse in them low self-image to make it easier to get own European moral and cultural superiority accepted, the first step to get royal authority accepted. Political pundits have said: "If you want to establish your rule over some people, you have to

---

[151] 3.Swami Prakashanand Sarswati, 'The True History of the Religion of India' (200, pp. 274-276).

weaken them by maligning their culture and heritage." So Britain did with the people they conquered. They were smart. They used to heavily bribe Sanskrit pundits to interpret words and sentences to suit their missionary agenda. They even got Sanskrit Vachaspatyam (dictionary) authored by some bribed Pundit. Max Müller wrote about the Vedas according to such dictionary[152]. Out of many, I am giving only two words –'*ashhvamedh*' and '*goghn*' – will explain my point.

Ashvamedh (Ashva = horse and medh means to kill) the horse to kill not be killed. How the king will order to kill the horse which made his mission successful.

The other word '*goghn*' has also been misinterpreted to demean Hinduism. In fact, in Sanskrit '*go*' means cow and '*ghn*' means receiver of cow in charity. But it has been miss-interpreted as the 'killer' of the cow. How would Hindus kill cow which is being worshipped as mother from the birth of Hinduism? Hindus adore cow as mother because it gives milk? In Hindustan slaughter a cow is crime.

Money can buy any thing, even conscience and religion. The renowned Pundit Taranath of Calcutta Sanskrit College, in his *Vachaspatyam* (Dictionary) defied the accepted meanings of the words, '*Ashvamedh*' and '*goghn*'.

Surprising, history professor Stanley Wolpert, in *A New History of India* (1997, p.25), miss-translates the word '*dasa*' as 'slave'. The professor of history should have known the history and antiquity of the slavery. It does not have a long history. The shameful inhuman slavery is mainly associated with the Western people of Europe and America. Only rich and strong man or nation can have courage to do such shameful thing. Moreover, Wolpert should have known the exact dictionary meaning of '*dasa*' and the education system of ancient India. In Hindu educational traditions, the word '*dasa*' means '*sewak*' or servant who voluntarily stayed at the residence of his guru for education during the first stage (ā*shram)*, known as *Brahmcharya*, of his life during which he was supposed to strictly observe celibacy to earn the knowledge of the Vedas and other sacred Vedic scriptures with uninterrupted guidance of his learned guru. He stays at Guru's house as a student, not as a slave. He returns home after his education is over to start the second ashram

---

[152] Ibid. p. 274.

of life, known as *'Grahastha'* (family). The Dasas were not slaves, sold and bought. They were shewaks (servants), rather students to learn Vedic knowledge. Their service to their guru was as if the tuition for their vidya (education).

Hindu life is divided into four *āshrams* – Brahamcharya, Grahastha, Vaishya and Sanyas. During his *brahamcharya āshram,* one is supposed to live at his guru's (teacher's) residence. Naturally he, as his student, would serve his guru at whose house he is staying as a member of the family. Misrepresentation of such an important historical institution of *Brahmcharya* as slavery is abuse of history.

Wolpert's (p.25) statement that the *Rig Veda* is "the world's earliest surviving Indo-European literature" contradicts his conviction in the theory of 'Aryan invasion of India', according to which Sanskrit, the language of the *Rig Veda,* came to India from outside.

Sacrifice: misunderstand, Sacrifice of animals within self

The word 'sacrifice' is being misinterpreted. Jain sage Jinabhadra[153] interprets the Vedic sacrifice as metaphorical figure of speech, one thing spoken for another:

"Body is the altar, mind is the fire blazing with the ghee of knowledge and burning the sacrificial sticks of impurities produced from the tree of karma."

Body for Altar
Mind for Fire
Ghee for Knowledge
Sticks for impurities
Tree for karma

It means that the sticks of impurities are to be burned out by the fire of mind, blazed with the ghee of knowledge, activated by Karma.

---

[153] Studies in Jain literature by Vaman Mahadeo Kulkarni, Śreshṭhī rabhāī Lālabhāī Smāraka Nidhi, p. 92.

Jinabhadra, in his *Visesavasyakabhasya,* cites a number of passages from the Upanishads which have been misinterpreted as animal sacrifice. In fact, it was sacrifice of **animals in human,** in form of five basic vices – *Kām* (lust), *Krodha* (Anger), *Lobha* (greed), *Moha* (attachments) and *Ahamkar* (ego, egoism, pride). Hindus perform *hawans* (fire ceremonies) in which they throw ghee and rice (as oblation) while singing mantras saying *"suhava"* meaning "we offer sacrifice of our vices, metaphorically animals within self. Sacrifice of human vices is misinterpreted as sacrifice of animals by some, particularly western scholars. It is unimaginable that a scholar would believe that God, who gives life and protects it, would like an animal be killed for His feast or would accept it as an offering. Such scholar may be an atheist or confused about the relationship between God and life. God is merciful not only to humans but also to all creatures who have life.

It is hard to understand why the word 'sacrifice' is used in prayer. The sacrifice[154] King Dasaratha was performing for progeny was not sacrifice, but prayer to God to bless him with children. Only ghee with grains of rice, not flesh of an animal, was being poured into the *hawan* (fire) while chanting holy religious mantras, praying to forgive the sins, symbolically represented by ghee and grains of rice.

Use of the word 'sacrifice' inappropriate, thus confusing

The word 'sacrifice' is confusing because its use in the context is not right. In Hinduism, such ceremony is not called *'balidan'* (sacrifice), but it is called *pooja,* praying for progeny or removal of the pains, the family has been suffering. It is hard to see any truth in this that the ritual is performed to offer sacrifice of an animal to please God. Man prays silently at home, go to temple to pray before deities, or arrange a *pooja* at home inviting family and friends. It is hard to understand that the 'pooja' is termed as 'sacrifice'. I, as a teenager, remember my grand father and grand uncles had arranged a two-day-long *pooja (Yagya)* (not sacrifice) at home in our home town Mehar in Sind (now in Pakistan). There seems colonial mischief to term 'Pooja' as sacrifice. During the days of *pooja,* no meat was served, though our family is basically non-vegetarian.

---

[154] Its wrong use, as explained in C. Rajagopalchari's, Ramayana, p.3.

The word 'sacrifice' does not mean sacrifice of slaughtered animals, but, of five animals (vices) within:

1. *kaam* (lust),
2. *krodha* (anger),
3. *lobha* (greed),
4. *moha* (attachments) and
5. *ahimkar* (ego or self-pride).

Vices (animals within) more ferocious than lion

Vices are more ferocious than even wild living animals. It is easy, rather possible, to tame animals, even the lion, but very difficult to regulate the above animals within self. For this man needs long tedious *tapasya* (meditated penance) under the guidance of a celebrated guru. During 90 years of my life, I have never seen, nor heard, serving meat during the day of *pooja*.

S. R. Rao[155] observes that Hindus worship goddess *Agni* (Fire) and Mother Goddess. He talks about Hindu veneration of animals and suggests that the Indus Valley did not know animal sacrifice. If animal sacrifice was practiced, it would have continued until today. Hindus are traditionalist. They continue their traditional practices. On the days of religious rituals, Hindus observe fast and strict vegetarianism. Such ceremony, known as '*hawan*' (offering an oblation with fire), is performed when Hindu family is praying to God for '*daya*' (mercy). Almost all Hindu ceremonies – celebrating nomenclature, wedding, *janeoo*, graduation, victory in any matter, *shanti* (peace of mind), or even death (praying peace for the departed soul) – are performed around *Agni* (fire), symbolically destroyer of enemies and all ills of life. Thus, India's missiles have been named as Agni-1, Agni-2, 3, 4, 5, 6.

In modern times, even non-vegetarian Hindus avoid eating non-vegetarian food on religious days. How then, would animal sacrifice be practiced among Hindus who venerate animals? Present Vedic people (Hindus) in general, even after millennia-years of Vedic customs, have retained their tradition of vegetarianism and *ahimsa*. Even in present

---

[155] S. R. Rao, in 'Dawn and Development of the Indus Civilization (1991, p.121).

times, non-vegetarianism is not considered a celebrated tradition among Hindus, Jains, Buddhists and Sikhs. Even Sikhs, though generally non-vegetarian, never serve non-vegetarian food in *langers* – meals served in Gurudwaras – or even at home on religious occasions. Vegetarianism is considered as a virtue. In matrimonial matter, the candidate groom, if vegetarian, earns more marks. I don't deny that non-vegetarianism has been there since the birth of the humanity in varying degree from society to society. Globalization, with its emphasis on healthy food, has been promoting vegetarianism.

Shrādha is the ceremony to remember and offer shradhanjali to the departed soul to give him/her loving homage and talk about the great things he/she did. There is a month during which all departed souls are remembered and offered loving homage. The tradition helps every body in the family, including friends, to remember the departed soul. To solemnize the pious *Shrādh* ceremony, a Brahmin or a girl, depending on the gender of the departed soul being remembered, is invited to a feast of sumptuous vegetarian meal, supplemented by fruits and milk-product sweets. I remember, in case of the Shrādha, remembering my grand mother, a girl, not a Brahmin, was invited to grace the occasion. Hindus view girl equal to one hundred Brahmins because of her innocence and purity. I am talking about the Shrādha, as perceived in my family. I have not experienced Shrādhs for over 40 years; I have been in America without my parents who passed away in 60s of twentieth century. I feel guilty for not observing our great traditions which, I see, has desirable lessons of life. Statements, related to some meat-eating people in the *Smriti*, were interpolated to show that meat was served at even the *Shrādha* ceremonies, which is wrong. It is difficult to believe that this can happen.

I remember, every year, we had *Shrādhs* in our family to remember our departed souls. We considered *Shrādha* as a sacred ritual when whole day we, though non-vegetarian, ate and served only vegetarian food, supplemented by sweets and fruits. This gave us a feeling that we were cleansed. Parents used to talk about the great things their parents had. This is way to let children know their heritage – which were our great-grand parents, what their attitudes, thoughts, were and what great things they did. History of family has lessons for children. Absence of such family ceremony will put end to the history of family. *Shrādha* enliven the continuity of the family, from its origin to its present.

Ashvamedh Yagya, Misperceived

Western historians – some due to their intentional ignorance and some because of their dedication to their missionary agenda – have abused their 'only child' history, by misinterpreting and mistranslating Sanskrit words to justify their intentionally biased perspectives on Hinduism. For example, the word *'Ashvamedh'* has been miss-interpreted as killing of *Ashva* (horse). *Ashvamedh* is a well known historical *Yagya*,[156] mentioned in various Vedic scriptures. It was a well-known royal custom in ancient times when country was divided into town-size small kingdoms. A horse – well adorned and ritually worshipped with Vedic Mantras – was let free by a mighty king to roam around in nearby small kingdoms to assert his lordship over them. The horse, driven by a brave soldier, was followed by a group of well-armed warriors. The king, in whose territory the horse entered, had two options – either to accept subordination or put up fight.

It is a well known historical fact that British colonialists used to translate or get translated histories and sacred scriptures of their colonized peoples, particularly of India, because they knew that Hindus were capable of rising up again. Political pundits have said: "If you want to establish your rule over some people, you have to weaken them by maligning their religion, culture, and heritage by distorting, misrepresenting and mitigating their history." So Britain did with the peoples they conquered. They were smart. They used to heavily bribe Sanskrit pundits to interpret words and sentences to suit their missionary agenda and strategy. They got Sanskrit Vachaspatyam (dictionary) authored by some bribed Pundit. Max Müller wrote about the Vedas according to such dictionary.[157] Out of many, I am giving only three words, *ashhvamedh, gogh'* and *dasa*. They will explain my point:

---

[156] 3. Ibid, (pp. 274-276).
[157] . Ibid. p. 274.

1. Ashvamedh (Ashva = horse and medh means to kill) the horse to kill not be killed. How would the king order to kill the horse which made his mission successful?

2. Goghn' has also been misinterpreted to demean Hinduism. In fact, *go'* means cow and *ghn'* means receiver of cow in charity. But, it has been miss-interpreted as the 'killer' of the cow. How would Hindus kill'cow', they have been worshipping from the day of the birth of Hinduism, too ancient to know. Hindus revere cow as mother, because she gives milk, as mother gives to her children, In Hindustan it is crime to slaughter cow.

3. 'Dasa' (devoted servant) has been mistranslated as 'slave', to malign ancient Hindus allegedly practicing shameful slavery. History professor Stanley Wolpert, in *A New History of India*' (1997, p.25), translates the word *'dasa'* as slave. A few other scholars also have done the same. Wolpert should have known the educational system in ancient India, so as to understand the meaning of the word *Dasa*, characterizing the student, serving his teacher (Guru) while staying at his residence. The word 'Dasa' literally means servant (sewak, naukar), not slave. But in the *guru-vidyarthi* (teacher-student) context during ancient Vedic period, student was not considered as a servant (naukar) who gets wages. He was considered *sevak* who did *seva*, meaning service to Guru for receiving knowledge from him. He stayed at Guru's residence, not in a hostel to receive education. That was the system, quite different from the present system, both are appropriate as per the circumstances, modern different from the ancient. For Europeans and even for several modern Hindus it may be difficult to differentiate *sevak* from servant. Sevak is graced with attributes of devotion and respect for Guru (teacher), which servant, in general, does not have, because he is paid wages.'Dasa' gets *gyān'* (knowledge, education) without paying any fee. In Hinduism, Guru (teacher) gets high regard. There is a couplet in a religious scripture: "If both Guru and God are standing in front of you, whose feet you will touch first? The answer is "I will first salute Guru, because I can meet God, only with help of Guru." Guru is medium between devotee

and deity. Guru is essential for self-realization and realization of oneness with Almighty God. Both systems of education are correct as per circumstances. Had Wolpert understood the teacher-student Guru-Vidyarthi) relationship in the ancient Vedic school system, he would have not taken 'Dasa' as slave.

Wolpert, before branding India as the culprit for history of slavery, should have known the antiquity and history of the slavery. Its history is not longer than a few centuries. The shameful inhuman slavery is mainly associated with the western peoples of Europe and America. Only Europe and America did enjoy the luxury of slavery.

I don't blame only Wolpert for mistranslating the word 'Dasa.' Several others have done the same. Even some Sanskrit dictionaries have been corrupted, in which *'Dasa'* has been translated as 'slave.'

Conclusion

Western scholars – because of their foggy understanding of Vedic rituals due to their limited knowledge of Sanskrit and more so because of their colonial mischievous agenda – have intentionally misinterpreted several Vedic rituals. At each *hawan*, religious ceremony for peace and tranquility holy mantras are sung, and the word *'suhawa'* is pronounced at each offering (throwing) of 'rice, ghee, etc' in the sacred *Agni kunda* (alter). The word 'suhawa' (offering) has been interpreted as a sacrifice of an animal. It is offering of ghee and rice, as thrown into the fire, not pieces of flesh of an animal to please of God, the giver of life (Brahma) and care protector of life (Vishnu). Shiva ends old and suffering life to be born as fresh child, as explained by the basic Hindu tenet, known as 'Rebirth and Reincarnation.' Shiva – because of His double role of both birth and death to enliven the continuity of life – is worshiped the most as the great mythological god.

Chapter Twentytwo

BHAGAVAD GITA, TORCH ON THE PATH TO TRUTH

Bhagvad Gita is a diagnostic as well as therapeutic conversation between Lord Krishna as therapist and Arjuna as a patient. Arjuna, because of his psychologically unresolved *moha* (attachments), had conflict between saving the lives of his kith and kin and the interest of the nation, rather humanity. Thus he refused to lift his arrow against his extended family of cousins, uncles and grand uncles and even his gurus. Lord Krishna helped Arjuna during the 18 days of the battle on the Krukshetra to understand the TRUTH and fight for justice. It is an objective story, as evidenced by both, the civilized as well as brutal dealings, like gambling wife, let her be sold and allow Kauras to unclothe her, which fortunately could not be done.

It seems, Lord Krishna had knowledge of psychoanalysis and skills of psychotherapy. It would be wrong to think that psychoanalysis has European origin. Knowledge, like humanity, has no earmarked known origin, nor any ethnicity. Knowledge (*gyan*) is secular without any known color or race. Knowledge has no borders to be confined within. It travels all over the planet without any identity and visa, as evidenced by the millennia ancient Vedic knowledge in all its departments – mentioning a few, such as sociology, psychology, psychotherapy, psychoanalysis, scientific, engineering, medical technology, etc, still alive and getting increasingly fresh. I am trying to emphasize that '**knowledge, like God, is origin-less and endless**'. Knowledge has still unending lot in store for man to identify and use it for the development and progress of humanity.

Sigmund Freud might have got knowledge or idea of psychoanalysis from Vedas and Mahabharata. It is also possible that Freud himself might have unconsciously sensed its vibrations within inner-self and theorized it as 'Freudian psychoanalysis'.

The Bhagavad-Gita is the eternal message of spirituality. The word Gita means song and the word Bhagavad means God. Often the Bhagavad-Gita is called the song of God. Vedavyasa was the divine saint who authored the Srimad Bhagavatam, Vedanta Sutra, the 108 Puranas, composed and divided the Vedas into the Rik, Yajur, Artharva and Sama Vedas, and wrote the great historical treatise Mahabharata known as the fifth Veda. His full name is Krishna Dvaipayana Vyasa and he was the son of sage Parasara and mother Satyavati. The Bhagavad-Gita is composed of 700 Sanskrit verses, of conversation between Lord Krishna and Arjuna, while on the Mahabharata battlefield Kurukshetra. It contains 18 chapters, one chapter on each day of the 18 days of Mahabharata war. It is divided into three sections, each consisting of six chapters:

(i)   They are Karma Yoga the Yoga of actions or activity
(ii) Bhakti Yoga the Yoga of devotion and
(iii) Jnana Yoga (Gyan Yoga) the Yoga of knowledge.

Gita is the eighteen-day conversation between Lord Krishna and Arjuna, while on the battle field, known as *Kuruksheshtra,* during the 18 days of the Mahabharata war (3137 BC). The basic theme of the Bhagvad Gita is that Arjuna was hesitant to fight against his blood cousins, uncles and grand uncles because of his unresolved *moha* (attachment) to be able to see the interest of the nation over the lives of his kith and kin. Lord Krishna helped him to rise and fight for the good of the nation. The knowledge of the Bhagvad Gita is practical and justifiably applicable in all human conflicts, irrespective their religious orientations.

Ancient history being delivered by millennia-long oral traditions

In those prehistory distant ancient times, there was neither writing nor printing facility. Gita – like Vedas, several *shastras* and the two epics,

Ramayana and Mahabharata – is being given down from generation to generation through millennia-long oral traditions. It is unbelievable, but the fact, as evidenced by the millennia-long ancient history, being shared through street Ram and Krishna *leelas* (plays, dramas), from generation to generation. Even the wisdom of Gita is being entertained since thousands of years.

Hindus believe that the true knowledge, like lotus, survives clean and clear, even passing through the human muddy mind. The flower LOTUS (Sanskrit *Padma, Kamal*) has great symbolical significance in Hinduism. It is rooted in mud, floats above in clean water. It represents beauty and non-attachment, meaning not attached to the dirt of evil thinking and of evil deeds. It gives the message: "Keep above the evils of humanity." According to the Bhagvad Gita:

> "One who performs his duty without attachments, surrendering the results to the Supreme Lord, is unaffected by sinful action, as the lotus leaf is untouched by water."

Attachment with dear ones can bring pain in case of loss or separation. Better remain concerned and do what you are expected to do for your dear ones, but don't get too emotionally attached and lose yourself. Several non-Hindu scholars have praised Bhagvad Gita, and even some non-Indians have translated Gita into the language of their country. The English novelist and essayist Aldous Huxley (1894-1963) has said that the Bhagvad Gita is for the whole world. He recommends to every one to read it to discover pearls, no where else one would find. He further says:

> "The Bhagvad Gita is the most systematic statement of spiritual evolution of endowing value of mankind. The Gita is one of the clearest and most comprehensive summaries of the spiritual thoughts ever to have been made."[158]

---

[158] T. C. Galav: 'Philosophy of Hinduism – An Introduction' (p.65).

The Greek Demetrios Galianos had translated the Bhagavad-Gita.

Prof. Fatehullah Mojtabai, former Cultural Counselor of the Embassy of Iran in India, was a noted scholar of Sanskrit and a well-known exponent of Vedic philosophy. He has translated Bhagvad Gita into Persian, the *Laghuyogavāsistha* and *Mahopanisad*. He was so much impressed by the philosophy of Hinduism, as contained in Gita, that he wanted his countrymen (Iranians) should also benefit from the Gita philosophy. May be his ancestors were Zoroastrians whose language Zend-Avestan was very similar to Sanskrit.

Henry David Thoreau (1817-1862) displayed fascination with Vedic spirituality, as reflected in the Bhagvad Gita:

"In the morning I bathe my intellect in the stupendous and cosmogonal philosophy of the Bhagavad Gita, since whose composition years of the gods have elapsed and in comparison with which our modern world and its literature seems puny and trivial."

Amazingly, Robert Oppenheimer, the very first Chairman of Atomic Energy Commission and the father of the Atom bomb was a great admirer of the *Bhagvad Gita*. Amazingly, he learnt Sanskrit to understand Gita. After witnessing the first atomic explosion, Oppenheimer read a couplet from Gita (Chapter 11: 12):

"If hundreds of thousands of suns rose up into the sky, they might resemble the effulgence of the Supreme Person in the universal form."

Westerners translated Bhagvad Gita

Sir Charles Wilkins, KH, FRS (1749 – May 13, 1836), was an English typographer and Orientalist, notable as the first translator of Bhagavad Gita into English, and as the creator, alongside Panchanan Karmakar, of the first Bengali typeface. He was born at Frome in Somerset in 1749. In 1770 he went to India as a printer and writer in the East India Company's service. His facility with language allowed him to quickly learn Persian and Bengali. He was closely involved in the design of the first type for printing Bengali. He published the first typeset book in the language, earning himself the name "the Caxton of India." He also designed type for publications of books in Persian. In 1781 he was appointed as translator of Persian and Bengali to the Commissioner of Revenue and as superintendent of the Company's press. He successfully translated a Royal inscription in Kutila characters, which were hitherto indecipherable. In 1784, Wilkins helped William Jones establish the Asiatic Society of Bengal. Wilkins moved to Varanasi, where he studied Sanskrit under Kalinatha, a Brahmin pundit. At this period he began work on his translation of the Mahabharata, securing strong support for his activities from the governor of British India, Warren Hastings. Though he never completed the translation, portions were later published. The most important was his version of the Gita, published in 1785 as *Bhagvat-geeta, or Dialogues of Kreeshna and Arjoon* (London: Nourse, 1785). In his preface Wilkins argued that the Gita was written to encourage a form of monotheist "unitarianism" and to draw Hinduism away from the polytheism he ascribed to the Vedas. His translation of Gita was itself soon translated into French (1787) and German (1802). It proved Gita's major influence on Roman literature and on European perception of Hindu philosophy. William Blake later celebrated the publication in his picture *The Bramins*, exhibited in 1809, which depicted Wilkins and Brahmin scholars working on the translation.

With Hastings' departure from India, Wilkins lost his main patron. He returned to England in 1786, where he married Elizabeth Keeble. In 1787 Wilkins followed the Gita with his translation of *The Heetopades of Veeshnoo-Sarma, in a Series of Connected Fables, Interspersed with Moral, Prudential and Political Maxims* (Bath: 1787). He was elected a fellow of the Royal Society in 1788. In 1800, he was invited to take up the post of the first director of the India House Library, which became over time the world famous 'India Office Library' (now British Library - Oriental Collections). In 1801 he became librarian to the East India Company, He was named examiner at Haileybury when a college was established there in 1805. During these years he devoted himself to the creation of a font for Devanagari, the 'divine script'. In 1808 he published his *Grammar of the Sanskrita Language*. King George IV gave him the badge of the Royal Guelphic Order and he was knighted in recognition of his services to Oriental scholarship in 1833.

The English novelist and essayist Aldous Huxley (1894-1963) has said that the Bhagvad Gita is for the whole world. He recommends to every one to read it and try to discover pearls, no where else available. He has further says:

> "The Bhagvad Gita is the most systematic statement of spiritual evolution of endowing value of mankind. The Gita is one of the clearest and most comprehensive summaries of the spiritual thoughts ever to have been made."[159]

Annie Besant has[160] also talked about the jewels in the Bhagvad Gita and Mahabharata:

> "Among the priceless teachings that may be found in the great Indian epic Mahabharata, there is none so rare and priceless as the Gita. ... For those who, though born for this life in a Western land, and clad in a Western body, can yet look back to earlier incarnations in which they drank the milk of spiritual wisdom from the breast of their true mother – they must feel ever the magic of her immemorial past, must dwell ever under the spell of her deathless fascination; for they are bound to India by all the sacred memories of their past; and with her, too, are bound up all the radiant hopes of their future, a future which they know they will share with her who is their true mother in the soul-life."[161]

---

[159] T. C. Galav: 'Philosophy of Hinduism – An Introduction' (p.65).

[160] Stephen Knapp, 'The Power of the Dharma' (2006, p.10).

[161] Annie Besant, 'India: Essays and Lectures' (vol. iv), London: The Theosophical Publishing Co. (1895, p.11).

Deathless Life

Annie Besant talks about India's amazing fascination for 'deathless life.' It is a fact of Hindu life. It is a continuous life without any death, like that of 'cycle of day and night' as suggested by Hindu belief in *'Punner-janma'* (rebirth). It is like an unending chain of 'birth → life → death →birth', the union of 'birth and death', like the union of 'day and night', 'light and darkness'. At higher level, it means the union of *'atma'* and *Parmatma* (soul and Supreme Soul). The words 'death' (English) and 'maot' (Arabic) mean end of life. The word *'Dehant'*, the Sanskrit word for death, means end of only body (*deh* = body + *ant* = end), not of soul. It explains the Hindu concept of death means 'unending continuous or deathless life'. According to the Bhagvad Gita and other shastras only the body dies, the soul transmigrates into another infant body. Such optimistic view of life dilutes the fear of death, as stressed by Mahatma Gandhi.

Sir Charles Wilkins (1749 – 1836), an English typographer and Orientalist, was the first translator of Bhagavad Gita into English. In 1770, he went to India as a printer and writer in the East India Company's service. His facility with language allowed him to quickly learn Persian and Bengali. He was closely involved in the design of the first type for printing Bengali. He published the first typeset book in the language, earning himself the name 'the Caxton of India'.

In 1784, Wilkins helped William Jones to establish the Asiatic Society of Bengal. Wilkins moved to Varanasi, where he studied Sanskrit under Kalinatha, a Brahmin pundit. At this period he began work on his translation of the Mahabharata, securing strong support for his activities from the governor of British India, Warren Hastings. Though he never completed the translation, portions were later published. The most important was his version of the Gita, published in 1785 as *'Bhagvat-geeta, or Dialogues of Kreeshna and Arjoon'*. In the preface, Wilkins argued that the Gita was written to encourage a form of monotheist "Unitarianism" and to draw Hinduism away from the polytheism he ascribed to the Vedas. His translation of the Gita was itself soon translated into French (1787) and German (1802). It proved to be a major influence on Romantic literature and on European perception of Hindu philosophy. William Blake later celebrated the publication in his picture *The Brahmins*, exhibited in 1809, which depicted Wilkins and Brahmin scholars working on the translation.

With Hastings' departure from India, Wilkins lost his main patron. He returned to England in 1786, where he married Elizabeth Keeble. In 1787 Wilkins followed the Gita with his translation of *The Heetopades of Veeshnoo-Sarma, in a Series of Connected Fables, Interspersed with Moral, Prudential and Political Maxims* (Bath: 1787). He was elected a fellow of the Royal Society in 1788. In 1800, he was invited to take up the post of the first director of the India House Library, which became over time the world famous 'India Office Library' (now British Library — Oriental Collections). In 1801 he became librarian to the East India Company. He devoted himself to the creation of a font for Devanagari, the "divine script". In 1808 he published his *Grammar of the Sanskrita Language*. King George IV gave him the badge of the Royal Guelphic Order and he was knighted in recognition of his services to Oriental scholarship in 1833. He died in London at the age of 86.

Demetrios Galianos translated the Bhagvad Gita and the French philosopher and historian Roger – Pol Droit has written in his classic 'L'oubli de l'Inde' (India Forgotten) "that there is absolutely not a shadow of a doubt that Greeks knew all about Indian philosophy."

Bhagavad Gita Quotes by Lord Krishna[162]

Here are about hundred Bhagavad Gita quotes, spoken by Krishna to Arjuna on the battlefield of the Kurukshetra (around 3138 BC). [163]They represent the essence of Gita, teachings of Lord Krishna who died around 3102 BC.

---

[162] Sunil Daman, Wikipedia
[163] These are taken from a translation by Eknath Easwaran.

Krishna Quotes from the Bhagavad Gita

- Whenever dharma declines and the purpose of life is forgotten, I manifest myself on earth. I am born in every age to protect the good, to destroy evil, and to reestablish dharma.
- As they approach me, so I receive them. All paths, Arjuna, lead to me.
- I am the beginning, middle, and end of creation.
- Among animals I am the lion; among birds, the eagle Garuda. I am Prahlada, born among the demons, and of all that measures, I am time.
- I am death, which overcomes all, and the source of all beings still to be born.
- Just remember that I am, and that I support the entire cosmos with only a fragment of my being.
- Behold, Arjuna, a million divine forms, with an infinite variety of color and shape.
- Behold the gods of the natural world, and many more wonders never revealed before.
- Behold the entire cosmos turning within my body, and the other things you desire to see.
- I am time, the destroyer of all; I have come to consume the world.
- That one is dear to me who runs not after the pleasant or away from the painful, grieves not, lusts not, but lets things come and go as they happen.
- Just as a reservoir is of little use when the whole countryside is flooded, scriptures are of little use to the illumined man or woman, who sees the Lord everywhere.
- They alone see truly who see the Lord the same in every creature, who see the deathless in the hearts of that entire die.
- Seeing the same Lord everywhere, they do not harm themselves or others. Thus they attain the supreme goal.
- With a drop of my energy I enter the earth and support all creatures. Through the moon, the vessel of life-giving fluid, I nourish all plants. I enter breathing creatures and dwell within

342

as the life-giving breath. I am the fire in the stomach which digests all food.

- There are three gates to this self-destructive hell: lust, anger, and greed. Renounce these three.
- Pleasure from the senses seems like nectar at first, but it is bitter as poison in the end.
- That which seems like poison at first, but tastes like nectar in the end – this is the joy of sattva, born of a mind at peace with itself.
- The Lord dwells in the hearts of all creatures and whirls them round upon the wheel of *maya*. Run to him for refuge with all your strength and peace profound will be yours through his grace.
- Whatever you do, make it an offering to me – the food you eat, the sacrifices you make, the help you give, even your suffering.
- I am heat; I give and withhold the rain. I am immortality and I am death; I am what is and what is not.
- Those who worship other gods with faith and devotion also worship me, Arjuna, even if they do not observe the usual forms. I am the object of all worship, its enjoyer and Lord.
- Those who remember me at the time of death will come to me. Do not doubt this. Whatever occupies the mind at the time of death determines the destination of the dying; always they will tend toward that state of being.
- When meditation is mastered, the mind is unwavering like the flame of a lamp in a windless place.
- They are forever free who renounce all selfish desires and break away from the 'ego cage' of "I," "me," and "mine" to be united with the Lord. This is the supreme state. Attain to this, and pass from death to immortality.
- They live in wisdom who sees themselves in all and all in them, who have renounced every selfish desire and sense-craving tormenting the heart.
- The meaning of Karma is in the intention. The intention behind action is what matters. Those who are motivated only by desire for the fruits of action are miserable, for they are constantly anxious about the results of what they do.

- You have the right to work, but never to the fruit of work. You should never engage in action for the sake of reward, nor should you long for inaction.
- Perform work in this world, Arjuna, as a man established within himself – without selfish attachments, and alike in success and defeat. Yoga is perfect evenness of mind.
- At the beginning of time I declared two paths for the pure heart: jnana yoga, the contemplative path of spiritual wisdom, and karma yoga, the active path of selfless service. There are the fundamental different types of yoga.
- Do your work with the welfare of others always in mind. It was by such work that Janaka attained perfection; others too have followed this path.
- There is nothing in the three worlds for me to gain, Arjuna, nor is there anything I do not have; I continue to act, but I am not driven by any need of my own.
- Ignore work for your own profit, Arjuna, Always work for the welfare of the world, without thought for yourself.
- It is better to strive in one's own dharma than to succeed in the dharma of another. Nothing is ever lost in following one's own dharma, but competition in another's dharma breeds fear and insecurity.
- The senses are higher than the body, the mind higher than the senses; above the mind is the intellect, and above the intellect is the Atman. Thus, knowing that which is supreme let the Atman rule the ego. Use your mighty arms to slay the fierce enemy that is selfish desire.
- You and I have passed through many births, Arjuna. You have forgotten, but I remember them all.
- My true being is unborn and changeless. I am the Lord who dwells in every creature. Through the power of my own maya, I manifest myself in a finite form.
- Those who know me as their own divine Self break through the belief that they are the body and are not reborn as separate creatures. Such a one, Arjuna, is united with me.

- Delivered from selfish attachment, fear, and anger, filled with me, surrendering themselves to me, purified in the fire of my being, many have reached the state of unity in me.

Bhagavad Gita Quotes on emotions

- Actions do not cling to me because I am not attached to their results. Those who understand this and practice it live in freedom.
- The wise see that there is action in the midst of inaction and inaction in the midst of action. Their consciousness is unified, and every act is done with complete awareness.
- The process of offering is Brahman; that which is offered is Brahman. Brahman offers the sacrifice in the fire of Brahman. Brahman is attained by those who see Brahman in every action.
- The offering of wisdom is better than any material offering, Arjuna; for the goal of all work is spiritual wisdom.
- Approach those who have realized the purpose of life and question them with reverence and devotion; they will instruct you in this wisdom.
- Even if you were the most sinful of sinners, Arjuna, you could cross beyond all sin by the raft of spiritual wisdom.
- As the heat of a fire reduces wood to ashes, the fire of knowledge burns to ashes all karma.
- Those who surrender to Brahman all selfish attachments are like the leaf of a lotus floating clean and dry in water. Sin cannot touch them.
- Those who renounce attachment in all their deeds live content in the "city of nine gates," the body, as its master. They are not driven to act, nor do they involve others in action.
- Those who possess this wisdom have equal regard for all. They see the same Self in a spiritual aspirant and an outcaste, in an elephant, a cow, and a dog.
- Pleasures conceived in the world of the senses have a beginning and an end and give birth to misery, Arjuna. The wise do not look for happiness in them. But those who overcome the

impulses of lust and anger which arise in the body are made whole and live in joy. They find their joy, their rest, and their light completely within themselves. United with the Lord, they attain nirvana in Brahman.

- Free from anger and selfish desire, unified in mind, those who follow the path of yoga and realize the Self are established forever in that supreme state.

- Knowing me as the friend of all creatures, the Lord of the universe, the end of all offerings and all spiritual disciplines, they attain eternal peace.

- It is not those who lack energy or refrain from action, but those who work without expectation of reward who attain the goal of meditation.

- Those who cannot renounce attachment to the results of their work are far from the path.

- Reshape yourself through the power of your will; never let yourself be degraded by self-will. The will is the only friend of the Self, and the will is the only enemy of the Self.

- To those who have conquered themselves, the will is a friend. But it is the enemy of those who have not found the Self within them.

- The supreme Reality stands revealed in the consciousness of those who have conquered themselves. They live in peace, alike in cold and heat, pleasure and pain, praise and blame.

- With all fears dissolved in the peace of the Self and all actions dedicated to Brahman, controlling the mind and fixing it on me, sit in meditation with me as your only goal.

- Arjuna, those who eat too much or eat too little, who sleep too much or sleep too little, will not succeed in meditation. But those who are temperate in eating and sleeping work and recreation will come to the end of sorrow through meditation.

- In the still mind, in the depths of meditation, the Self reveals itself. Beholding the Self by means of the Self, an aspirant knows the joy and peace of complete fulfillment.

- Wherever the mind wanders, restless and diffuse in its search for satisfaction without, lead it within; train it to rest in the Self.

- I am ever present to those who have realized me in every creature. Seeing all life as my manifestation, they are never separated from me.
- When a person responds to the joys and sorrows of others as if they were his own, he has attained the highest state of spiritual union.
- No one who does good work will ever come to a bad end, either here or in the world to come.
- Through constant effort over many lifetimes, a person becomes purified of all selfish desires and attains the supreme goal of life.
- Meditation is superior to severe asceticism and the path of knowledge. It is also superior to selfless service. May you attain the goal of meditation, Arjuna!
- Even among those who meditate that man or woman who worships me with perfect faith, completely absorbed in me, is the most firmly established in Yoga.
- With your mind intent on me, Arjuna, discipline yourself with the practice of Yoga. Depend on me completely. Listen, and I will dispel all your doubts; you will come to know me fully and be united with me.
- The birth and dissolution of the cosmos itself take place in me. There is nothing that exists separate from me, Arjuna. The entire universe is suspended from me as my necklace of jewels.
- Arjuna, I am the taste of pure water and the radiance of the sun and moon. I am the sacred word and the sound heard in air, and the courage of human beings. I am the sweet fragrance in the earth and the radiance of fire; I am the life in every creature and the striving of the spiritual aspirant.
- My eternal seed, Arjuna, is to be found in every creature. I am the power of discrimination in those who are intelligent, and the glory of the noble. In those who are strong, I am strength, free from passion and selfish attachment. I am desire itself, if that desire is in harmony with the purpose of life.

Bhagavad Gita Quotes on Life and Death

- The states of sattva, rajas, and tamas come from me, but I am not in them.

- The three *gunas* make up my divine *maya*, difficult to overcome. But they cross over this *maya* who takes refuge in me.

- Some come to the spiritual life because of suffering, some in order to understand life; some come through a desire to achieve life's purpose, and some come who are men and women of wisdom. Unwavering in devotion, always united with me, the man or woman of wisdom surpasses all the others.

- After many births the wise seek refuge in me, seeing me everywhere and in everything. Such great souls are very rare.

- The world, deluded, does not know that I am without birth and changeless. I know everything about the past, the present, and the future, Arjuna; but there is no one who knows me completely.

- Delusion arises from the duality of attraction and aversion, Arjuna; every creature is deluded by these from birth.

- Those who see me ruling the cosmos, who see me in the adhibhuta, the adhidaiva, and the adhiyajna, are conscious of me even at the time of death.

- The Lord is the supreme poet, the first cause, the sovereign ruler, subtler than the tiniest particle, the support of all, inconceivable, bright as the sun, beyond darkness.

- Remembering me at the time of death, close down the doors of the senses and place the mind in the heart. Then, while absorbed in meditation, focus all energy upwards to the head. Repeating in this state the divine name, the syllable Om that represents the changeless Brahman, you will go forth from the body and attain the supreme goal.

- I am easily attained by the person who always remembers me and is attached to nothing else. Such a person is a true yogi, Arjuna.

- Every creature in the universe is subject to rebirth, Arjuna, except the one who is united with me.

- The six months of the northern path of the sun, the path of light, of fire, of day, of the bright fortnight, leads knowers of Brahman to the supreme goal. The six months of the southern path of the sun, the path of smoke, of night, of the dark fortnight, leads other souls to the light of the moon and to rebirth.

- Under my watchful eye the laws of nature take their course. Thus is the world set in motion; thus the animate and the inanimate are created.

- I am the ritual and the sacrifice; I am true medicine and the *mantram*. I am the offering and the fire which consumes it, and the one to whom it is offered.

- I am the father and mother of this universe, and its grandfather too; I am its entire support. I am the sum of all knowledge, the purifier, the syllable Om; I am the sacred scriptures, the Rig, Yajur, and Sama Vedas.

- I am the goal of life, the Lord and support of all, the inner witness, the abode of all. I am the only refuge, the one true friend; I am the beginning, the staying, and the end of creation; I am the womb and the eternal seed.

- Those who follow the rituals given in the Vedas, who offer sacrifices and take soma, free themselves from evil and attain the vast heaven of the gods, where they enjoy celestial pleasures. When they have enjoyed these fully, their merit is exhausted and they return to this land of death. Thus observing Vedic rituals but caught in an endless chain of desires, they come and go.

- Those who worship me and meditate on me constantly, without any other thought – I will provide for all their needs.

- Those who worship the devas will go to the realm of the devas; those who worship their ancestors will be united with them after death. Those who worship phantoms will become phantoms; but my devotees will come to me. Those who worship the devas will go to the realm of the devas; those who worship their ancestors will be united with them after death. Those who worship phantoms will become phantoms; but my devotees will come to me.

349

- Fill your mind with me; love me; serve me; worship me always. Seeking me in your heart, you will at last be united with me.
- All the scriptures lead to me; I am their author and their wisdom.
- Bhishma, Drona, Jayadratha, Karna, and many others are already slain. Kill those whom I have killed. Do not hesitate. Fight in this battle and you will conquer your enemies.
- Neither by knowledge of the Vedas, nor sacrifice, nor charity, nor rituals, nor even by severe asceticism has any other mortal seen what you have seen, O heroic Arjuna.
- Better indeed is knowledge than mechanical practice. Better than knowledge is meditation. But better still is surrender of attachment to results, because there follows immediate peace.
- Some realize the Self within them through the practice of meditation, some by the path of wisdom, and others by selfless service. Others may not know these paths; but hearing and following the instructions of an illumined teacher, they too go beyond death.
- The brightness of the sun, which lights up the world, the brightness of the moon and of fire – these are my glory.
- Calmness, gentleness, silence, self-restraint, and purity: these are the disciplines of the mind.
- To refrain from selfish acts is one kind of renunciation, called *sannyasa*; to renounce the fruit of action is another, called *tyaga*.
- By serving me with steadfast love, a man or woman goes beyond the *gunas*. Such a one is fit for union with Brahman.
- When they see the variety of creation rooted in that unity and growing out of it, they attain fulfillment in Brahman.
- I have shared this profound truth with you, Arjuna. Those who understand it will attain wisdom; they will have done that which has to be done.
- I give you these precious words of wisdom; reflect on them and then do as you choose.

ANCIENT HINDU ASTRONAUTS: UNBELIEVABLE, BUT TRUE

"One of the world's oldest books on astronomy is the Hindu *Sut-ya Siddhanta*. It speaks of Siddhas and Vidyahatas, or philosophers and scientists, who were able to orbit the earth in a former epoch below the moon but above the clouds."

Andrew Tomas[164]

Tomas further says:

"Another book from India – the *Samara-nagana Sutradharna* – contains a fantastic paragraph about the distant past when men flew in the air in skyships and heavenly beings came down from the sky. Was there a sort of two-way space traffic in a forgotten era?"

Dr. Roberto Pinotti talks about this:

"The importance of such studies and investigations could prove to be shocking for today's man because the existence of flying devices beyond mythology can only be explained with a forgotten superior civilization on earth."

---

[164] David Hatcher Childress, in 'Technology of the Gods: The Incredible Sciences of the Ancients' Kempton, US: 2000, p.158.

This chapter will take its readers to the incredible sciences of ancient Bhārat and to the controversial and fascinating world of Pinotti's 'forgotten superior civilization' which is none but Bhārat's.

Will Durant[165] has said: "As we acquire knowledge, things do not become more comprehensible, but more mysterious."

Prof. H.L. Hariyappa[166] of Mysore University, in his essay on the *Rig Veda*, writes that in a distant epoch "gods came to the earth often times, and that it was the privilege of some men to visit the immortals in heaven." The tradition of Bhārat is insistent upon the reality of this communication with other worlds during the Golden Age. The book further writes that the god Garuda is thought by Brahmins to be a combination of man and bird who travels through space.

Garuda is the national airline of Indonesia. The Garuda[167] is a mythical bird or a bird-like creature that appears in both Hindu and Buddhist mythology. History tells that in ancient times Indonesia was colonized by Hindus and Buddhists, and its language Bahasa is very much influenced by Sanskrit. In Hindi, 'bhasha' (very comparable to 'Bahasa) means language. The names of several cities, like Jakarta, Surbaya, etc. and of individuals, like Sukarno, Suharto, Yudhoyona, Megavati, Sukarno-putri, (putri in Hindi means daughter) etc. seem to have their origin in Sanskrit. Its monetary unit Rupiah is very much comparable to Indian Rupaya.

Childress (p.168) writes about the Aerial warfare in Ancient India:

> "The ancient Indian epics go into considerable detail about aerial warfare over 10,000 years ago. So much detail that a famous Oxford professor included a chapter on the subject in a book on ancient warfare."

Childress (p.169) writes that Dikshitar, commenting on the famous Vimana text *'Vimanika Shastra'*, says:

---

[165] Ibid, p. 11.
[166] Ibid, p. 158
[167] Wikipedia.

"In the recently published 'Samarangana Sutradhara of Bhoja' a whole chapter of 230 stanzas is devoted to the principles of construction underlying the various flying machines and other engines used for military and other purposes. The various advantages of using machines, especially flying ones, are given elaborately. Special mention is made of their attacking visible as well as invisible objects, of their use at one's will and pleasure, of their uninterrupted movements, of their strength and durability, in short of their capability to do in the air all that is done on earth."

Sanskrit scholar Ramchandra Dikshitar,[168] in his book titled '*War in Ancient India*' (1944), writes:

"No question can be more interesting than in the present circumstances of the world than India's contribution to the science of aeronautics. There are numerous illustrations in our vast Puranic and epic literature to show how well and wonderfully the ancient Indians conquered the air. To glibly characterize every thing found in this literature as imaginary and summarily dismiss it as unreal has been the practice of both Western and Eastern scholars until recently. The very idea indeed was ridiculed and people went so far as to assert that it was physically impossible for man to use flying machines. But today what with balloons, aero planes and other flying machines, a great change has come over our ideas on the subjects."[169]

Col. Henry S. Olcott (1832-1907), an American philosopher and cofounder of the Theosophical Society, in a lecture in Allahabad in 1881, said:

---

[168] Ibid, p. 168.
[169] Ramchandra Dikshitar, 'Warfare in Ancient India', Madras: Oxford University Press, 1944.

"The ancient Hindus could navigate the air, and not only navigate it, but fight battles in it like so many war-eagles combating for the domination of the clouds. To be so perfect in aeronautics, they must have known all the arts and of the atmosphere, the relative temperature, humidity, density and specific gravity of the various gases."

Frederick Soddy[170] (1877-1956), a Nobel Laureate (1921, Chemistry of radioactive substance), had a great regard for the Indian epics Rāmāyanā and Mahābhāratā, from which he might have got the idea of the awesome power of the atom. Therefore, it seems he did not take the records, as contained in these ancient Hindu epics, as fables. Soddy, in 'Interpretation of Radium' (1909), wrote:

"Can we not read into them (the texts of the epics) some justification for the belief that some forgotten race of men attained not only to the knowledge we have so recently won, but also to the power that is not yet ours?"

Dr. Vyacheslav Zaitsev[171] has said that the holy Indian (Hindu) sages have mentioned in the Rāmāyanā that two storied celestial chariots with many windows roared off into the sky like comets. He adds that the Mahābhāratā and various Sanskrit books describe at length these chariots which were powered by winged lighting. He further remarks: "It was a ship that soared into the air, flying to both the solar and stellar regions."

Dr. Roberto Pinotti[172] – an Italian scientist who had made exhaustive study of the history of Indian astronautics – told the World Space Conference that India may have had a superior civilization with possible contacts with extraterrestrial visitors, and the flying devices 'Vimanas', as described in ancient Indian texts and that it may underline their possible connections with today's aerospace technology. He asked the

---

[170] Hindu Wisdom - Vimanas
[171] ibid
[172] ibid

delegates to examine in detail the Hindu texts instead of dismissing 'all the Vimana descriptions and traditions' as mere myths.

Dr. Pinotti asserted:

> "The importance of such studies and investigations could prove to be shocking for today's man because the existence of flying devices beyond mythology can only be explained with a forgotten superior civilization on earth."

Pinotti's "forgotten superior civilization" was none but the prehistory ancient Vedic civilization.

He pointed out that Indian (Hindu) gods and heroes fought in the skies using piloted vehicles with terrible vehicles. He further said that they were similar to modern jet propelled flying machines, and that certain descriptions of the Vimanas (airplanes) seemed "too detailed and technical in nature to be labeled as myth."

Dr. Pinotti cites various texts to amazing secrets related to the operation of Vimanas, some of which could be compared to modern day use of radar, solar energy and photography. It is amazing that the ancient Indians had scientific 'Airplane manual', known as 'Vymanika Shastra'. Quoting from it, Dr. Pinotti says that the ancient flying devices of India were made from special heat-absorbing metals named 'Somaka, Soundalike and Mourthwika.' He also writes that the *Shastra* also discusses the seven kinds of mirrors and lenses installed aboard for defensive and offensive uses. He explains that the so-called 'Pinjula Mirror' offered a sort of 'visual shield' preventing the pilots from being blinded by the 'evil rays', and the weapon 'Marika' used to shoot enemy aircraft does not seem too different from what we today call laser technology.

Dr. Pinotti had made an exhaustive study of the history of Indian astronautics. He talks about another text according to which ancient Hindus knew the use of element 'fire' as could be seen from their *Astra* (weapons) that included *Soposamhara* (flame belching missile), *Prasvapna* (which caused sleep) and four kinds of *Agni Astras* (fire weapons) that traveled in sheets of flame and produced thunder.

It should be noted that *'Agni'* (fire) is seen as a Hindu goddess. It contributes lot to human life in various ways from life-sustaining kitchen to high technology. Its prime use in technology – manufacturing, missiles, space, astronautics, nuclear and what not – is surfacing now meeting various multifarious demands of the present complex life.

Fire is purifier too. Thus, it is used in all Hindu religious ceremonies. The seven promises, made by bride and groom, are taken while circling around fire. Even the end of the Hindu life (death) is blessed by Agni. Cremation is environment-purifying. It saves space for several beneficial uses.

Dr. Pinotti said that depictions of space travel, total destruction by incredible weapons and the fact that Vimanas (Vimans) resembled modern unidentified flying objects would suggest that India had a 'superior but forgotten civilization.' Dr. Pinotti suggests: "In light of all this, we think it will be better to examine the Hindu texts and subject the descriptive models of Vimanas to more scientific scrutiny."

All this technical version of the construction and operation of the ancient flying machines (airplanes), as given in the ancient Hindu scriptures, can not be considered as mythology. Only the Western technologists may say so, because they fear that their Viman-related technology may be thought, as based on the knowledge given in Hindu *Shastras* (scriptures).

> The Mahābhāratā (3067 BC)[173] people did have knowledge of not only flying machines, but also of fire missiles (Agnibaans, meaning fire arrows), and TV. Sanjaya was narrating, step by step to the blind king Dhratrashtra in his palace what was happening on the Kurukshetra, while the Mahābhāratā War was in progress, just like watching cricket match on TV in living room in present times.

Ancient Hindus had knowledge and technology how to create dense clouds to cover the sun and let the day look dark as seen at the sunset.

---

[173] Kosla Vepa, 'Astronomical Dating of Events & Select Vignettes from Indian History', Pleasanton (Ca, USA): Indic Studies Foundation, 2008.

Such necessity arose when Jayadratha, the powerful Raja of Sindh, was hiding himself until the sunset. Arjuna had taken an oath to kill him before the sunset, and if he failed he would kill himself in blazing fire. Arjuna wanted to kill Jayadratha, because he, with help of his army, had held Pandavas from going ahead to protect Abhimanyu, the son of Arjuna and Subhadra. He was surrounded and then killed by six great Kaurava warriors including Drona, Kripa, Karna, Ashvatthama, Kritavarman, and Brihadvalla.

To bring Jayadratha out from his hide, Lord Krishna covered the sun with his mighty potencies. It looked like sunset. Jaydratha jubilantly came out from hide to enjoy seeing Arjuna being burnt. Krishna again used his power to disburse the clouds and let the sun come out. Then Krishna told Arjuna to go and kill Jayadratha, which he did.

The question arises how the Mahābhāratā people got the ideas about the things – fire missiles, airplanes, TV, etc. Ideas don't come from nothingness. Even the idea of 'zero' came from 'numbers,' because zero itself is a number. Some incidents must have prompted ideas why and how it happened. Thus, TVs, missiles, airplanes, etc. have been invented. They didn't copy the present-time inventions. The PAST can not copy the PRESENT.

It is possible that the present scientists got the ideas regarding the flying machines, nuclear missiles, TV, etc. from the ancient Hindu scriptures. UFOs might have given idea of flying in the air.

The infant Hindu scientific technology did not mature into its robust adulthood, only because of historically known self-centered mentality of Hindus – secrecy – not to share knowledge with others. Every new idea was secretly confined to family only. Thus it died with the family without its ultimate development.

The Indian Emperor Ashoka[174] started a 'Secret Society of the Nine Unknown Men'. Those nine men were great scientists. Each one wrote a book on his work. One wrote on "The Secrets of Gravitation." The work of the Society was kept so secret that only the name of the book was known to historians, but it was not read nor even seen by them. The book was kept in the secret library of the Secret Society. Where? No body knows if in India, Tibet or somewhere else.

[174] www.hinduwisdom.inf

It further says that only a few years back, the Chinese discovered some Sanskrit documents in Lhasa, Tibet. The documents were sent to the University of Chandrigath to be translated. Dr. Ruth Reyna of the University said recently that the documents contain directions for building interstellar spaceships. Their method of propulsion, Reyna said, was "anti-gravitational" and was based upon a system analogous to that of "laghima," the unknown power of the ego existing in man's physiological makeup, "a centrifugal force strong enough to counteract all gravitational pull." It further says that according Hindu Yogis, it is this "Laghima' which enables a person to levitate.

Dr. Reyna observes that according to the document which seems to be thousands of years old, the ancient Indians (Hindus) could use these flying machines, known by them as "Astras" (Weapons), for transporting some men onto any other planet. It seems it was kept secret so that its advanced scientific inventions are not used for evil purpose of war.

Dr. A.V. Krishna[175], professor of aeronautics at the Indian Institute of Science, Bangalore says:

> "It is true that the ancient Indian Vedas and other texts refer to aeronautics, space ships, flying machines, ancient astronauts. A study of the Sanskrit texts has convinced me that ancient India did know the secrets of building flying machines, and those machines were patterned after space ships coming from other planets."

Rāmāyanā[176] has a highly detailed story of a trip to the moon in a Vimana. It gives details about a battle with an "Asvin" (or Atlantean) airship. It further says that this is but a small bit of recent evidence of anti-gravity and aerospace technology used by Hindus. It suggests that in order to understand the technology, the 'Rama Empire' developed on the Indian sub-continent; we must go much further back in time, at least fifteen thousand years. It further says that Rama existed, apparently, parallel to the Atlantean civilization in the mid Atlantic Ocean.

---

[175] Ibid.
[176] The Hindu Wisdom – Vimanas

This puzzle can be solved only when we locate the planet from where the UFOs are coming. May be, Bharatvasis (Indians) had some relationship and communication with the residents of that planet, history of which has been lost or yet to be discovered. We do not know any other planet with human life.

The point that Hindu traditions call heroes as gods (*devas*) be stressed and understood. The gods, we are referring to as flying in the space above our planet, are merely humans with great divine powers. Or since we are unable to establish their factual identity, we may take them as mythological Hindu gods. Likewise the Greek mythology talks about Atlas, Titans, Olympian gods, and Zeus, the god of heavens.

Rama and Krishna were not mythological gods. Historically, it is known that both were born, lived and died. Both were great warriors with amazing vision and powers. Both were *Kshatris*, not *Brahmins*. They respected *Brahmins*. Hanuman, a disciple of Sri Rama, is worshipped as a god by most Hindus.

Hindu concept of time: Age of the humanity

It is fascinating to see comparative concept of time between the West and the East (Hindu). Shri Aurobindo Ghosh[177] (1872-1950), a great philosopher of modern India, has said:

> "European scholarship regards human civilization as a recent progression starting yesterday with the Fiji islander, and ending today with Rockefeller, conceiving ancient culture as necessarily half savage culture. It is a superstition of modern thought that the march of knowledge has always been linear. Our vision of 'prehistory' is terribly inadequate. We have not yet rid our minds from the hold of a one-and-only God or one-and-only Book, and now a one-and-only Science."

According to 'Hinduism Today'[178]:

---

[177]   Ibid.
[178]   Hinduism Today (April/May/June 2007, p. 14).

"Hinduism's understanding of time is as grandiose as time itself. While most cultures base their cosmologies on familiar units such as few hundreds or thousands of years, the Hindu concept of time embraces billions and trillions of years. The *Puranas* describe time units from the infinitesimal truti, lasting 1/1,000,0000 of a second to a *mahamantavara* of 311 trillion years. Hindu sages describe time as cyclic, an endless procession of creation, preservation and dissolution. Scientists such as Carl Sagan have expressed amazement at the accuracy of space and time descriptions given by the ancient *rishis* and saints, mystically awakened senses."

It is hard to believe all this. There are lot of commonalities and similarities in Greek and Hindu mythologies, so much that one may tend to believe that there is truth in what Pococke has written in his book *'India in Greece; or Truth in Mythology.'* If we objectively examine the mythologies of the world societies, we would find in them lot of history. We can not have solid evidences of the truths in mythologies of the remote past. Answer can be found in what two scholars have said – Dr. Carl Sagon: "Absence of evidence is not evidence of absence." And Aldous Huxley: "Facts do not cease to exist because they are ignored.".

Lynn Thorndike (1882-1965) – American historian, author of several books including *'A History of Magic and Experimental Science'* (8 vols) – remarked: "Thus we see that India's marvels were not always false."

John Burrows, in 'Ancient Vimana Aircraft, remarks: "Sanskrit texts are filled with references to gods who fought battles in the sky using Vimanas equipped with weapons."

It seems gallant 'heroes' were revered as 'gods'. A few of the different modes of transportation as used in pre-history ancient Bhārat:

- Jalayan – a vehicle designed to operate in air as well as on water (Rig Veda 6.58. 3).
- Vidyut Ratha, a vehicle that operates on power (RV 3.14.1).
- Tritala – a vehicle consisting of three stories (RV 3.14.1).

- Vaayu Ratha a gas or wind-powered chariot (RV 5.41.1).
- Trichakra Ratha – three wheeled vehicle designed to operate in air (RV 4.36.1).

It would be worth glancing over Vedas, Upanishads, Shastras and several other scriptures to mirror the lives of our ancestors for lessons to guide us.

TV, fire-and-clouds-maneuvering arrows in Mahābhāratā

Several devices – TV, agni-bāuns (fire arrows), and clouds-maneuvering arrows (arrows to make clouds and again to disperse them) – were used in Mahābhāratā war. They were in their infancy stage and were not research-based developed. But the idea and use of such instruments in their pre-mature stage talks lot about the ancient Hindu vision. Many do not believe in truth of such seemingly magical instruments in those times.

But it is true that *Sanjaya* did narrate the visual and audio happenings on the *Krukshetra* (battle field of Mahābhāratā) step by step to the blind king *Dhratrashtra* in the living room of his palace. Without TV, how could he do it? It was like watching cricket match at home.

If ancient Bhārat did not have that technology, how could he create night-like dark clouds to get Jaidratha, the Raja of Sind, out of his hide and then disperse them for Arjuna to kill him? Arjuna had taken oath that he would burn himself alive to death if he could not kill Jaidratha, the cause of the murder of his son Abhmanyu, before the sunset. Jaidratha went into hide, too secret for Arjuna. Jaidrath erected wall of brave soldiers to stop Pandwas from saving Abhmanyu who alone was being assaulted by a group of Kaurava warriors.

MAHABHARATA: BLOODY WAR BETWEEN COUSIN FAMILIES

Mahabharata (approx 3138 BC) was the bloody battle between two cousin-brother families, the Pandavas and the Kauravas. They were sons of two brothers, the Pandwas – Yudhishthira, Bhima, Arjuna, and twins, Nakula and Sahadev of Pandu – and Kauravas of Dhrirtarashtra who had 100 children and Duryodhana was their commander.

In ancient times, like in modern upper educated class, woman had right to select husband of her choice. Among some royal families, festivals like *swamvers* (self selection of husband) were organized and celebrated with pomp and dignity. Dhrishtadyumna arranged *swayamver* for his sister Draupadi. He told the host of assembled brave aspirants that the Draupadi will marry the brave warrior who would be able to bend the heavy bow and accurately shoot the designated target. She would prefer to live life alone, if she did not find any suitable. All the aspirants including Karna and Kauravas, excepting Arjuna failed. The arrow was too heavy for them even to lift it up from the floor. Arjuna, without any pause easily lifted the bow and accurately hit the target and won Draupadi. She loved it as she was eagerly waiting for Arjuna to win. But, unfortunately some thing happened, neither Arjuna nor Draupadi might have not liked.

When Arjuna, along with Draupadi, arrived at door of his house joyously shouted to tell his mother: "Maa! I have a great gift for you, I have won in the competition!" His mother, not knowing what he was talking about, innocently shouted back: "Divide it among your brothers." Thus, Draupadi became wife of all the five Pandwa brothers, though vicious, barbaric and uncivilized. As per circumstial evidence that though wife of five husbands for long, no pregnancy was reported. It can be presumed without any doubt that Draupadi, being a civilized woman, did not play as wife to any of the five men. Each one had a legitimate wife, as Arjuna had Subhadara.

In modern times, it looks ridiculous, but in ancient times the word (*vachan*), particularly by mother or father was respected, as evidenced by the word (*vachan*), given by Dashrata (in about 5114 BC) to his youngest wife Kekayee, who at the mischievous suggestion by her maid servant Manthara, asked Dashrata to exile Rama to forest for 14 years and make Bharata the king. Rama, though innocent, did not fight for the throne, but respected it because it was given by his father, though wrong, but right according to the Vedic traditions to respect father and his oaths, whatever.

Happily surprising, her civilized son Bharata for whom Kekayee did all this, defied it without any vocal anger against his mother. He went to forest to plead Rama to kindly return to glorify the throne after Dashrata retires. Rama refused to return only to honor father's word (*vachan*) to Kekayee. Bharata begged his *chakris* (chappals), to place on the throne, symbolically representing Rama as the ruler. It is hard to imagine the pain, his repenting mother might be having, losing the love and respect of her son Bharata and of the people.

Hinduism is wrongly considered as conservative. As the matter of fact, Hinduism is utmost progressive and liberal, always moving forward along with the changing times. Amazing! Now, modern Hindus, realizing the wrongs their ancestors did, can have only one wife to avoid jail.

There has been socio-cultural link between Ramayana (appox 5114 BC) → Mahabharata (appox 3138 BC) → and modern religion (2017 AD). It would be wrong to tightly bind the PRESENT to the PAST to break man's continuous run toward the Everest, which is all the times moving forward, further and further, making difficult to realize the golden gifts of imagination. This is the secret of man's never-ending continued effort chasing inventions, one after the other.

Hinduism, not conservative, but liberal and progressive

Hinduism, during its millennia years long life has never been conservative, to remain tied fast to the thoughts and ideas of their ancestors. Hindus feel free to think and mobilize their resources according to the demands of the changing times. Hindus believe that still water, unlike the water of a river, stinks and becomes unworthy to drink.

Very sorry for my unconscious helpless slip from Mahabharata to Ramayana, from Duraupadi to Kekayee. Quite natural, because this is the story of man, whose thinking, always riding over the fast galloping horse of imagination, can keep on changing to be able to meet the demands of the time, always moving and never still.

Mahabharata War

The bloody Mahabharata was born because of absence of any kind of democracy – Ram Rajya (approx 5,114 BC) or modern – which could regulate the deceitful misbehavior of the selfish, self-centered greedy Kauravas. They didn't feel any law to respect. It was like a jungle with beasts in human attire, seducing the ferocious Mahabharata, much worse than the World War 11, resulting loss of abundant resources and thousands of lives, according to some millions. The Mahabharata war was between two cousin families, involving killing of kith and kin – uncles and grand uncles and also Gurus fighting on the opposite side – made Arjuna feel sensitive how to kill own cousins, uncles, grand uncles, and gurus, once worshiped. He felt too depressed to fight. Keeping his *Dhanush* and arrows on the floor refused to fight, looking at Krishna for help.

Weapons used in Mahabharata War

The weapons used in Mahabharata war were a combination of both (i) ancient earthly weapons and (ii) the highly powerful and advanced futuristic weapons, being understood as provided by the Aliens, meaning gods, because they could not understand by whom and for what purpose. But, it is certain that those amazing weapons were used in Mahabharata war.

The weapons whose technology they could not understand, especially the various types of "Asthras" (like missiles) and various types of "Dhanush" (launchers) of Mahabharata are understood as provided by the Aliens (gods). It is illogical. Since Mahabharata provides detailed description of their construction, they should not be considered as received from sky. Nothing, excepting rain, snow and clouds, comes from above. European historians, in general, it seems do not have the grace to recognize the scholarship of others, particularly of Hindus. Amazing that some Mahabharata Asthras (weapons) would take U turn and go back to the person who launches them, for example, Karna's Nagaasthara and Krishna's Sudharsana chakra. These may be similar to the reusable missiles, the 'Indian Space Research Organisation' is working on.

Karna (करण), originally known as Vasusena, as one of the central actors in Mahābhārata Epic, was the king of Anga, present day Bhagalpur and Munger. Karna was known as one of the greatest warriors, whose martial exploits are recorded in the epic, as the only warrior, believed to be able to defeat Arjuna in any battle, and also admired by Lord Krishna and Bhishma. Karna is known for Digvijaya Yatra, a campaign in which he conquered the kings all over in the region. Karna, angry at Pandawas, was instrumental in establishing Duryodhana as the emperor of the region and to conduct the Vaishnava sacrifice.

Karna, as per mythology, was born of the ear of Kunti (therefore named 'Karna') or out of wind, as the son of Surya and Kunti, prior to her marriage with Pandu. It must be socio-culturally painful for Karna, being considered as an ill-legitimate child. It seems because of this, Karna, Pandawa turned as a friend of Dhristarashtra, adversary of Pandawas. This also is wrong (unnatural) to consider Karna born from Kunti's ear or wind. No child can be born like that. It is not scientific.

The nature – since its birth, may be of billions of years back or beyond or unknown – testifies that it has always been scientific and behaved accordingly. The belief that Karna was born of the ear (kaan, karna) of Kunti or of the wind is unnatural, unscientific, illogical and invalid. Such unbelievable unnatural story regarding the birth of Karna was framed only to cover up the misbehavior of Kunti to conceive out of wedlock and the black spot on innocent Karna to be seen as an illegitimate child.

Kauravas, the sons of Pandu's brother Dhritarashtra, envied the Pandavas for their bravery and the love they were getting from the people, particularly from Lord Krishna. Dhritarashtra, born blind, could not manage to restrain his son Duryodhana, who bitterly resented the achievements of his cousins, the Pandavas. Duryodhana arranged the deceitful dice gambling game by his vicious cunning cheating uncle Sakuni in which Yudhishthira lost every thing and got unavoidable exile for some time. On their return, Duryodhana, thinking himself too powerful, refused to give back any thing to Pandavas, invited the terrible bloody battle on Krukshtra which lasted for 18 days, losing thousands, some historians say millions of innocent lives, including all Kauravas. Krishna fought on the side of the Pandavas, as Arjuna's charioteer.

Krishna, charioteer of Arjuna's chariot

Arjuna, while fighting against Kauravas, was also protecting the charioteer Krishna by neutralizing the arrows from Kauravas, which could kill Krishna, if not protected. Arjuna was husband of Subhadra, the sister of Lord Krishna.

Arjuna was not only the warrior fighting against the mischievously unpredictable Kauravas, but also was responsible for providing protective umbrella over the chariot, neutralizing arrows from Kauravas to protect self and the charioteer Krishna.

It is amazing that the prehistory ancient Vedic people (Hindus) had the knowledge of the technology of arrow (like present missiles) war accurately shooting exactly the destined target from a fast running chariot. Such history they got from the prehistory Vedas, the most ancient scriptures of the humanity. Most modern school / college text books don't give such information, saying that all this is not history, but mythology. As a matter of fact, it was history because the notion of history came much later when stories were rightly recognized as history.

It is soul satisfying that the ancient Hindus thought 'Brahmacharya' (education) as the foundation of life, leading to the realization of the need of the lessons of Bhagvad Gita, the discourse between Lord Krishna and Arjuna to help Arjuna to develop self-awareness (*atmagyaan*) to peep deep within inner-self to understand the dynamics of his inner conflicts, which due to *moha* (attachment) with kith and kin and '*krodha*' (anger at self, not understanding why) might be preventing Arjuna to fight against them (*moha* and *krodha*), ignoring *Dharma* (his sacred responsibility) to fight against own kith and kin for the welfare of the whole society at any cost.

Man against himself

According to the Vedic philosophy there are five enemies, ironically all from within and against self, meaning '**man against himself.**' They are *kaam* (lust), *krodha* (anger), *lobha* (greed), *moha* (attachment), *ahamkaar* (self pride). In Mahabharata, greed of Kauravas was the most serious problem which led to war on Kurukhshetra. All the five man's enemies operate at soul level, hidden from self, thus too difficult for the vicious self-centered people, like Kauravas, to identify and understand them. Only psychoanalysis would help. Kauravas would resist because they thought that whatever they were doing was right.

It seems Lord Krishna had the knowledge of psychology and psychoanalysis and had the diagnostic and therapeutic skills, like those of a modern psychoanalyst. Sigmund Freud might have got the idea and knowledge of psychoanalysis and psychotherapy from the Bhagvad Gita, emphassaising '*Atmagyan*' (self awareness) meaning deep awareness of self. One can visit and know the world, but it is too difficult to know self, the inner-self, not visible to open eyes. One can feel God within self only with the help of Guru, like the psychiatric patient needs guidance and help of a qualified psychoanalyst.

The Bhagvad Gita, in short, is the wisdom of *karmas* (activity), rather than remaining lethargically inactive, caught in the self-created web of ignorance. The Bhavad Gita emphasizes *gyan* (wisdom, education) and *karma* (action, activity) and freedom from the suicidal thought of destiny. Opportunity can be created only by education and aim-related activity, not by remaining idle to wait for a gift of destiny. Only the persons of wisdom and action are loved by beautiful Miss Opportunity.

She lives not only in America, but all over the planet, in homes of education and activity as evidenced by the fact all Americans are not rich and all living in India are not poor.

Nuclear weapons in Mahabharata

According to history,[179] in the 18 day Mahabharata war the total death toll amounts to around 1.6 billion. This could not be possible unless and otherwise weapons of mass destruction, like nuke, were used. Modern archeological surveys have slowly started providing some information regarding the use of mass destruction weapons in Mahabharata war. The vast amount of devastation was found at the site of Mohenjo Daro, approximately corresponding to Nagasaki. Interestingly, the ancient texts refer repeatedly to the use of *Vimanas*, or the flying cars, which fly with their own power, intriguing with intense interest that it was a scientific community. Nationally known expert William Sturm said, "the melting of bricks at Mohenjo Daro could not have been caused by a normal fire". Professor Antonio Castellani, a space engineer in Rome commented "it's possible that what happened at Mohenjo Daro was not a natural phenomenon."

Mr. Oppenheimer's (architect of modern atomic bomb) believed that nukes were used in ancient India, most probably in the Mahabharata war.

---

[179] Wikipedia

SUDARSHANA CHAKRA (सुदर्शन चक्र)[179]

Sudarshana Chakra is a spinning disk-like weapon, literally meaning auspicious wheel, having 108 serrated edges used by god Vishnu. The Sudarshana Chakra is generally portrayed on the right rear hand of the four hands of Vishnu, who also holds a *shankha* (conch shell), a Gada (mace) and a *padma* (lotus). While in the Rig Veda the Chakra was Vishnu's symbol as the wheel of time by the late medieval period *Sudarshana Chakra* emerged as an ayudhapurusha as a fierce form of weapon, Vishnu used for the destruction of an enemy.

The word *Sudarshana* is derived from two Sanskrit words – *Su*(सु) meaning "good/auspicious" and *Darshana* (दर्शन) meaning "vision". In the Monier-Williams dictionary the word Chakra is derived from the root करम् (*kram*) or ऋत् (*rt*) or करि (*kri*) and refers among many meaning, to the wheel of a carriage, wheel of the sun's chariot or metaphorically to the wheel of time.

The Chakra finds mention in the Rig Veda as a symbol of Vishnu, and as the wheel of time, and in the Itihasas and Puranas. In the Mahabharata, Krishna, identified with Vishnu, uses it as a weapon. For example, he beheads Shishupala with the Sudarshana Chakra at the Rajasuya Yagna of Emperor Yudhishthira.

In Mahabharata, Jayadratha was responsible for the death of Abhimanue, the son of Arjuna and Subadra, Arjuna vowed to kill Jayadratha the very next day before sunset. Drona who was on the side of Kaurwas, created a combination of 3 layers of troops, to act as a protective shield around Jayadratha. Krishna created an artificial sunset

---

[180] Wikipedia

using his Sudarshan Chakra. Seeing this Jayadratha came out from hide to enjoy the vision of Arjuna's suicide, being burnt to honor his word. Instantly at that moment, Krishna withdrew his Chakra to reveal the sun. Krishna then commanded Arjuna to go to kill Jayadratha. Arjuna followed his orders and beheaded Jayadratha.

Two Vrishni silver coins[181]

There are several *Puranic* stories associated with the Sudarshana Chakra, such as that of Lord Vishnu granting King Ambarisha the boon of Sudarshana Chakra in form of prosperity, peace and security to his kingdom.

The chakra is found in the coins of many tribes with the word *gana* and the name of the tribe inscribed on them. Early historical evidence of the Sudarshana-chakra is found in a rare tribal Vrishni silver coin with the legend *Vrishni-rajannya-ganasya-tratasya* which P.L.Gupta thought was possibly jointly issued by the gana (tribal confederation) after the Vrishnis formed a confederation with the Rajanya tribe. However, there is no conclusive proof so far. Discovered by Cunningham, and currently placed in the British Museum, the silver coin is witness to the political existence of the Vrishnis. It is dated to around 1st century BC. Vrishni copper coins dated to later time were found in Punjab. Another example of coins inscribed with the chakra are the Taxila coins of the 2nd century BC with a sixteen-spoked wheel.

A coin dated 180 BCE, with an image of Vasudeva-Krishna, was found in the Greco-Bactrian city of Ai-Khanoum in the Kunduz area of Afghanistan, minted by Agathocles of Bactria. In Nepal, Jaya Cakravartindra Malla of Kathmandu issued a coin with the chakra. Among the only two types of Chakra-vikrama coins known so far, there is one gold coin in which Vishnu is depicted as the Chakra-*purusha* (man). Though Chandragupta II issued coins with the epithet vikrama, due to the presence of the kalpavriksha on the reverse it has not been possible to ascribe it to him.

The rise of tantrism aided the development of the anthropomorphic personification of the chakra as the active aspect of Vishnu with few

---

[181] Wikipedia

370

sculptures of the Pala era bearing witness to the development, with the chakra in this manner possibly associated with the Vrishnis. However, the worship of Sudarshana as a quasi-independent deity concentrated with the power of Vishnu in its entirety is a phenomenon of the southern part of India; with idols, texts and inscriptions surfacing from the 13th century onwards and increasing in large numbers only after the 15th century.

The chakra *purusha* in Pancharatra texts has either four, six, eight, sixteen, or thirty-two hands, with double-sided images of multi-armed Sudarshana on one side and Narasimha on other side (called Sudarshana-Narasimha in Pancharatra) within a circular rim, sometimes in dancing posture found in Gaya area datable to 6th and 8th centuries. Unique images of Chakra Purusha, one with Varaha in Rajgir possibly dating to the 7th century, and another from Aphsad (Bihar) detailing a fine personification dating to 672 AD have been found.

While the chakra is ancient, with the emergence of the anthropomorphic forms of chakra and shankha traceable in the north and east of India as the *chakra-purusha* and *shanka-purusha*; in the south of India, the Nayak period popularized the personified images of Sudarshana with the flames. In the Kilmavilangai cave is an archaic rock-cut structure in which an image of Vishnu has been hallowed out, holding the Shanka and Chakra, without flames. At this point, the Chakrapurusha with the flames had not been conceived in southern India. The threat of invasions from the north was a national emergency during which the rulers sought out the Ahirbudhnya Samhita, which prescribes that the king should resolve the threat by making and worshiping images of Sudarshana, and learn how to use.

Though similar motives induced the Vijayanagar period to install images of Sudarshana, there was a wider spread of the cult during the Nayak period, with Sudarshana's images set up in temples ranging from small out-of-the-way ones to large temples of importance.

The worship of Sudarshana Chakra is found among the Vedic and the tantric cults. In the Garuda Purana, the chakra was also invoked in tantric rites. The tantric cult of Sudarshana was to empower the king to defeat his enemies in the shortest time possible. Sudarshana's hair, depicted as tongues of flames flaring high forming a nimbus, bordering the rim of the discus and surrounding the deity in a circle of rays (prabha-mandala) are a depiction of the deity's aggressive destroying energy.

Various Pancharatra texts describe the Sudarshna Chakra as prana, maya, kriya, shakti, bhava, unmera, udyama and saṃkalpa. In the Ahirbudhanya Samhita of the Pancharatra, on bondage and liberation, the soul is represented as belonging to *bhuti-shakti* (made of two parts, viz., time (bhuti) and shakti (maya) which passes through rebirths until it is reborn in its own natural form which is liberated; with the reason and object of samsara remaining a mystery. Samsara is represented as the 'play' of God even though God in the Samhita's representation is the perfect one with no desire to play. The beginning and the end of the play is effected through Sudarshana, who in the Ahirbudhanya Samhita is the will of the omnipotent, omniscient, omnipresent God. The Sudarshana manifests in five main ways to wit the 5 Shaktis – creation, preservation, destruction, obstruction and obscuration – to free the soul from taints and fetters which produce *vasanas* causing new births; so as to make the soul return to her natural form and condition which she shares with the supreme lord, namely, omnipotence, omniscience, omnipresence.

According to the Ahirbudhanya Samhita, "Vishnu, in the form of Chakra, was held as the ideal of worship for kings desirous of obtaining universal sovereignty", a concept associated with the Bhagavata cult in the puranas, a religious condition traceable to the Gupta period, which also led to the chakravartin concept. The concept of universal sovereignty possibly facilitated the syncretism of Krishna and Vishnu and reciprocally reinforced their military power and heroic exploits; with the *kshatriya* hero, Krishna preserving order in the phenomenal world while the composite Vishnu is the creator and upholder of the universe supporting all existence. Begley notes the evolution of the anthropomorphic iconography of Sudarshana, beginning from early expansion of the Bhagavata sect thus: "In contrast to the relatively simple religious function of the cakra-purusa, the iconographic role of the medieval sudarsana-purusa of South India was exceedingly complex. The medieval Sudarsana was conceived as a terrifying deity of destruction, for whose worship special tantric rituals were devised. The iconographic conception of Sudarsana as an esoteric agent of destruction constitutes a reassertion of the original militaristic connotation of the chakra".

Chakra Perumal is the personified deification of Vishnu's Sudarshana Chakra. Though Chakraperumal or ChakkrathAzhwar shrines (sannidhis) are found inside Vishnu's temples, there are very few temples dedicated to Chakraperumal alone as the main deity (moolavar). The temple of Chakraperumal in Gingee on the banks of Varahanadi was one such temple. However, it is not a functioning temple currently. In present time, only two functioning temples with Chakraperumal as moolavar exist – Sri Sudarshana Bhagavan Temple, and Nagamangala Chakrapani Temple – located on the banks of the Chakra bathing ghat of the Cauvery river. Here, the god is Chakrarajan and his consort is Vijayavalli. The idols of Chakra Perumal are generally built in the Vijaya Nagar style. There are two forms of Sudarshana or Chakraperumal, one with 16 arms and another with 8 arms. The one with 16 arms is considered the god of destruction and is rarely found. The Chakraperumal shrine inside the Simhachalam Temple is the home of the rare 16-armed god. The one with 8 arms is benevolent and is the form generally found in Vishnu's temples in present time. Chakraperumal was deified as an avatar of Vishnu himself, with the Ahirbudhnya Samhita identifying the Chakra-purusha with Vishnu himself, stating *Chakrarupi svayam Harih*. The Simhachalam Temple follows the ritual of Baliharanna or purification ceremony. Sudarshana or Chakraperumal is the *bali bera* of Narasimha, where he stands with 16 arms holding emblems of Vishnu with a circular background halo. Beside his *utsava bera* are the *chaturbhuja thayar* (mother goddess), Andal and Lakshminarayana in the Bhoga mandir. In Baliharana, Chakra Perumal, the *bali bera* is taken to a yagnasala where a yagna is performed offering cooked rice with ghee while due murti mantras are chanted, along with the Vishnu Sukta and Purusha Sukta. Then he is taken on a palanquin around the temple with the remaining food offered to the guardian spirits of the temple.

RAM SETU: ENGINEERING MARVEL OF ANCIENT INDIA

The ruins of the Ram Setu, an engineering marvel of the 5076 BC, have been discovered. It is now a historical fact that it was built by Lord Rama and his army as a road in water to help them to reach Sri Lanka to rescue Sita from the clutches of Rawana, the cruel king of Sri Lanka. The ruins of the Ram Setu have been discovered to give reality orientation to the myth of Rama travel to Sri Lanka along with his huge broad-based army to tame Rawana.

European mind biased against ancient Indian technologies

Modern mind, particularly European, will boast of Alexander the Great (356-323 BC) with a thin army invasion of thousands miles distant unknown and culturally different India, but reluctant to accept Rama's with a large army invasion of nearby culturally well-acquainted Sri Lanka, only because European colonial mind is biased to believe in the ancient (6th BC) Hindu technological caliber. The following images will explain the Ram Setu, the ancient road Lord Rama used to reach Sri Lanka.

Adam's Bridge (Tamil: *ātām pālam*), also known as Rama's Bridge or Rama Setu (Tamil: *Irāmar pālam*, Sanskrit: *rāmasetu*), is a chain of limestone shoals, between Pamban Island, also known as Rameswaram Island, off the south-eastern coast of Tamil Nadu, India, and Mannar Island, off the north-western coast of Sri Lanka. Geological evidence suggests that this bridge is a former land connection between ancient India and Sri Lanka.

The bridge is 30 miles (48 km) long and separates the Gulf of Mannar (southwest) from the Palk Strait (northeast). Some of the sandbanks are dry and the sea in the area is very shallow, being only 1 to 10 metres (3 to 30 ft) deep in some places, which hinders navigation. It was reportedly passable on foot up to the 15th century until storms deepened the channel. Temple records seem to say that Ram Setu was completely above sea level until it broke in a cyclone in 1480.

The Ram Setu Bridge was first mentioned in the ancient Hindu Sanskrit epic *Ramayana* of Valmiki. The name *Rama's Bridge* or *Rama Setu* (Sanskrit; *setu*: bridge) refers to the bridge built by the Vanara (ape men) army of Rama in Hindu theology with instructions from Nala, which he used to reach Lanka and rescue his wife Sita from the Rakshasa king, Ravana. The *Ramayana* attributes the building of this bridge to Rama in verse 2-22-76, naming it as *Setubandhanam*, a name that persists until today.

The sea separating Bharat and Sri Lanka is called Sethusamudram meaning "Sea of the Bridge". Maps prepared by a Dutch cartographer in 1747, available at the Thanjavur Saraswathi Mahal Library show this area as *Ramancoil*, a colloquial form of the Tamil *Raman Kovil* (or Rama's Temple). Another map of Mughal India prepared by J. Rennel in 1788 retrieved from the same library called this area as "the area of the Rama Temple", referring to the temple dedicated to Rama at Rameswaram. Many other maps in Schwartzberg's historical atlas and other sources such as travel texts by Marco Polo call this area by various names such as *Sethubandha* and *Sethubandha Rameswaram*. The western world first encountered it in "historical works in the 9th century" by Ibn Khordadbeh in his *Book of Roads and Kingdoms* (c. 850), referring to it is *Set Bandhai* or "Bridge of the Sea". Later, Alberuni described it. The earliest map that calls this area by the name *Adam's bridge* was prepared by a British cartographer in 1804. Some early Islamic sources refer to a mountain in Sri Lanka as Adam's Peak, where Adam supposedly fell to earth, and describes Adam as crossing from Sri Lanka to India on what became known as Adam's Bridge.

Adam's Bridge starts as a chain of shoals from the Dhanushkodi tip of India's Pamban Island and ends at Sri Lanka's Mannar Island. Pamban Island is semi-connected to the Indian mainland by 2 km long

Pamban Bridge. Mannar Island is connected to mainland Sri Lanka by a causeway. The border between India and Sri Lanka is said to pass across one of the shoals constituting one of the shortest land borders in the world. Adam's bridge and neighboring areas like Rameswaram, Dhanushkodi, Devipattinam and Thirupullani are mentioned in the context of various legends in Ramayana.

Age of the bridge, known as Ram Setu

In a programme called "Project Rameswaram", the Geological Survey of India (GSI) concluded through the dating of corals that Rameswaram Island evolved beginning 125,000 years ago. Radiocarbon dating of samples in this study suggests that the domain between Rameswaram and Talaimannar may have been exposed sometime between 7,000 and 18,000 years ago. Investigation by the Centre for Remote Sensing (CRS) of Bharathidasan University, Tiruchi, led by Professor S.M. Ramasamy dates the structure to 3,500 years. In the same study, carbon dating of some ancient beaches between Thiruthuraipoondi and Kodiyakarai shows the Thiruthuraipoondi beach dates back to 6,000 years and Kodiyakarai around 1,100 years ago. Another study suggests that the appearance of the reefs and other evidence indicate their recency, and a coral sample gives a radiocarbon age of 4,020 ± 160 years BP.

The worldwide interest in Ram Setu was so much that a more detailed marine survey of Ram Setu was undertaken in 1837 by Lieutenants F. T. Powell, Ethersey, Grieve, and Christopher along with draughtsman Felix Jones, and operations to dredge the channel were recommenced the next year. However, these and subsequent efforts in the 19th century did not succeed in keeping the passage navigable for any vessels except those with a light draft.

ASTRONOMY AND ASTROLOGY, NOT STRANGE TO VEDIC HINDUS

Astronomy[182] deals with the study of celestial objects, moon, sun, stars, planets, and comets, their location and rotation. It was known to ancient Hindus, much earlier than to the West. *Rig Veda*, the oldest Veda and the oldest documents of the mankind, talks about astronomy. *Rig Veda* hymn LXXXV (earlier than 11,700 BC) talks about the *nakshtras* (constellations) – the sun, the moon, planets, in the center of stars. Ancient Hindus knew their position from one-an-other and the times of their rotations. It evidences that prehistory ancient Vedic people (present Hindus) had knowledge of Astronomy earlier than any other people on the planet. Brahmins were able to tell the day and time of lunar eclipse, long before the science of astronomy was formalized as a discipline. Europeans have been ahead of Hindus in formalizing sciences of astronomy and astrology because of two reasons:

1. Hindus treasured inner happiness which can be achieved only by the knowledge of self rather than of external world. This is the reason why in Bhārat, Mahatmas are worshipped and in the Western world great scientists are adored.
2. Europeans, unlike Hindus, because of colonization were financially able to afford scientific and technological research.

---

[182] Wikipedia

It would be wrong to say that the knowledge of astronomy and astrology went to Bhārat from Greece or from any other European country. Vedas are the oldest scriptures of the humanity and as said earlier, there is mention of *nakshtras* (planets) in *Rig Veda*, the oldest scripture of the mankind. The Vedas, the primary texts of Hinduism, have knowledge of astronomy which had gone to Greece with Hindus who had colonized Greece in about 2448 BC, as per Edward Pococke in *"India in Greece, Or, Truth in Mythology"* (1856).

Prof. David Frawley[183] talks about the Vedic astronomical references related to the calendar:

> "The Vedas contain various astronomical references relative to the calendar. Vedanga Jyotish, as referred to by Varsha Mihira in his Brihat Samhita (III.1), outlines a calendar wherein the summer solstice occurred in the middle of the Nakshatra Aslesha (23 20 Cancer), which yields a date of around 1400 BC. Yajurveda, Atharva (XIX.7.2), and several Brahamanas place the vernal equinox in the Krittik (Taurus), the summer solstice in Magha (Leo), and the winter solstice in Aquarius, a date of 2500-2000 BC. Such astronomical data reflect the Harappan and post-Harappan era, which one would expect to, have an adequate calendar."

In astronomy too, Indus people were precursors. The 17th century French astronomer Jean-Claude Bailly had noticed that the Hindu astronomic systems were much more ancient than those of the Greeks or even of the Egyptians and the movement of stars which was calculated by the Hindus 4500 years ago, does not differ from those used today by even one minute.

Rig Veda talks about astronomy (Jyotiṣh). But, it, as Vedic astronomy, historically developed as a discipline of Vedanga much later in Mauryan era – Chandragupta, Bindusara and Asoka – from 327 BC to 185 BC. Indian astronomy has very close association with Hinduism. Therefore, Brahmans are accepted as *Jyotshi* (astrologers). A *jyotshi* – who

---

[183] Prof. David Frawley (Sharma & Ghose, 1998, p. 140).

may be a *vashya* by caste, but in order to be accepted as a *jyotshi* – he would introduce himself as '*Pundit*' or '*Acharya*'.

Calendars

There are two types of calendars (i) lunar, based on moon and (ii) solar, on sun. In earlier times, particularly in the East (Hindus, Buddhists), it was based on moon. Now in modern era, for global uniformity it is solar system, based on sun. In Hinduism, time has its significance with religion and traditions. Therefore, almost all its religious festivals, like Divali, Holi, Janmashtmi, etc are dated according to Hindu (Lunar) calendar, therefore different from Christian calendar. Brahmins have knowledge of astronomy and are astrologers, hence able to know their *tithi* (religious date). Thus, Hindu calendar is a collective name for most of the luni-sidereal calendars.

The Hindu calendars[184] also change with region. Therefore, some times even the dates of main Hindu festivals are different from region to region. Mostly, difference is of a day or two. The difference may be due to different astronomers whose astronomical calculations may differ. Some of the more prominent regional Hindu calendars include Nepali, Punjabi, Bengali, Odia, Malayalam, Kannada, Tulu and Tamil.

Vikrama Samvat is used in Northern India, and Shalivahana calendar in the Deccan states of Karnataka, Telangana, Maharashtra and Andhra Pradesh. The common feature of many regional Hindu calendars is that the names of the twelve months are the same because the names are based in Sanskrit. The month, with which the year starts also, varies from region to region. All astronomers should jointly decide the year. History vouches that the Hindu ego has been too stubborn to yield to collectively think and work together in the interest of the nation, because of which Hindustan was dominated for centuries by few foreigners. Even in present times, how can the Parliament function smoothly by so many egos?

The Buddhist calendar and the traditional luni-solar calendars of Cambodia, Laos, Myanmar, Sri Lanka and Thailand are also based on an older version of the Hindu calendar.

---

[184] Wikipedia.

Most of the Hindu calendars are derived from Gupta era astronomy as developed by Āryabhaṭa and Varāhamihira in the 5th to 6th century BC. These in turn were based in the astronomical tradition of *Vedāṅga Jyotiṣa*, which in the preceding centuries had been standardized in a number of (non-extant) works known as *Sūrya Siddhānta*. Regional diversification took place in the medieval period. The astronomical foundations were further developed in the medieval period, notably by Bhāskara II (12th century, AD).

Differences and regional variations abound in these computations, but the following is a general overview of the Hindu lunisolar calendar. The Indian national calendar or "Saka calendar" was introduced in 1957 based on the traditional Hindu calendars. But there are different years, Islamic, Buddhist, Hindu, etc.

In astronomy, several kinds of year are distinguished, having slightly different lengths. But, in order to observe the uniformity in time all over the planet, the solar year has been recognized, divided into 12 months with some 31, some 30 and one (February) with 28 and every 4th year there is February of 29 days, known as 'Leap year' to complete the total journey of the sun of 365 days 5 hours 48 minutes 46 seconds. This is also called 'tropical year' or year of the seasons. 'Tropical Year' or known as 'Solar Year' has been accepted by the global family.

Tropical Year / Solar Year[185]

A tropical year, also known as a solar year, for general purposes, is the time that the Sun takes to return to the same position in the cycle of seasons, as seen from earth; for example, the time from vernal equinox to vernal equinox, or from summer solstice to summer solstice. Because of the precession of the equinoxes, the seasonal cycle does not remain exactly synchronized with the position of the Earth in its orbit around the Sun. As a consequence, the tropical year is about 20 minutes *shorter* than the time it takes Earth to complete one full orbit around the Sun as measured with respect to the fixed stars (the sidereal year).

Since antiquity, astronomers have progressively refined the definition of the tropical year. The *Astronomical Almanac Online Glossary* 2015

---

[185] Wikipedia

states that tropical year is the period of time for the ecliptic longitude of the Sun to increase 360 degrees. Since the Sun's ecliptic longitude is measured with respect to the equinox, the tropical year comprises a complete cycle of seasons, and its length is approximated in the long term by the civil (Gregorian) calendar. The mean tropical year is approximately 365 days, 5 hours, 48 minutes, 45 seconds.

An equivalent, more descriptive, definition is: "The natural basis for computing passing tropical years is the mean longitude of the Sun reckoned from the precessionally moving equinox (the dynamical equinox or equinox of date). Whenever the longitude reaches a multiple of 360 degrees the mean Sun crosses the vernal equinox and a new tropical year begins".

The mean tropical year on January 1, 2000, was about 365.2421897 ephemeris days according to the calculation of Laskar (1986); each ephemeris day lasting 86,400 SI seconds. By 2010 this had decreased to 365.2421891 (365 ephemeris days, 5 hours, 48 minutes and 45.14 seconds). This is about 365.242181 mean solar days, though the length of a mean solar day is constantly changing. Bhārat has produced several astronomers, introducing a few.

Astronomers[186]
Lagadha

Lagadha (1st millennium BC) was the 1st Astronomer from India, perhaps on the planet. The Vedāṅga Jyotiṣa is an Indian text on Jyotisha, redacted by Lagadha. The text is foundational to the Vedanga discipline of Jyotisha. As the text describes rules for tracking the motions of the sun and the moon, it's dating in the final centuries BCE seems implausible as the more sophisticated horoscopic astrology and advanced astronomical knowledge possessed by ancient Hindus. In the Vedanga Jyotisha, Lagadha praises Jyotisha as the crowning subject in the ancillary Vedic studies of human enlightenment. The Vedanga Jyotisha is available in two recensions: one of 36 verses associated with the *Rig Veda* and another of 45 verses associated with the *Yajur Veda*. There are 29 verses in common.

---

[186] Wikipedia

The earliest astronomical text, named Vedānga Jyotiṣha details several astronomical attributes generally applied for timing social and religious events. The Vedānga Jyotiṣa also details astronomical calculations, calendrical studies, and establishes rules for empirical observation. Since the texts written by 1200 BC were largely religious compositions. Vedānga Jyotiṣha has connections with Hindu astrology and it details several important aspects of the time and seasons, including lunar months, solar months, and their adjustment by a lunar leap month of *Adhimāsa*. *Ritus* and <u>*Yugas*</u> are also described. Tripathi (2008) holds: "Twenty-seven constellations, eclipses, seven planets, and twelve signs of the zodiac were also known at that time."

Aryabhata

Āryabhata (आर्यभट, 476-550 BC) was the author of the *Āryabhatīya* and the *Aryabhatasiddhanta*, which, according to Hayashi (2008) circulated mainly in the northwest of India and, through the Sāsānian dynasty (224–651) of Iran, had a profound influence on the development of Islamic astronomy. Its contents are preserved to some extent in the works of Varahamihira (flourished c. 550), Bhaskara I (flourished c. 629), Brahmagupta (598– 668), and others. It is one of the earliest astronomical works to assign the start of each day to midnight. Āryabhata was a major mathematician.

Aryabhata explicitly mentioned that the earth rotates about its axis, thereby causing what appears to be an apparent westward motion of the stars. Āryabhata also mentioned that reflected sunlight is the cause behind the shining of the moon. Āyrabhata's followers were particularly strong in South India, where his principles of the diurnal rotation of the earth, among others, were followed and a number of secondary works were based on them.

Brahamgupta

Brahamgupta (598-668 BC) correctly established Doctrine of *Brahmasphuta-siddhanta* and dealt with both Indian mathematics and astronomy. Hayashi (2008) writes: "It was translated into Arabic in

Baghdad about 771 AD and had a major impact on Islamic mathematics and astronomy." In *Khandakhadyaka* (A Piece Eatable, 665 CE) Brahmagupta reinforced Aryabhata's idea of another day beginning at midnight. Bahmagupta also calculated the instantaneous motion of a planet, gave correct equations for parallax, and some information related to the computation of eclipses. His works introduced Indian concept of mathematics based astronomy into the Arab world.

Varāhamihira

Varāhamihira (505 CE) was an astronomer and mathematician who studied Indian astronomy as well as many principles of Greek, Egyptian, and Roman astronomical sciences. His *Pañcasiddhāntikā* is a treatise and compendium drawing from several knowledge systems.

Bhāskara (629 CE)

Bhāskara authored the astronomical works *Mahabhaskariya* (Great Book of Bhaskara), *Laghubhaskariya* (Small Book of Bhaskara), and the *Āryabhatiyabhashya* (629 CE) – commentary on the *Āryabhatīya* written by Āryabhata. Hayashi (2008) writes 'Planetary longitudes, heliacal rising and setting of the planets, conjunctions among the planets and stars, solar and lunar eclipses, and the phases of the Moon are among the topics Bhaskara discusses in his astronomical treatises.' Baskara I's works were followed by Vateśvara (880 CE), who in his eight chapter *Vateśvarasiddhānta* devised methods for determining the parallax in longitude directly, the motion of the equinoxes and the solstices, and the quadrant of the sun at any given time.

Lalla

Lalla (8th century CE) was the Author of the *Śisyadhīvrddhida*, the Treatise Which Expands the Intellect of Students. This corrects several assumptions of Āryabhata. The *Śisyadhīvrddhida* of Lalla itself is divided into two parts: *Grahādhyāya* and *Golādhyāya*.

1) (*Grahādhyāya* (Chapter I-XIII) deals with planetary calculations, determination of the mean and true planets, three problems pertaining to diurnal motion of Earth, eclipses, rising and setting of the planets, the various cusps of the moon, planetary and astral conjunctions, and complementary situations of the sun and the moon.

2) The second part—titled *Golādhyāya* (chapter XIV–XXII)—deals with graphical representation of planetary motion, astronomical instruments, spherics, and emphasizes on corrections and rejection of flawed principles.

Lalla shows influence of Āryabhata, Brahmagupta, and Bhāskara I. His works were followed by later astronomers' Śrīpati, Vateśvara, and Bhāskara II. Lalla also authored the *Siddhāntatilaka*.

Bhāskara II

Bhāskara II (1114 CE) authored Siddhāntaśiromaṇi (Head Jewel of Accuracy) and Karaṇakutūhala (Calculation of Astronomical Wonders) and reported on his observations of planetary positions, conjunctions, eclipses, cosmography, geography, mathematics, and astronomical equipment used in his research at the observatory in Ujjain, which he headed.

Śrīpati

Śrīpati (1045 CE) was an astronomer and mathematician who followed the Brhmagupta School and authored the *Siddhāntaśekhara*.

The above is an article on Astronomy and astronomers, not to get confused with astrology and astrologers. An irregular galaxy of a star-forming region in the Large Magellanic Cloud[187] is so captivating!

Astronomy is a natural science that deals with the study of celestial objects, such as stars, planets, comets, nebulae, star clusters and galaxies, and phenomena that originate outside the atmosphere of Earth, such as cosmic background radiation. It is concerned with the evolution,

---

[187] Wikipedia

physics, chemistry, meteorology, and motion of celestial objects, as well as the formation and development of the universe.

Astronomy is one of the oldest sciences. Prehistoric cultures left behind astronomical artifacts such as the Egyptian monuments, Nubian monuments and Stonehenge, and early civilizations such as the Hindus, Babylonians, Greeks, Chinese, Iranians and Maya performed methodical observations of the night sky. However, the invention of the telescope was required before astronomy was able to develop into a modern science. Historically, astronomy has included disciplines as diverse as astrometry, celestial navigation, observational astronomy, the making of calendars, and astrology, but professional astronomy is nowadays often considered to be synonymous with astrophysics. The word 'astronomy' comes from the Greek words astron ἄστρον, "star" and -nomy from nomos (νόμος), "law" or "culture") literally means "law of the stars" or "culture of the stars", depending on the translation.

During the 20th century, the field of professional astronomy split into observational and theoretical branches. Observational astronomy is focused on acquiring data from observations of celestial objects, which is then analyzed using basic principles of physics. Theoretical astronomy is oriented towards the development of computer or analytical models to describe astronomical objects and phenomena. The two fields complement each other, with theoretical astronomy seeking to explain the observational results, and observations being used to confirm theoretical results.

Amateur astronomers have done many important astronomical discoveries, and astronomy is one of the few sciences where amateurs can still play an active role, especially in the discovery and observation of transient phenomena. Astronomy is not to be confused with astrology, the belief system which claims that human affairs are correlated with the positions of celestial objects, although the two fields share a common origin they are now entirely distinct.

Astronomy and astrophysics[188]

Generally, either the term "astronomy" or "astrophysics" may be used to refer to this subject. Based on strict dictionary definitions, "astronomy" refers to "the study of objects and matter outside the

---

[188] Wikipedia.

Earth's atmosphere and of their physical and chemical properties" and "astrophysics" refers to the branch of astronomy dealing with "the behavior, physical properties, and dynamic processes of celestial objects and phenomena". In some cases, as in the introduction of the introductory textbook *The Physical Universe* by Frank Shu, "astronomy" may be used to describe the qualitative study of the subject, whereas "astrophysics" is used to describe the physics-oriented version of the subject. However, since most modern astronomical research deals with subjects related to physics, modern astronomy could actually be called astrophysics. Few fields, such as astrometry, are purely astronomy rather than also astrophysics. Various departments in which scientists carry out research on this subject may use "astronomy" and "astrophysics," partly depending on whether the department is historically affiliated with a physics department, and many professional astronomers have physics rather than astronomy degrees. One of the leading scientific journals in the field is the European journal named Astronomy and Astrophysics.

In early times, astronomy only comprised the observation and predictions of the motions of objects visible to the naked eye. In some locations, such as Stonehenge, early cultures assembled massive artifacts that likely had some astronomical purpose. In addition to their ceremonial uses, these observatories could be employed to determine the seasons, an important factor in knowing when to plant crops, as well as in understanding the length of the year.

Before tools such as the telescope were invented, early study of the stars had to be conducted from the only vantage points available, namely tall buildings and high ground using the naked eye. As civilizations developed, most notably in India, Mesopotamia, China, Egypt, Greece and Central America, astronomical observatories were assembled, and ideas on the nature of the universe began to be explored. Most of early astronomy actually consisted of mapping the positions of the stars and planets, a science now referred to as astrometry. From these observations, early ideas about the motions of the planets were formed, and the nature of the Sun, Moon and the Earth in the universe were explored philosophically. The Earth was believed to be the center of the universe with the Sun, the Moon and the stars rotating around it.

This is known as the geocentric model of the universe, or the Ptolemaic system, named after Ptolemy.

A particularly important early development was the beginning of mathematical and scientific astronomy, which began among the Babylonians, who laid the foundations for the later astronomical traditions that developed in many other civilizations. The Babylonians discovered that lunar eclipses recurred in a repeating cycle known as a saros. Following the Babylonians, significant advances in astronomy were made in ancient Greece and the Hellenistic world. Greek astronomy is characterized from the start by seeking a rational, physical explanation for celestial phenomena. In the 3rd century BC, Aristarchus of Samos calculated the size of the Earth, and measured the size and distance of the Moon and Sun, and was the first to propose a heliocentric model of the solar system. In the 2nd century BC, Hipparchus discovered precession, calculated the size and distance of the Moon and invented the earliest known astronomical devices such as the astrolabe. Hipparchus also created a comprehensive catalog of 1020 stars, and most of the constellations of the northern hemisphere derive from Greek astronomy. The Antikythera mechanism (c. 150–80 BC) was an early analog computer designed to calculate the location of the Sun, Moon, and planets for a given date. Technological artifacts of similar complexity did not reappear until the 14th century, when mechanical astronomical clocks appeared in Europe.

During the Middle Ages, astronomy was mostly stagnant in medieval Europe, at least until the 13th century. However, astronomy flourished in the Islamic world and other parts of the world. This led to the emergence of the first astronomical observatories in the Muslim world by the early 9th century AD. In 964, the Andromeda Galaxy, the largest galaxy in the Local Group, containing the Milky Way, was discovered by the Persian astronomer Azophi and first described in his *Book of Fixed Stars*. The SN 1006 supernova, the brightest apparent magnitude stellar event in recorded history, was observed by the Egyptian Arabic astronomer Ali ibn Ridwan and the Chinese astronomers in 1006. Some of the prominent Islamic (mostly Persian and Arab) astronomers who made significant contributions to the science include Al-Battani, Thebit, Azophi, Albumasar, Biruni, Arzachel,

Al-Birjandi, and the astronomers of the Maragheh and Samarkand observatories. Astronomers during that time introduced many Arabic names now used for individual stars. It is also believed that the ruins at Great Zimbabwe and Timbuktu may have housed an astronomical observatory. Europeans had previously believed that there had been no astronomical observation in pre-colonial Middle Ages sub-Saharan Africa but modern discoveries show otherwise.

Galileo's sketches and observations of the Moon revealed that the surface was mountainous. During the Renaissance, Nicolaus Copernicus proposed a heliocentric model of the solar system. His work was defended, expanded upon, and corrected by Galileo Galilei and Johannes Kepler. Galileo innovated by using telescopes to enhance his observations.

Kepler was the first to devise a system that described correctly the details of the motion of the planets with the Sun at the center. However, Kepler did not succeed in formulating a theory behind the laws he wrote down. It was left to Newton's invention of celestial dynamics and his law of gravitation to finally explain the motions of the planets. Newton also developed the reflecting telescope. Further discoveries paralleled the improvements in the size and quality of the telescope. More extensive star catalogues were produced by Lacaille. The astronomer William Herschel made a detailed catalog of nebulosity and clusters and in 1781 discovered the planet Uranus, the first new planet found. The distance to a star was first announced in 1838 when the parallax of 61 Cygni was measured by Friedrich Bessel. During the 18–19th centuries, attention to the three body problem by Euler, Clairaut, and D'Alembert led to more accurate predictions about the motions of the Moon and planets. This work was further refined by Lagrange and Laplace, allowing the masses of the planets and moons to be estimated from their perturbations. Significant advances in astronomy came about with the introduction of new technology, including the spectroscope and photography. Fraunhofer discovered about 600 bands in the spectrum of the Sun in 1814–15, which, in 1859, Kirchhoff ascribed to the presence of different elements. Stars were proven to be similar to the Earth's own Sun, but with a wide range of temperatures, masses, and sizes. The existence of the Earth's galaxy, the Milky Way, as a separate group of stars, was only proved in the 20th century, along with the existence of "external" galaxies, and soon after, the expansion of the Universe, seen in the recession of most galaxies from us. Modern astronomy has also discovered many exotic objects such as quasars, pulsars, blazars, and radio galaxies, and has used these observations to develop physical theories which describe some of these objects in terms of equally exotic objects such as black holes and neutron stars. Physical cosmology made huge advances during the 20th century, with the model of the Big Bang heavily supported by the evidence provided by astronomy and physics, such as the cosmic microwave background radiation, Hubble's law, and cosmological abundances of elements. Space telescopes have enabled measurements in parts of the electromagnetic spectrum normally blocked or blurred by the atmosphere.

Chapter Twentyeight

BUDS OF MODERN TECHNOLOGIES IN RĀMĀYANĀ AND MAHĀBHĀRATĀ

I t is heartening to see that the origins of several modern technologies spring from the ideas, the Vedic *Rishis* entertained in pre-history ancient distant times of Rāmāyanā (5114 BC) and Mahābhāratā (3138 BC); but painful to see Hindu failure in translating them into desirable end products. Salute Europeans who translated them into enviable social, political, scientific and technological products to serve the mankind.

Frederick Soddy[189] (1877-1956), a Nobel Laureate (1921) in Chemistry of radioactive substance, had a great regard for the Hindu epics Rāmāyanā and Mahābhāratā, from which he might have got the idea of the awesome power of the atom. Therefore, it seems he did not consider the records, as contained in these ancient Hindu epics, as fables. Soddy, in *'Interpretation of Radium'* (1909), wrote:

> "Can we not read into them (the texts of the epics) some justification for the belief that some forgotten race of men attained not only to the knowledge we have so recently won, but also to the power that is not yet ours?"

Dr. Vyacheslav Zaitsev[190] has said that the holy Indian (Hindu) sages have mentioned in the Rāmāyanā that two storied celestial chariots with many windows roared off into the sky like comets. He adds that

---

[189]   Hindu Wisdom - Vimanas
[190]   ibid

the Mahābhāratā and various Sanskrit books describe at length these chariots which were powered by winged lighting. He further remarks: "It was a ship that soared into the air, flying to both the solar and stellar regions."

Rām Rājya, the oldest democracy

It is hard to believe that Americans consider theirs as the oldest democracy. They will know the truth when they understand the *Rām Rājya* democracy of the Rāmāyanā period (5114 BC). In *Rām Rājya* the voice of the poorest ordinary people was heard and respected by Lord Rama. It was not like the modern democracy in which the voice of the majority rules, even wrong. Politics, like a smart lawyer, can prove the right as wrong and vice versa. Cases of hanging of wrong persons are not rare because money can buy justice. But in ancient times of Rama it was not possible because truth was truth which could not be proved different by greedy unprofessional and unethical lawyers. The *Rām Rājya* democracy was different, in which votes were not taken to give authority to a majority by even a single vote to rule and make the laws. In *Rām Rājya,* all people – the rich and the poor – were regulated by one and the same loving and ethical stick, too delicate for a modern mind to understand.

Rama Setu - An Engineering Marvel of 5076 BCE

The Government of India has decided to go ahead with its plans for building a shipping channel by breaking the Rama Setu, the oldest man-made bridge of our civilization, a civil engineering marvel of 5076 BCE. This bridge is believed to have been built by Lord Rama and his team. Rama is a historical personality. His history is being shared from generation to generation by millennia-long Vedic (Hindu) oral traditions by street Ram *leelas*, temple *gathas*, school texts, cinema, etc. The Ram Setu Bridge has been proved to be man-made. For details about Ram Setu, please read the chapter on Ram Setu.

Lord Rama is being worshipped and Diwali is being celebrated for millennia to commemorate his return to his kingdom Ayodhya after completing his 14-year exile. Deepawali or Diwali is a festival of lights symbolizing the victory of righteousness and the lifting of spiritual darkness. The word "Deepawali" means rows of *diyas*, clay lamps. This is the most popular festival, celebrated by Hindus, Jain, Buddhists and Sikhs all over the planet. It is celebrated on the 15th day of Kartika. The stories about Rama and Ravana are told during another holiday, known as Dassehra[191] or Vijaya Dashami.

Vijayadashami literally means the celebration of righteousness over evil. It is celebrated on the tenth day of the Hindu lunar month of

Ashwin as Vijayadashami or Dassehra. It marks the end of the Maha Navratri or the nine days Durga Puja. The day is basically the celebration of the victory of the Mother Goddess over evil demons named Shumbh and Nishumbh. So it is a celebration of righteousness over evil and according to legends the day is marked by several other such victories of good over evil.

The festivity also marks the beginning of the harvest season and prayers are offered and rituals are observed to invoke blessings from Mother Earth for a good harvest, peace and prosperity to all.

Mythological legends refer to a number of stories related to Vijayadashami, meaning victory. Parvati (or Shakti) the wife of Shiva defeats and kills the demon called Mahishasura after a nine-day long battle. According to the Skanda Purana, this is the victory of the Mother Goddess who acquires power and energy to defeat and vanquish all evils from the face of the earth and protect her progenies from every misery.

The victory of Lord Ram over Ravana to rescue his wife Sita who was abducted by Ravana and imprisoned in Lanka is also celebrated as Vijayadashami. Effigies of Ravana are burnt on Dassehra to symbolically mark the victory of good over evil.

This chapter addresses itself to explain that the most modern technologies, scientific achievements, political and psycho-social institutions are based on the ideas the ancient Vedic people entertained in those pre-history distant ancient times, as described in Rāmāyanā and Mahābhāratā.

---

[191] Wikipedia

Technologies of planes and civil engineering

The legend that Ravana kidnapped Sita and flew her to Lanka suggests that they had technology of tiny planes, only good for short distance. Rama and his army prepared road in shallow water along the coast (Ram Setu) suggest that they had knowledge of civil engineering.

During the battle, when Lakshmana fainted, Hanuman brought a shrub from a mountain top, smelling which he regained senses. It suggests that the ancient Vedic people (Hindus) had knowledge of Aurvedic medicine.

Ayurveda, an ancient science of medicine

Ayurveda, known as the "science of life" in ancient Sanskrit, has been a key part of a comprehensive natural system of living in India and Sri Lanka for over 2000 years. The basic tenet of Ayurveda is that your health should be treated with holistic, natural therapies tailored to the needs of each individual. In addition to supplementing the physical body with Ayurvedic herbs, Ayurveda focuses on balancing the mind and spirit to achieve inner harmony.

Ayurveda teaches that each person is a blend of three doshas, or vital energies within the body - Vata, Pitta and Kapha. Each person is born with an optimal balance and a unique harmony among the three doshas. Later in life, negative health may arise from an imbalance in the three doshas - and the science of Ayurveda is used to bring back this essential harmony.

Unlike the Western approach to health which tends to be more reactive, Ayurveda is used to strengthen and nourish the body before the onset of negative health conditions. Ayurvedic practitioners typically recommend a natural course of herbs, diet, exercise and meditation to bring harmony back to the individual. This may be accomplished with a regimen of natural herbs which focus on bringing the three doshas back into balance. In returning the mind, body and spirit back to its original dosha balance, Ayurvedic practitioners believe that an individual is better able to strengthen the body's health while living a more pleasant, harmonious life.

Lakshmana Rekha, a mine bomb

Ravana did not dare to cross over the Lakshmana Rekha, Lakshmana had drawn when Sita insisted that he should go in search of Rama who was also forced by Sita to catch the golden shining deer for her. Rama went chasing the golden deer which actually was the Rakshasa Maricha in disguise. When Rama did not return for a long time, Sita coerced Lakshmana, particularly by suspecting him that he wanted Ram to die so that he could get her. Lakshmana reluctantly left her in search of his brother subject to the condition that she would not cross the protective line he drew which historically is known "Lakshman Rekha". Anybody other than Rama, Sita and himself attempting to cross the line would be singed by flames erupting from the line. It seems the modern idea of mining came from the Lakshmana Rekha. Once Lakshmana left in search of Rama, Ravana came disguised as mendicant begging alms. Ravana, knowing the danger in crossing the Lakshmana Rekha, begged Sita to come forward to give him alms. Innocent Sita not expecting the trick and sentimentally driven by the Vedic tradition of "अतिथि देवो भवः" (Atithi Devo Bhava), meaning that the guest is embodiment of a Deva (god) crossed the **Lakshman Rekha** to provide alms to him and Ravana kidnapped her in his Pushpaka Vimana to Lanka.

All this reflects the three technologies Vedic people had:

i. Lakshmana Rekha, as mining an explosive, and
ii. Flying a small plane (Pushpaka Vimana) Ravana flew Sita from Panchavati forest, near Nashik to Lanka and
iii. Art of make-up to disguise own identity.

Every thing grows from some thing of the past. No number would grow from zero if it has no numerological value. Zero is a number, the origin and the base of numerology. Vedic people had all this knowledge and belief in this. It seems difficult for the West to understand the 'eternal continuity of life' because non Hindus don't believe in 'rebirth and reincarnation.' Hindus don't believe in graves because grave buries body, not the soul which is remembered during the month of Shradhs.

Chapter Twentynine

MODERN V/S ANCIENT CIVILIZATION

C ivilization should improve with the time, but unfortunately the civilization in modern India, rathrer in whole world, has been declining. Honesty has been rare and so the Truth. Cheating is common, even between H and W, between friend and friend, between brother and brother, between neighbor and neighbor and in every relationship. Promises are not kept; oaths are ignored, as evidenced by increasing family court cases. In ancient times of Ramayana and Mahabharata times oathe even at the cost of life were honored. Jaidratha, the king of Sind along with his soldiers had mischievously stopped the Pandavas moving further to help Abhimanu, the son of Arjuna and Subhadra who was trapped in a *Chakraview*, mischievously formed by Kaurvas. He was killed. Arjuna swore that if he failed to kill Jaidratha before the sunset, he will get himself killed in fire. Jaidrath went in hide. Lord Krishna, just before the sunset, with help of his weapon created dark clouds to cover the sun. It looked like night. Jaidratha joyously came out of hide to enjoy the sight of Arjuna a blaze. Krishna with his weapon dispersed the clouds and told Arjuna to kill Jaidratha.

Respect for chasteness of woman, the mother of the humanity

The people of the Ramayana and Mahabharata times respected the chasteness of the woman, the mother of the humanity. There was no case of rape of a woman, as evidenced by the moral character of the Raksha Rawana who did not rape the charming beautiful Sita who spent a few months at his royal palace, completely under his control.

Has a teen-age young innocent intern been safe in White House? Can the modern society be called civilized like that of Vedic times? It is shame that even in the civilized societies a single day does not pass without rapes, not within roofed walls in privacy, but in open naked sunny environment, being watched, not only by humans, but by birds and animals. Rapes even by parents and siblings (fortunately rare) have been happening today. Should the modern be considered as a 'civilized civilization'? Modern civilization is measured by the material gains, not by the psycho-social and spiritual advanced mentality of man. It is shame that 'Money can buy any thing', even the integrity explains the shameless introduction of the modern civilized man. This is the reason why mistrust in all relationships. Mistrust all over explains the absence of happiness and peace of mind al over. In modern times "TRUST" has been a rare commodity, too expensive, rather too difficult, to get. Man is too sefish to find rarely one to be his friend because he is not friend of any one. Adversary of enemy, rather of a rival, is the most desirable friend, even expensive.

Chapter Thirty

GIFTS IND HAS GIVEN TO THE WORLD

A German magazine: Gifts by India to mankind

"I t is true that even across the Himalayan barrier India has sent to us such questionable gifts as grammar and logic, philosophy and fables, hypnotism and chess, and above all our numerals and our decimal system."

Mathematics

Aryabhata[192] invented the concept of *zero*. The decimal system was developed in India in 100 BC. Budhayana first calculated the value of pi. He explained the concept of what is now known as the Pythagorean Theorem. In 1999, British scholars published Budhayan's work, which dates back to the 6th century, long before the time of European mathematicians talked about Algebra, trigonometry and calculus. Sridharacharya formulated quadratic equations in the 11th century. According to Forbes Magazine, Sanskrit is a suitable language for computer software.

---

[192] Google-Aryabhata (476-550 A.D., approximate) mathematician, astronomer and scientist. About him, read Chapter. "Aryabhata: Mathematician, Astronomer and Scientist.

Education

Hindus had first idea of a university, not only within its compound, but worldwide spread, and various subjects to be taught – sociology, psychology, medicine, technology, architecture, navigation, shipbuilding and what not. The Taxila University, the ancient seat of learning, world's first university was established in 700 BC. More than 10,500 students from all over the world studied more than 60 subjects. It was in the Punjab region, northwest of India, now in Pakistan, where, it seems, it is resting in grave, because not that much fond of knowledge, as evidenced by the unfortunate history of the Nalanda University library at hands of a Muslim king. Nalanda University was founded in 427 AD in northeastern India, not far from what is today the southern border of Nepal, It flourished under the patronage of the Gupta Empire during the 5th and 6th centuries, and it survived until 1193.

Nālandā (नालंदा) University,[193] the second ancient center of higher learning was located in Bihar, about 88 kilometers south east of Patna. It remained as a center of learning from the fifth century CE to 1193 CE. The complex was built with red bricks and its ruins occupy an area of 14 hectares. At its peak, the university attracted scholars and students from as far away as Tibet, China, Greece, and Persia.

Nalanda University was built in Baragoan in 4th century. Nalanda (नालंदा) University was a higher learning center in Bihar, India. The university was an architectural and environmental masterpiece. It had eight separate compounds, 10 temples, meditation halls, classrooms, lakes and parks. At its peak, the university attracted scholars and students from as far away as Tibet, China, Greece, and Persia. Nalanda was one of the first great universities in recorded history. It was devoted to Buddhist studies, but it also trained students in fine arts, medicine, mathematics, astronomy, politics and the art of war. The university had a nine-story library where monks meticulously copied books and documents so that individual scholars could have their own collections.

Nalanda University, particularly its library, was ransacked and destroyed by the army under the Muslim king Bakhtiyar Khilji in 1193. The great library of Nalanda University was so large and vast with

---

[193] Wikipedia, Google

thousands of books that it is reported to have burned for three months after the invaders set it on fire. It is unbelievable that man could be against knowledge.

Mission for revival of the Nalanda University

Bhārat, the land of Vedas, can not let the knowledge be drained out. The first Ashram Brahamacharya emphasizes education. In 2006, Singapore, China, India, Japan, and other civilized nations proposed the plan to restore and revive the ancient Nalanda site as Nalanda International University.

At a summit meeting of the leaders in the Philippines, senior officials from India, Singapore, Japan and perhaps also from some other countries, decided to revive the ancient Nalanda University. It is expected that there would be significant potential benefits of this project to Asia, and on Asia's role in the world, and it could make revolutionary impact on global higher education, particularly in Asia and Africa.

Several Asian nations – Singapore, Japan, Bhārat, and some other – have been interested in reviving and rebuilding the university. Fortunately, on November 25, 2010 Nalanda University has been revived with former Singapore Foreign Minister George Yeo as its Chancellor and Gopa Sabharwal, as its Vice Chancellor. Nalanda University is located in Rajgir, near Nalanda, Bihar, India. The University's first academic session began on September 1, 2014 with 15 students including five women.

The project includes the revival of the ancient Nalanda School teaching various aspects of health, medicine and surgery and the most ancient school of Ayurvedic medicine. Sushruta is the father of surgery. Over 2600 years ago, Sushruta and a team of health scientists conducted surgeries such as cesareans, cataract, fractures and urinary stones. It is amazing that the usage of anesthesia was well known in ancient Bhārat.

Sports

The game 'Chess' was first introduced on the planet, in ancient Bhārat. Will Durant[194] has talked about India's gifts to Europe: "It is true that even across the Himalayan barrier India has sent to us such questionable gifts as grammar and logic, philosophy and fables, hypnotism and chess, and above all our numerals and our decimal system."

Navigation

The art of navigation was born in the river Sindhu (Indus), over 5000 years ago. The very word "navigation" is derived from the Sanskrit word Navgatih.

Communication

The pioneer of wireless communication was Prof. Jagdish Bose, not Marconi; Bose had announced his achievement later after Marconi.

Philosophical Gifts

Henry David Thoreau (1817-1862) displayed fascination with Indian spirituality, as reflected in the Bhagvad Gita:

> "In the morning I bathe my intellect in the stupendous and cosmogonal philosophy of the Bhagavad Gita, since whose composition years of the gods have elapsed and in comparison with which our modern world and its literature seems puny and trivial."

Sir Charles Wilkins, KH, FRS (1749 – 1836), was an English typographer and Orientalist, notable as the first translator of Bhagavad Gita into English, and as the creator, alongside Panchanan Karmakar, of the first Bengali typeface.

---

[194] Taken from 'The Power of Dharma' by Stephen Knapp (2006, p. 11).

Amazingly, Robert Oppenheimer, the very first Chairman of Atomic Energy Commission and the father of the Atom bomb was a great admirer of the *Bhagvad Gita.* Amazingly, he learnt Sanskrit to understand the Gita. After witnessing the first atomic explosion, Oppenheimer read a couplet from Gita (Chapter 11: 12):

> "If hundreds of thousands of suns rose up into the sky,
> they might resemble the effulgence of the Supreme
> Person in the universal form."

Several westerners translated Bhagvad Gita[195]

Prof. Fatehullah Mojtabai, former Cultural Counselor of the Embassy of Iran in India, was a noted scholar of Sanskrit and a well-known exponent of Hindu philosophy. He has translated Gita into Persian, the *Laghuyogavāsistha* and *Mahopanisad.*

Sir Charles Wilkins, KH, FRS (1749 – May 13, 1836), was an English typographer and Orientalist, notable as the first translator of Bhagavad Gita into English, and as the creator, alongside Panchanan Karmakar, of the first Bengali typeface. He was born at Frome in Somerset in 1749. In 1770 he went to India as a printer and writer in the East India Company's service. His facility with language allowed him to quickly learn Persian and Bengali. He was closely involved in the design of the first type for printing Bengali. He published the first typeset book in the language, earning himself the name "the Caxton of India". He also designed type for publications of books in Persian. In 1781 he was appointed as translator of Persian and Bengali to the Commissioner of Revenue and as superintendent of the Company's press. He successfully translated a Royal inscription in Kutila characters, which were hitherto indecipherable. In 1784, Wilkins helped William Jones establish the Asiatic Society of Bengal. Wilkins moved to Varanasi, where he studied Sanskrit under Kalinatha, a Brahmin pundit. At this period he began work on his translation of the Mahabharata, securing strong support for his activities from the governor of British India, Warren Hastings. Though he never completed the translation, portions were later

---

[195] Wikipedia, Google

published. The most important was his version of the Gita, published in 1785 as *Bhagvat-Geeta, or Dialogues of Kreeshna and Arjoon* (London: Nourse, 1785). In his preface, Wilkins argued that Gita was written to encourage a form of monotheist "Unitarianism" and to draw Hinduism away from the polytheism he ascribed to the Vedas.

His translation of Gita was itself soon translated into French (1787) and German (1802). It proved to be a major influence on Romantic literature and on European perception of Hindu philosophy. William Blake later celebrated the publication in his picture *The Bramins*, exhibited in 1809, which depicted Wilkins and Brahmin scholars working on the translation.

With Hastings' departure from India, Wilkins lost his main patron. He returned to England in 1786, where he married Elizabeth Keeble. In 1787 Wilkins followed the Gita with his translation of *The Heetopades of Veeshnoo-Sarma, in a Series of Connected Fables, Interspersed with Moral, Prudential and Political Maxims* (Bath: 1787). He was elected a fellow of the Royal Society in 1788. In 1800, he was invited to take up the post of the first director of the India House Library, which became over time the world famous 'India Office Library' (now British Library — Oriental Collections). In 1801 he became librarian to the East India Company, He was named examiner at Haileybury when a college was established there in 1805. During these years he devoted himself to the creation of a font for Devanagari, the "divine script". In 1808 he published his *Grammar of the Sanskrita Language*. King George IV gave him the badge of the Royal Guelphic Order and he was knighted in recognition of his services to Oriental scholarship in 1833. He died in London at the age of 86.

Bhagvad Gita, the most valuable gift to the West[196]

The English novelist and essayist Aldous Huxley (1894-1963) has said that the Bhagvad Gita is for all the peoples on the planet. He recommends to every one to read it and try to discover pearls, no where else available. He further says:

---

[196] Wikipedia

"The Bhagvad Gita is the most systematic statement of spiritual evolution of endowing value of mankind. The Gita is one of the clearest and most comprehensive summaries of the spiritual thoughts ever to have been made."[197]

Prof. Fatehullah Mojtabai, former Cultural Counselor of the Embassy of Iran in India, was a noted scholar of Sanskrit and a well-known exponent of Hindu philosophy. He has translated Gita into Persian as, the *Laghuyogavāsistha* and *Mahopanisad*. He was so much impressed by the philosophy of Hinduism, as contained in Gita, that he wanted his countrymen (Iranians) should also benefit from the Gita philosophy. May be his ancestors were Zoroastrians whose language Zend-Avestan was very similar to Sanskrit.

Annie Besant has[198] also talked about the jewels in the Bhagvad Gita and Mahabharata:

"Among the priceless teachings that may be found in the great Indian epic Mahabharata, there is none so rare and priceless as the Gita. ... For those who, though born for this life in a Western land, and clad in a Western body, can yet look back to earlier incarnations in which they drank the milk of spiritual wisdom from the breast of their true mother – they must feel ever the magic of her immemorial past, must dwell ever under the spell of her deathless fascination; for they are bound to India by all the sacred memories of their past; and with her, too, are bound up all the radiant hopes of their future, a future which they know they will share with her who is their true mother in the soul-life."[199]

---

[197] T. C. Galav: 'Philosophy of Hinduism – An Introduction' (p.65).
[198] Stephen Knapp, 'The Power of the Dharma' (2006, p.10).
[199] Annie Besant, 'India: Essays and Lectures' (vol. iv), London: The Theosophical Publishing Co.,(1895, p.11).

Deathless Life

Annie Besant talks about India's amazing fascination for 'deathless life.' It is a fact of Hindu life. It is a continuous life without any stop (death), like that of 'cycle of day and night' as suggested by Hindu belief in *'Punner-janma'* (rebirth). It is like an unending chain of 'birth → life → death → birth', the union of 'birth and death', like the union of 'day and night', 'light and darkness'. At higher level, it means the union of *'atma'* and *Parmatma* (soul and Supreme Soul). The words 'death' (English) and 'maot' (Arabic) mean end of life. The word *'Dehant'*, the Sanskrit word for death, means end of only body (*deh* = body + *ant* = end), not of soul. It explains that the 'Hindu concept of death' means 'unending continuous or deathless life'. According to the Bhagvad Gita and other *shastras* only the body dies, and the soul transmigrates into another infant body. Such optimistic view of life dilutes the fear of death. Gandhi stressed that transmigration – passage of the soul after death into another body – is not a theory, but it is the fact of life. It is a great contribution of Hinduism to the mankind.

Gita's influence on Roman and European literature

Sir Charles Wilkins (1749 – 1836), an English typographer and Orientalist, was the first translator of Bhagavad Gita into English. In 1770, he went to India as a printer and writer in the East India Company's service. His facility with language allowed him to quickly learn Persian and Bengali. He was closely involved in the design of the first type for printing Bengali. He published the first typeset book in the language, earning himself the name "the Caxton of India".

In 1784, Wilkins helped William Jones to establish the Asiatic Society of Bengal. Wilkins moved to Varanasi, where he studied Sanskrit under Kalinatha, a Brahmin pundit. At this period he began work on his translation of the Mahabharata, securing strong support for his activities from the governor of British India, Warren Hastings. Though he never completed the translation, portions were later published. The most important was his version of the Gita, published in 1785 as *Bhagvad-geeta, or Dialogues of Kreeshna and Arjoon*. In the preface, Wilkins argued that the Gita was written to encourage a form of monotheist "Unitarianism" and to draw Hinduism away from the polytheism he ascribed to the Vedas. His translation of the Gita was itself soon translated into French (1787) and German (1802). It proved to be a major influence on Romantic literature and on European perception of Hindu philosophy. William Blake later celebrated the publication in his picture *The Bramins*, exhibited in 1809, which depicted Wilkins and Brahmin scholars working on the translation.

With Hastings' departure from India, Wilkins lost his main patron. He returned to England in 1786, where he married Elizabeth Keeble. In 1787 Wilkins followed the Gita with his translation of *The Heetopades of Veeshnoo-Sarma, in a Series of Connected Fables, Interspersed with Moral, Prudential and Political Maxims* (Bath: 1787). He was elected a fellow of the Royal Society in 1788. In 1800, he was invited to take up the post of the first director of the India House Library, which became over time the world famous 'India Office Library' (now British Library) — Oriental Collections). In 1801 he became librarian to the East India Company. He devoted himself to the creation of a font for Devanagari, the "divine script". In 1808 he published his *Grammar of the Sanskrita Language*. King George IV gave him the badge of the Royal Guelphic Order and he was knighted in recognition of his services to Oriental scholarship in 1833. He died in London at the age of 86.

CENTRAL ASIA, ORIGINALLY
A PART OF ANCIENT INDIA

"It is a fascinating chapter in history, though we can study it only in the fine Greek-modeled coins of these rulers and in those sculptures of Graeco-Buddhist art which the ruined Buddhist shrines of the Swat and Peshawar valleys have preserved for us. Then when the great Indo-Scythian empire of the Kushan dynasty had replaced the small Hellenistic chiefships on both sides of Hindukush and had further extended its sway beyond the Indus, it was from the north-western borderland that fervent religious propaganda carried the Buddha's doctrine, together with Graeco-Buddhist art and Indian (Hindu)[200] literary culture, into Central Asia and thence into China. This spread of Buddhism right across Asia may well be considered India's greatest contribution to the civilization of mankind in general."

Aurel Stein[201]

Aurel Stein (1862-1943), a Hungarian archaeologist, who spent much of his life in the service of the British Empire in India, conducted a series of important Central Asian expeditions in the early years of

---

[200] The word 'Indian', in fact implies 'Hindu', and the 'Indian contribution' implies contribution of Hinduism and Buddhism.

[201] Aurel Stein (1862-1943), in his book 'On Alexander's Track to the Indus' (2001, preface, p. xi), writes about the presence of Buddhists and Indian (Hindu) literary culture in Central Asia.

the 20th century. He carried out explorations over the greater part of innermost Asia, and along the whole of those north-western borderlands of India.

Kulke and Rothermund[202] write that the transmission of Indian (Hindu & Buddhist) culture to distant parts of Central Asia, China, Japan, and Southeast Asia without military conquest is certainly one of the greatest achievements of Indian history or even the history of mankind.

Stan/istan countries in Central Asia

Most countries in Central Asia – particularly those with their names ending with 'stan' or 'istan,' such as Baluchistan, Afghanistan, Tadzhistan (Tajikistan), Turkmenistan, Turkistan or Turkestan, Kyrgyzstan, Uzbekistan, Kazakhstan, etc.. – could be part of Greater India in ancient times. '*Sthan/stan*' is a Sanskrit word, meaning place. According to the Dictionary,[203] '*sthanam*' means "A state, place, spot, site, locality, station, position, etc." Some say that "istan" is a Persian/ Iranian word. It is possible. Both Sanskrit and Avestan may have the same or similar word for land. It is known that ancient Sanskrit and ancient Avestan were linguistically very close to each other. History tells that in ancient times Iran was a culturally and administratively part of India. For more particulars, please read the Chapter, 'Iran: A Part of Ancient India.'

Research needs to ascertain if all these countries with suffix 'stan' or 'istan,' like Pakistan, were once part of India or not. According to Aurel Stein, the literary culture of most of the Central Asian peoples seems like Indian. For example University Takshashila[204] gets its name from Taksha, son of Bharat, brother of Lord Rama. Taksha ruled over the kingdom of Taksha dynasty which even extended beyond modern day Uzbekistan. Tashkent, the present day Uzbek capital, gets its name from Taksha.

---

[202] Kulke and Rothermund, in 'A History of India' (1986, p.152).
[203] The Practical Sanskrit-English Dictionary, by Vaman Shivram Apte (1992, p.1007),
[204] Wikipedia

The question arises: "What were the original names of these the most recent example of Pakistan will explain it. Prior to the partition of India in 1947, Pakistan, Baluchistan and Vaziristan were part of Bhārat (India). In the Chapter 'Afghanistan: A Part of Ancient India' it is shown with irrefutable documented historical evidences that Afghanistan was originally governed by Hindus and Buddhists before it was occupied by Afghans. All these 'istan' countries (refer to the map on the following page) are in the northwest of India, sharing border with India. When drawing a line around them, beginning at Kazakhstan in the extreme northwest and ending at Pakistan, including Iran, they make a block connecting with India. It suggests that all these or most Central Asian 'istan' countries, like Pakistan, might have been part of the ancient Bhārat. The alleged invading Aryans are said to be from Central Asia. In fact, they were Indo-Aryans – Vedic people or Hindus – originally from the extended India of those times. When in trouble, Hindus (Aryans) in those countries, like Hindus in Pakistan, migrated to the mainland India and some of them stayed there and got culturally absorbed.

History of the movement of ancient Aryans – 'India→ Central Asia→ India' – has been misinterpreted as 'Central Asia→ India' to validate the ill-founded theory *Aryan Invasion of India.*'

The north-west of India has always been vulnerable to foreign invasions. The ancient 'Greater India' (Vishaal Bharat) has been dismembered as a result of foreign invasions, excepting Pakistan which was created in 1947 by partitioning British India on the basis of religion. These 'istan' parts of ancient 'Greater India' must have been captured one by one by some tribes, such as Baluch, Afghan, Tadzh/Tajik, Turk, Kyrg, Uzbek, Kazakh, etc. They were renamed after the name of the tribe conquered it, for example, Kazakhstan after Kazakhs, Afghanistan after Afghans, etc.

Stephen Knapp in *'Proof of Vedic Culture's Global Existence'* (2000, pp. 68-69) shows Vedic connection of most of Central Asian countries:

> "In any case, not only are there many words connected with or derived from Sanskrit, there are many places around the world that also reflect their Vedic

connection. For example, the places that end with the suffix *sthan*, which is the Sanskrit *stan*, reflect their Vedic connection as found in Baluchistan, Afghanistan, Kurdisthan, Kafiristhan, Turkishan, Ghabulisthan, Kazaksthan, and others, such as Arvasthan which was corrupted to Arabia. Countries like Syria and Assyria show their Sanskrit connection through Sura and Asura communities mentioned in the Vedic epics. Those countries also spoke Sanskrit until they lost their connection with India or Vedic culture. Cities in England show their Sanskrit connection with their corrupted form of *puri* turned to 'bury' as in Shrewsbury, Ainsbury, and Waterbury."

J. P. Mallory, in *'In Search of the Indo-Europeans: Language, Archaeology, and Myth'* (1989, p.53), remarks:

"Moreover, the remains from these steppe Bronze Age sites provide us with some of the finest parallels with common reconstructions for Indo-Iranian culture. The settlement and cemetery of Sintashta, for example, although located far to the north on the Trans-Ural steppe, provides the type of Indo-Iranian archaeological evidence that would more than delight an archaeologist seeking their remains in Iran or India. Next to a small settlement occurs a cemetery of tumulus burials dating to the sixteenth century BC."

Indo-Iranian rituals in some 'istan' countries, as indicated by archeological finds, reflect very clearly the presence of Sanskrit-speaking Aryans in Central Asia. The name "Sintashta" of a cemetery seems to have its origin in Sanskrit, and the remains found there reflect Vedic rituals. The dating 16th century B.C. of such cemetery evidences that Indo-Aryans were in Central Asia before they might have started migrating back to the mainland India in about 1500 B.C.

Mallory (p. 53) continues to give more evidences to prove that Indo-Aryans were there in these 'sthan / istan' countries, before 16th century B.C.:

> "Indeed, it is in the eastern Andronovo variants such as the Bishkent culture of south Tadzhikistan that one encounters again the probable expression of Indo-Iranian ritual in the archeological record. At the cemetery of Tulkhar, male burials were provided with small rectangular hearths, reminiscent of the typical Ahavaniya, the rectangular fire-altar of early Indic priests, while females were provided round hearths, comparable to the Garhapatya, the female-associated hearth fire of the Indo-Aryan house."

History, unfortunately enslaved by rulers, has hidden the original names of these countries and the ethnic identities of the ancestors of their present natives. The contents of the book on Kazakhstan, authored by Dr. Alma Kunanbay, when objectively analyzed, implicitly would suggest that the ancestors and the heritage of Kazakhs seem to have very close religio-cultural association with none, but Hindus, and their philosophy of life similar to that of Hinduism. Research on the remaining "istan" countries, I am sure, would show that they, like Kazakhstan, have historical socio-cultural relationship with ancient Hindu India.

Traces of Kazakhstan: Its heritage in India

The flap of the jacket of 'The Soul of Kazakhstan' (2001),[205] authored by anthropologist and ethnographer Dr. Alma Kunanbay, reads:

> "This formerly nomadic country that sprawls nearly 2000 miles across the middle of Central Asia is rich

---

[205] The essays in "The Soul of Kazakhstan" are written by Dr. Kunanbay, photographs by Wayne Eastep, and edited by Gareth L. Steen. It is published by Easten Press, New York.

in culture, tradition and spirituality that date back thousands of years. Until recently, it was little known outside the region because it lost much of its identity and heritage under the 70-year domination of the Soviet Union, and before that, the Russian Empire. Since independence in 1991, Kazakhstan is reestablishing its own identity and making itself felt in world politics and the global marketplace. Kazakhs, who have been taught under the Soviet system that their nomadic heritage was worthless, are rediscovering their roots and an inherent richness that many of that generation had not known existed. *The Soul of Kazakhstan* is an attempt to help fill that void."

Dr. Kunanbay laments that "it (Kazakhistan) lost much of its identity and heritage under the 70-year domination of the Soviet Union ... who (Kazakhs) have been taught under the Soviet system that their nomadic heritage was worthless." Such brainwashing is done by the victors. Unfortunately, history has not been cooperative to help the subjugated people to know who originally they were. It has left a void, some, like Dr. Kunanbay, are trying to fill in, as much as possible. I think 'bay' suffix to 'Kunan' can be compared to 'bai' suffixed to a woman's name in the past, as well as in present India to show respect. Youngsters used call my mother 'Reejh' as 'Reejhibai.' Even now, in some parts of modern India 'bai' is suffixed to the name of an elderly woman, as a gesture of respect.

The book does not clearly mention who were the ancestors of the Kazakhs and what were their original culture and religion. But, the way Dr. Kunanbay has described the culture and religion of the Kazakhs; one can feel some of its grains similar to Hinduism:

"(Kazakhstan) is rich in culture, tradition and spirituality that date back thousands of years."

This can be interpreted with fair certainty that their religion and culture do not seem to have their origin in Islam, which is only about

1500 years old. Most of its elements, as described by Dr. Kunanbay (pp. 53, 60, 72), seem to be similar to those of the Vedic religion (present Hinduism):

- Rich in culture, tradition, and spirituality that dates back thousands of years.
- Kazakhstan, as "the spiritual cradle".
- Close relationship with nature and their response to nature's influences.
- Veneration of mountains, caves, rivers, and lakes.
- Burning incense at sacred places.
- Solar deities (*Surya Devta),* and "Mother Earth".
- Worship of the deities of fire, sky, earth, water, and fertility.

It is interesting to see that the name **'Umay'** of the 'protector 'of fertility' as noted by Kunanbay, is very close to *'Uma'*, the wife of *Shiva,* the god of fertility (*Shiva Lingam*). Dr. Kunanbay describes the heritage of Kazakhs as thousands years long. No religion, other than Vedic (Hinduism), has that longevity. Like Hinduism, spirituality and knowledge (*gyan*) are significant ingredients of the Kazakhstan's philosophy. All these philosophical ingredients of the Kazakh culture seem to be similar to those of Hinduism.

Dr. Kunanbay (p.60) remarks that Sufism is well known in the southern region of Kazakhstan, which is not far away from Afghanistan and pre-1947 India. It has been very much loved by Hindus in India, as evidenced by its significant ingredients, such as mysticism, agnosticism, love, spirituality and Urdu mystic poetic genres, which seem to be similar to Vedic philosophy. Thus Sufism in India may be a little different from that in Muslim countries, because in India, there has been mutual influence between Sufism and Vedanta.

Some feel that Sufism appears to be a blend of Hinduism and Islam. Some believe, Sufism is the result of the influence of Islam on Hinduism and some others believe the opposite. Sufism has lot of Vedanta in it. Swami Vivekananda was a disciple of mystic Ramkrishna (1834-86). Some Muslims do not accept Sufism as Islamic.

Columbia Encyclopedia notes:

"The development of various aspects of Islamic civilization (e.g. literature and calligraphy), many conservative Muslims disagree with many popular Sufi practices, particularly saint worship, visiting of tombs, and the incorporation of non-Islamic customs. Consequently, in recent centuries, Sufism has been a target for Islamic reformist and modernist movements."

Kabīr[206] (also Kabīra) कबीर, (c. 1440 – c. 1518) was a mystic poet and saint of India, whose writings have greatly influenced the Bhakti movement. The name Kabir comes from Arabic *al-Kabīr* which means "The Great" – the 37th name of God in Islam. Kabir's legacy is today carried forward by the Kabir Panth (Kabir's religious sect), a religious community that recognizes him as its founder and is one of the Bhakti Marg Sant (saint). Its members, known as *Kabir panthis*, are estimated to be around 9.6 million. They are spread over northern and central India, as well as dispersed with the Indian Diaspora across the world, up from 843,171 in the 1901 census. His writings include Bijak, Sakhi Granth, Kabir Granthawali and Anurag Sagar.

Kabir, particularly his *dohe* (couplets in poetry form) have secured a very popular place in Bollywood.

Rig Vedic Aryans in Anau, Turkmenistan

Dr. Premsukh Poonai[207] writes that excavations at the site of Anau on the plains of Turkmenistan have revealed that early emigrants from the Indus valley had settled there.

Tocharian, spoken by Central Asian people and in the NE Tarim Basin of West China in remote past is now extinct. Some Tocharian documents were found written in Brahmi script. Since Tocharian was written in Brahmi, it can be presumed that its speakers and their land had some relationship with the Indus Valley people who wrote in Brahmi script. The influence of Sanskrit on Tocharian suggests presence

---

[206] Wikipedia.
[207] Dr. Premsukh Poonai, Ph.D., M.D., in 'Origin of Civilization and Language' (1994, p. 66).

413

of Sanskrit-speaking Indo-Aryans in the land of Tochars in ancient times. Historical research is needed to tell if they were the natives, immigrants, or invaders of the Chinese Turkestan (Tarim Basin).

Dr. Poonai (p. 223) writes that Vedic Aryans, about 4,500 years back, were in the region of the Caspian Sea and the Black Sea, according to some historians, invading Aryans might have come from:

> "By about 2,500 B.C., the speakers and potential speakers of these Rig-Vedic Sanskrit-derived languages had reached the northern shores of the Caspian Sea and the Black Sea, the Anatolian coast on the Aegean Sea, the Phoenician coast on the eastern Mediterranean, the northern shores of the Adriatic Sea and the shores of the Gulf of Genoa."

This proves beyond any doubt that the some Sanskrit-speaking Aryans might have attempted to return to India, the abode of their ancestors, in about 1500 B.C. when their kingdoms might have been overpowered by other forces. Those returning Aryans were mistaken as invaders.

Indian (Vedic) culture in Central Asia, China, Japan, SE Asia

Kulke and Rothermund[208] talk about the wings of Indian (Hindu) culture flying over most of the countries in Central Asia, China and South-East Asia:

> "The transmission of Indian culture to distant parts of Central Asia, China, Japan, and especially Southeast Asia is certainly one of the greatest achievements of Indian history or even the history of mankind. None of the other great civilizations – not even Hellenic – had been able to achieve a similar success without military conquest. ...In this brief survey of India's history, there is no room for an adequate discussion of the development

---

[208] Kulke and Rothermund, in 'A History of India' (1986, p.152).

of the 'Indianised' states of Southeast Asia which can boast of such magnificent temple cities as Pagan (Burma; constructed from 1044 to 1287 AD), Angkor (Cambodia; constructed from 889 to c. 1300 AD), and the Borobudur (Java, early ninth century AD). Though they were influenced by Indian culture, they were nevertheless part of the history of those respective countries."

Burial Rituals in Central Asia: Similar to *Rig Vedic*

John L. Papanek (ed.)[209] talks about the resemblance of the Central Asian burial rituals to the *Rig Vedic:*

> "Interestingly, many details of the Central Asian burial rituals and sacrifices that emerged in the course of the excavations correspond to rites described in the *Rig Veda*, suggesting that the steppe graves may well contain the ancestors of the Vedic Aryans themselves."

The burial rituals among the people of the Central Asia – as reflected by the 4,000 years old graves, excavated by archaeologists show their resemblance to the rituals as described in the *Rig Veda* – evidence the presence of the *Vedic Aryans* in Central Asia who had gone there earlier than 1500 B.C. Aryans had established their kingdoms in Central Asia, Middle East, Egypt, and Asia Minor region. As a matter of fact, Central Asia was a part of India, before it was occupied by Kazakhs, Tadzhs, Turks, Uzbecs, Kyrgyz, etc. Takshashila university gets its name from Taksha, son of Bharat, the brother of Sri Ram.

Taksha ruled over the kingdom of Taksha Khandan which even extended beyond modern day Uzbekistan. Tashkent, the present day Uzbek capital, also gets its name from Taksha. This evidences that in ancient times, Hindus (Aryans) had kingdoms in 'istan' countries of

---

[209] John L. Papanek (ed.), in "Ancient India: Land of Mystery" (1994:55), Time-Life Books, Alexandria, Virginia.

Dr. Jagat K. Motwani

Central Asia from where, Aryans had allegedly invaded India. Central Asia was inhabited by Aryans (Hindus and Buddhists). Bharat has lost all *'istan'* countries in north-west of India, including Afghanistan and Pakistan.

IRAN, ORIGINALLY A PART OF ANCIENT INDIA

One would not need any more to get convinced that Iran was a part of ancient India. Max Müller[210] has talked abaut the origin of Iran:

"Most closely allied to Sanskrit, more particularly to the Sanskrit of the Veda, is the ancient language of the Zend-Avesta, the so called Zend, or sacred language of the Zoroastrians, or worshippers of Ormazd. It was, in fact, chiefly through the Sanskrit, and with the help of comparative philology, that the ancient dialect of the Parsis, or the so called Fire-worshippers, was first deciphered, The MSS had been preserved by the Parsi priests at Bombay, where a colony of Zoroastrians had fled in the tenth century, and where it has risen since to considerable wealth and influence."

Resemblance between Vedas and Persia's Avesta

Jawaharlal Nehru[211] talks about the resemblance between the Vedas and the Persia's Avesta and between their languages, Sanskrit and Avestan respectively:

---

[210] Max Müller, The Science of Language, (1891. pp.278-9).
[211] Jawaharlal Nehru, The Discovery of India, (1946, p.77).

"The Vedas were the outpourings of the Aryans as they streamed into the rich land of India. The brought their ideas with them from that common stock out of which grew the Avesta in Iran, and elaborated them in the soil of India. Even the language of the Vedas bears a striking resemblance to that of the Avesta, and it has been remarked that the Avesta is nearer to the Veda than the Veda is to its own epic Sanskrit."

I agree with Nehru that Persia's Avesta and its language Avestan resemble to Bhārat's Vedas and Sanskrit respectively. It has been historically proved that in ancient times Iran was a part of Bhārat, culturally as well as administratively. But I do not agree with Nehru that Aryans came to India from outside and that the Vedas were brought or composed by the alleged invading Aryans. Aryans were the original natives of Aryavarta (India), as evidenced by the historical fact that in most ancient time, India was known as Aryavarta (Max Müller (p.291). Secondly, Vedas were not composed by alleged invading Aryans. Vedas were composed long before alleged Aryan invasion of India in 1500 B.C. The *Rig Veda* was composed twelve thousand years ago, as evidenced by mention of melting of Himalayan glaciers in the *Rig Veda* which occurred long before ten thousands years back. This challenges the validity and reliability of the theory of 'Aryan invasion of India'.

Dr. Poonai[212] (pp. 168-170) writes:

"Iran was one of the first destination sites which came under the influence of the Rig-Vedic Aryan cultural impact. That was so because of its proximity to Aryavarta, the land of the Aryans as India was then called, and because of its location directly in the path of westward emigration from the land. Most emigrating groups were clans of Asura or Assur Rig-Vedic Aryans. One such group colonized an eastern region of the Iranian plateau. They referred to themselves as Ahuras

---

[212] Dr. Poonai, Premsukh. Origin of Civilization and Language. Dayton Beach (Florida): Pearce Publishers, Inc. 1994.

and to God as Ahura Mazda, a name most probably derived from the Sanskrit Asura Mehda, giver of the breath of life."

As a matter of fact, Iran was not colonized by India. Iran was from pre-history ancient times, culturally, linguistically and administratively, a part of Aryavarta (India).

In Persian 's' is pronounced as 'h'. Asura became Ahura.

Poonai (p.65) explains how the name Persia has been derived from Purusham Aryanam:

> "The Ahuras also called themselves Purushaspa Aryanam, a name most probably derived from the Sanskrit, Purusham Aryanam, the noble people, which later became abbreviated into Parsianam, Parsia, and Parthia."

In ancient times, India enveloped Iran and most of the Central Asian 'istan' countries. Iran, in its ancient times, was culturally and linguistically very similar to ancient India.

Geoffrey Bibby[213] (1969, p. 278) has said that "... so was Iran governed by India in ancient times."

Zend-Avesta and Sanskrit

Zend[214] is the language of the ancient sacred scripture 'Zend-Avesta' of Zoroastrians, as Sanskrit of the Vedas of Hindus. Max Müller (p.273) writes that according to J. Muller:

> "Avesta, or avastak, was, according to J. Muller, derived from the same root which in Sanskrit appears as ava-astha, the participle of which, ava-sthita, would mean laid down, settled. According to this etymology Avesta

---

213   Geoffrey Bibby, Looking for Dilmun, Alfred A. Knoof, new York, 1969.
214   Max Müller, 'The Science of Language,' (1891, p. 278).

would have been intended as a name for the settled text of the sacred Scriptures."

Max Müller (p.273) writes "Professor Haug preferred to derive it from 'a vid', taking Avesta in the sense of what has been known, knowledge, a title somewhat analogous to the Sanskrit Veda."

Will Durant, in *The Story of Civilization: Our Oriental Heritage* (1935, p. 391), describes the scene of the history of ancient India enveloping Ceylon (Sri Lanka), Afghanistan and Persia:

> "The scene of the history is a great triangle narrowing down from the everlasting snows of the Himalayas to the eternal heat of Ceylon. In a corner at the left lies Persia, close akin to the Vedic India in people, language and gods. Following the northern frontier eastward we strike Afghanistan, here is Kandahar, the ancient Gandhara, where Greek and Hindu sculpture fused for a while, and then parted never to meet; and north of it is Kabul, from which the Moslems and the Moguls made those bloody raids that gave them India for a thousand years."

Durant (p. 391, foot notes) writes that in 1805, Colebrooke's essay *on the Vedas* revealed to Europe the oldest literature of India, and also "Anquetil-Duperron's translation of a Persian translation of the *Upanishads* acquainted Schelling and Schopenhauer with what the latter called the profoundest philosophy that he had ever read."

Pococke, in '*India in Greece*' (p.47), talks about colonization of Persia, Colchis, Armenia, and Egypt by India:

> "The ancient map of Persia, Colchis, and Armenia, is absolutely full of the most distinct and a starling evidence of Indian colonisation and what is more astonishing, practically evinces, in the most powerful manner, the truth of several main points in the two great Indian poems, the Ramayana and Mahabharata.

The whole map is positively nothing less than a journal of emigration on the most gigantic scale. ... I have glanced at the Indian settlements in Egypt."

The Zoroastrianism of Iran can be understood better only in the light of the following ancient historical relationships:

- between India and Iran.
- particularly between Sanskrit and Avestan, and
- Vedas and Avesta.

The Avesta is close to the Vedas. Its language Avestan was too close to Sanskrit to distinguish one from the other as seen from the following few sentences.

| Avestan: | tem amavantem yazatem |
| Sanskrit: | tam amavantam yajatam |

| Avestan: | surem damohu sevistem |
| Sanskrit: | suram dhamasu savistham |

| Avestan: | mithrem yazai zaothrabyo |
| Sanskrit: | mitram yajai hotrabhyah |

Very close linguistic correspondence between Sanskrit and Avestan words (given by Burrow,[215] p. 4), as shown above, will puzzle many to think if Avestan and Sanskrit are two different languages.

Will Durant, in *'Our Oriental Heritage'* (p.406), remarks that Sanskrit was a near relative of the early Persian dialect in which the Avesta was composed.

Benjamin Walker[216] writes about inter-mixing of old Iranian and Indian (Hindu) gods and deities.

Max Müller, in *'The Science of Language'* (1891, p.289), remarks:

---

[215] Burrow, T. The Sanskrit Language. Delhi: Motilal Banarsidas Publishers,2001.
[216] 'The Hindu World: An Encyclopedic Survey of Hinduism' (vol. 2, p 353)

"Sanskrit and Zend share certain words and grammatical forms in common which do not exist in any other Aryan languages; and there can be no doubt that the ancestors of the poets of the Vedas and the worshippers of A*huro mazdao* lived together for some time after they had left the original home of the whole Aryan race."

Max Müller (p. 293) remarks: "Now *Airya* in Zend (like in Sanskrit) means venerable, and is at the same time the name of the people."[217] He (p. 292) remarks: "In India, as we saw, the name of Arya, as a national name."

'Gathas' (hymns of the Avesta) is a Sanskritic word, meaning stories. Both Hindus and Zoroastrians worship fire, and both wear sacred thread – *Janeoo* (Hindus) and *Kusti* (Zoroastrians). Hindus wear *Janeoo* hanging from the shoulder, and Zoroastrians wear *Kusti* around the waist. Zoroastrians, like Hindus, believe in 'after life.' Both Hindus and Zoroastrians, unlike Christians, sit on the floor to pray.

Avestan "Vohu Mana" means good mind. 'Mana', in Sanskrit, means mind. The Avestan 'Asha' (the spirit of truth) means 'hope' in Sanskrit.

History clearly explains that in ancient times, Iran, like Afghanistan, was a part of India. Iran was a land of Aryans.

Prof. Fatehullah Mojtabai, former Cultural Counselor of the Embassy of Iran in India, was a noted scholar of Sanskrit and a well-known exponent of Hindu philosophy. He has translated into Persian the Gita, the *Laghuyogavāsistha* and *Mahopanisad*. Translation of Gita into Persian suggests that Prof. Mojtabai was so much impressed by the philosophy of Hinduism, as contained in Gita, that he wanted his countrymen (Iranians) should also benefit from the Gita philosophy. May be his ancestors were Zoroastrians whose language Zend-Avestan was very similar to Sanskrit.

Name 'Iran' derived from 'Aryan"

Dr. Peter B. Clarke (ed.), in *'The World's Religions'* (1993, p.130), writes that the name 'Iran' is derived from 'Aryan'. He seems to suggest

---

[217]   Lassen, Ind. Alt. b. i. s. 6.

that Iran, in ancient times, was inhabited by Aryans. The old Iranian language Avestan was very close to Sanskrit. C.V. Vaidya, in *'History of Sanskrit Literature'* (vol. I, 1986, p.39), observes that there is significant similarity between Avestic *gathas* and *Rig Vedic mantras*. The word 'gathas' in Sanskrit/Hindi means stories. Some times, it looks as if both are identical. Clarke continues that there is no doubt that the Indo-Aryans and Iranians once formed one people and lived together.

Use of the word "ARYA" in Iran too

Max Müller (1891, pp.292-293) talks about the use of the word "Arya" in Iran and its Zend-Avesta:

> "In India, as we saw, the name of Arya, as a national name, fell into oblivion in later times, and was preserved in the term Arya-avarta only, the abode of the Aryans. But it was more faithfully preserved by the Zoroastrians who had migrated to the north-west, and whose religion has been preserved to us in the Zend-Avesta, though in fragments only. Now Airya in Zend means venerable, and is at the same time the name of the people."[218]

This evidences that in ancient times Iran was a significant part of Greater India, and the Avestan was very close to Sanskrit.

J. P. Mallory (1989, pp. 42-43) states that according to Burrow, Indo-Aryans were once the occupiers of Iran.

T. Burrow, in *'The Sanskrit Language'* (2001, p.4), writes:

> "The relations between this ancient Iranian and the language of the Veda are so close that it is not possible satisfactorily to study one without the other. ... It is quite possible to find verses in the oldest portion of the *Avesta*, which simply by phonetic substitutions according to established laws can be turned into intelligible Sanskrit."

---

[218] Lassen, Ind. Alt. b. i. 8. 6.

Burrow (p.1) observes:

> "In the greater part of India today languages are spoken
> which are derived from a single form of speech which
> was introduced into India by invaders from the north-
> west more than three thousand years ago. The invading
> peoples were known in their language as *arya*, a word
> which is also commonly used as an adjective meaning
> 'noble, honourable.'"

Burrow's statement – that the invading people were Aryans, and that the word 'Arya' (in Sanskrit) means 'noble' – clearly suggests beyond any doubt that those alleged invading people were originally Indo-Aryans from India. How then could it be invasion? It was their 'return' to, not 'invasion' of India. The Aryan invasion of India is a myth, a mischievously fabricated theory. Historians, like Burrow and others, who believe in 'Aryan invasion of India', have not been able to identify the country (other than India) which had Aryans as its natives and Sanskrit as its native language. Burrow, on the same page (p.1), writes that the modern name 'Iran' is ultimately derived from Arya. He further says:

> "In conformance with this usage, the term *Aryan*
> is now used as common name of these peoples and
> their languages; alternately the term Indo-Iranian is
> commonly used. To distinguish the Indian branch from
> the Iranian, the term *Indo-Aryan* has been coined."

This proves that none but Aryavarta (Bhārat, India) is the original home of the Aryans and of their language Sanskrit. As a matter of fact, Indo-Aryans must have been residents of also Iran whose language 'Avestan' was one of India's vernaculars. Very close linguistic correspondence between Sanskrit and Avestan words – given by Burrow, as shown below – will puzzle many to think if Avestan and Sanskrit were two different languages.

Sanskrit	Avestan	Meaning in English
Hiranya	Zaranya	Gold
Sena	Haena	Army
Rsti	Arsti	Spear
Asura	Ahura	Lord
Yajna	Yasna	Sacrifice
Hotar	Zaotar	Sacrifying priest
Soma	Haoma	Sacred drink Soma
Aryaman	Airyaman	member of religious sodality

Sanskrit 's' is pronounced as 'h' in Avestan and 'h' as 'z'. Likewise, 'Sindhu' became 'Hindu', soma became homa, and 'Sindhustan' became 'Hindustan.

Will Durant, in *Our Oriental Heritage* (p.406), remarks that Sanskrit was a near relative of the early Persian dialect in which the Avesta was composed.

Benjamin Walker, in *'The Hindu World: An Encyclopedic Survey of Hinduism'* (vol. 2, p 353), writes about inter-mixing of ancient Iranian and Indian (Hindu) gods and deities:

> "The Indo-Iranian tribal communities gave place to new territorial kingdoms situated on great rivers and the jungle retreats of the rishis. The old Iranian gods faded in importance and were substituted by deities of new dimensions, Brahma, Siva, Vishnu, Krishna, the Nagas, the Linga."

Benjamin Walker (vol. 1, p.70) talks about the Aryan language whose literary descendants were Avestic in Persia and Vedic in Bhārat. It suggests religious, cultural and linguistic closeness between Iranians and Indians (Vedic people) in ancient times. This explains who Aryans were and where they were from:

> "They (Aryans) spoke an Aryan language of which the literary descendants were Avestic in Persia and Vedic

in India. The immigrant Indian branch has left a vivid
glimpse of its faith and customs in the Vedas, which have
given their name to the period and their way of life. ...
In the country of their ancestors the Iranian Aryans and
the Indian Aryans lauded the same gods with the same
hymns, and worshipped them with identical rites. Their
relationship is today well established, and their 'original
home' is now believed to have been at least as far as west
as the wide plain between the Oxus and Jaxartes, the
cradle of some of the characteristic features of Indo-
Iranian culture and religion."

It clearly suggests that the Iranian Aryans and the Indo-Aryans
were one and the same people in ancient times when they "lauded the
same gods with the same hymns, and worshipped them with identical
rites." I don't think they were known as 'Hindus' and 'Persians'. All
the people of the subcontinent, including Indians, Iranians, Nepalese,
Bhutanese, Sri Lankans, Burmese, etc., must have been called Aryans,
as the country was known as Aryavarta, Aryadesh, or Aryabhoomi. The
unfounded theory of the 'Aryan invasion' – engineered in London and
guided by the world-known British policy "Divide and Rule" – seems
to have divided Indians and Iranians who, in ancient times, were one
and the same people.

From what Dr. Peter B. Clarke, Mallory, Burrow, and several other
scholars have talked about the co-habitation of both – the Indo-Aryans
and the Indo-Iranians – it seems they were one people and lived together
in ancient times when Iran was a part of Greater India. In my opinion,
the term 'Indo-Aryan' is linguistically fallacious, because there were no
Aryans other than of those of Indian origin.

Persia: Named after Parsooram, warrior with Axe:

E. Pococke, in his book *India in Greece* (p.45), has said that Persia was
named after Parsooram, the Mahābhāratā warrior with Axe:

"I have glanced at the Indian settlements in Egypt which again be noticed; and I would now resume my observations from the lofty frontier which is the true boundary of the European and Indian races. The Parsoos, the people of Parsoo-Rama, those warriors of the Axe, have penetrated into and given a name to PERSIA; they are the people of Bharata."

'Rama', suffixed to the name Parsoo, shows that Iran (Persia) was under the control of India from the days of Rāmāyanā which happened before 5114 B.C., the birth of Lord Rama and long before Mahabharata.

According to '*mahabharat@intelindia.com*,' the coastal area of Karnataka and Kerala state in India is known as Parashurama Kshetra:

"Parashurama Bhargava or Parasurama (Axe-wielding Rama), according to Hindu mythology is the Sixth Avatara (incarnation) of Vishnu, belongs to the Treta Yuga, and is the son of Jamadagni & Renuka. Parashu means axe, hence his name literally means Rama-with-the-axe. He received an axe after undertaking a difficult penance to please Shiva, from whom he learned the methods of warfare and other skills. He is a Chiranjeevin, who fought the advancing ocean back thus saving the lands of Konkan and Malabar (Maharashtra-Karnataka-Kerala coastline). The coastal area of Karnataka and Kerala state in India is known as Parashurama Kshetra (Parashurama's area). Some dispute this and say it extends all the way to Mumbai in Maharashtra."

Euphrates as Eu-Bh'rat-es?

Pococke (p.45) writes that the name 'Eu-Ph'rat-es (as Eu-Bh'rat-es) has been given to the principal stream that pours its water into the Persian Gulf.

Dr. Poonai, in *Origin of Civilization and Language* (1994, p. 170), explains the root of the name Persia which resembles to Parshurama:

> "The doctrines of the Vedas were therefore widely taught to the noble people of Iran also called Purusham Aryanam a phrase which can be abbreviated to Parsianam or Parthians or Persians."

The term 'Parsee' seems to have originated from Parsianam. Poonai (pp. 220,221) remarks:

> "The Ahuras were originally a colony of Asura Rig-Vedic Aryans who immigrated from Aryavarta or India into the land of the Purusham Aryanam or Persianam or Persia, as explained earlier. The Asura Rig-Vedic Aryans reached the Iranian plateau readily and in considerable numbers from the earliest times."

Herman Kulke and Dietmar Rothermund[219] do not seem to be clear about the originality of the Aryans:

> "A peace treaty of 1350 BC from Boghazkoi in Western Asia, which was then the capital of Hittites, is often quoted as the first document referring to the Aryans. In this treaty, which a king of the Hittites concluded with the ruler of the Mitanni kingdom, the Aryan gods Mitra, Varuna, Indra and the Nasatyas were invoked as witnesses. As these gods thereafter reappeared in the sacred literature of the Vedic Aryans or that this elite was a branch of a larger Indo-Aryan community which had migrated first to India and then to the west. The old Iranian language of the Mitanni, is closely related to the Indo-European language and Iran means 'Land of the Aryans'. Thus some Aryans may have come via Iran to India."

---

[219] Herman Kulke and Dietmar Rothermund in 'History of India' (1986, p.33).

Kulke and Rothermund seem to be confused, as seen by their two contradicting statements: (i) "Iran means 'Land of the Aryans', and (ii) "Thus some Aryans may have come via Iran to India." I think they must be talking about their returning to India. Mention of "Aryan gods Mitra, Varuna, Indra and the Nasatyas were invoked as witnesses" clearly shows that both Hittite and Mitanni kings were Indo-Aryans (Vedic people, Hindus).

As a matter of fact, Aryans didn't come to India or Iran from somewhere. They were originally from India who had gone out for trade and colonization. According to Aurel Stein, as said earlier, Indo-Aryans were already in Central Asia. They were returning. The Hittites and Mitanni were originally the natives of India and Iran. C.V. Vaidya, in *'History of Sanskrit Literature'* (1986, p.39), writes that Mitanni were Aryans from the Punjab. They were Vedic Indo-Aryans (Hindus) as evidenced by the names of the Vedic gods invoked in the treaty. These gods were already being worshipped, as evidenced by the *Rig Veda* in which their names appeared long before 4000 BC. Kulke and Rothermund's statement, "these gods thereafter (after 1300 BC) reappeared in the sacred literature of the Vedic Aryans", seems to be based on the ill-based theory of Aryan invasion of India, according to which the Vedas were composed by the alleged invading Aryans in 1000 BC or even later. But, the Vedas were composed long before that as explained in the Chapter on Vedas.

As explained earlier, Iran was a part of Greater India. Indo-Aryans, who had gone out of India and had established their kingdoms in Asia Minor region and beyond, were returning to India, when they were routed out by some other forces.

V. Gordon Childe, in *'The Aryans: A Study of Indo-European Origins'* (1926, p.19), writes that Mitannis were warriors *(Kshatries)* from India: "Finally we know that there existed among the Mitanni at this time a class of warriors styled *marianna* which has suggested comparison with the Sanskrit *marya,* young men, heroes."[220]

Childe further talks about the Aryan (perhaps Mitanni and Hittites) dynasts installed in the Mesopotamia region:

---

[220] Moret, 'From Tribe to Empire' in 'Cambridge Ancient History'.

> "So it is clear enough that the dynasts installed on the Upper Euphrates by 1400 B.C. was Aryans, closely akin to those we meet in the Indus Valley and later in Media and Persia. But their subjects were non-Aryan Asianics and the rulers had adopted the native language and the Babylonian script for their official correspondence, and apparently acknowledged local gods besides their own."

Similar traits we find among Indian emigrants, particularly Sindhis, the original natives of the Indus Valley (Mohenjo-daro, Sind), who would pick up the vernacular of their adopted country without going to school. I have seen in Jakarta, how fluently my host Mr. V. Ram (a Sindhi gentleman) was communicating with his maidservant in Bahasa, the local language of Indonesia. He had not gone to school to learn that Indonesian language.

Childe (p.19) underlines that the Aryan adventurous movement kept on advancing further and further:

> "And the movement which had brought them to the Euphrates did not stop there. During the same period the Tell-el-Amarna tablets mention Aryan princes in Syria and Palestine too – Biridaswa of Yenoam, Suwardata of Keilah, Yasdata of Taanach, Artamanya of Zir-Bashan and others.[221] These two were probably mere dynasts ruling over non-Aryan Semetic subjects."

The personal names of the Aryan princes – like Biridaswa, Suwardata, Yasdata, and Artamanya – look very close to Indic (Sanskritic) rather than Iranian. He explains that 'Birdaswa' has been plausibly compared to the Sanskrit 'Brhad-aswa', meaning owning a great horse – 'brahad = great, and 'aswa' = horse.

Childe (p.7) talks about close linguistic congruence between Sanskrit and ancient Iranian languages:

---

[221] Cambridge Ancient History, ii, p. 331.

> "Sanskrit of the *Rig Veda* and Iranian of the inscriptions of Darius the Great and the Gathas of Zoroaster are so much alike that they might almost be regarded as just dialectic varieties of a common stock."

Childe comments: "Such correspondences allow us to conclude that the Indians and Iranians are, indeed, two branches of one and the same people who had lived together long after their separation from the parent stem."

Iran means 'Land of Aryans'

Max Müller (1891, pp.292-293) talks about the use of the word "Arya" in Iran and its Zend-Avesta:

> "In India, as we saw, the name of Arya, as a national name, fell into oblivion in later times, and was preserved in the term Arya-avarta only, the abode of the Aryans. But it was more faithfully preserved by the Zoroastrians who had migrated to the north-west, and whose religion has been preserved to us in the Zend-Avesta, though in fragments only. Now Airya in Zend means venerable, and is at the same time the name of the people."[222]

Ariana or Aryana

The Columbia Encyclopedia (Fifth Edition) writes: that 'Ariana' or 'Aryana' was the general name for the Eastern provinces of the ancient Persian Empire, regions south of the Oxus River (modern Amu Darya). Ariana is included in present East Iran, N and E of Afghanistan, India, and the Indus River.

It may be erroneous to say that 'Arianism,' founded in 4th century AD by a Christian priest Arius in Alexandria, had any relationship with Indo-Aryans.

---

[222] Lassen, Ind. Alt. b. i. 8. 6.

Indo-Aryans and Iranians as one people

The authors of the Vedas and worshippers of Ahuro Mazdao did live together in early ancient times. Iran, as a significant part of India, was the original home of the Aryans. Because of military occupation of Persia (present Iran) by foreign powers, the worshippers of Ahuro Mazdao were separated from the mainstream Sanskrit-speaking Aryans of India. Because of their long separation, the Zend language got heavily influenced by the language of its occupiers. In about ninth century A.D., several Parsees (Zoroastrians) had to leave Persia (present Iran) because of religious persecutions. Some of them, not all, fled to India, the country, previously shared by both, Hindus and Zoroastrians. They were welcomed because the Vedic (Hindu) India is historically known as a kind-hearted shelter to refugees of various other ethnic peoples including Jews and Buddhists from Tibet.

Parsees, perhaps because of their traditional religio-cultural bond with Hindus, and more so because of historical close relationship their language Zend-Avestan had with Sanskrit, they have felt comfortable and secure in Hindustan. They have very well mainstreamed in all spheres of life. – Culture, language, food and ethnic dress Sari. They have advanced a great deal economically, educationally and technologically. Parsees have adopted Gujarati, as their language, because they first came to Navsari and Surat, big towns of Gujarat. They have been free to practice their religion and culture. Parsees, in general, are peace loving people. Most of them are well-educated and financially well off. If you want to be happy in your adopted home, heed the advice of the elders: "Behave, think, and feel like a Roman when you are in Rome."

Religiously also both seem to be close to each other. For example, both Hindus and Zoroastrians worship fire. Parsis, like Hindus wear Janeu. Hindus wear it from shoulders and Parsis tie it around the waist. They call it Kusti.

As a matter of fact, as explained earlier in this chapter, in remote ancient times, Iran was a part of Greater India (Vishaal Bharat), and their languages – Sanskrit and Zend-Avestan – were linguistically too close to be seen as two different languages.

Max Müller, in '*The Science of Language*' (1891, p.289), remarks: "Sanskrit and Zend share certain words and grammatical forms in common which do not exist in any other Aryan languages; and there can be no doubt that the ancestors of the poets of the Vedas and the worshippers of A*huro mazdao* lived together for some time after they had left the original home of the whole Aryan race." It is clear that Max Müller considered Aryavarta (India) as the "original home of the whole Aryan race." On p. 295, Max Müller wites the same:

> "That *Aryan* was used as a title of honour in the Persian Empire is clearly shown by the cuneiform inscriptions of Darius. He calls himself Ariya and Ariya-*kitra*, an Aryan and of Aryan descent; and Ahuramazda, or, as he is called by Darius, Auramazda, is rendered in the Turanian translation of the inscription of Behistun, 'the god of the Aryas.' Many historical names of the Persians contain the same element. The great-grandfather of Darius is called in the inscriptions Ariyaramna, the Greek Ariaramnes (Herod, vii. 90)."

The suffixes "*ramna*" or "*ramnes*" in the names of the grand father of Darius '*Ariyaramana*' or '*Ariaramnes*' need to be noticed which reflect the name of Hindu god Rama. This is also found in present Hindu names, like 'Venkatraman', 'Raghviraman', 'Sitaraman', etc.

Max Müller (1891, p. 296) remarks:

"The modern name of Iran for Persia still keeps up the memory of this ancient title." He (p.298) continues to tell about the presence of the element of Arya in the names of both the countries – Armenia[223] and Ireland. He clarifies: "And it's maintained by O'Reilly, though denied by others, that this *er* is used in Irish in the same sense of noble, like the Sanskrit *arya*."

Max Müller (1891, p.294) writes that some other countries in the region craved for Aryan title: "As the Zoroastrian religion spread westward, Persia, Elymais, and Media all claimed for themselves this

---

[223]   De Sacy, Memoire, p. 47; Lassen, Ind. Alt. i. 8.

Aryan title. Hellanicus, who wrote before Herodotus, knows of Aria as a name of Persia."

Max Müller (1891, p.297) traces the countries in the north-west of India, where the name of Arya has spread:

> "We have traced the name of Arya from India to the west, from Arya-avarta to Ariana, Persia, Media, more doubtfully to Armenia and Albania, to the Iron in the Caucasus, and some of nomad tribes in Transoxiana. As we approach Europe the traces of this name grow fainter, yet are not altogether lost."

Max Müller (1891, p.298) talks about the two roads open to the Aryas of Asia took to Northern Greece and along the Danube to Germany. It is now certain beyond any doubt that the Aryans from India (Aryavarta) were there in the Caucasus, Central Asia, and Europe, who, on their return to India in about 1500 B.C., were mistaken as invaders.

C.V. Vaidya, in *'History of Sanskrit Literature'* (1986, vol. 1, pp. 39-40), is attempting to give lingual (Sanskrit and Avestan) evidences to establish that in ancient times, the Indian Aryans and Iranians, not only lived together, but also were one people. He writes that the Avestic *gāthās* and *Rig Vedic mantras* were extremely similar and some times identical. By the way, *'gāthās'* is a Sanskrit word, meaning stories. Therefore, Vaidya feels:

> "Argument again in favour of a late date for the Rigvedic hymns is sought to be derived from the extreme similarity of Avestic gāthās and Rigvedic mantras which are sometimes identical. There is no doubt that the Indo-Aryans and the Iranians once formed one people and lived together. They naturally have some mantras in common. But we must remember that Zoroaster did not himself compose these *gāthās*. He only preserved what had come down for centuries and even if we take 550 B.C. as the date of Zoroaster that cannot be the date of those *gāthās*. Indeed, as the

Hindus have preserved the Vedic mantras intact for thousands of years, because they have become sacred, so also must the Avestic gāthās have been preserved intact for thousands of years before they were taken up by Zoroaster for his new religion."

The above is an irrefutable evidence that there was close relationship between India and Iran, and so between Sanskrit and Avestan, and so between Hinduism and Zoroastrianism.

V. Gordon Childe, in his book '*The Aryans: A Study of Indo-European Origins*' (1987, p. 20), writes that according to Eduard Meyer, "Indians and Iranians had lived together as one body and had worshipped these very deities in common before the Indians had occupied the Indus Valley."

In my opinion, Eduard Meyer is wrong in saying that Indians had occupied the Indus Valley. As a matter of fact, they were its natives.

AFGHANISTAN, ORIGINALLY
A PART OF ANCIENT INDIA

Almost all the Central Asian countries with suffix 'istan' or 'stan' – Afghanistan, Turkmenistan, Uzbekistan, Tajikistan, etc – like Pakistan were culturally as well as administratively part of Ancient Bhārat. The word 'sthan' in Sanskrit means land or territory.

Henri Stierlin, in *'Hindu India'* (2000, p.8): talks about the ancient India (Bhārat) that it was vast spread and was big like a continent:

"India is often referred to as the subcontinent. … In the historical sense of the word, 'India' referred to the territory bounded by the Hindu Kush and the Himalayas, and extended from modern Afghanistan and Pakistan in the west to Bangladesh in the east. South of the basins of the Indus and Ganges, rivers whose sources lie in the mountain barrier to the north, India includes the entire peninsula: the Deccan. This lies between the Gulf of Oman and the Bay of Bengal projecting like a triangle into the Indian Ocean."

Stierlin has described above the vast geography of ancient India. He continues: "The Greek influence (in 3rd century B.C.) was particularly noticeable, for example, in the treatment of the human figure by the Buddhist sculptors of Gandhara." The ancient name 'Gandhara' was changed to 'Kandhar' by Afghans. Gandhara has a marvelous history in Mahabharata (3138 B.C.). Gandhari, the wife of the blind king Dhritarashtra due to respect for her blind husband, blind-folded her eyes for ever.

Mahabharata attributes high moral standards to Gandhari, although Gandhari's sons were portrayed as villains. She repeatedly exhorted her sons to follow dharma and make peace with the Pandavas. Gandhari fostered a big-little sister relationship with Kunti. Famously, when Duryodhana would ask for her blessing of victory during the Kurukshetra war, Gandhari would only say "may victory find the side of righteousness".

Gandhari was an ardent worshipper of Lord Shiva and a student of Durvasa and various versions of the Mahabharata state that she was blessed by the lord himself to have 100 children. Gandhari's sacrifice of her eyesight and her austere life granted her great spiritual power, allowing her to grant powers and make curses.

Gandhari's major flaw was her love for her sons, especially her first born, Duryodhana, which often blinded her to his flaws. Unknown to her, Gandhari's marriage was a major reason for the story's central conflict. Her brother Shakuni, was enraged that Hastinapur, already having humiliated Gandhar in the war against Pandawas in which all his brothers were killed, would offer for his prized sister a blind man. Shakuni swore to destroy the Kuru dynasty, and played an instrumental role in fueling the flames of conflict between the cousins. Gandhari along with her husband Dhritarashtra, brother-in-law Vidura, and sister-in-law Kunti died in the Himalayas, in a forest fire.

Buddhist statues in Afghanistan, shattered by a Muslim king

Buddhist statues in Afghanistan tell the story of Buddhists and Hindus in ancient Afghanistan, originally known as Gandharadesh in the third century B.C. 'Hari Rud' river is another evidence of the Hindu presence in ancient Afghanistan. Hari is the name of the Hindu god Krishna.

Ancient Bhārat was much larger than a continent. It included Bangladesh, Pakistan, Baluchistan, Afghanistan, Iran, Asia Minor, Sri Lanka, Myanmar, Bhutan, Thailand, Cambodia, Indochina, Vietnam, Indonesia, Java, Sumatra, Bali, etc as reflected by Ramayana and Mahabharata; and several other countries in Central Asia with their names suffixed with 'istan' or 'stan' were also part of ancient Bhārat

History has been silent to identify their original names prior to their occupation by Tajiks, Turks, Kyrgs, Uzbeks, Kazakhs, etc.

The Columbia Encyclopedia (5th edition, p.27) makes a mention of the "rich valley of HERAT on the Hari Rud (Arius) river in the northwest corner of the country (the heart of ancient ARIANA)." The words Arius and Ariana reflect Aryan presence in Afghanistan. As a matter of fact, Aryans are Hindus, as explained in the Chapter *"Aryans, Who and from Where?"* Many historians have admitted that there are several evidences reflecting significant presence of Hindus and Buddhists in Afghanistan in its pre-Afghan period.

Iqbal Ali Shah (1938, p. 9) writes:

"Historians believe that the inhabitants of Afghanistan, prior to the Greek invasion, were Hindus. After the decline of the Indo-Scythians, the Hindus were governing and inhabiting the country. They ruled the country till the end of the seventh century when the Arabs conquered Afghanistan and the people of Afghanistan embraced Islam."

Abdul Ali Arghandawi (1984, p.136) writes:

"Buddhism and Hinduism were practiced in Afghanistan and its remains are still available in northern Afghanistan and other parts of the country. Buddha's 52 meter high statue in Bamian and many stupas dug up in different parts of the country represent Buddhist religion."

Phil Zabriskie, in *'The Outsiders'* (National Geographic, February 2008), writes:

"At the heart of Afghanistan is an empty space, striking absence, where the larger of the colossal Bamian Buddhas once stood. In March 2001 the Talibans fired rockets at the statues for days on end, then planted and detonated explosives inside them. The Buddhas had looked out over Bamian for some 1,500 years. ... The regimes rose and collapsed or were overthrown. The statues stood through it all. But the Talibans saw the Buddhas simply as non-Islamic idols, heresies carved in stone. They did not mind being thought brutish. They did not fear further isolation. Destroying the statues was a pious assertion of their brand of faith over history and culture."

Talibans declined offers from a few museums to remove and relocate them in museums. This reminds me of what I read in a history text about Mahmud Ghaznavi– known as *'But Shakan'*, meaning destroyer of Idols (*but* = Idol, shakan = destroyer) – who got Hindu idols smashed into pieces when he ruled over Afghanistan in about 10th century A.D. They ignorantly thought that the images of those Hindu idols would disappear from history.

Alexander Cunningham[224] writes that the people of whole Afghanistan spoke Indian language and practiced Hinduism and Buddhism:

> "For several centuries, both before and after the Christian era, the provinces of Northern India beyond the Indus in which the Indian language and religion were predominant, included the whole of Afghanistan from Bamian and Kandahar on the west to the Bholan Pass on the south. This large tract was then divided into ten[225] separate states or districts, of which Kapisa was the chief."

Cunningham (p.14) describes Afghanistan, as the country of Hindus and Buddhists:

> "In the following century, as we learn from the Chinese pilgrim, the king of Kapisa was a *Kshatriya*, or pure Hindu. During the whole of the tenth century the Kabul valley was held by a dynasty of Brahmans, whose

---

[224] Alexander Cunningham, 'The Ancient Geography of India' (1871, p.14)
[225] M. Julien's 'Hiouen Thsang,' 1.71.

439

power was not finally extinguished until towards the close of the reign of Mahmud Ghaznavi. Down to this time, therefore, it would appear that a great part of the population of eastern Afghanistan, including the whole of the Kabul valley, must have been of Indian descent, while the religion was pure Buddhism."

Max Müller (1891, p. 287) writes that Pushtu was more closely related with languages of India:

"The language of the Afghans, the Pushtu, and Paktyes of Herodotus, which was formerly classed as an Iranian dialect, has been proved by Trumpp to be more closely related with the vernaculars of India than of Persia. The large tract was then divided into ten."

The question whether Afghanistan's Pushtu is more related to Indian or Iranian language can be answered by the historical fact that Iran, in ancient times, was a part of India, as explained in the chapters *"Hinduism and Zoroastrianism"* and *"Iran, a part of ancient India."*

Peshawar, originally known as Parashawar

On p. 66, Cunningham writes that the present Peshawar was originally known as *Parashawar.* And that the kingdom of Gandhara was a dependency of Kapisa or Kabul. Nehru, in *'Discovery of India'* (p. 202), writes that the well- known town in ancient India "Gandhara (present Kandahar) must have been an important part of Aryan India." Thus, Nehru believed that India was an Aryan country, and didn't believe in "Aryan invasion of India."

Lahore, founded by Lav, son of Sri Rama

Cunningham (pp.166-168) talks about the originality of 'Lahore' and 'Kusawar (or Kasur):

"The great city of Lahore, which has been the capital of the Punjab for nearly nine hundred years, is said to have been founded by *Lava*, or *Lo*, the son of *Rama*, after whom it was named *Lohawar.* ... According to the traditions of the people *Kasur* was founded by *Kusa*, the son of *Rama*, after whom it was named *Kusawar*, which, like the contemporary city of *Lohawar*, has been slightly altered in pronunciation by the transposition of the vowels. The town stands on the high bank of the old bed of the Bias River, 32 miles to the south-south-east of Lahore, and is popularly said to have once possessed Bara *kilah*, or twelve forts."

Pushkalavati, Ancient capital of Gandhara: Alexander Cunningham, in *"The Ancient Geography of India"* (pp.41-42), talks about *Pushkalavati*, capital of Gandhara, which was under the administration of Pushkara, nephew of Rama:

"The ancient capital of Gandhara was *Pushkalavati*, which is said to have been founded by Pushkara, the son of Bharata, and the nephew of Rama.[226] ... The Greek name of *Peukelaotis*, or *Peucolaitis*, was immediately derived from *Pukkalaoti*, which is the Pali, or spoken form of the Sanskrit Pushkalvati."

Rama was the only son of the eldest queen Kaushalya of Maha Raja Dashratha. Bharat was the only son of the youngest queen Kekai. Sumitra had two sons, Lakshman and Shatrughan. Rama's son Kush or Cusha was given Africa to govern, as shown later in the chapter 'India in Africa' See in such ancient times Hindus ruled all over, including Africa.

John W. McCrindle[227] (pp.115-117) writes some similar things about Gandhara:

---

226 Wilson's 'Vishnu Purana', edited by Hall, b.iv.c.4.
227 John W. McCrindle, in 'Ancient India as described by Ptolemy' (2000, pp.116, 117)

"The Gandharai: – Gandhara is a name of high antiquity, as it occurs in one of the Vedic hymns, where a wife is represented as saying with reference to her husband, "I shall always be for him a Gandhāra ewe." It is mentioned frequently in the *Mahabharatā* and other post-Vedic works, and from these we learn that it contained the two royal cities of Takshasila (Taxila) and Pushkalavati (Peukelaotis) the former situated to the east and the latter to the west of the Indus."

The Mahabharata war was between the two cousin families – the Pandavas, headed by Yudhishtra, and the Kauravas, headed by Dhrutrashtra. On the battle field at Kurukshetra, the Kauravas were led by his eldest son Duryodhana. There has been controversy over the exact time of the Mahabharatā war, ranging from 1000 B.C. to 5,000 B.C. Consensus seems to be around 3,000 B.C. correct approximate year is 3067 B.C.[228] the date has been based on astronomical calculations.

John W. McCrindle (pp.116, 117), talks about Gandhara:

"Gandhara (present Kandahar) was one of the most flourishing seats of Buddhism. ... Proklais is the ancient capital of Gandhara situated to the west of the Indus, which was mentioned in the preceding remarks under its Sanskrit name Pushkalavati, which means 'abounding in the lotus.'"

Purushapura (present Peshawar)

On p.362, in notes, McCrindle writes that Pushkalavati was named after Pushkala, the son of Bharat, the younger brother of Rama. It means, Gandhara was under the control of the Vedic Aryans (present Hindus),

---

[228] Kosla Vepa (ed.), Astronomical Dating of Events& Select Vignettes from Indian History (2008, p. 35), as per Kota Venkatachelam The Plot in Indian Chronology (1954)

since the rule of Dashratha, the father of Rama (about 5114 B.C.). *Purushapura* (present Peshawar) was one of the capitals of Gandhara.

Dr. A. Foucher – in *"Notes surla géographieanccienne du Gandhāra"* (*Notes on The Ancient Geography of Gandhara*), in the October issue of the *Bulletin de l'École francaise d' Extreme-Orient* (1901) – talks about his scientific mission in India, when he visited in detail the Peshawar District, the territory of ancient Gandhara. He talks about Purushapura at Peshawar and Pushkaravati in the immediate neighborhood of Charasadda, where he saw Buddhist sculptures and the inscriptions of Asoka. Foucher (p.2) remarks that Pushtu was spoken in the birth place of Panini. Grammarian Pāṇini was born in Pushkalavati, Gandhara, in the modern-day Afghanistan.

Foucher further states: "But the worst invasions were yet to come and Gandhāra at least remained Indian in manners and language."

Panini was the most ancient (4th century B.C.) grammarian. The present grammars of most of the world languages seem to have been based on Panini's 'Ashtadhyayi' (8 chapter-long) grammar.

On p.2, it is mentioned:

> "In our days when under the rule of the Sikhs and their successors the English, Gandhāra again became part of India, it was all too late to revive the past. ... It is true, there seems to remain a residue of the Hindu population, *banya* families, scattered here and there, in the larger villages and whom for the sake of their trade, the Pathans unable to keep accounts and in consequence incapable of shop-keeping, have been obliged to tolerate."

Foucher (pp.10-13) talks about his tour with Chinese traveler Hiuan-tsang from Purushapura to Pushkaravati, and Hashtanagar. In the neighborhood of the town, they visited a Brahmanical temple, a stupa built by Asoka, and another stupa very high and flanked by its monastery.

Jawaharlal Nehru, in *Discovery of India* (p.107), writes about Gandhara, the present Kandahar:

"The great civil war, which occurred later, described in the Mahabharata, is vaguely supposed to have taken place about the fourteenth century B.C. That war was for the overlordship of India (or possibly of northern India), and it marks the beginning of the conception of India as a whole, of Bharatvarsha. In this conception a large part of modern Afghanistan, then called Gandhara (from which the name of the present city Kandahar), which was considered an integral part of the country was included. Indeed the queen of the principal ruler was named Gandhari, the lady from Gandhara."

Nehru (p.202) writes that the well-known town in ancient India "Gandhara (Afghanistan) must have been an important part of Aryan India."

Afghanistan and Baluchistan under Emperor Asoka

The Columbia Encyclopedia (p.164) remarks that the Emperor Asoka (232 B.C.), the grandson of Chandragupta, "brought nearly all India, together with Baluchistan and Afghanistan, under one sway for the first time in history." It also mentions that after his bloody conquest of Kalinga (261 B.C.), Asoka felt remorseful of the sufferings he had inflicted on the people. He resigned from the worldly life for the service of the people and accepted Buddhism and abandoned wars of conquest.

Pre-Afghan name of Afghanistan

Alexander Cunningham, in *The Ancient Geography of India'* (p.14), remarks that the Indian language and religion were predominant in whole of Afghanistan, and that the great part of the eastern Afghanistan, including the whole of the Kabul valley must have been of Indian descent, while religion was pure Buddhism.

McCrindle (pp. 81, 82) quotes Max Müller, from *India: What Can It Teach us?*, that Afghanistan was known as the land of the Paktys:

"In the *Vedas* we have a number of names of the rivers of India as they were known to one single poet, say about 1000 B.C. ... The Indus was known to early traders whether by sea or land. Skylax sailed from the country of the Paktys, i.e. the Pushtus, as the Afghans still call themselves, down to the mouth of the Indus."

But this name came in currency later after advent of Afghans and other tribes. Still its ancient name has not been ascertained. Ludwig, Lassen, and Whitney substitute *Kubha* (Kabul) for the Sarasvati and think the Oxus (present Amu Darya) also must have been one of the seven rivers.

Rig Veda and Afghanistan

R. C. Majumdar, in *'The History and Culture of the Indian People'* (1951, pp. 247-248), tells that the *Rig Veda* knew about Kubha (Kabul), that the *Rig Veda* mentions the Kubha (Kabul), Gomati (Gumal), Kruma (Kurram), and Suvastu (Swat), which lie to the west of the Indus. He adds that it is possible that the *Rig Veda* people knew of the existence of the Oxus. On the basis of all this, Majumdar asserts:

"We may thus conclude that the extent of the country, as reflected in the hymns, is Afghanistan, the Punjab, Sind and Rajputana, the North-West Frontier Province, Kashmir, and Eastern India up to Sarayu."

Hertel Brunnhofer, Hertel Husing, and others, however, argue that the scene of the *Rig Veda* is laid, not in the Punjab, but in Afghanistan and Iran.[229] Brunnhofer relies mainly on the identification of the peoples mentioned in the Veda, with tribes located in Afghanistan, in the inscriptions of Darius, or in later Greek authors. In my opinion, Afghanistan or Punjab or Iran does not make any difference, because Afghanistan and Iran, like Punjab, had been a part of ancient Bharat.

---

[229] Brunnhofer, Arische Urzeit, 1910; Hertel, Indo-Germ; Husing, MAGW, xivi; Winternitz, HIL, I, pp. 63-4; and Childe, Aryans, p.32 (Taken from Majumdar, R.C. et al, p.248).

According to the Vedic traditions and other historical, geological and archaeological evidences, it is an established fact that Afghanistan was a part of ancient India. Kandahar was originally Gandhara, named after Gandhari of Mahābhāratā. According to Dr. David Frawley,[230] a region in Afghanistan was known as Gandhara, whose name is mentioned in the *Rig Veda*.

Frawley (1991, pp. 82, 83) – referring to the names of some rivers, such as Sindhu, Kubha (Kabul), Gomati, Krumu, and Mehatmu in a Vedic hymn – rightly seems to have identified their relationship with the Vedic India, in other words the historic relationship between India and Afghanistan. Frawley (1991: 83) remarks:

> "John W. McCrindle,[231] in his work titled *'Ancient India as described by Ptolemy'* (p.82), seems to suggest that Afghanistan was the country of *Paktys* (Pushtus). He writes: "Klaudios Ptolemaios,[232] the celebrated astronomer, mathematician and geographer, was a native of Egypt. ... He was the first systematic writer on Greek astronomy, whose works are now extant; but his astronomical labours are chieflybased on those of Hipparchus." ....

Some scholars have used their designations to connect the Vedic people with some home in Afghanistan and Central Asia. Actually there is a more simple and obvious reason for their inclusion. They are the rivers of a region known as Gandhara, the western uplands of India. The name of this region can be found in the Rig Veda itself as associated with sheep (1.126.7). It is an important source for wool, as sheep do well in mountain areas. ... At the time of the Greek visits to India, which followed Alexander the Great, 356-323 B.C. Gandhara was inhabited by traditional Aryan peoples. They were not displaced until the Muslim invasion. Afghanistan itself was called 'the land of the Aryans' from ancient time.

---

[230] Dr. David Frawley, in 'Gods, Sages and Kings' (1991:83).
[231] John W. McCrindle, in "Ancient India as described by Ptolemy," p.82i.
[232] Ibid, p.xiii...

Chapter Thirtyfour

FAR SOUTH-EAST ASIA UNDER VEDIC INFLUENCE

Jawaharlal Nehru[233] describes that most SE countries had their roots in the Indian (Vedic) civilization:

"Indian civilization took root especially in the countries of South-East Asia and the evidence for this can be found all over the place today. There were great centres of Sanskrit learning in Champa, Angkor, Srivijaya, Majapahit, and other places. The names of the rulers of various states and empires that arose are purely Indian and Sanskrit. This doesn't mean they were pure Indian, but it does mean that they were indianized. State ceremonies were Indian and conducted in Sanskrit. All the officers of the state bear old Sanskrit titles and some of these titles and designations have been continued up till now, not only in Thailand but also in the Moslem states of Malaya."

Nehru further writes about the colonizing waves of Indians (Hindus and Buddhists) over the South-East Asia:

"From the first century of the Christian era onwards wave after wave of Indian colonists spread east and south-east reaching Ceylon, Burma, Malaya, Java,

---

[233] Jawaharlal Nehru, in 'Discovery of India' (1946, p. 202).098

447

Sumatra, Borneo, Siam, Cambodia, and Indo-China. Some of them managed to reach Formosa, the Philippine islands and Celebes. Even as far as Madagascar (whose) the current language is Indonesian with a mixture of Sanskrit words."

Nehru (p.202) remarks that "the names that were given to these settlements were old Indian names," for example 'Cambodia' for present Kambodia.

Nehru: The Influence of Hindu Art abroad

Nehru (p.207) talks about the influence of Indian Art abroad:

"These records of ancient empires and dynasties have an interest for the antiquarian, but they have a large interest in the history of civilization and art. From the point of view of India they are particularly important, for it was India that functioned there and exhibited her vitality and genius in a variety of ways. We see her bubbling over with energy and spreading out far and wide, carrying not only her thought but also her other ideals, her art, her trade, her language and literature, and her methods of government. She was not stagnant or standing aloof, or isolated and cut off by mountain and sea."

It would have been more clear and accurate if the words "Indian' and 'Indianized' were replaced by 'Hindu' and 'Hinduized' respectively. The word 'Indian' is a broader term which includes other present sections of the Indian society – Christians, Muslims, Jews, Zoroastrians, etc who were not there active in the historical process during the time we are talking about. In fact, Hindus and Buddhists had gone to the SE Asian region much earlier. They spread Bhārat's Sanskrit, Vedic culture, philosophy, ideals, art, and literature there much earlier. The words India and Indian came in use later, when Bhārat was named as

India, Bhāratiya as Indian, and Sindhu as Indus by Westerners. The words 'India', 'Indian', and 'Indus' are misnomer when you talk about the history of spread of the Bhāratiya culture all over in earlier times. Nehru adds:

> "Her (India's) people crossed those high mountain barriers and perilous seas and built up, as M. Rēnē Grousset says, 'a Greater India politically as little organized as Greater Greece, but morally equally harmonious'. ... But M. Grousset refers to the wider areas where Indian culture spread: 'In the high plateau of eastern Iran, in the oases of Serindia, in the arid wastes of Tibet, Mongolia, and Manchuria, in the ancient civilized lands of China and Japan, in the lands of the primitive Mons and Khmers and other tribes in Indo-China, in the countries of the Malayo-Polynesians, in Indonesia and Malay, India left the indelible impress of her high culture, not only upon religion, but also upon art and literature, in a word, all the higher things of spirit."[234]

René Grousset (1885 – 1952) was a French historian, curator of both the Cernuschi and Guimet Museums in Paris, and a member of the prestigious Académie française. He wrote several major works on Asiatic and Oriental civilizations.

The Khmers created Angkor Wat. Bill Harris[235] writes:

> "Angkor Wat still has power to command reverential silence and inspire wild flights of imagination. ... The great temple and more than seventy others covering twenty five square miles in what was once the capital city of Angkor seem more a monument to the culture of India than to either the Chinese or the Khmers.

---

[234] Civilizations of the East' by Rēnē Grousset, vol. II, p. 276.
[235] Bill Harris, "Lost Civilizations" (1993, p,84)

> They were built as Hindu temples and only much later became holy places for Buddhists."

Harris (p.90) writes that the images at Angkor are easily interpreted because there are so many representations of Hinduism and Buddhism all over Asia.

Stephen Knapp, in *'Proof of Vedic Culture's Global Existence'* (2000, p. 81), talks about the spread of Vedic influence over vast area in Southeast Asia and then it traveled to Europe too:

> "By studying some of these connections and similarities we can see how much how many of these cultures are connected to each other and related to the earliest traditions that came out of the Vedic Aryan civilization. We also recognize how the Vedic influence extended over a vast area and traveled west into Europe and other regions and affected these countries in greater or lesser degrees."

Knapp adds:

> "Ancient India no doubt covered a much larger area of land than it does today and spread much farther to the north and west. At least there are historical indications showing that the Aryan influence was felt over long distances. The Vedic gods, for example, were over a wide area."

Concept of Dev Raja (God King)

Garraty and Gay[236] (1972, pp.355-357) speak about influence of the Indian (Vedic) culture on SE Asia:

---

[236]   Garraty, John A. and Peter Gay. The Columbia History of the World. New York: Harper & Row.

"Culturally the strongest external influence on early Southeast Asia was exercised by India. Hinduism and Buddhism spread widely in the area, bringing with them the art of writing, along with new deities, epics, and mythologies. From India came the idea of a despotic God-King who must be supported by his subjects as their necessary link with the supernatural forces that control the world. Brahman priests were employed by ambitious Southeast Asian rulers hoping to expand their dominion and, through consecration as divine kings, to legitimize their conquests. ... The earliest state of which clear evidence survives was Funan, founded in the Mekong Delta not later than the first century A.D. by Kaundinya, the "King of the Mountain." Funan was a maritime state, and `maintained commercial relations with India, Persia, and China. Its greatest king was *Jayavarman (d.514), who lived in a palace with a tiered roof, rode on an elephant, and governed walled cities where inhabitants prized gold, silver, pearls, and engraved ornaments, and who delighted in cockfighting and pigfighting."

Garraty & Gay talk about its farther spread in the region:

"West of Annam and Champa arose in the ninth century the Khmer empire of Cambodia. It was the Khmers who elevated the principle of the *deva-raja*, or God-King, to the highest peak it attained in Southeast Asia. During the reign of *Suryavarman II (1113-c.1150) the building of the mighty temple complex of Angkor Wat began."

According to Nehru (p.205), the greatest of these states was the *Salendra Empire, or the empire of *Sri Vijaya, which became the dominant power both on sea as well as on land in whole of Malaysia by the eighth century. At the height of its power it included Malaya,

Ceylon (Sri Lanka), part of Java, Borneo, Celebes, the Philippines, and a part of Formosa, and probably exercised suzerainty over Cambodia and Champa (Annam), which was a Buddhist Empire. A great ruler, *Jayavarman, united the small states in the ninth century and built up the Cambodian Empire with its capital at Angkor. The Cambodian state lasted for nearly four hundred years under the succession of great rulers *Jayavarman, *Yashovarman, *Indravarman, *Sumatra and *Suryavarman (all the five were Hindu).[237]

*seem to be Hindu names

According to Nehru (p.205):

> "The capital became famous in Asia and was known 'Angkor the Magnificent,' a city of a million inhabitants, larger and more splendid than the Rome of the Cæsars. Near the city stood the vast temple of Angkor Vat. The empire of Cambodia flourished till the end of the thirteenth century, and the account of a Chinese envoy who visited it in 1297 describes the wealth and splendour of its capital. But it suddenly collapsed, so suddenly that some buildings were left unfinished."

Nehru (p. 203) remarks: "Trade and adventure and the urge for expansion drew them to these eastern lands which were comprehensively described in old Sanskrit books as the *Svarnabhumi*, the Land of Gold or as *Svarnadvipa*, the Island of Gold."

Nehru (p.203) praises ancient Bhārat as a naval power and for her well-developed and flourishing shipbuilding industry:

> "It is clear that shipbuilding was a well-developed and flourishing industry in ancient India. We have some details and particulars of the ships built in those days. Many Indian ports are mentioned. South Indian (Andhra) coins of the second and third centuries A.C. bear the device of a two-masted ship. The Ajanta

---

[237] All with mark (*) were Hindu.

Frescoes depict the conquest of Ceylon and ships carrying elephants are shown."

It is beyond believing what Nehru (p.203) talks about an interesting Tamil inscription in 1088 A.C. which refers to a Corporation of the Fifteen Hundred:

"This was apparently a union of traders who were described in it as brave men, born to wander over many countries ever since the beginning of the Krita age, penetrating the regions of the six continents by land and water routes, and dealing in various articles such as horses, elephants, precious stones, perfumes, and drugs, either wholesale or in retail."

According to Kulke and Rothermund[238] the transmission of Indian culture to distant parts of Central Asia, China, Japan, and Southeast Asia without military conquest is certainly one of the greatest achievements of Hindu history or even the history of mankind.

Philip Rawson[239] writes about Indian colonization of the Far South-East Asia:

"The culture of India has been one of the world's most powerful civilizing forces. Countries of the Far East, including China, Korea, Japan, Tibet and Mongolia owe much of what is best in their own cultures to the inspiration of ideas imported from India. The West, too, has its own debts. But the members of that circle of civilizations beyond Burma scattered around the Gulf of Siam and Java Sea, virtually owe their very existence to the creative influence of Indian[240] ideas. Among the tribal peoples of Southeast Asia these formative ideas took root, and blossomed. No conquest or invasion,

---

[238] Kulke and Rothermund, in 'A History of India' (1986, p.152).
[239] Philip Rawson, in 'The Art of the South East Asia' (1990, pp. 7-8).
[240] Better to be specific. Instead of "Indian," it should be "Vedic" or "Hindu".

no forced conversion imposed (upon) them. They were adopted because the people saw they were good and that they could use them."

Rawson further writes:

"The small colonies of Indian traders, who settled at points of vantage along the sea routes into the islands and around the coast of Indo-China, merely imported with them their code of living, their conceptions of law and kingship, their rich literature and highly evolved philosophy of life. They intermarried with prominent local families; and dynasties evolved capable of organizing extensive kingdoms within which their populations could live ordered and fruitful lives. ... But archaeology may yet reveal more about the history of Indian colonization in the more remote parts of the Southern Seas."

Rawson's remark "They intermarried with prominent local families; and dynasties" reminds me of its parallel to Akbar's marriage with Jodhabai of a Rajpoot royal family. It was a prudent political and diplomatic strategy to stay strong in the captured country. When in Rome, behave like a Roman. The same was true about the adaptability and flexibility of the character of the Hindu and Buddhist art in their adopted countries in SE Asia, as described by Nehru (p.204):

"Indian art was flexible and adaptable and in each country it flowered afresh and in many new ways, always retaining that basic impress which it derived from India. Sir John Marshal has referred to 'the amazingly vital and flexible character of Indian art' and he points out how both Indian and Greek art had the common capacity to 'adapt them to suit the needs of every country, race, and religion with which they came into contact."

Nehru further writes:

"Indian art derives its basic character from certain ideals associated with the religious and philosophic outlook of India. As religion went from India to all these eastern lands, so also went this basic conception of art. Probably the early colonies were definitely Brahminical, and Buddhism spread later. The two existed side by side as friends and mixed forms of popular worship grew up. This Buddhism was chiefly of the Mahāyāna type, easily adaptable, and both Brahminism and Buddhism, under the influence of local habits and traditions, had probably moved away from the purity of their original doctrines. In later years there were mighty conflicts between a Buddhist state and a Brahminical state but these were political and economic wars for control of trade and sea routes."

Adaptability has been the most significant acumen of the Indian traders and businessmen, particularly those who have been engaged in inter-civilization and international trade adventures. Necessity is the mother of invention. It also comes naturally to them, apparently in heritance. *'Vaishya'* (business men) is the third on the caste-ladder, after *Brahamin* and *Kshtriya*. It has been the most important and perhaps the largest caste-segment of the Hindu society, which has kept India vibrantly lucrative since her pre-history ancient times, excepting the dark period of her subjugation by Muslims and later by Britain. During Muslim period public money was squandered and spent on tombs, etc., and the Britain economically exploited India in various ways.

As a matter of fact, only Vaishya alone did not venture overseas to colonize countries far away from home. They did not have *Kshatri* muscle nor the *Brahmin* brain. All the three – *Brahmins, Kshatris* and *Vashyas* – were adventurous. Their joint coordinated effort was responsible for ancient India's overseas economic, political and colonizing fruits. All the three – *Brahmin, Kshatri* and *Vaishya* – have been embodied in every Hindu in varying degrees to use what is appropriately required in the situation, the person is confronted with. Caste (kind of occupation) is not hereditary. One's occupation depends on one's aptitude and the demands of the times. The needs make the man work (do karma) for survival. The fruit of the *karma* depends on one's caliber, use of the caliber, resources and the cooperation of the circumstances, which are not under one's control. It is wrong to understand the result depends on destiny. It is the man / woman who has responsibility to make his / her destiny. God does not have time nor interest in making every one's destiny. Man becomes meaningfully successful, only when he does *karma* diligently and when there is desired coexistence of all the four – knowledge, aptitude, circumstances and effort (*karma*) – to reach the coveted goal. Effective *Karma,* guided by relevant knowledge, can modify circumstances. The economic health of a society depends on the inter-occupation flexibility and mobility.

Hindu colonization, different from the European and Muslim

Indian (Hindu) colonization is unique and humane Hindus did neither use sword nor did economically lure the colonized people to change their religion. Hindus know that for everybody religion is sentimentally too precious to give up. Christians did not coerce them to get converted but lured them through baits of free education and health services. An educated young Muslim, knowing me as a staunch Hindu, came to me to help him to convert into Hinduism. I told him that all religions are good and faultless. I explained to him to believe, think and behave the way he wants without changing his religion. I explained to him that no religion believes in hurting any body. Change of religion will hurt his parents and every body in the family. Religion teaches how to be close to and be loved by God. So he should do what he feels would bring near to God without hurting any body. He seems disappointed, but a few days later he called me to thank me and tell me that he does and feel what he has learnt from Hinduism and Islam, without changing his religion.

Tagore[241] has said that India has never coveted new territory and that she has never sent out her forces for plunder but to carry out message of peace and goodwill.

---

[241] Tagore, in 'Towards Universal Man (1961, p. 64).

Rawson has rightly talked about the influence of Indian (Vedic) ideas which took root and blossomed in the countries of the South-East Asia. India culturally colonized peoples without conquest.

Hindus in Indochina and Indonesia

According to *the 'World Book Encyclopedia'* (1984, vol.10, pp.168-179), Hindus and Buddhists had established their kingdoms in Indochina and Indonesia. Indochina extends into the South China Sea from the mainland of Southeast Asia. It includes Kampuchea (Cambodia), Laos, and Vietnam. The WBE writes:

> "Indochina has long been a crossroads of peoples and cultures. It has been invaded from what is now Thailand on the west, from China on the north, and from the sea on the east. Most of the people of Indochina originally came from the plains and mountains of Central Asia. Some of the earliest tribes came from the islands now part of Indonesia. From the 900's to the 1700's, China and Thailand fought for control of Indochina. France gained control of the region in the 1800's and held it until 1954. The French called the region *French Indochina*."

According to the Geneva Agreement of 1954, the nations of Kampuchea, Laos, and North and South Vietnam were formed.

The WBE (p.169) writes that the Khmer people, who entered what is now called Kampuchea about 100 A.D., claimed that the peoples of India, China, and the Indo-Malay were their ancestors. The Khmer ruled most of Indochina from the Gulf of Thailand to China between the 800's and 1400's with Angkor as its capital.

Cultural similarities between India and Indonesia

The history has talked about lot of similarities between India and Indonesia, such as:

1. Similarity of the Indonesian language with Sanskrit, as reflected by the names, such as *Sumatra, Sukarno, Suharto, Jaya, Putri, Kalimantan, Jakarta (Jaya-karta), Yogiakarta, Surakarta, Madura, Sukabumi,* etc.
2. Worship of ancestors and nature.
3. Some of its traditional musical instruments similar to those of Bharat.
4. Puppet dramas playing stories from Hindu epics, Ramayana and Mahabharata.
5. Hinduism in Bali.
6. Dances, particularly in Bali, similar to Hindu classical dances.
7. Batic designs of clothes, etc.

All these seem to suggest the presence of Hindus and Buddhists in Indonesia prior to the advent of Muslims there in 1400's.

The WBE (vol.10, p.170b) remarks:

"Buddhism and Hinduism were significant religions on the islands, hundreds of years ago. One of its islands is called 'Irian Jaya' (WBE, p.171) which seems to compare with 'Aryan Jaya."

The WBE (vol.10, p.176) talks about Indian (Hindu and Buddhist) influence on Indonesians:

"Indian influence, especially Hinduism and Buddhism began to affect Indonesian life strongly during the A.D. 400's. Small kingdoms had begun to develop especially in Java and Sumatra. Indonesians, like Hindus, believed that a king was either a god in human form, or was descended from a god. Influences of Indian architecture show clearly in early Indonesian temples. In the villages, Indian legends became part of local puppet plays."

Hindu and Buddhist kingdoms in Indonesia became rivals for power for hundreds of years. The Hindu kingdom called Mataram was established in Central Java. (The word 'Mataram' in Sanskrit/

Hindi means mother.) It later fell to a Buddhist king Sailendra who later established the kingdom called Srivijaya in southern Sumatra. The kingdoms of Singosari and Madjapahit were ruled by Prince Widjaya. Buddhist kingdom of Srivijaya (600's-1200's A.D.) expanded from Sumatra and became a great sea power. The Hindu kingdom of Madjapahit controlled much of Indonesia in 1300's, before Islam began to spread in 1400's.

According to the WBE (vol. 10 p. 177), the trade in Indonesian waters was at first controlled largely by Srivijaya, the region's sea power. Their power generally came from the production of rice. Madjapahit became the first Indonesian kingdom to base its power on both rice production and commerce. The Indonesian islands were crossroads in expanding international trade, involving merchants of many lands, including Arabs, Indians, Chinese, Persians, etc. They traded several goods including porcelain, textiles, raw silk, spices and scented woods for Indonesian products. Such Asian goods were also traded in Europe. Marco Polo, the Italian traveler and merchant, visited the islands in 1292 to establish Italy-Indonesia trade relations. Muslim from Arabia and India came to Indonesia in 1400 A.D. as traders, and later established themselves as the rulers. Melaka gained control of the important trading route through the Strait of Malacca, between Malaya and Sumatra. Melaka became a major trading power. Its ruler converted to Islam spread to various regions of Indonesia.

Note: The names – Mataram, Sailendra, Srivijaya, Sumatra, Singasari, Maljapahit, and Widjaya – seem to have their origin in Sanskrit.

Maldives and the Indus Valley civilization

Maldives (formerly Maldive Islands) are in the Indian Ocean. Maldivians are of mixed Indian, Sinhalese and Arab stock. The Maldivians were originally from South Asia. In the 12th century, Islam was brought to the islands. The Maldives obtained complete independence (from Britain) as a Sultanate in 1965.

Graham Hancock[242] writes that Thor Heyderdahl[243] makes a case that there is real history behind the Redin[244] myth. Peter Marshal reports a Maldivian tradition about the phenomenal maritime abilities of the Redin with supernatural or even god-like powers flying swiftly across the sea in their boats with sails and oars.[245]

Hancock (p.286) remarks that this is "strangely reminiscent of the imagery of the *Rig Veda* (cited in chapter 7) concerning the Asvins – who are several times praised for having conducted a daring rescue in the deeps of the Indian Ocean."

According to Thor Heyerdahl (Hancock, p.287), the Redin probably originated in north-west India, the primary setting of the *Rig Veda*. Heyerdahl,[246] after visiting Gujarat and the great Marine dockyard of the Indus-Sarasvati civilization at Lothal where cowrie shells from Maldives (*Cyprea Moneta*) have been excavated amongst the ruins and are to be seen in the site museum. Thor Heyerdahl comments:

> "I was convinced that at least the Hindu element in the Maldives had come from the north-western corner of India. And probably the Hindus were not even the first to have made the journey straight south from the Gulf of Cambay to the Maldives. Perhaps earlier sailors in the days of Mesopotamian and Indus Valley seafaring had been led by the sun to the Equatorial Channel, and survived in legend as the Redin."[247]

---

[242] Graham Hancock, 'Underworld: The Mysterious Origins of Civilization' (pp. 286-287)

[243] Thor Heyerdahl, The Maldives Mystery, London: Unknown Paperbacks, 1988.

[244] Ancient oral traditions of Maldives speak of a mysterious people – the Redin –who, in the opinion of Heyerdahl, were 'a former people with more than ordinary human capacities'.

[245] Amin, Mohamed, Duncan Willets and Peter Marshal, Journey through the Maldives, 16, Camerapix Publishers International, Nairobi, 1992.

[246] Heyerdahl, op. cit., p.159.

[247] Ibid, p.312.

The north-western corner of India can not be other than Sindh and Punjab in the Indus Valley. The sculptures, *stupas* and pyramidal *hawittas,* excavated in the Maldives, are similar to those of the Buddhists of Sri Lanka and the Hindus of South India. Buddhism was extensively present on the Maldives before advent of Islam in 12th century.[248] A Sanskrit text of Vajrayana Buddhism dating back to the ninth or tenth century A.D. is the earliest surviving legible inscription thus far found in the Maldives.[249] It seems definitely Hinduism must have preceded Buddhism in the Maldives. According to the Encyclopedia Britannica, Micropaedia (vol. 10, 837), Dhivehi, the Maldivian language, belongs to the Indo-European family and is related to Sanskrit and thus also to Sinhalese, one of the two languages of Sri Lanka (the other being Tamil). Clarence Maloney[250] remarks that a Tamil/Dravidian sub-layer exists in Dhivehi, which suggests that Hinduism was present in the Maldives before the Buddhist period. Buddhism is an offshoot of Hinduism.

Phallic Sculptures in the Maldives

Hancock (p.280) talks about Siva Linga in the Maldives:

"Interestingly, large numbers of 'phallic' sculptures have been recovered in archaeological excavations in the Maldives – for example amid the ruins of a vast temple complex in North Nilandhoo Atoll.[251] I was able to study a collection of such objects from different parts of the archipelago, and in my opinion, despite some idiosyncrasies, they are nothing more nor less than Sivalinga."

---

[248] Kon Tiki Museum, 'Archaeological Test-Excavations on the Maldive Islands', Occasional Papers, vol. 2, 66, Oslo, 1992.
[249] Dhivehi Writing Systems, 5, National Centre for Linguistic and Historical Research, Maldives, 1999.
[250] Clarence Maloney, People of the Maldives Islands, Madras, 1980, cited in Kon Tiki Museum, op. cit., 70.
[251] Mohamed Amin et al. op. cit. p. 12.

It is amazing that India had colonized almost all South-East Asian countries, such as Malaya, Ceylon (Sri Lanka), Sumatra, Borneo, Celebes, Philippines, Formosa, Cambodia, Champa (Annam), China, Korea, Japan, Tibet, Mongolia, Indonesia, Siam, Java, Laos, and Vietnam. Some of them were administratively colonized, and some were only culturally influenced by Hindus and Buddhists.

HINDUS AND GREEKS: ANCIENT FRIENDS

Hindus and Greeks have a long history of mutual exchange of culture and linguistics from prehistory remote past. Wars must have been responsible for mutual exchange of enviable gifts of culture, language and philosophy. Enmity fans war and in return war aggravates enmity. But it is not true about Hindus and Greeks. Both have mature culture and civilization. They believed in 'Give & Take', not only in 'give' or 'take'. Such relationship between the two peoples is rare in history. Edward Pococke and others have talked lot about India in Greece, meaning India once colonized Greece.

History tells lot about Greek hostile invasions of India, particularly by Alexander the Great via Iran, when Iran was an integral part of India. As a matter of fact, Alexander was Macedonian, not Greek. Macedonia is in north of Greece. Alexander was the son of Philip II, King of Macedonia. Greece was later captured by Macedonia. Alexander had established Macedonian Empire covering Asia Minor (present Turkey), Babylon, Susa, Egypt, Persia, etc. Most of which was colonized by India in prehistory distant ancient times, which is not coming out clear in recent history books, as history has been distorted. Modern history is silent about India's remote worldwide colonizing adventures including related to Greece. First Greek hostile intrusions into India will be addressed, starting with those by Macedonian Alexander starting in about 327 B.C.

Alexander the Great[252] (356-323 B.C.) was son of Philip II, King of Macedonia, a great military power. The Macedonia, being talked about, was a kingdom in north of Greece, as present Republic of Macedonia. The following map will make it clear.

Macedonia[253]

Republic of Macedonia is a modern country in southeastern Europe. Alenxader's father arranged for his teenager son, not only training in warfare, but also schooling in geography, history and philosophy. He hired Aristotle, as his personal tutor. At age 16, Alexander was given post of commander to invade Greece. Macedonia, his father Philip II was king of, was not a part of Greece.

In 331 B.C., Alexander fought against the Persian King and crushed his army at the battle of Gaugamela in northern Mesopotamia, near the border of modern Iraq and Iran. Then Alexander marched further eastward into Iran on the way to India.

Alexander and King Porus (Puru)

Alexander had entered in India via Afghanistan's Hindu Kush Mountains in 327 B.C. when Afghanistan was an integral part of India, culturally as well as administratively. Afghanistan's relationship with ancient India will be explained in later pages. Alexander would not have been able to stay in Hindustan (India) even a day, rather would not have been able to enter, if rivalry-driven Hindu kingdoms were united to jointly and collectively fight back against the invaders from north-west. Unfortunately, north-western borders were left unprotected to welcome foreign intruders. Both powers – Nandas and Mauryans – were enough to seal the North-western borders to arrest any unwanted foreign intrusion. Nandas were a militarily powerful kingdom with large army of brave soldiers, elephants and horse-driven chariots. Mauryans, under Chandragupta were even stronger. Hindustan would have remained different and larger. Afghans and Baluchs would not have been able to

---

[252] Thomas R. Martin in 'Ancient Greece' (1996, pp. 198-201).
[253] Wikipedia

create Afghanistan and Baluchistan. The Raja of Takshashila (Taxila), feeling alone and insecure, yielded to Alexander without putting up a fight. He became a very generous host to Alexander and his army. Shamelessly, he provided food for his army and sizeable soldiers to help him fight against his rival neighboring King Porus[254], belonging to the Pauravas tribe, descending from the Puru. He has been mentioned in the *Rig Veda*. Alexander had fierce battle with King Porus, one of the most powerful Indian kings by the river Hydaspes (Beas) in the spring of 326 B.C. Porus was defeated although he fought with a large army, assisted by elephants. Alexander had never seen before elephants in battles. Porus was captured. Alexander allowed him to retain his kingdom, as he had done with other defeated Indian kings. His army, fatigued and strained by harsh circumstances, did not co-operate with him to retain those kingdoms. I have a faint remembrance reading some where that wife of Porus tied *rakhi* on Alexander's wrist. He knew its significance that the woman considers the man, on whose wrist she ties *rakhi*, as her brother. It may not be true because he did the same with other Indian kings, defeated by him.

Alexander got lot of success in India which would have given him fortunes, but he could not hold. Fierce battles in India with several kingdoms fatigued him and his army. In ancient times India was fragmented into hundreds of small kingdoms. Credit goes to Sardar Vallabhbhai Patel (31 Oct.1875 – 15 Dec. 1950) who tactfully with his iron fist consolidated and integrated all scattered states into a giant India. Patel was an Indian barrister and statesman, one of the leaders of the Indian National Congress Party.

Alexander was wounded several times during his violent confrontation with the Malli,[255] known to be one of the most warlike Indian tribes. He was most seriously wounded when an arrow pierced his breastplate and his ribcage. His army officers rescued him in a narrow escape. Alexander, seeing his army's shaken morale, gave up the pursuit of his next goal to reach about 250-miles-distant Ganges (Ganga) Valley because his army heard tales of powerful tribes, they had to fight against. India, as divided into hundreds of small kingdoms,

---

[254] Wikipedia, Free Encyclopedia
[255] Ibid, Wikipedia

looked as a weak country; but it became difficult for a foreigner invader to fight numerous battles, as happened with Alexander.

Moreover, with fatigued army and inadequate supplies, Alexander felt utterly disappointed. Indian Territory was unknown to him. Weather became too warm. Day by day increasing depletion of the supplies – food, entertainment, prostitutes, etc. – made the army unhappy. At the top of all this, Alexander's horse Bucephalus got wounded and died. He was very emotionally attached to his horse helped him in fierce battles. Its death severely depressed him. He loved Bucephalus so much that he founded a city in its name.

Being far away from his base, he could not get supplies adequately refilled. Fatigued army had to carry own armor, because Alexander could not financially afford to hire help to carry the armor. Perhaps, help became exorbitantly expensive because the coolies, though poor, because of their patriotism, did not want to help an invader. Unlike now, in ancient times, foreigners, though white and handsome, were considered *malechha,* meaning dirty and untouchable. Long accumulated fatigue from his ferocious series of battles with various kingdoms – compounded by war-related hardships and absence of adequate supplies particularly food – made his army angry and unhappy, and thus reluctant to march further. Above all this, over two months of heavy monsoon rains impacted as the last straw on camel's back. In 326 B.C., army mutinied on the banks of Hydaspes River (Beas) in the Punjab [province of five waters (Rivers)] in north-west of India. All these hostile circumstances, compounded by sinking morale of the army compelled Alexander to return home without achieving what he went to India for.

Thomas R. Martin (Ancient Greece, p. 195) writes: "As a climax to his frustrated rage, he flung himself over the wall of an Indian town to face the enemy alone like a Homeric hero. His horrified officers were barely able to rescue him in time; even so he received grievous wounds." It seems Martin is talking about his encounter with the Malli tribe, mentioned earlier. To me, it was his deliberate attempt to commit a heroic suicide as he felt lonely and helpless to cope up with the hostile circumstances, his life was confronted with. This took too heavy toll on his life. It is hard to believe that such a brave and strong man from a royal family with abundance of wealth would die a natural death at so young age of 33 years.

After Alexander's death in 323 B.C., his mother Olympias tried for several years to establish her infant grandson, Alexander's son by Roxane, as the Macedonian king under her protection. She could not succeed, as three of Alexander's most powerful commanders wanted to establish their own kingdoms. Antigonus (382-301 B.C.) and his son Demetrius (336-283 B.C.) established their kingdoms in Macedonia and Greece, Seleucos Nicator (358-281 B.C.) in Syria and the old Persian Empire, and Ptolemy (367-282 B.C.) in Egypt.

King Chandragupta, the founder of the Mauryan dynasty, defeated Seleucos, who after being defeated, ceded eastern territory of his kingdom to Chandragupta, who ruled from 323 until 299 B.C. Seleucos sent Megasthenes, as his ambassador in Chandragupta's court. Mauryan King Asoka proclaimed his Buddhist mission to Greeks.

European knowledge about India[256] was mostly based on the reports prepared by Megasthenes while he was Seleucos' ambassador in the court of Chandragupta. The originals[257] have been reported as lost. I feel that they could not be lost. They have been hidden or have been deliberately destroyed with some ethno-political agenda. I think Britain did not want that Chandragupta should be praised.

India and Greece prior to Alexander

Nehru[258] talks about India's contacts with Greece from prehistory ancient times: "It is interesting to note that Panini (4th century B.C.) mentions the Greek script. This indicates that there were some contacts between India and Greece long before Alexander came to the East (327 B.C.)." Other evidence is influence of Vedic philosophy on Plato (429-347 B.C.).

---

[256] Herman Kulke and Rothermund, 'A History of India' (1986, p.61).
[257] 'Ibid, p. 61.
[258] Jawaharlal Nehru, 'Discovery of India", p.115.

Talking about the triumph of the East and the Hellenistic Age, historian, Herbert J. Muller[259] has elaborated on how Greeks profited immeasurably from their spiritual trade with the East:

> "At the same time, Plato's own thought was so fertile because it was not a classically ordered system but an exploration of various possibilities, a sensitive response to various influences, including Oriental thought. Its historic influence has stemmed chiefly from his inclination to a transcendental idealism, another worldly kind of spirituality that is more typical of India than of Greece in its heyday."

Exact place and time of Plato's birth are not known. Based on ancient sources, most modern scholars believe that he was born in Athens or Aegina in about 424 B.C. and died in about 348 BC., much earlier than Alexander. He belonged to an aristocratic and influential family. His descent has been traced from the king of Athens. Plato was a Classical Greek philosopher and mathematician. He was a student of Socrates.

Plato seems to have been influenced by two primary Vedic doctrines of *'immortality of soul'* and *'rebirth/reincarnation'*. According to the 'World Book Encyclopedia' (1993, vol.15, p.504), Plato believed in the immortality of the soul and reincarnation:

> "Plato believed that though the body dies and disintegrates, the soul continues to live forever. After the death of the body, the soul migrates to what Plato called the realm of the pure form. After a time, the soul is reincarnated in another body and returns to the world. But the reincarnated soul retains the dim recollection of the realm of forms and yearns for it. Plato argued that people fall in love because they recognize in the beauty of their beloved the ideal form of beauty they dimly remember and seek."

---

[259] Herbert J. Muller, 'The Loom of History' 1958, P. 15).

M. P. Pandit has highlighted a study by Dr. Vassilis Vittaxis[260], a former Greek ambassador to India. Dr. Vittaxis brings to light the similarities and differences between Hindu philosophy and the philosophy of Plato. For example, he likens the *nous* (mind) of Plato to the *Atman* of the Upanishads. He further draws parallels between Plato's *Division of Society* and the caste system, 'Plato's Guardians, Warriors, Craftsmen have close resemblance to the Indian Brahmin, Kshatriya, Vaishya respectively.

It seems, Alexander had knowledge about the greatness of India which lured him to capture her. He made heroic attempt, but could not succeed. Circumstances did not cooperate with him.

The question, 'How did Alexander come to know India?' has been bothering me. I am certain there is history to answer the question. This is black gap in the history. Edward Pococke's book *"India in Greece or Truth in Mythology"* has given some answers. He has given an enormous number of evidences to prove that India was in Greece and that India had colonized Greece[261] in remote ancient times But he has not given the chronicled history of the events how and when Greece was colonized by India and how and when Greece became independent. History tells that Aryans from Greece came to India via Iran. But, it has not been explained who those Aryans were. I think it was return of Aryans (Hindus) from Greece to India. It should be seriously researched to know if Greece was colonized by India, if yes when, with what purpose, achievements and what happened later. Why is history silent about this or is ignoring such an important fact?

Edward Pococke, in his *'India in Greece or Truth in Mythology'* (preface, p. vii), seems helplessly rebuking the European scholarship for destroying the Temple of History:

"A gigantic mass of absurdities now lies exposed, for a sifting examination. It remains for the patient sagacity of European scholarship, working upon both Occidental and Oriental materials, to re-build I trust, upon no unstable foundation, that Temple of History

---

[260] M. P. Pandit, 'Traditions in Mysticism' (1987, p.121),
[261] Edward Pococke "India in Greece or Truth in Mythology."

which national vanity has destroyed, and whose ruins
national Bud'hism has obscured."

Pococke further writes (p. ix): "Our ignorance it is which has made a
myth of history; and our ignorance is a Hellenic inheritance, much of
it the result of Hellenic vanity." It explains why Pococke, has titled this
book as, *"Truth in Mythology."*

It is an important historical question whether India ever colonized
Greece answer. History books, in general, have not been clear about
this. There seems truth in what E. Pococke, Esq. has written in his
book *'India in Greece; or Truth in Mythology'* (1856). He has given lot of
evidences to prove that in remote ancient times, Hindus had colonized
Greece, and during their long stay there, they left distinct cultural,
philosophical and linguistic impress on Greeks. A few other scholars
also have written about India's cultural as well as linguistic impress on
Greece. If the years of the events were given, the story would have been
clearer and more convincing.

E. Pococke[262] has written:

"Clans, whose martial fame is still recorded in the faithful chronicles of North-Western India, as the gallant bands who fought upon the plains of Troy; and, in fact, the whole of Greece, from the era of the supposed god-ships of Poseidon and Zeus, down to the close of the Trojan war, as being Indian in language, sentiments, and religion, and in the arts of peace and war. Much I shall, I doubt not, incontestably establish; much must be left to a future period."

Pococke (pp.253-258), while talking about Hesiod's history of Greece, remarks that the geographical facts, as recorded on the mountains and rivers of Hellas (ancient name of Greece), seem to be "connected with those people who gave names to these rivers and mountains." His later statement, "the representative to Hesiod of words apparently Greek, but in reality Sanscrit, Thibetan, or the Pehlavi dialects," suggests that 'those people' were Hindus and Buddhists from Indian subcontinent who had gone there in ancient times and colonized Greece He seems to complain about "corrupt orthography, and corrupt history based upon that orthography." Later, Pococke talks about Lamaism, solar or Buddhist forms of worship among the primitive population of Hellas.

Pococke (p.254) remarks that the *Surya Vanshi* and the *Chandra Vanshi* have been the best colonists of Greece:

"The great aggregate of the colonists of Greece has already been shown to consist of those two great bodies, the Solar and the Lunar races; each following the peculiar tenets of that faith to which the heads of their respective races gave so strong a bias, viz., either the Solar or the Bud'histic forms of worship. The former was more ancient in its establishment, but the latter more durable. The Lamaic nations, springing up apparently upon the

---

[262] E. Pococke, Esq. in 'India in Greece or Truth in Mythology', published by Richard Griffin and Company, London (1856, p. 12).

frontiers of the kingdoms of Cashmir and Thibet, have
by the population, already shown in Thessaly, been
proved to have existed in the latter countries in high
antiquity, and the record of the life of Zeus, as drawn
by Hesiod, is but a garbled statement of plain facts,
in perfect harmony with existing state of Lamaism in
Tartary."

Pococke (p.130) writes: "… but that the province of Cashmir
and its neighbourhood, and its tribes, and its Mahabharatian history,
are transported to the Hella Nova with almost the faithfulness of
lithographic transfer from one material to another."

Pococke (pp. 131-2) remarks that Greece has practically become
as primitive as India, and that the people of India were primitive even
from the most ancient times.

Pococke (p. 131) talks about 'Rajatarangini', in his opinion, the
most authentic document, as an historical foundation on India-Greece
connection:

"The most authentic document which north-western
India possesses – (and north-western India is now
made synonymous with Greece, more especially
with northern Greece,) – is the Rajatarangini. The
Rajatarangini, written at Cashmir, the identical point
whence the Cassiopæi, or "people of Casyapa," set out
on their emigration into north-western Greece, is a
dynastic record of the princes of that far-famed valley,
whose chronicles ascend to the venerable antiquity of
B.C. 2448."

Pococke, in the footnote (p.131) tells that Raja Tarangini is not one
entire composition. It is a series of compositions written by different
authors at different times of different circumstances, as per Prof.
Wilson's very copious and learned treatise on the Hindoo History of
Cashmir, *Asiatic Researches* (vol. xv).

Pococke (p.9), talking about the evidences of Indian colonization of Greece, describes various things looking like Indian – such as beautifully embroidered shawls, numerous ornaments of ivory, tasteful ample produce of the loom, elegant workmanship on the golden jewelry, constant use of the war chariot both by Greeks and Asiatics. On p.255, Pococke talks about the presence of the people of the Himalayas and Buddhist priesthood. On p. 256, he talks about 'The High Lama Town and "a sect of Buddhists so ancient and so extensive as to give a name to a vast tract of country in which they had settled." He mentions that a village bore its name as "Grihya", which, it seems has its origin in Sanskrit word 'Griha' meaning house or habitation.

Pococke (p.12) gives more evidences of Indian (Hindu) presence in Greece:

> "Now, the whole of this state of society, civil and military, must strike every one as being eminently Asiatic; much of it specifically Indian. Such it undoubtedly is; and I shall demonstrate that these evidences were but the attendant tokens of an Indian colonization, with its corresponding religion and language. I shall exhibit dynasties disappearing from Western India, to appear again in Greece."

Pococke (pp.18-19), while referring to the identity of structure, of vocables, and inflective power, in the Greek and Sanskrit languages, remarks:

> "Every day adds fresh conviction produces fresh demonstration, of this undeniable fact. The Greek language is a derivation from Sanscrit; therefore, Sanscrit-speaking people – i.e., Indians, must have dwelt in Greece, and this dwelling must have preceded the settlement of those tribes which helped to produce the corruption of the old language; or, in other words, the people who spoke that language – i.e., the Indians, must have been the primitive settlers; or, at least, they

> must have colonized the country so early, and dwelt
> there so long, as to have effaced all dialectic traces of
> any other inhabitants; just as the Saxons displaced the
> feeble remains of the dialect of the ancient Britons, in
> this island, and imparted a thoroughly Saxons stamp to
> the genius of the English language."

Pococke explains that the long stay of Indians (Sanskrit-speaking Indo-Aryans) in Greece was cause of the impress, Sanskrit left on the regional dialects of Greece. It is clear that the philological similarities, Sanskrit has with Greek, are not genetic or cognate, as several linguists feel. Greek and Sanskrit can not be lingual genetic sisters because they are geographically too distant, and culturally and historically too different from each other.

Pococke (p.19) speaks high about the lofty effect, the Indo-Aryan colonization left on the language, philosophy, religion, political institutes, etc. of Greece:

> "But, if the evidences of Saxon colonisation in this
> island – (I speak independently of Anglo-Saxon
> history) – are, strong both from language and political
> institutions, the evidences are still more decisive in the
> parallel case of an Indian colonisation of Greece, – not
> only her Language, but her Philosophy, her Religion,
> her Rivers, her Mountains, and her Tribes; her subtle
> turn of intellect, her political institutes, and above all
> the Mysteries of that noble land – irresistibly prove her
> colonisation from India."

It would be interesting to analytically examine what Garraty & Gay (1981, p. 97) have said about the migratory journey of Aryans from Greece into India via Iran:

> "The Aryans ("noble ones") were part of a large Indo-
> European migration which left a common cultural
> heritage from Greece through Iran into India. The

religious and social institutions of these invaders are reflected in the oldest stratum of the Veda (sacred "knowledge") – the most revered sector of traditional Hindu religious literature. The tribes were led by an aggressive warrior aristocracy mounted on horse-driven chariots, and armed with copper and bronze weapons of good quality."

These invaders from Greece into India, whose religious and social institutions are reflected in the Vedas, can not be other than Vedic Indo-Aryans (Hindus) who had colonized Greece in about 2448 B.C., as talked about by Pococke in his book *'India in Greece or Truth in Mythology'.* The story would have been clear if Garraty & Gay had given the year of their trip to India. They can not be Greeks, nor any other Europeans. How would Vedas reflect their religious and social institutions, if they were not Indo-Aryans? Indo-Aryans (Hindus) were in Greece since long and they were known as charioteers and warriors (*Khshatries*). Later, they must have been in trouble. Therefore, they were returning to India, the country of their ancestors.

Stephen Knapp, in *'Proof of Vedic Culture's Global Existence'* (2000, p. 165), sheds some light on 'India in Greece':

"In looking at the Greek culture, we find many connections between it and the Vedic civilization. Many people and scholars tend to view Greece as a source of western civilization. However, it is seldom realized that the original Greek culture was itself Vedic. This is not to say that no one has recognized the similarities. Even as far as 1830 we can find on pages 61-2 from volume II of *Narrative of a Journey Overland from England to India* by Mrs. Colonel Eldwood, where she sees the Vedic influence in Greece."

Knapp (pp.165-166) tells what Mrs. Elwood has said about the relationship between Hindus and Greeks in remote ancient times:

"The striking analogy between some of the Hindoo fables with those of the Greeks, would induce us to believe that the Greeks and Hindus must, at an early age, have had intercourse, and possibly Pythagorus, with the doctrine of the Metempsychosis, may have imported some of the adventures of the Indian gods and ascribed them to the Greek deities."

Krishna, a god of Greeks?

It is interesting and seems convincing, though hard to believe what Knapp (p. 166) has said about Krishna, as a god of Greece:

"The fact that Krishna was the God of Greece is proved by the silver coins made by Agathaclose, a Greek ruler of the 2nd century B.C. These coins bear the imprint of Lord Krishna and His brother Balarama and are on display in several museums. Furthermore, a large mosaic of young Krishna playing the flute, standing cross-legged under a tree while grazing cows, hangs in the museum in Corinth. This was obviously salvaged from a local Krishna temple which proves this city was once a center of Vedic culture with temples of Krishna. We can recognize that as the Vedic culture moved from India to Egypt to Greece, etc., much of the philosophy stayed the same, although the names and artistic characteristics of the gods changed with time."

Knapp (p.167) explains how the Greek god 'Hera klessle' seems like the Vedic god "Hare-Krishna":

"Greek writers like Pliny referred to Hari Krishna as Heracles. This is traced back to the way the early Greek writers who visited India said that the city they called Klessleboro (Mathura) was the capital of Krishna worship. The Greeks pronounced the name Krishna as *klessle,* and Hare or Hari as *hera.* Thus came the name of Heraklessle, or Heracles and Hercules, who is the muscular man who played prominent roles in the Greek myths."

Lord Krishna loved cows and considered cow as mother, because like mother, cow gives milk, the first food the infant gets right from his/her birth. Therefore, Hindus don't eat cow (beef) meat. Krishna is known by some names connected with cow such as Gobind and Gopal, meaning protector of cows (Go = cows + pal = protector). In Sanskrit, cow is known as "go".

Jawaharlal Nehru, in *Discovery of India* (1946, p. 92), writes about the influence of Indian philosophy on Greece and Christianity, as contained in the Upanishads:

> "Early Indian thought penetrated to Greece, through Iran, and influenced some thinkers and philosophers there. Much later, Plotinus came to the east to study Iranian and Indian philosophy and was especially influenced by the mystic element in the Upanishads. From Plotinus many of these ideas are said to have gone to St. Augustine, and through him influenced the Christianity of the day."

Plato, influenced by the Vedic philosophy

Talking about the triumph of the East and the Hellenistic Age, Herbert J. Muller (1958, p.15) has elaborated on how Greeks profited immeasurably from their spiritual trade with the East:

> "At the same time, Plato's own thought was so fertile because it was not a classically ordered system but an exploration of various possibilities, a sensitive response to various influences, including Oriental thought. Its historic influence has stemmed chiefly from his inclination to a transcendental idealism, another worldly

kind of spirituality that is more typical of India than of Greece in its heyday."

Plato (429 B.C.) was a Classical Greek philosopher and mathematician. He was a student of Socrates,

According to the 'World Book Encyclopedia' (1993, vol.15, p.504), Plato believed in the immortality of the soul and reincarnation:

> "Plato believed that though the body dies and disintegrates, the soul continues to live forever. After the death of the body, the soul migrates to what Plato called the realm of the pure form. After a time, the soul is reincarnated in another body and returns to the world. But the reincarnated soul retains the dim recollection of the realm of forms and yearns for it. Plato argued that people fall in love because they recognize in the beauty of their beloved the ideal form of beauty they dimly remember and seek."

Both – immortality of the soul and reincarnation – are the ancient basic doctrines of Hinduism and also of its offshoots Jainism, Buddhism and Sikhism. Buddhism was founded by a Hindu prince Siddhartha Gautama (563 to 483 B. C.). He was known as Buddha (enlightened), at the age of 35 when he attained supreme enlightenment.

A popular love song from an Indian movie echoes the belief in reincarnation, *"Aisa lagta hai ki ham agle janam men kahin mile honge."* (It seems we must have met somewhere in our previous life).

M. P. Pandit – in his book, *'Traditions in Mysticism'* (1987, p.121), has highlighted a study by Dr. Vassilis Vittaxis, a former Greek ambassador to India. Dr. Vittaxis brings to light the similarities and differences between Indian philosophy and the philosophy of Plato. For example, he likens the *nous* (mind) of Plato to the *Atman* of the Upanishads." He further draws parallels between Plato's *Division of Society* and the caste system, 'Plato's Guardians, Warriors, Craftsmen have close resemblance to the Indian Brahmin, Kshatriya, Vaishya.'Vedic philosophy left impress also on the rest of Europe.

It is heartening to know that in prehistory distant ancient times our ancestors maintained cultural and linguistic relations with distant Europeans, particularly Greeks, to share happiness and sorrows together.

Captain F. Wilford[263] has talked about *Swetadweepa,* or the White Island in the West:

> "The sacred Isles in the West of which *Swetadweepa* or the White Island, is the principal and the most famous. In fact, it was the holy land of the *Hindus.* There the fundamental and mysterious transaction of the history of their religion, in its rise and progress, took place. The White Island, this holy land in the West, is so intimately connected with their religion and mythology that they can not be separated and of course, divines in *India* are necessarily acquainted with it, as distant *Muselmans* with *Arabia.* This I conceive to be a most favorable circumstance; in the present case, the learned have little more to do with than to ascertain whether the White Island be England, and the Sacred Isles of the Hindus, the British Isles. After having maturely considered the subject, I think they are."

I wish Wilford had explained how the White Island, the holy land in the West, was so intimately connected with the religion and mythology of Hindus. He (p.249) has made an interesting observation:

> "But in the course of conversation, my pandit, and other learned natives, often mentioned most interesting legends, bearing an astonishing affinity with those of the western mythologists."

Benjamin Walker, in *'The Hindu World: An Encyclopedic Survey of Hinduism'* (1968, p.468), talks about the *Svetadvipa* (White Island):

---

[263] 8th volume, Chapter VII, of Asiatic Researches, (ed) Sir William Jones (1787: 246).

"Svetadvipa (Sveta-dvipa, White Island) in Hindu cosmology represents the sixth island continent surrounding Jumbu encircled by an ocean of … Frequently mentioned in Sanskrit literature, it clearly refers to a place, the exact location which is not known. The *Mahabharata* speaks the white people of Svetadvipa on the northern shores of the Ocean as worshippers of Narayana, a thousand-rayed god. …There has been much speculation about this place, which remains the mysteries of ancient Indian geography. It has been variously identified with Greece, with Greek kingdoms of Parthia, and with Scythia, the country of the Sakas, because an alternative name for Svetadvipa was *Sakadvipa*. *An ancient Brahmin* caste of India known as *sakadvip* are traced to the maga priests of Persia. Others identify Svetadvipa with Tibet, China, Japan, Palestine, even with Britain, since the name of the island suggests white-skinned inhabitants."

Benjamin Walker also in the end thinks that it would be "Britain, since the name of the island suggests white-skinned inhabitants."

Harry H. Hicks and Robert N. Anderson,[264] in *'Ancient India and Vedic Aryans: New Discoveries, Scientific Procedures and Implications for History'*, talking about Asiatic migrations, write: "Druids and their priests are believed to have arrived in the British Isles ca. 3000 to 2500 B.C. according to British archeological calculations."

John Bently, in Asiatic Researches (pp.377- 497) talks about the influence of the *Vedas* in Europe and Persia.

Nehru (*Discovery of India*, p.92) writes:

> "The rediscovery by Europe, during the past century and a half, of Indian philosophy created a powerful impression on European philosophers and thinkers."

---

[264] Sharma and Ghose (ed.), "Revisiting Indus-Sarasvati Age and Ancient India" (1998, p.353)

Aryan (Hindu) contribution to Russia and Europe

Childe, in the Chapter *'Role of the Aryans in History'* of his book *'The Aryans'* (1926, pp. 210-212), has written:

1. "… graves covering the remains of a people, who, whether they were come from South Russia or represented a section of the pre-dolmenic population, were, we believe, Aryan in character."
2. "The gulf between French and Scandinavian culture at the beginning of the 2nd millennium is enormous. The superiority of the former is the measure of the contribution made by the Aryan element to European civilization."
3. "Thus the Aryans do appear everywhere as promoters of true progress and in Europe their expansion marks the moment when the prehistory of our continent (Europe) begins to diverge from that Africa or the Pacific."
4. "Aryan genius found its true expression in Greece and Rome."
5. The lasting gift bequeathed by the Aryans to the conquered people was neither a higher material culture nor a superior physique, but a more excellent language and the mentality it generated.

Childe, in the First Chapter *'Language and Prehistory'*, emphasizes the significance of spiritual unity, and the concept of Divine Law or Cosmic Order in Aryan culture which was bequeathed to Europeans through their language (I believe Sanskrit) which has ability of abstract thinking. Spirituality, the gem of the Aryan (Vedic or Hindu/Buddhist/Sikh) culture, is too complex for most European thinkers. This was the reason why the scientist Albert Einstein wrote to Nehru that the first part of his book *'Discovery of India'* was not easy reading for a Westerner.

Chapter Thirtysix

HUMAN TRANQUILITY = SPIRITUALITY + MATERIALISM

Man unhappy, when in search of only either

The West, as in general seen, more interested in body comforts, has been more engaged in scientifically exploring the ways to make life more comfortable. The East is very much indebted to the West for research to make body comfortable. Neither the West's riches of materialism for comforts of body, nor the East's wealth of spirituality **alone** can give optimal happiness and tranquility, man needs. Body and soul are two inseparable compartments of life; unfortunately man seems to have been ignorant of. Man, in general, has been actively engaged in pursuit of only the either and ignoring the other. Mostly, the man of the East or of the West has been seeking all the comforts of body, ignoring the solace of the soul. Foolishly, man does not go for the solace of soul which is hundred percent free and body comforts are expensive.

Man is unhappy because he does not know and does not want to understand that happiness lies in the union of both, not in separation of body from soul. Like wise, happiness lies in marriage of man and woman, divorce gives pain. Both body and soul are born as twins, live as twins and would be unhappy if and when separated. Man's happiness lies in well-balanced union of materialism and spirituality, not in their loneliness. There will be peace in the mind, body and heart, only when man seeks it in a well-balanced manner, which is very difficult, but not impossible. Man himself is responsible for 180 degree pulls from both – materialism and spirituality.

Globalization has been working to bring W and E closer to each other, as evidenced by the changing demography of the well-developed West, particularly, America, UK and Australia, and also of the Gulf region, having unending heavy influx of Indians there and reverse trend, quite thin and not physical migration in all cases, from the West, particularly of increasing number of philosophers who have been looking to India to quench their spiritual thirst by their deep dip into the ocean of Vedic and Gita wisdom, to mention a few – Amos Bronson Alcott (1799-1888), Ralph Waldo Emerson (1803-1882), Edward Eldbridge Salisbury (1814-1901), Henry David Thoreau (1817-1862), Herman Melville (1819-1891), Walt Whitman (1819-1892), Sir Charles Eliot (1862-1931), Romain Rolland (1866-1944), Albert Einstein (1879-1955), Plato (427-347 B.C.), Sir William Jones (1764-1794), Friedrich Max Müller (1823-1900), Dr. Sheldon Pollock (Arvind Raghunathan), Stephen Knapp ('Sri Nandanandana Dasa, 1947-), Dr. David Frawley (1950- Vāmadeva Śāstrī वामदेव शास्त्री), Dr. Diana L. Eck (1945-), Alain Daniélou, Will Durant, Dr. Annie Besant (1847-1933), Helena Blavatsky (1831-1891), Sister Gargi (Marie Louise Burke, 1912-2004), Arthur Schopenhauer (1788 – 1860), Gene D. Matlock, Fatehullah Mojttabai (Iran) – and many others. Some have migrated to India.

It is a complicated puzzle. The East craves for the wealth in the West for the comfort of body. The rich there are not happy because of the poverty of spirituality, seeking tranquility of soul in the East.

Man, needs to understand that he can get both – comfort of body and the tranquility of soul – at any place of his residence because soul is not separate from body. One has not to travel to America to get rich. There is numerous numbers of rich in India and America has several poor. Are wealthy people happy? Why should a spirituality-soaked *sadhu* wander around to get happiness? As a matter of fact, happiness can not be secured by only too much of money, or by only too much of spirituality. Both – money and spirituality, in desirable blend – are necessary for a happy life. Neither can be ignored while hunting of the other. Too much of either – money or spirituality – is not going to make man and his family at peace.

Man psycho-sociologically needs to understand, that he can be happy only when he is with the family and concerned about the family, not by being selfish and self-centered, wandering around alone in search of money or spirituality only for self. Man has responsibilities and duties to others, not only to self. Such individual is lost not only for self, but lost for family and lost for the society. Conscience will bite him and God will not forgive him for neglecting such responsibilities. Social service is the best worship of God, as prescribed by Swami Vivekananda.

Several western philosophers have settled in India in search of wealth of spirituality, because they think that spirituality can not be secured in America. They are wrong. Soul, the home of spirituality, is in every man, irrespective of his residence, New York or Mumbai. But, it is difficult for a confused man to understand this truth. This also is true that atmosphere helps. People in New York in general may have been more driven to chase money, and the people in *Haridwar* in general, may have been more driven to get the peace of soul. Both, money and tranquility of soul are available every where, in New York as well as in *Haridwar*, depending on seeker's understanding. Man needs to understand that for happiness both are needed in desired blend. Only either is not going to make man happy. Therefore, both *sanyasi* monk and wealthy man are unhappy.

It is paradoxically perplexing that Hindus are learning significance of spirituality from the Westerners who have come to India for spirituality. Both passengers – one bound for India for only spirituality and the other one for America to earn resources for only body comfort – are wrong. Both money and spirituality, like God, are available everywhere, depending on the kind of the pursuit of the seeker. The key lies in 'Self Contentment'. Be happy with what you can have. There is no limit to what the man would like to have.

Neither too much of spirituality, nor too much wealth can give happiness; desirable practical blend of the two is required. Even healthy food, if eaten in too large quantity, can give problem.

Lessons are to be learnt from the lives of the westerners who have come to India in search of spirituality and also from the lives of those who have gone to America, suffering from its effect on marriage and children.

Annie Besant

Dr. Annie Besant[265] (1847-1933), daughter of William Wood and Emily Morris was born in London in 1847 and died in India on 20th September, 1933. She left her husband Rev. Frank Besant who was a conservative religious man. Annie was revolutionary, heretic, social reformer, free thinker, very much involved in women causes. She rejected Christianity in 1874, and became like an atheist. In 1877, she was elected as an MP of the House of Commons. In 1890s, she became supporter of Theosophy, a religious movement founded by Helena Blavatsky in 1875. Theosophy was based on Hindu-Buddhist ideas of *karma*, reincarnation and *Nirvana*. She went to live in India. She got actively involved in the 'Indian Home Rule' movement.

She continued to write letters to British newspapers arguing the case for women's suffrage and in 1911 she was one of the main speakers at an important NUWSS rally in London. While in India, Annie joined the struggle for Indian Home Rule.

Annie Besant became the second President of The Theosophical Society from 1907 to 1933. She was described as a 'Diamond Soul' for she had many brilliant facets to her character. She was an outstanding orator of her time, a champion of human freedom, educationist, philanthropist, and author with more than three hundred books and pamphlets to her credit.

Sister Gargi[266]

Sister Gargi (1911-2004), born as Marie Louise Burke, was an eminent researcher on Swami Vivekananda. Burke is known for her six volume work '*Swami Vivekananda in the West: New Discoveries*' highly acclaimed in India and in Vedanta circles worldwide. Burke was initiated into the Ramakrishna-Vivekananda movement in 1948 by Swami Ashokananda, the abbot of the Vedanta Society of Northern California in San Francisco. Burke took her first vows in India from the Ramakrishna Order in 1974. In recognition of her brilliant accomplishments as researcher and writer

---

[265] Wikipedia
[266] Wikipedia

she was given the monastic name "Gargi" after the Vedic scholar Gargi Vachaknu. In 1983, the first Vivekananda Award was given to her by the Ramakrishna Mission for her research on Vivekananda. Later on, she took her final vows of "sanyas" and was given the name Pravrajika Prajnaprana. Gargi did significant research on the life and philosophy of Swami Vivekananda, as contained in her books.

Gargi's books are based on the teachings of Vivekananda and Vedanta. They are valuable gifts from Westerners to mankind, and eye-openers particularly to Hindus to enjoy the hidden diamonds of the Vedic knowledge to guide self to improve the quality of life. Hindus should be grateful to Gargi for giving us back in effective way the knowledge she received in India to awaken Hindus. Now I understand why one girls' hostel of my alma mater the M.S. University, Baroda is named as Gargi Hall.

European scholars influenced by Vedic philosophy

There are several European philosophers, influenced by Vedic philosophy who did not come to India. Arthur Schopenhauer (1788 – 1860), a German philosopher is best known for his book, '*The World as Will and Representation* (German: *Die Welt als Wille und Vorstellung*),' in which he claimed that our world is driven by a continually dissatisfied will, continually seeking satisfaction. Influenced by Vedic philosophy, he maintained that the "truth was recognized by the sages of India" consequently, his solutions to suffering were similar to those of Vedantic and Buddhist thinkers (i.e., asceticism). His faith in "transcendental ideality" led him to accept atheism.

Schopenhauer at age 25 published his doctoral dissertation, *On the Fourfold Root of the Principle of Sufficient Reason*, which examined the four distinct aspects of experience in the phenomenal world; consequently, he has been influential in the history of phenomenology. He has influenced many thinkers, including Friedrich Nietzsche, Richard Wagner, Otto Weininger, Ludwig Wittgenstein, Erwin Schrödinger, Albert Einstein,[10] Sigmund Freud, Otto Rank, Carl Jung, Joseph Campbell, Leo Tolstoy, Thomas Mann, and Jorge Luis Borges, among others.

'One has to lose some thing to gain some thing' is the rule of life. The East→West migration has caused disintegration of Indian family and has adversely affected the culture, particularly institution of marriage, and inter-generation relations, impacting respect for and security of seniors. Inter-ethnic marriages have been changing the face of the Indian family abroad, in terms of language, cuisine, dress, inter-generation and inter-spousal relations and roles. Because of internet and fast and economical transport and communication, NRI influence has been significantly echoing back in India, as evidenced by bazaars of changing fashions, cosmetics, restaurants, use of cutlery, table manners, etc. Such changes have distanced ultra urban families from their rural relatives who have been living modest traditional life.

Globalization has impacted both, the East and the West. Western man is also interested in the internal universe of self where peace of mind can be more easily enjoyed. The West loves body more than the soul. The West prefers comforts for body to the tranquility of the soul. This is the reason why the West has difficulty in understanding the fruits of spirituality, the treasure of the East, particularly of Hinduism, Buddhism, Jainism and Sikhism.

I don't mean that all Westerners are crazy about comforts of only body and that all Hindus of only soul. Body and soul are inseparable and the line between the two is too slim to demarcate them. But it is true that man – western or eastern – is more sensitive to physical discomfort. Man can have total happiness only when his both – body and soul – are healthy and are in tune with each other.

INDIA'S SPIRITUAL & SCIENTIFIC GIFTS TO THE WORLD

Nehru (Discovery of India, p. 92) talks about Arthur Schopenhauer who praises sublime thoughts given in Upanishads:

> "From every sentence (of the Upanishads) deep, original and sublime thoughts arise, and the whole is pervaded by a high and holy and earnest spirit. ... In the whole world there is no study ... so beneficial and so elevating as that of the Upanishads. ... (They) are products of the highest wisdom. ... It is destined sooner or later to become the faith of the people. ... The study of the Upanishads has been the solace of my life it will be the solace of my death."

Max Müller[267] has talked about Schopenhauer who, according to him, was the last man to write at random, or to allow himself to go into ecstasies over so-called mystic and inarticulate thought:

> "I am neither afraid nor ashamed to say that I share his enthusiasm for the Vedanta, and feel indebted to it for much that has been helpful to me in my passage through life. ... The Upanishads are the sources of the Vedanta philosophy, a system in which human speculation seems

---

[267] Ibid, p.93.

to me to have reached its very acme. ... I spend my happiest hours in reading Vedantic books. They are to me like the light of the morning, like the pure air of the mountains – so simple, so true, if once understood."

Nehru (1946, pp. 92-93) has further discussed the spread of Indian philosophy beyond the borders of India in very early times. Early Indian thought penetrated Greece, through Iran. Plotinus traveled to the East to study Indian and Iranian philosophies, which influenced Christianity of the day. It spread throughout Europe.

Romain Rolland[268] (1866-1944) has given a note on *'The Hellenic-Christian Mysticism of the First Centuries and its relationship to Hindu mysticism'* that "a hundred facts testify to how great an extent the East was mingled with Hellenic thought during the second century of the era."

Spirituality: Gift from India to the West

India's philosophy and spirituality are too abstract to understand and least financially attractive for common Westerners, who, unlike Easterners, are more materialistic and less spiritualistic. Spirituality has attracted the upper echelon of American and European philosophers of the 19th and 20th centuries – Amos Bronson Alcott (1799-1888), Ralph Waldo Emerson (1803-1882), Edward Eldbridge Salisbury (1814-1901), Henry David Thoreau (1817-1862), Herman Melville (1819-1891), Walt Whitman (1819-1892), Sir Charles Eliot (1862-1931), Romain Rolland (1866-1944), Albert Einstein (1879-1955) – among many others. It has influenced several European philosophers – Plato (427-347 B.C.), Sir William Jones (1764-1794), and Friedrich Max Müller (1823-1900).

Albert Einstein[269] (1879-1955) wrote in his letter to Nehru on Feb.18, 1950, expressing his inability to understand the spirituality and intellectuality of India:

---

[268] Ibid, (p.92), footnote.
[269] Ibid, back cover.

Dear Mr. Nehru:

I have read with extreme interest your marvelous book The Discovery of India. The first half of it is not easy reading for a Westerner. But it gives an understanding of the glorious intellectual and spiritual traditions of your great country. The analysis you have given in the second part of the book of tragic influence and forced economic, moral and intellectual decline by the British rule and the vicious exploitation of the Indian people has deeply impressed me.

My admiration for Gandhi's and your work for liberation through non-violence and non-cooperation have become even greater than it was already before. The inner struggle to conserve objective understanding despite the pressure of tyranny from the outside and the struggle against becoming inwardly a victim of resentment and hatred may well be unique in world history. I feel deeply grateful to you for having given to me your admirable work.

With my best wishes for your important and beneficent work and with kind greetings,

Yours cordially,

Albert Einstein

It is hard for westerners (Europeans and Americans) to understand spirituality in its real sense, because they, in general, prefer and practice materialism. Albert Einstein was born in Ulm, Germany. Later he became a Swiss citizen. He received the 1921 Nobel Prize in Physics. He became an American citizen in 1940.

Oriental Spirituality in the Hellenistic Greece

Max Müller[270] has observed that it was difficult to admit that so much influence was exercised by Hindus on Greek philosophers:

"But when Alexander went to converse with Brahmans, who were even then considered by the Greeks as the guardians of a most ancient and mysterious wisdom, their answers had to be translated by so many interpreters that one of the Brahmins themselves remarked, they must become like water that had passed through many impure channels."

Talking about the triumph of the East and the Hellenistic Age, Herbert J. Muller (1958, p.15) has elaborated on how Greeks profited immeasurably from spiritual trade with the East, more typical of India:

"At the same time, Plato's own thought was so fertile because it was not a classically ordered system but an exploration of various possibilities, a sensitive response to various influences, including Oriental thought. Its historic influence has stemmed chiefly from his inclination to a transcendental idealism, another worldly kind of spirituality that is more typical of India than of Greece in its heyday."

Plato,[271] like Hindus, Buddhists, Jains and Sikhs, believed in the immortality of the soul, rebirth and reincarnation:

> "Plato believed that though the body dies and disintegrates, the soul continues to live forever. After the death of the body, the soul migrates to what Plato called the realm of the pure form. After a time, the soul is reincarnated in another body and returns to the world. But the reincarnated soul retains the dim recollection of the realm of forms and yearns for it. Plato argued that people fall in love because they recognize in the beauty of their beloved the ideal form of beauty they dimly remember and seek."

A popular love song from an Indian movie echoes the Hindu belief in reincarnation, *"Aisa lagta hai ki ham agle janam mein kahin mile honge."*

---

[270] Max Müller, in his book 'The Science of Language' (1891, p.95).
[271] World Book Encyclopedia (1993, vol.15, p.504).

(It seems we must have met somewhere in our previous life). Both doctrines, immortality of the soul and reincarnation, are the ancient basic doctrines of Hinduism and of its offshoots – Jainism, Buddhism and Sikhism. Buddhism was founded by a Hindu prince Siddhartha Gautam (563 to 483 B.C.). He was known as Buddha (enlightened) at the age of 35 when he attained supreme enlightenment.

Plato and the Upanishads

M.P. Pandit[272] has highlighted a study by Dr. Vassilis Vittaxis a former Greek ambassador to India Dr. Vittakis brings to light the similarities and differences between Hindu philosophy and the philosophy of Plato. For example, he likens the *nous* (mind) of Plato to the *Atman* of the Upanishads. He further draws parallels between Plato's *Division of Society* and the caste system, "Plato's Guardians, Warriors, Craftsmen have a close resemblance to the Indian Brahman, Kshatriya, Vaishya."

According to the Columbia Encyclopedia (p.2171), Plotinus (205-270), a Neoplatonist philosopher, traveled in the Eastern expedition of Gordian III, the Roman emperor in c.242 to study the philosophies of India and Persia:

> "The theories of Plotinus were fundamentally those of Plato, but included elements of other Greek philosophies as well, all drawn together into an original system that rapidly won followers and had considerable influence on the thinkers of the Christian church, although Plotinus himself opposed Christianity."

There is persuasive evidence that his cosmological conception, which is the chief tenet of Neo-Platonism, was influenced by the *Vedanta* philosophy.

The influence of Vedic thought on Plato and Plotinus is one example of India's philosophical contribution to America via Europe. Unlike America's material and technological contribution to India, India's contribution to America has been intangible, abstract and philosophical.

---

[272] M.P. Pandit, in his book, 'Traditions in Mysticism' (1987, p.121)

History has been hostile, unkind and indifferent to Eastern civilizations, making it difficult for present generation to know and appreciate their (of Eastern civilizations) contribution to the mankind.

Present trend seems to be focused on soul's solace rather on bodily pleasures. Developing awareness that man's psychological pain is caused by family disintegration due to his over-indulgence in bodily pleasures and material pursuits. This has led many Westerners to look toward the East for answers. Meditation, Yoga, and vegetarianism are gaining popularity amongst Americans and Europeans. Indians, like Deepak Chopra, are gaining attention of the West. This also is true that increasing number of Hindus are being attracted by non-vegetarian food.

During one of his lectures at the University of Cambridge in 1882, Max Müller[273] talks about what India can do for mankind:

> "If we were to look over the whole world to find out the country most richly endowed with all the wealth, power, and beauty that nature can bestow – in some parts a very paradise on earth – I should point to India.

> "If I were asked under what sky the human mind has most full developed some of its choicest gifts, has most deeply pondered on the greatest problems of life, and has found solutions of some of them which well deserve the attention even of those who have studied Plato and Kant, I should point to India. .....

> "And if I were to ask myself from what literature we, here in Europe, have been nurtured almost exclusively on the thoughts of Greeks and Romans, and of one Semitic race, the Jewish, may draw that corrective which is most wanted in order to make our inner life more perfect, more comprehensive, more universal, in fact more truly human, a life, not for this life only, but

---

[273] Friedrich Max Müller (India: What Can It Teach Us? (1999, p. 24).

493

a transfigured and eternal life – again I should point to India."

The 'Bhajan Belt': Serenity In The Catskills[274]

Mark Healy in "The 'Bhajan Belt', Serenity in the Catskill" (NY Times, Oct.18, 2002, Escapes section) has said about the Bhajan Belt in the Catskills:

> "Everything you need to know about the spiritual rhythms of the Catskill Mountains (in north New York State) is spray-painted on a rock face along Route 28. It is the sign for 'OM' – the mystic syllable of Hinduism.

Healy[275] writes that OM is not a word. It is rather an intonation, which, like music, transcends the barriers of age, race, culture and even species. There is harmony, peace and bliss in this simple but deeply philosophical sound. By vibrating the sacred syllable OM, the supreme combination of letters, if one thinks of the Ultimate Personality of Godhead and quits his body, he will certainly reach the highest state of "stateless" eternity, states the *Bhagavad Gita*.

During meditation, when one chants OM, viabrations are developed within self that attune sympathy with the cosmic vibration and he/she starts thinking and feeling universally, not lonely. The momentary silence between each chant becomes palpable. Mind moves between the opposites of sound and silence until, at last, it ceases the sound. In the silence, the single thought – OM – is quenched; there is no thought, he is absorbed within. This is the state of trance, where the mind and the intellect are transcended as the individual self merges with the Infinite Self in the pious moment of realization. It is a moment when the petty worldly affairs are lost in the desire for the universal. Such is the immeasurable power of OM,

Healy explains:

---

[274] Wikipedia.
[275] Wikipedia, Subhamoy Das

"It's a subtle suggestion of the energy that vibrates throughout the region. Some call it the bhajan (devotional song) belt, applying a word derived from Sanskrit for devotional song to an area that stretches from the holistic enterprises of New Paltz to a yoga ranch in Woodbourne."

East-leaning academics, musicians and authors, like Mark Healy, Sharon Gannon, David Life and Robert A.F. Thurman (a Buddhist author and scholar, who had a home in Woodstock) have founded a home at Woodstock, upstate New York. They call it "Bhajan Belt." It provides solitude and energy to move man within self. Now they have established "Jivanmukti Yoga Center" to teach Yoga, called as 'Jivanmukti' Yoga, meaning, freedom from the miseries of life.

Talking about 'Jivanmukti Yoga Center' is not to suggest that one can attain serenity and peace of mind only at this center. Serenity can be realized any where through spirituality, meditation, Yoga and singing *bhajans* (devotional songs). The rhythm of *bhajans* in Hindi, Sanskrit or any Indian vernacular has a peculiar soothing effect.

Albert Einstein: India's contribution to science

Several great Western scholars have emphasized India's contribution to the world. Albert Einstein (1879-1955) – American theoretical physicist, known for the formulation of the general theory of relativity – has praised India's contribution to science: "We owe a lot to the Indians, who taught us how to count, without which no worthwhile scientific discovery could have been made."

India has given to America several scientists, technologists, Nobel Laureates, doctors, nurses, engineers, academics, economists, managers, administrators, politicians and entrepreneurs including some in key positions.

Max Müller (1999, p.22) talks about the European charm connected with India and fancy for the wisdom of Brahmans:

"And, strange to say, this feeling exists in England more than in any other country. In France, Germany, and Italy, even in Denmark, Sweden, and Russia, there is a vague charm connected with the name of India. One of the most beautiful poems in the German is the *Wiesheit der Brahmanen,* the "wisdom of the Brahmans," by Rückert, to my mind more rich in thought and more perfect in form than even Goethe's *West-östliecher Divan.*"

Historian Will Durant (1885-1981) thought that the West should learn from India its tolerance and gentleness and love for all living things.

Eminent French philosopher Victor Cousin[276] (1792-1867) praises India as the cradle of the human race and highest philosophy:

"When we read with attention the poetical and philosophical monuments of the East – above all those of India, which are beginning to spread in Europe – we discover there many a truth, and truths so profound, and which make such a contrast with the meanness of the results at which European genius has some times stopped, that we are constrained to bend the knee before the philosophy of the East and to see in this cradle of the human race the native land of the highest philosophy."[277]

Stephen Knapp (p.10) has cited Will Durant in praise of India and its race, Sanskrit and philosophy:

"India was the motherland of our race, and Sanskrit the mother of Europe's languages: she was the mother of our philosophy, mother through the Arabs, of much of our mathematics; mother, through the Buddha, of the ideals embodied in Christianity, mother through the village community, of self-government and democracy. Mother India is in many ways the mother of us all."

---

[276] Ibid, p. 11.

[277] Sir John Woodroffe, 'Is India Civilized: Essays on Indian Culture'.

HINDU INVENTIONS

O rigins of some important products of common use have been historically misconceived and some if Indian, have been ignored:

- **Ink for writing:** India was the original source of carbon pigment used in Indian black ink (called musi). Since 4th century BC, the practice of writing with ink with a sharp pointed needle was common in South Bhārat. This suggests that the pre-history ancient Hindus were not only fond of knowledge, but also of writing that the knowledge be preserved for ever.

- **Chess** was developed out of Chaturanga, which is an ancient strategy board game. It was developed in Bhārat during the Gupta Empire in Bhārat around the 6th century AD. Later it spread to China and all over the world.

- **Rulers** were first used by the Indus Valley Civilization, long prior to 1500 BCE. Most rulers, found during excavations, were made of ivory. Rulers reveal the amazing accuracy of decimal subdivisions on it. All this reflects their importance in mathematics and geometry, the science of measurements.

- The game, 'Snakes & Ladders', was invented in Bhārat as a game of morals. Later it spread to England and eventually introduced in the USA by game pioneer Milton Bradley in 1943.

- The ancient Greeks used to wear animal skins and were not even aware of cotton. But Hindus were sort of cool and started cultivating cotton during the 5th – 4th millennium BCE in the

Indus Valley Civilization. The word spread to the Mediterranean and beyond and soon everyone was ordering one from Flipkart.

- Hindus were pioneers in Plastic Surgery too. It was carried out in Bhārat as early as 2000 BCE. So, we've always been a **cool** country. History is testimony to it. So what's stopping you from being innovative? Go, win the world.

- Worldwide, Bhārat was the only source of diamonds until the discovery of mines in Brazil in the 18th century. Almost 5000 years ago, diamonds were first recognized and mined in central Bhārat.

- ISRO's Chandrayaan-1 made the startling discovery that the moon is not a dry ball of rocks. The discovery of lunar water is attributed to the Chandrayaan mission.

- We all know that Marconi received a Nobel Prize in Physics in 1909 for contribution to the development of wireless telegraphy. But the first public demonstration of radio waves for communication was made by Sir Jagdish Chandra Bose in 1895, two years prior to Marconi's similar demonstration in England. Sir Bose was posthumously credited (more than a century later) for his achievement. The fact remains that this discovery truly shaped the face of modern wireless communication.

- It was in 7th century CE when Brahmagupta found the first general formula for solving quadratic equations. The decimal system (or the Hindu number system), which was a precursor of the Arabic numeric system, was developed in India between the 1st and 6th centuries CE.

- Ancient Hindus were pioneers in metallurgy. High quality steel was produced, almost two thousand years before it was understood by the West. One of the most remarkable feat in metallurgy: creating a seamless celestial globe, was invented in Kashmir. It was earlier considered impossible to create a metal globe without seams. So thanks to Bhārat, Iron Man can wear cotton suit now.

SUNKEN ANCIENT INDIA
DISCOVERED278

About 21,310 years back India's territory was larger because her some part was not drowned. In that epoch India's coastal plains were every where more extensive than they are today. Particularly, in two areas – north-west Gujarat near Dwarka, and Tamil Nadu south-east near Mahabalipuram – coasts were so much extensive as to make ancient India virtually unrecognizable. In these two coastal areas there was dramatic marine encroachment due to heavy floods as the result of the Ice Age meltdown. Cities – Dwarka (Gujarat) and Mahabalipuram, Poompuhar and Kumari Kandam along the coasts of Tamil Nadu – were swallowed up the Arabian Sea in the west and the Bay of Bengal in the east.

Dwarka

According to the BBC News, oceanographers from the India's National Institute of Ocean Technology by chance, while conducting survey of pollution in 2002 discovered archaeological remains of a sunken civilization about 120 feet under water in the Gulf of Cambay, off the western coast of Gujarat, India.

Using side scan sonar, which sends a beam of sound waves down to the bottom of the ocean, they identified huge geometrical structures which looked like a city. The remains, found in the sunken city were

---

278   Graham Hancock, 'Underworld: The Mysterious Origins of Civilization' (2002, p.151).

scattered around in the area of five miles long and two miles wide. The remains found there seem to predate the oldest known remains in the subcontinent by more than 5,000 years. The recovered debris, included construction material, pottery, walls, beads, sculpture and human bones, and teeth. As carbon dated, they were 9,500 years old, much older than the Indus cities – Harappa and Mohen-jo-daro (Mooan-jo-daro) which were about 5000 years old. Mohen-jo-daro is a misnomer. It should be 'Mooan-jo-daro' which is a Sindhi word. Mooan means dead, Jo = of, and daro = mound, meaning the 'mound of the dead'.

The area must have been submerged as ice melted at the end of the last ice age about 10,000 years ago. Or, it could be a tsunami. Large areas of the Indian subcontinent experienced severe oceanic flooding at the end of the ice Age, particularly between 15,000 and 8000 years ago.

Graham Hancock in *"Underworld, the Mysterious Origins of Civilization"* (2002, p.109) has talked about this. He writes that in about 3102 B.C., the ocean arose and submerged the whole of Dwarka. Lord Krishna died around that time. According to Hancock, it seems the sunken city was earlier Krishna's Dwarka, now on this sits new Dwarka, has been built in memory of Lord Krishna.

The grandeur of the ancient civilization of India seems like a mystery. Thanks to oceanographers like Graham Hancock, who have dived deep into oceans and have discovered several underwater mysteries and have introduced them by way of believable historical documents. Discovery of the drowned cities, like Dwarka, Mahabalipuram, Poompuhar and Kumari Kandam has added numerous significant pages to the ignored, buried, hidden and forgotten history of prehistory ancient India including Ramayana, Mahabharata, Bhagvad Gita, the book of philosophy as a torch on the path to self-realization. It has been mischievously branded as myth by colonial historians. Thus, it has not been taught as history in schools and colleges. Hope, several other towns, yet underwater, will be surfaced.

Mahabalipuram, "The Shore Temple"

Graham Hancock[279] describes his fascination for diving into oceans to trace the ruins of gigantic towns – with extensive and impressive ruins, seem to have been drowned by angry tsunami. He read Captain Carr's anthology of travelers' journals and reports, so as to identify the spots where to dive to find the drowned towns. He himself, along with other divers, including with his wife Santha and Trevor Jenkins, has discover several sunken towns, like Dwarka, Mahabalipuram shore temple, Poompuhar and Kumari Kandam and some other. There must be several other towns still hiding underwater to be discovered by some other Graham Hancock. History of his interest traces back to 1956 when he was only six year old. He was with his father in Mahabalipuram, where his father was working as a surgeon at the Christian Medical College in a nearby town Vellore, Tamilnadu, in Bay of Bengal, south-east coast of India.

In April 2002, Hancock,[280] diving through the murky waters of the Bay of Bengal, only a mile far from Mahabalipuram, "found amongst huge submerged walls, plazas and pinnacles emerging out of the gloom – structures that seemed more like the work of gods or titans than of men and to belong more in the world of myth than that of history."

Hancock (p.678) writes:

> "Sinking down through the murky waters of the Bay of Bengal a mile offshore of the southeast Indian town of Mahabalipuram, I found myself amongst huge submerged walls, plazas, and pinnacles emerging out of the gloom – structures that seemed more like the work of gods or titans than of men and to belong more in the world of myth than that of history. With a kick of my fins I slowly turned around, and in every direction that I looked I saw extensive and impressive ruins stretching away. Involuntarily my heart began to pound and my breathing speeded up. Because for more than five years

---

[279] Grahm Hancock, pp. 678-679).
[280] Ibid, p.678/

I had been diving the world's oceans searching for evidence just such as this – the hard evidence that I had long believed must lie behind mankind's collective inheritance of more than 600 ancient 'flood myths'."

On the same page, he cites one paper of Captain Caar's anthology, in which J. Goldingham, Esq. writing in 1798, spoke of the part of Mahabalipuram – the "Shore Temple" which was carved out of solid granite:

"The surf here breaks far out over, as the Brahmins inform you, the ruins of a city which was incredibly large and magnificent. ... A Brahmin, about 50 years of age, a native of the place, whom I had opportunity of conversing with since my arrival in Madras, informed me his grandfather had frequently mentioned having seen the gilt tops of five pagodas in the surf, no longer visible."

Hancock, (p.681) talking to fishermen, heard various stories of their experiences seeing underwater structures near the shores of Mahabalipuram, some of magnificent temple. He also talks of his own dives along with his wife Santha who was shooting underwater stills. He talks about one dive with Trevor Jenkins, the expedition's videographer, following "a superb, curved wall that ran unbroken for more than 16 meters." On another dive he says: "I was able to expose the core masonry on a different length of wall, revealing the fine jointing between blocks."

Hancock (p.682) talks about the NIO's (National Institute of Oceanography) press statement proposing a possible date and function for the submerged ruins and citing the same 'lion figure' as evidence:

"Based on what appears to be a Lion figure, of location 4, ruins are inferred to be parts of temple complex. The possible date of the ruins may be 1500-1200 years before present (2002, year of the book publication). Pallava dynasty, ruling the area during the period, has constructed many such rock-cut and structural temples in Mahabalipuram and Kanchipuram."

Trever Jenkins (pp. 683-4) discovered what he thought might be a stone carving of a lion. Hancock was not sure that it was of a lion. Later he felt happy to see NIO's (National Institute of Oceanography) press statement proposing a possible date and function for the submerged ruins and citing this very same **'lion figure'** as evidence. I think it was a part of a Hindu temple which got submerged by angry waters. Hindu temples in ancient times were and even now are culturally fond of lion and elephant. Lion was the *vahan* (vehicle) of Goddess Durga.

Durga is considered as the goddess of power and moral order. She protects the mankind from evil, misery and tyranny. Agni is also the goddess of power. Hence India missiles are named as *Agni*. The word 'Agni' means fire which can destroy enemies. India successfully test-fired its surface-to-surface inter-continental ballistic missile 'Agni V' on 19th April, 2012 and joined the elite missile club, with America, Russia, France and China as its members. The Agni V has range of over 5,000 km (3,106.8 miles) and can reach almost whole China, Eastern Europe, East Africa and the Australian coast.

Hindus believe that power lies with women. In pre-history ancient times, all the three main portfolios – defense, finance and education – were assigned to women Durga, Lakshmi and Sarasvati respectively for India's optimal functioning. It seems it answers the question 'Why these ministries in present times are not functioning well, may be because women are not in command. In ancient times, women were rightly seen as honest, more systematic, sincere, shrewd and hard working administrators than men. The present government has been thinking, thinking and thinking how to resolve border issue involving Kashmir. Indira Gandhi, a brave, fearless and courageous lioness with a verbal stroke made Bangladesh independent and frees it from the tyranny of the East Pakistan and completely removed it from the map.

Poompuhar and Kumari Kandam discovered under water

Hancock (pp. 683-4) tells that the mystery doesn't stop at Mahabalipuram. He talks about *Poompuhar* and *Kumari Kandam*. They were also drowned by angry waters in three terrible deluges, the first of which took place 11,500 years ago. The NIO, during its marine archaeological survey off *Poompuhar,* discovered in March 2002 a very large apparently man-made structure more than 5 kilometers from shore at a depth of about 70 feet. Hancock thinks that the depth of the submergence of the structure suggests that it could have been under water for 11,000 years. It is evident that the people had know-how of building houses. They have been under water for about 11,500 years. Therefore, it is difficult to know what sort of houses they were and what the quality of their structure was. Hancock himself, along the NIO team, had participated in these expeditions.

Hancock, along with his diving team including his wife Samantha was exited to watch the interesting geometrical setup of the structure and lay out of the walls under water. The material of which these blocks were made was lateritic. Stone, like the same as was used in ancient south India during times immemorial, seems to have been used in the common construction. Large symmetrical slabs (approx 1.5 meters x 1.5 meters x 0.5 meters) were found scattered on the seabed. In March 2002, a straight wall approximately 100 meters in length was found lying in 25 meters of water and almost 7 kilometers from land.

Hancock (p.685) states that he himself and majority of the team including divers of the NIO and Britain's led by Monty Halls of the Scientific Exploration Society are of the confirmed opinion that these structures at Mahabalipuram and Poompuhar were man-made. The walls were made of laterite stone, not of burnt bricks, as houses of the 4th millennia Harappa and Mohen-jo-daro cities were built of. 'U-Shaped' structure and parallel walls suggest that those ancient people had some knowledge of geometry and sense of measurement. It is amazing to see Hindus of such early age, 9,478 B.C. (11,500 – 2002 = 9, 478) lived in such houses, built of parallel stone walls and had temples with carved lions. It is more amazing that they had sense of religion. According to Hancock there are still much more underwater ruins to be discovered.

Culture and religion of Mahabalipuram and Poompuhar

'Lion figure' as seen by Trever Jenkins suggests that the people living at Mahabalipuram and Poompuhar were Hindus, worshipping goddess Durga, riding lion. Durga as a mythological goddess and 'lion' as her *vahan* (vehicle) suggest that the Hindus of ancient times worshipped goddess '*Shakti*' (power) for protection. India should learn from history that the defense should be strong and the officers should be honest like Durga, not to fatten their pockets at the cost of the protection of Bharat Mata (Mother India).

It seems Hancock's open-mind-encounters – with Hindu temples while diving into waters around Hindustan and studying some sacred Vedic scriptures, some through David Frawley's writings, perhaps his book *"Gods, Sages and Kings"* – have opened his inner eyes to think what should be the basis to history, materialism or spiritualism and also to see who are more happy, sages or kings. The choice is between comfort of body and tranquility of the soul. Hancock writes that "most historians and archaeologists today more or less automatically project the materialist basis and structure of modern society." However, a thought-provoking counterview by David Frawley has begun to emerge that "our political and economic interpretations of history cannot be true if enlightenment or spiritual realization is the real goal of humanity."[281] Unfortunately, materialism will remain as the basis for the modern society, because spirituality, though prime goal for happiness, is very difficult to realize. Even in prehistory remote society sages were very few among a great mass of humanity. Through sincere effort, modern man can earn and practice some spirituality which can bring happiness, not only for self, but also for family, community and nation. However, it is pleasing to note that both Yoga and transcendental meditation have been getting increasingly more attention in India as well as all over the planet. Yoga has been increasingly more popular in the West (America and Europe) than in its cradle India.

---

[281] David Frawley, 'Gods, Sages and Kings' (1991, p. 41.

Chapter Forty

HINDU CULTURE IN EARLY AMERICA

M any students of Theosophy have desired more information about the connection between ancient India and ancient America than is given by H. P. Blavatsky in the few references she makes to the subject. We are glad to find that a learned Hindu scholar, Mr. Chaman Lal, has at last taken it up and presented a mass of evidence in his deeply interesting volume of 247 pages entitled Hindu America[282], published by the New Book Co., Hornby Road, Bombay, in 1940. We are indebted to Dr. W. Y. Evans-Wentz for drawing our attention to this valuable corroboration of H. P. Blavatsky's claim of an intimate connection between America and India some thousands of years before either the Norse or the Columbian rediscovery of the New World. Unfortunately, I have not been able to get a copy of the book which would have helped me to describe its related contents adequately and appropriately.

Mr. Chaman Lal's evidence for the similarity of the ancient Hindu and the native American religions and cultures, as well as for the historicity of the traditions in both the Old and the New Worlds wherein the voyages and connecting links between them are recorded under more or less allegorical forms or even in plain language, is strong and well-selected, though we regret the inclusion of a citation from Churchward among those from serious and recognised scholars.

Most Western writers have ignored the possibility of pre-Columbian travel between India and America by civilized expeditions by either

---

[282]   I in vain tried my best to get the copy of 'Hindu America' by Mr. Chaman Lal. published by the New Book Co., Hornby Road, Bombay, in 1940.

the western or the eastern sea route or by both, but have concentrated attention on the possible emigration of early savage tribes from northern Asia across the Bering Straits perhaps more than 30,000 years ago. H. P. Blavatsky, however, and the ancient traditions mentioned, indicate that highly civilized persons came over to America from India at a later date, some even as recently as 5,000 years ago.

Mr. Chaman Lal's evidence includes the sculptural and pictorial representations in America of the **Indian** elephant with their unmistakably Hindu artistic "feeling." These elephants do not resemble the prehistoric American types. The American god Tlaloc was elephant-headed, as was the Hindu Ganesha, a derivative of Indra, and both were rain-gods. The author gives a large number of quotations from various sources illustrating the close resemblance between American and Indian cultures and ideas, such as religious traditions and myths, cosmical concepts, the knowledge of the four Yugas and of the races preceding the present Fifth Race, identical social systems and customs, and yoga meditation methods. He discusses the use of the zero in mathematics among the Mayas, unknown elsewhere in the ancient world except in India; the symbols common to India and America such as the cross, the swastika, the thunder-bird (the latter being stylized at Ocosingo in Mexico so as to be practically identical with the Egyptian Winged Globe) and the traces of food-plants being transported across the Pacific, etc. He mentions the recent discovery of stone wheels at Tiahuan-aco in Bolivia, but does not refer to the unexpected revelation that America knew the principle of the true arch. These examples of Old World culture in ancient America were unknown till quite recently.

Mr. Chaman Lal pays considerable attention to the curious identity between certain Indian and American games, but he does not mention the fact that when the Spaniards arrived in Arizona they found the Pima Indians playing a game which required a pattern exactly duplicating the elaborate plan of the Labyrinth of ancient Crete as shown on the Cretan coins! This pattern is so uniquely specialized that it seems impossible for it to have been independently invented in places so remote as Crete and our Southwestern States; but Mr. Chaman Lal traces a powerful Hindu influence in Greece and the Mediterranean and quotes significant evidence about the extensive maritime trade carried on by India with foreign countries.

Many pages are devoted to the Snake or Dragon (Naga) Cult of Hinduism and its close resemblance to the widespread Snake Cult of ancient America, which is still extant in places, even in the United States. Students of Theosophy know the importance that is attached to the snake as a symbol of Wisdom and of the Initiate, which is found in every ancient religion, even in Christianity, for Jesus uses the word when sending forth his twelve trained apostles: "Be ye therefore wise as serpents, and harmless as doves." Moses healed the people by setting up the Brazen Serpent under direction from his God. How different the story of the European penetration into and domination of America might have been if the pure teachings of Jesus had been followed by the professed Christians!

The Theosophical student feels that Mr. Chaman Lal is right in his insistence upon the importance of the similarity between the ancient Hindu and American religious philosophies, and in doing so he is supporting a fundamental teaching of The Secret Doctrine, i. e., the former existence of a universal "Wisdom-Religion," Theo-sophy as we now call it, widely diffused over the earth, the origin and fountain of the partial presentations of the One Truth which have arisen as specialized religions, and which have mostly become more or less degenerated or superstitious. This, however, is no obstacle to the probability that the Hindu "colonists" brought to America many new ideas and methods which were engrafted into the prevailing forms of belief.

In explaining that many of the difficulties in tracing the religious practices of ancient America arise from the almost complete destruction of records by fanatical bigots, Mr. Chaman Lal speaks plainly of the horrifying cruelties perpetrated on the American tribes by the so-called "Christians," but he firmly believed "the Indian culture will revive again and will redeem America. There are already clear signs to that effect. The most advanced and scientifically brought up Americans are already looking for a philosophy that will "save their souls."

In this he (I think Mr. Chaman Lal) would sympathize with Dr. Gregory Mason, Americanist, who in his recent South of Yesterday asks if we, modern Americans of all types, shall not carry on the

American traditions that have come down from antiquity and build a real civilization in all respects suitable to the Western conditions, and in which we shall no longer depend upon European culture.

The following quotations from H. P. Blavatsky will suffice to prove that Mr. Chaman Lal's main principle is well-founded. Speaking of the Chaldean, Assyrian and Indian "Nargals" or chiefs of the Magi, and the Hindu "Nagas" or "Wise Men," she writes:

> "Such similarity cannot be attributed to coincidence. A new world is discovered, and we find that, for our forefathers of the Fourth Race, it was already an old one. That Arjuna, Krishna's companion and chela, is said to have descended into Patala, the "antipodes," and therein married **Ulupi**, a Naga (or Nagini rather), the daughter of a king of the Nagas, Kauravya – The Secret Doctrine, II, 213-4. (Also see footnotes 406, 407)."

In H. P. Blavatsky's Theosophical Glossary we read: ULUPI (**Sk.**) A daughter of Kauravya, King of the Nagas in Patala (the nether world, or more correctly, the Antipodes, America). Exoterically, she was the daughter of a king or chief of an aboriginal tribe of the Nagas, or Nagals (ancient adepts) in pre-historic America — Mexico most likely, or Uruguay. She was married to Arjuna, the disciple of Krishna, whom every tradition, oral and written, shows travelling five thousand years ago to Patala (the Antipodes). The Puranic tale is based on a historical fact. Moreover, Ulupi, as a name, has a Mexican ring in it, like "Atlan," "Aclo," etc.

And again in The Secret Doctrine: Exoterically, the Nagas are semi-divine beings. . . . Yet there was a race of Nagas, said to be a thousand in number only, born or rather sprung from Kadra, Kasyapa's wife, for the purpose of peopling Patala, which is undeniably America.— II, 132.

There is no doubt that America is that "far distant land into which pious men and heavy storms had transferred the sacred doctrine" . . . the Secret Doctrine of the land which was the cradle of physical man, and of the Fifth Race, had found its way into the so-called New World ages and ages before the "Sacred Doctrine" of Buddhism.

ANCIENT INDONESIA: HINDU-BUDDHIST KINGDOMS

The names of some Indonesian islands reflect their origin in ancient Sanskrit. The name "Bandar Seri Begawan" linguistically compares to "Bandar = Port, Seri = Sri, Begawan = Bhawan (God)", meaning the 'port of God'. There are several Hindu-Buddhist stupas and sculptures in Indonesia. The names of several towns, cities and islands reflect Sanskrit touch, as evidenced by the few names, such as Bali, Jakata (even the capita), Jaya, Irian Jaya, Sulavasi, Sumatra, Kalimantan, Singapore (Sing=lion+pore (place), etc. All this suggests that Indonesia, originally was the territory of Sanskrit-speaking people, Hindus and Buddhists. After foreign bondage its demography has changed, most of its population being Muslims, changed from Hindus and Buddhists due to conversions by various ways, mostly painful.

Indonesian state philosophy.

Indonesia is praise worthy for remaining secular, unlike most other Muslim-majority nations, respecting its ancestry and basic Hindu religious philosophy, surprising not Muslim. Pancasila {(panca = panch (five), sila = principles} is the official motto of Indonesia. Pancasila comprises two Old Javanese words originally derived from Sanskrit: 'pañca' (five) and 'sila' (principles). It is composed of five principles which are inseparable and interrelated, such as:

i.   Divinity worship of God

ii. ultimate unity of the people
iii. just and civilized humanity
iv. democracy, predicated on the inherent wisdom of unanimity arising from deliberations among popular representatives
v.   social justice for all Indonesian people

There will be peace on earth when all peoples, particularly Muslim-majority nations follow the godly wisdom of the Muslim Indonesia. It is difficult to understand the 'why' of Muslim terrorism when Islam, the terrorists feel proud of, is a peace-loving religion. All Muslims are not terrorist, very few are, but shockingly almost all terrorists are Muslim. All main religions – Hinduism, Judaism, Christianity, Islam – preach love and peace. God is One, so all religions preach love and peace. Only few religiously misguided persons divide God as per various religions and create problems.

Hinduism and Buddhism are original religions of Indonesia and Islam came later as the religion of the invaders. Indonesian archipelago has witnessed the rise and fall of Hindu-Buddhist empires. Jakarta and several temples in Indonesia will testify the presence of Hindus in aancient times.

The world's largest Borobandur Buddhist Temple is considered as one of the masterpieces among the Seven Wonders of the World. It is located in the Borobudur Village, Borobudur district, approximately 3 km from Mungkid city. The Borobudur Temple was built by King Samaratungga, one of the kings of ancient Mataram Kingdom, from the descendant of Wangsa Syailendra. Based on the Kayumwungan inscription, an Indonesian named Hudaya Kandahjaya revealed that Borobudur is a place of worship which was completely built on May 26th, 824, almost a hundred years since they first started its construction. According to several sources the name of "Borobudur" means as a mountain with terraces (budhara), while some others say that it means monastery located on the high ground.

The Borobudur Temple, popular as one of the seven wonders of the world, was designed as staircase consisting of 10 levels. Before Borobudur was renovated, the height of the temple was 42 meters and 34.5 meters after the reconstruction. Its height decreased because the lowest level functioned as a barrier, therefore was removed when being renovated. The six lowest square and top three circle and one of the highest levels of Buddhist stupa is facing to the west. Each level represents as one of the stages of human life. According to the Mahayana Buddhism, every person who wants to reach the level as the Buddha, must pass through every level of human life. Kamadhatu, the lowest part of Borobudur (basement) symbolizing human beings that are bound by lust.

Early kingdoms in Indonesia

Rock inscriptions on Java dating from the 5th or 6th century talk about Taruma, as an extensive Javanese kingdom that was centered near the present day Jakarta. The people of Taruma observed Hindu religious rites as in India and promoted irrigation works. By the beginning of the 7th century Java was home to several important kingdoms, and a harbor kingdom was also apparently well established on the southeastern coast of Sumatra. The kingdoms of this time fell into two main types of political unit: the seafaring trading states along the coasts of Sumatra, northern Java, Borneo, Sulawesi, and some of the other eastern islands; and the rice-based inland kingdoms, particularly of eastern and central Java. The greatest maritime empire was Sri Vijaya, a Mahayana Buddhist kingdom on Sumatra's southeast coast. In the late 7th century Sri Vijaya was a center of trade with India and China and for the next five centuries controlled much of China's trade with the western archipelago. Little archaeological evidence of the Kingdom of Sri Vijaya remains on Sumatra.

In contrast, the Hindu-Buddhist kingdoms of central and eastern Java have left extensive temples, buildings, and inscriptions. These monuments and artifacts show that the Hindu culture had vast influence on the religion and state organizations of the Javan kingdoms. The central and eastern kingdoms relied on rice agriculture and had a complex hierarchy headed by a god-king. Inscriptions reveal that under the Sanjaya family the Hindu kingdom of Mataram flourished on the Dieng Plateau in the early 8th century. In the second half of the 8th century a new Buddhist kingdom under the Sailendra dynasty developed in the nearby Kedu Plain; Mataram declined as the Sailendra kingdom rose. The Sailendras built the massive temple monument of Borobudur in the mid-9th century.

Also by the mid-9th century, rulers claiming descent from King Sanjaya (ruled 732-778) of central Java founded a new kingdom of Mataram, whose rule extended from central to eastern Java. In the early 10th century, for unknown reasons, the kingdom's center shifted to the east, where Hindu influence on the state weakened. First under Sindok (ruled 929-947) and later under Airlangga (ruled 1019-1042), who united the eastern kingdom with Bali, Mataram became increasingly interested in overseas trade. A period of division followed, after which the new kingdom of Singosari was founded on Java in 1222. Its founder and first ruler was Angrok, a commoner. Under the Buddhist king Kertanagara (ruled 1268-1292), Singosari controlled many of the Sumatran areas formerly ruled by Sri Vijaya. Kertanagara's successor, Vijaya (ruled 1293-1309), repelled a Mongol invasion of Java and in 1293 founded Majapahit, the greatest Javanese empire. Majapahit, under Hayam Wuruk, claimed sovereignty over much of what is now Indonesia and Singapore and parts of Malaysia.

The arrival of Buddhism started with the trading activity that began in the early of first century on the Silk Road between Indonesia and India. According to some Chinese source, a Chinese traveler monk on his journey to India, witnessed the powerful maritime empire of Srivijaya based on Sumatra. The empire also established a Buddhist learning centre in the region. A number of historical heritage monuments are found in Indonesia, including the Borobudur Temple in Yogyakarta and statues or prasasti (inscriptions) from the earlier history of Buddhist empires. Following the downfall of President Sukarno in the mid-1960s, Pancasila was reasserted as the official Indonesian policy on religion to recognize only monotheism. As a result, founder of Perbuddhi (Indonesian Buddhists Organisation), Bhikku Ashin Jinarakkhita proposed that there was a single supreme deity, Sanghyang Adi Buddha. He was also backed up with the history behind the Indonesian version of Buddhism in ancient Javanese texts, and the shape of the Borobudur Temple.

Archeological evidences suggest that Tarumanagara is one of the earliest known Hindu kingdoms in Indonesia and that the geographic spread of Hinduism in West Java in the 5th century CE has been significant. Hinduism in Indonesia is as old as Indonesia itself. Historical evidence is unclear about the diffusion process of cultural and spiritual ideas from India. Java legends refer to Saka-era, traced to 78 AD. Stories from the Mahabharata Epic have been traced in Indonesian islands to the 1st century. However, the versions mirror those found in southeast Indian peninsular region (now Tamil Nadu and southern Andhra Pradesh). The Javanese prose work *Tantu Pagelaran* of the 14th century, which is a collection of ancient tales, arts and crafts of Indonesia, extensively uses Sanskrit words, Indian (rather Hindu) deity names and religious concepts. Similarly ancient *Chandis* (temples) excavated in Java and western Indonesian islands, as well as ancient inscriptions such as the 8th century Canggal inscription discovered in Indonesia, confirm widespread adoption of Shiva lingam iconography, his companion goddess Parvati, Ganesha, Vishnu, Brahma, Arjuna, and other Hindu deities by about the middle to late first millennium AD. Ancient Chinese records of on his return voyage from Ceylon to China in 414 AD mention two schools of Hinduism in Java, while Chinese documents from 8th century refer to the Hindu kingdom of King Sanjaya as *Holing*, calling it "exceedingly wealthy" and that it coexisted peacefully with Buddhist people and Sailendra ruler in Kedu Plain of the Java island.

The two major theories regarding the arrival of Hinduism in Indonesia include that South Indian sea traders brought Hinduism with them, and second the Indonesian royalty welcomed Hindu religion and culture, and it is they who first adopted these spiritual ideas followed by the masses. Indonesian islands adopted both Hindu and Buddhist ideas, fusing them with pre-existing native folk religion and Animist beliefs. In the 4th century, the kingdom of Kutai in East Kalimantan, Tarumanagara in West Java, and Holing (Kalingga) in Central Java, were among the early Hindu states established in the region. Excavations between 1950 and 2005, particularly at the *Cibuaya* and *Batujaya* sites, suggest that Tarumanagara revered deity Wisnu (Vishnu) of Hinduism. Ancient Hindu kingdoms of Java built many square temples on the islands with the names of the rivers such as Gomati and Ganga, as major irrigation and infrastructure projects.

Several notable ancient Hindu kingdoms in Indonesia, known as Mataram, were famous for the construction of one of the world's largest Hindu temple complexes, known as the Prambanan temple, followed by Kediri and Singhasari. Hinduism along with Buddhism spread across the archipelago. Numerous shastras and sutras of Hinduism were translated into the Javanese language, expressed in art form. For example, Rishi Agastya is known as the principal figure in the 11th century Javanese text *Agastya parva.* The text includes *puranas,* and a mixture of ideas from the Samkhya and Vedanta schools of Hinduism. The Hindu-Buddhist ideas reached the peak of their influence in the 14th century. The last and largest among the Hindu-Buddhist Javanese empires, Majapahit, influenced the Indonesian archipelago.

Sunni Muslim traders of the Shafi'i fiqh, as well as Sufi Muslim traders from India, Oman and Yemen brought Islam to Indonesia. The earliest known mention of a small Islamic community amidst the Hindus of Indonesia is credited to Marco Polo, about 1297 AD, whom he referred to as a new community of Moorish traders in Perlak. Over 15th and 16th centuries, a Muslim militant campaign led by Sultans attacked Hindu-Buddhist kingdoms and various communities in the Indonesian archipelago, with each Sultan trying to carve out a region or island for control. Four diverse and contentious Islamic Sultanates emerged in north Sumatra (Aceh), south Sumatra, west and central Java, and in southern Borneo (Kalimantan).

These Sultanates declared Islam as their state religion and pursued war against each other as well as against the Hindus and other non-Muslim, viewed as infidels. Hindu, Buddhist, Confucian and Animist communities in these Indonesian Sultanates bought peace by agreeing to pay Jizya tax to the Muslim ruler, while others began adopting Islam to escape the Jizya tax. For example, Jizya was imposed on unbelievers of Islam in Sumatra, as a condition for peace by the local Sultan. In some regions, Indonesian people continued their old beliefs and adopted a synergetic version of Islam. In other cases, Hindus and Buddhists left and concentrated as communities in islands that they could defend. Hindus of western Java, for example, moved to Bali and neighboring small islands. While this era of religious conflicts and inter-Sultanate warfare was unfolding, and new power centers were attempting to consolidate regions under their control, European colonialism arrived. The Indonesian archipelago was soon dominated by the Dutch colonial empire. The Dutch colonial empire helped prevent inter-religious conflicts, and it slowly began the process of excavating, understanding and preserving Indonesia's ancient Hindu-Buddhist cultural foundations, particularly in Java and western islands of Indonesia.

Chapter Fortytwo

ANCIENT THAILAND SOAKED IN HINDU CULTURE

H istory of Thailand[283] talks about its ancient kingdoms such as Sukhothai Kingdom, Ayutthaya Kingdom, Thonburi Kingdom, Rattanakosin Kingdom, etc. The names of the kingdoms of Thailand reflect their origin in Sanskrit, suggesting its relationship with Vedic culture, similar to the culture of the countries in its vicinity, like Vietnam, Cambodia, Sri Lanka, Malaysia, Myanmar (Burma), Bharat and others.

The Tai peoples originally lived in southwestern China. Later over a period of several centuries, they migrated into the mainland Southeast Asia. The oldest known mention of their existence in the region is given by the eponym *Siamese* in a 12th century A.D. inscription at the Khmer temple complex of Angkor Wat in Cambodia, which refers to *syam* (shyam is a Sanskrit word, meaning light dark) or "dark brown" people. *Siam* is derived from the Sanskrit word *syam*, or brown race, with a contemptuous signification. During the reign of Rama III (1824–1851), a Scottish trader had experimental coins struck in England at the king's behest. Though not adopted for use, the name of the country put on these first coins was *Muang Thai*, not Siam. Also spelled *Siem*, *Syâm* or *Syâma*, it has been identified with the Sanskrit *Śyâma* (श्याम, meaning "light dark" or "brown"). The country's designation as Siam by Westerners likely came from Portuguese, the first Europeans to give a coherent account of the country. Portuguese chronicles noted that the king of Sukhothai (seems Sanskritic) had sent an expedition to

---

[283] Wikipedia, Google

Malacca at the southern tip of the Malay Peninsula in 1455. Following their conquest of Malacca in 1511, the Portuguese sent a diplomatic mission to Ayutthaya (Ayudhya). A century later, on 15 August 1612, '*The Globe*', an East India Company merchantman bearing a letter from King James I, arrived in "the Road of Syam". By the end of the 19th century, *Siam* had become so enshrined in geographical nomenclature that it was believed that by this name and no other would continue to be known and styled.

Indianized kingdoms such as the Mon, Khmer and Malay kingdoms had ruled the region. Thai people established their own states starting with Sukhothai, Chiang Saen and Chiang Mai and Lanna Kingdom and then Ayutthaya kingdom. These states fought each other and were under constant threat from the Khmers, Burma and Vietnam. Much later, the European colonial powers threatened in the 19th and early 20th centuries, but Thailand survived as the only Southeast Asian state to avoid European colonial rule because the French and the English decided that Thailand would be a neutral territory to avoid conflicts between their colonies. After the end of the absolute monarchy in 1932, Thailand endured sixty years of almost permanent military rule before the establishment of a democratic elected-government system.

Prior to the southwards migration of the Tai people from Yunnan in the 10th century, the Indochina peninsula had been a home to various indigenous animistic communities far as far back as 500,000 years ago. The recent discovery of Homo erectus fossils such as Lampang man is but one example. The remains were first discovered during excavations in Lampang province, Thailand. The finds have been dated from roughly 1,000,000–500,000 years ago in the Pleistocene. There are myriad sites in Thailand dating to the Bronze (1500 BC-500 BC) and Iron Ages (500 BC-AD 500). The most thoroughly researched of these sites are located in the country's northeast, especially in the Mun and Chi River valleys. The Mun River in particular is home to many 'moated' sites which comprise mounds surrounded by ditches and ramparts. The mounds contain evidence of their prehistoric occupations.

Around the 1st century AD, according to Funan epigraphy and the records of Chinese historians, a number of trading settlements of the South appear to have been organized into several Malay states, among the earliest of which are believed to be Langkasuka and Tambralinga. Some trading settlements show evidences of Roman trade: a Roman gold coin showing Roman emperor Antoninus Pius (161 AD) has been found in southern Thailand.

Ancient civilizations

Prior to the arrival of the Tai people and culture into what is now Thailand, the region hosted a number of indigenous Mon-Khmer and Malay civilizations. Yet little is known about Thailand before the 13th century as the literary and concrete sources are scarce and most of the knowledge about this period is gleaned from archeological evidence.

The 13 meter long reclining Buddha in Nakhon Ratchasima, Chao Phraya valley in Central Thailand reflects Buddhism had once been the home of Mon Dvaravati culture, which prevailed from the 7th century to the 10th century. The existence of the civilizations had long been forgotten by the Thai when Samuel Beal discovered the polity among the Chinese writings on Southeast Asia as "Tou-lo-po-ti". During the early 20th century the archeologists led by George Coedès made grand excavations on what is now Nakorn Pathom and found it to be a center of Dvaravati culture. The constructed name Dvaravati was confirmed by a Sanskrit plate inscription containing the name "Dvaravati".

Later on, many more Dvaravati sites were discovered throughout the Chao Phraya valley. The two most important sites were Nakorn Pathom and Uthong (in the present Suphanburi Province). The inscriptions of Dvaravati were in Sanskrit and Mon using the script derived from the Pallava script of the Indian Pallava dynasty. The religion of Dvaravati is thought to be Theravada through contacts with Sri Lanka, with the ruling class also participating in Hindu rites. The Dvaravati art, including the Buddha sculptures and stupas, showed strong similarities to those of the Gupta dynasty of India. The most prominent production of Dvaravati art are the *Thammachakra*s or the Stone Wheels signifying Buddhist principles. The eastern parts of the Chao Phraya valley were subjected to a more Khmer and Hindu influence as the inscriptions are found in Khmer and Sanskrit.

Dvaravati was not a kingdom but a network of city-states paying tributes to more powerful ones according to the *mandala* model. Dvaravati culture expanded into Isan as well as southwards as far as the Isthmus of Kra. Dvaravati was a part of ancient international trade as Roman artifacts were also found and Dvaravati tributes to the Tang court are recorded. The culture lost power around the 10th century when were submitted by a more unified Lavo-Khmer polity.

In what is considered as present day Isan another Indianized kingdom of Si Kottaboon rose with the capital of Nakhon Phanom. The territory of Si Khottaboon covered mostly northern Isan and central Laos.

Below the Isthmus of Kra was the place of Malay civilizations. Primordial Malay kingdoms are described as tributaries to Funan by 2nd century Chinese sources – though most of them proved to be tribal organizations instead of full-fledged kingdoms. From the 6th century onwards, two major mandalas ruled Southern Thailand – the Kanduli and the Langkasuka. Kanduli centered on what is now Surat Thani Province and Langasuka on Pattani. Southern Thailand was the center of Hinduism and Mahayana. The Tang dynasty monk I Ching stopped at Langkasuka to study Pali grammar and Mahayana during his journey to India around 800 AD. At that time, the kingdoms of Southern Thailand quickly fell under the influences of the Malay kingdom of Srivijaya from Sumatra.

From about the 10th century to the 14th century Thailand was known through archeological findings and a number of local legends. The period saw the Khmer domination over a large portion of Chao Phraya basin and the Isan. The expansion of Tai people and culture southwards also happened during the classical era.

According to the Jamadevivamsa, the city of Hariphunchai (modern Lamphun) was founded by the hermits. Jamadevi, a Lavo princess, was invited to rule the city in around 700 AD. However, the date is considered too early for the foundation of Hariphunchai as Jamadevi brought no Thammachakras to the north. Hariphunchai may be a later (about the 10th century) offshoot of the Lavo kingdom or instead related to the Thaton kingdom.

Hariphunchai was the center of Theravada in the north. The kingdom flourished during the reign of King Attayawong who built the Dhatu of Hariphunchai in 1108. The kingdom had strong relations with another Mon kingdom of Thaton. During the 11th century, Hariphunchai waged lengthy wars with the Tai Ngoenyang kingdom of Chiang Saen. Weakened by Tai invasions, Hariphunchai eventually in in 1293 fell to Mangrai, the Great, king of Lanna, the successor state of the Ngoenyang kingdom.

Arrival of the Tais[284]

The most recent and accurate theory about the origin of the Tai people stipulates that Guangxi province in China is really the Tai motherland instead of Yunnan province. A large number of Tai people, known as the Zhuang, still live in Guangxi today. Around 700 AD, Tai people who did not come under Chinese influence settled in what is now Dien Bien Phu in modern Vietnam according to the Khun Borom legend. From there, the Tais began to radiate into northern highlands and founded the cities of Luang Prabang and Chiang Saen.

The *Simhanavati legend* tells us that a Tai chief named Simhanavati drove out the native Wa people and founded the city of Chiang Saen around 800 AD. For the first time, the Tai people made contact with the Indianized (Hindu) civilizations of Southeast Asia. Through Hariphunchai, the Tais of Chiang Saen adopted Theravada Buddhism and Sanskrit royal names. The Dhatu of Doi Tung, constructed around 850 AD, signified the piety of Tai people on the Theravada religion. Around 900 AD, major wars were fought between Chiang Saen and Hariphunchai. The Mon forces captured Chiang Saen and its king fled. In 937, Prince Prom the Great took Chiang Saen back from the Mon and inflicted severe defeats on Hariphunchai.

Around 1000 AD, Chiang Saen was destroyed by an earthquake with all inhabitants killed. A council was established to govern the kingdom for a while. Then a local Wa man, known as Lavachakkaraj, was elected as the King of the new city of Chiang Saen or Ngoenyang. The Lavachakkaraj dynasty ruled over the region for about 500 years.

---

[284] Wikipedia

The overpopulation might have encouraged the Tais to seek their fortune further southwards. By 1100 AD, the Tai had established themselves as *Po Khun*s (ruling fathers) at Nan, Phrae, Songkwae, Sawankhalok, Chakangrao, etc. on the upper Chao Phraya valley. These southern Tai princes faced Khmer influence from Lavo. Some of them became subordinates to the Lavo-Khmer polity.

Lavo kingdom's temple

Around the 10th century, the city-states of Dvaravati (looks Hindu name) merged into two *mandalas* (Sanskrit word) – the Lavo (modern Lopburi) and the Supannabhum (modern Suphanburi). According to a legend in the Northern Chronicles, in 903, a king of Tambralinga invaded and took Lavo and installed a Malay prince to the Lavo throne. The Malay prince was married to a Khmer princess who had fled away from an Angkorian dynastic bloodbath. The son of the couple contested for the Khmer throne and became Suryavarman I, thus bringing Lavo under Khmer domination through personal union. Suryavarman I also expanded into the Khorat Plateau (later styled Isan), constructing many temples. Suryavarman, however, had no male heir and again Lavo was independent. King Anawratha of Bagan invaded Lavo in 1058 and took a Lavo princess as his wife. The power of the Lavo kingdom reached the zenith in the reign of Narai (1072–1076). Lavo faced Burmese invasions under Kyanzittha, whose mother was the Lavo princess, in 1080 but was able to repel. After the death of Narai, however, Lavo was plunged into bloody civil war and the Khmer under Suryavarman II took advantage by invading Lavo and installing his son as the King of Lavo. The repeated but discontinued Khmer domination eventually "Khmerized" Lavo. Lavo was transformed from a Theravadic Monic Dvaravati city into a Hindu Khmer one. Lavo became the entrepôt of Khmer culture and power of the Chao Phraya river basin. The bas-relief at Angkor Wat showed a Lavo army as one of the subordinates to Angkor. However, one interesting note is that a Tai army was shown as a part of Lavo army, a century before the establishment of the Sukhothai kingdom.

South-East Asian Hindu Empires

Hindus had established several empires in ancient SE Asian region as seen in the above picture. States were small because of absence of all basic services such as, motor mobility, telephone and post-office services, financial resources and most important knowledge and technology of community organization would be required for administratively managing large states.

Southeast Asia c.1300 CE, showing Khmer Empire in red, Lavo kingdom in light blue, Sukhothai empire in orange, Champa in yellow, Dai Viet in blue and Kingdom of Lanna in purple.

Thai city-states gradually became independent from the weakened Khmer Empire. It is said that Sukhothai was established as a sovereign, strong kingdom by Pho Khun Si Indrathit in 1238 AD. A political feature which "classic" Thai historians call "father governs children" existed at this time. Everybody could bring their problems to the king directly, as there was a bell in front of the palace for this purpose. The city briefly dominated the area under King Ramkhamhaeng, who established the Thai alphabet, but after his death in 1365, Sukothai fell into decline and became subject to another emerging Thai state, the Ayutthaya Kingdom in the lower Chao Phraya area.

Another Thai state that coexisted with Sukhothai was the eastern state of Lanna, centered in Chiang Mai. King Phya Mangrai was its founder. This city-state emerged in the same period as Sukhothai. Evidently, Lanna became closely allied with Sukhothai. After the Ayutthaya kingdom had emerged and expanded its influence from the Chao Phraya valley, Sukhothai was finally subdued. Fierce battles between Lanna and Ayutthaya also constantly took place and Chiang Mai was eventually subjugated, becoming Ayutthaya's 'vassal'. Lanna's independent history ended in 1558, when it finally fell to the Burmese. Thereafter it was dominated by Burma until the late 18th century. Local leaders then rose up against the Burmese with the help of the rising Thai kingdom of Thonburi of king Taksin. The 'Northern City-States' then became vassals of the lower Thai kingdoms of Thonburi and Bangkok. In the early 20th century they were annexed and became part of modern Siam, the country now called Thailand.

Chapter Fortythree

BALI A PURELY HINDU STATE IN INDONESIA[285]

After Indonesia gained its independence from Dutch colonial rule, it officially recognized only monotheistic religions under pressure from political Islam. Further, Indonesia required an individual to have a religion in conformity with Islam to gain full Indonesian citizenship rights. Indonesia officially did not recognize Hindus as its citizens. It considered Hindus as *orang yang belum beragama* (people without religion), and as those who must be converted. In 1952, the Indonesian Ministry of Religion declared Bali and other islands with Hindus as needing a systematic campaign of proselytization to accept Islam. The local government of Bali, shocked by this official national policy, declared itself an autonomous religious area in 1953. The Balinese government also reached out to India and former Dutch colonial officials for diplomatic and human rights support. A series of student and cultural exchange initiatives between Bali and India helped in formulating the core principles behind Balinese Hinduism (Catur Veda, Upanishad, Puranas, Itihasa). In particular, the political self-determination movement in Bali in mid 1950s led to a non-violent passive resistance movement and the joint petition of 1958 which demanded Indonesian government to recognize Hindu Dharma. This joint petition quoted the following Sanskrit mantra from Hindu scriptures: "*Om tat sat ekam eva advitiyam*", explaining that 'Om, thus is the essence of the all pervading, infinite, undivided ONE, asserting that Hindus worship only One Almighty God representing

---

[285] Wikipedia, Google

Himself through His various manifestations, known as gods and goddesses known as saints.

On June 14, 1958, Hindus of Bali filed a Joint petition expressing the "undivided one" to satisfy the constitutional requirement that Indonesian citizens have a monotheistic belief in one God. The petitioners identified *Ida Sanghyang Widhi Wasa* as the undivided one. In the Balinese language, this term has two meanings: the Divine ruler of the Universe and the Divine Absolute Cosmic Law. This creative phrase met the monotheistic requirement of the Indonesian Ministry of Religion in the former sense, while the latter sense of its meaning preserved the central ideas of in ancient scripts of Hinduism. In 1959, Indonesian President Sukarno supported the petition and a Hindu-Balinese Affairs section was officially launched within the Ministry of Religion. Indonesian politics and religious affairs went through turmoil from 1959 to 1962, with Sukarno dissolving the Konstituante and weakening the impact of communist movement in Indonesia along with political Islam. Nevertheless, officially identifying their religion as Hinduism was not a legal possibility for Indonesians until 1962, when Hinduism became the fifth state-recognized religion. This recognition was initially sought by Balinese religious organizations and granted for the sake of Bali, where Hindus were in majority. Between 1966 and 1980, along with Balinese Hindus, large numbers of Indonesians in eastern Java, as well as in parts of South Sulawesi, North Sumatra, Central and South Kalimantan officially declared themselves to be Hindus. They politically organized themselves to press and preserve their rights. The largest of these organizations, Parisada Hindu Dharma Bali, changed its name to 'Parisada Hindu Dharma Indonesia' (PHDI) in 1986, reflecting subsequent efforts to define Hinduism as a national religion, rather than just a Balinese concern.

While Hindus in Bali, with their large majority, developed and freely practiced their religion in other islands of Indonesia they suffered discrimination and persecution by local officials as these Hindus were considered as those who had left Islam, the majority religion. However, the central government of Indonesia supported Hindus. In 1960s, Hinduism was an umbrella also used by Indonesians whose faith was Buddhism and Confucianism, but neither of the two was officially recognized. Furthermore, Hindu political activists of Indonesia worked to protect people of those faiths under rights they had gained at the 'Indonesian Ministry of Religion'.

Currently, Hindu Dharma is one of the five officially recognized monotheistic religions in Indonesia. Folk religions and animists with a deep concern for the preservation of their traditions of ancestors declared their religion to be Hinduism, considering it a more flexible option than Islam, in the outer islands, seeking shelter for their indigenous ancestor religion under the broad umbrella of 'Hinduism', followed by the Karo Batak of Sumatra in 1977. In central and southern Kalimantan, a large Hindu movement had grown among the local indigenous Dayak population which led to a mass declaration of 'Hinduism' on this island in 1980. However, this was different from the Javanese case, in that conversions followed a clear ethnic division. Indigenous Dayak were confronted with a mostly Muslim population of government-sponsored (and predominantly Madurese) migrants and officials, and deeply resentful at the dispossession of their land and its natural resources.

Compared to their counterparts among Javanese Hindus, many Dayak leaders were also more deeply concerned about Balinese efforts to standardize Hindu ritual practices nationally; fearing a decline of their own unique 'Hindu Kaharingan' traditions and renewed external domination. By contrast, most Javanese were slow to consider Hinduism at the time, lacking a distinct organization along ethnic lines and fearing retribution from locally powerful Islamic organizations like the Nahdatul Ulama (NU). Several native tribal peoples with beliefs such as Sundanese Sunda Wiwitan, Torajan Aluk To Dolo, and Batak Malim, with their own unique syncretic faith, have declared themselves as Hindus in order to comply with Indonesian law, while preserving their distinct traditions with differences from mainstream Indonesian Hinduism dominated by the Balinese. These factors and political activity have led to a certain resurgence of Hinduism outside of its Balinese stronghold.

The general beliefs and practices of *Agama Hindu Dharma* are a mixture of ancient traditions and contemporary pressures placed by Indonesian laws that permit only monotheist belief under the national ideology of *panca sila*. Traditionally, Hinduism in Indonesia had a pantheon of deities and that tradition of belief continues in practice; further, Hinduism in Indonesia granted freedom and flexibility to Hindus as to when, how and where to pray. However, officially, Indonesian government considers and advertises Indonesian Hinduism as a monotheistic religion with certain officially recognized beliefs that comply with its national ideology. Indonesian school text books describe Hinduism as having one supreme being, Hindus offering three daily mandatory prayers, and Hinduism as having certain common beliefs that in part parallel those of Islam. Scholars contest whether these Indonesian government recognized and assigned beliefs reflect the traditional beliefs and practices of Hindus in Indonesia before Indonesia gained independence from Dutch colonial rule.

Hindus out of joy started constructing new temples of various kinds of 'East-West' and 'Ancient-Modern' blended architecture, mostly rich in nature, a marvelous tourist attraction, the Bali economy depends on.

Hindus believe in one supreme Almighty God with His various manifestations, known as gurus, saints and pegamgers with various responsibilities to serve the humanity.

Hindu believe in the Trimurti, consisting of: Brahma, the creator, Vishnu, the preserver and Shiva, the destroyer. Lord Shiva, like death, is being misunderstood. Death is unavoidable. Shiva gives death to terminate the continuing suffering of the old decayed life. It is terrifying to imagine what would happen if death was not there. Hindus believe in eternal life, only to be understood by the Hindu doctrine "rebirth and reincarnation" according to which death is the beginning of a new fresh life. Hinduism is optimistic, sees good in every thing, created by God.

The sacred texts found in Agama Hindu Dharma are the Vedas and Upanishads. They are the basis of Hinduism including Balinese Hinduism. Other sources of religious information include the Universal Hindu Puranas and the Itihasa (history) of the oral traditions as recited mainly in Ramayana (approx 5000 BC) and Mahabharata (approx 3000 BC). The epics *Mahabharata* and *Ramayana* became enduring traditions among Indonesian Hindus being expressed through shadow puppet (*wayang*) and dance performances.

As in India, Hinduism in Indonesia recognizes four paths (Chatur marg) of spirituality leading to ultimate union with God:

(i) *bhakti mārga* (path of devotion to deities),
(ii) *jnana mārga* (path of knowledge),
(iii) *karma mārga* (path of activity and effort) and
(iv) *raja mārga* (path of meditation).

Bhakti marga has extremely large following in Bali.

Similarly, like Hindus in India, Balinese Hindus believe that there are four proper goals of human life, known as *Chatur Purusartha:*

(i) *dharma* (pursuit of moral and ethical living),
(ii) *artha* (pursuit of wealth and creative activity),
(iii) *kama* (pursuit of lust, joy and love, and
(iv) *moksha* (pursuit of self-knowledge and liberation.

Balinese Hinduism is an amalgamation of Indian religions and indigenous animist customs that existed in Indonesian archipelago before the arrival of Islam and later Dutch colonialism. It integrates many of the core beliefs of Hinduism with arts and rituals of Balinese people. In contemporary times, Hinduism in Bali is officially referred by Indonesian Ministry of Religion as *Agama Hindu Dharma*, but traditionally the religion was called by many names such as Tirta, Trimurti, Hindu, Agama Tirta, Siwa, Buda[286], and Siwa-Buda. The terms Tirta and Trimurti emanate from Indian Hinduism, corresponding to Tirtha (pilgrimage to spirituality near holy waters) and Trimurti (Brahma, Vishnu and Shiva) respectively. I think Buda refers to Buddha.

Like in India, Hinduism in Bali grew with flexibility, featuring diverse ways of life. It includes most of the Hindu spiritual ideas, legends and myths of *Puranas* and Hindu Epics, as well expressed through unique set of festivals associated with a myriad of hyangs – the local and ancestral spirits, as well as forms of animal sacrifice that are not common in India. As a matter of fact, there was no custom of

---

[286] Buda means Buddha

animal sacrifice, meaning slaughter of animals to please vegetarian God. Such has been historical European mischief to misinterpret to defame Vedic civilization. Human vices like theft, cheating, greed, dishonesty, adultery, etc, are symbolically considered as animals in human attire. Colonial historians, despite knowing all this, tend to literally translate them for Indians to infuse in them inferiority complex to enable them to rule longer. This may affect only a thin minority of western educated urbanites. The mass Hindus get really true Vedic history from millennia-ancient oral traditions in temples and street plays.

Spirituality is one of the central vibes of Bali and it is no surprise that the place is dotted with many temples. The main religion here is Balinese Hinduism and a Hindu temple here is known as pura. Most of the pura (known as temple) in Indonesia is concentrated in Bali though one may find some in other parts where many Balinese people live. The term pura is originated from the Sanskrit word which means "walled city" or "palace" but now the word had evolved to be known as a temple complex in the Balinese language. Here in Bali, the most important pura (temple) is the Mother Temple of Besakih, known as the largest and holiest of all temples in Bali. Since there are so many puras built here on Bali, it had been aptly called "the island of thousand puras." Bali temples are a great gift of a fountain of spirituality, paradoxically a millionaire can not afford, but a penniless poor can enjoy.

BESAKIH TEMPLE (MOTHER OF TEMPLE)

Pura Besakih is the most well-known and the holiest temple in Bali and being the mother of all temples as aptly named, this pura so one of the oldest in Bali. It is revered for its importance and being over 1000 years old. Mount Agung that stood nearby erupted in 1963 but the lava flows jut off the temple by few meters, and people had taken it as a sign from the gods. The temple's main axis align with the peak of Gunung Agung, which is the tallest mountain in Bali, making them significant. Besakih temple complex consists of 23 separate temples, with some dating back to the 10th century.

Uluwatu Temple, also known as Pura Luhur, is a famous Balinese sea temple. It is one of the nine directional temples of Bali which are meant to protect it from the evil spirits. This spectacular temple is perched at the edge of the rock overlooking the raging sea. The word Luhur means "something of divine origin" and ulu means "land's end" while watu means "rock" in the old language, and as you can see it is aptly describing this inspiring temple. It is one of the six most important temples after Besakih temple. Most travelers enjoy the view of the temple from two different vantage points – northern and southern.

This temple is known as the "land in the middle of the sea" (meaning island) as it sits off the coast on a majestic rock. It reminds me of the temple "Sadh Bela" in the Indus river (Sindhu river in Sukhar, Sindh, now in Pakistan.

Pura Tanah Lot is another very popular temple in Bali, being well known for its serenity and cultural significance. It is part of the seven temples that form a ring at the southwest of Bali. Traveler's tip is to go there during low tide so that one can walk across the water to the temple, an experience, one would not like to miss. This temple dates back to the 15th century AD and believed to be the work of the priest Nirartha, whereby after spending a night on that same place, he instructed the local fishermen to build a temple there.

PURA TIRTA EMPUL TEMPLE

Another one of the six important temples of Bali, Pura Tirta Empul is known for its sacred spring water with healing properties. This temple dates back to 926 AD and well revered by the locals. Many people climb up to the temple for a bath and meditation in the long main pool because it is believed to bring good fortune and health. The legend around this temple is that this spring is created by the god Indra as an antidote to the poisonous spring by an evil demon king.

The above very famous temple, especially among the rice farmers in Bali, at Bedugul is situated on the shores of Lake Bratan. It is the primary temple of the many temples that is for the popular Bali's subak irrigation system. The temple is dedicated to the goddess of lakes and rivers. Its one section seems floating on the lake just off the mainland of the temple complex. It also has a towering pagoda over the beautiful placid lake.

Goa Lawah, which means "bat cave" is located in the southeast of Bali. It was founded in 1007 AD. Its name, is filled with thousands of bats. It is also one of the directional temples that is protecting Bali from the evil spirits. The temple is a popular site for post-cremation purification that is culturally important to the Balinese people. It is believed that the Javanese priest Nirartha had visited the cave before and that the interior of the cave extends over to connect with Pura Besakih.

TAMAN AYUN TEMPLE

This royal temple of Mengwi empire is located in Mengwi village. Not exactly a well-known temple to travelers, but it is well worth a visit as off the beaten tracks. It is a family temple, built back in 1600 by King of Mengwi. Now it survives as a beautiful example of a royal public temple. Taman Ayun means beautiful garden, and this complex stands surrounded by a moat that makes it appear as if floating on water. The front courtyard has an ornamental gate while the inner courtyard has a number of multi-tiered pagodas (meru).

This temple, known as the "valley of the Kings' is located in the cliffs between rice fields at the south of Tampaksiring, Bali. The Pakerisan river flows through the ravine and flanking the river is the shrines and carved stones that are meant to commemorate the 11th-century kings and queens. Though technically not a temple, it is still revered as a holy place by the locals. This site is more of an actual tomb for the royalties that are cremated here based on Balinese customs.

PURA LUHUR LEMPUYANG

This temple is one of the most obscure of the lot but not lacking in importance as a eligious site. It is one of the six sad kahyangan (temples of the world) which is dedicated to the supreme God – Sang Hyang Widi Wasa and also one of Bali's nine directional temples to protect from evil spirits. Visiting this temple requires a bit of an effort as you need a serious 1.5 hours hike to the top of 1,700 steps, which cuts into the mountainside jungle. At the peak, you also get a grand view of Gunung Agung with the temple gate framing it. One of the best time to visit here is the day after Galungan to see the Lempuyang during its odalan.

The Pura Saraswati, though small in size, is beautiful in its own right, surrounded by beautiful lotus ponds. The temple of 19th century was built by the royal family of that time to dedicate it to the Goddess of Saraswati (Goddess of Knowledge and Learning). The temple has exquisite exterior design while the interiors resemble the typical Balinese temples with stone carvings. The splendor of this temple is because it stood amidst the beautiful lotus pond lined with trees. Pura Saraswati is also used for many dance performances on Thursday (Guruwar) evenings. In Hindi Thursday means Guruwar, the day of guru. Admission to the temple is free, but there is a fee for watching the dances.[287] The Balinese temple is called *Pura*. These temples are designed on square Hindu temple plan, as an open air worship place within enclosed walls, connected with series of intricately decorated gates to reach its compounds. Each of these temples has a more or less fixed membership; every Balinese belongs to a temple by virtue of descent, residence, or affiliation. Some house temples are associated with the family house compound (also called *banjar* in Bali), others are associated with rice fields, and still others with key geographic sites. In rural highlands of Bali, *banua* (or *wanwa*, forest domain) temples in each *desa* (village) are common. The island of Bali has over 20,000 temples, or about one temple for every 100 to 200 people. Temples are dedicated to local spirits as well as to deities found in India; for example, Saraswati, Ganesha, Vishnu (Vishnu), Siwa, Parvati, Arjuna, and others. The temple design similarly amalgamate architectural principles in Hindu temples of India and regional ideas. Each individual has a family deity, called Kula dewa, who resides in the temple called the family temple that the individual and his family patronize. Balinese Hindu follow a 210-day calendar (based on rice crop and lunar cycles), and each temple celebrates its anniversary once every 210 days. Balinese have unique rituals and festivals that are not found in India, include those related to death of a loved one followed by cremations, cockfights, tooth filings, Nyepi and Galungan. Each temple anniversary, as well as

---

287 Wikipedia, Photo credits from top: nerdwithoutglasses, Ricky Qi, Madeleine Holland, Christ06, Jesus Abizanda.

festivals and family events such as wedding include flowers, offerings, towering bamboos with decoration at the end and a procession. These are celebrated by the community with prayers and feast. Most festivals have a temple as venue, and they are often occasions for prayers, celebration of arts and community. Some traditions, in contrast, involve animist rituals such as *caru* (animal blood sacrifice) such as *Tabuh Rah* (lethal cockfighting) or killing of an animal to appease *buta kala* (spirits of the earth) - however, the animal sacrifices are conducted outside the premises of a temple.

Balinese Hindu arts

Dance, music, colorful ceremonial dresses and other arts are a notable feature of religious expression among Balinese Hindus. As in India, these expressions celebrate various mudra to express ideas, grace, decorum and culture. Dance-drama is common. Various stories – mythical as well historical – are expressed through dance and music. For example, one involves a battle between the mythical characters Rangda the witch (representing adharma, something like disorder) and Barong the protective spirit represented with a lion mask (representing dharma), in which performers fall into a trance, the good attempts to conquer evil, the dancers express the idea that both the good and the evil exist within each individual, and that conquering evil implies ejecting evil from oneself. The dance-drama regularly ends undecided, neither side winning, because the primary purpose is to restore balance and recognize that the battle between dharma and adharma (good and evil) is within each person and a never ending one. Barong, or dharma, is a major symbolic and ritual paradigm found in various festivities, dances, arts and temples.

Rituals of the life cycle are also important occasions for religious expression and artistic display. Ceremonies at puberty, marriage, and, most notably, cremation at death provide opportunities for Balinese to communicate their ideas about community, status, and the afterlife.

Hinduism in Java

Both Java and Sumatra were subject to considerable cultural influence from the Indian subcontinent. The earliest evidences of Hindu influences in Java can be found in 4th century Tarumanagara inscriptions scattered around modern Jakarta and Bogor. In the sixth and seventh centuries many maritime kingdoms arose in Sumatra and Java which controlled the waters in the straits of Malacca and flourished with the increasing sea trade between China and India and beyond. During this time, scholars from India and China visited these kingdoms to translate literary and religious texts. From the 4th to the 15th century, Java had many Hindu kingdoms, such as Tarumanagara, Kalingga, Medang, Kediri, Sunda Singhasari and Majapahit. This era is popularly known as the Javanese Classical Era, during which Hindu-Buddhist literature, art and architecture flourished and were incorporated into local culture under royal patronage. During this time, many Hindu temples were built, including 9th century Prambanan near Yogyakarta, which has been designated as a World Heritage Site. Among these Hindu kingdoms, Majapahit kingdom was the largest and the last significant Hindu kingdom in Indonesian history. Majapahit was based in East Java, from where it ruled a large part of what is now Indonesia. The remnants of the Majapahit kingdom shifted to Bali during the sixteenth century after a prolonged war by and territorial losses to Islamic sultanates.

The heritage of Hinduism left a significant impact and imprint in Javanese art and culture. The wayang puppet performances as well as wayang wong dance and other Javanese classical dances are derived from episodes of Hindu epics Ramayana and Mahabharata. Although the majority of Javanese now identify as Muslim, these art forms still survive. Hinduism has survived in varying degrees and forms in Java; in recent years, conversions to Hinduism have been on rise, particularly in regions surrounding a major Hindu religious site, such as the Klaten region near the Prambanan temple. Certain ethnic groups, such as the Tenggerese and Osing, are also associated with Hindu religious traditions.

Hinduism elsewhere in the archipelago

The Tamil Hindus walking around the Sri Mariamman Temple, in Medan Among the non-Balinese communities are considered as Hindu by the government, for example, the Dayak adherents of the Kaharingan religion in Kalimantan Tengah, where government statistics counted Hindus as 15.8% of the population as of 1995. Many Manusela and Nuaulu people of Seram follow Naurus, a syncretism of Hinduism with animist and Protestant elements. Similarly, the Tana Toraja of Sulawesi have identified their animistic religion as Hindu. The Batak of Sumatra have identified their animist traditions with Hinduism. Among the minority Indian ethnic group, Tamils and Punjabis of Medan, Sumatra and the Sindhis in Jakarta practice their own form of Hinduism which is similar to the Indian Hinduism. Hindus in Jakarta are celebrating Hindu holidays as commonly found in India, such Divali, Holi and Thaipusam. The Bodha sect of Sasak people on the island of Lombok are non-Muslim; their religion is a fusion of Hinduism and Buddhism with animism; it is considered Buddhist by the government. The Hindu organization Ditjen Bimas Hindu (DBH) carries out periodic surveys through its close connection with Hindu communities throughout Indonesia. In 2012 its studies stated that there are 10,267,724 Hindus in Indonesia. The PHDI (Parisada Hindu Dharma Indonesia) along with other some other religious minority groups claim that the government undercounts non-Muslims in census recording. The 2010 census recorded the number of Hindus at 4,012,116, some 80% of them residing in the Hindu heartland of Bali.

I can not forget Deepavali I enjoyed in Jakarta. Deepavali is the day when Hindus all over the world celebrate to commemorate the day when Lord Rama (born Jan10,5114 BC) returned to Ayodhya, his birth place after completing 14 years of his exile. It is celebrated with lights, exchange of sweets, music and dances. All wear new clothes and children wear colorful dresses to dance.

Holidays celebrated in Bali

People in Bali celebrate the victory of dharma over adharma (right over wrong). Hari Raya Galungan occurs every 210 days and lasts for 10 days. It celebrates the coming of the gods and the ancestral spirits to earth to dwell again in the homes of their descendants. Festivities are characterized by offerings, dances and new clothes. The ancestors must be suitably entertained and welcomed, and prayers and offerings must be made for them. Such ancestors-remembrance festivity looks similar to festivity in India, known as 'Shradha – remembering ancestors and giving homage to them. The eldest person in the family may talk about the family recalling the great matters of the heritage, the juniors may feel proud of. Families whose ancestors have not been cremated yet, but remain buried in the village cemetery, must make offerings at the graves. Kuningan is the last day of the holiday, when the gods and ancestors depart until the next Galungan.

Hari Raya. Saraswati is the goddess of learning, science, and literature. She rules the intellectual and creative realm, and is the patron goddess of libraries and schools. Balinese Hindus believe that knowledge is an essential medium to achieve the goal of life as a human being, and so honor her.

Saraswati, the goddess of knowledge, is celebrated first because she helps man to succeed in taming his wandering and lustful mind, always preoccupied with the goddess of material wealth. On this day, offerings are made to the lontar (palm-leaf manuscripts), books, and shrines only talking about Saraswati (knowledge), starting from the knowledge of self (self-awareness) which is most difficult. According to Vedas the knowledge of self means 'knowledge' of the path to Almighty God. For this, man needs a well-versed Guru.

In Bali, Saraswati Day is celebrated every 210-days on Saniscara Umanis Wuku Watugunung and marks the start of the New Year according to the Balinese Pawukon calendar. Ceremonies and prayers are held at temples allover, in family compounds, villages and businesses from morning to noon. Prayers are also held in school or any other learning institution temples. Teachers and students abandon their uniforms for the day in place of bright and colorful ceremony gear, filling the island with color. Children bring fruits and traditional cakes to school for offerings at the temple.

Hari Raya Nyepi ('Hari' refers to god Krishna) is a Hindu Day of silence, peace of mind as the Hindu New Year in the Balinese Saka calendar. On this day, several largest celebrations are held in Bali as well as in Balinese Hindu communities around Indonesia. On New Year's Eve the villages are cleaned, food is cooked for two days and in the evening as much noise is made as possible to scare away the devils. On the following day, Hindus do not leave their homes, cook or engage in any activity. Streets are deserted, and tourists are not allowed to leave hotel complexes. The day following Nyepi night, everything stops for a day except emergency services such as ambulances. Nyepi is determined using the Balinese calendar, the eve of Nyepi falling on the night of the new moon whenever it occurs around March/April each year. Therefore, the date for Nyepi changes every year. Nyepi night is a night of community gatheringe and burning of effigies island-wide (similar to Holika in India), while the next day is the day of total peace and quiet (unlike Holi which is full of dancing, coloring, merry making and noise).

ANCIENT MEDICAL AND SURGICAL TRADITIONS

During the Ramayana war (about 5114 BC) between Lord Rama and Rawana in Sri Lanka to get Seeta free from the barbaric clutches of Rawana, Laksmana got hurt and fainted. Hanuman went up a mountain to trace the shrub, they knew would help him to regain consciousness. In prehistory ancient Vedic times, people had knowledge about organic therapeutic means to various illnesses and diseases to avoid hospitalization and the side effects of biochemical medicines. Such organic knowledge even in modern times is being used and passed over down from generation to generation through the millennia-long oral traditions. Happily surprising, several families have been practicing the grandma prescriptions to deal with several common illnesses – fever, cold, running nose, arthritic aches, constipation, etc.

True story, let me share that a few days back (July 2017 morning) I myself 91 yr old felt too weak, to walk even a few feet. I couldn't understand what happened overnight. If I had rushed to hospital, I would have gone under few diagnostic tests, futile finding nothing. I am telling this because this has happened two times in USA and one time in India, no diagnosis established for treatment. Recalling what my father had said that rest has therapeutic agents to try first before taking any major step. After rest of a day I regained my healthy yesterday.

Other example of grandma's surgical prescription is amazing, hospitals would feel scared to use. I myself 12 year kid while playing cricket within walls hit a stone-like sharp wooden material and started heavily bleeding. If taken to hospital I would have lost blood too much to survive. I my mother immediately stopped bleeding by a wall of I think of 'kajal', in my Sindhi language known as *'surma'*, always available and reachable to women. Wish my mother was alive to make this story authentic.

The knowledge of the medicinal value of plants and other substances and their uses go back to the prehistory Vedic times. The 'Medical Today' has learnt lot from the 'Medical Past' to teach the 'Medical Future'. The medical knowledge, like other kinds of knowledge, runs like a river not only quenching the needful thirst of each generation, but also researching to identify new avenues to better, sharpen and supplement the medical and surgical science to make the life of the humanity healthier. To achieve all this, more attention should be given to ancient models – Ayurveda, Unani and Siddha – unfortunately have been sidelined because of biomedicine model which gives comparatively quicker relief, more suitable for employed and students, but unfortunately ignoring detrimental side effects of biomedicine. The organic medicine is good for maintaining good health – longer and free of pains associated with biomedicine. Better to have organic, domestic and economical medical model, free from the side effects of biomedicine, friendly to national purse by minimizing import costs and economical to reach the poor. In present times there are several Vaidas practicing Vaidic and Homeopathic medicines. Please, refer to the Chapter 18 pages 280-289 for Ayurveda and more important "Yoga" (Chapter Fifteen, pp 257- 268).

As based on linguistic and philological evidence, the Rig Veda is the oldest surviving literature (1700-1100 BC) of the Vedic religion, now known as Hinduism[288], God Rudra (Shiva) is mentioned in the Rig Veda (RV 2.33) . Shiva is described as the "Father of the Rudras", a group of storm gods. Furthermore, the Rudram, one of the most sacred hymns of Hinduism is found both in the Rig and the Yajur Veda. The term *Shiva* is used as an epithet for Indra, Mitra and Agni many times.

---

[288] Wikipedia.

Chapter Fortyfive

CAVES: WINDOWS TO THE MORNING OF HINDU LIFE

Caves have silent tongue

Writing came much later. So the description about the construction of the houses for God and for His assistants (gods and goddesses) appeared much later. God initially lived in a cave. The most ancient cave has been traced back at Amarnath, situated at the ultimate north tip of Jammu and Kashmir where the Temple of "Baba Amarnath" is being worshipped as His holy birth place. Lord Shiva, along with his beautiful dedicated consort Parvati, has been enjoying His life at the naturally evolved cave (अमरनाथ गुफा) in Jammu and Kashmir. It is now worshiped as the Temple of Baba Amarnath.

Amarnath: The morning of Hindu Life

The temple is dedicated to Lord Shiva[289]. The cave is situated at an altitude of 3,888 m (12,756 ft), about 141 km (88 mile) from Srinagar, the capital of Jammu and Kashmir. It can be reached via the Pahalgam town. The shrine reflects the initial stage of Hinduism, and is considered to be one of the holiest Hindu shrines. The cave is surrounded by snowy mountains. The cave itself is covered with snow most of the year, except for a short period of time in summer when snow starts melting and makes it easy for thousands of pilgrims to travel to visit the abodes of

---

[289] Information is taken from the Website of Wikipedia.

their beloved gods and goddesses. Thousands of Hindu devotees brave an annual challenging pilgrimage to Amarnath Temple on high snowy mountain.

The ancient history of Hinduism is also inscribed in several caves, like those at Ajanta, Elora and several other caves. Painters, like Ludovico Pisani, have been making beautiful paintings to weave the stories of gods and their messages:

According to Walter M. Spink, this painting from Cave 1 features superb murals and is of imperial quality.[290]

The above painting from Cave 2, is showing extensive paint loss in its many areas. It was never completely finished by its artists.

It is interesting that unlike all modern ways of preserving history, the history of the pre-history ancient Vedic world was preserved in caves, later expressed by their silent non-literal symbolic ways. Caves have mind to symbolically express volumes, only Vedic Rishis and Munis can interpret what the caves talk about the gods within.

One can understand how history – though mercilessly misinterpreted, hidden and even buried – has been important to the modern generations to know their ancestors.

Thanks to the caves, the windows to our lofty PAST!

---

[290] Wikipedia

Scholars in Discovery of Pre-history Ancien India

Adigal, Elango
Alcott, Amos Bronson
Anderson, Robert N.
Apte, V. S.
Arghandawi, Abdul Ali
Arjuna
Arnold, Sir Edwin
Arrian
Arunachalam, V.S.
Arya, Dr. Ravi Prakash
Asoka, King
Baldi, Philip
Banerji, R.D.
Benveniste, Emile
Besant, Annie
Bibby, Geoffrey
Blavatsky, Helena
Burke, Marie Louise
Burns, Bill
Burrows, John
Burrow, T
Bush, President George W.
Butterfield, Herbert
Captain Carr
Castellani, Antonio
Childe, Prof. V. Gordon
Childress, David Hortcher
Chopra, Deepak

Clarke, Dr. Peter B.
Coedoux, Pere
Coomaraswamy
Cousin, Victor
Cunningham, Alexander
Cunningham, Major Gen.
Daniélou, Alain
Demoule, Jean-Paul
Dikshitar, Ramchandra
Will, Durant,
Eck, Diana L
Eldbridge, Edward
Einstein, Albert
Eliot, Sir Charles
Embree, Ainslie T
Emerson
Feuerstein
Foster, Donald
Foucher, Dr. A
Frankfort, Dr. Henry
Frawley, David
Freud, Sigmund
Galav, T. C.
Galianos, Demetrios
Gandhi, Indira
Gandhi. Mohandas
Gandhi, Rahul
Gandhi, Sonia

Müller, Max

Munshi, Dr. K.M.

Narayanan, K. R.

Nehru, Jawaharlal

Nietzsche, Friedrich

Nivedita, Sister Nivedita

Oak, P. N.

Obama, President Barack

Olcott, Col. Henry S

Oppenheimer, Robert

Orlov, Oleg

Pandit, M.P.

Panini

Philip, Rev. Morris

Pinotti, Dr. Roberto

Plato

Plotinus, Pliny

Poonai, Dr. Premsukh

Pococke, Edward

Pollock, Dr. Sheldon

Radhakrishna, B.B.

Radhakrishnan, Sir S.

Rao, P.V. Narasimha

Roy, Raja Ram Mohan

Rao, S. R

Rawson, Philip

Renfrew, Colin

Reyna, Dr. Ruth

Robinson, Andrew

Rolland, Romain

Rothermund, Dietmar

Rückert, Friedrich

Russell, G.L.

Sagan, Dr. Carl

Sagar, Rāmānand

Salisbury

Sassetti, F.

Schelling

Schildmann, Kurt

Schlegel, August Wilhelm von

Schlegel, Frederick

Schopenhauer, Arthur

Schulze, B.

Shah, Iqbal Ali

Shih, Hu

Shirer, William L

Singh, Dr. Manmohan

Smith, Vincent

Soddy, Frederick

Stevenson, Victor

Swaraj, Sushma

Starr, Chester G

Strachey, John

Sturm, William

Tagore, Rabindranath

St. Rain, Tedd

Thorndike, Lynn

Thompson, Gunnar

Thoreau, Henry David

Thurman, Robert A.F.

Tilak, B.G.Lokmaniya

Tomas, Andrew

Trubetskoy, N.S.

Twain, Mark

Trager, James

Trumpp

Twain, Mark

Vaidya, C.V.

Vajpayee, Atal Bihari

Vittaxis, Dr. Vassilis

Vivekananda, Swami

Voltaire, Francois

Waldo, Ralph
Wagner, Richard
Walker, Benjamin
Wheeler, R. E. M.
Wheeler, Sir Mortimer
Whitman, Walt
Wilford, Lieut. Col. F.
Wilkins, Charles
Winternitz,
Wolpert, Prof. Stanley
Wood, Michael
Woodroffe, Sir John
Yeats, W.B.
Zabriskie, Phil
Zaitsev, Dr. Vyacheslav

Printed in the United States
By Bookmasters